COMPARATIVE GOVERNMENT AND POLITICS SERIES

Published

Maura Adshead and Jonathan Tonge
Politics in Ireland

Rudy Andeweg and Galen A. Irwin
Governance and Politics of the Netherlands (3rd edition)

Tim Bale
European Politics: A Comparative Introduction (3rd edition)

Nigel Bowles
Government and Politics of the United States (2nd edition)

Paul Brooker
Non-Democratic Regimes (2nd edition)

Kris Deschouwer
The Politics of Belgium: Governing a Divided Society (2nd edition)

Robert Elgie
Political Leadership in Liberal Democracies

Rod Hague and Martin Harrop
* Comparative Government and Politics: An Introduction (9th edition)

Paul Heywood
The Government and Politics of Spain

Xiaoming Huang
Politics in Pacific Asia

B. Guy Peters
Comparative Politics: Theories and Methods
[Rights: World excluding North America]

Tony Saich
Governance and Politics of China (3rd edition)

Eric Shiraev
Russian Government and Politics (2nd edition)

Anne Stevens
The Government and Politics of France (3rd edition)

Ramesh Thakur
The Government and Politics of India

Forthcoming

Tim Haughton
Government and Politics in Central and Eastern Europe

* Published in North America as **Political Science: A Comparative Introduction** (7th edition)

Comparative Government and Politics
Series Standing Order ISBN 978–0–333–71693–9 hardback
Series Standing Order ISBN 978–0–333–69335–3 paperback
(*outside North America only*)

You can receive future titles in this series as they are published by placing a standing order. Please contact your bookseller or, in the case of difficulty, write to us at the address below with your name and address, the title of the series and one of the ISBNs quoted above. Customer Services Department, Macmillan Distribution Ltd, Houndmills, Basingstoke, Hampshire, RG21 6XS, UK

This book is dedicated to Jackie, Javier, Belén
and Jack – and to Peter, Wendy and Simon

3rd Edition

European Politics

A COMPARATIVE INTRODUCTION

TIM BALE

 macmillan education palgrave

First edition 2005
Second edition 2008

Third edition published 2013 by
PALGRAVE

Palgrave in the UK is an imprint of Macmillan Publishers Limited, registered in England, company number 785998, of 4 Crinan Street, London, N1 9XW.

Palgrave Macmillan in the US is a division of St Martin's Press LLC, 175 Fifth Avenue, New York, NY 10010.

Palgrave is a global imprint of the above companies and is represented throughout the world.

Palgrave® and Macmillan® are registered trademarks in the United States, the United Kingdom, Europe and other countries

ISBN: 978-0-230-36293-2 hardback
ISBN: 978-0-230-36294-9 paperback

This book is printed on paper suitable for recycling and made from fully managed and sustained forest sources. Logging, pulping and manufacturing processes are expected to conform to the environmental regulations of the country of origin.

A catalogue record for this book is available from the British Library.

A catalog record for this book is available from the Library of Congress.

Printed in China

Contents

List of Illustrative Material

Country profiles

Debates

Maps

Boxes

Figures

Tables

List of Abbreviations and Acronyms

General terms

A-2	Bulgaria and Romania
A-8	eight CEE states joining EU in 2004
ACP	African, Caribbean and Pacific
ADB	*algemene bestuursdienst* (Netherlands)
AMS	alternative member system
AMM	(EU) Aceh Monitoring Mission
ASEAN	Association of South East Asian Nations
ASEM	Asia-Europe Meeting
BBC	British Broadcasting Corporation
BME	black and minority ethnic
CAP	Common Agricultural Policy (EU)
CEE	Central and eastern Europe
CEEP	European Centre of Enterprises with Public Participation and of Enterprises of General Economic Interest
cefic	European Chemical Industry Council
CET	Common External Tariff
CFSP	Common Foreign and Security Policy
CH	*Confoederatio Helvetica* (Switzerland)
CIA	Central Intelligence Agency (US)
CIS	Commonwealth of Independent States
CoE	Council of Europe
CoR	Committee of the Regions
COPA	Committee of Agricultural Organizations
COREPER	Committee of Permanent Representatives (EU)
COSAC	Conference of Community and European Affairs Committees
CPHR	*See* ECHR
CSTO	Collective Security Treaty Organization
CSDP	Common Security and Defence Policy (EU)
DDR	German Democratic Republic – (Communist) East Germany
DG	Directorate General (of the European Commission)
DOM	*Département d'Outre-Mer* (French Overseas Department)
EAJ-PNV	*Eusko Alderdi Jeltzalea – Partido Nacionalista Vasco*
EBA	'everything but arms'
EC	European Community
ECB	European Central Bank
ECHR or CPHR	European Convention for the Protection of Human Rights and Fundamental Freedoms (European Convention on Human Rights)
ECJ	European Court of Justice
ECOFIN	Economic and Financial Affairs Council
ECSC	European Coal and Steel Community
EDC	European Defence Community
EDF	European Defence Fund
EEA	European Environmental Agency
EEAS	European External Action Service
EEC	European Economic Community
EFPIA	European Federation of Pharmaceutical Industries and Associations
EFTA	European Free Trade Area
EMU	European Monetary Union
ENP	European Neighbourhood Policy
ENPP	effective number of parliamentary parties
EP	European Parliament
EPC	European Political Cooperation
ESDP	European Security and Defence Policy
ETA	*Euskadi Ta Azkatasuna* (Basque Homeland and Liberty – paramilitary organization)
ETUC	European Trade Union Confederation
EU	European Union
EUFOR–RDCongo	European Union Force – Democratic Republic of Congo
EUMS	EU military staff
EU-3	France, UK and Germany
EU-15	European Union of fifteen member states (1995–2004)
EU-25	European Union of twenty-five member states (2004–7)
EU-27	European Union of twenty-seven member states (2007–)
EVS	European Values Survey
FDI	foreign direct investment

FRG	Federal Republic of Germany (West Germany)
FPP	first-past-the-post
FSU	former Soviet Union
FYROM	Former Yugoslav Republic of Macedonia
G-8	group of the world's richest industrialized countries (Britain, Canada, France, Germany, Italy, Japan, Russia, US)
GATT	General Agreement on Tariffs and Trade
GDP	gross domestic product
GDR	German Democratic Republic (Communist East Germany)
GHGs	greenhouse gases
GM	genetically modified/modification
GNI	gross national income
GNP	gross national product
ICT	information and communication technology
ID	party ID (party identification)
IGC	Intergovernmental Conference
IMF	International Monetary Fund
IRA	Irish Republican Army
IRU	International Romani Union
IT	information technology
JHA	Justice and Home Affairs
JNA	Yugoslav Army
LDC	least-developed country
LIS	Luxembourg Income Study
M&As	mergers and acquisitions
MEDEF	*Mouvement des Entreprises de France* (French employers' organization)
MEP	member of the European Parliament
MMP	mixed member proportional
MP	member of Parliament
NATO	North Atlantic Treaty Organization
NELF	New European Left Forum
NFU	National Farmers' Union (UK)
NGO	non-governmental organization
NI	Northern Ireland
NIC	newly industrializing country
NIS	newly independent states
NPM	New Public Management
ODA	overseas development assistance
OECD	Organisation for Economic Cooperation and Development

OPZZ	*Ogólnopolskie Porozumienie Związków Zawodowych* (All-Polish Alliance of Trade Unions)
OSCE	Organization for Security and Cooperation in Europe
p.a.	per annum
PCA	(EU-Russia) Partnership and Cooperation Agreement
PFI	Private Finance Initiative
PPC	Permanent Partnership Council (EU and Russia)
PPP	purchasing power parity
PR	proportional representation
QMV	qualified majority voting
R&D	research and development
RRF	Rapid Reaction Force
RSPB	Royal Society for the Protection of Birds
SEA	Single European Act
SEM	Single European Market
SGP	Stability and Growth Pact
SIS	Schengen information system
SME	small and medium-sized enterprises
SOE	state-owned enterprise
SSA	sub-Saharan Africa
STV	single transferable vote
TACIS	Technical Assistance to the CIS (EU)
TEU	Treaty on European Union (Maastricht Treaty)
TOM	*Territoire d'Outre-Mer* (French overseas territory)
TRNC	Turkish Republic of Northern Cyprus
UK	United Kingdom
UN	United Nations
UNHCR	United Nations High Commissioner for Refugees
UNICE	Union of Industrial and Employers Confederations of Europe (from 2007, *BusinessEurope*)
USA	United States
USSR	(Union of Soviet Socialist Republics) Soviet Union
VAT	Value added tax (sales tax)
WEU	West European Union
WMD	weapons of mass destruction
WTO	World Trade Organization

Political parties and groupings

AKEL	*Anorthotikon komma Ergazemenou Laou* (Progressive Party of Working People – Cyprus)
ALDE	Alliance of Liberals and Democrats for Europe (European Parliament)
AN	*Alleanza Nazionale* (Italy)
AOV	*Algemeen Ouderen Vorbond* (Pensioners' Party – Netherlands)
AP	*Alianza Popular* (Popular Alliance – Spain)
ATAKA	*Ataka* (Attack Coalition – Bulgaria)
AWS	*Akcja WyborczaSolidarno* (Solidarity Electoral Action – Poland)
BNP	British National Party
BZO	Alliance for the Future of Austria
C	*Centerpartiet* (Centre Party – Sweden)
CDA	*Christen Democratisch Appèl* (Christian Democratic Appeal – Netherlands)
CDC	*Convergència Democrática de Catalunya* (Democratic Convergence of Catalunya – Spain)
CDS/PP	*Centro Democrático Social/Partido Popular* (Social Democratic Centre/Popular Party – Portugal)
CDU	*Christlich-Demokratische Union* (Christian Democratic Union – Germany)
CiU	*Convergència i Unió* (Convergence and Union – Catalunya, Spain)
CSSD	*eská strana sociálné demokratická* (Czech Social Democratic Party)
CSU	*Christlich Soziale Union in Bayern* (Bavarian Christian Social Union – Germany)
CU	*Christen Unie* (Christian Union – Netherlands)
D66	*Democraten 66* (Democrats 66 – Netherlands)
DC	*Democrazia Cristiana* (Christian Democracy – Italy)
DF	*Dansk Folkeparti* (Danish People's Party)
DS	*Democratici di Sinistra* (Democrats of the Left – Italy)
DUP	*Democratic Unionist Party* (Northern Ireland)
ECR	European Conservatives and Reformists
EFD	Europe of Freedom and Democracy
EPP	European Peoples' Party
FDP	*Freie Demokratische Partei* (Free Democratic Party – Germany)
FLNC-UC	National Liberation Front for the Liberation of Corsica – Union of Fighters
FN	*Front National* (National Front – France)
FpL	*Folkpartiet Liberalerna* (People's Party Liberals – Sweden)
FPÖ	*Freiheitliche Partei Österreichs* (Austrian Freedom Party)
FrP	*Fremskrittspartiet* (Progress Party – Norway)
GL	*Groen Links* (Green Left – Netherlands)
GUE-NGL	European United Left - Nordic Green Left
IU	United Left (Spain)
K	*Kristdemokraterna* (Christian Democrats – Sweden)
KESK	*Suomen Keskusta* (Finnish Centre)
KS M	*Komunistická Strana ech a Morava* (Communist Party of Bohemia and Moravia – Czech Republic)
LAOS	La kós Orthódoxos Synagermós (People's Orthodox Rally-Greece)
LN	*Lega Nord* (Italy)
LPF	*Lijst Pim Fortuyn* (Pim Fortuyn List – Netherlands)
LPR	*Liga Polskich Rodzin* (League of Polish Families)
M	*Moderata Samlingspartiet* (Moderate Rally Party Sweden)
MP	*Mijöpartiet de Gröna* (Green Environmental Party – Sweden)
ODS	*Ob anská Demokratická Strana* (Civic Democrats – Czech Republic)
ÖVP	*Österreichische Volkspartei* (Austrian People's Party)
PASOK	*Panell nio Sosialistikó Kin ma* – Greek Socialist Movement – Greece
PCF	*Parti Communiste Français* (French Communist Party)

PCI	*Partito Comunista Italiano* (Italian Communist Party)	SLD	*Sojusz Lewicy Demokralycznej* (Democratic Left Alliance – Poland)
PDS	*Partito Democratico della Sinistra* (Democratic Party of the Left – Italy) or *Partei des Demokratischen Sozialismus* (Party of Democratic Socialism – Germany)	SNP	Scottish National Party
		SNS	*Slovenská narodná strana* (Slovakia)
		SP	*Socialistische Partij* (Socialist Party – Netherlands)
PiS	*Prawo i Sprawiedliwo* (Law and Justice – Poland)	SPD	*Sozialdemokratische Partei Deutschlands* (German Social Democratic Party)
PP	*Partido Popular* (Popular Party – Spain)	SPR-RS	*Sdružení pro republiku* (Czech Republican Party)
PRM	*Partidul Rômania Mara* (Greater Romania Party)	SVP	*Schweizerische Volkspartei* (Swiss People's Party)
PS	*Parti Socialiste* (Socialist Party – France)	TOP 09	*Tradice Odpov dnost Prosperita 09* (Tradition, Responsibility, Prosperity 09 party – Czech Republic).
PSL	*Polskie Stronnictwo Ludowe* (Polish Peasants' Party)		
PSOE	*Partido Socialista Obrero Español* (Spanish Socialist Workers Party)	UCD	*Unión Centro Democrático* (Union of the Democratic Centre – Spain)
PvdA	*Partij van de Arbeid* (Labour Party – Netherlands)	UDF	*Union pour la Démocratie Française* (Union for French Democracy)
PVV	*Partij voor de Vrijheid* (Freedom Party – Netherlands)	UKIP	United Kingdom Independence Party
		UMP	*Union pour un Mouvement Populaire* (Union for a Popular Movement – France)
S & D	Progressive Alliance of Socialists and Democrats		
SAP	*Arbetarepartiet-Socialdemokraterna* (Social Democratic Labour Party – Sweden)	V	*Vänsterpartiet* (Left Party – Sweden)
		VB	*Vlaams Blok,* now *Vlaams Belang* (Flemish Interest Belgium)
SDLP	*Social Democratic and Labour Party* (Northern Ireland)	VV	*Věci Veřejné* (Public Affairs party – Czech Republic)
SGP	*Staatkundig Gereformeerde Partij* (Political Reformed Party – Netherlands)	VVD	*Volkspartij voor Vrijheid en Democratie* (People's Party for Freedom and Democracy – Netherlands)
		WASG	Electoral Alternative for Labour and Social Justice (Germany)

Introduction

So much has happened in (and, indeed, to) Europe since the last edition of this book was published five years ago that it is hard to know where to begin. Not since the collapse of communism in 1989 has the media paid the continent so much attention, and what quickly became obvious from its coverage was how closely all the economic problems that preoccupied journalists and citizens alike were inextricably bound up with politics. Without some understanding, for example, of the way things work (or don't work) in Greece or Italy or Germany, it would be impossible to understand the Eurozone crisis that began to dominate headlines from 2011 onwards. On the other hand, without understanding something about Europe more generally, the goings-on in those countries make much less sense. All of this, it would seem, supports the approach taken by this book.

The country-by-country approach taken by other books has the merit of teaching you a great deal about a few very important states. But even the best of such books (and there are some very good ones) can leave you not knowing that much about how politics works in the continent as a whole. Such an approach makes it hard to compare and contrast because it cannot help but stress particularity. A second set of books organize things not by country but by theme, hoping to get over this problem by being explicitly comparative. But this can leave you feeling both overloaded and a little detached from the living, breathing Europe that less abstract, country-by-country texts are better able to evoke and convey. This book aims to combine the strengths of both approaches in order not to lose sight of the wood for the trees or the trees for the wood – to capture, if you like, commonality but also diversity.

Why European politics?

This book is intended to be user-friendly enough for the general reader but is aimed at those studying politics for their degree or as part of their degree. Anyone doing that needs to be able to 'demonstrate knowledge and understanding of different political systems, the nature and distribution of power in them; the social, economic, historical and cultural contexts within which they operate, and the relationships between them' (QAA, 2000). Studying European politics is clearly one way of doing this. Europe also provides us with comparative material on political institutions, processes and issues – the kind of things that anybody with an interest in politics *per se* is naturally going to be keen to find out more about. Even if you are primarily interested in your own country, you can hardly avoid making comparisons, even if you do it only implicitly. Political science is inherently comparative because it has pretensions to building and testing theories (if not laws) that work *across time and space*; even when its focus is the unique, it attempts generalizable (and therefore) comparative explanations. Europe is in some ways a fantastic laboratory in which to develop and test a whole host of educated guesses about how politics works, all the more so because the European Union – a collection of nearly thirty states that together form the world's largest economy – also constitutes the biggest experiment in (peaceful!) regional integration ever attempted. Moreover, the study of politics takes in political philosophy as well, and few would argue that many of the big ideas about how societies should be organized not only originated in Europe but continue to play out there. By the same token, simply because Europe likes to bill itself as the 'cradle of democracy', the quality and health of that democracy cannot be taken for granted – it needs interrogating, deconstructing, measuring against its pretensions and ideals.

But the rationale for studying European politics goes wider than the intellectual. It may, for instance, be quite practical: even those readers who do not currently live or work in Europe may well do so at some time in the future. At the very least, they may pursue careers that involve some passing contact either with European companies or even European governments and the EU. Knowing what makes the continent tick politically, and having some handle on the social and economic issues that preoccupy it, is culturally and practically useful. Nor should we necessarily play down the emotional reasons. Having lived and taught outside Europe for five years at the turn of the century, I am as aware as anyone that more and more of us are born and/or brought up outside our family's 'country of origin'. If that country is European, then studying the continent helps achieve a sense of connection to your roots. This obviously applies to students in the so-called 'settler societies' – the USA and Canada, Australia and New Zealand, Israel, and South Africa. But it can just as easily apply if, say, you were born and brought up in one European country but your family (or a part of it) has its origins or still lives in another.

There is also a democratic and, if you like, political purpose to studying the politics of other countries.

Wherever we live, we are generally given to believe by our own politicians that the way things are done in our country is either in tune with what goes on elsewhere, or probably even better. But when we look abroad we soon realize several things. The first is that 'it doesn't have to be this way': governments that do things differently to the way your own government does them do not necessarily go to hell in a handcart, and while it is not for me to pronounce on which precise form of organizing the state or running elections is better than the rest, you need not shy away from making such judgements. Second, many of the challenges faced and the solutions offered by the politicians you voted (or did not vote) for bear a remarkably strong (and only sometimes depressing) resemblance to the challenges faced and the solutions offered by their European counterparts. And, third, wherever you are, the picture of European and EU politics painted by the media is almost guaranteed to be highly partial – in both senses of the word. Ample reason, then, to dig a little deeper.

Why this book?

Persuading you that European politics is something worth studying in general is one thing. Persuading you that this book in particular is worth using is another. One reason why it might be is because it is founded on experience in the classroom and is therefore based on what works. What works is providing you with a good balance of breadth and depth, simplicity and complexity, overview and detail. In other words, providing you with a book that will tell you not only what you need to know but also introduce you to issues that you might like to find out more about. A book that communicates the enthusiasm of the author but does not blithely assume you share it – at least at the outset, anyway! A book that you can understand but refuses to talk down to you. A book that avoids jargon when it is unnecessary but is not afraid to use it and explain it (either in the text or in the definitions emboldened in the text) when it is. A book that does not pretend that absolutely everything can be broken down into predigested, bite-sized chunks, but which also realizes that it needs to be accessible. A book that uses up-to-date examples from the real world of

European politics, allowing and encouraging you to make connections between what you study in the classroom or the library and what you watch, listen to and read in the media. A book that realizes that, unless it helps you better understand and function in the world as you perceive it, then education – an increasingly expensive commodity – is pretty pointless.

The media has a considerable advantage over an academic work, of course. It may on occasion be more simplistic and one-sided, but it is a good deal less time-consuming and much less time-bound. It rarely tells us more than we need to know – even if sometimes that is not quite enough. It is almost always well crafted and presented, with the accent on the visual and a style that aims to grab the attention of busy people who, by and large, can take it or leave it. Paradoxically, the media may also be quite influential: it helps to construct a common wisdom that by definition many of us buy into whatever our political convictions – assuming we have any in the first place. This book is unapologetic about seeking to question at least some of that common wisdom. Part of its point, without trying to sell you a particular world-view, is to interrogate some of the popular assumptions – be they conservative or right-on and radical – about European politics and Europe's politicians. That will almost certainly include some of the (half-) truths you yourself hold to be self-evident, whether they concern, for instance, the supposed iniquity, inevitability and impact of globalization, the apparently all-pervading electoral power of the media, or the much-trumpeted shortcomings and sell-outs of self-interested politicians.

You should expect, then, to disagree – and anyone who is teaching you to disagree – with quite a bit of what this book says. Some of those disputes, indeed, are crystallized for you in a 'Debate' feature in some chapters. At the very least, this book may make you think twice. Even if you do not change your mind, your opinions are likely to be the stronger for being tested. Maybe – indeed, probably – you can prove me wrong. Time itself might well do so, too. Part of the mix of fascination and frustration of studying politics is that things never stand still, hence the need for a new edition now and then. A new edition also allows an author to do some of the things he or she has since realized should have been done before.

As a result, every chapter has been extensively revised in the light of new research and more up-to-date stats and examples included.

Keeping it real – and up to date

This book is full of tables and figures that, hopefully, will give you some helpful facts at your fingertips. Even though each chapter mentions all sorts of countries, focusing here and there on particular states that seem particularly relevant to the discussion in hand, I have made the decision to concentrate in the tables and figures on just nine countries. These run from Sweden in the north, down through the UK, the Netherlands, France, and Spain, then over, via Italy, to Germany, and east through the Czech Republic and Poland. Each country is given its own profile, providing an overview of its history, economy and society, governance, foreign policy, and contemporary challenges it faces, along with some further reading and – because it can give an insight into a nation's self-image – a bit of information on its national anthem. Some headline statistics are also provided but, since absolute numbers for things like area, population and GDP can easily be found elsewhere, I have tried to add a dash of comparative value by expressing each as a share of the EU total.

These countries are chosen because they are some of the biggest and because they represent variety. They can never, of course, represent every country in Europe. But there is always a trade-off in terms of focusing on a manageable core and doing everything. I have chosen the former, well aware that in so doing I am bound to disappoint some people who hoped to see more of their favourite countries – or at least the ones on which they had decided (or been asked) to write an essay or term paper. Not everybody who seeks to improve European understanding is faced with such a choice. Each of the seven banknotes that make up Europe's embattled single currency, the euro (€), contains a picture of a bridge. The intention is to emphasize links and communication between the different countries of Europe and between the continent and the rest of the world. But the banknote bridges, though apparently prompted by actually existing structures, are imaginary. They represent, if you like, an attempt to inspire without offending those who are left out. On the other hand, they avoid the sometimes messy reality which this book – admittedly a slightly lesser project than the forging of a functioning currency union! – tries to encompass and make sense of.

To that end, this book is also full of boxes. They are not there just to break up the text, though if they help do that, all well and good. They are there to provide you with vignettes designed to provide (hopefully) vivid examples of the points the surrounding paragraphs are trying to make. You do not actually have to look at them if you do not want to. But if you do, they should add a lot not just to your enjoyment, but also to your understanding and your ability to recall what you have read – something that can make all the difference when you are in the exam room or trying to pull that paper, essay or dissertation together from scratch. Think of the boxes like hyperlinks on a webpage. You do not have to click on them but it is often worth it when you do; and even when it turns out not to be, you can get back to where you were by hitting the Back button, or in this case just by turning over the page.

These boxes, as well as the book's tables and figures, have been brought up to date for this third edition – and many are brand-new. Of course there are other ways of keeping things current namely, the use of the web and other electronic and print media. This book refers to websites and has one of its own (www.palgrave.com/politics/bale) which will provide selective update material and function as a gateway to other websites. Some of them may be academic or, as with the admirable http://blogs.lse.ac.uk/europp blog/ or http://ideasoneurope.eu/, attempts to communicate academic work in a more accessible form. Some may be hybrids, featuring academics, policy makers and researchers, and media pundits: http://www.europesworld.org is a great example. A regular glance at the electronic contents pages of a few politics journals (many of which offer free, downloadable articles via libraries) is often worthwhile, too. Indeed, with the electronic subscriptions so many campus libraries now hold, many of the journals mentioned in the References are as easy to access as the Internet itself, especially if you use Google Scholar rather than Google's generic search page. This allows you to search all the journals at once, get the citations and often, if you are at college or university, click straight on to what you want to read (normally in pdf) should you want to print it off and maybe scribble all over it.

Many websites will, of course, be run by media organizations who make it their business to keep us informed and are becoming increasingly good at providing searchable archives: the BBC's is an excellent example. Other sites, it is true, shut you out just when things get interesting. If you are studying at a university or college, however, you are very likely to find that your library actually gives you free and full access to the premium content that others who are less fortunate would have to pay for. Again, if you use a database (*Nexis* is one, but there are others) you can search many newspapers and news magazines at once and save time doing it. Even if you are not at college or university right now and cannot take advantage of the reduced prices often offered to students, you might want to think about a trial subscription to a news magazine like *The Economist*. Notwithstanding its slightly off-putting title (and, for some, its off-putting editorial line!), it has to be one of the best (and definitely the best-written) concise sources on European (and indeed global) political developments. Subscribing also gives you access to its very useful archive on the web. *Time* magazine, which is also a good source for in-depth articles on aspects of European society and politics, has a similarly useful searchable archive online – again, a subscription (or campus access) helps. You can, though, get news and opinion free at sites like euractiv.com, and openDemocracy.net. I should also, of course, mention Wikipedia, regarded by some as a blessing and others as a curse. I fall, I confess, into the former group – it is a great source for politics facts, figures and history, and for more besides: I would certainly like to acknowledge here and now the assistance given me by its backgrounders on national anthems.

Where is it going?

Having explained this book's rationale and suggested other places you can go to supplement its content, it is time to give you a broad overview of how the book is organized and to explain why it is done the way it is. What is needed is a route-map, a rationale and a taster all rolled into one.

This text does not assume any prior knowledge of European history. Rather, it starts by providing a brief but systematic overview intended to help both the novice and the person who just needs to fill in a few gaps to appreciate how we got where we are today. It also stresses the need to get to grips with contemporary Europe economically, demographically and socially – and with where it might be heading on all three counts.

Once it gets into the politics, this book takes a distinctive approach. Most textbooks begin, very democratically but perhaps rather idealistically, with citizens and then take readers on up through groups, parties, elections, parliaments, governments until they reach the top, the state itself. This book, however, begins at the top. After all, before there were citizens who could vote and groups they could belong to and parties they could vote for, before there were parliaments those parties could sit in and elected governments they could hold to account, there was the state. So, the state – historically if not always logically prior to other democratic institutions – is our starting point. As we show, though, it is an increasingly problematic one; under attack, as some would have it, both from below and from 'above' in the shape of the EU – a body we introduce early on but whose institutions and influence are deliberately woven throughout the chapters on the grounds that they are now woven throughout European politics. This **Europeanization** is an overarching and persistent concern (but never an automatic assumption) in this book.

> **Europeanization** is an observable process – ongoing and contested, more or less voluntary, but neither inevitable nor uniform – by which the policies, institutions, norms, goals and actors of the EU and/or other European countries have a perceptible and significant impact on those of individual European countries; policies, institutions, norms, goals and actors can be 'uploaded' to Europe, just as those from Europe are 'downloaded' to and by individual countries.

Europeanization is a recent and much contested field of enquiry in political science, and there are ongoing arguments concerning its definition and scope (for recent reviews, see Graziano and Vink, 2006; Ladrech, 2010). Consonant with the working definition supplied above, the following chapters look not for convergence on some imagined 'European model', although many of them find evidence of patterned variation which often allows us usefully to group states. Rather, they look for evidence (and sometimes explanations) of this process of incremental and interactive influence – a process that is always mediated by national variations in political economy (Chapters 1 and 9), public policy (Chapter 3) and, of course, politics, be they bureaucratic politics (Chapter 3), parliamentary politics (Chapter 4), party politics (Chapter 5), mediated politics (Chapter 7), participation and pressure group politics (Chapter 8), or international politics (Chapter 11). The same interactive influence can be seen in the two chapters that concentrate on particular issues. (Chapter 9) discusses the oft-noted (but not always accurate) extent to which left and right in Europe are becoming so similar that politics no longer really matters, especially when economic necessity seems to force the same set of policies on governments of whatever stripe. The other (Chapter 10) focuses on what the media often see as one of the biggest concerns facing European politics – immigration and integration.

The way politicians are handling these and other issues, and the way the institutions they work within and create seem to be moving, involves what is sometimes called **multilevel governance**. This, like Europeanization, is a persistent theme in this book. The idea of multilevel governance originated in academic work on European integration (see Hooghe and Marks, 2001). It combines two things. First, it comprises criticism of academic work that explains integration as the product either of bargaining between self-interested governments or, in contrast, the role of EU institutions. Second, it contains insights derived from research into individual states on the fragmentation of formerly top-down government. Like Europeanization, multilevel governance

> **Multilevel governance** refers to the fact that the allocation of resources, the delivery of services, and the making of law and policy in Europe is characterized – perhaps increasingly so – by a dispersal or diffusion of power, a multiplication of (sometimes overlapping) sites of authority and policy competence, as well as a mixture of cooperation and contestation between tiers of government that would formerly have been considered more separate and hierarchically ordered.

is thus a portmanteau – and not altogether uncontested – term, but one that arguably describes (and perhaps even helps to explain) the complex reality created by decentralization and the impact of the EU. Unlike Europeanization, the extent of which perhaps varies much more according to the institutions and issues under discussion (indeed, part of understanding European politics nowadays is about getting some idea of where the EU matters more and where it matters less), we are likely to see multilevel governance in evidence in almost all the areas that we explore.

Getting started

Every chapter, then, is self-contained, but – to the extent that they are relevant in each case – each one touches on Europeanization and multilevel governance. Also, every chapter follows its predecessor in a more or less logical manner. Each one also contains lots of references to the other chapters so you can (to pursue the hyperlink metaphor one more time) click (or in this case flick) from one to the other. In other words, this is a book that can be read cover-to-cover, but one that realizes this is not normally the way things work. If you, or your lecturers, instructors and tutors are anything like me, you are pretty much guaranteed to create your own order to fit either the way your particular course runs or the way your own mind works. Use the contents pages, the definitions, tables, figures, boxes, as well as the index, and the sub-headings, the key points and the summaries contained at the beginning and end of the chapters, to help you 'pick and mix'. Take a look, too, at some of the suggestions in the Learning Resources section which concludes every chapter. And maybe check out some of the citations in the references in the back of the book: most of them are there not just to acknowledge the author (although that is always important in academic work, including student essays and term papers!), but also

because I think they are worth chasing up. The web is all very well, but it cannot give you the depth and range provided by the experts who commit their words to the printed page (even if that printed page is available electronically, too). Much of what I cite, though, is chosen with an eye to approachability as well as credibility.

So, there you have it. A book that tries to be a one-stop shop if that is all you want it to be, but also one that provides you with a gateway to other, more detailed and sophisticated takes on European politics. You can use it just for self-directed study. But more likely you will use it as part of a course that someone else has designed. If so, it hopes to sit neatly between the general overview that lectures are normally intended to give you and the more detailed stuff you will discuss in small group classes and read in the library. Hopefully, it will give you enough of what you need, something you might even like and, if you are of an argumentative cast of mind, something you can disagree with as well. If so, neither my time nor your time will have been entirely wasted. And nor will the time of all those whose work, support and generosity has helped me over the years.

Any writer of a textbook inevitably depends, like Blanche DuBois in Tennessee Williams's play, on 'the kindness of strangers' as well as friends. That means that there are way too many people who have responded to my requests for help – often by way of an email out of the blue from some strange guy in England – to mention by name. Most will, I hope, see their work cited in the References. Special thanks, though, should go to all those involved in the annual Political Data Yearbook produced by the *European Journal of Political Research*, to my colleagues and students at Sussex and Queen Mary, University of London and to the legendary Steven Kennedy and his staff, including Stephen Wenham, Helen Caunce and Cecily Wilson, at Palgrave Macmillan. I owe most of all, of course, to my family – all three generations of them. This third edition is dedicated, once again and as always, to them.

Chapter 1
Europe – a continent in the making

Covering around 10 million square kilometres or just under 4 million square miles, Europe is the second smallest of the world's seven continents. But it is number three in terms of population: over 725 million people live there, some thinly spread in the cold of the far north or the heat of the far south, but most packed closely together in towns and cities. That population density, combined with centuries of international trade and the fact that it was the home of the industrial revolution, has made Europe one of the richest and most powerful parts of the globe. In times past, it was also one of the most violent. Its turbulent history was crowned in the twentieth century by two world wars, after which it was divided during nearly fifty years of Cold War into the capitalist 'West' and the communist 'East'. With the collapse of the latter, however, Europe now contains more genuinely democratic states than any other continent on earth.

But Europe, like most continents, is not just a place, a geographical container for those states. It is also an *idea* and an *identity* (see Pagden, 2002). Indeed, because of this, it is actually quite difficult to define it as a place. Our notions of where it begins and ends are fuzzy: they change to suit our conceptions of who should be in and who should be out. The Europe covered in this book is as much of a conventional and convenient fiction as any other. For instance, it excludes some states like Russia, Ukraine, Georgia and indeed Turkey, despite the fact that all of them pop up in the European section of newspapers and news magazines and despite the fact that they could claim (and in the case of Turkey are claiming) to be sufficiently European to join the EU. The Europe covered here basically encompasses those states located between the Mediterranean in the south and Arctic in the north, and between the Atlantic in the west and the Urals and the Caspian Sea in the east. Most of our focus will be on the 27 states that make up the EU, as well as inveterate non-joiners like Norway and Switzerland. This means there is less focus on the Balkan countries of the former Yugoslavia – although, as we shall see below, they have played a dynamic part in European history and provide an extreme example of what can happen when, as is the case in several European countries, multiple nations and/or ethnicities are obliged to live together in just one state.

The first aim of this chapter, however, is to provide some historical background to those concerns. It hopes to show not only how Europe got where it is today, but also how some of what happened to it along the way still resonates with and helps to structure the contemporary continent. The latter then becomes the chapter's main focus as it explores what Europe looks like now and how is it changing – economically, demographically and sociologically. All three aspects play a huge part in political processes, preoccupations and possibilities, not least because they help structure what political scientists call **cleavages**.

> **Cleavages** are splits or divisions in a society that give rise to conflicts that may well be expressed in political form – often, though not necessarily, via the formation of opposing parties representing people on either side of the split.

Exploring the 'then and now', and indeed the 'where next?' helps us to question and qualify some of the common wisdom surrounding social and economic (and so, perhaps, political) change. For instance, the welfare state appears to be alive and well but neither it nor mass education have brought about a classless society – social mobility and equality may even be decreasing. Certainly, women are not doing as well as some of their mothers and grandmothers might have hoped – a continued inequality that is remarkable not just because (as we shall see in, say, Chapter 4) it is reflected in a similar lack of progress in political institutions, but also because (unlike class inequality which continues to some extent to mobilize voters and parties) it does not seem to lead to much political discontent or expression on the part of those who suffer it (see Chapters 5 and 6). Conversely, a phenomenon that, as we note in this chapter, is often assumed to be on the wane – namely, religion – would still appear, at least in some countries, to help structure, say, the party systems and voting behaviour we examine in Chapters 5 and 6. Meanwhile, the ethnic minorities and identities we also deal with below not only have an impact on representative politics but, as we will see in Chapter 2, can threaten the integrity of states in which that representative politics largely takes place, as well as (see Chapter 10) creating political tensions between those living in them.

More generally, the chapter shows that European countries, and the people who live in them, may be growing a little less unlike each other. But it also gives us little reason to think that either Europeanization (which we defined in the Introduction) or *globalization* (discussed in Box 1.1), necessarily entail convergence, let alone homogenization. Europe may be coming together literally as well as figuratively in the guise and under the umbrella of the EU. As a result, it is already more than simply the sum of its parts. But, at the beginning of the twenty-first century, the contrasts and contradictions between those parts – contrasts and contradictions that emerged over hundreds and thousands of years of often overlapping development – are not disappearing quite as fast as we might think.

This chapter, then, provides the context for what we will find in later chapters whose focus is more expressly political: namely, some shared (but rarely identical) challenges faced by countries with sometimes remarkably different cultures, conflicts and bureaucratic and representative arrangements (see Chapters 3, 4 and 6). By recounting in some detail the continent's sometimes bloody history and economic variation that led to such differences, it also indicates why a European integration project that seems to hold out peace and prosperity (see Chapter 2) has proved so attractive to so many countries. At the same time, it hints at why such a project may be more popular with the citizens of some countries than with those of others, as well as at the continued challenges faced on the foreign policy front by both individual countries and the EU acting collectively – challenges we deal with in Chapter 11.

People into empires

People have been around in Europe since the first Stone Age. From around 6000 BC, nomadic hunter-gathering began to give way to farming. And by the time the first Indo-Europeans began arriving in the southern and western part of the continent after 2500 BC, people were already working bronze, trading, and practising religious rites. Early civilizations included the Minoans of Crete and the Indo-European Mycenaeans, who by 1500 BC not only controlled most of Greece but had also supplanted the Minoans. In more central parts of Europe, a rapidly expanding population was beginning to work iron and had already begun to form (language) groups with which we are still familiar today. Celts lived at the western borders of the continent, Slavs in the east and the Germanic peoples in the north. In the south, the Greeks had recovered from the decay of the Mycenaean culture and now formed a number of powerful city-states. They were also

BOX 1.1

Globalization or globaloney?

Globalization has got to be the biggest buzzword of the twenty-first century so far. But, like many buzz-words, its meaning is a little fuzzy and the proof of it not always as solid as those who bandy it about seem to assume (see Martell, 2010 for a thoughtful and accessible summary of the evidence and arguments). In short, the fact that the concept is used so often – as well as blamed or praised for almost all the woes and the wonders of contemporary life – does not make it true or mean that it explains that much.

As far as meaning goes, there are many versions. But the most popular ones are encapsulated in the following definitions:

> The intensification of worldwide social relations which link distant localities in such a way that local happenings are shaped by events occurring many miles away and vice versa. (Giddens, 1990: 64)

> A process (or set of processes) which embodies a transformation in the spatial organization of social relations and transactions – assessed in terms of their extensity, intensity, velocity and impact – generating transcontinental or inter-regional flows and networks of activity. (Held *et al.,* 1999: 16)

> A social process in which the constraints of geography on economic, political, social and cultural arrangements recede, in which people become increasingly aware that they are receding and in which they act accordingly. (Waters, 2001: 5)

Apart from this apparent collapse of time, space and national and regional difference, other writers see globalization as western capitalist imperialism by another name and/or as heralding the end of the nation state and the rise of transnational states. As far as evidence goes, there are, however, many analysts who are sceptical, claiming the rhetoric surrounding globalization may be more important than the reality, which is nowhere near as all-encompassing and transformative as many of us now routinely and casually assume. One recent study (Ghemawat, 2011) notes, among other things, that only 2 per cent of the world's university students attend institutions outside their home countries and that exports only comprise 20 per cent of global GDP. It also notes that, all other things being equal, two countries will engage in nearly 50 per cent more trade with each other if they share a common language and over twice as much more if they share a common currency. And it finds that less than a fifth of internet traffic actually crosses national borders.

expanding into what we now call southern Italy – a land whose northern half was peopled by the Villanovans and then the Etruscans, who, soon after it was founded, took control of Rome.

In the fifth century BC, however, it was the city-state of Athens which, after fighting off Persia

KEY POINT

The continent's early history was characterized by pan-European enterprises, like the Roman Empire, that rose to prominence and then, unable to maintain a grip on their far-flung territories, fell into disrepair.

(modern-day Iran), was the foremost power in Europe. It was also home to many of the classical political philosophers, such as Aristotle and Plato, whom we read even today. Its ambitions proved too strong for its own good, however. Greece descended into a series of wars between the various cities, the devastating consequences of which made it relatively easy prey for Macedonia, to the north. Macedonia's Alexander the Great then proceeded to forge an empire from both Greece and Persia. By the middle of the second century BC, however, that empire was controlled by the Romans. Previously, they had taken not only all of Italy but also that part of Europe that bordered the Mediterranean Sea, as well as much of North Africa and the Middle East. Although Greek culture was allowed to thrive by the Romans, they insisted that all those living under their protection become citizens of Rome and encouraged the use of the Latin language. This, and their commitment to building a transport infrastructure, facilitated trading and other contacts among the peoples of Europe (and North Africa and the Middle East). This helped usher in a period of prosperity and economic development throughout the continent.

Despite a series of civil wars, the Roman Empire persisted into the fourth century AD. By then, Christianity had become what amounted to its 'official religion, and the political and administrative centre of gravity had shifted east to Constantinople (now Istanbul). By the fifth century, however, Germanic peoples such as the Franks, the Visigoths and the Vandals (famous for their sackings of Rome) had first undermined and then destroyed the western part of the empire. What they did not undo, though, was the widespread use of Latinate languages and Christianity, with the latter increasingly under the sway of the head of the Roman Catholic church, the Pope. By the beginning of the ninth century AD, this religious power combined to mutual advantage with the military and political power of the Franks to form what became known as the 'Holy Roman Empire', under Charlemagne.

Empires into nations

This new empire, however, was a rather loosely coupled affair, with overlapping authority exercised by various kings and princes. It also proved no more immune to invasion and division than its Greek and Roman predecessors. The Vikings came from Scandinavia and settled in mainland Europe, including the northernmost part of France, eventually producing a duke, William of Normandy, who became the conqueror of England in 1066. Elsewhere, too, monarchs other than the emperor, as well as lesser nobles, monastic orders such as the Benedictines, and eventually the papacy itself, dominated their own territories, wherein the 'feudal system' (the granting, from the king downwards, of land and rights in exchange for military and political support) gradually took hold. At the same time,

Europe's economy and population expanded prodigiously, as did the towns and cities which, despite the power of the feudal nobility who often continued to live in less urban areas, became centres of commerce, religion and education. These developments provided the resources and the rationale for the Christian Crusades in the Holy Land (now the Middle East) of the eleventh, twelfth and thirteenth centuries. They also financed the overseas voyages of exploration to more far-flung continents, all of which were to provide new sources of wealth and raw materials and eventually empire and colonies.

KEY POINT

Later pan-European empires, such as the Holy Roman Empire, were even more loosely coupled and gave way to smaller nations run more effectively by monarchs. Some of these – with Spain in the vanguard but Britain not far behind – began to seek their own empires in the New Worlds of America and India.

The earliest beneficiaries of overseas expansion were Portugal and, in particular, Spain. Since the expulsion of the Moors of North Africa in the late fifteenth century and the subordination of the country's component kingdoms to that of Castile, Spain had become a firmly Christian country. It also became the foremost upholder of Roman Catholicism against the threat posed to it by what became known as Protestantism. This dissenting movement – aided by the invention of the printing press and the ambitions of German princes who chafed against the Holy Roman Empire – had grown up in central and northern parts of Europe at the beginning of the sixteenth century in both spiritual and political opposition to what it saw as the corrupt papacy. This role as defender of the faith helped put Spain on a collision course with its commercial rival, England which, after breaking with Rome over the Pope's refusal to acquiesce in its king's divorce plans, had adopted a non-Roman Catholic hybrid known as Anglicanism as a state religion. Spain's Armada, a sea-led invasion fleet, was defeated, and the country slipped into its long-term decline, its apparently endless access to the gold of South America stymieing economic dynamism. The religious question in the British Isles, however, was

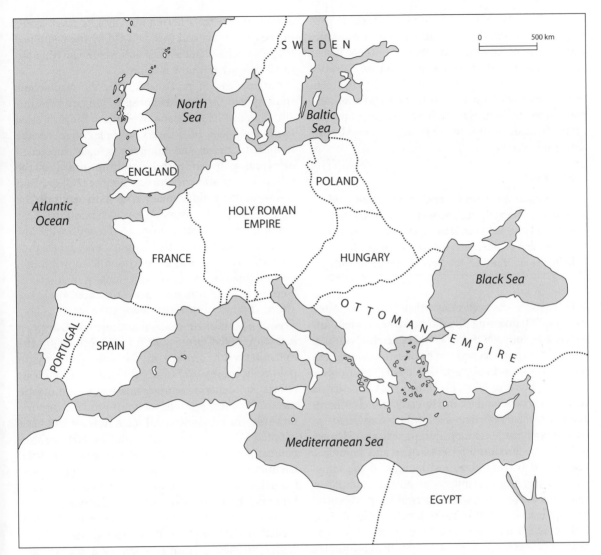

Map 1.1 Europe c.1500 – on the eve of two centuries of religious wars

by no means decided and, as it did all over Europe, played a part in politics in the run up to and long after the country's civil war in the 1640s (see Map 1.1).

Nations into states

In fact, religious conflict and political self-interest and expression combined to cause wars not only between but also within countries throughout late sixteenth- and early seventeenth-century Europe –

and not just in the west. Hungary, for example, had been one of central Europe's strongest powers but spent much of its strength on successive wars against the Islamic Ottoman empire, centred in what we now call Turkey. By the sixteenth century, however, its former rulers, the Habsburg dynasty of Austria, who also held the crown of the rather fragmented Holy Roman Empire, took advantage of Hungary's weakness to restore Roman Catholicism to a country that had – officially anyway – become Protestant. Struggles such as this culminated in the so-called Thirty Years' War. Fought between 1618 and 1648, it brought the Scandinavian countries into a prolonged armed conflict that also involved the kings and princes of central and western Europe. It also saw France emerge not just as mainland Europe's strongest rival to English power, but also as a centralized state with a large bureaucracy and a military maintained to fight wars, many of them aggressive rather than defensive, in what was supposedly the national interest.

KEY POINT

Competition between Europe's monarchies, and conflicts over religion, encouraged warfare that needed to be paid for, leading to greater centralization and to international treaties that established some if not all the borders we know today.

This model was copied by other European states, so France's pioneering role did not grant it predominance for long. By the late eighteenth century, Europe was characterized not by one 'hegemonic' (all powerful) nation but by a so-called **balance of power** between countries such as France, Britain, Austria (and its unstable empire in Hungary and elsewhere) and Prussia, part of what we now know as Germany. By the nineteenth century, Europe was also characterized by a mixture of monarchies and republics. France had become the most famous of the latter, with its revolution acting as a shining example to some and a dire warning to others of the possibilities and the risks inherent in turning political ideals into reality. After what amounted to ten years of permanent upheaval from 1789 onwards, that revolution succumbed to the dictatorship of Napoleon Bonaparte. Napoleon declared himself emperor and proceeded to centralize the French state even further. He also unleashed a succession of aggressive military campaigns against other countries, on to which he attempted, quite successfully, to graft the French

The **balance of power** is an equilibrium existing between states (or groups of states) when resources – especially military resources – are sufficiently evenly distributed to ensure that no single state can dominate the others. The concept was an essential part (and, indeed, aim) of European diplomacy and warfare from at least the seventeenth century onwards.

administrative model. That was until he overreached himself in Russia and was defeated by the combined might of Britain and Prussia at the battle of Waterloo in 1815, in what is now Belgium.

Nationalism, in part inspired by the Napoleonic wars, spread throughout Europe. Hungary continually chafed at its Austrian domination; Bulgaria tried (with the help of Russia) to break free of the Ottoman empire; and Romania actually succeeded in winning its independence from not just the Ottoman but also the Russian empire. Nationalism was soon competing, however, with demands on the part of the public of many European countries for political participation commensurate with what liberals suggested were their rights and what they themselves argued was their economic contribution. Such demands grew stronger among workers to whom industrialization and urbanization now afforded the concentrated power to organize collectively to press their case. In continental Europe, a series of failed proto-socialist revolutions in the mid-nineteenth century in the end gave way to politically more successful (if socially less radical) efforts to achieve representation by democratic means. By the beginning of the twentieth century, universal (or near-universal) male suffrage had been adopted in many European countries. Nationalism, however, continued apace, and Europe entered the twentieth century with the hitherto fragmented Germany and Italy now unified nation states, bringing the number of states on the continent to around 25, compared to the 500 or more that had existed in 1500 (see Tilly, 1975). To a greater or lesser degree, all these turn-of-the-century states assumed an increasingly active role in their national economies, not least in order to raise the tax revenue that could be used to boost military strength, as well as to improve control over the increasingly industrialized population, be it through coercion through an expanded police apparatus or through education, much of which aimed at the reinforcement of national identity (see Tilly, 1993).

States into blocs

As Germany began to use its new-found unity to claim an overseas empire, Europe's always fragile balance of power began to harden into the military alliances that ended up driving the continent into the First World War. Germany's ambitions were opposed by its imperial rivals, France and Great Britain. They allied with Russia, a country whose association with Slavic national independence movements in Serbia set it on a collision course with Germany's ally, Austria-Hungary. Other countries were sucked into the war once it broke out in 1914: Italy, Japan and, eventually, the USA on the side of the self-styled 'Allies' (Britain, France and Russia); Bulgaria, and Turkey's Ottoman empire, on the side of Germany and Austria-Hungary. Only Scandinavia, Spain and Portugal, and Switzerland (which had pursued a policy of neutrality since it came together as a confederation in the early sixteenth century) escaped involvement. For most of the four years which followed, the combatants fought each other to a standstill at the cost of millions of human lives lost or blighted. But such a war of attrition eventually favoured the side with the greatest resources in terms of men and *materiel*. True, the Allies suffered a loss when, in 1917, Russia was seized by communist revolutionaries under Lenin, who saw the war as benefiting only the old ruling class and its capitalist allies and ended Russia's participation accordingly (Box 1.2). Nevertheless, in the autumn of 1918, Germany and Austria-Hungary were basically starved into signing an armistice.

KEY POINT

With the coming of industry (and industrialized warfare) the tendency of states to seek protective alliances combined with the ideological struggle between capitalism and socialism to produce the Cold War – a stand-off between blocs led by the USA and the USSR that split Europe between a Soviet-ruled east and a west that sought peace and prosperity through European integration.

After the World War, the map of Europe was literally redrawn. First, came the creation of the *Soviet Union* (or USSR), through which Russia extended its empire (Box 1.2). Second came the Treaties of Versailles and Trianon. The Austro-Hungarian and Ottoman empires were broken up and Turkey forced out of Europe. Hungary lost territory to the new countries created for Slavic peoples in the artificially

BOX 1.2

The Soviet Union and communism

The Union of Soviet Socialist Republics (USSR) was established in 1922 by the *Bolshevik regime* that came to power under its first leader, Lenin, during the Russian revolution of 1917. The Bolsheviks were communists, believing in a state supposedly run on behalf of the working class and with equality and social justice for all. It was dominated by Russia, but also came to include the republics to Russia's south, including Georgia and Ukraine, and the Baltic states of Latvia, Lithuania and Estonia (now EU members).

Under the leadership of Lenin's successor, Stalin, it undertook the industrialization of vast swathes of eastern Europe, as well as the collectivization of its agriculture – projects that delivered economic growth but at a terribly high price: tens of millions died, most from starvation but also as a result of forced labour and the political repression needed to maintain the dictatorial regime. Millions of people also lost their lives during the desperate fight against Germany in the Second World War. The postwar period, during which the nuclear-armed Soviet Union faced off but never actually fought against the capitalist West, offered some respite, though the communist regime remained essentially intact until the late 1980s. With its collapse came the collapse of the Soviet Union, and its population of nearly 300 million people found themselves living in either Russia (population 145 million) or what are sometimes referred to as the newly independent states (NIS).

constructed states of Czechoslovakia and Yugoslavia, the latter created not just at the behest of Slav nationalists, but also to provide Serbian protection to small countries such as Slovenia and Croatia against larger powers such as Italy (which despite territorial gains continued to believe it had been short-changed). Further north, Germany – now a republic – lost territory to France and Poland and was forced not only to admit guilt for the war but also to pay financial compensation ('reparations') to France. The resentment thus created was cleverly

Fascism and socialism

European fascism of the 1920s and 1930s was in many ways defined by its opposition to communism, and to socialism or social democracy, which believed in achieving public ownership and redistributionary policies and seemed destined to win over many working-class voters. Although fascism was also about the supremacy of the ethnically exclusive state over the interests and rights of individuals, the private sector was allowed to profit from its activities. Fascist leaders promised easy solutions to the worldwide economic depression of the 1930s – solutions based not just on totalitarian politics and increasingly racist, anti-Semitic policies, but also on the sort of military rearmament and an aggressive, expansionist foreign policy that socialists and social democrats (some of them pacifists as well as 'internationalists') abhorred.

exploited by nationalistic, fascist dictators, such as Hitler and Mussolini (see Box 1.3).

Other states, also coping with the economic depression, proved unable or unwilling to quash fascism's territorial ambitions, despite the existence of the 'League of Nations' (the forerunner of the postwar United Nations). Emboldened by its success in grabbing back Austria and much of Czechoslovakia, and determined to act before potential enemies such as Great Britain and France could fully prepare themselves, Germany signed a non-aggression pact with the Soviet Union. This pact basically delivered the Baltic republics of Estonia, Latvia and Lithuania to Russia, along with half of Poland. In September 1939, Germany invaded Poland to take its half, thereby provoking war with Britain, France and, in the end, also the Soviet Union. The USA, which was attacked by Germany's ally, Japan, at Pearl Harbor in 1941, joined the fight against the so-called 'Axis' powers (Germany, Japan and a not altogether enthusiastic Italy) in the same year.

It took the use of nuclear weapons to bring Japan to surrender in the summer of 1945. But the Second World War ended in Europe with the occupation of first Italy and then Germany in the spring of that year. However, if anyone thought that the continent's problems were solved, they were sadly mistaken. Although spared a re-run of the postwar influenza outbreak that had killed millions in the aftermath of the 1914–18 conflict, Europe was on its knees. Millions of Jews, as well as political opponents, Roma (gypsies) and other minorities, had been put to death or worked to death by the Nazis – a tragedy now known as the Holocaust. In addition, the physical destruction and economic misery wrought by six years of total war involving civilian populations as well as armed forces was calamitous.

Any chance that the victorious Allies would continue their cooperation in peacetime was quickly dashed. The Soviet Union was determined to maintain a military presence in the eastern part of the continent and used its occupation to facilitate the seizure of power by communist parties in Poland, Czechoslovakia, Hungary, Romania and Bulgaria. Only Austria and Finland were allowed to remain free, and over time Finland became fully integrated with a Scandinavia that included neutral Sweden as well as Denmark and Norway, occupied in the war by Germany. In the face of the developments in central Europe, the USA quickly reverted to the strongly anticommunist stance that it had pursued since the Russian revolution and had softened only during the war. It took steps to ensure that the Soviet 'sphere of influence' (the area where its dominance could not be challenged) would not expand to include the western part of Germany. That nation had been divided into two states: the liberal capitalist Federal Republic of Germany (FRG), which most outsiders called West Germany, and the communist German Democratic Republic (GDR), routinely labelled East Germany. By the same token, the USA put considerable effort (and cash) into ensuring that the home-grown (but Soviet-aided) communist parties did not take power, even by ostensibly democratic means, in Italy and Greece (which endured a short civil war) (Map 1.2).

The other side of this anti-communist, anti-Soviet 'containment' strategy included the establishment of NATO and the stationing of American military capability throughout Europe. This included bases in Spain, which, like Portugal, had succumbed to right-wing authoritarian dictatorship in the interwar period but had remained neutral between 1939 and 1945. Another important part of the

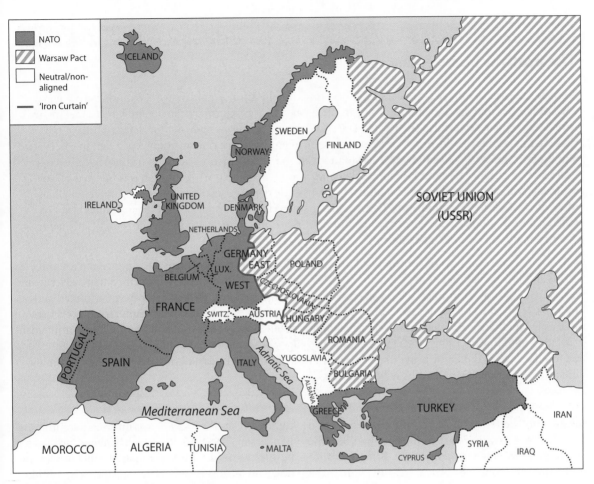

NATO

Warsaw Pact

Neutral/non-aligned

'Iron Curtain'

ICELAND

SWEDEN

NORWAY

FINLAND

IRELAND

UNITED KINGDOM

DENMARK

SOVIET UNION (USSR)

NETHERLANDS

GERMANY EAST

POLAND

BELGIUM

LUX.

WEST

CZECHOSLOVAKIA

FRANCE

SWITZ.

AUSTRIA

HUNGARY

PORTUGAL

SPAIN

ITALY

Adriatic Sea

YUGOSLAVIA

ROMANIA

ALBANIA

BULGARIA

Mediterranean Sea

GREECE

TURKEY

IRAN

MOROCCO

ALGERIA

TUNISIA

MALTA

CYPRUS

SYRIA

IRAQ

Map 1.2 Europe during the Cold War

strategy was economic, with the US 'Marshall Plan' (named after the former general who initiated it) providing much-needed aid to most countries in its sphere of influence. European democracies spent it not just on American goods, but also on redeveloping their industrial base, on establishing welfare states and, in time, participating in the consumer booms of the 1950s and 1960s.

US efforts to secure a peaceful western Europe as a bulwark against communist expansion and as a prosperous trading partner also led it to support moves among some European governments to create a mechanism for increasing interstate cooperation that would lock in their economic interdependence and, along with unity in the face of the Soviet Union, make war between western European powers a thing of the past. These moves began in 1952 with the European Coal and Steel Community (ECSC) and eventuated in the founding of the European Economic Community (EEC) by the Treaty of Rome in 1957. Having played a massive part in helping to preserve peace and, for the most part, prosperity, it has since relabelled itself the European Union, commonly known as the EU. In 2004 and 2007, it expanded to take in a total of 27 members, including former dictatorships in southern and central and eastern Europe that are now functioning market democracies (see Map 2.4).

Notwithstanding the EU's importance, it was by no means the only thing that helped western Europe become such a secure and prosperous place. Other factors helped, too. A generation of politicians was determined not just to avoid the mistakes of the interwar period but also to prove that liberal capi-

---

BOX 1.4

The postwar boom – east and west

To many in western Europe, the years 1950–73 represented a kind of 'golden age'. Economic growth averaged over 4 per cent a year, with catch-up countries such as West Germany, Spain and Greece making up for relatively poor performers such as the UK and Belgium (see www.ggdc.net for details). Inflation was present, but rarely rose above 3–4 per cent. Europe's unemployment rate was only 3 per cent in the 1950s and dropped below 2 per cent in the 1960s. European countries began to catch up technologically. Energy was also very cheap. Moreover, consumer demand, already pent-up during the war, was boosted by governments willing to spend to avoid a return to 1930s-style depression and to meet the military challenge of Soviet and Chinese communism. The American-supervised system of stable exchange rates also provided liquidity within a secure institutional framework for international trade, while the EEC helped to facilitate trade between member states.

Interestingly, the economy of communist Europe actually grew even more rapidly (7 per cent p.a.) in the 1950s and 1960s than that of the capitalist west. As the Soviet bloc countries transformed themselves from largely agricultural economies to basically modern, industrial nations, national income quadrupled and industrial output in 1970 was seven times that of 1950! An overemphasis on heavy industry, however, as well as the inefficiencies inherent in central planning, meant a poor environmental outlook, a continued curtailment of human rights, and only a very poor range and quality of consumer goods. However, eastern Europeans did enjoy heavily subsidized housing, essential foods and other goods. And unemployment was 'abolished', or at least heavily disguised.

talism was better than communism. They also presided over a withdrawal from what had become costly overseas entanglements, with Britain, France and smaller countries such as Belgium, the Netherlands and Portugal letting go of the bulk of their colonial empires (see Chapter 10). The American-led postwar boom (Box 1.4), and the fact that consumers were kept spending both by vastly expanded leisure and mass media markets and the extension of the welfare state, meant that, compared to the prewar period, even the bad times were good. Nor, as Box 1.4 also shows, were they as bad as we might think (at least when it came to the essentials) in what became known as the 'Soviet Bloc'.

CEE countries, in fact, were transformed during the postwar period from agricultural backwaters into modern industrial economies in which income inequalities were narrow and access to health, welfare and education was impressively wide. For all this, however, it remains true that instead of 'burying' capitalism, as one Soviet leader had famously promised, communism proved incapable of matching either the technological progress, the prosperity or the freedom enjoyed by those living under liberal

capitalism in 'the West' – an 'imagined community' (Anderson, 1991: 5–7) which seemed to stretch beyond western Europe through North America and down to Australia and New Zealand. The problem was there seemed to be nothing that those who lived in eastern and central Europe could do about it. Any time they came close to trying to liberalize their regimes, reformists were crushed by Soviet tanks.

The new Europe

Yet at the same time as it looked as if things would never change in Europe, something had to give. The Soviet Union found itself financially unable both to deliver its population a basic standard of living and to compete with the Americans militarily – particularly if it meant holding on as firmly as ever to its satellites in eastern Europe. This analysis persuaded Mikhail Gorbachev, who took over the leadership of the Soviet Communist Party in 1985, to signal to those countries that they could pursue their own course without fearing military action on his part. Gorbachev clearly hoped that this would mean merely a reform of the existing system, in whose basic principles he still believed. But it rapidly became clear that his famous policies of *glasnost* (openness) and *perestroika* (restructuring) gave the CEE populations the green light to overthrow communist dictatorships in favour of democracy and market-based economies.

The year 1989 saw revolutions all over eastern Europe, symbolized for many by the fall of the Berlin Wall that had for so long and so cruelly kept apart those living in the capitalist and communist halves of the city. Most of these revolutions, barring the one in Romania and the events which followed the break-up of Yugoslavia (see Chapter 2), were, mercifully, peaceful. Yugoslavia aside, border changes in what was now post-Cold War Europe were limited to the surprisingly swift reunification of Germany in 1990, and the slightly more drawn out and not entirely amicable 'velvet divorce' of the Czech and Slovak republics. The biggest changes on the map actually occurred in the former Soviet Union, which itself dissolved in 1991, after a failed coup by communist hardliners. What became the Russian Federation, under Boris Yeltsin, initially tried to hold on to its regional hegemony by getting even large former Soviet republics like Georgia and Ukraine to join the so-called 'Commonwealth of Independent States' (CIS), although it soon became clear that the CIS would not allow it to exert anything like the control Russia had in the Soviet era (see Malgin, 2002 and Olcott, *et al.*, 2000). Moreover, Russia failed to exert any control whatsoever over the former Soviet republics of Estonia, Latvia and Lithuania, all of which joined the EU and NATO in 2004 (see Map 2.4).

KEY POINT

With the collapse of the Soviet Union, CEE countries were free to determine their own destiny and overwhelmingly plumped for liberal capitalism. Many of them also joined what has become the European Union (EU).

To those so-called 'Baltic states', and to the other CEE postcommunist countries that joined the EU (and NATO) alongside them, accession was a symbolic 'coming home'. As we have seen, for centuries up until the end of the Second World War they were intimately connected to those countries which, as the Cold War wore on, sometimes forgot that they were part of the same continent. Now that they have assumed their rightful place, Europe has in effect reassumed the shape it had for hundreds, even thousands, of years. And it has done so in a manner that seems likely to forestall the kind of intra-European (and indeed intercontinental) warfare that characterized so much of its history, but also helped make it what it is today. It is to the task of describing this current reality – economic, demographic and social – that we now turn.

Europe's economy – rich in variation

Europe is the home of most of the world's great trading nations. As the industrial revolution that began in the UK in the late eighteenth century gained momentum all over Europe, these nations imported raw materials from the rest of the world in order to manufacture finished goods for export, as well as for the burgeoning home market. Yet Europe is by no means devoid of natural resources of its own. Norway, Finland and Sweden all have large forests. France and Sweden were traditional sources of iron ore. Coal could be found in quantity in Britain, Germany, Poland and even Spain. The North Sea between the UK and Scandinavia contains oil and natural gas fields. Europe has also been more than self-sufficient in most agricultural products for many decades. Although mixed farming predominates, the further north one goes, the more meat and dairy feature; the further south, the more citrus, olives and grapes one finds; the further east, the more cereal and other arable crops there are.

The differing extent to which Europe's states are blessed with access to this or that natural resource,

KEY POINT

European economies vary according to size, resources and history: size isn't everything but the richest countries tend to be bigger, to have industrialized relatively earlier and to have escaped communism. Although most European countries are richer than they have ever been, unemployment has returned to haunt them.

however, combines with differing access to international trade routes and areas of expertise and comparative advantage, to make for a great deal of economic variation between their economies. Size matters, too. A quick glance at Figure 1.1 shows us that Germany's gross domestic product (GDP) dwarfs not only that of the neighbouring Czech Republic (as one would expect) but is also nearly twice the size of Spain's. To some extent, a country's wealth is a function of its population: Germany's population is currently twice that of Spain. But size isn't everything, as we can see if we control for population size by looking at wealth per person – or, to use the jargon, *per capita* (Figure 1.2). By dividing wealth by population, we can see that people in some countries are considerably better off than others, even if we take into account the cost of living.

At one end of the scale are the postcommunist countries whose *per capita* wealth means that, while they are clearly much richer than those living in

Figure 1.1 GDP ($US billion), 2010 (adjusted for PPP)

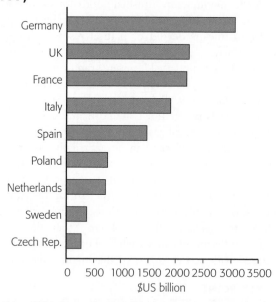

Note: GDP is the overall market value of goods and services produced in a country during the year. It comprises the country's consumer, investment and government spending, along with the value of everything the country exports, minus the value of what it imports. It is the generally accepted measure of a country's economic worth. All figures use purchasing power parity (PPP), which takes into account what money can buy in each country in order to make a more meaningful comparison.

Source: Data from *OECD Factbook 2011*.

Figure 1.2 GDP (adjusted for PPP) *per capita* ($US), 2010 – Europe's range and its competitors

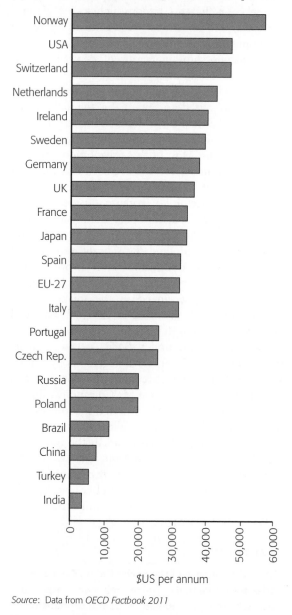

$US per annum

Source: Data from *OECD Factbook 2011*

developing or 'Third World' nations (or for that matter an EU candidate country like Turkey), they do not enjoy anything like the living standards of many of their fellow Europeans. Certainly the gap, between the richest and the poorest European states is considerably greater than is the gap between, say, the richest and the poorest states of the USA: Mississippi's *per capita* income is around half of Connecticut's, but Poland's is less than a third of, say, Norway's (which incidentally is greater than that of the USA). For the most part, this relative poverty is a characteristic of former communist countries, particularly Bulgaria and Romania which, due in part to their comparative backwardness, did not join the EU until 2007. However, there are also differences between traditionally 'western' countries, with Portugal lagging some way behind the other pre-accession EU members (the so-called EU-15) and now 'overtaken' by a postcommunist country, the Czech Republic. Note also that Turkey, now a candidate to join the EU, lags some way behind current member states.

Behind the figures, however, lie all sorts of other measures of how well or badly a country is doing, many of which impact more directly on the public, who will be only dimly aware of things like GDP. The most obvious of these are *inflation* (a measure of rising prices, normally expressed as an annual percentage) and of course *unemployment* (Figure 1.3). During most of the postwar period, European (and American and Australasian) governments operated on the assumption (labelled 'Keynesian' after British economist John Maynard Keynes) that there was a trade-off between the two. In other words, if economic demand outstripped supply, then there would probably be plenty of jobs around (so-called 'full employment') but inflation would rise; if, however, government acted to reduce demand (by, say, reducing its own spending or that of consumers and business by raising taxes or the interest rates which banks charged people for borrowing money) then inflation would fall but unemployment would rise. But, in the late 1960s-early 1970s, many advanced industrial economies began to suffer 'stagflation' – high inflation (i.e. rising prices) *and* higher unemployment.

From the late 1960s onwards, a number of influential 'neoliberal' or 'monetarist' economists persuaded many governments that trying to boost demand to tackle unemployment was making the situation worse. Their answer was to stop allowing trade unions to use full employment to bid up wages, to stop subsidizing loss-making industries and generally to leave things like monetary policy (i.e. interest rates) to the free market. As governments moved towards these policies, there was what was euphemistically called a 'shake-out' of inefficient

Figure 1.3 Average annual unemployment rates, 2007–2010

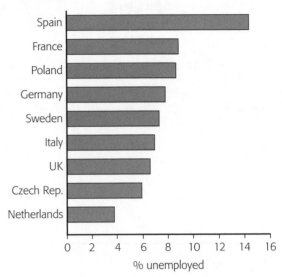

Source: Data from Eurostat, *EU Economic Data Pocketbook*, 4-2010.

manufacturing firms (especially those involved in or connected to 'heavy industries' such as steel, shipbuilding, mining, etc.). This accelerated the end of the postwar boom and heralded the return of the kind of mass unemployment that postwar generations had assumed was a thing of the past. This unemployment is 'structural' as much as 'cyclical' (i.e. it will not completely disappear in times of economic growth) and, because different European countries have different economies, labour markets and policies to regulate and improve them, it also varies considerably between them notwithstanding the economic downturn which has affected the continent as a whole (see Figure 1.3). GDP figures, then, do not tell the whole story.

Regions

Just as importantly, there are big regional variations between different parts of the same country (see Box 1.5). Germany, for instance, contains some of the richest regions of Europe; but, having absorbed the formerly communist East Germany (GDR) in 1990, it also contains some of the poorest. It is by no means alone in this, for these national and regional variations are inherent in the very different ways in

Table 1.1 Towards the postindustrial economy in Europe?

	Agriculture, forestry mining and fishing			Manufacturing and Construction			Services		
	1970	1991	2008	1970	1991	2008	1970	1991	2008
UK	3	2	2	42	25	18	55	73	81
Netherlands	6	4	3	36	24	17	58	72	80
France	15	6	3	37	26	20	48	69	77
Sweden	8	4	2	39	28	23	53	68	75
Germany	8	3	2	48	35	25	44	62	73
Spain	25	10	4	37	31	27	48	69	69
Italy	16	8	4	42	29	28	42	63	68
Czech Rep.	14	10	4	49	46	38	37	44	59
Poland	n/a	25	14	n/a	32	31	n/a	44	55

Source: Data from *OECD Factbook* 2007.

which the economies of European states are structured. Traditionally, wealth and development were associated with industrialization, which, after the Second World War, was concentrated in Southern Scandinavia (Gothenburg, Malmo and Copenhagen), England, eastern France, northern Italy, Belgium and the Netherlands, Germany, the Czech and Slovak Republics and Poland. In the latter half of the twentieth century, however, this relationship began to break down as wealth became more closely connected with services.

KEY POINT

There are big disparities within nations as well as between them.

'Postindustrialism'?

Most European states, such as the UK and other advanced countries, can be labelled 'postindustrial' because the service sector has overtaken the manufacturing sector as the biggest employer in the economy, with agriculture shrinking still further (Table 1.1): in the EU as whole around 6 per cent of people are employed in agriculture, forestry, mining and fishing, 25 per cent in manufacturing and construction, and 69 per cent in 'services.' This is not,

however, to deny that the labels may be a little misleading in view of the fact that many so-called 'service jobs' are no less routinized, low-status, low-skilled and low-paid than the production-line jobs traditionally associated with industrialization (see Wilensky, 2002: 186–90). Nor should we forget that some European nations still have large farming sectors. Greece and Portugal in the west and Romania and Poland in the east are examples. This is why agriculture, which still takes up almost half the EU's total spending (see Chapter 2), has always been an issue when it comes to expanding the EU. Although there are exceptions, a large agricultural (or primary goods) sector tends to be associated with poorer states, a large service sector tends to be associated with wealthier states.

KEY POINT

The relationship between industrialization and wealth no longer holds – Europe's future lies in the service economy.

In the decades following the Second World War, there was also a strong association in Europe between wealth and industrial development. With the rise of the service sector in most advanced economies, however, this relationship began to break

BOX 1.5

Poverty amid plenty – Europe's huge regional variations in wealth

There are regional disparities in many European countries. Some of the most glaring gaps, not surprisingly, occur in the richest states. For example, in 2008 (the latest year for which we have reliable figures from Eurostat) residents of London (the richest region in the UK) had a GDP per capita of two-and-a-half times that of the poorest part of Wales. The same was true if one compared those living in Hamburg in Germany with those living in North East Brandenburg (which was part of communist East Germany before the fall of the Berlin Wall) and those living in Prague with the poorest region in the Czech Republic. Spain, and especially Italy, also have big regional imbalances, characterized by a north–south divide. In 2008, residents of rich regions like Madrid, the Basque Country and Catalunya (the latter two being parts of the country where there are demands of independence from Spain) were one-and-a-half times better off than those who live in Andalucia. In Italy, people living in Calabria (the southernmost point of the Italian peninsula) were doing only half as well as those living in the rich north of the country, with those in its German-speaking regions being the best off of anyone. Of course, those figures are only averages: there are plenty of poor people, for instance, in London and some rich people living in southern Spain. And in Germany, there is also a good deal of resentment in the run-down parts of supposedly wealthier western *länder* that some of the taxes they pay go to provide their eastern counterparts with the sort of development aid and infrastructure that they could only dream of.

down. Nowadays, with the exception of Germany, which still benefits from its traditionally high-quality industrial base, Europe's wealthiest countries are those in which services – be they predominantly private (and profit-generating) or public (and welfare-creating) – are strongest.

Transition

One factor, then, in the disparity between western Europe, where two-thirds now work in services, and CEE, where fewer of the workforce are similarly employed, is the fact that much of the latter has yet to move into the postindustrial age. At a regional level in the west, it is those parts of a country historically associated with primary production, mining and/or heavy industries such as steel-making or shipbuilding which, after the agricultural regions, are least prosperous. This means that CEE states, where these sectors were key to communist postwar modernization right up until the late 1980s, are at a big disadvantage. That industrialization – and the lack of attention paid to its environmental consequences – also explains why the region's relatively backward economies are no less polluting than their

more developed western counterparts (see Figure 1.4). It is worth noting, too, that countries with a green reputation (for example, Sweden) do not necessarily use less oil than others that have no such reputation (see Figure 1.5). Moreover, simply because one country pumps less carbon dioxide into the atmosphere than another, it doesn't mean it is any less polluted: indices like population-weighted concentration of particulate matter (the environmental pollutant most hazardous to health) are considerably higher, for instance, in Spain, Poland and Italy than they are in Germany and the UK.

KEY POINT

Europe's postcommunist countries have made huge – if not always unfaltering or even – strides towards catching up with their western counterparts economically, although it will still be a long haul.

The economic backwardness associated with communism is not a disadvantage that can be overcome overnight. It will take decades – at least. Nevertheless, the so-called 'transition' economies of postcommunist Europe have made considerable

Figure 1.4 CO$_2$ emissions *per capita*, 2008

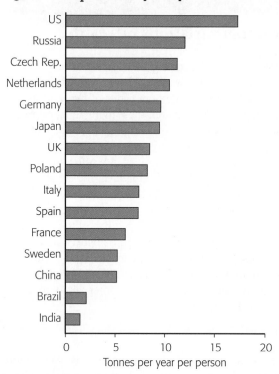

Tonnes per year per person

Source: Data from *UN Development Report*, 2011,
http://hdr.undp.org/en/statistics/.

progress. That progress has not, of course, been even. Some countries were already closer to the West to begin with. And, although most decided early on that capitalism, and the privatization of the massive state sector, was where they wanted to go, there has been considerable variation in the route chosen to get there. Hungary, for instance, which actually had already begun market-style reforms under its communist regime, pursued a fairly cautious strategy. Poland, and to a lesser extent the Czech Republic, chose to move more quickly: both devalued their currencies to a realistic level, removed price subsidies and tolerated a degree of unemployment and (what they hoped would be) short-term contraction in order to achieve manageable inflation and respectable growth in the long term.

Privatization proceeded in different ways and at a varying pace (see, for example, Hopkins, 1998; and Klich, 1998; see also Chapter 10). Generally speaking, however, with the exception of Romania

and Bulgaria, most CEE countries largely managed to avoid the overnight creation of a semi-criminal oligarchy that occurred in Russia. Still, the process was not without its problems (see Iatridis and Hopps, 1998). Governments did little to dampen expectations early on and, especially in Poland, they suffered a backlash as the public caught on to the fact that privatization would make very few people wealthy and a lot of people unemployed. They were also so keen to get rid of state assets that they not only failed to realize their true value, but, in selling off rather than breaking up dominant firms, they also failed to create truly competitive markets. There were undoubtedly cases where entrepreneurs obtained profitable parts of state-owned enterprises (SOEs) with large market share at knock-down, never-to-be-repeated prices. And legitimate criticisms can be made of the extent to which the 'creative destruction' of some of communism's industrial inheritance was really that creative, even (and perhaps especially) in East Germany.

Generally, however, to have transferred so much in so short a time without causing utterly unbridled corruption, mass poverty or disruption to the supply of goods and services has to be seen as a major achievement. Given that speed and the creation of a viable market economy were by far the most important priorities of early postcommunist governments (much more so than preserving a relatively equitable distribution of wealth, for instance), then privatization in the region has to be judged a success on its own terms. In the Czech Republic, Poland and Hungary, by far the bulk of the economy is now in private hands. Because there is a lot of catching-up to do (and a relatively large amount of foreign direct investment (FDI) coming in) growth is, or is likely to be, slightly higher than in the former West. Inflation is similarly low. Unemployment, however, remains a persistent problem, especially in Poland, Slovakia and (to a lesser extent) the Baltic states (Latvia, Lithuania and Estonia). Meanwhile, Slovenia, formerly part of Yugoslavia – always rather closer to the West than countries in the Soviet bloc – boasts one of the best-performing economies of all the postcommunist states and, although it was later joined by Malta, Cyprus, Slovakia and Estonia, it was the first of those 'accession states' to join the 'Eurozone' – the group of EU members with the euro as their single

Figure 1.5 Per capita oil consumption, 2009

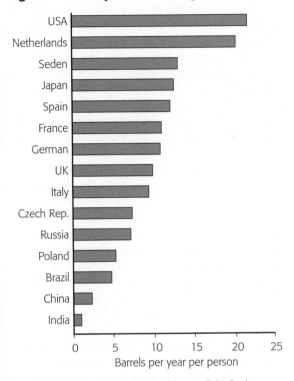

Source: Data from nationmaster.com and UN Population fund.

currency. The proverbial wooden spoon goes to Bulgaria and Romania, where liberal reform has been slow and continues to stutter.

Globalization and/or Europeanization?

The economic picture in Europe, then, is complex, and even in some cases quite negative, at least in the short term. Some accounts make it seem even bleaker by suggesting that jobs in manufacturing and even services are leaking away to developing countries, leaving Europe destined to be 'overtaken' by growth economies such as China and other east and south Asian economies. According to this view, Europe's corporates will, like their American counterparts, benefit from globalization, but its population will end up as victims. In fact, there is as little evidence to support this pessimistic view, however fashionable, as there is to support some of the more

ambitious versions of globalization itself. Both of them buy too heavily into the idea that things are fast changing beyond recognition and that space, time, existing patterns and cultural inertia may not matter much any more. Arguably, however, they do. Even if we ignore the obvious argument that a great deal of European countries' economic activity is (as it is in the USA) domestic, and concentrate on the international sector, it is (a) not clear that European countries are doing badly; and (b) obvious that all of them spend more and more time and more and more money with each other than with anyone else.

KEY POINT

Globalization does not spell doom for European economies, although some are adjusting better than others.

Take, for instance, the argument that industry, and therefore jobs, will abandon Europe in favour of the 'Tiger' economies of South East Asia. Statistics do show that, like the USA, some European nations (often traditional trading nations such as the UK and the Netherlands) seem to be running large deficits in manufacturing trade with newly industrializing countries (NICs) such as Korea and Taiwan. But they also show that others, notably Italy and Sweden, export far more goods (at least in terms of value) to those countries than they import from them. And, bluntly, none of this may matter if a country's 'comparative advantage' is in services rather than in manufacturing (as is undoubtedly the case with the UK). Moreover, despite the common fallacy, there is no finite number of jobs out there in the world that means if one country loses them, it cannot grow them again: a high- or low-tech plant in Shanghai or yet another call-centre in Mumbai does not spell the end of the road for Europe. In any case, rising trade with the rest of the world – which, if it were done fairly, should help all concerned – is not half so important for many as the steady rise in the extent to which European countries trade with each other. Interestingly, the EU seems to be less important as a destination for exports for those countries that are traditionally more wary about European integration like Sweden and the UK, although the position of Italy (traditionally very 'pro-Europe' but a worldwide exporter) and the

Table 1.2 The growth and current importance of intra-European trade

| | Percentage growth in trade (1960–2000) | | Intra-EU exports as a percentage of total exports |
	Rest of World	Intra-EU	
Czech Rep.	n/a	n/a	84
Poland	n/a	n/a	79
Netherlands	862	1485	77
Spain	1909	2591	68
EU	734	1221	65
France	743	1666	61
Germany	755	902	60
Sweden	1043	711	57
Italy	1166	1720	57
UK	342	1000	54

Sources: Data from Badinger and Breuss (2003); Eurostat , *External and Intra EU Trade*, (2011).

Czech Republic (very dependent on Europe but also relatively 'Eurosceptic') should make us wary of drawing too many easy conclusions from this (Table 1.2). The myriad connections this trade is built on are long-standing (centuries old, indeed) and increasingly institutionalized by EU membership and cooperation. At the very least, then, 'Europeanization is sufficiently deeply embedded to act as a filter for globalization' (Wallace, 2000: 381).

National and patterned variation

But just because European countries trade with each other and are all moving towards postindustrial economies, albeit at varying rates, we should not take Europeanization to mean some kind of uniformity. History matters in economics as much as it does in politics and policy. Obviously, there are some basic similarities. Notwithstanding some of the postcommunist outliers, European countries have relatively advanced and – compared with, say, the USA – relatively 'mixed' economies. Within a largely capitalist framework that sees most goods and services produced by the private sector, there is public sector involvement in areas such as defence and law and order, education and welfare provision and, not uncommonly, in the ownership of utilities and other industries. Even where state involvement is relatively low, it is probably crucial to the continued health of a nation's economy. The state, whether local or national, is a big customer for many private firms. Moreover, by maintaining transport and networks, and building and staffing schools and hospitals, it helps supply the infrastructure and the human resources those firms need. Its welfare payments help to ensure that as many consumers as possible have money to buy the goods and services produced by the private sector. Its stewardship of the economy, via tax and spending decisions and the legal and regulatory framework it maintains, contribute to the creation of an environment in which, hopefully, business will thrive.

KEY POINT

Europe's economies and its welfare states can be more or less neatly divided up according to the extent to which government plays an active role and the extent to which welfare is intended as living expression of egalitarian solidarity or a form of social insurance or merely a safety net.

But the distinctions between Europe's mixed economies are arguably every bit as important as the similarities. This need not mean we give up the search for some kind of patterned variation, however. Hall and Soskice (2001), for instance, put together a stimulating case, which others continue to argue about and build on (see Hanké, 2011) that (west) European countries' economies can be characterized as 'liberal' (UK, Ireland) or 'coordinated' (Germany, Scandinavia and Benelux) or hybrids where the state is still quite a prominent actor (France, Greece, Italy, Portugal and Spain). Analysts also routinely draw distinctions between Europe's welfare state regimes, with the 'three worlds' typology pioneered by Gøsta Esping-Andersen (1990) the most popular – if no longer undisputed (see Scruggs and Allan, 2006a) – choice (see Box 1.6).

It is still too soon to place Europe's postcommunist countries precisely and firmly into such schemas. But

Figure 1.6 Social spending levels per capita, 2007

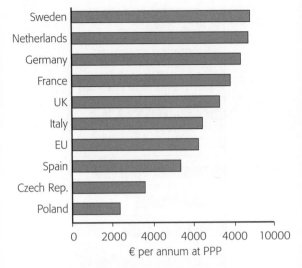

Source: Data from Mau and Verwiebe, 2010: 57.

Europe's various welfare state regimes

Stressing variations in the extent to which political and trade union representatives of ordinary working people were able to wring concessions from states that were essentially pro-capitalist, Swedish expert, Gøsta Esping-Andersen (1990) posited the existence of the following three 'worlds of welfare':

▸ *Social-democratic*: Extensive high-quality services, open to all irrespective of income; generous (and income-related) transfer payments to those out of or unable or too old to work; strong public support; exemplified by Scandinavian countries such as Sweden.

▸ *Liberal*, Anglo-Saxon: Basic services, many available only via means-testing; limited transfer payments; safety net for the poor so middle-class use and support is limited; both the UK and Ireland are examples, but (compared to, say, the USA) only imperfect ones because they have been influenced by the other traditions.

▸ *Conservative*, corporatist: Insurance-based welfare schemes, many of which are administered by unions and employers; strong bias towards support for traditional family structures; Austria, Germany, the Netherlands and the other Benelux countries fit neatly into this category, though France and Italy (and rather less easily Spain, Portugal and Greece) can also be included.

the early signs are there. When it comes to which type of capitalism predominates, for instance, we are beginning to see a pattern emerge – one best summed up in the work of Bohle and Greskovits (2012) which identifies three basic variants of capitalism in the region: neoliberal, embedded neoliberal, and neocorporatist. The first, which has taken hold in the Baltic states, is characterized by fewer controls on capital, more open markets, and less state provision for social welfare. The second is also export-focused but there is more state intervention and a bigger welfare safety net (Poland, Hungary, and the Czech and Slovak republics). Slovenia is the outlier, blending competitive industries and social inclusion. Other analysts, it should be said, would question the degree to which even the supposedly neoliberal states are in reality such champions of the free market as they might have been. They point out, for instance, that vested interests in western Europe exploited the desire of postcommunist countries to join the EU to foist the kind of rules and regulations on them that would ensure that they didn't become utterly cut-throat competitors (Jacoby, 2010). This did not altogether prevent a drift of manufacturing to the east – a development that has seen Slovakia (to take just one example) become a continental centre for car production.

When it comes to welfare specifically, many postcommunist states took their initial inspiration from the USA, via the recommendations of the International Monetary Fund (IMF) and the World Bank (see Ferge, 2001), and (see Figure 1.6) they remain less generous in terms of per capita social spending (defined here as spending to meet the costs of adverse circumstances affecting individuals and/or households) than their west European counterparts. However, many of them (notably the Czech

Republic) have moved towards systems that pick and mix elements of both the social democratic and the 'corporatist' or 'conservative' model' (see Cerami, 2010; Cook, 2007, 2010; Deacon, 2000, Fenger, 2007, Fuchs and Offe, 2008, Keune, 2006; see also Chapter 9). The findings of the most recent review (see Aidukaite, 2011) of postcommunist countries' welfare states stresses their variability but notes some common characteristics, namely 'insurance-based programs that played a major part in the social protection system; high take-up of social security; relatively low social security benefits; increasing signs of liberalization of social policy; and the experience of the Soviet/communist type of welfare state, which implies still deeply embedded signs of solidarity and universalism.' As for their effects, it notes that 'despite some slight variation… the new EU countries exhibit lower indicators compared to the EU-15 [when] it comes to the minimum wage and social protection expenditure… However, when it comes to at-risk-of-poverty rate after social transfers or inequality, some eastern European outliers especially the Czech Republic, but also Slovenia, Slovakia and Hungary perform the same or even better than the old capitalist democracies.' Countries like Latvia, Lithuania, Estonia, Romania, Bulgaria, Poland, have a great deal in common, including the fact that they do not perform anywhere near as well on these indicators.

The fact that some of Europe's postcommunist states are tending toward at least some aspects of Esping-Andersen's conservative or corporate welfare regimes, relying as they do on social insurance rather than tax-funded welfare, might not be a good thing for their populations, especially those who are unemployed. In west European countries whose welfare states rely on social insurance paid by employers and, to a lesser extent, employees (such as France, Germany, Italy and Spain), employers are reluctant to take on new (and that often means young) workers when the costs to them are so high. This is especially the case if what they see as 'red-tape' (but others see as worker protection) makes them difficult to offload if things do not work out – one reason (though not the only one) why Germany, which undertook significant reforms at the turn of the century, seems to have ridden the global economic downturn far better than Spain, which failed to reform during the good times and by 2012 had close to half of all 18–25-year-olds out of work. At

Figure 1.7 Social expenditure as a proportion of GDP, 1995 and 2007

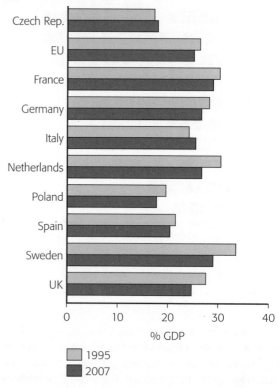

Source: Data from Mau and Verwiebe, 2010: 57 (For Poland and EU, 1995 figure is for 2000).

the same time, the relative generosity shown by both countries (and Spain and France) to pensioners places a much greater burden on those in work than is the case in other countries. These 'residual Anglo-Saxon' welfare states, such as the UK or egalitarian 'Scandinavian' welfare states such as Sweden, are not only a little less generous to pensioners but load more of the burden of taxation on to the individual (via income tax) and their consumption, since they regard insurance-based levies as 'a tax on jobs' which hurts those looking for one.

If Europe's new democracies do adopt this insurance aspect of the conservative or corporatist (some use the term 'Bismarckian' after the founder of the system in Germany) welfare regime, it might mean that once the comparative advantage they enjoy over western economies in terms of cheap labour wears off they, too, run into some of the same problems. On the other hand, because that advantage is likely

BOX 1.7

Births, deaths – and a lot more in between

Europe – both west and east (see Chawla *et al.*, 2007) – has probably reached its peak as far as population is concerned. This is primarily because, after a postwar boom, its birth rate has declined markedly below the 2.2 replacement rate required to keep numbers stable. In Poland, Spain, the Netherlands and Germany', for instance, women in 2008 were on average having one or even two babies less than they would have done in 1960. In 1950, 548 million people lived in Europe and this increased to 740 million by 2011. But by 2050, Europe's population is projected to decline, although (contrary to earlier projections that suggested a decline to under 600 million) it should stay above 700 million. In some countries, despite their rising fertility rates slowing after 2008, the population is expected to rise (the UK, for example, is projected to grow from 63 million to 76 million by 2050), while in others it will fall (Germany, for instance, is projected to shrink from 82 million to 69 million over the same period). On the other hand, life expectancy is expected to increase everywhere. Life expectancy at birth in Europe currently stands at just under 75 years of age. By 2050 it is likely to be around 80.

Putting these two things together leads to the obvious conclusion that Europe has an 'ageing population'. Take the median age – the age you would pick in order to divide a country's population into two equal halves. In 1950, this would have been 29.2, in 2000 it would have been 37.7 and in 2050 it is expected to be 49.5! In fact, Japan aside, it is in Europe where population ageing is at its most advanced. The proportion of children in Europe, for instance, is projected to decline slightly to around 15 per cent in 2050, while it is estimated that the proportion of older people (those over 60) will almost double by 2050. By then, there will be two-and-a-half older people for every child and more than one in every three people will be aged 60 years or over. Obviously, owing to improved healthcare etc., those in their sixties by the middle of the century will seem, comparatively speaking, less 'elderly' than they do nowadays. But there will also be many more people in their eighties, and therefore highly dependent: on current projections, Germany and Italy are going to have real problems, as will some central and eastern European countries (and Poland in particular), whereas countries which have seen more immigration and whose birth-rates (only partly as a consequence) have held up better (for instance France, Sweden and the UK) may find things slightly easier see Table 1.3)

Sources: Data from UN Population Division, Eurostat, and Crouch (1999).

to last for at least a decade or more, they have plenty of time to adjust, and adjustment clearly is possible. Given a certain amount of political will (and perhaps a perceived 'fiscal crisis'), European states can and have moved from one category to the other or at least turned themselves into hybrids. The restructuring of social security in the Netherlands, which in the 1980s seemed to be trending to the 'welfare without work' model, shows that, even faced with public opposition (over one million joined street protests in 1991), politicians are capable of turning things around (Green-Pedersen, 2001; and see van Kersbergen *et al.*, 2000). Whether they have turned them round enough – and whether the so-called 'Dutch model' is really one to be followed – is another matter (see Keman, 2003).

Debates about *how* European countries should best finance their welfare states should not, however, obscure the main point that they do still finance them. There is a lot of hype surrounding 'the end of the European welfare state', but, as we show in more detail in Chapter 9, it is not well supported by the facts: the era of 'tax and spend' is by no means over. Just prior to the recent financial crisis, for example, they were not spending much less than a decade or so previously (see Figure 1.7 and Crouch, 1999: 368–74), with any decline due (at least in part) to a booming economy and with only slight (though not altogether

Table 1.3 **The coming squeeze: Europe's aging population, 1960–2060**

	1960		2010		2060 (projected)	
	% over 80	Dependency Ratio	% over 80	Dependency Ratio	% over 80	Dependency Ratio
Poland	0.7	9.5	3.3	19	12.3	64.6
Germany	1.6	17	5.1	31.4	13.5	59
Italy	1.3	14	5.8	30.8	14.1	56.7
Spain	1.2	12.7	4.9	24.7	14.2	56.4
Czech Rep.	1.3	14.6	3.6	21.6	12.2	55
Europe	1.4	15	4.1	23.6	11.5	52.4
Netherlands	1.4	14.6	3.9	22.8	11.1	47.5
France	2	18.7	5.2	25.6	11	46.6
Sweden	1.8	17.8	5.3	27.7	9.9	46.2
UK	1.9	18	4.6	24.9	9.3	42.1

Notes: Europe consists of the EU plus Norway, Switzerland and Iceland. The dependency ratio is a standard measure which divides the population over 65 by the population aged 15–64: the higher the figure the fewer people of working age there are to support those in retirement.

Source: Data from Lanzieri, 2011.

insignificant) variations in what each country spends its money on. For instance, France and Germany spend (per capita) a little more than most on health, but Sweden spends (per capita) more than other countries on education; postcommunist countries do not spend significantly more or less (at least per capita) than the rest; all spend a good deal on the elderly – and will continue to do so (see Box 1.7).

Whatever happened to 'the classless society'?

In both the former West and East, however, there are systematic differences in the distribution of employment, income and wealth. This, many analysts would suggest, is because European societies remain (or in the case of postcommunist countries are becoming) 'class societies'. There is plenty of room for argument about the precise make-up of these classes. Sociologists disagree and different countries employ different means of categorization, and it may be true that the traditional categories are becoming somewhat blurred (see Crouch, 1999: Chapter 5). There is also considerable dispute, as we shall see in Chapter 6,

about the precise and changing impact of class on political behaviour. However, it is difficult to refute the general proposition that the circumstances into which a child is born and the work an adult finds him or herself doing (or, in the case of the unemployed, not doing) strongly influence his or her income, lifestyle and life-chances.

KEY POINT

While their governments are still committed to relatively high social spending, and while poverty – at least until the current economic crisis – has been decreasing, most European countries are far from being classless societies. Indeed, inequality and social mobility may well be increasing rather than decreasing in some of them. Education is certainly no panacea.

In Europe, the manual working class – at nearly one-third to almost one-half of European countries' populations – is still the largest group (especially if we were to confine our figures to men). It is, though, in decline, as jobs in manufacturing and mining decrease relative to jobs in the often non-manual

Figure 1.8 Changes in real household incomes from the mid 1980s to the late 2000s

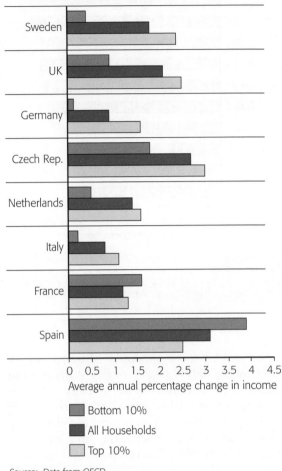

Average annual percentage change in income

■ Bottom 10%

■ All Households

□ Top 10%

Source: Data from OECD,
http://www.oecd.org/dataoecd/40/12/49170449.pdf
No figures available for Poland.

along with Italy, Ireland, Spain and France was historically one of the continent's most unequal societies), saw inequality increase from the early 1980s onwards. In east-central Europe, this increase began slightly later and occurred because of the collapse of the communist economic system and the move toward marketization; it has, however, been notably less extreme than in the countries of the former Soviet Union (see Heyns, 2005), and at least some governments – and here the Czech Republic would seem to be in advance of its counterparts in Hungary and Poland (see Ferge, 2001) – are taking the problem of poverty seriously.

In the west, the increase in inequality was largely because (with the exception of the late 1980s/early 1990s when some workers lost out as unemployment affected them directly or indirectly by lowering wages), the rich got richer (as they benefited from more deregulated economies) rather than because the poor got poorer (see Table 1.4, which also shows the extent to which welfare states operate – to varying degrees – to relieve poverty via transfer payments). The rise in inequality even occurred in egalitarian bastions like Sweden, although that country, with its Nordic neighbours, nevertheless remains one of the most equal in Europe (Figure

Table 1.4 Percentage of population at risk of poverty in selected European countries

	At risk before transfers			At risk after transfers		
	1995	2000	2008	1995	2000	2008
Czech Rep.	n/a	18	20	n/a	8	9
Netherlands	24	22	20	11	11	11
Sweden	n/a	17	28	n/a	9	12
France	26	24	23	15	16	13
Germany	22	20	24	15	10	15
EU	26	23	26	17	16	17
Poland	n/a	30	25	n/a	16	17
Italy	23	21	23	20	18	19
UK	32	29	29	20	19	19
Spain	27	22	24	19	18	20

Notes: EU is EU-15 in 1995 and EU-27 in 200 and 2008.

Source: Data from Mau and Verwiebe (2010: 215).

service sector. Because many of the jobs in the latter are not necessarily well paid (especially if they are occupied by women), the so-called 'growth of the middle class' has not been accompanied by a trend toward growing equality of incomes or wealth. Indeed, in some countries, it is quite the opposite (see Figure 1.8, which compares the growth in real household incomes since then for the top and the bottom 10 per cent of households). With the prominent exception of France and Spain, most European countries, including in Scandinavia and the post-communist states (the two regions in which traditionally there was most equality) and the UK (which

1.9). Nowhere in Europe, however, is inequality as evident as it is in the USA or, closer to home, Russia. Recently, social scientists have argued that people who live in more equal countries enjoy better lives (Wilkinson and Pickett, 2010). By no means all their colleagues agree with them but it is noticeable that when it comes to people's self-perception of their life satisfaction, as measured by the OECD's Better Life Index (2012), Denmark (#1), Norway (#2), Finland (#7) and Sweden (#10) are all in the top ten – along, it must be said, with four other, less equal but also prosperous, European countries, namely the Netherlands (#3), Switzerland (#4) and Austria (#5).

The extent and growth of income inequality differs between European countries. But its continued existence would seem to contradict the claim that the so-called 'classless society' has finally arrived, brought about, ironically, not by communism but by the capitalism it set out to destroy. Yet inequality does not stop at income. Take education, which is said by many to be one of the factors contributing to the blurring of class distinctions. Throughout Europe, an individual's progress and performance is influenced most not by the school she attends but by the educational attainment (and to a lesser extent the socio-economic position) of her parents. Like the USA, though later on, Europe has seen a massive expansion in university and other tertiary education provision. But research suggests that across the continent the main – or at least the first – beneficiaries were those sorts of families who were already consumers of such provision. Rather than many more working-class children going on to university, for example, places have been found for the siblings whose gender or limited ability would have ruled them out in the more sexist and selective days of old. In the UK, for instance, '[y]oung people from the poorest income groups have increased their [university] graduation rate by just 3 percentage points between 1981 and the late 1990s, compared with a rise in graduation rates of 26 percentage points for those with the richest 20 per cent of parents' (Blanden *et al.,* 2005: 11).

In short, while there has been a considerable closing of the gender gap (and in many European countries the opening of a new one as more women gain degrees than men) education is as much influenced by class distinctions as ever. It is, therefore, unlikely to have as big an impact on eroding such

Figure 1.9 Inequality in Europe compared

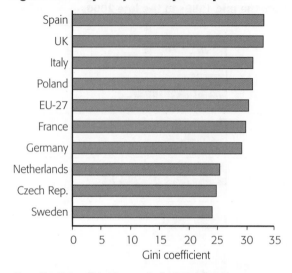

Note: The Gini coefficient is a standardized measure of income inequality, with zero being complete equality and 100 its opposite: good examples of a higher-scoring, more unequal developed countries include Russia and the USA (which hover around 40).

Source: Eurostat

distinctions as some optimistic advocates suggest (see Crouch, 1999: 238–41). In fact, it may well be making things worse: social mobility in some European countries (see Breen, 2004) may even be declining because of the increasing relationship between educational achievement (now more vital than ever in the labour market) and family income.

Nor should too great a faith be placed in the capacity of social policy more génerally to reduce inequality. There is some evidence to support the idea that reductions in inequality in former dictatorships such as Spain, Portugal and Greece may have had something to do with big increases in social spending (particularly in the last two countries). We can also say that efforts to curb welfare spending in the UK, which in the 1980s saw it swing toward the 'Anglo-Saxon' model and away from the social democratic one, probably exacerbated its relatively high level of poverty. At the other end of the scale, however, the Scandinavian countries that consistently emerge as having the most equal societies normally do so not just after, but also before we take taxation and transfers into account – though this is not to discount completely the redistributionary effect of welfare states, including the one that operates in a postcommunist country like the Czech Republic (see Table 1.4). Interestingly (and perhaps surprisingly to those who argue that, as in the USA, inequality and national wealth go hand-in-hand), this is a reminder that in Europe there appears to be a positive correlation between how rich and how equal a country is (see Conceição *et al.,* 2001; see also Kenworthy, 2004 and Pontusson, 2005).

Glib predictions about the coming of the classless society, then, are at the very least premature. On the other hand, this should not prevent us from acknowledging that the proportion of the population that can be called, or calls itself, working class is on the decline. In short, while there are just as many workers on wages or salaries out there, far fewer of them are wearing blue collars and far more are wearing white. This is partly because, as we go on to discuss, more and more of them are wearing skirts (as well as trousers!), too. But it is also because of a move away from large-scale extraction and industrial production and into services. Fewer mines and large factory settings means fewer places where large numbers of (traditionally) male manual workers work, live and play together and in so doing sustain a sense of themselves as having different (and competing) interests to those who employ them. As we shall see in Chapters 5 and 6, this has had a major impact on voting and party politics, posing particular problems for parties of the left, which historically were able to count on such people as their core supporters.

Women – working but not yet winning?

If class remains an important source of differences between people, so too does gender. This is despite the fact that one of the clearest European social trends of the latter half of the twentieth century was a move into the paid workforce by women, particularly married (or, increasingly, cohabiting) women. As we can see from Figure 1.10, the rate at which this move has occurred actually varied between countries. Some western European nations, particularly those such as Italy and Spain, in which the Roman Catholic church exercised a strong influence, historically had low levels of female participation in the paid workforce: the increase in the latter may seem impressive, but rates overall are still lower.

Although comparable figures are not available, former communist countries deliberately and successfully encouraged women to enter the workforce by providing easily accessible childcare and promoting gender equality as official policy. But they, like other European states, are now well behind

Figure 1.10 More and more women in the (paid) workforce, 1960–2008

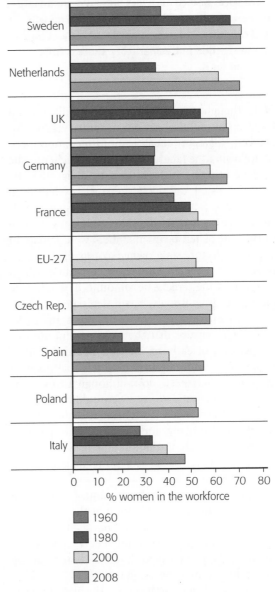

Sources: Data from Pissarides *et al.* (2004) and Mau and Verwiebe (2010).

Scandinavian countries, which seem to have achieved a permanent culture-shift to which feminists in other countries can, for the moment at least, only aspire.

KEY POINT

Gender inequality continues to be the norm in Europe, although Nordic countries have made more progress on this score than most. Despite increased participation in education and in the workplace, women earn less and do more unpaid domestic work – possibly because of childbirth and childcare. Progress is partly dependent on political action but, remarkably, there is little demand for it.

Note, though, that culture shifts are built on and backed up by political action: in January 2006, for instance, Norway's equality minister announced that, following the failure of a voluntary scheme, she would be bringing in legislation to oblige the 500 companies listed on the Oslo stock exchange to ensure at least four out of ten people in their boardrooms were women. At the time, only between one and two out of ten board members were female in the private sector; state-owned companies already adhere to a 45 per cent rule. Those companies which did not meet the target, she announced, would face winding-up. Interestingly, Spain, legislated in 2007 and called on quoted firms with more than 250 employees to ensure that they had a minimum of forty per cent of each sex on their boards by 2015. No sanctions were stipulated, which may explain why progress has been slow, although firms complying will be given priority when bidding for state business. Measures are also being debated in the Netherlands, Germany, and in Italy, where particularly few women are in the top jobs in the business world (see Figure 1.11). The same debate led to France, sometimes seen as a bastion of workplace sexism, to legislate for quotas in January 2011. The next step, begun in 2012, is action at the EU level – another initiative 'from Brussels' that the UK (where businessmen and politicians still believe they can do something about the woeful levels of women at the top by exhortation alone) is set to resist.

The so-called 'feminization' of the workforce is relative as well as absolute. The increase in female

Figure 1.11 The proportion of women on the board of Europe's top businesses

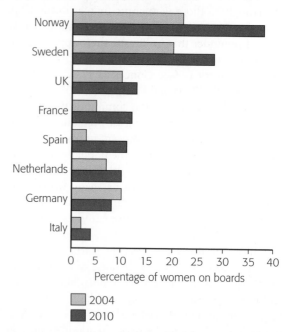

Percentage of women on boards

☐ 2004
■ 2010

Sources: European Women's Professional Network http://www.europeanpwn.net/files/europeanpwn_boardmonitor_2010.pdf

participation in paid employment has occurred alongside a decrease in the proportion of men working (see Figure 1.12). This decrease is mainly explained by the steep rise in unemployment experienced by almost all European countries as the 'long' or 'postwar' boom came to an end at the same time as technological advance really began to impact on jobs. Much of this unemployment is long-term, affects the less skilled, is often geographically concentrated and occurs in the manufacturing sector. The service sector, however, has remained very much a growth area, and it is clearly this sector that has provided the bulk of the jobs that women, in increasing numbers, have moved into. Many of these jobs are part-time. There are, though, considerable national variations in the supply of, and demand for, this kind of work: it is popular in the Netherlands, Norway, Denmark and the UK, for instance, but less so in, say, France and southern Europe. Perhaps as a result, women in these countries are more likely to be unemployed than men.

Figure 1.12 Male and female labour force activity rates – towards convergence, 1960–2003

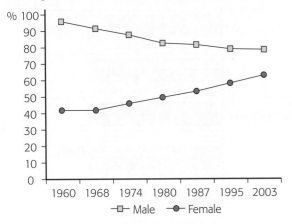

Source: Data from MacInnes (2006: 229).

In some European states, most notably in the Nordic countries, many of these jobs are also in the public sector, particularly in welfare (although men, it should be noted, continue to dominate the higher grades even here). There, so many women work that their need for childcare – a responsibility few European men seem willing to take on – cannot be met informally (through family or friends) and instead is met by the state. Those whom the state employs to perform that and other tasks (such as looking after the elderly) are mainly women. More women therefore work, and so on in circular fashion. Whether this circle is 'vicious' or 'virtuous' is a moot point. Some see emancipation and empowerment. Others see the traditional segregation of male and female roles simply transferred from the domestic to the paid economy, with Europe's women no less exploited. And, although there is evidence that Europeans are moving away from traditional attitudes about gender roles at the level of rhetoric (see from MacInnes, 2006) and to some extent reality (see Gimenez-Nadal and Sevilla, 2012), working women still do far more domestically than working men, and are therefore weighed down by the 'dual burden' or 'double shift' of work and family (see Figure 1.13).

Whether any real difference will occur as the result, for example, of a change made in 2005 to the civil marriage contract in Spain that obliges men to do their fair share of housework and childcare

(failure to do so being taken into account in any subsequent divorce settlement) will, however, be interesting to watch. As with the same government's action on boosting women's presence in the board-room – and its explicit promotion of women into the cabinet (see Chapter 4) – the measure represents a conscious attempt to achieve cultural change through political means. What is remarkable, however, is the fact that in most countries, there is the absence of organized pressure, either through groups or party politics (see Chapters 5 and 8) to emulate such measures.

Responses to this burden vary, but they seem to be more personal than political. Most obvious is the avoidance or at least the postponement of marriage and of childbearing and/or childrearing – activities that interrupt careers and account for a significant proportion of the persistent pay gap between men and women (see Figure 1.14). Certainly, there are strong trends in European countries (trends often led by Scandinavia and picked up last in southern Europe) toward having fewer children and having them later on in life and toward later marriage or no marriage at all (though

Figure 1.13 The end of traditional gender roles? Time spent on domestic chores by twenty-first century working men and women in Europe

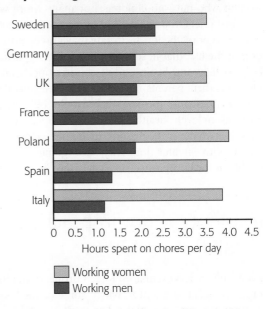

Sources: Data from Eurostat, *Statistics in Focus*, 4/2006.

headline figures here can be misleading because of the rise of cohabitation). Divorce is also on the rise in Europe, although, outside the UK and Scandinavia, it is nowhere near the levels seen in the USA. Indeed, in countries with a Roman Catholic (and Orthodox) tradition, it is still low, internationally speaking. This, though, may begin to change as religious constraints on the legal (i.e. divorce) regime, as well as on the thinking and behaviour of the population begin to decline.

Clearly, however, there are areas in which papal prohibitions on contraception have long since lost their influence. Roman Catholic countries like Spain, Italy and Poland have the some of the lowest birth rates in Europe (and indeed the world), and are therefore doing nothing to prevent the remorseless ageing of Europe's population (see Box 1.7) Interestingly, birth rates in the Nordic countries, where women participate more fully in the labour force, are nearer (though not at) replacement level. This is possibly because childcare and other welfare provision is easily accessed by working women in Scandinavia. It may also be because, as surveys consistently show, people in southern Europe continue to place a higher priority on family obligations. Since they are committed to carrying out what they see as their duties (which, more often than in the north, also include looking after resident elderly relatives as well), they are more careful about adding to them. There are still few women who have no children, but many more who have just one. On a lighter (but by no means entirely frivolous) note, the low birth rate may also be a function of the fact that in southern Europe (and particularly in Italy and Spain), adult children increasingly live with their parents far longer (i.e. well into their late twenties and thirties) than would be deemed 'normal' or even 'healthy' in other European countries. But whatever the reasons, such rates, when combined with greater longevity, are going to pose problems for Europe's welfare states (see Chapter 9).

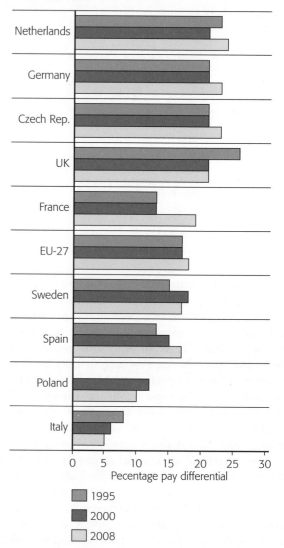

Figure 1.14 Europe's persistent gender pay gap, 1995 to 2008

Note: The pay gap is the difference between men's and women's gross earnings as a percentage of male earnings.

Source: Data from Mau and Verwiebe (2010: 202).

In theory if not in practice – religion in Europe

Even this brief excursion into European demography reveals the extent to which some of the broad distinctions we can make between countries, or groups of countries, are influenced by religion. Indeed, some argue quite convincingly that religion has been crucial in structuring the varieties of capitalism and especially the worlds of welfare that we have talked about above (see van Kersbergen and Manow, 2009). Democracy, too, would appear to be similarly influenced (see de Vreese and

Boomgaarden, 2009). The same goes for public policy and for public opinion. For example, there seems no other plausible explanation for the highly restrictive laws covering abortion, and the widespread (though not total) support for those laws, in, say, Poland and Ireland, other than the grip traditionally exerted over national life by the Roman Catholic church. No survey of Europe, then, would be complete without exploring the continent's religious life a little more deeply, not least because doing so can sometimes see our stereotypes overturned rather than confirmed: to take just one instance that we talk more about in Chapter 8, one might not have expected that Spain, generally (if not always accurately) seen as a deeply Roman Catholic country, would be at the forefront of moves towards institutionalizing gay marriage (unthinkable at the moment in Poland, for instance) and female representation in politics and business.

First and foremost, until very recently at least, Europe has been a bastion of Christianity. Yet the history of each country has been profoundly shaped according to which branch or branches of the Christian faith were important within its territory (see Table 1.5). The earliest divide in the Christian church was the eleventh-century breach between Roman Catholicism and the Orthodox church, which split Europe in an east–west fashion from (Catholic) Poland in the north down to (Orthodox) Greece in the south. This split left most modern states on one side or the other. In the sixteenth and seventeenth centuries, Protestantism either overcame Roman Catholicism (as in Lutheran Scandinavia) or (as in the UK, Germany, Switzerland and the Netherlands) came to exist alongside it. The latter continued to dominate the Irish Republic, Belgium, Austria, France and, of course, Italy, Spain and Portugal.

In some countries, the influence of the dominant branch of Christianity went beyond society and was reflected at the level of the state. In the postwar period, of course, things changed, especially in the east where communist states displayed various levels of hostility towards organized religion, ranging from the obstructive (Bulgaria, Hungary, Romania and Poland) to the overtly antagonistic (Czechoslovakia). In the west, however, most states continued to provide subsidies to churches, whether direct or indirect (for example, by funding faith-based schools and hospitals).

KEY POINT

Europe is not quite as Godless as some people assume: large numbers still profess to believe and, although, fewer people attend places of worship regularly, many still use them to mark births, marriages and deaths, etc. Christianity is still dominant, but Muslims (and Jews) make up an important part of Europe's religious identity.

In the middle of the twentieth century, Europe still seemed to be a religious place. Although regular attendance could be patchy, the church continued to play a part in the life of most Europeans as the place where rites of passage – births, marriages and deaths – were marked. As the new millennium approached, things had changed, but perhaps less than might be imagined. Research (see, for example, Halman and Riis, 2002; and Norris and Inglehart, 2011) suggests that the numbers of people who in censuses and surveys declare themselves adherents of no religion has increased, particularly in France and Belgium (where Roman Catholicism has been the big loser) and in the Netherlands (where Protestantism lost even more heavily than Catholicism). In addition, although religious baptism and marriage are still the norm for most western Europeans, there has been a continental decline in the former and a decidedly mixed picture as regards the latter. Eight out of ten couples still have a church wedding in Italy, Spain, Portugal, Greece and Finland – the 'western' states which historically took longest to move from the agricultural into the industrial age. But only around half of couples in other western states do the same. Moreover, while there is still a tendency to 'marry in' rather than 'marry out', it is very small – far smaller than among, for instance, some of Europe's non-Christian ethnic communities.

As for church attendance, problems with obtaining accurate information from either churches or their parishioners make it difficult to say anything conclusive or precise about change over time. However, the evidence we do have both from World Values Surveys and the big opinion polls regularly conducted by the EU known as *Eurobarometer* surveys suggests a general decline in western Europe (see Norris and Inglehart, 2012). Until recently we might have had the confidence to say that Roman

Figure 1.15 Europeans saying that, weddings and funerals aside, they never attend religious services, 2010

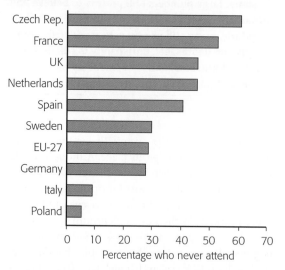

Source: *Eurobarometer* 73.1 (Special Report on Biotechnology), 2010.

Table 1.5 Religious adherents in Europe in the twenty-first century

Percentage of country's population who are:			
	Catholic	Protestant	Jewish	Muslim
Czech Rep.	40	3	–	–
France	82	2	1	7
Germany	35	37	–	4
Italy	97	1	–	1
Netherlands	35	27	–	4
Poland	92	1	–	–
Spain	98	0	–	1
Sweden	2	95	–	2
UK	10	53	1	2

Note: 1. Percentages are given only if the proportion of the population identifying with a particular religion reaches 1 per cent; the absence of a figure does not mean the total absence of a community (the Jewish community is a good example).
2. Note also that, because of the methodology used, Protestants in predominantly Catholic countries may be slightly underrepresented. The figure for Protestants in the UK includes Anglicans.

Source: Data from Barrett *et al.*, (2001).

Catholics, at least outside France, were much better at actually going to the church than Protestants, particularly those Protestants belonging to the official state churches of the UK and Scandinavia; however, although recent surveys suggest that Poland and Italy continue to live up to this stereotype, Spain does not (see Figure 1.15). Interestingly, some argue – not without contradiction it must be said (Norris and Inglehart, 2011: 111–132) – that decades of communist anti-clericalism seem to have been followed by something of a bounce-back for religion in central and eastern Europe (Tomka, 2011) and official suppression seems to have had only limited impact on a tendency for most people to believe in some kind of higher power. Outside the former East Germany, atheism (believing that no spirit or God or life force beyond mankind exists) is not noticeably higher than in 'western' countries such as Denmark, although (as Figure 1.15 shows) there are many people in the Czech Republic in particular who state that they never go to church except for weddings and funerals. On the other hand, agnosticism (not knowing either way) would appear from surveys to be widespread.

Generally, however, there appears to be no evidence that either atheism or agnosticism is on the rise, even if these attitudes are much more openly admitted to – even by public figures (including politicians) – than they are in the USA. A Eurobarometer poll in 2005, for instance, found that just over half of those living in EU countries believed in God – a figure which fell to around a fifth in Sweden and the Czech Republic but rose to over three quarters in Italy and Poland. And the number of people still identifying with one religion or another is still significant (see Table 1.5). That does not, however, prevent large minorities and even majorities – particularly where one church occupies a privileged position, as it does in Ireland and the UK, in Scandinavia and southern Europe and, in post-communist Europe, in Poland, Romania, Estonia and Lithuania (see Madeley, 2011 and Stan and Turcescu, 2011) – who worry that religion is accorded too much importance in their country (see Figure 1.16). Certainly, as we suggest in Chapter 8, some churches can be (and maybe should be) seen as successful pressure groups, maintaining their traditional privileges despite a considerable decline in their pulling power.

What some label 'secularization', then, is real – and almost certainly related to the fact that, especially in the latter half of the twentieth century, rising (economic) security meant that fewer people felt in need of the consolation and support that religion can bring (see Norris and Inglehart, 2011). However, the number of people still believing in God, even if they do not attend religious services, is still considerable, even if it pales in comparison with the figure in the USA. Where Europe differs from the latter – dangerously so claim some commentators (see Chapter 10) – is in the rapid growth and increasing visibility of the continent's other main religion, Islam. Most estimates (and that is all they are) suggest over 15 million people in Europe are Muslim – a total that is projected to rise significantly over time (see Table 1.6). Unlike most of their Christian compatriots, many of them are relatively new immigrants and members of ethnic minorities. This makes them far more prone to discrimination, as well as to poverty. Many European towns and cities, however, contain mosques, and it does seem as if more Muslims attend worship than their Christian counterparts: Klausen (2005: 138, 142) calculates that around nine out of ten people who are nominally Muslim profess a belief in God (as opposed to between six and eight nominally Protestant Christians and seven and nine Catholics), and although only three in ten attend Mosque this is higher than the two in ten who go to church anything like regularly.

However, the stereotype of non-integration in the face of supposedly decadent western values, on the one hand, and reactionary moral and doctrinal conservatism, on the other, is just that – a stereotype (see al-Azmeh and Fokas, 2007; and Klausen, 2005). That the stereotype is stronger than ever, however, is clearly one of the consequences of the terrorist attacks in New York, Madrid and London. But it merely builds on what one writer, in view of the crusades and expulsions touched on above, justifiably calls 'a thousand years of myth making in Europe' (see Reeves, 2003). On the other hand, there are increasing media reports of European Muslim involvement in an apparent rise in anti-Semitic attacks – attacks on Jews or Jewish property – especially in France, which, according to the US State Department's 2010 international report on religious freedom, has, along with the UK (where an estimated 280,000 Jews live), Europe's largest Jewish

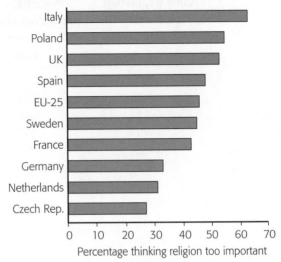

Figure 1.16 People thinking that 'the place of religion in our society is too important'

Source: Data from *Eurobarometer*, 66 (2006).

community (some 600,000). There are Jewish communities in other countries but, as Table 1.5, indicates, they are very small relative to the population. In absolute terms, of course, there are large numbers of Jewish people living in Germany (200,000) Italy (30,000), the Netherlands (30,000), Sweden (20,000) and Spain (48,000). In Poland and the Czech Republic, the population is no more than a few thousand, due mainly to the Holocaust. To give some idea of scale, the Jewish community of the USA is four to five times bigger than the Jewish community of all the countries listed in Table 1.4. In contrast, the Muslim community in the USA is only just over a third of that living in the European countries listed. This may or may not help explain some of the foreign policy differences we explore in Chapter 11.

Composition and identity: multi-ethnic, multi-national – and European?

But if the proportion of people in European countries who can be clearly and conventionally identified as religious, or working class, is shrinking, there

Table 1.6 European countries with significant Muslim populations, 2010 and 2030

	Muslim population (millions) 2010	Percentage of population which is Muslim 2010	Increase 2010–30 (millions)	Percentage of population which is Muslim 2030
Bulgaria	1.0	13.4	1.0	15.7
France	4.7	7.5	2.2	10.3
Belgium	0.638	6.0	0.5	10.2
Austria	0.475	5.7	0.3	9.3
Switzerland	0.433	5.7	0.2	8.1
Netherlands	0.914	5.5	0.5	7.8
Germany	4.1	5.0	1.4	7.1
Sweden	0.451	4.9	0.5	9.9
Greece	0.527	4.7	0.25	6.9
UK	2.9	4.5	2.7	8.2
Denmark	0.226	4.1	0.1	5.6
Norway	0.144	3.0	0.2	6.5
Italy	1.6	2.6	1.6	5.4
Spain	1.0	2.3	0.8	3.7

Source: Data from Pew Centre, *The Future of the Global Muslim Population*, 2011, available at http://www.pewforum.org/The-Future-of-the-Global-Muslim-Population.aspx.

seem to be increasing numbers whose self-definition now includes some element of nationality and/or ethnicity (distinctive group characteristics rooted in history and/or race). In fact, Europe provides plenty of opportunity for people to feel and claim multiple and divided loyalties because, as we explore in more detail in Chapters 2 and 10, the continent contains far more ethnic groups than states. Many people, even those who could be officially classified as citizens of one or other country, think of themselves as belonging (either solely or simultaneously) to some other entity or identity. Because of the way the map of Europe has been drawn and redrawn over the centuries, and because of migration, there is almost no country that is completely unaffected by such currents, or by the backlash against them. But some are more affected than others (see Box 1.8 and Chapter 2).

While outright hostility to the EU is low in most member states and attitudes to European integration are more complex than either/or–yes/no surveys suggest (see Gaxie *et al.*, 2011), there is limited evidence that the populations of the conti-

nent's various countries are developing an explicitly (even less, an exclusively) European identity. On the other hand, many people seem comfortable with both national and European identity (see Risse, 2010). *Eurobarometer* surveys consistently suggest that just over half of people in the EU member states are happy to describe themselves both as a national of a particular country and European, while under half identify exclusively with their own country. The demographic analyses show that people who left full-time education at the age of 20

KEY POINT

Many European states contain ethnic and national minorities. This means a large number of people have multiple attachments. There is also some, albeit limited, evidence of the emergence of a European identity, although this varies between countries. The basic values that many deem necessary for the survival of capitalist liberal democracy, however, seem to be present in almost all countries, whatever their history.

BOX 1.8

Politically significant ethnonational minorities in Europe

Belgium	60 per cent Dutch-speaking Flemish in the north; 30 per cent French-speaking Walloons in the south: considerable rivalry (see Chapter 2).
Bulgaria	10 per cent Turkish; 8.5 per cent Roma (gypsies).
Czech Rep.	Moravians (13 per cent), but most identify as Czech; 2 per cent Roma.
Cyprus	12 per cent Turkish minority, living in officially unrecognized independent state.
Estonia	Formerly part of the Soviet Union: 25 per cent Russians, 3 per cent Ukrainian and Belarusian.
Finland	6 per cent Swedish.
France	Mediterranean island of Corsica. On mainland, sizable ethnic and racial minorities from former African colonies, many of whom are of Arab descent and practising Muslims.
Germany	Some regional identity in former East Germany and in Bavaria. Large immigrant community, made up of various European groups plus Turks (2.5 per cent).
Hungary	4.5 per cent Roma, 2.5 per cent German, 2 per cent Serb, 1 per cent Slovakian.
Italy	Two small linguistic minorities: German-speaking *Alto Adige,* and French-speaking *Valle d'Aosta.* Significant. north v. south divide.
Latvia	Formerly part of the Soviet Union: 28 per cent Russian, 6 per cent Ukrainian and Belarusian.
Romania	Collection of very small minorities from surrounding states, plus 6.5 per cent Roma, as well as 7 per cent Hungarian concentrated in Transylvania.
Slovakia	10 per cent Hungarian, 9.5 per cent Roma.
Spain	Several more or less self-conscious regions, two of which (Catalunya and Euzkadi or the Basque country) see themselves as separate nations (see Chapter 2). Roma population could be up to 2 per cent
Switzerland	Patchwork of cantons with majorities whose mother-tongue is German (64 per cent of the Swiss population) or French (20 percent) or Italian (7 per cent). But no separatism.
UK	Sizable national minorities in Scotland and Wales, though separatism is non-violent and not as intense as in Northern Ireland where a large proportion identify with the Irish Republic to the south (see Chapter 2). Significant ethnic minorities from former colonial possessions in the Indian subcontinent (4.4 per cent) and the West Indies (2 per cent).

Sources: Data from CIA *World Factbook* and Barany (2002: 160).

or older, those who are still studying and managers are most likely to feel European as well. They are also most likely to feel 'proud to be European'. Retired people and people who look after the home are most likely to identify with their own nationality only. In other words, education, class (and age) make quite a difference. Breaking things down by country, however, reveals even bigger differences, with the British standing out as less 'European' than their counterparts in other countries (see Figure 1.17). There seems, however, to be no correlation between pride in one's own country and not feeling

Figure 1.17 Mixed feelings (for some) – European and national identity

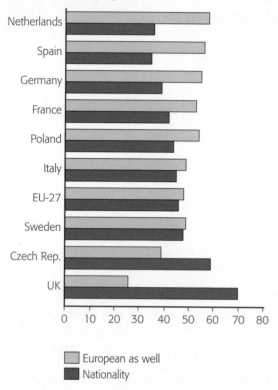

Note: Question asks if people see themselves as a national of their country only or as European as well.

Source: Data from *Eurobarometer* 73 (2010).

so European: according to Eurobarometer 66 (conducted in 2006), national pride is high (80–90 per cent) all around Europe (outside Germany, where it still seems to be associated with excessive nationalism) and the British do not stand out on this score.

People in some countries are clearly much more willing than others to identify with something called 'Europe (see Figure 1.17). The fact that some people are quite reluctant Europeans while others are comfortable with multiple or 'nested' identities, be they local, regional, national and supranational, is interesting (Checkel and Katzenstein, 2009). But it could also prove politically problematic: it may divide an educated cosmopolitan elite from an undereducated parochial mass. There are clearly national differences which may have their origins in the extent to which European identity is portrayed in public debate as a

threat or a complement to national identity (see Díez Medrano and Gutierrez, 2001; and Smith, 1992). However, there are very tangible symbols of greater integration – travel, a common passport, a flag, a currency, for instance – that now exist independent of that debate and may over time be contributing to what some analysts clearly believe is 'the emergence of a mass European identity' (Bruter, 2005), even if it is stronger in some nations and some demographics than in others (see Outhwaite, 2008: 122–3 for a useful summary of research findings on the differences). Certainly, as the same analysts show, using survey and focus group evidence, there is no simple 'zero-sum' game between Europe and the nation: sometimes they are seen as opposed; in other places the one is constitutive of the other (see Kriesi *et al.*, 2003; and Stråth, 2001). This interaction and debate is destined to continue. As we suggest in Chapter 2, 'Europe' can no longer be thought of as existing outside or even above the state, while state and nation are no longer as commensurate as some countries tried to pretend they were.

But we need to be careful not to think that limited, or at least variable, levels of identification with an abstract called 'Europe' means that Europeans do not share some – and possibly enough – attributes in common. Clearly sharing the same problems does not mean they share the same perspectives on those problems or on, say, the merits of 'European' solutions (see White, 2011). It is also true that one can draw systematic distinctions between groups of European countries with regard to democratic and liberal values (e.g. self-responsibility and work ethic, solidarity with the disadvantaged and trust in others, ethnic tolerance, support for and confidence in democracy and the political system, rejection of violence). And it is true that these differences may be traceable to countries' religious and imperial histories, as well as their level of economic development. But it is also true that there seem to be systematic differences between (broadly speaking) the countries that currently make up the EU-25 and, on the one hand, the USA and, on the other, countries further to the east (i.e. the Former Soviet Union, FSU). And it is true that the differences between the old and new member states of the EU are nowhere near as significant as we sometimes think. Indeed, in

Figure 1.18 Net public debt in selected countries, 2010

Source: Data from nationmaster.com. Figures in brackets indicate world ranking.

the realms of religion, ability to speak English as a *lingua franca,* and popular culture, there are often more differences between the fifteen member states that made up the EU before 2004 than there are between those fifteen and the states that joined in that year (see Laitin, 2002). As Fuchs and Klingemann (2002: 52) put it, 'Between the countries of Europe there is little difference in the political values and behaviours that are essential to a democracy.'

Shared political values and behaviours, however, do not necessarily result in identical political institutions: as we shall go on to see, the latter are to some extent the product of particular histories and reflections of social and economic differences. In turn, they presumably help produce those differences – and in so doing present those charged with running each country with sometimes unenviable challenges. One such (and one that is much talked about in the midst of the global financial crisis) is public debt (Figure 1.18). Amidst all the talk of the irrationality of the markets and the iniquities of credit rating agencies, it is worth noting that those European countries in most trouble were for the most part the ones that owed most. It is also worth asking what it was about their political systems, as well as their economies, that allowed (or caused) their governments to end up in such a mess.

Learning Resources for Chapter 1

Further reading

Contemporary histories of Europe abound: the best reads are Mazower (2008), *Dark Continent: Europe's Twentieth Century* and Judt (2007), *Postwar: A History of Europe Since 1945*. See also Gaddis (2007), *The Cold War*, Davies (2007), *Europe East and* West, Stone (2011), *The Atlantic and its Enemies* – and, for a provocatively pessimistic take by one historian on Europe's past, present and future (if, indeed, it has one!), see Laqueur (2012), *After the Fall*. See also Bongiovanni (2012), *The Decline and Fall of Europe* and Marquand (2011), *The End of the West*. For those particularly interested in postcommunist Europe, the collected edited by Ramet (2010), *Central and Southeast European Politics since 1989* is superb value. So too is the collection edited by White, Lewis and Batt (2013), *Developments in Central and East European Politics 5*. There are also plenty of reference works covering the whole of Europe (and, indeed, the world) country-by-country: Turner (2012), *Statesman's Yearbook 2013* is particularly comprehensive. Perhaps the best work on the sociology and economics of western Europe remains Crouch (1999), *Social Change in Western Europe*, but see also the introduction to the collection edited by Hall and Soskice (2001), *Varieties of Capitalism*, as well as Mau and Verwiebe (2010), *European Societies: Mapping Structure and Change*. For a stirring (but also empirically persuasive) call for (welfare) states to focus on improving children's life chances, see Esping-Andersen (2009), *Incomplete Revolution: Adapting Welfare States to Women's New Roles*. On (the lack of) social mobility or 'fluidity' in Europe, see the collection edited by Breen (2004), *Social Mobility in Europe*. On the gender dimension, see the collection edited by Krook and Mackay (2010), *Gender, Politics and Institutions*. On the ethnic minorities of Europe, the best reference book remains Cordell and Wolff (2004), *The Ethnopolitical Encyclopaedia of* Europe, but see also Hsu (2010), *Ethnic Europe: Mobility, Identity, and Conflict in a Globalized World*, which contains fascinating contributions on ethnicity, identity and Europe's diasporas. On values, *see* Arts *et al.*, (2004), *The Cultural Diversity of European Unity* and, on the way they are influenced (and possibly brought closer together) by the EU, see Kurzer (2001), *Markets and Moral Regulation*. On religion, see the edited volumes by Motzkin and Fischer (2008), *Religion and Democracy in Contemporary Europe*, by Haynes (2009), *Routledge Handbook of Religion and Politics*, by Foret and Itçaina (2011), *Politics of Religion in Western Europe*, by al-Azmeh and Fokas (2007), *Islam in Europe* and, in order to set Europe in its global context, see Norris and Inglehart (2011), *Sacred and Secular*. Jenkins (2007), *God's Continent* is useful, too. See also, for a fascinating take on the relationship between different types of democracy and state-church relations, Minkenberg (2011), 'Church-state regimes …' (online). Finally, for a brilliant rejoinder to those who insist (despite the facts) that America and Europe are as different as Mars and Venus – and a reminder of quite how much variation there is between European countries, too – see Baldwin (2009), *The Narcissism of Minor Differences*.

On the web

www.worldatlas.com – maps and basic country information

https://www.cia.gov/library/publications/the-world-factbook/wfbExt/region_eur.html – detailed country information

http://hdr.undp.org/en/ – country facts and figures from the UN

www.nationmaster.com – make your own charts and tables

epp.eurostat.ec.europa.eu and www.oecd.org – country and EU statistics

ec.europa.eu/public_opinion – Europe-wide survey research

http://vlib.iue.it/history/index.html – History of European countries and the EU on the web

http://www.coldwar.org/ and http://besthistorysites.net/index.php/modern-history/cold-war – all things Cold War

Discussion questions

1　Different countries have risen and fallen in pre-eminence in Europe over the last five hundred years. Pick one or two examples: why and how do you think status was gained and then lost?

2　What do you think drove Europe toward two world wars in the first half of the twentieth century? And how, in your opinion, has it managed to avoid something similar happening since then?

3　There may have been no world war after 1945 but there was a Cold War. Was such a conflict inevitable and why do you think did it came to an end?

4　Why is there so much economic variation between, but also within, European countries? And what does it mean to say that they are almost all 'post-industrial'?

5　The new democracies of central and eastern Europe (CEE) have had to adapt to life after communism: can you point to particular successes and failures?

6　How would you define globalization and what impact, if any, is it having on Europe? If you are opposed to it, why?

7　Europeanization doesn't mean that all the continent's countries are becoming more like each other. How does the organization and extent of welfare in different states, for instance, illustrate this point?

8　It's often assumed that Europe is becoming more classless, gender-blind, and secular. Do you think that's the case?

9　Why do some inequalities seem to mobilize people politically and others, which are just as glaring and have political ramifications, apparently excite little interest?

10　Why might it always be unrealistic to talk about Europeans, or, for that matter, about, say, Britons or Spaniards or Belgians or Cypriots or Slovaks or Estonians or Latvians?

ONLINE RESOURCES AVAILABLE

Visit the companion site at **www.palgrave.com/politics/bale** to access additional learning resources.

Chapter 2
The end of the nation state?

A **nation state** is a country where the boundaries of the political and administrative system are presumed – rightly or wrongly – to coincide with those that contain a population with a supposedly shared culture, history and (probably) language.

The possession of **sovereignty** implies the ultimate right, free from external hindrance, to decide and control how a state will be run and the direction it will take.

As we saw in Chapter 1, the late nineteenth and early twentieth century confirmed Europe as a continent of states. These were constructed on the basis – sometimes firm, sometimes more fictional – that they were the institutional embodiment of a nation, of a community living (and in most cases born) in a territory and amongst other people with whom they felt a binding affinity. These **nation states** were presumed to be *sovereign* in the sense of exercising supreme political authority within their territorial boundaries and remaining free from hindrance from outside bodies.

In fact, the reality has rarely matched the presumption. There are two reasons for this. First, many European countries contain 'stateless nations' (Keating, 2001). These are minorities that consider themselves to be, or to belong to, nations other than that on which the state claims to be founded – either because what they see as their nation has been denied statehood or because they believe they are part of a nation that does have a state, just not the one in which they themselves reside. In recent years, many have become politicized and, as we shall see below, have obliged states to respond to their demands. Secondly, few states could claim complete freedom from outside 'interference' Those in CEE formerly (if not formally) controlled by the Soviet Union are only the most blatant example. Many of their Western counterparts, by joining what is now the EU, have also pooled (some would say) or (according to others) compromised their **sovereignty**.

This chapter explores, in turn, both facets of what some are bemoaning as the end of the nation state in Europe. It begins, first, by looking at how the phenomenon of **minority nationalism** is helping to make historically unitary states (in which sub-national government traditionally enjoyed no real power) look more like those federal states where (as we shall see in Chapter 3) local autonomy has long been important. And it asks whether the hybrid forms that they have taken on will be enough to save them from eventual break-up. Second, it looks at how the nation state is apparently being undermined both 'from above' and even 'from within' by the European Union – a political project which (as much by stealth as by fanfare) is changing the everyday lives of Europeans: so much more than an international organization but not yet the 'federal super-state' that is the dream of some but a nightmare for others.

Minority nationalism is the feeling on the part of one community within a state that they belong to a separate nation that should therefore be accorded some kind of autonomy, special rights or even independence.

Stateless nations

Identifying strongly with the region as well as or more than the country you live in is not uncommon in Europe – particularly, research suggests, if you live somewhere that speaks its own language, which doesn't border the country's capital city, which is well-off compared to other parts of the country, and which displays distinctive voting behaviour (see Fitjar, 2010). But for some people, this identification runs even deeper. They have an emotional attachment – sometimes only latent or dormant, sometimes vociferously and even violently manifest – to what they regard as a nation even though, officially, it is simply part of another state. In some European countries there is a clear territorial, as well as historical, cultural (and possibly linguistic) demarcation between these 'national minorities' and the majority population, even if the minority is effectively surrounded in its 'enclave' (a smaller territory within, yet distinct from, a larger territory) by the majority. In other places, the minority may assert there is a clear territorial demarcation, but so many people from the majority live inside what they claim to be their 'borders' that the pattern is, in fact, complex and confused. Complexity and confusion can also arise when a minority in one state sees itself as part of a nation, but the majority of their fellow 'nationals' live in a neighbouring state – a situation which can give rise to 'irredentism' (the pursuit of reunification with the homeland). This situation occurs (outside Northern Ireland, anyway) far more frequently in CEE than in the west: the Hungarian populations of Slovakia, Serbia and Romania mentioned in Chapter 1 are obvious examples (see Csergo and Goldgeier, 2004). In the west (again, with the exception of Ireland), states that could have laid claim to some common identity showed no interest in interfering in the politics of their neighbours: examples include Sweden with Swedish-speaking Finns, or Austria with German-speaking Italians, or the Netherlands with Dutch-speaking Belgians.

That said, European history provides plenty of examples of the bloody consequences of minority nationalism. As we saw in Chapter 1, the First World War itself was sparked by Serbian nationalists anxious to throw off what they saw as the yoke of the Austro-Hungarian empire. Ironically, however, the treaties that followed the war were so intent on dismembering the latter that they established artificial borders which, in CEE, often left linguistic minorities stranded in a state they did not regard as their own. This was not something the architects of the peace after the Second World War did much about, the exception being their complicity in the forcible repatriation of the (Sudeten) German minority in Czechoslovakia, one of the many 'artificial' states created in the aftermath of the 1914–18 conflict. After 1945, an already broad consensus on borders in western Europe was effectively locked into place by the need for collective solidarity against the threat from the Soviet Union. This threat also ensured that Spanish dictator Francisco Franco would be given free rein to suppress those Spaniards who insisted on asserting the ancient autonomy of their regions. Moreover, the rush to join in the consumerist prosperity that seemed to be the natural accompaniment to peace and democracy also seemed to have helped reconcile minorities to living alongside the similarly materially preoccupied majority. Meanwhile in the east, communist regimes that were widely thought of as permanent seemed to have effectively kept the lid on, and perhaps extinguished, any lingering disputes between and within the member states of what became the Warsaw Pact (see Chapter 1).

KEY POINT

Some states contain people who feel either that the territory they occupy should be part of a neighbouring country or that they are a nation that deserves a state of its own. This combination of grievance and aspiration was previously suppressed by dictatorship or lay dormant under wider concerns to secure material well-being. This changed with the coming of democracy, with socio-economic development and with a trend toward decentralization. Outside the Balkans, fears that the rise of minority nationalism may spark calls for radical revisions of borders and widespread abuses of human rights have not been realized.

Partly as a result, few texts on European politics written in the three decades following the Second World War considered 'minority nationalism' of sufficient contemporary interest to bother affording it much, if any, space. As a cleavage it was a has-been, a relic of a bygone age which would supposedly slip into history. Yet the loyalty and identity we call nationalism, the need to belong to an 'imagined community' with whom we feel meaningfully connected (Anderson, 1991: 5–7), only *appeared* to have burned itself out. In fact, the embers could quite easily be fanned into life. Whatever states did to 'deal with' such loyalties – trying to ignore them (France), gradually acknowledging them (the UK and Belgium), or forcibly repressing them (Spain) – clearly did not deprive them of the oxygen they needed to exist, even if only in latent rather than in manifest form.

The transition of minority nationalism from latency to relevancy seems to have resulted, in the main, from two developments. First, the concept of democracy itself seems to have undergone considerable stretching from the 1960s onwards. It began to include notions of 'subsidiarity' (decisions being taken at the lowest appropriate level) and participation, not least as a response to the idea that 'big government' was bad government and that the political system was suffering from 'overload' (see Chapter 3). Instead of trying and failing to keep up with and balance too many demands by too many people wanting too much money (especially in 'lame duck' peripheral regions), states would be better advised to let them get on with it themselves. Such advice applied as much to their treatment of national minorities as any other group. Second, democracy, or voting at least, seemed less hung up on class (see Chapter 6): clearly, there is no necessary trade-off between class and ethnic and/or regional identity, but as the intensity of one declined, the intensity of the other seems to have increased.

This is partly explained by politics and economics as much as by sociology. For instance, in the UK the Scots' increased sense of themselves as distinct is likely to have been influenced by the imposition of unpopular policies by a largely English Conservative government during the 1980s. That decade saw 'London' widely blamed for an economic recession that hit Scotland's heavy manufacturing base hard – and all this as nationalists (increasingly prepared to stand candidates in all electoral contests) were claiming that Scotland's oil wealth, among other things, could make it a viable independent state within the EU. In Spain and Belgium, too, the desire

for more autonomy on the part of at least some of the nations that made up those states was likewise driven by a mixture of economics and politics. And it, too, developed in a context where European integration seemed to offer the chance for small states to prosper. On the other side of the equation, some state-wide parties were (perhaps misguidedly) willing to concede devolution and decentralization in order to protect their own electoral interests and, in so doing, not simply entrench it but in many cases – as we see below – actually prompt demands for further autonomy (see Alonso, 2012).

But material interests and institutions do not explain everything. Nowadays, only the most antediluvian Marxist or 'institutionalist' zealot would claim that people's identity, political or otherwise, can be 'read off' from their position in the market place or the political structures in which they are embedded. Clearly, we are all social and emotional, as well as economic, actors and are capable of storing, accessing and displaying multiple loyalties – not necessarily at will, but certainly when inspired by events, or at least the construction put on those events by inspirational and/or demagogic leaders. And the consequences of such politicization can be tragic. In the early 1990s, in the former Yugoslavia, latent minority nationalism was so whipped up by gangster politicians that it spilled over into civil war and the murder and forcible removal that was euphemistically labelled 'ethnic cleansing', with political and international consequences that are still with us today (see Box 2.1 and Ker-Lindsay, 2011).

The terrible events in the Balkans in the early 1990s seemed to provide proof of a latent tendency toward potentially aggressive nationalism, and heightened fears that states in CEE might celebrate their release from imperial bonds by attempting the kind of centralizing, majority 'nation-building' that characterized western Europe in the nineteenth century. The kind of nation-building, in other words, that ignored the wishes of often quite substantial minorities by privileging 'ethnic nationalism' over the sort of 'civic nationalism' that may have originated with a dominant ethnic core but saw it more or less peacefully co-opt, first, the elites and, then, the people of more peripheral regions (see Péteri, 2000; Schöpflin, 1995; and Smith, 1991). Fortunately, such fears were not, in the main, borne out.

BOX 2.1

Is it or isn't it? Kosovo as an independent state

Yugoslavia was a federal state created after the First World War. It consisted of six republics – Bosnia and Herzegovina, Croatia, Macedonia, Montenegro, Slovenia and Serbia, with the latter containing two autonomous provinces (Kosovo and Vojvodina) with non-Serb populations (Albanian and Hungarian respectively). After World War II it fell under communist (but not Soviet) control, but the end of dictatorship brought with it not just democracy but a bloody civil war and, by 1995, a break-up of the state into its component parts. When, four years later, the nationalist Milošević regime in Serbia attempted to 'ethnically cleanse' Kosovo of its Albanian population, the Americans and the Europeans – working together as NATO – brought the campaign to a halt by aerial bombardment between March and June 1999. Their action also hastened the fall of Milošević and the accession of politicians keen to end their country's isolation by pursuing membership of the EU – a prospect that seems at least possible now that they have cooperated with the arrest of fugitives either suspected or convicted of war crimes carried out in the early 1990s.

In 1999 Kosovo was placed under UN administration, after which a series of elections were held, in spite of the fact that they were in the main boycotted by its Serb population. In February 2008, Kosovo declared itself independent and has since been recognized as such by over 80 states, as well as by institutions like the World Bank and the IMF. Kosovo is not yet, however, a member of the United Nations and is unlikely to become one unless and until Russia, together with all the states keen to stay in its good books, withdraws its objections – objections based not just on solidarity with the Serbs but which also concern the precedent that recognition might set for its own potential 'breakaway republics'. These objections are also shared by the handful of EU countries who have refused to join other member states in recognizing the Republic of Kosovo, including Greece, which (like Russia) has long seen itself as an ally of orthodox Christian Serbia, and Spain, which (again like Russia) is worried about the ramifications of recognition for its own territorial integrity given demands for independence by the autonomous communities (and they themselves would say nations) of Catalunya and the Basque Country.

There were certainly some concerns, especially in the early 1990s, about the Baltic states (Estonia, Lithuania and especially Latvia). They were understandably reluctant, after winning their freedom from the Soviet empire by precipitating its collapse, to think much about the rights of the many Russians that had settled there during the previous half-century. Attempts to restrict their rights – particularly in the field of language and education – did not, however, survive a combination of pressure from the newly-formed Russian federation and the EU, which made it crystal clear that any state with a poor record on minority rights might as well forget trying to join. In central Europe, individual politicians and parties have tried to make capital by harking back to a time when all their 'countrymen' were united in the one homeland, particularly in Hungary, whose government in 2010 changed the

law in order to offer citizenship to those living outside its borders but who were familiar with the language and could claim Hungarian ancestry. This went down particularly (and predictably) badly in Slovakia (where many ethnic Hungarians live) and the country's new government responded in kind by passing legislation allowing it to remove Slovak citizenship from anyone voluntarily taking on citizenship of another state, unless through birth or marriage. Arguably, however, all this had more than a whiff of hypocrisy given that many Slovak politicians in the early 1990s were known for both exclusionary rhetoric and public policy decisions – until that is, as in the Baltic states, such populism suddenly seemed to soften in the face of their own possible exclusion from the EU (see Kelley, 2004; and Tesser, 2003). Just as importantly, perhaps, most of Europe's newest democracies could see for themselves that their western counterparts were beginning to accommodate rather than ignore or suppress what seemed to be a resurgence of minority nationalism from the 1960s onwards. This 'territorial management strategy' (Keating, 2006) is one that we now go on to explore in more detail.

Belgium – federal solution or slippery slope?

It used to be easy to sort European states into two categories. The majority were centralized, **unitary states** – a category which included, first, former imperial powers and their ex-colonies; second, the then communist countries; and third, Scandinavian states. Traditionally, only a handful of European states were **federal states** (Germany, Austria and Switzerland) although such a bald distinction always had its critics, not least because the federalism of Germany is very different to the federalism of, say, the USA and also different to the federalism of Switzerland (see Chapter 3). But, recently, the distinction has become even more blurred, as some former unitary states under pressure from minority nationalism, even where the justification and support for it is risible (see Box 2.2), are adopting federal or quasi-federal forms in response. The question is, in the long term, whether this will save them from break-up.

Unitary states are those in which regional government is really only local administration of centrally determined (and often financed) services, and where any power exercised by regional government is ultimately dependent on the consent of the central state.

Federal states are those in which territorial subnational government enjoys constitutionally guaranteed autonomy and functional competence – in other words; regional government really is government and is not simply administration under delegated authority from the centre.

In one former unitary state, Belgium, federalism is now fully fledged, even if (as in other federal states in Europe) it is not federalism US-style. Ever since it was, to all intents and purposes, conjured up by

Padania – an 'imagined community'?

Italy's *Lega Nord* (Northern League) is a political party that has participated in national governments and is also renowned for its xenophobic rhetoric. For almost a quarter of a century, its leaders have been arguing for increased autonomy for some of the richest of Italy's regions, notably Lombardy, Veneto, Piedmont, Emilia-Romagna and Liguria, which, taken together, account for around 40 per cent of Italy's population (and an even greater proportion of its GDP). Although the grounds for their claim to independence seem in the main to be economic (resentment at the supposed drain on dynamism caused by the South's relative poverty), they have tried to bolster it by dreaming up a nation, *Padania*, that is supposedly united by history and culture – and which the Lega accorded both a flag and a national anthem.

Once in government, the Lega Nord pared back its demands, making the case not for independence but for federalism, but its proposals failed to find favour with Italian voters in the referendum held on them in June 2006. According to opinion polls taken in 2010 and 2011, only a minority of Italians are persuaded of Padania's existence, and it has yet to join Italy's five existing 'special regions' (Sardinia, Sicily, Val d'Aosta, Trentino–Alto Adige and Friuli–Venezia), all of which have been accorded a degree of autonomy since the 1970s. But the *Lega's* utility as a coalition partner, and the threat it poses to the votes and ability to govern of other political parties, lent momentum to a rather less ambitious campaign for a federal Italy – a state which, after all, did not exist until 1861. In response, successive Italian governments have, since 2002, passed measures devolving power, although many of them are contested and remain to be implemented. *Padania* may be more fiction than fact, and Italy is, in reality, far from being a federal country yet. Whether the economic difficulties it has faced during the Eurozone crisis will push it further in that direction remains to be seen.

foreign powers in 1830, the country has been linguistically divided between the Walloon, French-speaking, south and the Flemish, Dutch-speaking, north. However, well into the postwar period its government and administration was conducted in French, even if many of those who ran it were from Flanders, their main link with their Walloon fellow-coutrymen being Roman Catholicism. The capital, Brussels, although located in the Flemish region was (and continues to be) predominantly French-speaking. This French-speaking control was facilitated not just by an essentially Francophone monarchy, but also by the fact that the more industrialized Wallonia provided the greater part of the nation's wealth. But the decline of heavy industry from the 1950s onwards reversed the situation and turned the political tide: as the Flemish north began to outstrip the French-speaking south economically, its people and their representatives began to demand autonomy from a community that, in their view, had not only dominated them unfairly for over a hundred years but was now also a drain on their resources. They were not, however, alone: a number of Walloon politicians believed their region would be better off without the Flemish. By 1993, this push for autonomy resulted in Belgium becoming a federal state, albeit one rendered unconventional because the ensuing **devolution** involved the transfer of powers not just to three geographical regions – *Wallonie, Vlaams* and *Brussel* or *Bruxelles*) but also to three 'communities' – French-, Dutch- and German-speaking.

> Literally, **devolution** is the transfer of competences from national to sub-national government. However, it has taken on a particular meaning in the UK where it is used in order to make it clear that the transfer of powers is not the forerunner of federalism, let alone complete independence for Scotland and Wales.

What is significant is that when the process of disaggregation began, as far back as the early 1960s, it started out as a way of defusing tensions, not as a conscious first step on the road to federalism. Yet Belgium seemed to slide inexorably towards the latter, spurred on by the continuation of inter-communal tension and, some would argue, encouraged by the possibility that separate development would be easier inside the EU (for a discussion of which,

KEY POINT

Belgium – arguably something of an artificial nineteenth-century creation – has adopted a federal structure in order to accommodate the demands for autonomy of its most assertive, Dutch-speaking linguistic community. But this seems to not to have halted but rather to have fuelled calls for more (or even complete) independence.

see Dardanelli, 2012). Laws passed in 1962 and 1963 defined the boundaries of the linguistic groups. Constitutional reform in 1970 set up linguistically based communities with responsibilities in 'cultural' areas such as broadcasting and education. Further constitutional reform in 1980 not only granted executive status to these communities (which were given additional responsibilities in health and welfare), but also gave executive and legislative powers to the regions of Wallonia and Flanders in economic planning, environment and transport, as well as setting up a court to arbitrate disputes between the regions, the communities and central government. More reforms in 1988 and 1989 added to the powers and responsibilities already devolved, and granted the same to Brussels.

Equally significant is the fact that 1993 did not bring an end to the process. The so-called 'Lambermont Accord' of June 2001 saw even more devolution of powers to the regions and the latter now have the right, where they have such powers, to negotiate with other member states in the EU instead of leaving it up to the federal government. Indeed, beyond taxation, social security, the monarchy, sports and the location of predominantly Francophone Brussels in Dutch-speaking Flanders, there seems to be little holding the country together. Belgian parties have long since split into Dutch- and French-speaking organizations. An agreement that the federal government should be linguistically balanced makes government formation (see Chapter 4) possible but sometimes very tricky. After the general election of June 2007 the parliamentary arithmetic made things so complicated that it took until 2008 to form a coalition government bridging the linguistic divide and, not for the first time, people began openly to discuss the possibility of a split – with the idea gaining momentum again when, after a general election in 2010, it took the parties in the federal parliament an incredible 541 days to form a government under the leadership of the (French-speaking) Elio Di Rupo, the first openly gay man to become Prime Minister of a European country. In the event the parties which negotiated the coalition agreement (partly, it should be said, out of fear that a downgrading of the country's credit rating might trigger a sovereign debt crisis), not only managed to avoid a split by transferring yet more powers to the regions but finally, it seems, settled a long-running, bad-tempered argument between French and Dutch speakers over the Brussels–Halle–Vilvoorde district.

If, however, Flanders and Wallonia do eventually go their separate ways, it would not be unprecedented, even in recent times. In 1993, the Czech Republic and Slovakia underwent a largely uncontested, 'velvet divorce', ending a federation that had first been put into place in 1969, some fifty years after the state's creation after the First World War. The divorce came about more as the result of the people accommodating the politicians rather than the latter finally agreeing to give the former what they appeared to want, whereas in Belgium politicians have arguably reflected popular will as much as they have shaped it. Also, things were made easier for the erstwhile Czechoslovaks than they would be for the disgruntled Belgians because each region had its own recognized capital: it is hard to see Flanders breaking away and leaving Brussels (which may be French-speaking but which is located firmly in Flanders) to Wallonia. Another difference between Czechoslovakia and the Belgian case lies in the fact that the main impetus for the break-up of the state came from Slovakia, the smaller, poorer and economically backward region, where politicians did their best to whip up fears over (among other things) language concessions to its Hungarian-speaking minority. By and large, Czech politicians were initially reluctant to dissolve the federation and consented only when it became clear that progress on other fronts would be blocked by the Slovaks until they did so. Given the often turbulent nature of politics in Slovakia in the 1990s, and the much slower economic progress it has made relative to the Czech Republic, it seems clear who got the best of the deal.

'Asymmetrical' federalism – Spain

The lesson from Belgium, surely, is that decentralization, rather than satisfying calls for more autonomy, can whet the appetite for even more. Yet this has not discouraged politicians in other European states – most notably in Spain, the UK and more recently Italy (see Box 2.2) – proffering devolution as some kind of 'solution' to the 'problem' of minority nationalism (Map 2.1).

Since its emergence from authoritarian dictatorship at the end of the 1980s, Spain has transferred increased powers and competences to its *Comunidades Autónomas* (literally, autonomous communities or regions). Many of these continued, as historic kingdoms, to maintain a sense of themselves as distinct, despite forming part of what for hundreds of years was one of the most centralized unitary states in Europe. However, this transfer of powers has proceeded on an incremental basis depending on negotiations between the central government and each of the seventeen autonomous

KEY POINT

Spain is a state composed of several historic kingdoms, some of which have never been entirely reconciled to rule from Madrid. Since its return to democracy in the mid-1970s, it has accordingly granted some of its regions extra autonomy. Whether this flexible response can save Spain from separatist violence or even eventual break-up remains to be seen.

communities established under the 1978 constitution, all of which now have an elected assembly and government. According to the statutory agreement each community has made with the state, each has a unique range of powers on issues excepting defence and foreign policy, key aspects of social security and macroeconomics, all of which are reserved for the centre. They can exercise these powers in any way they see fit provided they do not conflict with the constitution which, although it created what some see as a hostage to fortune by acknowledging and guaranteeing 'the right to autonomy for the *nationalities* and regions' (author's italics), also committed itself to 'the indivisible unity of the Spanish Nation'.

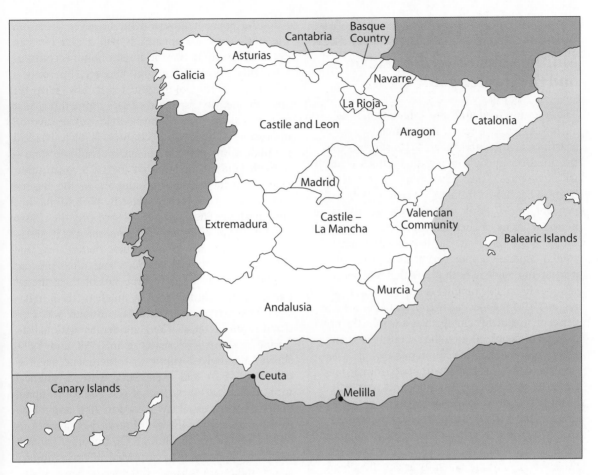

Map 2.1 Spain's autonomous communities

However, not all of Spain's autonomous communities have chosen (or been able) to assert their autonomy to the extent seen in, say, the Basque country and Catalunya. This has led to Spain being labelled as a practitioner of 'differentiated' or 'asymmetrical' federalism (see Agranoff, 1996). Under this hybrid system, most of the country still seems to operate as a unitary state, albeit with some devolution to the regions. But at the same time, there are parts of the country that look, to all intents and purposes, as if they are part of a federal state, or even independent nations. Theoretically (that is to say, constitutionally) Spain is not a federal state – the powers enjoyed by some of its regions, some might argue, are not defined as such by the constitution. But the idea that they can be taken back or that, as far as many in the regions are

concerned, they are not actually inalienable rights, is fanciful to say the least. The question now is not so much whether Spain is or is not federal or on the way to federalism, but whether the latter – hybrid or pure – will be enough to prevent its eventual break-up.

In the three and a half decades of the campaign of violence by the Basque separatist organization, *Euskadi Ta Azkatasuna* (ETA) over 800 people were killed. Millions of euros were paid out by businesses in what is one of Spain's wealthiest regions in protection money, extorted as a 'revolutionary tax' by an organization whose less high-profile *kale borroka* (or 'street struggle') caused millions of euros' worth of damage to property. ETA demanded the independence of what Basque speakers call *Euskadi* and Spanish speakers call *el País Vasco,* with its most

BOX 2.3

Multiple identities: the evidence – and the way forward?

The common wisdom is that minority nationalism is growing in Spain. Yet research (see Martinez-Herrera and Miley, 2010) suggests that the number of people in, say, the Basque Country who refuse to see themselves as in any way Spanish has halved from 43 per cent in 1983 to 21 per cent in 2007, while in Catalunya over the same period it has never risen much above 15 per cent, dropping at times nearer to 10 per cent. Since 1990, when the question was first asked, the proportion of people in both places that see themselves as living in a nation (as opposed to, say, a region) has remained fairly constant at around 35 per cent. Meanwhile, in Spain as a whole, the proportion of people rooting their identity in their region more than in the country as a whole has, over the same time period, dropped from around a quarter to a fifth – around the same proportion as those who now see themselves as more Spanish than anything else (a category which, at the end of the 1970s, mind, would have covered about a third of all those asked). The real growth has been in those who regard their identity as equally regional and Spanish – up from around four in ten people at the end of the 1970s to nearly six out of ten in thirty years later. In short, it looks as the future lies in people not feeling that they have to choose. How politics, which in a democracy, after all, revolves around people being asked to make choices (at elections, in referendums etc.), copes with this will be interesting to watch.

To the Spanish government, however, secession was not – and nor apparently will it ever be – an option. The region may be an autonomous community with a unique cultural heritage, but only a minority of its population reject any form of Spanish identity (see Box 2.3) – something that would make a Czechoslovak-style 'velvet divorce' impossible. The Basque country is also, Madrid maintains, but one part of an indissoluble state – notwithstanding the fact that the 1978 constitution failed to achieve majority support in the Basque country after calls for a boycott by peaceful nationalist parties. These parties – notably the *Eusko Alderdi Jeltzalea–Partido Nacionalista Vasco* (EAJ–PNV) – continue to do much better than the extremists in regional elections and often prevent candidates from the local branches of the national parties governing the region, much to their irritation. That irritation, not to say outrage, was rendered even greater when moderate nationalists, during a short-lived ceasefire in 1998 and 1999, showed themselves willing to contemplate negotiations with ETA and even work with its political wing, *Batasuna* – a party that was banned in Spain under a controversial law passed in 2002 and which is also on the EU's list of proscribed organizations (see Bale, 2007, forthcoming). On the other hand, it would be a mistake to see 'Madrid' as a unitary actor: there are serious differences between the centre-right *Partido Popular,* which traditionally took a hard-line stance, and the centre-left PSOE, which showed itself more willing to talk when and if ETA was prepared to renounce violence. After a number of false starts, which reflected growing tensions between ETA's irreconcilables and its modernizers, the organization finally declared what most observers now hope will indeed be a permanent cessation of the armed struggle in October 2011.

ETA has not, however, renounced the struggle for independence; nor have more mainstream Basque nationalists. Since 2003, the EAJ–PNV has been flirting with the idea of an amendment to the 'statute of Guernica' (the law governing the relations between the Basque region and the Spanish government) that would create 'a free state associated with Spain'. This would then supposedly be presented for approval by the Spanish parliament and then, in a referendum, by the Basque region's voters. Despite polls suggesting that such a referendum would be

ardent supporters subscribing to a 'catastrophist' belief that unless it is achieved, the Basque 'race' will be wiped off the face of the earth by a 'genocidal' Spanish government. As a result, hopes that the coming of democracy would see the swift end of ETA were dashed. The Basque country may have had its own parliament and police force, it may have controlled education and even taxation, but in relative and not just absolute terms, more terrorism occurred after Franco's death than before it.

BOX 2.4

Catalunya – nationality and nation

Along with the Basque country, Catalunya, whose capital, Barcelona, is one of Europe's most widely admired cities, is at the forefront of claiming and exercising its rights as an autonomous community. Its wealth, linguistic differences (6 million speak Catalan as well as Spanish, although only an estimated 40 per cent of the population as their 'first language') and history of independence give it a good claim to nationhood – or at least to special treatment compared with other autonomous communities whose poverty, history, and the fact that they speak *Castellano* (the Spanish spoken all over the country) mean they are far more dependent on Madrid.

Catalan nationalism may not have taken a violent turn, but it has profound ethno-linguistic roots (Miley, 2007) and has to be taken every bit as seriously as its Basque counterpart. Catalunya takes its independence very seriously: the *Generalitat* – its government – not only promotes the Catalan language and negotiates some agreements direct with the EU (see Roller, 2004), it also conducts its own 'foreign relations' with other governments. Catalan parties have achieved this by lending the support of the elected representatives they send to the national parliament in Madrid to governments of both right and left.

Cynical or skilful, the strategy has been successful to the point that Catalunya enjoys more power and prestige than many regions in formally federal states, especially in the light of the *Estatut d'autonomia* – a revision of the charter establishing the rights and powers of the region vis-à-vis central government in Madrid that was ratified in a referendum in June 2006 (see Keating and Wilson, 2009). On a practical level, the statute saw Catalunya gain more control over taxation and justice and home affairs, and even its ports and airports. The fact that its preamble referred to the fact that Catalans saw themselves as a *nation* was one of the reasons (along with fears about Catalunya reneging on its responsibilities to contribute funds to poorer regions) that the centre-right *Partido Popular* (then in opposition) sought to challenge the constitutionality of the charter. In June 2010 Spain's Constitutional Court ruled some of its articles as unconstitutional, and declared that the word "nation" had only historical and cultural rather than legal standing. This provoked outrage among Catalan nationalists who went on to organize a series of unofficial local referendums, culminating in one held in Barcelona in April 2011 where nine out of ten of those who took part voted for independence – a victory rendered slightly less impressive by the fact that only one in five who could have voted bothered to do so. Opinion polls taken since the Court's judgement generally show support for independence has grown, but doesn't yet constitute a sure-fire majority.

popular but would not necessarily produce a vote for more independence, Madrid continues to remind the Basque government that there is no chance of any Spanish parliament accepting such an amendment and that the Constitutional Court (see Chapter 3) would be asked to (and in all likelihood would) annul it. Outrage was not the only emotion, however. Some saw Madrid's rejection of these calls for 'shared sovereignty' as hypocritical, given that this is precisely the solution it currently favours for the British colony of Gibraltar on the southern coast of Spain – a territory it continues to lay claim to in spite of the clear preference of Gibraltar's population to remain British, and in spite of Madrid's insistence on maintaining its own possessions (Ceuta and Melilla) in Morocco.

An additional difficulty for the Spanish government is that any accession to the demands of those who want more autonomy for one region will be pounced on by others who want more autonomy for their own region. In the wake of moderate Basque nationalists' demands for a referendum on shared sovereignty, their Catalan counterparts called again for Catalunya to be recognized as 'a nation' and for a single administration in Catalunya which, in addition to the control it already enjoyed over education, culture, health and policing, would have the final say on public finances and be represented separately from Spain in the EU and at other international bodies. The centre-right government in Madrid immediately rejected this idea, pointing out once again that Spain was indivisible and that there were millions of people living in Catalunya who considered themselves (at least partly) Spanish. However, the centre-left PSOE government elected in 2004, partly because it was a minority government (see Chapter 4) reliant on the support of some nationalist parties, proved more accommodating (see Box 2.4).

But whatever the ideological complexion of the government in Madrid, it has to face the fact that further privileges handed to so-called 'fast-track' autonomous communities (the 'nationalities' of Catalunya, the Basque Country and Galicia) will prompt further demands for equal treatment by what were originally considered mere 'regions' (such as the Canary Islands and Andalusia). If these demands are acceded to, then (a) Spain could end up fully federal; and/or (b) the 'nationalities' may, in the event that they enjoy no more autonomy than the 'regions', demand independence. On the other hand, given the numbers of people living in the 'nationalities' who are clearly comfortable with being Spanish as well as Basque or Catalan, and so on (see Núñez, 2001: 22–5), there is no reason to assume support for independence would be sufficient to secure it even if a vote were allowed. This may, however, be changing. In September 2012, over half a million people attended a peaceful demonstration for independence in downtown Barcelona, while opinion polls began to show majority support for a split from Spain – a shift many claimed was confirmed at the early elections called by Catalunya's self-styled 'sovereigntist' regional government for November. The reason? Catalans were outraged that the government in Madrid insisted that they stick to tough deficit and debt targets when between 5 and 10 per cent of Catalan GDP is taken by central government and redistributed to Spain's poorer regions.

The UK – another hybrid

The only European country outside the Balkans that rivals Spain in terms of the potential for violence associated with minority nationalism is the UK, and

Map 2.2 The British Isles – the UK and Ireland

in particular Northern Ireland. It, too, has taken considerable steps towards a quasi-federal solution under which different regions are accorded different rights. We deal with Scotland and Wales below, but begin with Northern Ireland (Map 2.2).

The UK province of Northern Ireland (or Ulster) came into being because, although Ireland achieved independence from Great Britain in the 1920s, the majority Protestant population of the north-easternmost six counties of the island remained committed to the Union. Northern Ireland had its own government and parliament but, its largely Protestant 'unionist' population insisted, it was nevertheless very much part of the UK. Only a small minority of Roman Catholics thought the same way, with most looking forward, as 'nationalists' to 'a united Ireland' in the long term, most obviously achieved by pulling the province of Northern Ireland into the Irish Republic, hence the label 'republican'. The pursuit of this goal by violent means by the Irish Republican Army (IRA), however, attracted little support until the late 1960s and early 1970s when, following sectarian violence triggered by attempts to address the civil rights grievances of Catholics, the British government initially sent in troops and then imposed direct rule from London. There followed two decades of high-profile terrorist attacks in the province and on the mainland (in part funded by republican sympathizers in the USA), as well as lower-profile (but seemingly relentless) sectarian 'tit-for-tat' killings, not only by the IRA but also by Protestant paramilitary organizations – some allegedly with the collusion of the official security forces.

By the mid-1980s, it had become clear to many republicans that, despite the huge cost to the UK in terms of loss of life, security and, above all, tax-payers' money, the 'armed struggle' was not going to kick the 'Brits' out of Northern Ireland as long as the majority of its population remained committed to the Union. Meanwhile, the commitment of the Irish Republic and the UK to put an end to violence resulted first in the Anglo-Irish Agreement' (1985) and then in the 'Downing Street Declaration' (December 1993), which sought to institutionalize intergovernmental and cross-border cooperation, and created a new *quid pro quo*. London (declaring it had 'no selfish strategic or economic interest in Northern Ireland') now recognized the possibility of a united Ireland, while Dublin acknowledged that this could come about only with the consent of the majority in the North. These confidence-building measures, although they alarmed hard-line unionists, were enough to tempt what is widely regarded as the political wing of the IRA, Sinn Féin, into talks with the British – talks that eventually led to a cease-fire and to the creation (backed up by a referendum, by the release of paramilitary prisoners and by a

promise on the part of the IRA and others that they would 'decommission' their weapons) of an elected Northern Ireland Assembly and an executive on which all parties would serve depending on their share of the vote.

To some this political progress looked ephemeral. The parties could not, it seemed, work together and, in October 2002, the power-sharing Northern Ireland Executive at Stormont was suspended and direct rule from Westminster re-imposed by a frustrated British government. Equally depressingly, but not perhaps surprisingly, the day-to-day sectarian divide between Protestants and Catholics – always a matter not so much of doctrinal nitpicking as cultural identity and social networks – seemed if anything to have deepened, reinforced by the long-term decline of mixed neighbourhoods and intermarriage. This deepening of, rather than decrease in, hostility between the two communities was also reflected at the political level. In elections held in November 2003, support for the more hard-line Democratic Unionist Party (DUP) and Sinn Féin grew at the expense of the official Ulster Unionists and Social Democratic and Labour Party (SDLP), respectively. The moderates, it appeared were losing out, to the extremists. Yet there was another, more optimistic, way of looking at it: if a deal were to be secured, it would be more likely to hold if it were done by parties who could claim to be truly representative – either of the unionism that understandably feared being 'sold-out' by the British and losing its majority status to the expanding Catholic population, or of the republicanism intent both on defending Catholics from Protestant attacks and bringing about a united Ireland sooner rather than later. This analysis, it seems, was correct (see Box 2.5).

Interestingly, 'the troubles' in Northern Ireland have clearly taken a toll on the UK population outside the province, too. If opinion polls are to be believed, the majority blames both sides of the sectarian divide for the problem, and the numbers supporting a united Ireland, while not quite reaching a majority, are considerably higher than those favouring keeping the province part of the UK indefinitely.

Polls suggest that many English people would now be content to see the end of the union with Scotland, which was granted a parliament in 1997 – partly, some argue, in order to head off calls by nationalists for independence even though, at the time, the latter

KEY POINT

The UK has, like Spain, offered its component countries varying levels of autonomy in order to contain minority nationalism. Its situation is rather more complicated because some in Northern Ireland would like to see the province absorbed into the Irish Republic and have taken up arms to achieve this outcome. This violent conflict appears to be over, but it is by no means certain that in the long term the UK will retain its present shape.

BOX 2.5

Sworn enemies sit together in Northern Ireland

By 2004 things did not look hopeful for the Northern Ireland peace process. The power-sharing government at Stormont remained suspended, with agreement between the parties elected to the Assembly foundering on the refusal of the IRA to allow release of photographic evidence of arms decommissioning. Worse was to come when the organization was widely blamed for a multi-million pound bank robbery towards the end of the year. Things looked up, however, towards the end of 2005, when the body in charge of decommissioning concluded the IRA had indeed put its weapons beyond use – a conclusion it confirmed in October 2006.

Meanwhile, the British and Irish governments decided it was time to try and force the parties back into talks, and also (successfully, it turned out) put pressure on Sinn Féin to declare its support for the Northern Ireland police and criminal justice system. Fresh elections held in the spring of 2007 confirmed the leading role of Sinn Féin on the nationalist side and the DUP on the loyalist side, while a deadline imposed by the British government for the formation of a power-sharing executive seemed to concentrate minds. In May 2007, finally convinced that the nationalists were serious about never returning to violence and that a place in history was his, the DUP leader, the octogenarian Ian Paisley, took up the post of First Minister, with Martin McGuinness, a former IRA commander, as his Sinn Féin Deputy. Paisley retired from frontline politics in June 2008 and was replaced by another former hardliner, Peter Robinson.

In January 2012 Northern Ireland's New First Minister made what his Deputy called 'another little piece of history' by accompanying him to a Gaelic football match – a highly symbolic gesture because of the sport's association with the nationalist cause, albeit one made much easier by the visit made the year before by the Queen of England to the home of Gaelic sports, Croke Park in Dublin, a stadium where 14 people were shot dead by British soldiers during a football match in 1920. More history was made when McGuiness was photographed smiling and shaking hands with the Queen. Local hardliners on either side, however, are taking longer to reconcile – as the nights of sectarian rioting which suddenly flared up in September 2012 illustrated.

---

was rejected as an option by most Scots. Support for independence in Wales (which was absorbed much earlier and which could never really establish such a clear claim for itself as a self-governing nation) has always been much lower, evidenced by the very narrow majority (on a very low turnout) that, in 1997, approved the setting up of an assembly without the tax-varying powers granted to Scotland's new legislature. Opponents of devolution claimed that it represented a 'slippery slope' toward a more thorough-going federalism and possible threat to the British state itself – fears which, some would say, seem not to have been entirely misplaced. The legislatures and executives of both Scotland and Wales have gradually added to their powers, most recently after a referendum in Wales held in March 2011.

If the purpose of devolution from the Labour Party's point of view was to stop nationalist parties like the Scottish National Party and the Welsh nationalists, Plaid Cymru, from 'stealing' votes from it at Westminster (i.e. general) elections, it seems to have worked to some extent: support for nationalist parties at UK general elections has not risen appreciably. Elections to the legislatures in Scotland and Wales, however, are another matter. Although Plaid has recently suffered something of a setback after sharing power in the Welsh Assembly in Cardiff, the SNP has gone from strength to strength – so much so that in May 2011 it won an overall majority in the Edinburgh Parliament (by no means an easy thing to do in an election using proportional representation). Afterwards its leader, Alex Salmond, confirmed that what the SNP calls the 'Scottish Government' would be holding a referendum on independence sometime in the following five years. Even if the

BOX 2.6

What's in a name? The Scottish Government

One of the first official moves of the Scottish National Party (SNP), once it had formed an administration after the elections of 2007, was to declare that the Scottish Executive would hence-forth be called the Scottish Government – a move that, some alleged, would cost a small fortune as letterheads, publicity, documents and signs would all need to be changed. But the re-branding, some noted, was only skin deep. The government's legal name would continue to be the Scottish Executive, in order to escape the need to amend the Scotland Act that first established devolution. This may have been difficult because the SNP took power as a minority administration (see Chapter 4), meaning it would find it difficult to legislate on anything too contentious. With the party forming a majority government after May 2011 this con-straint no longer operates, but the party is focusing its efforts on a much bigger prize – full independence via a yes/no referendum in 2014 in which, very unusually in the UK and, indeed, in Europe as a whole (see Chapter Six), 16- and 17-year-olds will be allowed to vote.

Scottish people vote no, it is highly doubtful that the national parliament (i.e. Westminster) will ever seek to exercise its technical sovereignty to take back rights and powers it has granted to sub-national legislatures and executives. The one con-ceivable exception would be (as with the deadlocked Northern Ireland Assembly) action *in extremis*. Given this, it is not surprising that some constitutional experts argue that the UK is now a quasi-federal system (albeit one operating Spanish-style 'differentiated' or 'asymmetrical' federalism). Moreover, especially given the result of the refer-endum – to be held in 2014 – is currently too close to call, there is no guarantee that, when it comes to Scotland, where comparisons with Catalunya can fruitfully be drawn (Greer, 2007), that federalism (of whatever variant) will stave off rather than lead to disintegration.

France – no longer quite so indivisible

In view of this risk, those who wish to preserve the nation state intact sometimes look to France – sup-posedly *une et indivisible* (one and indivisible) – for inspiration. Despite movements for more inde-pendence for historic nations such as Bretagne (Brittany) in the west, Occitanie (modern-day Languedoc) in the south and Pays-Basque (Basque Country) in the south-west (see Map 2.3), France continues to protest its indivisibility – even to the extent of preserving the myth that its overseas pos-sessions (in, for example, the South Pacific) are simply extensions of mainland France. Closer to home, however, France has recently had to be rather more flexible. Nationalists on the Mediterranean island of Corsica (population just over 250,000) have not resorted to large-scale violence to anything like the same extent as their Irish and Basque coun-terparts, although empty holiday homes on the island have been fire-bombed. This reluctance to take life (and scare off the two million people who visit the island as tourists rather than as 'colo-nizers') possibly accounts for the relatively low profile of their struggle. The latter may also have something to do with the fact that in Corsica the

Map 2.3 France

relationship between nationalist terrorism and organized crime, by no means unimportant in Northern Ireland and Euskadi, is so close: violence there tends to be more surgical than spectacular, with lots of small incendiary explosions damaging (mainlanders') property and the line between mafia-style and apparently political assassinations very blurred. Due to this, perhaps, and to the awareness that the island depends economically on the mainland for tourism and aid, there would appear to be rather less support for full-blown independence among Corsica's quarter of a million inhabitants than in, say, the Basque country. Certainly, peaceful nationalist parties do less well in elections than their Basque counterparts.

KEY POINT

France has never been quite as united as it likes to think of itself and has taken its first faltering steps towards granting additional autonomy to its island province of Corsica in order to respond to separatist feeling there.

Yet following the murder of its prefect (local governor) in 1999, the French government made a bold move to break with its self-image as 'one and indivisible', putting together a staged autonomy package known as the 'Matignon Accords'. The island would be granted greater self-government and allowed to place greater emphasis on the teaching and use of its own language in return for progress on law and order that, if secured, would see a constitutional revision allowing for proportional representation (PR) elections and an assembly and executive with (albeit limited) lawmaking powers. Predictably, critics on the nationalist side declared that the Accords had not gone far enough, while critics in Paris declared it could be a Pandora's box that would not just lead to independence for Corsica, but also encourage claims for more autonomy by mainland regions. Nevertheless, the plan was adopted by the Corsican Assembly in July 2000 and given an initial green light by the National Assembly in May 2001. Notwithstanding a truce declared by the Corsican National Liberation Front, the murderous feuding between separatist organizations continued. Opinion polls also seemed to suggest that far from dampening enthusiasm for independence, the

Matignon Accords may well have encouraged it and, as in the case of British attitudes to Northern Ireland (and, increasingly, English attitudes to Scotland), the number of 'mainlanders' happy to see the back of the island is also rising.

With the election of a centre-right government in 2002, hopes of action on the Accords looked as if they had been dashed, as the new government's rhetoric suggested a reassertion of the Gaullist unitary state tradition. But while the new prime minister withdrew his predecessor's promises of a tailor-made autonomy package for Corsica, he sweetened the pill considerably, first, by making it clear that Corsica could be at the cutting edge of plans for limited decentralization throughout France and, second, by not reneging on the previous government's promise of almost €2 billion in development aid over the next decade-and-a-half. By July 2003, the government's devolution plans – which centred on a merger of the island's multiple elected bodies into one in return for enhanced powers – were ready to put to the islands voters in a referendum. Some of the largest separatist parties, such as *Corsica Nazione,* were prepared to go along with the plan as the first step; others rejected it as inadequate. Frustratingly for the French government, and those prepared to give it a chance, the plan was narrowly rejected.

There seemed to be no 'Plan B' and the situation was made even more tense in April 2004 by the arrest, on racketeering charges, of Jean-Guy Talamoni, leader of the pro-independence party *Unione Nazionale.* He was acquitted but another nationalist, Charles Pieri of the National Liberation Front for the Liberation of Corsica–Union of Fighters (FLNC–UC), was jailed on similar charges in the spring of 2005, upon which the organization broke off a ceasefire it had declared two years earlier. Later on that year, nationalist feeling was further inflamed by the decision of the French government to privatize the island's loss-making ferry service – and to send in troops to remove unions who were blockading the country's main port and effectively holding thousands of tourists to ransom. Things then quietened down but January 2007 saw small bombs go off in the Corsican port of Ajaccio. Nicholas Sarkozy, beginning his successful run for the Presidency, visited the island and argued that the way out of violence was to expand opportunities for the young: to this end he promised another billion-euro investment programme in the island's economy, suggesting once again that throwing money at the problem rather than granting greater autonomy would continue to be the main strategy. Whether this will eventually be enough to see off the island's small band of militant separatists is hard to tell. So far, the news is relatively good. The car bomb that they exploded outside a police station in July 2009 (the first since 2006) did not signal the start of a new campaign – and fortunately inflicted no injuries even if it reportedly blew the son of a gendarme off his bike. Nor did things escalate when, in June 2011, a court in Paris confirmed the life sentence handed down to the man convicted of killing the island's Police Chief back in 1998. That said, there was appreciable nationalist protest at NATO's use of French airbases on the island to bomb Libya in 2011. Moreover, moderate nationalists could point to the fact that, fighting as an alliance called *Femu a Corsica*, they managed to garner just over a fifth of the vote at regional elections held the previous year.

The EU and the end of sovereignty?

An argument put forward by those campaigning for the independence of nations with aspirations to statehood in twenty-first-century Europe is that (arguably anyway) it is rendered more feasible than ever by the existence of the EU (see McGarry and Keating, 2006). It may have been true, once upon a time, runs the argument, that Scotland or Catalunya (to take two of the most obvious examples) would have found it difficult to survive, given the costs of mounting, for instance, an independent foreign and trade policy. Now, the argument continues, so many of these expensive tasks can, in effect, be 'contracted out' to the EU. To some observers, the latter already promotes a degree of autonomy, via a 'Committee of the Regions' (COR), which advises (though it cannot compel) other EU institutions on policy and legislation that affect local or regional government. More importantly, the EU operates an 'internal market' which supposedly helps ensure that even the smallest state (Malta, Cyprus or Luxembourg, for example) can survive economically by being able to market its

goods and services freely in other, much bigger economies. It is also possible to argue that the EU's preference for distributing financial assistance to poorer regions (sometimes referred to as cohesion policy, sometimes as structural funding) has contributed to, if not necessarily driven, the tendency for some of the those regions to see themselves as nations, Scotland being an obvious example. Or the EU can just be one more forum in which stateless nations choose to insist on their right not to have everything decided for them by the national and/or federal government: the sub-national governments of Belgium, for example, not only have direct representation in certain EU institutions but their advice is routinely sought when they do not; in Spain, Catalunya and the Basque country have similar rights, although in most cases they are exercised collectively with the other autonomous communities in a manner reminiscent of the way things work with regard to the *länder* (states) which make up the Federal Republic of Germany (see Ladrech, 2010: 99–106).

The irony is, of course, that while some who aspire to independence look to the EU to underwrite it, many of the latter's existing member states worry about the EU (a) eroding their territorial integrity by bypassing national government and dealing direct with regions, and (b) undermining their independence by telling them what to do and what not to do – a threat that has grown particularly acute in the light of new rules first mooted in 2012 to control the budgets of those countries in which the euro has replaced national currencies. This final part of the chapter explores the extent to which the EU in general, and some of its institutions, policies and processes in particular, may be impacting negatively on the sovereignty of its member states.

Origins, enlargement and institutions

The forerunner of the EU, the European Economic Community (EEC), began life in 1958 after the signing of the Treaty of Rome by six western European nations: France, Germany, Italy, the Netherlands, Belgium and Luxembourg. All had been cooperating with each other since the USA had encouraged them in the late 1940s to work together to make the most of the aid granted to the continent by what became known as the Marshall Plan. The 1950s had seen that cooperation reinforced by the formation in 1952 of the European Coal and Steel Community (ECSC) – a project which aimed, by locking together those industries across the different member countries, not only to boost their economic fortunes but to tie them together in the hope that this might prevent yet another European war. Success in the economic and industrial realm contrasted with the failure of an ambitious attempt to bring together former enemies in defence cooperation. Economic cooperation was also limited somewhat by the reluctance of the UK to become involved, on the basis of its perception that its interests were global rather than regional and that both its sovereignty and freedom of action might be put at risk. Joining the EEC committed 'the six' to very practical measures such as a customs union with a 'common external tariff' (CET), and a 'common agricultural policy' (the now infamously expensive CAP) to ensure both plentiful food and a reasonable standard of living for farmers by providing them with a mixture of subsidies, protective tariffs and guaranteed prices.

KEY POINT

What has become known as the European Union has expanded since its birth in the late 1950s to include most of the continent's states. Since, in large part, they wish to combine continued sovereignty with collective action and a common market, the EU experiences a more or less creative tension between intergovernmental and supranational impulses – impulses that are embodied by its component institutions. So far, this has not prevented increased integration, even if the latter (and the alteration in decision-making rules it has required) has proceeded in fits and starts.

The Treaty of Rome, building on ECSC structures, also set up the *European Commission* and the *European Court of Justice* (ECJ) (see Box 2.8). Both were supranational rather than intergovernmental institutions (see Box 2.7) and, as such, were to prove instrumental in the drive to what the Treaty called 'ever closer union.' This notwithstanding, the UK soon changed its mind about joining, realizing quite quickly that it would suffer economically if it stayed out. After the failure of two applications in the

---

BOX 2.7

Balancing the intergovernmental and the supranational

Most international organizations are *intergovernmental*: those states that belong to them cooperate in search of better outcomes but reserve the right and maintain the power to block, or at least ignore, decisions that they feel are contrary to their interests. Such intergovernmentalism has always been one side of the story of European integration. But there is another, *supranational*, side. This is the agreement on the part of member states, on some matters at least, to forgo the right to a veto and be bound by decisions with which they do not always agree. Arguably, the history of the EU is the history of the tension between *intergovernmentalism* and *supranationalism*. It is also a tension embodied in (if not always effectively tamed by) its institutional structure. No EU body is completely and utterly intergovernmental or supranational in both composition and role, but (as Boxes 2.8 and 2.9 suggest) all display a bias one way or the other.

1960s, it became a member in 1973, along with Denmark and Ireland. Although global recession in the early 1970s took some of the shine off the initially impressive economic performance of the EEC, further expansion followed, most recently with the admission of ten postcommunist countries and two small islands (see Map 2.4). The political security reasons behind expansion are dealt with in more detail in Chapter 11. The economic arguments are also important. A bigger union provides a bigger and, over time, a wealthier market for European goods and services; it should also encourage the kind of mergers and acquisitions (M & As), and economies of scale, that will allow European business to compete more effectively across the globe.

The EU also provides a limited degree of redistribution from Europe's richer to Europe's poorer states. It gets (according to European Commission figures for 2011) approximately 13 per cent of its revenue from tariffs and duties (a proportion that is bound to go down over time as world trade is lib-

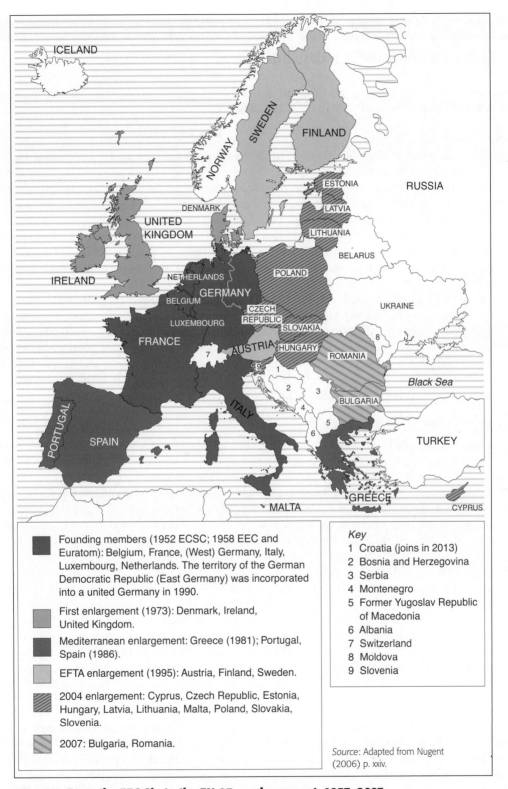

Founding members (1952 ECSC; 1958 EEC and Euratom): Belgium, France, (West) Germany, Italy, Luxembourg, Netherlands. The territory of the German Democratic Republic (East Germany) was incorporated into a united Germany in 1990.

First enlargement (1973): Denmark, Ireland, United Kingdom.

Mediterranean enlargement: Greece (1981); Portugal, Spain (1986).

EFTA enlargement (1995): Austria, Finland, Sweden.

2004 enlargement: Cyprus, Czech Republic, Estonia, Hungary, Latvia, Lithuania, Malta, Poland, Slovakia, Slovenia.

2007: Bulgaria, Romania.

Key
1 Croatia (joins in 2013)
2 Bosnia and Herzegovina
3 Serbia
4 Montenegro
5 Former Yugoslav Republic of Macedonia
6 Albania
7 Switzerland
8 Moldova
9 Slovenia

Source: Adapted from Nugent (2006) p. xxiv.

Map 2.4 From the EEC Six to the EU-27 – enlargement, 1957–2007

BOX 2.8

The EU's supranational institutions

These bodies may be appointed by governments or elected by their voters, but those who are chosen go on to work for the EU, not for member states. They include:

European Commission
Based in Brussels, with a staff of some 27,000 people, the Commission is headed by a President and European Commissioners appointed by member states. It is made up of over twenty Directorate Generals (DGs) which report to those Commissioners and are charged with preparing and administering policy in a particular area – agriculture, environment, internal market, regional policy, etc. Most EU law is based on proposals from the Commission, which are then discussed and adopted (or not!) by the Council of Ministers (see Box 2.9), and increasingly the European Parliament (EP), too (see below). The Commission is also involved in overseeing the implementation of laws and ensuring that they (and the Treaties more generally) are obeyed in and by member states. This task sometimes involves the Commission in initiating legal proceedings against states, and sometimes commercial concerns as well, for non-compliance. It has a particularly strong role in competition policy, where it can investigate, decide on guilt and levy fines without recourse to courts. As a result, the Commission is often in the news and – despite the fact that it is headed up by politicians from different countries and different parties who focus on particular issues and so is prone to national, partisan, and sectoral squabbles (Wonka, 2008) – it is often portrayed by domestic politicians and media as a single-minded predator intent on gobbling up national sovereignty. Less often commented on, but just as important (see Chapter 11), is the Commission's role as the sole trade negotiator for all EU states at the World Trade Organization (WTO).

European Court of Justice (ECJ)
Based in Luxembourg, the ECJ is staffed by judges appointed by member states. It hears cases involving disputes between member states and the Commission and also cases referred to it by domestic courts for clarification of European law which may be relevant to cases those courts are trying. Early on its life, the ECJ successfully persuaded member states (or, at least, their courts) that European law was supreme and could enjoy 'direct effect' within them. This led to a body of case law that has had important ramifications within member states, most obviously with regard to the free movement of goods, services and labour, and sex discrimination. As with the Commission, the ECJ is often in the news because it says things that companies and governments do not want to hear. Even worse, because there is no higher court, it can legally oblige them to go along with its rulings. Not surprisingly, then, the ECJ is seen as one of the EU's most supranational institutions. Its critics argue that, because it has to adjudicate disputes in the light of treaties designed to promote 'ever closer union, it has a built-in bias toward integration. They also complain that this bias, along with the fact that it often has to operate where no court has gone before, leads it not so much to interpret as actually make law. As we see in Chapter 3, however, this accusation is also levelled against national courts, as well as at the European Court of Human Rights in Strasbourg, France (which, by the way, is a completely separate institution and has nothing to do with the EU). ➡

---

eralized), 11 per cent from a share of the value added tax (VAT) receipts of member states, and 75 per cent of it from member states who contribute an essentially fixed proportion of their GNP but are keen, when the budget (or 'financial perspective') is periodically renegotiated to haggle at the margins in order to show voters that they are not a soft touch. The EU then spends this money (equivalent to between 1 and 2 per cent of the GNP of all its members or less than 5 per cent of all their government spending put together) on, among other things, agricultural support (which accounts for

European Parliament (EP)
Since it was first directly elected by voters in member states in 1979, the EP (which meets in both Brussels and Strasbourg) has been transformed from a body that was merely consulted to one that – at least, in certain circumstances – really counts. Its approval is required for the EU's budget and accounts, and under the 'co-decision' procedure it now has equal say with the Council of Ministers on most legislation, although it has very little impact on areas where the EU is most powerful, namely trade, agriculture and competition policy. The Commission has to pass an investiture vote in the EP and this is no longer a foregone conclusion. In September 2004, objections to a conservative Catholic nominee from Italy forced him to stand down and delayed matters considerably. The EP also has the power to dismiss the entire Commission – a possibility that prompted that body's resignation in 1999 after corruption allegations. Individual commissioners, the European Central Bank (ECB) and the European Council have to appear before and report to the EP, although practically there is little it can do if it dislikes what it hears. The EP tends to be seen as a supranational institution for three reasons: most of those who work in it are broadly in favour of European integration; they do not continually seek to uphold the views of the states from which they come; and they have an institutional interest in seeking to reduce (or at least match) the power of the body that most obviously represents those member states, the Council of Ministers. Members of the European Parliament (MEPs) are elected country-by-country (see Chapter 6), but they sit (and, for the most part, vote) in party groups based on ideology not nationality: the Party of European Socialists, for instance, contains members from all Europe's socialist and social democratic parties; the European People's Party is its centre-right equivalent (see Chapter 4). On the other hand, much of the real work done by the 754 MEPs is done in over twenty subject-specific committees where there is a premium put on cross-party cooperation. The problem all MEPs face, however, is that, despite their getting more and more power, those whom they claim to represent – the citizens of Europe – are less and less interested in them: turnout at European elections is at spectacularly low levels and has declined over time (see Chapter 6).

European Central Bank (ECB)
The ECB, based in Germany's financial capital, Frankfurt, is possibly the EU's most supranational institution. It sets an interest rate which applies across the member states that operate with the euro (irrespective of whether it is as high or as low as they or their populations would like or need it to be) in order to keep inflation below its 2 per cent target. The ECB is, to all intents and purposes, beyond the reach of individual member states even though they fund it, their contributions varying according to the size of their economies. They may appoint its president, its executive board and the national central bank presidents that make up its governing council, but that council is not practically accountable to them or to any other European institution. This has been a particular source of frustration during the European banking and sovereign debt crisis, which some politicians argue might have been better dealt with by obliging the ECB to act as a 'lender of last resort', guaranteeing the debt of member states 'under attack' by 'the markets'. In fact, the Bank did eventually assume what amounted to that role (see Chapter 9). And even before that, it acted to help out by, for example, making cheap loans to commercial banks and, in so doing, expanding the money supply and hopefully boosting growth. On the other hand, its message to the countries in most trouble was a tough one: prioritize debt-servicing and repayment, liberalize, and cut spending.

around 45 per cent of spending) and structural funding (help for poorer regions, which takes up about 35 per cent of spending), with administration taking up around 5 per cent of the total budget. This spending, particularly on poorer regions (see Chapters 1 and 3), as well as spending on countries that are hoping to join the EU, effectively takes money from the richer parts of the Union and gives it to their poorer counterparts. This is clearly not simply an act of generosity: in the longer term, making the backward regions better off should provide those that currently help

Figure 2.1 EU budget – net contributors and recipients *per capita*, 2010

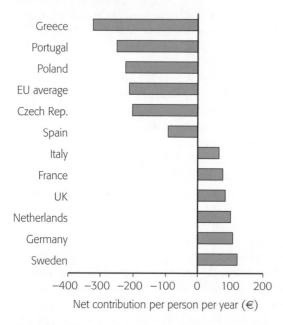

Net contribution per person per year (€)

Source: http://www.guardian.co.uk/news/datablog/2012/jan/26/eu-budget-european-union-spending#data

fund them with more lucrative markets for their goods and services.

After a decade of relative inactivity after the recession of the mid-1970s, European integration got going again in the 1980s. The case law of the ECJ, the activism of the Commission and fears that, without an end to intra-European trade barriers and the encouragement of bigger companies, Europe would lose out to Japan and America, all combined to produce the Single European Act (SEA) of 1986. The SEA was an intergovernmental treaty which committed what became known as the European Community (EC), and then (after 1991) the EU, to further legislation enshrining the 'four freedoms' of goods, services, capital and labour.

The European project aimed from the outset to give its member states access to a common market. Member states also become part of a customs union, charging a CET on goods coming from outside the EU, although these are often moderated or even removed as a result of trade deals, most obviously with those countries belonging to the European Free Trade Association (or EFTA), namely, Iceland,

Liechtenstein, Norway and Switzerland, states which are unwilling to join the EU on the grounds that the political integration entailed by full economic integration is too much for them. Not joining may not mean much of a loss in trade terms, but it does mean that they are unable to take advantage of any of the financial support on offer from the EU for things such as farming or the development of poorer regions. On the other hand, EFTA members, as relatively well-off countries, would in all likelihood join the ranks of the EU's net contributors (see Figure 2.1), so it is understandable if such incentives pale beside the costs of membership.

These costs are not only financial but logistical, legal and political. For instance, as the 2004 accession states found, any state wishing to join has to bring its administrative and legal system into what is known as the *acquis communautaire* – the corpus of legislation in force in the EU that is binding on member states, either directly or indirectly, via national laws that must be passed to give it expression. Largely because of the renewed push by the EU to make the common (or single) market a reality, the number of laws making up the *acquis* doubled between 1983 and 1998 (see Maurer *et al.*, 2003: 57).

Just as importantly, the SEA introduced procedural changes, such as the expansion of Qualified Majority Voting (or QMV) in one of the EU's most important and most intergovernmental institutions, the *Council of Ministers* (see Box 2.9). If every piece of European legislation required unanimity, it would be continually prone to deadlock or blackmail as member states exercised or threatened to exercise their veto. On the other hand, simple majority voting – where each member state was accorded one vote – would risk the possibility of legislation being passed against the wishes of governments representing the bulk of Europe's population. Under

The EU's **acquis communautaire** is the body of accumulated law currently in force that must apply in every member state if the EU is to function properly as a legally based and regulated community. Laws include **directives** (rules that must be turned into, or 'transposed' into, domestic law in national parliaments), **regulations** (which are automatically binding on all member states without any parliamentary discretion on their part as to their precise form), and the case law of the ECJ.

BOX 2.9

The EU's intergovernmental institutions

These bodies, in which member states are directly represented by national governments and civil servants, exist to ensure that the interests of those states play an important role in the decisions and direction of the EU.

Council of Ministers

Rather confusingly, the Council of the European Union (to give it its formal title) is, in fact, made up of a number of different councils, each dealing with a particular portfolio and each of which is attended by the relevant minister from each member state: hence transport, for instance, is dealt with by the transport ministers who meet regularly (around five times per year) in Brussels with their counterparts. Some sets of ministers meet much more regularly than others: for instance, the General Affairs Council, the Foreign Affairs Council and the Economics and Financial Affairs Council (dubbed ECOFIN) meet thirteen or fourteen times a year, whereas those in charge of education and health (subjects the EU is largely kept out of) meet only two or three times. At council meetings, ministers debate and amend, approve or reject proposed legislation from the European Commission, although often this is done on the nod after agreement has already been reached in the Committee of Permanent Representatives (COREPER), the committee made up of each member state's permanent representative (a senior diplomat each appoints) to the EU. The Council is, then, effectively the EU's legislature. Although this is increasingly a role it shares with the EP under the co-decision procedure, the Council remains more powerful because it grants final approval on legislation under other procedures in which EP's wishes can be overridden. It also plays an influential role in initiating proposals, even in those areas for which the Commission supposedly has the sole right of initiation. The Council is often thought of as a bastion of intergovernmentalism, although voting procedures mean that member states are not always in a position to block unwelcome developments.

European Council

Although it got going only in the early 1970s, this originally informal meeting of heads of government and foreign ministers from the member states can lay claim to being the most powerful body in the EU. It is, for instance, free from any of the quasi-constitutional checks and balances that, because they were set up by treaties, constrain the other institutions. Over the years, the European Council has developed into an institution that sets the overall political direction of the EU, determining, for instance, that there should be monetary union and enlargement, or deciding that, for example, migration and the promotion of deregulation and economic dynamism should be key goals. Its summit meetings also deal (though not always satisfactorily) with those issues that have proved too difficult to solve within the EU's formal structure, such as CAP and constitutional reform. The power of the European Council symbolizes to some the fact that, ultimately, the member states control the EU rather than the other way around

QMV, therefore, voting strength is adjusted according to the size of the state, although (as is also the case when it comes to sharing out members of the European Parliament) the weightings massively favour the smaller states. It was adjusted (largely at the expense of medium-sized countries) by the Nice Treaty of 2000 in order to reassure larger member states that they would not be overwhelmed by the increased number of small states after the accessions of 2004 and 2007. And larger member states do even better out of the Lisbon Treaty (see below) – at least, when it comes to getting legislation they want passed. Blocking legislation, however, may be more difficult. The ostensible aim of such changes may have been to ensure the swifter passage of that legislation. But they have also had the effect of under-

GERMANY (Deutschland)

Area: 349,300 km² (8.3% of EU-27)
Population: 81.8 million (16.3% of EU-27)
Religious heritage: Roman Catholic and Protestant
GDP (2011): €2,499 billion (20% of EU-27)
GDP *per capita* as percentage of EU-27 average (2011): 120
Female representation in parliament and cabinet (end 2011): 33% and 31%
Joined EU: founder member, 1957
Top 3 cities: Berlin – capital city (3.5 million), Hamburg (1.8 million); Munich (1.4 million).

History: Present-day Germany has its origins in the Holy Roman Empire that, a thousand years ago, covered much of central Europe. It developed into a loose collection of principalities that, in the sixteenth century, spawned the religious break-away from Roman Catholicism that became known as Protestantism. These small states, plus the much larger states of Prussia and Austria, were melded into the German Confederation in the early nineteenth century and finally united, minus Austria, as one country (initially known as the German Empire) in 1871. Germany became a constitutional monarchy with a parliament under Bismarck, a statesman famous for building the first welfare state and maintaining a European balance of power that, for a few years at least, delayed all-encompassing war.

With its large population and industrializing economy, Germany rapidly threatened to overtake the UK and France – a challenge that helped to usher in the First World War (1914–18).

The harsh peace settlement embodied in the Treaty of Versailles, along with the rise, rearmament programme and imperial dreams of Adolf Hitler's dictatorial *Nazi* regime, precipitated the Second World War just two decades later. Once again, the Germans (in alliance this time with the Italians and the Japanese) were pitted against the French, the British and, in time, the Russians and Americans. As well as inflicting (and suffering) enormous casualties in what became known as 'total war' (especially on the 'Eastern front' with Russia), Germany shocked the world by systematically putting to death some 6 million Jews across occupied Europe in what became known as the *Holocaust*.

The country's total defeat in 1945 saw it divided into the liberal capitalist Federal Republic (FRG, known as West Germany and the communist Democratic Republic (GDR, known as East Germany). The latter was easily eclipsed by the 'economic miracle' that saw its much bigger western counterpart become the powerhouse of the European economy from the 1960s onwards. In 1990, just a year after the fall of the communist-constructed wall that had separated them for decades, the two states were reunified – or more, accurately, East Germany was reabsorbed by the Federal Republic. This new Germany was governed by the centre-right Christian Democrats, under Helmut Kohl, until 1998, and then by a 'Red–Green' coalition led by the centre-left SPD. The 2005 election saw the formation of a 'grand coalition' between the SPD and the Christian Democrats under Germany's first woman Chancellor (Prime Minister) Angela Merkel. She was re-elected in 2009 this time at the head of a centre-right coalition with the market-liberal FDP and played the dominant role in the EU's response to the crisis in the Eurozone after 2009.

Economy and society: Since reunification, western Germany has not only extended its very generous welfare state to the east, but poured billions of euros into its economic development. Yet the east still remains comparatively depressed, with very high unemployment. Germany as a whole saw its formerly world-beating economy run into

WHAT'S IN AN ANTHEM?

Das Deutschlandlied has the distinction of a score written by classical composer, Joseph Haydn, who penned it as the anthem for the old Austrian empire at the end of the eighteenth century. The current lyrics were supplied in the middle of the nineteenth century and it was officially endorsed as the German national anthem in the 1920s. During the Nazi period, the stress was very much on the stirring (but in hindsight rather menacing) first verse – 'Germany above everything in the world ... Standing together as brothers for protection' etc. After that, the more idealistic and less bombastic third verse became the official version: it still mentions that staple of many an anthem, 'the Fatherland', but the emphasis is on striving 'with heart and hand' for 'unity, law and freedom', which are apparently the foundation for 'the glow of happiness'.

trouble during the 1990s but it has begun to recover, mainly through its high-quality manufacturing exports. It remains one of Europe's richest countries: its 81 million people (nearly 2 million of whom are Turks drawn into the country during the boom years) enjoy a standard of living a significant notch above the EU-27 average. Some regionalist sentiment is evident in eastern Germany, as well as in the predominantly Roman Catholic region of Bavaria in the south.

Governance: Germany is a parliamentary democracy, elected under proportional representation (PR). It is also a federal system, with considerable autonomy granted to its regions or states (called *Länder*) by the constitution, which is policed by a powerful federal constitutional court. The federal government is presided over by a prime minister (called the Chancellor), elected by a majority in parliament. The latter, which also elects a president as a ceremonial head of state, is divided into two houses: the popularly elected *Bundestag* and a second chamber, the *Bundesrat*, made up of *Länder* representatives, who (unusually in Europe) have the power to make or break a large proportion of legislation. Outside parliament, there is an extensive network of consultative bodies – involving regional government, employers and trade unions – that regulate the social and economic life of the country.

Foreign policy: Germany spent most of the second half of the twentieth century persuading its neighbours that they had no need to fear a repeat of the first half. It placed a great deal of emphasis on the country's membership of multilateral organizations such as the UN and NATO

A KEY CONTEMPORARY CHALLENGE
INCORPORATING THE FORMER EAST GERMANY

The absorption of the formerly Communist German Democratic Republic (GDR) by what had come to be known as West Germany was a triumph of hope and aspiration. Underneath it lay a grim reality of huge disparities in wealth and (to a lesser extent) values. After nearly twenty years, and despite massive transfers of taxpayers' money, later these disparities remain – and in some cases are glaring: the Oberbayern region in Bavaria has a GDP *per capita* rate as much as 70 per cent above the EU average and Mecklenburg–Vorpommern in the former GDR around 20 per cent below it. And the disparities appear to be having serious demographic consequences which politics seems to be powerless to offset. A disproportionate number of women, enabled by their superior educational performance to find jobs more easily than their male counterparts, have gone west, raising fears of an Eastern underclass of jobless and alienated men and a shrinking population for whom it is hard to justify continued government investment in infrastructure and housing. Certainly, Germany's wealthier states have been arguing for some time that they should not have to pay so much in fiscal transfers to their poorer eastern counterparts, the combined total of which, covering the fifteen years after 2004, is put at just over € 150 billion. Any attempt to forge yet another 'solidarity pact' to replace the one that runs out in 2019 will be difficult.

and, until the latter's military intervention to remove Serbian troops from Kosovo in 1999, was very reluctant to send its armed forces abroad, even on peacekeeping missions. Also, crucially important to Germany's rehabilitation was its membership of what is now the EU, in which the country effectively ceded political leadership to France in exchange for the right to be able to rebuild economically. This fraying 'Franco-German axis' was somewhat revived by the two countries' shared opposition to the US invasion of Iraq in 2003, although Germany did not back action in Libya. Germany has recently upped its involvement in EU peacekeeping without attracting too much controversy at home. It has also attempted to play a positive role in Europe's relations with Russia, though this has meant criticism from those – espe-

cially in Poland – who think it is placing its energy needs above collective security.

Contemporary challenges
● Doing more to integrate the country's large Turkish population.
● Incorporating the former East Germany so that the Federal Republic is genuinely socially, economically and psychologically united (see box above).
● Re-tooling the 'social market' model so that it provides jobs and helps pay for a welfare state facing pressure from an ageing (and falling) population.
● Freeing up its services sector so it becomes as dynamic and efficient as its manufacturing base.
● Pursuing a bigger role in global affairs without alarming either pacifists at home or friends abroad.

Learning resources. For overviews, go for Green *et al.* (2007), *The Politics of the New Germany*, and Anderson and Langenbacher (2010), *From the Bonn to the Berlin Republic*. Russell Dalton, in a real service to students, also provides his continually-updated textbook online for free at http://www.socsci.uci.edu/~rdalton/Pgermany.htm . For native insight into the mores and psyche of the Federal Republic, try Zeidenitz and Barkow (1999), *The Xenophobe's Guide to the Germans.* Keep up to date with the news at http://www.dw.de/dw/0,,1432,00.html .

mining the ability of individual member states (at least on topics where QMV applies) to veto proposals that they object to. According to 'Eurosceptics' – the nickname given to those who want to reverse or slow the pace of integration (see Hooghe and Marks, 2007) – this seriously, even fatally, undermines or, at the very least, compromises state sovereignty.

Some member states, notably (but not exclusively) the UK and Denmark, were sensitive to what they saw as a diminution of their sovereignty. Their concerns fed into the agreement which turned the EC into the EU – the Maastricht Treaty (or 'Treaty on European Union', (TEU)) signed in 1991. Maastricht narrowed the range of topics on which a state could veto a proposal from the Commission. But it also attempted to 'ring fence' those issues that most directly touched on sovereignty. It did this by assigning them to the second and third of what was to become known as the 'three-pillar' structure. Broadly speaking, the first 'European Community' (or EC) pillar would include economics and trade and be subject to 'community procedures' that in the main ruled out a veto; the second ('Common Foreign and Security Policy', CFSP) and third ('Justice and Home Affairs', JHA) pillars would remain intergovernmental rather than supranational. This would allow any single member state to prevent progress on an issue if it objected. Matters deemed to be part of the second and third pillars would also be excluded from the jurisdiction of the ECJ. This lessened the chance that member states would see their preferences and their domestic legislation, on those matters at least, overridden by European law.

These concessions to intergovernmentalism were, however, somewhat balanced by Maastricht giving the supposedly more supranational *European Parliament* (see Box 2.8) much more say in lawmaking. Previously it had been very much the inferior of the Council of Ministers, in which each member state was represented equally and that alone could pass or block new laws proposed by the Commission. Henceforth (at least in some areas), the EP would have the right of 'co-decision' with the Council of Ministers. The EP was further empowered a few years later when, in 1997, the Amsterdam Treaty (much of which was an attempt to codify and simplify previous treaties) expanded the range of issues to which the co-decision procedure would apply.

Integration via economics and law

The EU has long encouraged integration by offering its member states not just security but also prosperity. True, it is the poorer southern, central and east European states rather than the wealthier western European states that directly benefit in net terms from its spending (see Figure 2.1). But all get to sell into and buy from a single market that massively expands opportunities and cuts transaction costs for business – and is therefore capable of delivering tangible benefits to ordinary citizens, with cheap flights, so-called 'health-tourism' (the ability to seek treatment in other countries but paid for by one's domestic provider), and the freedom to live and work 'abroad' only some of the most trumpeted achievements of recent years.

What seemed at the time like another tangible benefit – at least, for holidaymakers and businesses trading in other countries – was added to the list in 2002 when twelve of the then fifteen member states gave up their separate currencies in favour of a single currency, the euro (€). The economic arguments for the move were not necessarily clear-cut (see Chapter 9), but the political rationale and ramifications are clearer (see Jones, 2002). First and foremost, Germany gave up its currency, the *Deutsche Mark* – at the time, by far the strongest and most stable currency on the continent – for the cause of integration. This acted to calm concerns (especially in France) that it would demand a role in European and global affairs to match its increased size after unification in 1990 (see Chapter 11).

The coming of the euro, then, was not only an economic but also a huge political development. EU

KEY POINT

Although they originated in political decisions, two of the key drivers of European integration are not overtly political. The euro is both the culmination and the spur to completion of a single market that locks member states into 'an ever closer union' – one that is underpinned and constantly reinforced not only by the supremacy of EU law but also by the fact that it is directly applicable by domestic courts.

member states had agreed not only to a symbolic but also to a very substantial loss of political control over their economies – and arguably their destinies. True, control of interest rates had often been a matter for central banks in each member state. But governments had ways of exerting leverage over their decisions. The *European Central Bank* (ECB) (see Box 2.8), however, was presumed to be immune to political pressure – certainly from individual member states, for whom the Europe-wide interest rate might be so low it encouraged a boom (as happened in Ireland and Spain) or so high that it choked off growth and (by making the euro too strong against, say, the US dollar) rendered exports uncompetitive. Individual governments could console themselves with the fact that they could employ fiscal measures (tax and spending) to help control their economies. But some observers argued even before the crisis that hit the Eurozone in 2011 that, in order to prevent some member states taking advantage of others and/or living beyond their means, such measures would eventually have to be coordinated with other member states, creating a pressure for the Europeanization of fiscal policy (tax and spending) as well as monetary (mainly interest rate) policy. Once the crisis hit, Germany and other member states refused simply to bail out countries like Greece and Portugal and insisted instead that they get their act together by introducing austerity programmes while the EU as a whole got on with finding a way to force fiscal and monetary rectitude, ideally on all member states but at the very least on those inside the Eurozone.

This, predictably, did not go down well with the UK which, like Denmark and Sweden (who shared its strong tradition of parliamentary sovereignty and desire to control its own economic destiny) had chosen not to join the euro – so badly, indeed, that (unlike Denmark and Sweden) it refused to sign up to 2012 fiscal compact (agreed by all other member states bar the Czech Republic) which committed signatories to passing a balanced budget rule into domestic law, allows the ECJ to fine states who subsequently break the rule and grants unprecedented powers to the Commission to keep an eye on member states' economic policies.

Europe's newest member states, of course, already had firsthand knowledge of the extent to which the EU could override domestic practices and prefer-

ences even before they joined. In order to do so, after all, each had to demonstrate that they were capable of adopting the *acquis communautaire*. Indeed, inasmuch as there is clear evidence of Europeanization anywhere, it is the way candidate countries are obliged – though not always unwillingly – to bring their domestic policies into line, and not necessarily just in those areas (such as the environment) in which the EU has competence (see Börzel and Sedelmeier, 2006). This 'conditionality' does not, of course, apply to states once they have joined. But the legal implications of joining are never over. Since the 1960s, the Court's decisions not only have 'direct effect' (i.e. they do not need to be embodied in domestic legislation before being enforced by government and the courts) but are also 'supreme'. This means that in the event of a conflict between the existing law of a member state and European law, the latter will be upheld. Moreover, domestic courts, even at a low level, can go direct to the ECJ for a ruling, effectively bypassing the normal national hierarchy of courts and courts of appeal. Even more so than in the economic sphere, then, it is obvious that the sovereignty of member states, inasmuch as it involves the right to make the ultimate decision (via parliament) on its own laws, has been compromised. Moreover, the ability to use European law to achieve a desired outcome against either local or national government, or, for instance, employers and other businesses, provides another tangible benefit of European integration for its citizens.

Tidying-up exercise or step towards a super-state? The Lisbon Treaty

One thing that struck many observers about the crisis in the Eurozone was how it took virtually everyone by surprise – in spite of the fact that critics of the single currency had from the outset predicted it would run into trouble. One reason was that, while the global (and European economy) seemed to be firing on all cylinders for most of the first decade of the twenty-first century, it was all-too-easy to believe that the critics had been crying wolf. Another reason was that Europe's politicians and bureaucrats took their eye off the ball because they were too busy thinking about how best to manage the institutional implications of the other big event in European integration, namely the expansion of the EU to include twelve new countries. In June 2004, the member states, following tough negotiations on a draft produced by a Convention including national delegations and EU institutions, finally agreed on the 66,000 word text of a *Treaty Establishing a Constitution for Europe.* Their ostensible aim was to provide a single document to replace the various treaties (Rome, the SEA, Maastricht, Amsterdam, Nice, etc.) that over time have laid down how the EU is to be governed and, in so doing, adjust a system originally designed for just six member states so that it could cope with 27. Eurosceptics, of course, saw this merely as a ruse and accused some countries of forcing the pace towards some kind of superstate. In the event, the Treaty had to be abandoned when French and Dutch voters – for a range of reasons that had as much to do with a distrust of their political elites as the content of the document itself – voted against it in ratification referendums held in the spring of 2005.

KEY POINT

Like the EU Constitution that could not be ratified, the Lisbon Treaty that replaces it is seen by some as merely a necessary tidying-up exercise to allow the EU to cope with 27 (and possibly more) members and by others as a major step (for good or ill) along the road to some kind of federal superstate. A balanced assessment suggests that the irritation of its proponents is understandable but so, too, are the suspicions of its opponents.

The Treaty was not, however, abandoned. Instead it was reworked as a 'Reform Treaty' that amended the EU's existing treaties – something which made it look very different but actually kept a good deal of the substance of the proposed Constitution. The Treaty got rid of the 'three-pillar' structure set up by the Maastricht Treaty in 1992, although special procedures were left in place for foreign, defence and security policy. It also reduced the number of ways in which EU law can be made, tried to streamline the institutions (by, for instance, reducing the number of European Commissioners), and created, if not a full-blown EU minister of foreign affairs, then a 'High Representative of the Union for

Foreign Affairs and Security Policy' chosen by the member states who would sit in both the Commission and the Council of Ministers. The Lisbon Treaty, like the putative constitution, augmented the role of the EP by extending the 'co-decision' procedure (renamed the 'ordinary legislative' procedure) to around 95 per cent of all legislation, as well as attempting to improve decision-making in the Council of Ministers by extending QMV to more policies and changing its rules slightly. Lisbon introduced a new system for voting by members where legislation passes if 15 out of 27 member states agree and those agreeing represent 65 per cent of the EU's population. Member states who are outvoted, however, have the option of applying an 'emergency brake' and trying to persuade the European Council that their 'vital national interests' must be protected.

As the result of the Lisbon Treaty (and as proposed by the constitution), the EU has a full-time 'President of the European Council' chosen (by QMV) by the European Council to oversee the agenda and work of the European Council and hence the general approach and priorities of the EU, thereby providing more continuity than the previous 'rotating presidency' held by each member state for six months. Just as importantly the EU was also granted a 'legal personality', allowing it to negotiate international treaties and agreements on behalf of its members; before it could really only do this on trade. And, as under the proposed constitution, the writ of the ECJ was extended to justice and home affairs issues (including immigration and asylum) where previously it did not run, although two countries (the UK and Denmark) can claim 'opt-outs' on this score. Whether, however, the UK could, as it claimed, opt out of the Treaty's formal incorporation of a 'Charter of Fundamental Rights', including the right to life and liberty, and the right to take industrial action, is debateable. So, too, is the extent to which national parliaments, as under the proposed constitution, really will be able to get the Commission to think again about any policy to which at least a third of member states' legislatures object. Similar doubts apply to the fact that a petition signed by one million European citizens from a significant number of member states can invite (not, note, oblige) the Commission to submit proposals to the Council and the EP.

Finally, those sceptical about European integration were pleased that the Lisbon Treaty followed the proposed constitution in providing, for the first time, an explicit 'exit option' for any member state that decides to leave. Anyone opposed to a European superstate was also pleased to see that Lisbon abandoned the constitution's idea of making the hitherto *de facto* anthem (from Beethoven's Ninth Symphony) and flag (blue with twelve gold stars) official. On the other hand, they were clearly very worried indeed about the so-called 'ratchet-clause', simplifying the process of treaty revision in the future. This opens up the possibility that potentially fundamental changes, while still having to be made unanimously (unless all member states decide that henceforth they can be made by majority voting), can in the future be made without the fanfare (and therefore the visibility) of an intergovernmental conference (IGC).

The end of the nation state?

Given what we have learned about both minority nationalism and the EU, it is easy to present a picture of Europe's historical nation states menaced, on the one hand, by sub-national pressures that may one day lead to the creation of new nation states and, on the other, by European integration. Indeed, as we have already noted, there is a sense in which the two threats to state integrity and sovereignty are complementary. National minorities take control of cultural and educational affairs and service delivery, while the EU handles (among other matters) monetary policy, agriculture, trade and the environment, supposedly leaving little for the state to do. But this is too simplistic.

For one thing, by no means the majority of European states find themselves under pressure from national minorities, and are unlikely to institute changes that undermine their status as relatively homogeneous unitary states. Scandinavia is an obvious example, notwithstanding the autonomy granted by Nordic countries to Greenland and the Faroe Islands (Denmark), the Swedish-speaking Aaland Islands (Finland) and the Sami (Laplanders). Moreover, the collapse of communism has brought back into the European fold a handful of countries that, at first glance, are both unitary and linguisti-

KEY POINT

By no means all European states face a threat to their territorial integrity from minority nationalism, although where it exists that threat is serious. However, all the states involved in European integration have incrementally compromised their sovereignty, even though they continue to command the primary loyalty of their (majority) populations and could, in theory, reassert their authority by leaving the EU.

cally homogeneous and unlikely to want to compromise a sovereignty that was so long suppressed by Soviet domination. Any list would include on it Poland and the Czech Republic, as well as the much smaller Slovenia.

That said, however, the new members of the EU also include countries, such as Slovakia and Hungary and the Baltic states, that contain minorities who (like Northern Ireland's nationalist community, although less violently) could feel more loyalty to neighbouring states. Whether, though, they will allow those minorities more autonomy is another matter – and will partly depend on the behaviour of those neighbouring states. Some are careful not to push things too far, relying on common EU citizenship to make things easier over time, although the fact that some countries involved look unlikely to join in the foreseeable future renders this strategy problematic (see Scott, 2006): Romania, for example, cannot apply this soothing logic to the Romanian minority in Moldova; but other states, like Hungary, have provoked concerns by granting special privileges to 'Hungarians' living in surrounding countries (Csergo and Goldgeier, 2004: 27–9).

Those concerns may put off those countries from ever following the UK, Spain and Belgium down the (quasi-) federal or devolutionary route, pushing them instead towards France's example and to cling to the constitutional ideal of being 'one and indivisible' in spite of the historic claims of certain regions for more autonomy. But they need to be careful. For one thing, as we have seen, France is not quite as inflexible as it presents itself. For another, France can get away with more because it is a country with clout. New EU members, such as Romania and Bulgaria (with Turkish minorities), might well need to make more effort under the watchful eye of fellow member states. On the other hand, pressure on such matters can prove counterproductive: Greek Cypriots clearly felt 'bounced' by the EU and the UN into accepting a federal solution to end the partition of their island and bring the Turkish-occupied north into Europe with them, and promptly voted 'no' to the plan in a referendum in April 2004 (see Box 2.10) – a decision which leaves the island in a kind of limbo and renders Turkish accession even more problematic than it would have been anyway (see Chapter 11).

We should also remember that, while the EU boasts – if not formally, then informally – many of the outward symbols we traditionally associate with a state like a flag and a passport, it still lacks a good deal of the substance. The EU's parliament is not sovereign, executive authority is blurred and it fails to command the primary loyalty of those it likes to call citizens. On the other hand, anyone supporting European integration can point, on the evidence of this chapter, to the fact that many member states, too, fail to inspire loyalty or affection among all those living within their borders. And, as we shall see in Chapters 3 and 4, few European states can boast a genuinely independent or powerful parliament – or, for that matter, an executive whose competence is clear, unencumbered and unchallenged.

Yet even if there is no clear 'pincer movement' against Europe's historical nation states, they are no longer quite what they were. Only some of them are under threat from below; but all of them have ceded the final say in some areas of policy and law to the EU. Indeed, such is the reach of the EU into the economics, policy making (see Chapter 3) and particularly the legal life of its member states, that it cannot be said merely to present a threat from above. Instead, it is embedded within and woven into each and every member state. Whether this represents an end to sovereignty, however, is a moot point. Practically, European states that join the EU no longer have complete control or freedom of action: they have swapped full sovereignty for the arguably greater security provided by an institution whose original purpose, after all, was to render states interdependent so they would not and could not wage war against each other ever again (see Debate 2.1). On the other hand, there is nothing – beyond the enormous costs that would presumably be involved

BOX 2.10

Cyprus – where the EU and minority nationalism meet

The internationally recognized Republic of Cyprus joined the EU in 2004 but, following the failure to win consent among Greek Cypriots for a re-unified federal state, the whole of the island of Cyprus did not. The area controlled by the self-styled Turkish Republic of Northern Cyprus (TRNC) – which has existed in various forms since. Turkey invaded, ostensibly to protect the Turkish population of the island against Greek nationalists in 1974 – is still excluded. The population of the TRNC wants to rejoin the Republic but with a level of autonomy and continued (military) links with Turkey (which has spent much of the last three decades encouraging migration of mainland Turks to Cyprus) that is unacceptable to the Greek majority. Despite the occasional confidence-building measure from the leaders of both communities, the situation remains deadlocked and a thin strip of no-man's land – the demilitarized zone – still stretches across the island from east to west. Notwithstanding the commitments it made when it became a candidate for EU membership, Turkey refuses to open up its ports and airports to the Republic of Cyprus until the EU (which now grants aid to the TRNC) allows direct flights from its member states into the Turkish north. Meanwhile, the Republic of Cyprus threatens vetoes left, right and centre should any quarter be given. This stand-off has hampered negotiations on Turkish membership, parts of which have been frozen until progress on this and other issues is made. It was hoped that EU membership for Cyprus and, eventually perhaps, Turkey would help solve one of Europe's most persistent and dangerous minority nationalist problems. Right now it doesn't look that way – not surprising perhaps in view of academic research which suggests that in these situations institutional cooperation between the states involved is the ultimate source of progress (Tannam, 2011).

DEBATE 2.1

Is EU membership a good idea?

<table>
<tr><th>YES</th><th>NO</th></tr>
<tr><td>

- Countries' businesses gain unrivalled and unlimited access to a market of nearly half a billion well-off consumers. Joining the 'Eurozone' reduces costs even more.
- Poorer member states gain from the money redistributed from their richer counterparts via 'structural funds' aimed at developing backward regions. Richer ones benefit in the short term by being able to locate production in poorer counterparts where costs are lower. In the long term, redistribution produces more consumers with more money.
- Citizens gain the theoretically unhindered and legally-enforceable right to travel, live, work, set up businesses, and (to a limited extent) access social security in 26 other countries. As consumers, they benefit from competition legislation.
- Common standards – for example, on the environment – help promote the collective good and prevent 'free-riding'. They can also be used to spread best-practice.
- Many modern challenges – the environment, terrorism, immigration, organized crime and trafficking – make a nonsense of borders and are better tackled in unison.
- For many states, being represented in foreign policy and trade negotiations by a large and powerful player gives them more influence than they would otherwise have.
- The EU helps lock in democracy, links economies and promotes cultural and diplomatic understanding and interchange – a recipe for peace as well as prosperity.

</td><td>

- The economic future is global not regional, with India and China rather than Europe being the markets of the future. The EU is inherently protectionist, giving aid to the developing world instead of opening up trade. It also subsidizes inefficient businesses – particularly in agriculture – and backward, sometimes corrupt countries.
- Some citizens – affluent and mobile cosmopolitans – benefit more than others from all these freedoms, but all have to put up with legal obligations imposed by institutions that they have not elected and therefore cannot hold directly accountable.
- Common standards put up costs for business and prevent it competing globally. The EU is biased towards a consensus model that stymies liberal economic reform.
- Countries could still co-operate on transborder issues and form coalitions in international fora without surrendering their sovereignty on vital issues like immigration, currency, and foreign and defence policy. Why should larger, more powerful nations have their freedom of manoeuvre limited by minnows?
- To credit the EU with fifty years of peace and prosperity is to confuse correlation with causation: those who have stayed outside it, like Norway and Switzerland, have also avoided war and grown rich – in fact, even richer.
- The new rules allowing EU institutions unprecedented control over Eurozone members' budgets means the end of economic independence for national governments and their citizens.

</td></tr>
</table>

– to stop a state that has forgotten (or no longer believes in the necessity of) that basic bargain from leaving and reasserting whatever control and freedom it feels it has lost.

Yet, while in many European countries the nation state as an institution is under threat, if not siege, it continues to exercise considerable cultural sway over many, perhaps even the majority, of Europeans. As we have seen in Chapter 1, people still see themselves as Czech or German or Dutch or Swedish or even Spanish or British or Belgian. This sense of identity is reinforced daily, not just by poli-

tics but, perhaps more powerfully by the 'banal nationalism' (Billig, 1995) of linguistic and spatial familiarity and popular culture, be it sport or prime-time television (see Chapter 7). The challenge for Europe is to reconcile its population's persistent attachment to nation states with its movement toward a 'multilevel governance' that, institutionally anyway, can override and undermine those states. Failure to do so risks delegitimizing democratic politics as a whole: people will feel governed (and indeed be governed) by an institution over which they seem to have little or no observable control. Success might help pave the way for the co-existence of national and European identity that is by no means impossible (see Smith, 1992) and some would argue is desirable. Whether such developments are, in reality, crucial to people working effectively with each other across borders – and therefore blurring those borders – is another matter: there are plenty of Europeans living in one state and journeying to work (often daily) in another (so many that the EU has had to introduce legislation to regulate their tax, social security pension arrangements), while there are EU-facilitated INTERREG programmes which encourage border regions to work with each other in promoting trade and business networks (see Harguindéguy, 2007). Whether, in turn, this is seen as sensible or some kind of threat depends ultimately on whether one believes sovereignty is absolute or relative – or, presuming it has been either lost or compromised, whether that process is irreversible and unqualified. In 2009, Germany's Constitutional Court effectively declared that it was neither: although it decided that the Treaty of Lisbon was compatible with the Federal Republic's Basic Law (the *Grundgesetz*), the Court made it clear that the EU's institutions lacked the legitimacy of their domestic counterparts, which should therefore retain a right to a say on certain crucial issues in what, in the end, remained 'an association of sovereign national states' – all slightly ironic perhaps in view of Germany's determination, in the wake of the Eurozone crisis, a couple of years later, to insist on a fiscal compact which would supposedly hardwire sound finance into the constitution of member states, arguably putting it beyond the reach of national parliaments.

Learning Resources for Chapter 2

Further reading

On the nation state and minority nationalism, the first port of call is still Keating (2001), *Nations Against the State*, and Guibernau (2007), *The Identity of Nations* or, if you want something very short, Keating's chapter in the collection edited by Heywood *et al.* (2006), *Developments in European Politics*. The collection edited by McGarry and Keating (2006), *European Integration and the Nationalities Question*, is also very useful, as is (for anyone seeking an up-to-date comparative book focusing on the party politics surrounding the issue) Alonso (2012), *Challenging the State*. See also Panayi (1999), *An Ethnic History of Europe since 1945*. O'Leary's chapter in the collection edited by Paul *et al.* (2003), *The Nation State in Question*, and Schmitter's chapter in the book edited by Gustavsson and Lewin (1996), *The Future of the Nation State*, provide typically stimulating essays on some of the issues raised here. On why conflicts do and do not spill over into violence, both in and outside Europe, see Wolff (2007), *Ethnic Conflict*.

Work on the EU is voluminous to say the least. A justifiably popular introductory text is McCormick (2011), *Understanding the European Union*, after which one can go into more detail by reading Cini and Perez-Solorzano Borragan (eds) (2009) *European Union Politics*, Wallace *et al.* (2010), *Policy making in the European Union*, and Bache, George and Bulmer (2011), *Politics in the European Union*. An advanced, but very approachably presented, guide is Hix and Høyland, (2011), *The Political System of the European Union*, while there is plenty of contemporary and historical food for thought in the collection edited by Meunier and McNamara (2007), *Making History*. The same goes for Schulz-Forberg and Stråth, (2012), *The Political History of European Integration*, Bartolini (2007), *Restructuring Europe*, Schmidt (2006), *Democracy in Europe*, and the collection edited by Thomson *et al.* (2006), *The European Union Decides*. Ross (2011), *The European Union and its Crises: Through the Eyes of the Brussels Elite* brings things bang up to date and conveys brilliantly how those on the inside of the EU's recent triumphs and travails see things. Anyone seriously interested in the EU should also check out the *Journal of Common Market Studies* (JCMS), the *Journal of European Public Policy* and the journal, *European Union Politics*.

On the web

http://www.ethnologue.com/country_index.asp?place=Europe – minority languages and cultures in Europe

www.expatica.com – twists and turns of Belgian politics

www.lehendakaritza.ejgv.euskadi.net – Basque Country

www.gencat.net – Catalunya

cain.ulst.ac.uk – Northern Ireland

http://www.guardian.co.uk/politics/scottish-independence – Scotland's referendum

www.moi.gov.cy and www.trncinfo.com – both sides of the Cyprus question

europa.eu – official overview of EU

http://www.cvce.eu/ – multimedia resource on European integration

www.euractiv.com – in-depth EU (and European) news, discussion and debate

www.epc.eu and www.cer.org.uk – EU think tanks

www.brugesgroup.com and www.openeurope.org.uk – Eurosceptic perspectives

www.europeanmovement.org and www.fedtrust.co.uk – Europhile perspectives

http://navigatingtheeu.wordpress.com/resources/journals-2/ – academic journals

Discussion questions

1   What are the historical roots of minority nationalism, and why do you think it has become more important in recent years?

2   Why have states like Belgium, Spain and the UK become (or made moves toward becoming) federal countries? Do you think these moves are a rational solution – and one that will last – to the problems they face? Or are these problems (and, indeed, the solutions) actually very different from each other?

3   In your opinion, can there be any justification for Europe's minorities to employ violence in order to make their case and impose their solutions? Why is the resort to violence for political ends relatively rare in Europe compared to other parts of the globe?

4   There are lots of criticisms of the EU. Yet in less than fifty years it has gone from a group of six to a group of 27 countries. Presumably, then, it has some attractions for the countries that have joined. What do you think explains its growth?

5   Why are some EU institutions thought of as *supranational* and some as *intergovernmental*? Do you think this is a useful or a false distinction? Is the tension between them creative or destructive?

6   What role have law and decision-making rules played in increasing European integration? Do you think they have eroded, or even ended, the sovereignty of EU member states?

7   Were the arguments over the proposed EU Constitution and the Lisbon Treaty really that important compared with the political implications of the Eurozone crisis which occurred a couple of years later?

8   Has the European nation state had its day?

ONLINE RESOURCES AVAILABLE

Visit the companion site at **www.palgrave.com/politics/bale** to access additional learning resources.

Chapter 3

From government to governance – running the state, making policy and policing the constitution

In Chapter 2, we looked at challenges to the supposed integrity and impermeability of the traditional European nation state. We discovered that the latter was under pressure from both within and without. Not every country was affected by minority nationalism, but all had conceded important powers to the EU, not least in the economic and legal domains. Those worried by such developments can perhaps derive some comfort from the fact that, notwithstanding such concessions, each country still retains its unique constitution. This formal legal framework sets out the rules of the game for politicians, citizens and the institutions by which they govern and are governed. As well as defining the rights (and sometimes the duties) of the citizen, the fundamental feature of most constitutions is a so-called 'separation of powers' between the legislature, the executive and the judiciary (see Box 3.1).

This chapter focuses primarily on the bureaucratic side and the policy making of the second of the 'three branches', the executive. This is the body that traditionally 'runs the country' or 'governs', albeit under the supposed direction of democratically elected politicians who form the government of the day and who are themselves meant to be under the watchful eye of parliament (see Chapter 4). But this chapter also considers the increasing importance of the third branch – the judiciary and the courts.

It has two main themes. The first is that, once again, we see some commonalities, but also the persistence of national differences. The second main theme is that governing in Europe, inasmuch as it was ever easy, is not as easy – or as easy to describe – as it used to be. As with the nation state, the scope, and even the size, of the executive is everywhere questioned. Authority, even where it is accepted, is more diffuse or spread out. What we used to talk of simply as government, it seems, is giving way to what is now termed *governance* (see Peters and Pierre, 2000). The former conjures up an image of institutions run by or on behalf of the state delivering, in more or less top-down fashion, those public goods which citizens (and the groups we examine in Chapter 8) are presumed to need. The latter implies a more complex process by which executive institutions – public and private, central and local – combine more or less smoothly to deal with the demands of increasingly less deferential individuals and interests. In short, '[the] top-down use of authority which characterizes government has given way to persuasion, incentivization and other forms of mobilization characteristic of networks' (Page and Wright, 2006: 4). It is this development, when combined with the growing impact of the EU, that has led political scientists to talk of the spread throughout Europe of the multilevel governance we defined in the Introduction – namely, the dispersal of power, a multiplica-

Separation of powers

The political philosopher Charles de Secondat, Baron de la Brede et de Montesquieu (1689–1755), known to us simply as Montesquieu, published his *On the Spirit of Laws* in 1748. In it, he famously argued that the 'checks and balances' required to safeguard a country against tyranny were best embodied in the 'separation of powers' between the following 'three branches of government'. These were a legislature to pass laws and agree taxation, an executive to administer those laws and take decisions where appropriate and a judiciary to broker disputes. In his time, Montesquieu believed that this division of labour was best exemplified by England. Since then it has become better entrenched – albeit with a rather more active executive than Montesquieu may have envisaged – in the USA. It also helps structure politics in Continental Europe, and is an important part of an ideal that emerged in German constitutional theory but spread throughout the continent – namely, the *Rechtsstaat*, a state whose acts must conform with laws enshrining fundamental rights.

tion of sites of authority and policy competence, and a mixture of cooperation and contestation between tiers of government that would formerly have been considered separate and hierarchically ordered.

This chapter begins by looking at how and why power has allegedly passed downward toward lower levels or tiers of government – a process often labelled 'decentralization' or, more specifically, 'devolution' (see Chapter 2) or 'regionalization'. It then returns to the topmost level – to the so-called **core executive**. It explores whether (and if so why) the core executive has shrunk, yet also possibly

The **core executive** is a label given by political scientists to the heart of government. It comprises both the political part of the executive – normally Cabinet and Prime Minister – and its bureaucratic support, as well as key civil servants from the most important departments, ministries and intelligence chiefs. The core executive normally operates out of the national capital.

gained in strength, via measures to improve coordination between a formerly more fragmented bureaucratic machine. Have recent developments such as the establishment of arm's-length 'agencies' (running things *on behalf of* government but not run *by* government) helped to 'hollow out' the state (Rhodes, 1997) to a degree that undermines one of the key branches of government? Or have they simply allowed it 'more control over less'? The chapter then goes on to show how the authority of the executive (and possibly parliament) is now constrained by the activism of the judiciary to such an extent that we should perhaps see the latter, too, as a part of the multilevel governance emerging across the continent.

Passing power downwards – decentralization

In Chapter 2, we referred to the classical distinction between unitary and federal states (see Elazar, 1997) and noted that it was breaking down as some former unitary states moved toward federalism. This move between classical categories, however, has been made only by the handful of countries we discussed in Chapter 2 – namely, Belgium, Spain, the UK and (possibly) Italy. Apart from Germany, Austria and Switzerland, all the others remain unitary states: no CEE state chose to become a federation or to stay in one. Yet that binary distinction between unitary and federal has always been as much analytical as real. In 'unitary' Scandinavia (especially Denmark) local government has long collected (relative to other non-federal states) a large proportion of state revenues (see Table 3.1). It has also been quite a big spender and runner of services, all of which has allowed room for regional variation. And even outside Scandinavia, local authorities in Europe are responsible for a raft of things that in some countries would be the preserve of central government (or private companies). These include public housing, public utilities, welfare and health. Consequently, even if they do not collect much of their country's revenue, they account for quite a high proportion of its spending (Table 3.2).

Spain, as we saw in Chapter 2, is not a 'normal' federal country, but even the supposedly more conventionally federal Switzerland and Germany are by

Table 3.1 The central/regional/local split of taxation, 2000 and 2009

	2000 (%)				2009 (%)		
	Central	**Regional**	**Local**		**Central**	**Regional**	**Local**
Spain	48.7	7.8	9.1		29.0	22.1	9.4
Germany	28.4	22.7	7.0		30.3	21.2	7.6
France	42.1	0.0	9.7		32.9	0.0	12.5
Poland	51.8	0.0	9.1		50.7	0.0	13.2
Italy	55.6	0.0	14.4		53.2	0.0	14.1
Sweden	60.6	0.0	28.9		57.6	0.0	35.6
EU-27 average	60.4	15.2	10.4		58.0	20.1	10.7
Netherlands	55.9	0.0	3.4		59.2	0.0	3.7
Czech Rep.	75.9	0.0	12.0		68.4	0.0	14.2
UK	94.3	0.0	4.0		94.0	0.0	5.2

Note: The remainder of taxes are taken by social security funds.

Source: Data from Eurostat, *Taxation Trends in the EU*, 2011.

Table 3.2 The central/regional/local split of spending, 2000 and 2009

	2000 (%)				2009 (%)		
	Central	**State/Region**	**Local**		**Central**	**State/Region**	**Local**
USA	48.4	51.6	0.0		53.5	46.5	0.0
Switzerland	20.1	31.7	20.9		14.0	36.9	19.1
Spain	25.8	28.3	12.6		20.8	35.7	13.7
Germany	14.2	23.6	15.5		19.2	21.0	15.7
Netherlands	31.3	0.0	35.4		30.5	0.0	34.0
Italy	34.2	0.0	30.0		31.9	0.0	31.1
Poland	41.3	0.0	24.1		33.0	0.0	32.5
France	38.1	0.0	18.3		34.0	0.0	20.7
Sweden	45.8	0.0	43.0		39.6	0.0	47.5
Czech Rep.	64.6	0.0	22.8		59.7	0.0	27.0
UK	71.6	0.0	28.4		72.3	0.0	27.7

Note: Remaining expenditure is accounted for by social security funds.

Source: Data from OECD, *Government at a Glance* 2011.

BOX 3.2

Alpine exceptionalism – the Swiss confederation

Each of the 26 cantons that make up the *Confoederatio Helvetica* (CH), or Switzerland, is linguistically homogeneous. They comprise German-speakers (who make up 64 per cent of the population) or French-speakers (20 per cent) or Italian-speakers (8 per cent). Each tends, as well, to be dominated by either Protestants (who make up 40 per cent of the population) or Catholics (who make up 45 per cent), though by no means all German-speaking cantons are Protestant, nor all French-speaking cantons Catholic. Little surprise, then, that the state forged from this religious and linguistic patchwork is federal rather than unitary. Survey evidence suggests that, in contrast to Germans, who do not feel much emotional attachment to their *Länder* (regional states), the Swiss root both their cultural and political identity in their canton rather than in the nation. Why else, one could argue, would they tolerate a federal government that has places all but reserved for a handful of the biggest parties, pretty much irrespective of results, with senior politicians almost automatically getting a turn to be president? The federal government may control more areas of day-to-day life than some suppose. But its growth is limited by the constitutional requirement that any new powers must be agreed by the cantons, as well as a referendum of all citizens, Switzerland being one of the world's biggest fans of *direct democracy* (Chapter 6). Cantons largely determine their own taxes. They have a big say in federal legislation, too. Not only do they have an 'upper house' of parliament all to themselves, but this *Council of States* knows that its veto cannot be overridden in the lower house, no matter how many MPs are ranged against it.

---

no means replicas of US-style federalism (see Box 3.2 and Linder, 2010; see also Kriesi and Trechsel, 2008). German *Länder* (regional states) have less power and autonomy than their American counterparts (see Box 3.3). They do, though, have considerable influence on national politics via the *Bundesrat* (the upper house of parliament) and on political outputs more generally because (along with local government and social insurance funds) they control two-thirds of Germany's budget and employ over half of all the country's public servants. In Switzerland, the competence of the federal (i.e. central) authority has been growing. The Swiss states (called cantons) are still the prime source of identity and (under the third article of the constitution) the ultimate authority when it comes to giving more power to the centre. But they are too frag-

KEY POINT

A variety of pressures – practical, financial and ideological – have ensured that it is not only in federal countries that powers are devolved from central to regional and/or local government. The EU has also played a part, although its influence – like the downward transfer of powers itself – is not quite as great as some assume.

mented to deliver all services and functions efficiently or effectively.

If, however, those countries moving toward federalism (full-blown or otherwise) are in the minority, they are by no means alone in pursuing decentralization. A variety of political, economic and institutional pressures have pushed – or are likely to push – all but the smallest European states in the same direction. From at least the 1970s onwards, central government finances in many unitary states were coming under pressure as the postwar boom began to tail off. This prompted the idea that they were suffering from 'overload' – too much responsibility for too many aspects and activities (see King, 1975). Policy makers wanted to offload some of this overload (and some of the blame for cutbacks to services) onto lower tiers of government. But they were nevertheless aware that efficient and effective service delivery and economic planning were just too big a job for the lowest level of local administration (normally called 'the commune' or district in Europe) – a level that is notoriously fragmented (Italy and France, for example, have over 8,000 and 36,000 communes, respectively). They were also coming to terms with the fact that development aid from the EU was increasingly targeted at the level of the

Germany's *Länder* – not quite as autonomous as they look

Unlike most of Switzerland's cantons, Germany's 16 *Länder* are largely artificial creations, designed not so much to reflect traditional regional identities as to disperse power efficiently in a country that the Allies of the Second World War felt they needed to neuter. Under the 1949 Basic Law (Germany's constitution), every *Land* government is accountable to a separate parliament, is elected in different ways, and operates according to its own constitution. The split with regard to responsibilities is broadly as follows:

	State (*Land*)	Federal (*Bund*)
Exclusive responsibility	Broadcasting Transport Police and judiciary Education (incl. curriculum)	Defence Foreign and trade policy National budget
Shared responsibility	Environmental policy, business and labour market regulation	

However, the federal government also has the ultimate say on anything judged to require uniformity throughout the country. The federal government also delegates a good deal of the implementation and administration of the policy areas in which it has competence. Interestingly, the *Länder* can deal direct with the European Commission on issues for which they have competence and, following arguments over ratifying the EU's Maastricht Treaty, they have a constitutionally guaranteed right to a say on any transfer of sovereignty that may affect them. They are also allowed to make their own agreements with foreign states – but only with the consent of the federal government.

In short, there is a good deal more functional overlap and interdependence in the so-called 'co-operative federalism' that distinguishes Germany (and Switzerland) from the 'dual' federalism that operates in the USA – and, therefore, still plenty of room for tension. An example is the *Finanzausgleich* – the constitutionally backed obligation on the most wealthy *Länder* to subsidize their poorer counterparts (especially those in the former East Germany). Disputes, ultimately, must be adjudicated by the Constitutional Court (see Table 3.4) but reforms passed in 2006 aim to reduce conflict by granting the *Länder* more autonomy in some areas in return for reducing their ability to block federal legislation in the powerful second chamber of Germany's bicameral parliament, the *Bundesrat* (see Chapter 4).

region rather than the state (see Keating and Hooghe, 1996).

This combination of ideological change and institutional pressure (domestic and to some extent European) drove a rationalization of central and local government. It also led to the setting up or strengthening of so-called 'meso-level' or regional government that sits between the local and the central state (see Table 3.3). In many (though not all) countries this level has, accordingly, progressed from being appointed to being elected (see Keating,

2000). This incremental trend toward 'functional decentralization' (the parcelling out of tasks and competences previously assumed by central government) first affected western Europe, including some of its administratively most centralized states. France, for instance, began by setting up appointed regional authorities to coordinate economic investment and planning in the 1970s, and the 22 in mainland France became elected bodies (assemblies chosen by voters which then go on to nominate executives) in 1986 as part of a general process of

Table 3.3 Levels of government – three examples

UK	France	Poland
Government	gouvernement	rząd
English region + Scottish government, Northern Ireland executive and Welsh Assembly government	région	województwo
County council or 'unitary authority'	département	powiat
City, town, borough, district council	commune, & municipalité	gmina

Note: Multilevel governance implies all levels communicating with each other simultaneously rather than a 'nested' chain of command or hierarchical division of labour. Note also that in England, after a failed referendum in 2004, plans were abandoned to move towards elected regional authorities. In France, four regions and departments are overseas.

both *décentralization* (decentralization) and *déconcentration* (the transfer of discretion to central government officials who are located outside Paris, or occasionally the physical relocation of government bodies) pursued by governments of both left and right (see Box 3.4).

Likewise, Italy, which had a similar so-called 'fused' system where provinces were overseen by prefects who reported directly to Rome, shifted to a system of 20 popularly elected councils representing its historic regions, although subsequent moves towards full-blown federalism (itself just one piece in a jigsaw of reforms to the governance of the country) foundered in 2006 (see Bull and Pasquino, 2007). Romania has an even more byzantine and overlapping system, which many argue promotes corruption. Greece, on the other hand, bit the bullet in 2010 and abolished its 57 prefectures, at the same time getting rid of nearly 700 municipalities and creating 13 elected regional governments. The situation in the Netherlands is more complicated (see Andeweg and Irwin, 2009). The country maintains its system of twelve provinces, with elected governments and legislatures, dealing mainly with transport and environmental matters. These are much

smaller than most European regions, hence a not altogether convincing recent attempt to group them into four 'Eurosized' *landsdelen* or 'country-parts' which some argued were set up primarily to adjust to the fact that, from the late 1980s onwards, the EU's 'structural funds' would no longer simply compensate member states for their own regional spending but supposedly go straight to the regions themselves. A similarly instrumental process of regionalization occurred in Ireland, too (Ladrech, 2010: 108). The extent to which this support for regions involves bypassing and therefore undermining the nation state (see Chapter 2), however, has to be set against the fact that many of the areas in which the EU assumes competence are precisely those which regions themselves have always had or have taken on or wish to get hold of (Panara and De Becker, 2010).

These moves toward regionalization arguably provide concrete evidence of Europeanization – and even more so perhaps in central and eastern than in western Europe. In CEE, many states (except for the very small ones) proceeded to carve themselves up into sometimes quite artificial regions (Poland has 16, the Czech Republic eight) in order to qualify for the €200 billion plus of EU funding that goes to deprived regions within countries (see Chapter 1) – just as happened in the Nertherlands and Ireland, and Greece, too (see Sotiropoulos, 2004: 417). That said, it is important not to ignore domestic pressure, the doggedness of domestic political and administrative actors, and the considerable diversity of outcomes (Hughes *et al.*, 2004). Still, the accession states of central and eastern Europe there is evidence that regionalization is having an impact in, for example, Poland and (after a difficult start) the Czech Republic, where (according to OECD data) the number of government workers employed by central government has dropped from 68.5 per cent in 2000 to just 46.4 per cent in 2008, making it the only country outside Spain (which saw a drop from 41.2 to 20.3 per cent) to register much change in that respect over the last decade. That said, the impact of regionalization in central and eastern Europe is an uneven one (see, for useful case studies, Baun and Marek, 2006, Dobre, 2009, and Scherpereel, 2010a); there is certainly no uniform pattern of multilevel governance in the region (see Bruszt, 2008). And from Brussels' point of view, con-

---

BOX 3.4

France: *plus ça change* – perhaps not

France is routinely portrayed (and sometimes ridiculed) as one of the most inveterately centralized, 'statist' (and, indeed, elitist) states in Europe, or perhaps the world. This portrayal always needed some qualifications. Centralization, for example, was traditionally mitigated by the fact that so many of France's national politicians held (and continue to hold) elected positions (for example, as mayors) at, the local level, guaranteeing that state policy took sub-national needs into account. But the portrait is also increasingly outdated. True, its civil servants or its politicians have not rushed to embrace what they see as the neoliberal tenets of new public management (NPM). But there has been a concerted attempt by governments of both right and left, beginning in the early to mid-1980s, to transfer powers from Paris (and its agents, the *préfets* or prefects) to local and regional government, which now controls almost half of government, expenditure. These lower tiers of government have responded positively to being given extra responsibilities, and governments have seen fit to add to them over the years. Nor have civil servants at the centre, as well as at local level, resisted reform completely (see Clark, 1998 and Rouban, 1995).

---

cerns about adequate financial control led the Commission to change its tune after 2000 and recommend that accession states manage their regional development programmes and policy centrally rather than letting a thousand flowers bloom at sub-national level (Keating, 2006). In both western and central and eastern Europe, it would also appear that central governments are using the advantages afforded to them by their greater presence and involvement in decision-making in Brussels to maintain a gate-keeping role between the EU and regions (Wessels *et al.*, 2003). Many regions, however, continue to lobby for themselves in the so-called capital of Europe, although this 'sub-state paradiplomacy' sometimes involves working with, as well by-passing, the national government (see Tatham, 2010; see also Moore, 2008a and b).

We should, then, be cautious not to overstate the case for 'regionalization' as an aspect of multilevel governance irrespective of whether it is or is not driven by Europeanization (see Bache, 2007). For one thing, as Tables 3.1 and 3.2 make clear, money does not follow structure in any simplistic way. In Spain, there has, since the mid-1990s, been a clear (but by no means complete) shift toward regions raising revenue themselves (Toboso and Scorsone, 2010), but central governments in many other countries – even the post-devolution UK – continue to keep a tight hold on sources of revenue and, where possible, spending. National politicians are aware of the impact on the macro-economy (and perhaps

their electoral chances) if they cede control of revenue-raising to sub-national government. Moreover, we need to be careful about treating the regions they are keen to keep an eye on as cohesive entities 'when the reality is that they are composed of diverse groups with multiple interests' (Keating, 2006: 151). Likewise, it is tempting (and not altogether incorrect) to see the EU's funding and efforts to diffuse best practice creating a network of increasingly assertive regions. But we should acknowledge that those regions which are keen and effective players at the EU level (such as the German *Länder*) are able to play that role not simply because of the EU but because they had already asserted themselves and gained recognition domestically (Keating, 2006: 152).

In any case, as Tables 3.1 and 3.2 hint, regionalization is not the whole story when it comes to decentralization. Beneath the level of the region there have also been significant developments in local government, whose service delivery role still dwarfs that of regions (for details, see Dollery and Robotti, 2008, Heinelt and Bertrana, 2011, and the chapter on Europe in Kersting *et al.*, 2009) Most notable in this respect is the extension – on the grounds of improving both management and accountability – of personalized political control (see Box 3.5). 'Regionalization' also masks the potential for conflict between local and regional authorities: in Italy, for instance, regions took over some of the supervision of local authorities from centrally appointed

---

BOX 3.5

The trend towards direct election in European local government

According to the UN, over half of Europeans lived in cities in 1950. By the first decade of the twenty-first century, that figure had risen to nearly three-quarters. In some countries, big cities are the powerhouses of the economy. Little surprise, then, that some of them want a politician who is the face of the city. Little surprise either that some smaller cities and towns, not wanting to be left behind, want the same thing. In the UK, London's Boris Johnson is only the best known of a number of directly-elected mayors. Even in those towns and cities which have not moved toward direct election, local councils have moved away from the traditional system of an appointed chief executive overseen by committees of elected councillors toward a system of a council leader with a cabinet (see Wilson and Game, 2006).

But the UK has a long way to go to catch up with Italy. There, as in France and Germany, there is a stronger tradition of an individual (elected or not) exercising administrative powers on behalf of the state. Since 1993, any of Italy's 8,000 *comuni* (local councils) with a population of more than 15,000 can hold direct elections for their mayor. Some local authorities have also been able to take advantage of a new property tax, the rate of which they can determine, to enhance their autonomy.

On the other hand, both the UK (which, in the jargon, is traditionally a *monist* country, emphasizing collegial, elected and local supervision of council activities) and Italy (a Napoleonic or *dualist* country where elected bodies traditionally worked alongside an individual executive answerable to the state) are part of a European trend toward 'de-collectivization' in local government (Wollmann, 2008; see also Borraz and John, 2004). The rest of Germany has been catching up fast with the southern *Länder*, which have a strong tradition of directly elected executive mayors. Meanwhile, the countries of Scandinavia, as in Britain, have been experimenting with more powerful council leaders and cabinets, and, in the case of the latter, directly elected mayors.

The aim of direct election has been to increase the responsiveness of services to local demands, and hopefully to offset declining voter turnout. Doubtless, it will enhance the prestige (and perhaps the accountability) of mayors and council leaders, especially in the biggest cities, vis-à-vis regional and national government. However, the extent to which greater powers for the locality have accompanied this enhanced prestige is less easy to gauge. Nor must we assume that any trend is universal. For instance, a move toward direct election seemed certain to take place in the Republic of Ireland, beginning in Dublin. But with a change of government in 2011 the idea seems to have died a death. Still, there are now directly elected mayors in twelve European countries (Loughlin *et al.*, 2011: 736), and more may follow.

---

prefects. This, and the failure of the regions to devolve some of their powers to the local level, has caused considerable tension. Indeed, some larger European towns and cities (especially in Italy) have even tried to bypass the regions by forming a more direct relationship with central government. And rarely are these conflicts merely institutional in the sense of an objective, if contested, search for the most rational and/or democratic way of running the country. Most reorganizations of local (and regional governments) will have a political tinge (if not a political motive) to them: the central governments that pursue them are made up of party politicians

who may well be hoping to disadvantage their opponents or even do away with them altogether – as was the case when the UK's Conservative government abolished London-wide government in the 1980s, only for it to be reinstated when Labour took over in 1997.

We should note, however, that this kind of local-regional (and central) conflict is not endemic in Europe. True, in countries with more adversarial styles of politics (such as Spain, the UK, France and Italy) parties in opposition at the national level use their occupation of local or regional office to 'grand-stand' against the government. But in countries with more consensual political styles (e.g. Germany, the Netherlands and the Nordic countries) cooperation tends to win out over conflict. In Sweden, for example, decentralization is taken for granted and runs relatively smoothly, albeit not utterly without tensions. Each of its 24 counties (*landsting*) has an elected council, but also a governor appointed from the centre. He or she leads an administrative board, but one made up of members chosen by the county council. The administrative board fulfils a planning role alongside not only the county councils but also the municipal authorities. The municipalities look after day-to-day service delivery according to goals set for them by government agencies. More generally, some 70 per cent of the total revenue of local government in Sweden is raised locally – a higher proportion than in most other European countries, including France (around 50 per cent), Germany (around 40), Italy (35 per cent), the Netherlands (25 per cent), Spain (less than 5 per cent) and Poland (where virtually no revenue is raised locally). Local authorities in Sweden also have a fair amount of discretion to decide how exactly they spend their centrally determined bloc grants (see Heinelt and Bertrana, 2011: 243–268, 311). Meanwhile in Germany, the fact that the *Länder* and the federal government, irrespective of party differences, effectively have to work together via the *Bundesrat* (the upper house of parliament) in order to avoid gridlock (see Chapter 4) also means that when conflict does flare up it eventually gives way to cooperation. This does not always happen in Spain (see Chapter 2), where the autonomous communities play only a minor role in Spain's upper house, the *Senado*.

'More control over less' – central government reform

Although many of its functions (and at least some of its funding) have been devolved downwards to regional and local authorities, the central state in Europe has by no means withered away. Many analysts, however, suggest that it has been 'hollowed out' (Rhodes, 1997). According to them power has passed upwards (to the EU), outwards (via the privatization we deal with in Chapter 9) and downwards (to arm's-length agencies, for example). At the same time as devolving responsibilities (if not always

KEY POINT

There is considerable variation in the extent to which Europe's central governments have embraced the ideas associated with new public management (NPM), although most have been concerned to improve political coordination of, and control over, the bureaucracy. Convergence toward one model, however, is not on the cards and – as is the case with regionalization – seems unlikely to be driven any further as a result of states adjusting to deal with the EU.

control), central governments across Europe have, to a greater or lesser degree, been changing how they do the things that are left. Influenced in part by **new public management** (NPM) ideas (Christensen and Lægreid, 2011) many have sought to separate policy making and setting (the advisory and supervisory function) from policy implementation (the administrative function). But they have also taken steps to offset the potential fragmentation involved in this effort. This has been done by maintaining and, indeed, improving political control of the non-elected part of the core executive.

New public management is as much an ethos as a doctrine. It rests on the notion that the public sector can learn a lot from the private sector in terms of its competitive focus on efficiency, value for money and responsiveness to clients or customers. Indeed, it should actually be re-structured to resemble a market wherein, ideally, the purchasers of a service are split from its providers, with managers given more autonomy but also clearer targets.

For Europe's top civil servants, NPM may well be a double-edged sword. Ostensibly, it provides a choice between a career in policy advice or more hands-on management, thereby ending any confusion between the two roles. But it also poses a risk: if, for example, politicians seek to expand the range of advice they receive, they will no longer rely so much (or at least so exclusively) on their top civil servants, and the latter may not appreciate the advantages of becoming '"network managers" rather than the wielders of public authority' (Page and Wright, 2006: 4) – especially if they face competition for such posts from executives with valuable private-sector experience. The same goes for Europe's politicians. NPM offers the chance to reduce their day-to-day operational responsibility (and, indeed, accountability) and therefore free up time for a more political role. However, NPM poses risks, both for politicians and for democratic legitimacy and control. At least in theory, politicians will be blamed for policy failures over which they have less direct control. On the other hand, if a politician can reasonably claim NPM-style separation between their function and implementation, they may escape accountability, whether 'formally' enforced by electors, parliament, the head of state or the judiciary or more informally policed by the media and the interest groups we deal with in Chapters 7 and 8 (see Helms, 2006). It is already rare for policy failure to prompt individual ministerial resignation in contemporary Europe, even though there is some evidence that such resignations do actually boost government popularity (Dewan and Dowding, 2005). In the August heatwave that hit France in 2003, over 10,000 people, mainly elderly, died of heat-related illnesses, prompting the resignation of the Surgeon General but not that of the Health Minister, who denied responsibility and stayed on in his job until a cabinet 'reshuffle' in 2004. If NPM makes such denials even more plausible, it may be more efficient (and some would say more realistic) but it might not be good for democracy.

In fact, the extent to which NPM ideas are seen as common sense in a particular country is, research suggests, heavily dependent on cultural and institutional practices that have built up over time (see Pollitt *et al.*, 2007b; and also Wright and Hayward, 2000). NPM is not irresistibly inevitable and, because of the strength of each country's 'administrative tradition' (see Painter and Peters, 2010) is always adapted rather than adopted wholesale – something which (along with an alarming lack of hard data) contributes to the difficulty of evaluating whether NPM has actually worked or not (van de Walle and Hammerschmid, 2011).

For instance, in Germany (where around half of all graduates in the civil service have law degrees) public service is more about administering according to legal procedure than managing service delivery, while the power of the *Länder* in the *Bundesrat* (see Chapter 4) has always meant that rapid change is difficult to achieve politically. Not surprisingly, then, Germany, while it may not have

completely rejected what is referred to there as the 'new steering model' has not swallowed NPM hook, line and sinker (Kuhlmann, 2009). On the other hand, the British civil service values pragmatism, bargaining and flexibility; nor is it either compartmentalized or governed by a separate civil service law. This, and the relative absence of constitutional and legal constraints on a majority government, means that NPM could be imposed relatively effectively from the late 1980s onwards (see Pollitt and Bouckaert, 2011). A Scandinavian country like Sweden, which combines a respect for legalism with an enthusiasm for decentralization and autonomy (see below) seems to lie midway between the two – not as resistant to the idea of management as Germany but not quite so gung-ho as the UK (see Christensen and Lægreid, 2011). Interestingly, there appears to have been little attempt by outside bodies (such as the IMF or the OECD) or the EU to make the adoption of NPM (as it did with privatization) a condition of assistance to the new democracies of east-central Europe (Goetz, 2001).

National history, tradition and culture, then, play a big role in governance. Indeed, it can sometimes seem that the only structural feature that European executives share is the tendency (particularly when it comes to the civil service and particularly at the highest levels) for them still to be staffed almost exclusively by white, largely middle-class and usually highly-educated, middle-aged men! While there may be a common thrust, and even common pressures (fiscal, political and otherwise), each country adapts to them in ways that – unlike, say, their parties and party systems (see Chapter 5) – do not always fit obvious patterns. For example, we cannot simply fall back (as the media often does) on easily assumed differences between the practices and responses of 'northern' and 'southern' Europe: differences do exist, but only some of them (the 'Mediterranean' tendency towards large-scale political appointments to civil service jobs and the 'over-production' of formalistic regulations) can be said to be systematic (see Sotiropoulos, 2004). And the national stereotypes that inform not only journalistic but also academic analysis are only sometimes useful (see Box 3.6). Comparative research on public administration rightly lays great stress on the strength and explanatory power of national traditions. But we should not allow this to trap us into automatic acceptance of

---

BOX 3.6

Living up to the stereotype? The civil service in Italy and Greece

Lazy, offhand and wedded to interminable bureaucratic procedure which will be set aside only if you know him personally or pay him if you do not: such is the stereotype of the southern European civil servant. Unfortunately, it is a stereotype that many familiar with the byzantine world of the Italian civil service would argue holds true (see Lewanski, 2000). Historically, many civil servants (a disproportionate number of whom were recruited from the poorer south of the country) saw their posts not so much as a passport to progression or a vocation but, rather, as a slowly rising means of subsistence that could be supplemented either by kickbacks or by holding down another job outside of the notoriously short opening hours. The administrative culture is highly legalistic, which ensures that there are myriad opportunities for those involved to charge a private premium for anyone wanting to move things along. Of course, all this applies most to 'street-level' bureaucrats. But the senior levels of Italy's civil service also come in for criticism (see Cassese, 1999) for excessive legalism, reform-resistant culture (though see Lewanski, 1999) and a tendency towards little empires ruled over by men who are there because of their staying-power and social networks rather than their talent. Traditionally, none of this mattered too much because – in a manner that in some ways paralleled the situation in communist east-central Europe before 1989 – the grip of Italy's political parties on society was so strong that politicians could effectively by-pass the civil service in order to get things done. Since the collapse of the old party system in the early 1990s, however (see Chapter 5), this is no longer the case, strengthening the case for reform. While the extent and scope of administrative change has not necessarily matched that in the electoral arena, Italy (along with other 'Napoleonic' southern European countries) has not been immune to reforms, some of which are consistent with the new public management (see Ongaro, 2011). That said, as so often in Italy, it depends where you look. In 2012 a report by the national audit court found that Sicily in the south, which has more autonomy than most of its regional counterparts, still had five times as many civil servants as Lombardy in the north, despite only having half its population.

Interestingly, probably the most significant reforms were introduced by 'technocratic' governments of non-politicians formed in the wake of a political crisis. The swearing in of such governments in the wake of the crisis in the Eurozone therefore gave advocates of reform some cause for optimism, not only in Italy but in Greece, where bringing in NPM-style reforms has not proved particularly easy in the past: attempts – led, for example, by the Ministry of Finance – to rationalize and retool the central state that had come to be seen as routine in many other European countries fell victim to the highly conservative and 'clientelist' system supported by both left and right (see Spanou and Sotiropoulos, 2011). On the one hand, the resultant 'bloated public sector' was one reason why markets, credit ratings agencies and other European governments began to pile the pressure on Greece as the Eurozone crisis began to unfold. On the other, it may mean that it is possible (though by no means painless for those directly affected) that the country can make big cutbacks in numbers of staff without hitting provision of services – something the Greek government had proved unwilling or unable to do until 2012.

outworn stereotypes that caricature countries rather than capture a more complex and dynamic reality.

The fact that comparison in this area is difficult might explain (and to some extent be caused by) the relative paucity of truly cross-national research in public administration (though see Ongaro, 2009; Peters, 2001; Pollitt and Bouckaert, 2011; Raadschelders *et al.*, 2007; and Weller *et al.*, 1997 for honourable exceptions), even though there are several useful collections of single-country descriptions (see Bekke and van de Meer, 2000; Bevir *et al.*, 2003; Page and Wright, 2006; Peters and Wright, 2000; Pierre, 1995; Verheijen, 1999). Many of these begin by estimating the number of 'civil servants' employed by each state. But even a cursory glance makes it clear that using these to compare the size of central states or core executives is highly problematic, because what counts as a civil servant varies so much between countries. What does emerge, however, is the fact that since the 1980s civil service numbers across Europe seem to have stopped expanding. This is especially the case if we accept the assertion that employees transferred, say, to regional governments or to bodies that used to be part of the central state but now exist at arm's length from it in, say, agencies (see Verhoest *et al.*, 2010) are no longer, strictly speaking, civil servants.

The state that regards itself as the pioneer of separating policy making and policy implementation is the UK. Since the late 1980s the British government has been steadily 'hiving off' operations and delivery to what are known as 'agencies'. There are now around one hundred, employing around three-quarters of what would traditionally have been called civil servants. Perhaps the most visible example is the 'Benefits Agency' which is responsible for social security payments and employs tens of thousands of people all over the country. Each agency is a more or less (see Gains, 2003) autonomous unit responsible for a particular function or service. It is headed by a chief executive reporting to a minister who, advised by senior civil servants, determines the agency's resources and goals.

Both fans and critics of 'agencification' in Britain point (either in sorrow or sceptically) to the fact that the model has not always been enthusiastically adopted elsewhere in Europe, with the exception, perhaps, of Denmark and, more recently, the Netherlands (see Pollitt *et al.*, 2007a), as well as the EU itself (Williams, 2005). Yet they miss an important point. In fact, the 'hiving off' of policy implementation has long been taken for granted in many other countries, especially in Scandinavia, even if few of them expressed much explicit enthusiasm for the NPM ideas that held sway in Britain (see Box 3.7). In Germany and the Netherlands, for instance, the delivery (and to some extent, via their collection of insurance premiums, the funding) of much of the welfare state has traditionally been left to so-called 'parastatal' or 'parapublic' bodies. The Federal Employment Service (*Bundesanstalt für Arbeit*) in Germany, for instance, runs most of the country's job centres, while most healthcare is provided via

---

BOX 3.7

Neither new nor neoliberal – government agencies in Sweden

The hiving off of government business from ministries to agencies is often associated with Thatcherite Britain in the 1980s. In fact, social democratic Sweden was the pioneer of the notion that the formulation of policy should be institutionally separated from its implementation. Indeed, the separation is formalized in its constitution, which charges government departments (overseen by cabinet ministers) with policy formulation while implementation rests with around 80 legally autonomous agencies (*ämbetsverk*). This means ministers cannot be held accountable for bureaucratic mistakes, but it also means that, potentially, they have much less control than some of their counterparts in other countries (for example, the UK) over what is done in the name of the government by agencies (see Ziller, 2001). In fact, ministers are able to exert influence via informal contacts between civil servants and, more formally, via the *Riksdag* (the Swedish parliament), which can vote to reorganize agencies and which determines their budgets. Interestingly, the latter have shrunk in recent years as agencies' service delivery roles have passed to local government. The response of agencies has been to turn themselves into supervisors rather than providers of local services (see Pierre, 1995).

---

insurance premiums collected by its *krankenkassen* – bodies organized either by sector or by geography and with the involvement of unions and employers. In the Netherlands, many of the institutions that originated in the days when the country was divided along the lines of its religious subcultures continue to deliver services (often organized regionally), albeit in a much more secular age.

Spain, it must be said, has less of an 'agency' tradition, and has been too preoccupied with territorial decentralization to develop one along NPM lines. Nor has there been much enthusiasm in France for agencies. On the other hand, agencies have played a part in reforms to the public service in Italy, possibly because they have long had a role there, even if, in

Table 3.4 Joined-up government – compartmentalized civil services

The compartmentalized rule	The interdepartmental exceptions
NL: Highly autonomous departments with own specialized recruitment; consequent lack of joined-up government has given rise to reforms in the 1990s, among them the ABD (*algemene bestuursdienst*) designed to improve horizontal mobility among senior civil servants.	**UK:** Emphasis on centrally recruited generalists; good horizontal mobility; cross-ministerial committees.
Germany: Very specialized departments with own career patterns.	**France:** generalist administrators with good networks often based on highly sought after membership of a *grand corps* (functionally oriented groups of high-flyers), shared educational background in one of the *grandes écoles*, and movement between departments and ministerial staff, and in and out of politics.
Sweden: As in most Scandinavian countries, the civil service is highly sectoral.	
Spain: Departments and ministries colonized by particular and specialized functional structures, called *cuerpos*, which seem to have survived an attempt by centre-left governments in the 1980s to loosen their grip.	
Italy: Historically fragmented with low horizontal mobility but changing after reforms introduced in 1998.	
Poland and **Czech Republic:** Little central recruitment or horizontal mobility.	

Sources: Bekke and van der Meer (2000), Page and Wright (1999), Verheijen (1999).

times past, they proliferated largely as means of providing patronage opportunities for politicians and bureaucrats alike – something which did nothing to ameliorate the unimpressive reputation of the country's public servants (see Box 3.6). It is also worth pointing out that, as those who make the case for Europeanization would expect, agencies in individual countries all over Europe also share best practice and even cooperate above the level of the nation state, sometimes facilitated in their efforts by EU bodies: this may mean that they end up being even more arm's-length than the (national) politicians who created them and/or are supposed to supervise them would like (Egeberg, 2008; Martens, 2008).

Hiving off the job of implementation has its potential downsides. The most obvious is that the creation of more structures (and arm's-length structures at that) will make it harder for the government of the day to coordinate, let alone control, policy and delivery (see Wright and Hayward, 2000) just as the latter may be becoming all the more important to voters who are no longer so tribal or hung up on ideology (see Chapter 6). This task is already rendered difficult in some states by a tendency toward compartmentalization on the part of ministries and departments (see Table 3.4) – a tendency that is only partly mitigated by the existence of finance ministries that oversee spending (and therefore all departments) and, in some countries, the appointment of a 'minister-without-portfolio' tasked with achieving what in the UK (a prime example of the trend) is called 'joined-up government'.

Partly in response, to these problems, potential and actual, Europe's politicians have recently looked for ways to help them at least steer their state machinery, even if – because of the fragmentation inherent in functional and territorial decentralization – they can no longer control it. It is this that explains what those who cling to the ideal of a neutral civil service believe is a damaging trend toward the politicization of bureaucracy. This trend (see Peters and Pierre, 2004) encompasses two things. First, there is an increased willingness on the part of senior civil servants to acknowledge that they need to be politically sensitive networkers rather than dry-as-a-bone administrators (see Pierre, 1995: 207, and Rhodes and Weller, 2001). This may explain why, despite it being increasingly possible to do so, not that many top civil servants are parachuted in from the private sector. Second, this notwithstanding, politicians seem ever keener to appoint to senior positions people they can trust.

No European country has anything like the 'spoils system' that sees incoming administrations in the USA make wholesale and overtly partisan changes at the top of the civil service. But Greece and (to a slightly lesser extent) Spain, where incoming governments can make sweeping changes at the top of the civil service and state-owned corporations, come some way towards it (see Sotiropoulos, 2004: 410). And there are other states which are more accepting of party involvement than some. In Austria and Belgium, for example, it has long been a convention that political parties were granted a number of civil service positions according to their relative strength, to which they would appoint their members. At the other end of the spectrum lie countries such as the UK and Denmark, where (in contrast to its Nordic counterparts in Sweden and Finland, whose top civil servants often belong to political parties) there is a strong cultural norm toward neutrality. Here, top civil servants are expected to switch seamlessly from outgoing to incoming governments of a different stripe. Indeed, in the UK it is difficult for a minister to replace bureaucrats whose attitudes are not conducive to his or her aims with better-disposed staff. It is, however, increasingly accepted (as it is in the Netherlands) that ministers will supplement existing staff with a handful (and no more) of people who are acknowledged to be political appointments but join the civil service as temporary 'special advisors'. Often, they provide political or media management advice that would be considered beyond the pale for permanent civil servants, who may well find their advice is overridden or that they are left out of key discussions. This so-called 'sofa government' – the taking of vital decisions by small groups of ministers

and advisers outside of formal meetings – came in for severe criticism during the Labour government that ran the country between 1997 and 2010. The Conservative–Liberal Democrat coalition that replaced it made much of its promise to cut down the number of so-called 'SpAds' (special advisors), although many ministers soon confided that they would have appreciated more help.

Other countries lie along this spectrum. In the Netherlands and in Germany (see Derlien, 2008: 188), openly political appointments to senior civil service posts, especially by new governments, are increasingly common: notwithstanding its reputation for legal formalism, the German civil service saw significant changes at the top when the CDU–CSU joined the SPD in government after the 2005 election and took the Chancellorship. In France, ministers, in addition to the departments they run, where they may, and often do, reshuffle the top posts, are also allowed what is called a *cabinet* (pronounced *cab-ee-nay* to distinguish it from the English term for the gathering of top ministers and head of government). This is a group of, at the very least, ten high-fliers, some of whom will be plucked from departments and some of whom will come from outside the civil service altogether, to help them supervise and drive their ministries, as well as to keep an eye on the work of their ministerial colleagues – a system that also operates in Italy. This practice of appointing advisory *cabinets* was copied in Poland, but not altogether successfully (see Zubek, 2006: 104). France's powerful president (see Chapter 4) also has a *cabinet*, in addition to his own general secretariat of civil servants who coordinate the work of the government. It is not surprising, perhaps, that many French ministers (who do not have to be – and while they serve cannot be – parliamentarians) have previous experience as civil servants, often working in a *cabinet*, before they become politicians and part of the elected government.

The governments of CEE also face the challenge of establishing political control over a bureaucracy that tends toward legal formalism without returning to (or failing to escape from) the profound party politicization of the civil service that characterized the communist era's *nomenklatura* system. They are not helped by the continuing antagonism between the centre-right and what, outside the Czech

Republic, is a centre-left that more often than not rose from the ashes of the Communist Party itself. This antagonism tends to see new governments try to bring in their own more trusted servants which, in turn, militates against the development of the neutral civil service that observers in, say, Scandinavia and the UK, assume (wrongly) is (or should be) the norm everywhere. On the other hand, we should beware of too negative a portrayal: extensive interviews with hundreds of ministers from CEE suggest that by far the majority of them were not only happy with the work of their civil servants but saw them essentially as (neutral) administrators (Blondel *et al.*, 2007: 147–8).

Europeanization – as well as **lustration** – almost certainly played some part in this, since accession represented a countervailing force to what might have become clientelism or cronyism and accelerated (or at least facilitated) the sometimes agonizing transition from state socialism (see Scherpereel, 2008). 'Brussels' needed a professional set of administrators that it could deal with during negotiations and which could implement change, a demand which dovetailed with the recommendations of external bodies like the OECD, even if the speed with which it was translated into reality depended, at least in part, on the character of the communist regime that preceded democratization: the formerly hard-line Czech Republic, for example, took longer to get its act together than Hungary, which had been relatively reformist (Camyar, 2010). There is also considerable evidence emerging that, once accession had been achieved, only some countries (for example, the three Baltic states) kept up the pace of reform, while others (notably Poland, Slovakia, Slovenia and the Czech Republic) let things slide (see Meyer-Sahling, 2011). The result of all this has sometimes been, as in Poland for instance, a gap between what is formally the case – the apparent erosion of politicians' ability to appoint their favourites to the civil service – and the informal reality on the ground, namely, 'tampering with the regulatory framework' so that 'far-reaching politicization' continues (Zubek: 2006: 116; see also O'Dwyer, 2006). This may, at least in part, explain why trust in civil servants is particularly low in Poland (see Figure 3.1), although it has to be said that that particular commodity is in short supply in most European countries, even (rather surprisingly perhaps given its relatively high levels of social trust

Lustration is the legal process by which formerly Soviet bloc countries have tried to reveal, regulate and in some cases ban the employment in the public sector of people who worked in (or for) the repressive apparatus of the communist regime – for example as secret policemen or their informants. The scope, pace and effectiveness of the laws passed has varied between countries but does seem to have contributed at least a little to increased trust in public institutions, if not in the governments that have passed and implemented the legislation (see Horne, 2012).

and internationally well-regarded public service) in Sweden.

Interestingly, closer analysis of these figures suggests that those countries whose civil services are most trusted (and in Europe they include Denmark, Switzerland, Ireland, Finland and Norway) are rated

Figure 3.1 Trust in civil servants

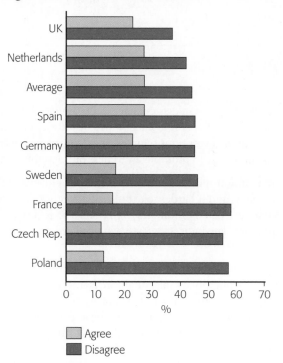

Note: Percentages are for those agreeing and disagreeing with the statement 'Most civil servants can be trusted to do what is best for the country'.

Source: Data from International Social Survey Programme, 2006 (Role of Government IV): this includes 33 countries; Italy, unfortunately, is not one of them

BOX 3.8

Freedom of information in Europe

In September 2011, the pressure group Access Info Europe and the Centre for Law and Democracy produced a comprehensive analysis of the legal framework for the right to information (RTI) across the world. Partly because it was the world's newest democracies which tended to have the best laws on freedom of information, most European countries scored poorly by comparison, as the table below (which scores countries on a range of indicators and out of a total of 150 shows).

	Date of Law	Right of Access	Scope	Request procedure	Exceptions & Refusals	Appeals	Sanctions and Protections	Promotion Measures	Overall score
UK	2000	2	25	20	12	23	7	6	95
Netherlands	1978	4	20	22	16	14	4	2	82
France	1978	1	20	17	14	16	0	2	70
Czech Rep.	1999	2	28	13	12	10	0	4	69
Poland	2001	2	26	19	10	4	1	0	62
Italy	1990	2	21	7	6	15	2	7	60
Sweden	1866	5	19	15	14	4	0	2	59
Germany	2005	0	19	7	13	15	0	0	54

Data from http://www.rti-rating.org/

In most European democracies, according to the analysts, 'typical weaknesses were the limited scope (the right not applying to the legislative or judicial branch or private bodies performing public functions), over-broad exceptions regimes, shortcomings in oversight and appeals mechanisms, and lack of legal requirements to promote awareness of the public's right of access to information.'

In reality, it is difficult to believe that the citizens of Sweden, which has a worldwide reputation for transparency, find it harder to get information out of their government than the citizens of Serbia, which came first out of all 89 countries examined. The RTI scores, after all, relate to the legal framework, not to actual practice. The indicators may also need refining and in some cases properly validating by country experts.

highly not so much because they actually produce better public policy (although, in fact, the evidence suggests that they do) but primarily because those working for the government in those countries are good at 'getting the process right by treating people fairly, avoiding favoritism, and containing corruption' (van Ryzin, 2011: 755). Just as interestingly, there appears to be only a weak relationship between the amounts government spend on public services and citizens' evaluations both of those services and those who work for them: for instance, the UK spends much less per capita than France but seems to be rated very similarly (if not particularly impressively) by its citizens; meanwhile Sweden, which spends almost as much as France, is more highly-regarded, though not as well-regarded as Finland, which spends significantly less (with the same being true of Ireland); Greece, not a particularly high- or low-spending country, although a highly centralized one when it comes to the location of its civil servants, performs poorly on virtually every measure (SCP, 2004: 268–9, 290).

Once again, then, cultural and institutional differences seem set to persist – and not just in this sphere (see Box 3.8). Although we can identify a European tendency toward trying to tighten political control over a state machine that is now more 'loosely coupled', there is no such thing as conformity. But what of one potentially crucial force for such conformity – namely, the need to improve the 'fit' between national and European administrative structures (see Cowles *et al.*, 2001)? It is certainly common to hear suggestions (from both federalists and anti-federalists alike) that the differences between east and west, and north and south, and between individual countries, will gradually grow smaller as their executive structures are somehow brought into line by the demands of dealing with the EU.

Clearly, there is evidence of Europeanization in this respect: for instance, the *grands corps* (high-ranking civil service organizations) in France have arguably lost some of their self-confidence and grip on the policy process in recent years as a result both of European integration and the way reformers have used it to bolster their case (see Cole and Drake, 2000: 29–30). More generally, member states have had to develop mechanisms for interministerial and departmental coordination, not an easy thing given the extent to which civil servants can make direct contact with their functional counterparts in other countries, often via the some 1,000–1,500 EU working groups and committees operating at any one time. The member states have done this, however, in strikingly different ways. Traditionally centralized states such as the UK and France have tried (not altogether successfully) to maintain central coordination of the European involvement of ministries, often via ad hoc committees, while other states – Sweden is an example – prefer a more formalized coordination and decision-making process that takes place at cabinet level. Meanwhile, some traditionally more fragmented, less streamlined states find coordination on issues with a European dimension more of a trial (see Maurer *et al.*, 2003: 69 and the individual country chapters in Wessels *et al.*, 2003).

This divergent response to a common adaptational challenge is confirmed in a useful summary of the research on the issue in western Europe; Klaus Goetz (in Hix and Goetz 2000) observes that 'the gap between expected adaptive reactions and the often rather modest effects that empirical analyses

uncover' is wide. Most studies, he notes, testify to 'the importance of national context and the capacity of national administrative traditions to modify, accommodate . . . and, perhaps, even neutralize European pressures'. The signs, Goetz goes on, are little different in the newer members of the EU from east-central Europe – and anyway the impact of Europeanization would be difficult to disentangle from the effects of the wider changes that postcommunist countries have undergone (though see Zubek, 2008). By the same token, Europeanization, cannot be seen as a silver bullet or cure-all for problems that seem to afflict some countries more than others, political corruption being one obvious example (see Box 3.9). More generally, as Page and Wouters (1995) observe, the survival of profound differences in structures and procedures in the bureaucracies of the component states of the USA – a fully federal system – should make us very cautious about predicting that the EU will somehow make Europe's state bureaucracies look more like each other.

Policy making – sectors and styles

As for structures, so for policy making – what actually goes on in those structures and emerges out of them. As Wessels *et al.*, (2003: xv–xvi) conclude from their comparative study of all 15 states that made up the EU until May 2004, although 'the head of government, governmental administrations and interest groups ... have increased their role as strong and active multi-level players' compared to 'weak adaptors' like parliaments (see Chapter 4) and (interestingly) regional administrations, '[f]unda-

KEY POINT

EU membership may have strengthened some actors and organizations relative to others, but it has not erased fundamental cultural and institutional differences in the way policy is made in individual states. These policy styles can be compared but they are only approximations, because sectors within countries vary and because contingencies always play a part. So, too, does Europeanization, but its effects are not uniform.

BOX 3.9

Political Corruption in Bulgaria and Romania

There are few, if any, European countries that could say, hand on heart, that they have rooted out corruption at every level of government, central, regional and local. But it is likely that some countries have state sectors which are less are less corrupt than in other countries – not so much perhaps because they have taken special measures but because the lack of corruption among civil servants is a symptom of a lack of corruption in the society in which they operate.

If, for the sake of argument, we accept that real levels of corruption bear some relation to perceived levels as measured by, say, Transparency International's Corruption Perception Index (see http://www.transparency.org/policy_research/surveys_indices/cpi) then civil servants in Nordic countries like Finland, Denmark and Sweden (which all routinely score over 9 and come second to top-performer New Zealand) will be much less likely, for example, to do special favours for money and/or for friends and relations, than their counterparts in Greece, Italy, Romania and Bulgaria (which score under 4 and rank in the seventies and eighties in the global league table). The latter two – countries which in the first few years of the collapse of the Soviet bloc experienced incomplete revolutions which left elements of the previous regimes in power – have found themselves the focus of efforts by the EU to use both publicity and sanctions to persuade them to do something about corruption on the part of politicians and civil servants, some of it linked to organized crime.

While it would be untrue to characterize all of those efforts as a waste of time, they have not been conspicuous by their success: in the end, research suggests, it is domestic rather than external pressure that makes the difference, although in Europe it would be a mistake to suggest too rigid a separation between the two (see Vachudova, 2009 and Gugiu, 2012). It would also be mistake to forget, however, that political corruption in Europe is not limited to places like Bulgaria and Romania. Indeed, it can occur – and quite spectacularly – in countries usually thought of as shining examples. Finland, for example, was rocked by a party funding scandal in 2009 that involved both private and public sector companies and eventually led all the way up to the Prime Minister, Matti Vanhanen, forcing him to step down in 2010. So, too, in the same year was Norway, when it was revealed that the Centre Party – one of the ruling coalition partners – had accepted illegal cash contributions, while some of its leading figures had failed to declare personal gifts, leaving them open to accusations of bribery.

---

mental patterns of national policy making have not changed'.

This firm rejection of the idea of 'Europeanization-as-convergence' when it comes to policy making raises the question of what those patterns are in the first place. Is it possible to talk about each European state having some kind of identifiable **policy style**? The answer seems to be probably, but not without considerable qualifications. The first of these is the extent to which policy making in nearly all advanced societies is 'sectorized', with each area engendering its own, more or less permeable, **policy network**. These involve, at the very least, government and those interest groups trying to get it to do something that could benefit them or prevent it

from doing something that they see as detrimental (see Chapter 8 for more detail on such groups). This means that there might be more in common between the making of, say, energy policy between two countries than there is between policy making

A state's **policy style** can be defined as the interaction between a characteristic problem-solving approach covering each stage of the policy cycle – initiation and formulation, implementation, evaluation and review – and a characteristic relationship between those involved, including (though not exclusively) politicians, bureaucracy and those groups affected by and/or seeking to effect change (see Richardson *et al.*, 1982: 13).

A **policy network** is a range of actors (including, for instance, organized groups, national and European civil servants, regulators, firms and academics) that interact, more or less systematically, in a given policy area. Tight knit networks are labelled 'policy communities', more loosely coupled ones 'issue networks'.

in, for instance, health and education within the same country, making generalizations misleading if not meaningless.

The second qualification to the idea of national policy styles is that the reality of policy making may differ considerably not just from the 'ideal type' or simplified model analysts use to understand it (the same is true for policy networks, as we note in Chapter 8), but also from the 'standard operating procedures' or 'norms' that those involved might prefer to adhere to – or, alternatively, might need to appeal or resort to if a deal cannot be worked out (see Hayward, 1982). Three examples of this – historical principles acting as a fallback, if you like – spring immediately to mind. First, there is the tradition of the state overriding objections in the public interest in France. Second, there is the insistence on 'parliamentary sovereignty' (a majority of the House of Commons ultimately trumping any intransigence by, say, interest groups) in the UK. Third, there is the *Rechtsstaat* tradition in Germany, whereby anyone proposing a policy, even on a relatively unimportant topic, should be able to show it is consonant with the constitution.

The point, though, is that on a day-to-day basis these principles are not brought into play: most of the time consultations and negotiations lead to deals. We therefore need to be careful about using these normative traditions to characterize (or caricature) a country's policy style. This still happens, as one of the examples just given illustrates: we now have ample evidence that French policy makers are no longer elitist apostles of *dirigisme*, directing things from the top because they assume they have all the answers as well as the right to do so; instead, they work with (and are sometimes severely constrained by) interest groups and local and regional governments (see Cole *et al.*, 2008). Yet it is still not uncommon to see the country labelled, indeed almost dismissed, as 'statist'. The potential, and possibly the propensity, that has always existed for such statism may still be there, but it is rarely drawn on

lest it waste political capital which politicians and bureaucrats might need in future policy making.

This brings us to the third qualification to the idea of national styles – one which opens up a classic debate in political (and all social) science – namely, the relationship between 'structure' (institutions, procedures, processes and norms) and 'agency' (individual and group action). The paradigmatic European example of agency triumphing over structure is the Conservative government under Margaret Thatcher that governed the UK from 1979 until 1990. Possibly some of those triumphs were as rhetorical as they were real, but they ruthlessly exposed the fact that the policy style widely associated with that country (and, indeed, that party) before it came to power in 1979 – pragmatic, consultative, compromising – was in some ways misleading, relying on what had been done before, not on what could be done if politicians were determined enough. Ironically, it also demonstrated that the notion of 'parliamentary sovereignty' alluded to above might indeed be important when comparing the UK with other countries where political circumstances, culture, processes and institutions made this kind of untrammelled power highly unlikely (see Table 3.5). Then again, parliamentary sovereignty can tell us little about how UK governments (in fact, all European governments) have fared when dealing with matters that demand policy but in which parliament plays only a bit part, such as economic policy – which is why, incidentally, one cannot really cover policy making by drawing a few standard diagrams of 'how a bill is passed' in various countries' legislatures. Nor does the concept (or the diagrams) help us much when it comes to governments having to deal with crises that demand immediate administrative action rather than parliamentary process – whether these crises are real (such as the imminent collapse of banks in 2007 and 2008) or one of the less tangible matters that temporarily achieves prominence in the media-primed 'issue attention cycle' (Downs, 1972, and see Chapter 7).

Even the strongest agents, then, may find themselves undone by structures not of their own making (like the oil or credit markets) or by sheer contingency (most obviously, the weather). Or, as we have suggested, they might sometimes find it convenient to recall an idealized version of their role in policy making rather than act, as they do on most days,

Table 3.5 Policy styles and their institutional and normative influences

Limits to action	France	Germany	Italy	Netherlands	Spain	Sweden	UK
Federal states / devolved regions?	No	Yes	No (may change)	No	Some	No (but increasingly decentralized)	Some
Accessible / assertive constitutional court?	Can be	Yes	No	No	Not often	No	No
Relatively powerful parliament?	No	Yes	Potentially	No	No	Yes	No
Institutionalized interest group participation?	Some	A lot	Some	A lot	Little	A lot	Little
Powerful coalition partners?	Rarely	Always	Always	Always	Rarely	Rarely	Never
Coalition agreement that really counts?	No	Yes	No	Yes, very much so	No	Sometimes	Occasionally
Interest groups required for implementation?	Sometimes	Often	Sometimes	Often	Sometimes	Often	Sometimes
Fragmented departments?	Occasionally	Often	Often	Often	Often	Often	Sometimes
Procedure over flexibility?	No	Yes	Yes	No	Yes	Yes	No
Intervention over 'hands-off'?	Yes	Yes	Yes	No	Yes	Depends	No
Consensus over majority rule?	No	Yes	No	Yes	No	Yes	No
Overall policy style characterized by:	Consultation within limits, then action	Interconnection and incrementalism risking immobilism	Disconnection and heavy going	Consensus where possible, action if not	Consultation within limits, then action	Consultation without immobilism	Consultation within limits, then action

more prosaically. Or, as we have also said, different 'standard operating procedures' may apply in different policy sectors. Nevertheless, it may still be worth essaying some broad generalizations about individual countries' policy styles. These should take into account the institutional influences on them (i.e. the other actors governments must deal with) and the normative influences on them (i.e. their problem-solving approach), since they help to explain how essentially similar policy goals often produce sharply differing outcomes (Héritier *et al.*, 2001). The generalizations are illustrated in Table 3.5, the aim being to provoke discussion and promote comparison rather than to present an all-encompassing account.

An all-encompassing account of policy making in Europe would prove impossible anyway, given how little we know as yet about policy making styles in east-central Europe. In fact, these styles are probably still very much in the making, just as they have been in older 'new democracies' like Portugal, Greece and Spain (on which see Magone, 2008). An exhaustive account would be equally difficult owing to the caveats already discussed above. Any comparative schema or shorthand characterization will inevitably fail to explain exceptions to what, in any case, are tendencies rather than rules.

For instance, the incrementalism and 'interconnectedness' that the Germans label *politikverflechtung* does not rule out major reforms being pushed through, often in the face of considerable doubts and opposition. One only has to think of the decision during reunification to allow East Germans to swap their weak communist currency one-for-one with the powerful Deutsche Mark then used in West Germany, or, more recently, the Schröder government's 1999 reform making it easier for 'foreigners' to claim citizenship. On the other hand, one could argue that both examples show the dangers of departing from the norm: currency union is included in a fascinating comparative study of European 'policy disasters' (see Gray and t'Hart, 1998), while the political arm-twisting required to get the citizenship law saw it rapidly struck down by the Federal Constitutional Court, obliging the production of an amended version.

In other words, just as policy styles that potentially brook no compromises need not preclude them, styles that emphasize consensus are equally capable of fostering innovative solutions. Indeed, because they eventually achieve 'buy-in' from all concerned, they may even be better at producing policy that works and lasts. The welfare reforms in the Netherlands and Sweden that we touch on in Chapter 9 are good examples. The latter country's policy system is famously consensual to the point of being cumbersome. Governments wanting to do something routinely appoint a state commission (*statsutredningar*) composed of experts, interest groups, agencies and representatives of (other) parties to examine their ideas and produce a report. At the same time, a wide variety of opinion is canvassed under the pre-legislative *remiss* consultation procedure. All these views feed into legislative proposals that are then intensively debated in parliamentary committees, often resulting in cross-party agreement. Yet for all this, Sweden is one of the few countries in western Europe that has 'grasped the nettle' on the pension reforms that many think Europe's ageing population make vital (see Chapters 1 and 8). France, with its more 'heroic' policy style has achieved some reform, but more is needed – and has, in 2007, already occasioned more of the protest that occurred when it was last tried in 1995.

Amid all this talk of national variations, what of Europeanization, as defined in the Introduction? Is policy making right across the continent increasingly interconnected, with state and non-state actors 'downloading' the prescriptions of the EU and/or other European countries at the same time as seeking to 'upload' their own? Studies seem to suggest a good deal of variation, with two things standing out as important. The first is the extent to which involving or invoking EU institutions and initiatives presents opportunities to domestic actors to speed up or slow down change as they see fit (see Héritier *et al.,* 2001: 288). In other words, Europeanization occurs or does not occur in part because its occurrence or non-occurrence suits policy makers: it need not be an unstoppable force but can just as often prove a valuable resource.

The second thing determining the extent of Europeanization is whether the EU has policy competence in the policy area concerned (see Zeff and Pirro, 2001; and especially Wallace *et al.*, 2010). So, for instance, policy making on agriculture and fisheries, or on the environment, does, of course, go on at the domestic level, but those involved (across all

COUNTRY PROFILE

FRANCE

History: Present-day France is composed of various regions centralized in the seventeenth century by a monarchy that was then overthrown in a revolution which began in 1789. In the following two decades, the country emerged (under dictator Napoleon Bonaparte) as an imperial power. After Napoleon's defeat, the monarchy was restored, only to be overthrown once again in 1848. Following two decades of dictatorship and the loss of a war with what became Germany, France finally settled, albeit fractiously, into democracy, although under this 'Third Republic' it rapidly began to lose its status as a world power.
During the Second World War the northern half of France was occupied by Germany, while the southern half ('Vichy') was ruled by a collaborationist regime under Marshal Petain. After an initially unstable period (the so-called 'Fourth Republic') during which both its constitution and its colonial policy were called into question, France pulled itself together under President Charles de

Gaulle. After De Gaulle bowed out at the end of the 1960s, the centre-right held on to power in what was (and still is) known as the 'Fifth Republic' until 1981, when Francois Mitterrand constructed the first fully centre-left government since the 1930s. Its radical economic programme soon came unstuck, however, forcing a policy U-turn. Until 2002, government alternated between multiparty blocs of the left (including a much weakened Communist Party and the Greens, as well as the more mainstream Socialists) and the right (made up of conservatives and liberals who, for the moment, continue to shun the well-supported far-right National Front). But this pattern was broken when, in 2007, the centre-right was returned for a second term, its leader Nicolas Sarkozy having managed to build, after years of fragmentation, an unusually large single party – the UMP. Sarkozy, however, was granted only one term by French voters who, in the midst of economic crisis turned to a Socialist, electing François Hollande in 2012.

Economy and society: France is still one of Europe's most powerful economies, and a notable exporter, especially of agricultural goods. With a generous, insurance-based welfare state but plagued by relatively high unemployment driven in part by relatively high labour costs, the French enjoy a standard of living on a par with that of their German neighbours – and one which is more evenly distributed in geographical terms. That said, Paris remains by far the richest city, although some of its suburbs

Area: 545,600 km² (13.0% of EU-27)	
Population: 65.4 million (13.0% of EU-27)	
Religious heritage: Roman Catholic and Protestant	
GDP (2010): €1,193 billion (15.5% of EU-27)	
GDP *per capita* as percentage of EU-27 average (2011): 107	
Female representation in parliament and cabinet (end 2011): 19% and 27%	
Joined EU: founder member, 1957	
Top 3 cities: Paris – capital city (2.2 million), Marseilles (0.8 million); Lyon (0.5 million).	

are notoriously blighted by crime and poverty. Some 4.5 million people in France are Muslim (most of whom have their origins in France's former colonial possessions in North Africa). There is some regionalist sentiment in the west and south, but it is only problematic in the Mediterranean island of Corsica.

Governance: France's elections are fought, unlike anywhere else in Europe, under a two-ballot, majoritarian system rather than under PR: the only other country which shuns the latter is the UK. France is also Europe's main 'semi-presidential' system. Its president is directly elected every five years and then appoints a prime minister and

WHAT'S IN AN ANTHEM?

Probably one of the most instantly recognizable anthems on the planet, *La Marseillaise* was made famous throughout Europe by the French Revolution and its defence against invading German and Austrian armies. So much so, indeed, that it became something of an anthem for radicals everywhere, and may well have been one of the first ever 'samples', making an appearance in Tchaikovsky's famous 1812 Overture. It is essentially a stirring (if slightly gory) call to arms against 'tyranny's bloody banner' and 'savage soldiers' from foreign lands who would 'cut the throats of your sons, your wives' but whose 'impure blood' will end up watering the fields of France.

cabinet who are accountable to a notoriously weak parliament, although a recently convened commission has called for the strengthening of the latter. This means that the French sometimes experience divided government if parties other than those who support the president win the parliamentary elections. In that case, the president has little choice but to appoint political opponents as prime minister and to cabinet. This so-called *cohabitation* should, though, become less common now that parliamentary elections are likely to follow hard on the heels of the presidential contest. France's Constitutional Court is an increasingly powerful player in the political process, and potentially important interest groups include (despite their small membership) the public sector trade unions and the farmers. Notwithstanding its reputation for being one of the continent's most 'statist' countries, France has pursued a policy of decentralization for more than two decades. Its national and its local politics are, in any case, intimately connected by virtue of many national politicians – again, unusually so in Europe – continuing to hold positions as local mayors or heads of regional government.

Foreign policy: After 1945, France dedicated itself to locking its old enemy Germany into Europe via an integration process that it was determined to lead and exploit. It has also attempted (much like the UK) to hang on to its former glory: France may have lost most of its overseas possessions by the 1960s (including, most bitterly, Algeria), but it still has far-flung colonies in the Caribbean and the South Pacific, still has its own nuclear weapons, and is still one of the five permanent members of the UN security council. France fell out badly with the USA over the Iraq war, for which it could see no sound justification.

A KEY CONTEMPORARY CHALLENGE
MAINTAINING FRANCE'S GLOBAL ROLE

Although relatively small in global terms, France – still one of only five 'permanent members' of the UN Security Council – continues to see itself as more than simply a medium-sized European power with a foreign and defence policy to match. As a result, and owing also to its colonial history and its desperate desire to gain the goodwill of regimes installed in the wake of the Arab uprisings against dictators it was previously happy enough to prop up, the country has been involved in a number of military conflicts in recent years. France has fielded forces in Afghanistan, in Côte d'Ivoire, and, most assertively, in Libya, where, after shaking off its initial reluctance and joining with the UK, it led NATO's successful air-campaign against the Gaddafi regime. Set against all this is the fact that France, like many other European countries, is in a tight spot economically and financially. Nor does it want to be seen to be running too far ahead of its EU partners, especially Germany, which is notably more reluctant to embark on overseas adventures. On the other hand, France wants to be seen as a solid ally within NATO, especially since it only properly reintegrated itself into that organization in 2009. One way forward is closer defence ties with the UK, which, like France, is looking for a way to continue punching above its weight in straitened times (see Chapter 11).

The one-term presidency of Nicolas Sarkozy, however, along with a shared concern over the nuclear ambitions of Iran, saw a significant rapprochement. Differences remain, however, on 'Anglo-Saxon capitalism' and climate change.

Contemporary challenges

- Attacking persistent disadvantage and discrimination suffered by citizens of immigrant origin, many of them young, unemployed and concentrated in *les banlieues* like Clichy-sous-Bois outside Paris – run-down suburbs dominated by public housing projects which are geographically close to, but seemingly cut off from, France's major cities.
- Maintaining support – financial and moral – for a foreign and defence policy with global pretentions (see box below)
- Ending what some see as the featherbedding of (unionized) public sector workers and labour market 'insiders' – whether they remain in work or benefit from relatively generous and no-strings welfare payments if they lose their jobs – in order to reduce the government's deficit, tackle high levels of unemployment and insecure employment among young people, and regain competitiveness relative to other European countries.
- Ensuring, through collective European action, that French banks' huge holdings of debt in Italy and Spain (worth around 21 and 8 % respectively of France's GDP) are not wiped out by widespread defaults by private and public sector lenders (and banks) in those countries.

Learning resources. A really useful introduction is provided by Drake (2011) *Contemporary France*. Then try Cole *et al.* (2008), *Developments in French Politics 4* and Brouard *et al.* (2008), *The French Fifth Republic at Fifty*. Keep up to date with the news at http://www.expatica.com/fr/main.html.

member states) exhibit a 'coordination reflex' which means they are attuned to and involved in (and therefore thinking of the consequences for) the policy process at the EU level. Perhaps, for instance, they participate in an EU *groupe d'experts* (preparatory committee) and therefore meet fairly frequently in Brussels with their sectoral counterparts from other countries – the kind of activity that, incidentally, makes it harder and harder for foreign ministries to maintain their gatekeeping and coordinating role over the interaction of supposedly 'domestic' departments. In other areas – including, say, health and education where governments have not ceded much to the EU – policy makers could well be learning from other countries, and they might well have a special 'desk' that deals with European affairs, as well as a man or woman on the ground in Brussels (in the government's permanent representation if they are a civil servant or, if they work for an interest group, at its office in the city). But they are not looking over their shoulders at other countries or seeking to anticipate their actions in anything like the same way. It is because of this variation between policy areas that we need to be careful before we assume that Europeanization necessarily disrupts or undermines the traditional (if informal) hierarchy that means some ministries tend to be seen as more important than others.

The booming third branch of government – the judicialization of politics

Talk of 'disruption' and 'undermining' brings us rather neatly to the extent to which the executive's job in Europe is made more difficult these days by the role of what in the USA is traditionally a powerful 'third branch of government': the judiciary. Theoretically, its role is not just to enforce criminal sanctions, but also to adjudicate disputes by applying the civil law to particular cases. These might be between private parties, or between individuals and the state, or perhaps between central and local government. In so doing, the judiciary is meant to provide another 'check and balance' by ensuring that government and the state operate under the rule of law and do not exceed their powers

The **judicialization of politics** refers to 'the ever-accelerating reliance on courts and judicial means for addressing core moral predicaments, public policy questions, and political controversies' – a phenomenon that has, in recent years, 'expanded beyond rights issues or transnational cooperation to encompass... matters of outright and utmost political significance which often define and divide whole polities', ranging from 'electoral outcomes and corroboration of regime change to matters of war and peace, foundational collective identity questions, and nation-building processes pertaining to the very nature and definition of the body politic.' In as much as its causes can be identified, it is not simply due to the growth of the state or the increasing prevalence of rights discourse or judges' own desire for more impact, but also to 'concrete choices, interests or strategic considerations by self-interested political stakeholders', sometimes motivated by a desire to avoid blame in 'no-win' situations, sometimes by the belief that they cannot get what they want by 'normal' political means (Hirschl, 2008: 94, 106).

and/or violate fundamental liberties laid out in the constitution. To some observers, however, the courts have taken things too far: their interventions have become so profound and frequent that we are moving, they claim, toward 'juristocracy' (Hirschl, 2004).

All European states, with the exception of the UK, which prefers the flexibility of tradition and precedent, have codified constitutions. At least in the eyes of the ordinary citizen, these constitutions – even though they are almost all the product of popular regime change and new-found independence – rarely attain the sanctified and sacred status enjoyed by the US Constitution, and they have been amended or (more often than is commonly thought) replaced by new, improved versions (see Elkins *et al.*, 2009). They are nonetheless important, helping as they do to structure politics by laying down the powers and roles of the various institutions (president, government, parliament, regions, etc.) involved in running a country. Many political 'rules of the game' can be rewritten pretty easily by the players; constitutions less so. There are a handful of states wherein any change requires a referendum, sometimes with the proviso that a certain proportion of those eligible to vote must do so: Romania, which made changes to its 1991 constitution in

2003, for example, stipulates a 50 per cent plus one turnout – the reason why, ultimately, a referendum that attempted to force out the country's president was declared invalid in 2012, despite it being passed by a large majority (see Chapter 4). Many other states allow minor changes to be made by parliament but require a referendum or at the very least a supermajority (e.g. the approval of both houses of parliament and/or, say, two-thirds of MPs) before making any major changes; still others require parliament to approve the change twice, once before and once after a general election. Constitutions, then, may not be totally fixed objects around which the executive is obliged to work, but they are seriously heavy pieces of scenery – very difficult to shift, and best not bumped into too often.

KEY POINT

To talk of 'juristocracy' is going too far, but it is apparent that the judges do play a role – and perhaps an increasing one – in the politics of European democracies, even where judicial review is restricted. And the ECJ is undoubtedly both influential and a driver of Europeanization, not least because (like those of the ECHR) its rulings are then applied by domestic courts. The judicial branch of government seems more popular than the executive or legislative branches – but this isn't saying much.

The UK is not only unusual in that its constitution is 'unwritten', although, since some documents are vital to it, it would be more accurate to say uncodified (see King, 2009). With the exception of Scotland, its legal system is based on what are called 'common law' principles, whereas the bulk of European countries (including Scotland) operates systems based on 'Roman' or 'code' law. In England and Wales, and also Ireland (and to some extent former dependencies like Malta and Cyprus), statutes passed through parliament are important (especially for criminal law), but so, too, are precedents set by judges' decisions in past cases. These establish principles – based on notions of equity and individual rights (for example, to free enjoyment of property) that are binding on lower courts

In other European countries, however, civil law is much more likely to be codified – systematically written down so it can be applied to particular cases by judges. These judges therefore enjoy rather less discretion than their counterparts in the common law system and are often seen (and, indeed, recruited and trained) as highly specialized civil servants rather than lawyers who have served their time arguing before other judges before going on to become one themselves. Roman law systems are generally less adversarial (and more 'inquisitorial') than common law systems. They also tend to have more of a division of labour between various specialist courts set up to deal with, for instance, criminal, financial or administrative law (although we should note that over the last two or three decades, the British legal system has also developed a network of more specialized administrative tribunals).

This is not to suggest that all Roman law systems are the same. For instance, Germanic countries (and now most CEE countries) place more stress on a logical progression from general principles – the *Rechtsstaat* idea we referred to when defining separation of powers – than do 'Napoleonic' countries (France, the Belgium, Italy, Portugal and Spain) even though they rely heavily on codified law. In Scandinavia, codes are slightly less rigid and detailed – and public servants see themselves as managers as much as mere implementers of the law – but process is important. Nor should we fail to note that many countries are hybrids – Poland and Greece, for instance, sit somewhere between the Germanic and the Napoleonic style, while Scotland even mixes in common law influences, as does the Netherlands. Generally, though, the distinctions between Roman and common law systems have traditionally been more important than the differences within them.

Anyone with a nodding acquaintance with US politics will be familiar with the idea of a Supreme Court that provides the ultimate insurance against government, be it central or local, undermining the rights guaranteed to citizens by the constitution. Similar courts exist in many European countries. The obvious exceptions are Britain, the Nordic countries and the Netherlands, though this by no means guarantees that politicians are free from judicial constraints (see Box 3.10). Where such courts do exist, the main difference between Europe and America is that in the USA, any judge in any court, can declare a law or government action or decision unconstitutional. This ruling can then be tested in

---

BOX 3.10

What, no constitutional court?

Just because they do not have a constitutional court does not make politicians in the UK, the Netherlands and Sweden immune from legal intervention – or, just as importantly, the fear of it. Although judicial review is only rarely resorted to in Sweden, the 'Council on Legislation, made up of senior judges, can be asked by the government or by a parliamentary committee to rule on government proposals. This usually takes place prior to the bill being brought before the *Riksdag,* which also appoints *ombudsmen.* These are officials to whom ordinary people can appeal if they feel due process has not been followed – an idea that has been copied in the Netherlands and the UK (as well as in other Scandinavian countries, Portugal and Austria).

In the UK the highest court in the land is now called the Supreme Court but it still cannot pronounce on the constitutionality or otherwise of acts of parliament. However, while the latter cannot be overturned by judges, the actions of the authorities can be challenged on the grounds that they are taken without due authority, or are irrational and unreasonable, or not in accordance with proper procedure. And, while it is true that no court can actually strike down a statute as unconstitutional, it has for some time been open to a judge either to rule illegal the executive action required to carry it out or to declare that parts of it are unlawful to the extent that they deprive an individual (or company) of their rights under EC law. Statutes can also be judged incompatible with the European Convention on Human Rights (ECHR or CPHR).

This also holds true in Sweden and in the Netherlands. The Dutch constitution may explicitly deny the courts any right to constitutional review, but this has not prevented them considering many matters that many would consider political, most famously euthanasia and (more mundanely) employment issues (see Andeweg and Irwin, 2009). And, as in many other European countries, certain high-profile cases inevitably drag the courts into politics, as happened when Geert Wilders, the leader of a radical right-wing populist party, was tried on charges of hate speech and discrimination – charges of which he was acquitted in June 2011.

---

other courts right up to and including the Supreme Court. In Europe, this kind of **judicial review** has traditionally been rejected, on the grounds that ultimate power rests with the people and is therefore invested in a democratically elected parliament rather than in appointed judges.

Alongside this belief in the supremacy of statutes, however, runs an enthusiasm for constitutionally backed rights, freedoms and principles which – logically, anyway – would seem to constrain and take priority over parliament. Many countries have resolved this potential contradiction by setting up special constitutional courts that are – supposedly, at least – 'above politics' (see Table 3.6). Countries that have set up such courts include Germany, France and Italy and, more recently, Spain, Poland and the Czech Republic (see Procházka, 2002 and Sadurski, 2005), all of which emerged from dictatorship wanting an extra bastion against any return to arbitrary rule. Italy and Germany were, of course, in a similar position in the 1940s, and the latter would in any case have needed some kind of umpire to settle

> **Judicial review** is the process by which legislation, regulations and administrative acts of the state are examined by the judiciary in order to check, among other things, that they are in accordance with the constitution and other law, and that neither the executive nor the legislature is going beyond its powers, breaking its own procedural rules or acting unreasonably.

disputes between federal and state authorities.

However, unlike the US Supreme Court, which sits at the apex of the ordinary court system and is, in effect, that system's final court of appeal, Europe's constitutional courts sit outside that system (the only exception being Ireland, where the High Court and Supreme Courts do the job of a constitutional court). It is possible in most countries that have a constitutional court for that court to hear cases referred to it by ordinary courts concerning laws that are already in force – a process known as 'concrete review'. But it will also spend much of its time, responding to requests by politicians (local or national) to decide on the constitutionality of laws that have already been passed by parliament but that are not yet in force. This process – because no particular case is involved – is known as 'abstract' review.

From sometimes small beginnings, these constitutional courts have expanded the role of the third branch of government. For the most part, the expansion was largely unforeseen and, because it crept up on politicians only gradually, went largely unnoticed. In France, for example, the Constitutional Court was seen as a tool of or prop for the executive and few made much of its 1971 decision henceforth to take into account the wideranging preamble to the constitution. This decision, along with a constitutional amendment in 1974 that extended the right to refer matters to the court to any 60 members of either legislative chamber, paved the way for a massive (and creative) increase in its competence and importance. Now, it may well have taken on a self-sustaining momentum of its own (see Stone Sweet, 2000). From March 2010, other courts were granted the right to appeal for a ruling from the Constitutional Court on cases before them. Moreover, the use by opposition politicians of abstract review to try to strike down legislation and policy that they are unable to vote down in parliament is increasing.

In France, constitutional veto has become a feature of everyday electoral politics (see Brouard, 2009): virtually every contentious bill (and budgetary measure) is re-fought in this way and, because it takes time for judges appointed by previous administrations to be replaced by those more favourable to the present government, such bills stand a 50 : 50 chance of being declared in some way unconstitutional. Governments and parliaments, in the face of possible defeat during what amounts to an extra final reading of bills, and knowing that changes to constitutions require big majorities (especially if the article covers basic rights), are already obeying what political scientists call 'the law

---

Tampering with the courts in Hungary

Among many other controversial changes brought about by the right-wing, single-party Fidesz government which took office in April 2010, after winning just over half of the total vote, was to bring the retirement age for judges, including those serving in Hungary's Supreme Court, into line with other workers. The effect of this seemingly innocuous move was to remove over 250 judges whose replacements, critics noted, would then be nominated by a single individual sympathetic to the government. The government, stung by the Court's striking down of its plans for a 98 per cent tax on severance payments to wealthy ex-employees, also brought forward a constitutional amendment to limit the Court's right to decide on fiscal issues. It also used its huge parliamentary majority to appoint trusted friends to two vacant posts. This, plus what was seen as an attempt to boost the government's control over the media and the central bank, as well as the reining back of human rights and anti-discrimination rules, provoked demonstrations in Budapest and in January 2012 prompted the European Commission, apparently with the backing of other member states, to threaten legal proceedings in the European Court of Justice.

---

of anticipated reactions'. They are watering down their legislation to improve its chances of either avoiding or passing judicial scrutiny – something that calls into question the idea of a separation of powers. The latter is in any case blurred by the fact that politicians can (and do) interfere with judicial appointments, although they rarely do so in quite so obvious a fashion as recently occurred in Hungary (see Box 3.11)

Also being called into question are the differences between Roman and common law systems – a development that provides considerable potential for, as well as evidence of, Europeanization. Concrete review – whereby courts (and sometimes individuals or ombudsmen) can ask their national constitutional court for a ruling which they can then apply

Table 3.6 Europe's constitutional courts

Country/Name	Membership	Reputation	Role	Record
Germany: Federal Constitutional Court	Sixteen members (half appointed by Bundestag, half by Bundesrat, both needing a two-thirds majority).	Highly regarded as 'above politics' or at least balanced.	Considers constitutionality before and after legislation has come into force. Pre-legislation ('abstract review'), applied for by federal or Länder governments, or one-third of MPs, and can therefore be a means by which oppositions try to over-turn a parliamentary defeat. 'Concrete' (i.e. post hoc) review initiated by courts or, most commonly, by individuals claiming violation of rights by a public body. Adjudicates between federal government and Länder, and civil liberties/human rights.	1993 rejects challenge to Maastricht Treaty, but stresses limitations on EU's power; 1993 makes publicly funded abortion harder; 1994 clears way for German military participation overseas; 1998 clears way for Germany to adopt the euro; 2001 grants equal legal treatment of 'gay marriages'; 2002 forces government to rethink liberalization of citizenship law; 2002 upholds military conscription; 2003 rejects legal ban on neo-Nazi parties; 2011 rules that 5% electoral threshold can no longer be used for EP elections; 2012 allows Federal government to contribute to EU bail-out funds but stresses need for parliamentary approval.
France: Constitutional Council	Nine members (three each chosen by President, National Assembly and Senate), including many former politicians.	Highly partisan: appointees of right-wing governments tend to oppose left-wing successors and vice versa.	Abstract review possible on request of the President, presidents of the two chambers of parliament, or 60 MPs. Concrete review (by referral from Conseil d'Etat or Cour de Cassation) also became possible in 2008 and was extended in 2010. Covers wide range of issues, but rarely involved in human rights cases. Seen by many as almost a third chamber, given the propensity of opposition parties, having lost the votes in parliament, to refer virtually all important bills and budgets to it.	1982 insists on adequate compensation for nationalizations; 1982 strikes down an attempt to boost the number of women candidates in local elections; 1984 blocks Left's plans to regulate media ownership; 1986 interferes with Right's plans to deregulate media; 1993 limits Right's attempts to tighten immigration and asylum regime; 1998 overturns Socialist by-election win over National Front because of media bias; 1999 grants same-sex couples full legal rights; 2011 upholds the civil code's prohibition of full marriage for gay and lesbian couples.
Italy: Constitutional Court	Fifteen members (five chosen by President, five by parliament and	Only moderately partisan, and normally reasonably balanced	Carries out pre-legislation abstract review (usually on the initiative of national or regional government) and concrete review (i.e. post hoc referrals from courts). Wide	1971 allows sale of and information on contraception; 1970s strikes down sexist adultery laws; 1970-4 upholds constitutionality of divorce liberalization; 1976 breaks up government monopoly of

Table 3.6 Europe's constitutional courts (continued)

Country/Name	Membership	Reputation	Role	Record
	five by judges in higher courts).	between partisans of the various parties.	range of activity but particularly active as gatekeeper for requests for referendums.	media 2009 struck down laws granting immunity to top politicians, not least Prime Minster Silvio Berlusconi.
Czech Rep.: Constitutional Court	Fifteen members, appointed by President and parliament.	Seen to favour government's establishment of liberal capitalism, notwithstanding social costs; early clashes with centre-left.	Abstract and concrete review – the former initiated by the President, or government or parliament; the latter by courts or individuals.	1993 upholds retrospective punishment for crimes under Communist regime and right to restitution of property, but strikes down criminal prosecution for defaming political institutions; 2000 strikes down rent controls; 2009 cancels early general election since the condition that there be three failed attempts to form a cabinet before one could be called had not been met.
Poland: Constitutional Tribunal	Fifteen members, appointed solely by parliament.	Seen initially as subservient to parliament and government's liberalizing agenda, but beginning to be more assertive	Before 1999, it could be overridden by two-thirds majority in parliament, but now its say is final. Very accessible – abstract review on the initiative of political institutions at the national and local level, judges and even on its own initiative. Concrete review via referrals from courts.	1989–94 strikes down some of Poland's 'shock therapy' economic reforms; stymies President's attempts to extend powers; upholds rights of former regime officials to pensions; upholds rights and privileges of the church; keeps abortion ban; 2007 strikes down 'lustration' law; 2009 declares that it is the PM rather than the President who has ultimate authority to represent Poland in the EU; 2011 strikes down new law prohibiting parties from buying paid TV and radio spots.
Spain: Constitutional Court	Twelve members, two each appointed by the Judiciary and the government and eight by parliament	Partisan appointments (especially under Socialist governments), but not sufficiently so as to undermine its legitimacy.	Abstract review on application by Prime Minister, president of parliament, 50 parliamentarians, regional governments, ombudsman. Concrete review via referral from court or requests by ombudsman or individuals. Can also rule on the text of international treaties.	1983 counteracts legislative move to slow down (for fear of antagonizing conservatives) granting of regional autonomy and declares that state law prevails over regional law; 2010, after case pressed on it by conservative opposition, declares Catalunya's new Statue of Autonomy constitutional but strikes down some of its provisions.

to their particular case – is being extended (as in France) and is blurring the formerly hard and fast distinction between ordinary courts and constitutional courts which, as a result, are arguably becoming more like a US-style Supreme Court. And the increasing stress on the interpretation of constitutional principles (as opposed to merely applying a code) may not differ that much from the use of precedent and the notion of the supremacy of decisions of higher courts that are already associated with common law systems. At the same time, common law systems, by developing specialized administrative tribunals and increasingly taking into account codified EC law, are becoming more like Roman law systems.

Law, and its contribution to governance, is one area in which Europeanization is without doubt important (see Cichowski, 2007). True, there are big differences in the extent to which European countries transpose European law into domestic legislation, and in the frequency with which they are hauled up in front of the ECJ for lagging behind or non-observance (see Figure 3.2). There is also considerable variation in the extent to which a judgement against a member state will induce it to comply – a large member state like Italy, for instance, may well ignore rulings for some time, while a smaller one like Portugal will try to put things right as soon as possible (Börzel *et al.*, 2012). Sometimes, then, bringing the rules into line is one thing, actually implementing them and policing them is another (Versluis, 2007 and Falkner, 2010), at least in part because national politicians will often go for the most flexible interpretation of EU rules. Those same politicians will also try to square the Commission, which is responsible for policing them and referring cases to court: government provision of 'state aid' to ostensibly private firms (which we touch on in Chapter 9) is a good example.

However, as the decline in state aid can be said to show, the fact is that in most cases compliance eventually occurs (see Zürn and Joerges, 2005), even if it is sometimes contingent on attention being drawn to non-compliance by powerful interested parties (see Conant, 2002) and the Commission (see Thomson, 2010) or demanded by the ECJ (see also Stone Sweet and Brunell, 2012). This is because, as we noted in Chapter 2, both

Figure 3.2 The non-compliance naughty-list: annual average of new actions taken by the ECJ for member states' failure to fulfil their obligations since year of joining

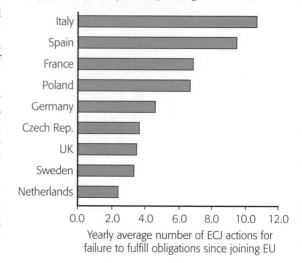

Yearly average number of ECJ actions for failure to fulfill obligations since joining EU

Note: States joining later are more likely to have a higher average since in earlier years there were fewer obligations to fulfil.

Source: Data from ECJ Annual Report, 2010.

national politicians and national courts have accepted the supremacy of European law and, where appropriate, acknowledged that it has direct effect on their countries without needing transposition. Indeed, the alleged enthusiasm of some national courts (especially lower courts) for the ECJ – combined with the willingness of businesses, individuals and pressure groups to bring actions based on European law (see Chapter 8) – has been a major factor in blunting any incipient resistance to its power on the part of national politicians. So, too, has the seemingly inexorable trend for the ECJ to expand the role of the EU into areas where many states would regard it as having no business, such as welfare and immigration (Martinsen, 2011). Financial services, which some countries are particularly protective of, will almost certainly follow: after a ruling in 2011, the insurance industry in the UK (and by implication other EU countries) will no longer be allowed to charge larger premiums on male drivers than their female counterparts – although most people expected the latter to rise rather than the former to fall!

Saving us from ourselves or a sick joke? UK judges and human rights law

The Labour government that ran the UK between 1997 and 2010 was not much loved by liberals. Even they, however, were happy with two particular pieces of legislation. One was the Freedom of Information Act of 2000 (see Box 3.8) and the other the Human Rights Act of 1998, which made it much easier for people wanting to make use of the European convention by effectively embedding it in UK law and reducing the necessity for them to go the European Court in Strasbourg. The flip-side of this has been a number of decisions in British courts and in Strasbourg itself which appear to many ordinary people (most of whom are not particularly liberal) to flout common sense.

One of the longest-running sores is a decision obliging the UK to overturn its long time prohibition on prisoners voting in elections. Another is interference in the UK government's efforts to detain terrorist suspects without trial or to deport them to their country of origin. But there have been even more emotive cases. On December 10 2010, for instance, British judges blocked a bid by the government to deport a failed asylum seeker from Iraq with criminal convictions in the UK for offences involving drugs, theft, burglary, criminal damage and harassment who, seven years earlier, had been involved in a hit-and-run traffic accident that cost a 12 year-old girl her life. In so doing, they supported an earlier finding that, since the man in question had formed a stable relationship, and had fathered children with his British partner in the meantime, his deportation would breach his right to a family life under the European Convention. The father of the girl who the man had run over before fleeing the scene was understandably angry. 'I work hard, play by the rules, pay my taxes and this is how I get treated', he protested. 'What does that say about politicians, our leaders and the legal system? It's a joke.' His words were all the more pointed in view of the fact that David Cameron, the UK's Conservative prime minister had, when in opposition, written to him implying that once in government, his party would make legislative changes that would supposedly ensure something like this would never happen again.

At least in those areas where their predecessors have granted competence to the EU, then, Europe's elected politicians and the states they run find their room for manoeuvre restricted by non-elected judges, either sitting in Strasbourg or – every bit as importantly (see Alter, 2003) – in domestic courts applying EU law or passing on cases to Strasbourg. It is worth noting, however, that domestic courts do not always speed the course of integration: Germany's Federal Constitutional Court, indeed, is well-known for periodically sticking a spoke in the wheels; in 2011, for instance, the government, obliged by a previous decision to ensure that the Bundestag was consulted on the new European Stability Mechanism (see Chapter 9), attempted to speed things along by confining discussion to a parliamentary committee – until that is, the Court stepped in and insisted it be dealt with in plenary.

While Europe's politicians do not like being 'named and shamed' via the ECJ, they do not always object to being bound by European-level law. ECJ decisions, like those of domestic courts, can sometimes provide political opportunities as well as constraints. A good example would be the series of decisions that helped build momentum for the Single European Act (SEA) (see Chapter 2), which accelerated progress on the single market (see Chapter 9) – something most of Europe's politicians (even reluctant Europeans such as the UK's Margaret Thatcher) were keen to see. Another would be the ECJ's ruling that pension ages for men and women should be the same – something that allowed European governments to raise the age of entitlement for women which will, in the long-term, save them money. States also exploit the power of the ECJ in disagreements they have with each other: ECJ rulings (backed up by the possibility of large fines) were said to be instrumental in getting France to drop what the UK claimed was an illegal ban on the import of British beef. In judicial matters as in

DEBATE 3.1

Would rule by judges be better than rule by politicians?

YES

- Judges in established liberal democracies are normally appointed on merit and are highly objective and intelligent professionals without an axe to grind.
- Judges make decisions based on rational argument and the evidence in front of them, not according to ideology or facts selected to support their prejudices. They respect well-established principles rather than appease or whip up emotive public opinion.
- While judges announce (and often justify) their decisions publicly, they take them away from the glare of publicity, meaning the media are less influential.
- Because they are not subject to election, judges have longer time horizons: they can do what is best in the long-term rather than what will get them into, or keep them in, power in the next three or four years.
- Not having to worry about what the majority wants, judges do a better job of protecting the rights and interests of minorities.
- The judiciary in established liberal democracies is free of corruption and well trusted.

NO

- Judges are often recruited from a social elite with a very narrow experience of the real world, unlike politicians who come from a variety of backgrounds and occupations. In some countries (notably Italy, France and Spain) judges also belong to unions and professional associations according to whether they are left- or right-wing.
- Emotions, symbols, and identity are important to people and their instincts and desires have to be respected. Society also changes faster than the law, which is inherently conservative.
- The idea that there are objective facts or evidence is a nonsense. Society is full of conflicting interests, ideas, and institutions: only if they are properly represented can they be peacefully reconciled and scarce resources efficiently allocated.
- When it comes to almost any decision, it is better to trust to the 'wisdom of crowds' rather than the judgement of a handful of people: 'millions of people can't be wrong' is not merely a phrase; it's a probability.
- The more the media scrutinize the decision process, the more open and fair it will be. Judges often come to their decisions behind closed doors
- Politicians who live with the knowledge that they will be held accountable every so often tend to act in the interests of the majority.
- The 'tyranny' of that majority can be avoided by, for instance, choosing an electoral system based on proportional representation.
- Politicians in democracies are, in fact, rarely corrupt and a lack of trust is healthy scepticism.

many other aspects of European politics, then, the EU 'lives' inside as well as outside the state and can be an opportunity and not just a threat.

Some claim to see in both domestic and EU affairs, and the blurring of the boundaries between them, the beginnings of a slide down a slippery slope they call the 'judicialization' of public life and politics. At the bottom lies a homogenized European legal system that, they argue, takes no account of national traditions which, supposedly at least, are culturally appropriate and have done the job well

enough for centuries. Parliamentary government, they claim, is giving way to 'rule by judges' who owe their positions partly to their professional colleagues, mostly to politicians and not to the supposedly sovereign people. It is all too easy to assume that constitutional and other courts are inevitably 'a good thing'. The record, however, is more mixed. The experience of central and eastern Europe, some suggest, is a case in point (see Sadurski, 2005). So, too, it can be argued, is what many see (particularly in the UK) as the growing and unwarranted interfer-

Table 3.7 Net trust in the legal system, government and parliament

	Legal system	Regional/ Local authority	Parliament	Government
Sweden	48	31	44	24
Netherlands	33	26	3	−6
Germany	26	29	−9	−30
UK	5	−7	−46	−53
EU-27	−1	−3	−39	−46
France	−5	15	−40	−53
Spain	−7	−29	−55	−64
Italy	−10	−49	−62	−68
Poland	−15	2	−43	−37
Czech Rep.	−28	−6	−76	−68

Source: Data from *Eurobarometer*, 66 (2006).

ence by judges seemingly willing and able to use European law (whether it stems from the EU or the European Convention on Human Rights) to frustrate the will of the people and parliament – or at least the government of the day (see Box 3.12).

As we have seen, however, judicialization, inasmuch as it is occurring, is not uniform throughout the continent (see Guarnieri and Pederzoli, 2002). Nor, we should remind ourselves, does it necessarily go against the wishes or the interests of either politicians or people in general. A number of the issues the courts deal with, such as anti-discrimination and the right to life, are seen by the former as 'too hot to handle' and by the latter as best kept free of partisan party politics. The same may be true of disputes between central, local and regional government, which will undoubtedly become more frequent with the popularity of decentralization, devolution and even federalization (hybrid or otherwise). In dealing with them, the judicial branch of government is, in effect, doing everyone a favour. It is also contributing a great deal to the governance not only of each country, but, especially with regard to EC law and the ECHR, Europe as a whole. Even if one disagrees that judges might do a better job than politicians (see Debate 3.1), and notwithstanding research which suggests that Europe's top judges may be no less influenced by their political views than their counterparts on the US Supreme Court (Hönnige, 2009), it does seem to be the case that people trust the legal system in general far more than they do their elected parliaments and governments – though, as Table 3.7 shows, this is sometimes not saying much. It is to these supposedly venerable but clearly much maligned institutions that we now turn.

Learning Resources for Chapter 3

Further reading

On regions, see Keating *et al.* (2005), *Culture, Institutions and Economic Development* and for a comparatively-attuned review of the state of play in central and eastern Europe, Pitschel and Bauer (2009), 'Subnational Governance Approaches on the Rise'. On local government, see the collections edited by Dollery and Robotti (2008), *The Theory and Practice of Local Government Reform*, Heinelt and Bertrana (2011), *The Second Tier of Local Government in Europe*, and especially Loughlin *et al.* (2011), *Oxford Handbook of Local and Regional Democracy in Europe*. For a discussion of governance, see Torfing *et al.* (2012), *Interactive Governance: Advancing the Paradigm*. Peters and Pierre (2004), *The Politicization of the Civil Service in Comparative Perspective*, also provides plenty of insights into how politicians are trying ensure they steer the bureaucracy instead of vice versa. Demmke and Moilanen (2010), *Civil Services in the EU of 27: Reform Outcomes and the Future of the Civil Service* is also invaluable. On the central state in Europe, see Page and Wright (2006), *From the Active to the Enabling State*. The collection edited by Pollitt *et al.* (2007b), *The New Public Management in Europe,* is the must-read if you are interested in this phenomenon. On the extent to which 'Europe' and the 'domestic' have (and have not) become enmeshed both bureaucratically and in terms of policy, see Wessels *et al.* (2003), *Fifteen into One?* On policy making, try the collection edited by Moran *et al.* (2008), *The Oxford Handbook of Public Policy.* For more on service delivery, see the collection edited by Wollman and Marcou (2010) *The Provision of Public Services in Europe.* For policy making in the EU, the first port of call has to be the collection edited by Wallace *et al.* (2010), *Policy making in the European Union.* See also Compston (2006), *King Trends and the Future of Public Policy.* On the interface between law and politics, especially in those countries operating constitutional courts, see Stone Sweet (2000), *Governing with Judges,* and Sadurski (2009), *Twenty Years After the Transition: Constitutional Review in Central and Eastern Europe.* On law and the EU, see Stone Sweet (2004), *The Judicial Construction of Europe,* and a special issue of the *Journal of European Public Policy* on the European Court of Justice edited by Kelemen and Schmidt (2012); see also Kelemen (2011), *Eurolegalism.* On the judges themselves, see Bell (2010), *Judiciaries within Europe.*

On the web

http://www.politicsresources.net/const.htm or http://www.servat.unibe.ch/icl/ – constitutions in English

http://www.confcoconsteu.org – constitutional courts

www.nispa.sk – CEE public administration and civil service

www.oecd.org – reports on governments and governance throughout Europe

http://www.local.gov.uk/european-and-international – local and regional governments in Europe

curia.europa.eu – the EU's European Court of Justice

http://www.echr.coe.int/ECHR/homepage_en – (non-EU) European Court of Human Rights

Discussion questions

1   Why do some analysts think it makes more sense to talk about governance rather than government? And why talk about multilevel governance?

2   Why does decentralization seem to be the trend across Europe? Does the trend mean that traditional distinctions between unitary and federal countries are now a little outdated and/or overstated?

3   What are new public management ideas and have they triumphed all over Europe?

4   The neutrality of the civil service is valued in some European states but less so in others: can you think of any advantages of a more politicized bureaucracy?

5   Why might trust in civil servants vary between countries?

6   Is transparency the cure for political corruption?

7   How do you think that Europeanization has affected the state machinery of European countries?

8   Some talk about national policy styles. How can we explain them? Why and to what extent do they persist?

9   Why do you think most European states have written constitutions and judicial review? Is it possible – or advisable – to do without them?

10 Has 'rule by judges' been made more or less likely by European integration?

ONLINE RESOURCES AVAILABLE   **Visit the companion site at www.palgrave.com/politics/bale to access additional learning resources.**

Chapter 4

Governments and parliaments – a long way from equality

Chapter 3 looked at governance, but, in addition to looking at policy making, it concentrated on the changing architecture of the state and the non-elected people who help to run it, be they civil servants or judges. Now, we turn to governments – the representative part of the executive.

The elected government in almost all European countries must enjoy 'the confidence of parliament', normally expressed in a vote when it takes office – a vote it has to win or, at the very least, not lose. Europe's parliamentary governments are led by a prime minister and a group of colleagues, which political scientists call the **cabinet**. The fact that cabinet members very often sit in, and in all cases are responsible to, parliament blurs the distinction between the executive and the legislature that constitute two parts of the classical three-part 'separation of powers' outlined in Chapter 3. This clear division of labour is considered sacrosanct by some Americans, yet its blurring in Europe does not seem to exercise many Europeans. Conversely, Americans see nothing strange in the head of state and the head of government being one and the same person – namely, the president. However, nearly all European countries, more or less successfully, keep the two functions separate.

This chapter begins by looking at the largely attenuated role of the head of state in European countries. It then focuses on governments and, in particular, prime ministers and cabinets. Who and what are they made up of? Do they always command a majority in parliament? How long do they last? How is it decided who controls which ministry? What do they spend their time doing? Next, the chapter turns to Europe's parliaments. Most European legislatures have two chambers: we look at whether it makes much difference. The chapter then moves on to the basic functions of legislatures – hiring and firing governments, making law, and scrutiny and oversight. It explores whether and why some of Europe's parliaments are weak and some are stronger. It looks at why, despite the fact that some parliaments are relatively powerful, they are rarely a match for governments. And it also considers whether parliaments and governments are representative of the societies which elect them, particularly when it comes to gender.

Cabinet, which may be known in particular countries by a different name (for instance, in France it is called the Council of Ministers) is the final democratic decision-making body in a state. In Europe, the cabinet is made up of party politicians who are, more often than not, chosen from the ranks of MPs and are collectively (as well as individually) responsible to parliament.

The head of state

All European countries have a head of state. In the continent's monarchies (Belgium, the Netherlands, Denmark, Norway, Sweden, Spain and the UK), the head of state will be the king or queen. In republics, it will be a president, either elected directly by the people (as in Austria, Bulgaria, Cyprus, Finland, France, Ireland, Lithuania, Poland, Portugal, Romania, Slovakia, Slovenia, and now the Czech Republic) or 'indirectly' by an electoral college (as in Germany, Italy, Greece, and Estonia) which is normally the parliament. The title of 'president', however, does not mean the post-holder is, like the US President, both head of state and head of government. In Europe the two roles – rightly or wrongly (see Debate 4.1) – are normally kept separate. The only clear exceptions to the rule are Cyprus, the only fully presidential system in the EU-27 (see Ker-Lindsay, 2006), and France (see Box 4.1), although a number of other countries (among them Romania and Portugal) can perhaps claim to be, like the latter, 'semi-presidential' (see Elgie, 2011; Elgie and Moestrup, 2008; Passarelli, 2010). By far the bulk, then, of Europe's presidents, like its monarchs, do not wield executive power but are instead supposed to be above day-to-day politics. As such, they are trusted not just to represent the state diplomatically but also neutrally to carry out vital constitutional tasks such as the official appointment of a prime minister as head of government, the opening of parliament and the signing of its bills into law.

KEY POINT

By far the majority of Europe's heads of state do not wield or even share executive power, even if they are directly elected. This does not, however, mean they have no role or influence.

It is, therefore, tempting to write off Europe's presidents and monarchs as playing a merely ceremonial role. They are a reminder to people (and, more importantly, to elected governments) that, underneath the cut and thrust of inevitably partisan politics, something more steady and solid endures. And, like the flag and certain unique traditions, they can be rallied round by all sides in times of trouble. Yet heads of state – and not necessarily just those who

BOX 4.1

Monsieur le Président – France's executive head of state

Under France's 'semi-presidential' system, the president has executive (and especially emergency) powers that go well beyond those given to other heads of state in Europe, other than in Cyprus – the EU's only fully presidential regime. Not only is he head of the armed forces and the negotiator of international agreements, he can also dissolve parliament for fresh elections without consultation and can call a referendum on policy put forward by parliament or the government. Very often, he is also in charge of domestic policy – but not always. As in most other European countries, the French president appoints a prime minister who must command the confidence of the lower house of parliament, *l'Assemblée Nationale.* The prime minister and cabinet ministers are then collectively and individually responsible to parliament, which is what differentiates semi-presidential from full-blown presidential systems. This means that French presidents can exercise anything like full executive power only when the prime minister and cabinet are drawn from his or her own party, or (as is often the case in France) an alliance of parties. Since the mid-1980s there have been several periods (1986–8, 1993–5, 1997–2002) where this has not been the case, obliging the president to 'cohabit' with a prime minister and cabinet drawn from a party or parties on the other side of the political fence. While the tension and conflict arising from cohabitation has not always been as bad as it might have been, the situation certainly obliges the popularly elected president to take more of a back seat – though less so in foreign and defence policy and diplomacy than in domestic policy. Now that French presidential elections have been re-timed to take place every five years, and in all likelihood just before parliamentary elections, *cohabitation* should become much less common.

are directly elected (see Tavits, 2008a) – do constitute an alternative locus of potentially countervailing power that can constrain the actions of governments seeking to push their mandates a little too far or, for instance, promote their friends inappropriately. Italy's President is a case in point (see Box 4.2).

This countervailing power is supposed to be used sparingly and for the good of the country. It is no bad thing that even elected governments are made to think twice once in a while: the right enjoyed by some presidents, for example, to refer controversial legislation to some kind of supreme court (see Chapter 3) probably does no harm if it is used sparingly, as it is in, say, Ireland. Frequent intervention of this or any other kind, however, leaves those heads of state who indulge in it open to the accusation that they are simply trying to undermine or obstruct an elected government with whom they (or their party) have policy disagreements. Postcommunist democracies which began life as semi-presidential regimes (see Sedelius and Ekman, 2010) have more problems on this score than other states – especially (but not exclusively) when it comes to foreign affairs. For instance, before he was killed in a plane crash in April 2010 Lech Kaczyński, Poland's president, confessed during a visit to Serbia that he had been unhappy about the decision of his country's government (no longer run by his twin brother but by their political rival, Donald Tusk) to recognize Kosovo (see Chapter 2). Disputes between the two over who should ultimately speak for the country at EU summits ended up in the TK, the Constitutional Court of Poland (see Chapter 3). In general, however, the situation has resolved itself (formally and conventionally at least) in favour of parliamentary government: in Poland, for example, the constitution still allows the president a veto over legislation, but the veto does not apply to the budget and can be overridden by a three-fifths majority in parliament.

There are, however, states which still experience serious conflict between the president and the legislature over who is entitled to do what. Bulgaria in 2010 saw an attempt by MPs to impeach President Parvanov after he had, in their view, breached confidentiality by publishing the transcript of a private meeting with the deputy prime minister and the finance minister in the wake of the disrespect they had displayed towards him during a television appearance. In Latvia in 2011, President Zatlers triggered a successful referendum to dissolve parliament (the *Saeima*) when he fell out with the government over what he saw as foot-dragging over corruption allegations. In Romania, things became so serious in

BOX 4.2

The country's (non-partisan) conscience? Italy's President

In the early 1990s, Italy's Francesco Cossiga made it clear that, like the public, he thought little of some of his fellow politicians who were at the time mired in the scandal that brought about major electoral and party system change (see Chapter 5). In 1994, his successor, Oscar Luigi Scalfaro, appointed a non-party 'technocratic' administration which lasted just over a year instead of dissolving parliament at the request of Silvio Berlusconi, whose first attempt at being prime minister ended after just a few months. Carlo Azeglio Ciampi, who came into post in 1999, provoked the outrage of Berlusconi (prime minister once again) by exercising his right, in December 2003, to veto a bill passed by parliament which many claimed gave Berlusconi *carte blanche* for a media monopoly in Italy (see Chapter 7). He was, however, constitutionally barred from vetoing the bill a second time when a slightly amended version was passed in April 2004. In 2006, a former communist, Giorgio Napolitano, became President. Relations with Berlusconi were predictably problematic and in early 2009 the two clashed when Napolitano refused to sign an emergency decree rushed through by Berlusconi in order to overturn a court decision permitting the family of a road accident victim finally to allow her to die after 17 years in a coma with no hope of recovery: a constitutional crisis was avoided only because the patient died at the height of a drama which inevitably involved the Vatican. After that, and in keeping with his attempt to play a straight bat at all times, Napolitano was careful not to be seen to be trying to push Berlusconi out of the Premiership as Italy's financial situation became increasingly critical towards the back end of 2011. But he was quick to follow the precedent set by some of his predecessors and appoint a technocratic, non-party government run by former European Commissioner, the economist Mario Monti, when, on 12 November, Berlusconi eventually jumped.

the summer of 2012 that the centre-left majority in parliament voted to suspend President Traian Basescu (who at one point managed to provoke the resignation of a well-known doctor by spontaneously calling into a television talk show to criticize his 'leftist views') with a view to triggering his impeachment. Even this finale to what was a series of long-running arguments over public spending, judicial manipulation, and even the academic record of the prime minister descended into fiasco, however. Some 88 per cent of those voting in the impeachment referendum in July 2012 called for Basescu to go, but the whole thing was ruled invalid by the Constitutional Court because the requisite turnout of 50 per cent was only reached as a result of the government excluding a large number of those Romanians living abroad (but still entitled to vote) from the total.

These sometimes debilitating (or at least headline-grabbing) conflicts between prime ministers and presidents whose powers arguably continue to entitle them to an influence beyond that enjoyed by most of their European counterparts are not limited to postcommunist countries. Aníbal Cavaco Silva, a former prime minister of Portugal, was elected its president in 2006 and then re-elected in 2010. As PM between 1985 and 1995, he had to endure criticism from the then president (and another former PM) Mário Soares. But this did not prevent him, after he took over as head of state ten years later, irritating not just the government but also parliamentarians more generally by criticizing their chronic absenteeism. This sort of conflict supports the idea that Portugal and Poland (and Slovenia) continue to merit the label 'semi-presidential' along with, say, France, Romania, and Lithuania. Arguably, however, parliamentary government has become the convention, with presidential assertiveness depending more on the character, experience and political position of the incumbent than his or her formal rights, even if the latter do appear to be more than ceremonial.

Prime minister, cabinet and parliamentary government

In all European states except France and Cyprus, the person charged with the running of the country is clearly the prime minister. He or she is normally the leader of (or at least one of the leading figures in) a political party that has sufficient numerical strength in parliament to form a government, whether on its own or (more usually) in combination with other parties. This does not necessarily mean he or she will be from the largest party after an election. Indeed, recent research covering 28 European countries (as well as, incidentally, noting that presidents play more of a role in deciding who the prime minister will be than is often thought) finds that the largest party by no means always secures the premiership – and that being the incumbent is no advantage unless your previous government ended reasonably amicably and your performance wasn't too badly thought of (Glasgow *et al.*, 2011). Once appointed, however, as long as the government he or she leads retains the confidence of parliament, and subject of course to how his or her party fares in general elections (and the inter-party bargaining that goes on after them in most countries), a prime minister can serve multiple terms: unlike most presidents, they are not time-limited.

Broadly speaking, the power of a prime minister depends on two things. The first is the power of the executive in general: this is facilitated, for example,

KEY POINT

Executive power in Europe is wielded by governments which are accountable to and rely on the support of parliament. They are led by cabinets comprised of ministers from one or more parties, many of whom retain their parliamentary seats. In theory, they are coordinated, if not controlled, by a prime minister whose power – which some argue is on the rise – varies between countries but also according to circumstances.

by a strong central state and limited judicial oversight of government actions (see Chapter 3), as well as a weak parliament (see below). The second is his or her power within that executive itself. Helms (2005: 14) provides a helpful checklist of factors that contribute to this:

the right to decide upon appointments and dismissals of members of the cabinet as well as on the major political appointments below the cabinet level; the right to determine the number and terms of reference of ministerial departments; a superior position within the cabinet; ... the uncon-ditional right to dissolve parliament (through an official proclamation of the head of state) without the need to secure the cabinet's approval[; being] the leader of the (dominant) governing party ... [and governing] in single-party governments [rather] than in coalitions.

Not surprisingly, and although we must recognize the extent to which he has to satisfy the preferences of his party when appointing colleagues (see Kam *et al.*, 2010), the UK prime minister (strong executive, plenty of powers within that executive, and – until recently – leading a single-party majority govern-ment) can claim to be one of Europe's most pow-erful (see Helms, 2005: 12–13). Meanwhile, his Italian counterpart (relatively weak executive, few advantages within the executive, and leading a large coalition with an often insecure majority) is one of the continent's weakest, although, as Silvio Berlusconi showed, there is a lot an individual whose power derives from other sources (see Chapter 7) can do to overcome these formal disad-vantages. Other countries combine strong executives with limited prime ministerial power within the executive (e.g. the Netherlands) or vice versa (e.g. Germany), or they find that their strength on some dimensions is at least partially limited by running a minority government (which we go on to talk about below), albeit one that normally involves a single party (as has often been the case – at least until recently –in Sweden and Spain).

Because of their ultimate dependence on the con-fidence of parliament, it may seem at first glance that European prime ministers enjoy less autonomy than, say, an executive who is also head of state, such as the president of the USA. In fact, this is far from being the case. First and foremost, unlike the US president, they can normally count on winning votes in the legislature. This is not only important domes-tically but at a European and global level, too. If a prime minister signs an international agreement at summit meetings – the increased frequency of which is said by some observers to contribute to a rise in prime ministerial prominence – his co-signa-tories can generally regard ratification (where it is required) as a done deal.

Back at home, prime ministers may well have a great deal of say in the appointment of their cabinet

Table 4.1 Country size and cabinet size

	Population (millions)	Total Cabinet Members
Sweden	9.4	22
Czech Republic	10.5	15
Netherlands	16.7	12
Poland	38.2	19
France	65.1	31
Italy	60.6	24
UK	62.4	23
Spain	46.1	15
Germany	81.7	16
EU27 average	–	17

Notes: Rank ordered according to how many cabinet posts there are per head of population, with the highest first. Data as of 31 December 2010.

Source: Caramani *et al.*, 2011: 873.

– the group of people (the size of which, as Table 4.1 shows, is fairly random) tasked both with running particular ministries and coordinating government policy as a whole (Blondel and Müller-Rommel, 1997). Moreover, the fact that they typically chair cabinet meetings means that they can wield consid-erable influence on what cabinet does and does not discuss, as well as over the conclusions and action points emerging from those discussions. Ultimately, too, most of them have the power to fire as well as hire cabinet colleagues (see Dowding and Dumont, 2008), the exceptions being the Dutch and French prime ministers. The latter, though he can oblige ministers to resign, can also have ministers all but forced on him if operating under a president from the same party.

In general, prime ministers also have power-bases in their party and may be so popular with the general public that ministers dare not risk deposing such a figure, even if they feel that his or her treat-ment of them verges on the dictatorial. In fact, inter-views with hundreds of ministers across Europe suggest that most of them accept prime ministerial authority and even prefer a strong prime minister, as long as he or she is also willing to listen to and involve his or her cabinet (Blondel *et al.*, 2007: 202). Even if this weren't the case, ministers would be at a comparative disadvantage because it is the prime minister, by dint of his or her coordinating function, who knows – inasmuch as any one person can know – what is going on across the whole range of government activity. They, on the other hand, may well be reluctant to intervene in the business of fellow ministers (unless of course it directly affects their own portfolio) for fear of getting a taste of their own medicine at a later date. This does not necessarily allow the prime minister to interfere as much as he or she might like to in the business of the ministry. Indeed, in Germany, for instance, there are strict conventions precluding such interference, notwithstanding an equally powerful convention (also included in Germany's, constitution, the *Grundgesetz* or 'Basic Law') concerning the Chancellor's right to set the overall direction of government policy – something with which a well-staffed Chancellor's Department helps considerably (which may explain why it was emulated, for instance, in Hungary, where Viktor Orbán, PM between 1998 and 2002 and then again after 2010 has shown himself particularly keen to assert his power). But the prime minister's overview does allow him or her to play one minister (or set of ministers) off against another.

A prime minister's prominence in the media may also be a source of power, and is one more thing that leads some to argue that European countries are undergoing what they call 'presidentialization' (see Poguntke and Webb, 2004) or, at the very least, witnessing a strengthening of the position of the prime minister relative to his cabinet colleagues. This represents not so much presidentialization as a move towards what some comparativists would call a 'centralized-prime ministerial core executive' and away from the 'centralized-cabinet' model or (in cases where ministers have considerable independence from their colleagues) the 'decentralized-ministerial' model (see Goetz, 2006, for more detail on this schema). This shift, many argue, has been accelerated by Europeanization and in particular the role of the European Council and its decision-making summits that bring together prime ministers (plus a few presidents) to make decisions which not only affect the EU but often have big (and sometimes immediate) implications for politics back at home (see Johansson and Tallberg, 2010).

Notwithstanding all this (and to a much greater extent than is the case with an executive president),

the prime minister of a European country must also engage in collective decision-making with his or her cabinet – even if this often takes place outside and prior to the cabinet meeting which is then used simply to formalize decisions. Ultimately, he or she cannot function (or, indeed, continue in office) without the cabinet's collective consent to his or her being *primus inter pares* or 'first among equals'. Inasmuch as it exists in its own right, then, 'prime ministerial power' is constrained not just by contingencies of time and chance and personality, but the multiple and mutual dependencies between the prime minister and his or her cabinet.

This is not to say, of course, that the extent of this interdependence is the same in all European countries (see King, 1994). And it clearly varies according to political circumstances: for example, in Poland 'the strength of prime ministerial leadership has been chiefly determined by political and personal factors, such as party standing, the nature of parliamentary support, the presence of important leaders outside the cabinet, personal style and the popularity of government policies' rather than the Prime Minister's relatively strong formal powers over his cabinet ministers (Zubek, 2006: 96). For instance, a prime minister trying to hold together a potentially fissiparous coalition of different parties will probably be less powerful than a textbook account suggests. At the very least, he or she will need to rely not so much on constitutional-cum-administrative means of coordinating his or her cabinet as on party-to-party relationships and mechanisms that are supplementary to formal processes (for which see Strøm *et al.*, 2010, especially Chapters 5 and 8).

That said, formal (or at least conventional) powers, accumulated over time and varying between countries, cannot be discounted. The UK prime minister, presiding over a single-party government and armed with the traditional prerogatives of the Crown, is more powerful, for instance, than his or her Dutch counterpart. This is because the latter is hemmed in by both a closely worded coalition agreement with other parties – something that is more and more common across Europe (see Strøm *et al.*, 2010: 159–199, 409–10) and a tradition of ministerial equality. On the other hand, even the most powerful UK prime ministers of recent years have had to defer to their finance minister. Indeed, in most European countries – west and east (see

Blondel *et al.*, 2007: 176) – the latter is especially powerful: his (and it is almost always his) resignation would give markets and voters cause for alarm, while inside government the frequent contact his ministry has with all other departments gives him not only control and coordination capacities that rival those of his 'boss' but also a similarly bird's eye view of the work of the government as a whole.

The relative lack of personal autonomy enjoyed by the prime minister of a European country, however, has its upside. Compared to, say, a US president, whose hold over the legislature might be tenuous or even non-existent, the prime minister and the cabinet of a European country can generally feel confident that their decisions will, where necessary, be translated into legislation. European governments are, above all, party and parliamentary governments. The political face of the executive more or less accurately reflects the balance of power between the parties elected into the legislature and will often (though not always) be a multiparty coalition. The ministers who make up the cabinet formed from that coalition might or might not be MPs (Box 4.3). But they are there first and foremost because they represent a political party whose presence in the government is required in order to secure an administration able to command – at least for the time being and on crucial pieces of legislation (such as budgetary matters) – what is routinely referred to as 'the confidence' of parliament. Although confidence is understood by most people in, say, the UK to necessitate a stable majority of the MPs in parliament, this is by no means always the case.

Permutations of parliamentary government in multiparty systems

Many European governments do indeed command such majorities – some even when they are made up of just one party, although this is unusual outside the UK, Malta and Greece (though see Figure 4.2). But, as Table 4.2 shows, a significant number qualify as minority governments, i.e. administrations made up of one or more parties which together control less than half (plus one) of the seats in parliament. Such a prospect would be anathema in some coun-

---

BOX 4.3

The Netherlands' non-parliamentary executive

In the majority of European countries, ministers are also parliamentarians, though in only a few (the UK, Ireland and Lithuania are good examples) do they, in effect, have to be. The Netherlands (like Belgium, Bulgaria, Estonia, France, Slovakia, Sweden and Norway) is more unusual in the sense that, there, members of the *Tweede Kamer* are constitutionally obliged to give up their role in parliament while they are ministers. Their place is taken by substitutes from their own party so as to maintain the balance of party power in parliament. They can still appear in parliament to answer questions – and do so much more frequently than their cabinet counterparts in the USA, for example. Whether this formally enhanced separation between executive and legislature increases the willingness of the latter to stand up to the former is a moot point: there is no doubt that, based on an assessment of its formal rights, the *Tweede Kamer* is one of Europe's most powerful legislatures (see Table 4.5); whether it is as assertive in practice as it is in theory is less certain.

---

tries, inside as well as outside Europe. But in others it is a far from frightening prospect. To understand why, we need to look a little deeper into the process and outcomes of government formation.

This is something that political scientists all over the world have been looking into for decades, some even pursuing the holy grail of a model or models that would allow us to predict, given the strength and the positions of the parties in parliament, which would make it into office and which would be left out – a quest that so far has only resulted in us being able, at best, to guess correctly around half of the time. This doesn't mean that we need to abandon the attempt, simply that we need to factor in more and more of the considerations that, in the real world (see Strøm *et al.*, 2010 and Andeweg *et al.*, 2011), seem to make a difference as to which type of government eventually emerges from nego-

Table 4.2 Types of government across Europe, 1945–2010

Percentage of postwar administrations that were:	Single-party majority	Minimal winning coalition	Oversized coalition	Minority government
UK	92	4	0	4
Germany	3	70	17	10
Netherlands	0	48	40	12
France	4	27	42	27
Europe	11	33	21	34
Italy	0	7	50	43
Poland	0	44	6	50
Czech Republic	0	44	0	56
Sweden	7	21	0	72
Spain	27	0	0	73

Notes: Europe is EU-27, minus Cyprus plus Norway.

Source: Calculated from Gallagher *et al.*, (2011: 434).

tiations. These negotiations, incidentally, can sometimes take an awfully long time (see Figure 4.1), with Belgium taking so long (541 days) in 2010/11 that at one point a senator suggested the spouses of the party leaders involved in the standoff deny them sex until they had cut a deal! Rather more common real-world considerations which need factoring into our analyses clearly include, to take just one example, the proven tendency for parties to try to avoid working with other parties which have – in

Figure 4.1 Average number of days taken to form a government

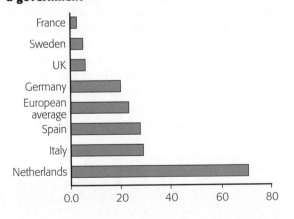

Source: Golder, 2010. Covers 17 governments in Western Europe 1944–1998.

their eyes anyway – let them down in the past (Tavits, 2008b) but, by the same token, to partner up with parties with which, in the immediate or none-too-distant past, they have managed to govern reasonably harmoniously (Martin and Stevenson, 2010).

Minimal (connected) winning coalitions

Few political scientists, even when conducting thought experiments, think of democratic politicians as purely 'office-seekers', interested in power either for its own sake or because of the personal profile, wealth, comfort and travel opportunities it can bring them. However reluctant the fashionably cynical among us might be to acknowledge it, the fact is that most people prepared to represent a political party are also 'policy-seekers'. They want to see some real progress (however limited) made toward realizing their vision of the good society. Even if we forget all the other aspects that might be involved (from the psychology of bargaining to the personal relationships between party leaders), this dual motivation is enough to ensure that government formation is very rarely simply a matter of putting together what political scientists call a

**Figure 4.2 Single-party majority government –
Hungary 2010**

MSZP	LMP	Fidesz/KDNP	Jobbik
Social Democrats	'New Politics'	Conservative	Radical Right
59	16	262	47

Notes: 1. Shading indicates government.
    2. Seats required for overall majority = 194.

minimal winning coalition. True, around one in three governments in postwar western Europe have been minimal winning coalitions, while only around one in ten have been single-party majorities. But most of these coalitions have also been what political scientists call **minimal connected winning coalitions** (see Figure 4.3 for an example).

KEY POINT

The majority of European governments are coalitions between two or more parties. Most command a majority in parliament – sometimes a much bigger one than they actually need. A surprising number, however, are minority administrations. Which type of government forms is partly a product of parliamentary arithmetic but also of institutionally influenced cultural norms.

Given that in most countries such a coalition would be theoretically, and often practically, possible, how then do we account for the fact that so many parties in Europe hold office, either singly or together, as **minority governments**? In fact, the answer is quite simple: they do it because they can.

Figure 4.3 A minimal connected winning coalition – Portugal 2011

BE	CDU	PS	PSD	CDS-PP
Left	Greens & Communists	Social Democrats	Conservatives	Conservatives
8	16	74	108	24

Notes: 1. Shading indicates government.
    2. Seats required for overall majority = 116.

A **minimal winning coalition** is a government made up of parties that control as near to just over half the seats in parliament as they can manage in order to combine their need to win confidence votes with their desire to have to share ministerial portfolios between as few claimants as possible.

Minimal connected winning coalitions are made up of parties with at least something in common ideologically, even if governing together means having more parliamentary seats than would be strictly necessary and/or could be formed by doing deals with less like-minded parties (Figure 4.3).

Minority governments

In some countries minority government is difficult, if not impossible. These are countries that operate what political scientists call 'positive parliamentarism'. This refers to the fact that their governments have to gain at least a plurality (and sometimes a majority) of MPs' votes before they are allowed to take office – something that is normally tested in what is called an 'investiture vote' on a potential government's policy programme and cabinet nominations. Examples include Germany, where minority government is made less likely still by a rule that insists that no government can be defeated on a vote of no confidence once it has been allowed to form unless the majority voting against it is ready to replace it immediately with another government. Other examples of countries insisting on investiture votes include Belgium, Ireland and Italy. So, too, do Poland and Spain which, like Germany, have a 'constructive' vote of confidence, where a successor government has to be ready to take over before one can be called. But Spain also reminds us that 'politics' can often trump 'institutions': after the 2004 general election, the social democratic PSOE managed, in spite of the rules and conventions, to construct a minority government!

A **minority government** is made up of a party or parties whose MPs do not constitute a majority in parliament but which, nevertheless, is able to win – or at least, not lose – the votes of confidence that are crucial to taking office and/or staying there.

Figure 4.4 A minority government – Sweden 2010

V	S	MP	FP	C	KD	M	SD
Left	Social Democrats	Green	Liberal	Centre Democrat	Christian	Conservative	Radical Right
19	112	25	24	23	19	107	20

Notes: 1. Shading indicates government.
2. Seats required for overall majority = 175.

Other European countries, however, are characterized as operating 'negative parliamentarism'. Governments do not need to undergo an investiture vote or, if they do (Sweden, where the prime minister and by implication the government has to step up to the plate, is an example), they are not obliged to win the vote, merely not to lose it. In other words, they can survive as long as those voting against them do not win over half the MPs to their cause. Likewise, to lose office the government has to be defeated rather than actually win a majority on motions of no confidence. This makes it much easier for minority governments to form and to stay in power once they have formed. It therefore comes as little surprise that a list of countries operating negative parliamentarianism includes (as well as Finland, Portugal and the UK), countries such as Sweden, Norway, and Denmark, where minority government has, since the 1970s, become the norm.

These countries are all the more likely to experience minority government because elections, historically anyway, have often produced what political scientists refer to as 'strong' parties. These may well be the largest party in the parliament. Moreover, they are 'pivotal' in the sense that any minimal connected winning coalition would have to include them, and would, if you filled all the seats in parliament in left–right order, have one of its MPs occupying the middle seat and therefore known in the jargon as the 'median legislator'. Around three-quarters of all postwar European governments contain parties which contain this coveted position in parliament (Andeweg *et al.*, 2011: 193). Pivotal parties are always at an advantage, even if they are not large: for example, the liberal FDP in Germany managed to turn its position midway between the SPD (social democrats) and the CDU–CSU (Christian democrats) into almost 31 years of government in the 49 years between 1949 and 1998. But when a pivotal party is also parliament's largest, it is often in a great position to run a minority government. This is particularly the case when, as in Scandinavia, parties on their immediate flank (say, ex-communist or green parties in the case of the social democrats, or a far-right or zealous market-liberal party in the case of the conservatives) would not dream of teaming up in government with parties on the other side of the left–right divide or bloc (see Figure 4.4). Unless these smaller, less mainstream parties are willing to increase what political scientists refer to as their 'walk-away value' by, say, threatening to support the other side or precipitate a new election, they become, in effect, 'captive parties', whose support (or, at least, abstention) in confidence motions can be pretty much guaranteed.

In any case, life as what political scientists refer to as a 'support party' rather than a coalition partner might suit all concerned. This is especially the case if it involves some kind of deal – an understanding (possibly written and public) that may fall short of a full-blown coalition agreement but provides some promises on policy and consultation. This 'contract parliamentarism' (see Bale and Bergman, 2006) allows the party or parties in government not just to limit the extent to which they have to share power, but also to affect a 'respectable' distance from the parties that are helping them get into or stay in office. Those other parties might benefit, too. First, if they are relatively small and/or inexperienced, full-blown membership of a coalition might thrust too much responsibility onto them before they are ready to accept it. Appointing ministers who are not really up to the job and subsequently have to resign can be very damaging, as the parties that made up the Polish government between 2005 and 2007 discovered – so much so, indeed, that two of the three lost all their MPs at the subsequent election. Not entering the government, on the other hand, but simply providing support, might have allowed them to go into the next election combining a claim to be contributing to political stability with a claim not to be responsible for all those things the government did that voters disliked. That election, or future elections, might have delivered them more seats by which time they would not only be more experienced but also better able to drive a hard bargain with a potential coalition partner. These agreements have occurred in the Czech Republic, Sweden and in Lithuania.

There is another reason why minority governments are more common than we might first suppose, and more common in some countries than in others (see Strøm, 1990). It is that in some systems being 'in opposition' is not nearly so thankless a task as it is in others, notably the UK. As we go on to show, some parliaments – particularly those with strong committee systems – offer considerably more scope for politicians whose parties are not in the government to influence policy and legislation. Again, it is the Scandinavian countries that experience frequent minority government where this so-called 'policy influence differential' between government and opposition is smallest. Finally, it is probably also the case that once a country has experienced minority government on a number of occasions and has lived perfectly well to tell the tale, it is more likely to embrace the possibility in the future. This does not mean it will never experience majority government, just that it will not be the default setting. For example, the centre–right coalition that took office in Sweden in 2006 was the first majority administration in that country for 25 years.

In short, the tendency toward minority or majority government has to be seen as cultural, as well as mathematical. There are few institutional barriers to minority government in the Netherlands, for instance. Even though the government has to get parliament to approve the often very detailed policy agreement the coalition parties spend months negotiating, there is no formal investiture vote, for example. Yet, because of a cultural trend toward achieving consensus, minority government rarely occurred until one formed in the wake of the 2010 election. Then, the sheer number or parties, their spread right across the left–right spectrum, the

ramped-up rhetoric of the radical right, and the reluctance of the centre-right and centre-left to work together lest they lose support to their flanks, made another solution practically impossible. Despite being backed by a contract, the arrangement (which never had particularly strong support from all of the parties to it) did not last long and was terminated by the radical right PVV in the spring of 2012, obliging the country to hold another election in the early autumn – one which saw voters turn decisively back to the mainstream and a majority Liberal–Labour coalition.

Hungary just doesn't seem to 'do' minority government either: unlike any other country in central and eastern Europe, all its governments in the post-communist period have commanded majorities. Conversely, and rather uniquely in a PR system, Spain's two main political parties seem to be so wedded to the idea of single-party government that, if it also means minority government, then so be it. This almost certainly has something to do with not wanting to court accusations that they are 'selling out' the unity of Spain to the regional parties with which they would have to coalesce in order to form a majority administration. Cultural 'hangovers' and cultural realities also help to explain a tendency in some countries toward the last type of parliamentary government, **oversized** or **surplus majority coalitions**.

> **Oversized** or **surplus majority coalitions** are governments that contain more parties than are needed to command a majority in parliament, to the extent that if one (or possibly more than one) party were to leave the government, it might still control over half the seats in the legislature.

Oversized or surplus majority coalitions

The traditional home of oversized or surplus majority coalitions in Europe is Finland. Because of the delicacy of its proximity to the old Soviet Union, the country got used to putting a premium on national unity, on consensus, and on including the left so as not to anger its bigger neighbour. So entrenched was the mindset that, until 2000, legislation that in most countries would have required

Figure 4.5 An oversized or surplus majority government – Finland 2011

VAS	VIHR	SDP	Åland Islands	SFP	KESK	KD	KOK	PS
Left	Green	Soc. Dem.	Ind.	Swedish Minority	Centre	Ch. Dem.	Con	Radical Right
14	10	42	1	9	35	6	44	39

Notes: 1. Shading indicates government.
2. Seats required for overall majority = 101.

only a simple majority in parliament required two-thirds of MPs to vote for it.

In Italy, too, there were institutional reasons for oversized coalitions. Until parliament stopped voting – at least, routinely – by secret ballot, governments needed a stockpile of extra votes because they could not trust enough of their highly factionalized MPs to toe the party line! The tradition of including more parties than a coalition really needs also built up over decades during which the main aim of most parties was to stand together in order to prevent the Communist Party sharing power. Nowadays, it is reinforced by an electoral system that encourages parties into 'pre-electoral' pacts with each other.

These occur in many countries (see Debus, 2009 and Allern and Aylott, 2009). They do not necessarily result in an oversized coalition, but they might well do so: pacts are generally honoured and the winning combination of parties will form a government even if it is composed of more parties than, strictly speaking, are needed. This was not the reason for the surplus majority government that formed in Finland in 2011: as well as the tradition referred to above, that had more to do with the refusal of the radical right wing party, which did well in the elections, to compromise, and the insistence of the social democrats that the Left party (which might otherwise have reaped the benefits of opposition if tough decisions had to be taken) be allowed to join the coalition (see Figure 4.5).

None of this is to suggest, however, that such governments are impossible, or even unlikely, in other countries. This is especially the case where, for example, parties are worried that excluding a close competitor means giving them carte blanche to mop up the votes of the disaffected should the government become unpopular or where, as may be becoming more common, there are parties – maybe smaller, maybe newer or perhaps former 'pariahs' –

keen to prove that they are ready to take responsibility and play with the big boys (see Andweg *et al.*, 2011: 197–8; see also Bale and Dunphy, 2011). There is even research to suggest that terrorist incidents make surplus majority governments (and indeed ideologically better-spread) governments more likely (Indridason, 2008). In other words, under certain circumstances surplus majorities can turn out to be the best, or even the only, option (see Volden and Carrubba, 2004). A case in point is Belgium. There, the contemporary need to ensure a balance of parties from both the Dutch- and French-speaking communities may make oversized coalitions increasingly necessary. But other classic 'institutional' reasons also come into play. The federalization of the country we explored in Chapter 2 requires two-thirds of MPs' votes because it entails changes to the constitution. But Belgium, of course, is by no means unique in presenting parties with a game which operates on more than one level – regional and national – making for a bargaining situation which is complex and for solutions that do not fulfil the predictions of models formulated before 'multi-level governance' became a fact of life (see Ştefuriuc, 2009).

This reminds us that a country's 'preferred solution' to government formation can change over time as institutions and cultures change. The Netherlands is a case in point. True, it still prefers majority governments, but as the differences have blurred between religious and ideological groups – differences that traditionally encouraged broad-based coalitions – the country has moved from preferring oversized to minimal winning coalitions and, finally, in 2010 to having to submit to a minority government made up of two centre-right parties with support from the far right PVV. The latter reminds us that, ultimately, preferred or conventional options are trumped by a combination of mathematics and

Figure 4.6 A 'grand coalition' – Austria 2008

Die Grünen	SPÖ	ÖVP	FPÖ	BZÖ
Green	Social Democrat	Christian Democrat	Radical Right	Radical Right
20	57	51	34	21

Notes: 1. Shading indicates government.
2. Seats required for overall majority = 92.

ideological incompatibility. The Austrian election of 2008, for example, like the German election of 2005, produced a 'grand coalition' between the SPÖ (social democrats: and the ÖVP (Christian democrats) – one which neither party really wanted but was inevitable once the latter made up its mind not to get into bed again with the far right (see Figure 4.6).

Government duration and stability

Much of the fear of minority government in countries with a more or less institutionalized preference for majorities results from the conviction that it is somehow less stable. In fact, this does turn out to be the case. Taking all the governments formed in western Europe between 1945 and 2010, the average government lasted 743 days (see Gallagher *et al.*, 2011: 447). Single-party majority governments, however, lasted on average 1017 days and minimal winning coalitions 910 days. Oversized or surplus majority coalitions lasted on average just 582 days – less than single party minority governments (608 days) but slightly more than minority coalitions (523 days). In central and eastern Europe between 1990 and 2010, the figures were 533 (average for all governments), 878 (single party majority), 610 (minimal winning coalition), 659 (surplus majority), 365 (single party minority) 372 (minority coalition).

But there are qualifications to this pan-European pattern. The ideological affinity or 'connectedness' of the various parties that go to make up a government is important. A government composed of those who are politically close will be more stable than one which is not. Nor, of course, should we forget the influence of institutional rules. For

instance, the rules we have already mentioned on votes of no confidence are bound to make a difference. Governments will often last longer where these are hard to lose or (as in Germany, Spain and Poland with their 'constructive' confidence votes) hard to stage in the first place. On the other hand, political culture or system traditions are also important. In western Europe, for example, minority governments in Scandinavia last longer than minority governments elsewhere: the average duration of minority governments in Sweden was 908 days for those formed by just one party and 785 days for those made up of two or more; in Italy the figures were 223 and 353 days respectively (Gallagher *et al.*, 2011: 447). In eastern and central Europe, governments in Bulgaria and Hungary last longer than most of their western counterparts, but governments in Poland (until recently) and Latvia have been notoriously short-lived (*ibid.*). Also important is the existence or absence of comprehensive and more-or-less binding coalition agreements. In some countries, like the Netherlands, these generally work well, although tradition offers no guarantees, of course. In others where they are uncommon (such as Italy) they might actually undermine stability by removing the flexibility that particular system seems to demand. The new democracies of eastern and central Europe have, of course, had less time to develop traditions and it may be that some countries which earlier looked as if they were doomed to unstable short-lived governments might not be stuck in that groove forever: Poland is a good example.

> **KEY POINT**
>
> **Multiparty systems do not necessarily produce unstable, short-lived governments. In fact, their duration and stability varies considerably – and not just according to type of government (majority or minority). Some countries routinely suffer from instability; some rarely, if ever, do so.**

But national political culture and institutions do not explain everything: there is after all a considerable degree of 'within-country variation' (see Saalfeld, 2010). Another qualification is that the 'durability' of European governments to some extent depends on the number of parties that actually make up (or potentially could make up) a coalition. A parliament with a large number of small parties presenting each other (and larger parties) with multiple options can mean that relatively minor shocks caused by policy or personality conflicts, or by unexpected 'critical events', are enough to precipitate a collapse of the government. This is especially the case when such a collapse does not necessarily entail fresh elections. Interestingly, very recent research (Warwick, 2012) shows that, irrespective of whether elections do or do not precede a new government, those parties which are responsible for a coalition collapsing – whether because their leader has the power of dissolution, or because they resign from it, or because they cause rows that lead to its break-up – tend not to benefit from that collapse, either in terms of votes at subsequent elections or in terms of participation and securing plum portfolios in any new government. This suggests (presuming for a moment that parties are aware of this) that either they are not acting rationally (not altogether unlikely) or that they believe that things would be even worse for them if they were to keep the coalition together – perhaps because to do so would alienate their activists (and possibly their funders), perhaps because to do so would harm their reputation for sticking to their principles or at least for competent management.

It is worth making the point, however, that frequent collapses of and (re)formation of coalitions, while they are easily portrayed in the media as denoting chaos and confusion, do not necessarily mean that the country concerned should be seen as the proverbial 'basket case'. In recent years, governments in Italy have actually lasted a reasonably long time, but for half a century after the end of the Second World War the country was notorious for the seemingly endless succession of administrations that came and went, even if most of them revolved around one 'core party', the now-defunct DC (Christian democrats). However, those were also the years in which the Italian economy raced ahead (although more so in the prosperous north than in the poorer south), suggesting that there is no clear correlation between political 'instability' and economic progress. In a similar vein, research on central and eastern Europe suggests that factors that supposedly make for weak governments – lack of a solid majority, large numbers of ideologically dissimilar parties in coalition together – have no negative impact on economic policy (Jahn and Müller-Rommel, 2010).

Dividing the spoils – 'portfolio allocation'

Putting together a coalition, of course, entails coming to some agreement both on policies and on the division of ministerial rewards. 'Who gets what, when and how?' is one of the classic political questions, and no more so than when it comes to what political scientists call 'portfolio allocation' – deciding which party gets which ministries. Except in the case of single-party governments, which in Europe tend to be the exception rather than the rule, this happens in two stages. First, the parties haggle over which ministries and departments they will occupy in the coalition cabinet. Next, they decide who in the party will take up the portfolios they manage to get. Actually, of course, the two stages are not quite so separate: which ministries a party wants may well be conditioned in part by the need to accommodate particular politicians. Indeed, sometimes the size of the cabinet will be increased in order to make a deal easier (Strøm *et al.*, 2010: 412), although over time, it should be said, the size of cabinets appears to be decreasing marginally – possibly in response to the decline of nationalized industries and enthusiasm for bigger ministries that can cut across ancient and unhelpful departmental divisions (see Chapter 4; see also Peters, 2007: 242).

KEY POINT

Which party gets which ministry partly depends on their preferences. But the number of ministries each party in a coalition gets normally equates to the strength of parliamentary support it can contribute relative to its partners in government – although sometimes those parties that are absolutely necessary to the formation of that government are given a disproportionate share of portfolios.

In theory, there are basically two methods governing the first stage of portfolio allocation: according to *bargaining strength* (which depends on what some political scientists call a party's 'walk-away value') or according to some kind of rule of *proportionality*. In the first instance, parties that are part of the coalition can use their importance to that coalition as leverage with which to gain the highest number of seats around the cabinet table as possible – even if this number is disproportionate to the number of MPs they bring to the government benches. The other way is simply to give each party in the coalition the number of cabinet places that best reflects the proportion of MPs with which it provides the coalition. For instance, a party which provides 30 per cent of the MPs on the government benches should be entitled to claim around a third of the cabinet positions.

In the real world, both these systems of allocation operate, although for the most part (and with the proviso that small parties holding the balance of power often receive slightly more than their 'fair share' of cabinet seats) proportionality is the norm. However, other factors can erode that principle. In central and eastern Europe, for instance, it seems clear that other parties are biased against former communist parties, even though they now claim to have transformed themselves into social democratic parties (see Chapter 5). The latter often participate in coalitions nowadays, but often with fewer seats around the cabinet table than they might expect (see Druckman and Roberts, 2007), even though their participation actually seems to result in longer-lasting government (Tzelgov, 2011). And, right across Europe, it is often the case that certain parties have certain favourite ministries. For example, a party representing agricultural interests might ask for, and almost always get, the agriculture portfolio. Likewise, social democrats tend to want health and social security, and greens the environment. This risks sclerosis, as the party in control has little incentive for fresh thinking. On the other hand, it does avoid damaging policy swings and can give the party a chance to make a difference.

Making a difference (as we go on to explore in much more detail in Chapter 9) is not that easy. Yet there does seem to be some link between which particular party in a coalition controls a particular ministry and the policy direction of that ministry. Political scientists Ian Budge and Hans Keman (1990) looked at labour and finance ministries and found, for instance, that they tended to pursue policies to avoid unemployment more strongly when they were controlled by social democrats rather than conservatives, who in turn were more interested in reducing the role of the state. But even if no such effects were perceptible, one suspects that parties

would still lay claim to particular ministries. Even if a particular portfolio is not part of a party's traditional brand, it may well have featured heavily in recent campaigns and therefore have become important to it: cross-national research (Bäck *et al.*, 2011) strongly suggests that 'parties prefer, and aim to gain control over, ministries with a policy area of competence that was stressed in their election manifestos.' Moreover, Bäck *et al.* also suggest that, along with longer-term associations with particular policy areas and being seen to have a reasonably moderate stance on them, these preferences and aims are good predictors of which party actually gets which ministry.

Governing

The formation of a government via the naming of a cabinet and the swearing-in of ministers to whom particular portfolios have been awarded is, of course, merely 'the end of the beginning'. Most politicians in Europe, even the most mainstream centrists, see themselves as having a particular job to do, above and beyond merely keeping the state ticking over. Normally, this involves the translation of policy into practice. More precisely, it involves ministers overseeing the drafting of legislation and the progress of civil servants in implementing the policies that have made it through the government formation process – the policies that are included in the coalition agreements that are becoming an increasingly common phenomenon in Europe (see Müller and Strøm, 2000). This, as we suggested in Chapter 3, has become more difficult. Most European states are no longer simply 'top-down' affairs although, as we also saw in Chapter 3, steps have been taken to tighten the hold of politicians over non-elected parts of the 'core executive'.

Ministers also have to meet with and take on board (or, at least, absorb) the views of pressure

> **KEY POINT**
>
> Being a cabinet minister involves balancing the goals of the party with the constraints imposed by other ministers, who may be from other parties, and the existing policies of one's department, as well as taking into account ongoing engagement with EU partners. It also involves both collective and individual responsibility.

groups, particularly those on whom they might rely to some degree for the implementation of policy (see Chapter 8). In addition to interest groups and parties, another source of policy (and possible trouble) is the EU. As we noted in Chapter 2, ministers in some departments may spend two or three days a month consulting with their counterparts in the other member states. In these consultations, they are assisted both by their home departments and by their country's permanent representative in Brussels. This 'ambassador to the EU', along with his or her 26 colleagues on the intergovernmental committee routinely referred to as COREPER, works to achieve compromises that will protect and promote the 'national interest' and, quite frankly, ease the burden of work for ministers. Not everything can be 'fixed' beforehand, however. A trip to Brussels can often, therefore, involve ministers trying to get something done or, alternatively, trying to stop something happening. This might be at the behest of other departments, whose civil servants meet in inter-departmental committees with those of the department concerned, or it might come from pressure groups or the cabinet, or even, in Denmark, parliament (see Box 4.8). Ministers, therefore, play a vital linkage role between the national and the supranational. Indeed, they are the embodiment of the blurring of the boundaries between them that is so important a part of contemporary European politics.

In Europe's parliamentary systems, ministers, even when they are not themselves MPs, also play a vital linkage role between citizens and the state by being individually answerable and, in most cases, collectively responsible to parliament. Being individually answerable means that they can, at least theoretically, be held to account for the actions of their department. This is vital if there is ultimately to be democratic control of the state, although not all countries follow Poland, for example, and allow parliament to officially vote 'no confidence' in an individual minister, thereby forcing him or her to resign. Being 'collectively responsible' means that ministers are expected to support government policy or else resign. This cabinet collective responsibility is also important in democratic terms because parliaments express their confidence (or maybe their lack of confidence!) in the government as a whole. The fiction that ministers are all pulling in the same direction

has therefore to be maintained, in order to preserve the political accountability of the executive in a system where the buck stops not with one individual (as it does in presidential systems), but with government as a whole.

This supposedly constitutionally necessary convention does not, in fact, hold everywhere. Belgium's cabinet ministers, for instance, are under no such obligation (Keman, 2002a: 229) and, notes one expert (Sanford, 2002: 165), their Polish counterparts certainly *feel* under no such obligation! Nor, of course, even where the convention has developed, does it preclude genuine and sometimes bitter disagreement within cabinet. Studies of cabinets across western and eastern Europe suggest that many governments (though not all governments, Sweden being an obvious exception) employ networks of cabinet committees to pre-cook and filter out issues different departments can agree on so as not to disrupt cabinet itself – although this technique cannot always prevent cabinet from becoming a court of last resort between disputatious ministers rather than a collegial and collective decision-making enterprise. But those same studies also show that cabinets themselves are mostly still meaningful forums: their deliberations actually change policy (Blondel and Müller-Rommel, 1997, 2001). The extent to which cabinets actually control ministers and prevent them from 'going native' (becoming more interested in protecting their departments than the interests of the government as a whole), however, is another matter (see Andeweg, 2000).

It is also one that feeds into another thorny issue – the extent to which cabinets made up of politicians from different parties, as is the norm in many countries, can actually work together. In fact, coordination often takes place outside the cabinet room itself. In an increasing number of countries, the formation process produces a written agreement which is used to bind the coalition partners (and their ministers) into a common programme: the most detailed study we have comes from the Netherlands, and suggests it is quite an effective technique (see Thomson, 2001). In a few countries, the cabinet as a whole is encouraged to 'bond' by spending time with each other (whether they like it or not!) at 'working lunches' and the like – this is famously the case in Norway, for instance. Whether or not some sort of bonhomie

COUNTRY PROFILE

United Kingdom (UK)

History: The United Kingdom of Great Britain (England, Wales and Scotland) and Northern Ireland took some time to assume its present shape. Wales was all but assimilated into England in the 1540s. But the union of the two with the kingdom of Scotland, long an ally of France, was not achieved until 1707. A seventeenth-century civil war established the supremacy of parliament over the crown. By then, after centuries of religious dispute that began in the sixteenth century when the English king broke with the Roman Catholic church, Britain was a largely Protestant country.

Across the sea, however, the island of Ireland, which Britain had conquered but found hard to subdue, was predominantly Catholic. There was, however, a Protestant minority in the north – one deliberately transplanted there (mostly from Scotland) in order to strengthen colonial power. When, in the wake of the First World War, Ireland began to regain its independence, this minority rejected a place in what (in 1948) finally became the sovereign Irish Republic, remaining part of the UK.

By the beginning of the twentieth century, Britain had become the world's greatest commercial and imperial power, using the wealth generated by its pioneering role in the Industrial Revolution to establish control of huge swathes of the Indian subcontinent and Africa. This imperial expansion helped put the country on a collision course with Germany. Although the ensuing First World War resulted in a British (and French) victory, it proved a big drain on the country's resources, just as its other ally, the USA, began to supersede it economically. The Second World War (1939–45), from which Britain also emerged victorious, confirmed this relative decline, as did its inexorable surrender of its overseas empire. On the domestic front, however, the aftermath of the war saw the building by a Labour government of a comprehensive welfare state. Since then, power has alternated between Labour, on the centre-left, and the Conservatives, on the centre-right, with the former, under Tony Blair, winning a landslide victory in 1997 after eighteen years out of office. Blair finally handed over to his long term collaborator and rival, Gordon Brown, who, after a disappointing premiership, lost the general election of 2010. Very unusually, however, the Conservatives, while emerging as the largest single party in parliament did not claw back enough seats to win an overall majority, obliging them to join the Liberal Democrats in the UK's first peace-time coalition government for over seventy years.

Area: 241,600 km² (5.8% of EU-27)	
Population: 63.0 million (12.5% of EU-27)	
Religious heritage: Mainly Protestant	
GDP (2010): €1,697 billion (13.6% of EU-27)	
GDP *per capita* as percentage of EU-27 average (2011): 108	
Female representation in parliament and cabinet (end 2011): 22% and 22%	
Joined EU: 1973	
Top 3 cities: London (capital) (8.2 million), Birmingham (1.0 million), Glasgow (0.6 million).	

Economy and society: The UK economy underwent severe restructuring under the free market policies of Conservative Prime Minister Margaret Thatcher during the 1980s but then did well until the global crisis. The service sector – particularly finance – is especially strong. As a result, the country's 63 million people – around 6.5 per cent of whom came (or their parents or grandparents came) as immigrants from the Caribbean and the Indian subcontinent – enjoy a *per capita* annual income of about 8 per cent above the EU average. The south-east of the country, especially around London, however, is notably better off than some of the more peripheral regions. Tackling that disparity plus persistent

WHAT'S IN AN ANTHEM?

No one is quite sure where the tune of the turgidly monarchical *God Save the Queen* came from, although the words date from the eighteenth century. Indeed, the anthem was probably the first to be consciously adopted as such. The first verse conveys the hope that Her Majesty will be around as long as possible and that the deity will ensure she is 'victorious, happy and glorious'. The less-often-sung second verse is slightly less unctuous: said deity, it hopes, will see not only to the scattering of enemies but will also 'confound their politics' and even 'frustrate their knavish tricks'. It is not just Scotland and Wales that prefer to use a different anthem at sporting events: the England cricket team has experimented with *Jerusalem* – a hymn to 'England's green and pleasant land'.

inequality (and child poverty) is proving tricky – and got trickier still when the coalition's much vaunted commitment to deficit reduction helped push the country back into recession.

Governance: The UK employs not a PR but a 'first-past-the-post' (FPP) electoral system to elect MPs to its Westminster parliament. Historically, this resulted in single-party majority governments and made things difficult for the third largest party, the Liberal Democrats. It does, however, afford representation to nationalist parties from Northern Ireland, Scotland and Wales. As a result of the Labour government's pursuit of decentralization and devolution, these components of the UK now have their own legislatures, elected under more proportional systems. The UK government pioneered the privatization of formerly state-owned utilities. And it still likes to think of itself as at the cutting edge of new approaches to governance, contracting out civil service work to public agencies and promoting public-private initiatives. The Conservative-led coalition continued this trend.

Foreign policy: The UK proved sceptical about European integration until the late 1950s, when it realized its days as a world power were numbered and that its economy was stagnating. It finally joined what was then the EEC (now the EU) in 1973. It retains its reputation as 'an awkward partner', and chose not to adopt the euro. EU membership is not seen as contradicting either the country's continuation of its self-styled 'special relationship' with the USA (with which it retains close defence, intelligence and trade links) nor its contacts with its former colonies via the British Commonwealth. The special relationship came under fire fol-

A KEY CONTEMPORARY CHALLENGE
PROVIDING SUFFICIENT HOUSING

Despite a double-dip recession, a reduction in numbers coming to the UK from central and eastern Europe, and endless international surveys suggesting that the British housing market is seriously overvalued and due a big correction, property prices held up surprisingly well. One reason for this was the Bank of England keeping interest rates unprecedentedly low in order (not very successfully) to kick-start the economy. But it was also because the demand for housing far outstrips the supply. In part that is because a combination of increased longevity, family breakdown and large-scale immigration has increased the number of households. However, there are three further reasons. First, UK investment in public sector housing collapsed in the 1980s and has never recovered. Second, the country has very strict (some think too strict) planning laws which make it too easy for existing residents to object to new residences being built by either the public or the private sector. Third, the relatively robust market disguises massive regional disparities: houses are cheap to buy and hard to sell in the more depressed parts of the UK (most obviously, former manufacturing and mining areas in the North and in Scotland and Wales) but the opposite is the case in many parts of the South East where the bulk of the population lives and which has, by and large, coped better with the recession than other regions. Some economists argued that the economic downturn was the ideal time for the government to begin building 'council housing' once again but the coalition government preferred to leave it to the private sector and instead to try to ease planning constraints. Whether this characteristically supply-side solution will work remains to be seen. So far housing has not become the big political issue some think it should be, mainly because, while voters know that there is a problem, they don't want to see the value of their own houses fall. One of the perils of the 'property owning democracy' perhaps?

lowing the invasion of Iraq, with politicians and commentators on both left and right calling for a healthier distance with Washington. But continued concerns over terrorism, Iran's nuclear ambitions and a newly assertive Russia suggest links will remain close.

Contemporary challenges
● Fighting Islamist terrorism without alienating Muslim citizens and sacrificing civil liberties.

● Coping with the prospect of Scottish independence.
● Freeing local government to decide (and raise funds for) its own priorities whilst ensuring that access to services does not become 'a postcode lottery'.
● Meeting climate change targets in the face of concerns about keeping the lights on.
● Providing sufficient housing and infrastructure to cope with migration and population growth (see box above).

Learning resources. A good all-round starting point is McCormick (2007), *Contemporary Britain*. Good textbooks include Moran (2005), *Politics and Governance in the UK* and Garnett and Lynch (2012), *Exploring British Politics*. The latest in the series *Developments in British Politics* is always worth reading. On the UK's first peacetime multiparty government for over half a century, see Hazell and Yong (2012), *The Politics of Coalition*. Keep up to date with the news at www.bbc.co.uk/news/uk/.

is achieved, parties in a coalition also like to keep tabs on each other's cabinet portfolios by having one of their people appointed as a junior minister (and therefore a 'watchdog' in the ministries that they do not control (Strøm *et al.*, 2010: 412; Lipsmeyer and Pierce, 2011).

Often, coordination (some would call it conflict management) between coalition partners involves not just ministers but other party political actors and arenas that are expressly set up for the purpose (see the chapter by Andeweg and Timmermans in Strøm *et al.*, 2010). Sometimes this kind of coordination goes on in so-called coalition committees. The three-way coalition that took over in Bulgaria in 2005 and saw the country safely into the EU in 2007 established a 'coalition council' of the chairmen of the parties concerned which helped smooth over disagreements between them (Spirova, 2007). But more often than not, it occurs informally. This might involve bilateral contacts by ministers or their political appointees to the civil service. In the case of disputes that are harder to resolve, it could involve troubleshooting by the prime minister and deputy prime minister, who are very often from different parties. But it might also involve meetings between party leaders, especially when, as occurs surprisingly often in Europe, those leaders do not actually play a formal role in government or even parliament (see Gibson and Harmel, 1998). In Belgium, for example, party chairmen meet frequently (often weekly) with 'their' ministers (see Keman, 2002a: 228) and thus exercise a kind of 'outside' influence on Cabinet that would be considered intolerable in a country such as the UK, for example.

British politicians, of course, have recently had to come to terms with managing a government made up of more than one party – a challenge they had not had to face since 1945 and one that sent them scurrying to learn lessons from overseas (and Scotland and Wales) even if, in the end, there was a fair amount of re-inventing the wheel amidst the innovation (Hazell and Yong, 2012). Moreover, the use of parliamentary scrutiny of legislation by the parties involved (particularly by the coalition's junior partner, the Liberal Democrats) in order to police each other's actions was also in line with what recent research suggests is common practice in European democracies – even if the efficacy of using the legislature to settle arguments between coalition

partners depends on whether a country has (unlike the UK!) a powerful parliament with committees able to stand up to (and even to override) the wishes of the executive (Martin and Vanberg, 2011).

Excessive ministerial autonomy (or 'departmentalitis') and intra-coalition coordination are not, however, the only problems facing the political part of a state's executive branch. Limited time is clearly a major – if largely overlooked – constraint. And a government's capacity to do what it wants to do may be constrained by events beyond its control such as war, terrorism, recession, by opposition from important interest groups (Chapter 8) and/or the media (Chapter 7) and, of course, by the need to retain the confidence of the financial markets and the credit-referencing agencies which they rely on (Chapter 9). One would also expect, on both a strict interpretation of the separation of powers doctrine and the assumption that they owe their very existence in most European countries to parliament, that governments would be constrained, too, by the second 'branch of government', the legislature. Interestingly, however, the influence of Europe's parliaments over their executives – their governments – is widely dismissed as illusory. According to common wisdom, they are (or have over time been reduced to) talking shops and rubber stamps, while the prime minister and the cabinet call the shots. Indeed, the supposed 'decline of parliament' is often a given in media discussion. Academic contributions, however, question, first, whether there ever really was a golden age of parliamentary power and independence and, second, the extent to which any decline has actually taken place (see Martin and Vanberg, 2011). A comparative approach, which reveals significant variation in both the structure and the operation of parliaments around Europe, suggests a similarly nuanced picture.

Parliaments – one house or two?

In many European countries, as in the USA, the legislature is 'bicameral', with an 'upper house' that sits in addition to a 'lower house': out of the 15 'older' democracies that constituted the EU before the accessions of 2004 and 2007, nine had parliaments made up of two houses – an arrangement traditionally favoured in particular by larger, as well as federal states. However, out of the 27 countries now in the EU the majority (14) are 'unicameral' – an arrangement traditionally favoured by smaller and unitary states (a definition that fits most of the EU's new joiners). Unicameral parliaments have only one chamber. In bicameral systems, the lower house (as in the sole chamber in unicameral systems) is filled by MPs or 'deputies' who are directly elected by all adults entitled to vote. Upper houses, on the other hand, are not always directly elected (see Table 4.3). A couple have appointed members, including the British House of Lords. Many are composed of democratically chosen representatives from local, regional or, in federal countries, state governments.

With the exception of Switzerland (where the upper house, the Council of States, has a veto that the lower house, the National Council, cannot overturn), Germany and Italy (see Boxes 4.4 and 4.5), there is no doubt that in Europe's bicameral systems it is the lower house that is the more powerful, and therefore the focus of public attention. In short, where bicameralism prevails in Europe, it is normally what political scientists label 'weak' as (opposed to 'strong') bicameralism. There are, however, some upper houses in Europe which are more than capable of thwarting the desires of the majority of the supposedly more powerful (and, its members sometimes argue, more democratic and responsive) lower house. This contrast between the weak and the strong has led more than one political scientist to recall the words of the French revolutionary philosopher and statesman, Sieyès, who famously observed that an upper house that agreed with the lower house was superfluous, while one that dissented was mischievous.

In most countries with two chambers, the power of the upper house lies primarily in its ability to amend and/or delay, rather than actually to block,

KEY POINT

Around half of all Europe's parliaments have just one chamber; the other half have two, although rarely is this 'upper house' – normally chosen on a different basis to the 'lower house' – as powerful as the latter. Hopefully, however, they improve the representativeness of the legislature and the quality of its legislative output.

Table 4.3 The upper house – who decides who sits there?

	Basis of upper house
Czech Rep.	Directly elected.
France	Electoral colleges of mainly local politicians, and overseas territories.
Germany	Delegates from state governments (Länder).
Italy	98 per cent directly elected, all (apart from six members who represent Italians overseas) on a regional basis; 2 per cent lifetime appointments.
Netherlands	Elected by provincial councils
Poland	Directly elected on a regional basis.
Spain	85 per cent directly elected; 15 per cent indirectly elected by regional authorities
Sweden	Sweden is unicameral: it has no upper house.
UK	80 per cent appointed for life; 15 per cent hereditary; 5 per cent church.

bills passed by the lower house. However, in some countries even this power is very limited. This might be because the lower house has the ability to bring things decisively to a head, as in France, where the Senate can be overruled. Or it may be because the power is little used since the party composition of the upper house is so similar to that of the lower house, as in Spain. But the general point is that outside Germany, Switzerland, Belgium and Italy, the rules favour the lower house of parliament by limiting the number of times a bill can go back and forth and giving the lower house what is in effect the last word. Despite this relative weakness, however, there seems to be no movement to dispense with them altogether in favour of unicameral systems: in the Czech Republic, where debate about the need for such a body and its composition was initially so heated that it almost failed to get off the ground, people seem reconciled to its existence, if not exactly enthusiastic; meanwhile in Romania, a call for abolition of the Senate which was approved by voters in a referendum in 2009, has yet to be put into effect.

However, upper houses are not powerless. The power of delay is not to be sniffed at. Moreover, on

The Italian *Senato* – powerful or pointless?

With the exception of a handful of senators-for-life, the vast bulk of the Italian *Senato* is directly elected to an upper house that has equal standing with the lower house, the *Camera dei Deputati.* Italy, therefore, would appear to have one of the most powerful second chambers anywhere in the world. But, as in Spain, because elections to the two houses take place simultaneously, the party complexion of each is remarkably similar. Consequently, there is far less of the partisan friction witnessed in Germany (see Box 4.4). This does not, however, prevent disagreements between the two chambers on particular pieces of legislation, not least because local and national interest groups lobby both assiduously. Because both houses have equal power, some bills can be batted back and forth between them for so long that they perish when new parliamentary elections are held. Given this tendency to delay legislation, Italians can be forgiven for wondering quite what the point of bicameralism is in their country. On the other hand, after reforms made to Italy's electoral system (see Chapter 6), the *Senato* is now elected on more of a regional basis, which should mean it takes on a more specific representative function and that it will contain a different balance of forces than the *Camera,* which is now supposed to provide a majority to whichever pre-electoral coalition wins the election – at least at the outset of the government it goes on to form.

proposed constitutional changes supported by the lower house, a number of Europe's upper houses possess a power of veto. This makes sense given that their raison d'être – especially in federal systems – is often to protect the rights and interests of subnational government. And even where such a role is denied them, one can argue that upper houses still, potentially at least, have a valuable role to play. For instance, they provide a forum that, because it is less of a focus for media attention, is somewhat less charged and therefore somewhat more conducive to clear-headed, expert consideration of issues. The UK House of Lords, for example, might be ridiculed as a bastion of entrenched conservatism, but its European Union Committee is often acknowledged as performing a useful role in scrutinizing EU legislation that will impact the UK (see, for example, Neuhold and de Ruiter, 2010). The Lords was also the venue used by dissatisfied members of the country's Conservative–Liberal Democrat coalition to get the government to amend its controversial health legislation in 2011 and 2012, although they found that some of the defeats they (together with the opposition) inflicted in the upper house were simply overturned in the lower house. This so-called 'ping-pong' almost certainly confirmed opponents of Liberal Democrat plans to make the Lords more democratic in their belief that do so would give the two chambers near-equal legitimacy, thereby setting the scene for constant battles and even a constitutional crisis.

Parliaments – hiring and firing

Generally, however, when most Europeans think of parliament, they think of the directly elected lower house. This is the place that not only passes laws, but makes and breaks – and in between hopefully scrutinizes – governments. As we have seen, running European countries rests on a party or a coalition of parties being able to command a majority in confidence and supply votes in parliament. Theoretically, then, parliaments are ultimately the most powerful branch of government. When it comes to the crunch, it is they who retain the right to hire and fire the executive, thereby translating the results of elections into a government and forcing that government to account to those whom electors elect, and perhaps the electors themselves. But how powerful does this make them in practice?

KEY POINT

Europe's governments require the support of their legislatures and, as such, can normally be dismissed by them. This power – easier to exercise in some countries than in others – is rarely used in practice but is almost certainly a constraint.

BOX 4.5

The upper house with the upper hand? The German *Bundesrat*

Germany's upper house, the *Bundesrat,* is made up of 68 members belonging to delegations from the governments of each of the Federal Republic's 16 states (*Länder*), with delegations varying in strength from three to six members depending on the size of the state. These representatives of the *Länder* have quite a large role in the passing of federal (i.e. national) legislation. The *Bundesrat* has veto power over legislation impacting on states – which until recently meant that over half of all legislation had to be voted on and approved there. And even when a bill does not fall into this category, it is open to the *Bundesrat to* reject it. This obliges the lower house, the *Bundestag,* to produce a 'yes' vote as big as the. *Bundesrat's* 'no' vote in order to overrule it. The extent to which this makes things awkward for the government depends, more than anything, on whether the party controlling it also controls the upper house. As in the USA, this depends on it being able to win those state elections that take place in between federal elections. If the opposition win these (and they very often do as the government bears the brunt of 'midterm blues'), the party composition of one or, more states' delegations changes, causing the government to lose its control of the *Bundesrat.* When this happens, 'divided government' prevails and the upper house comes into its own. Perhaps through negotiation in the *Vermittlungsausschuß* (the mediation committee formed by representatives from both houses), the *Bundesrat* often obliges the government in the lower house to modify those aspects of its legislative programme that opposition parties do not support. It is this need to take account of the views of opposition parties that makes Germany's parliament (and perhaps its politics in general) so consensual. According to critics, though, it also makes radical reform practically impossible (see Chapter 9). Frustration on both sides led to the setting up in 2003 of a bicameral commission to look into modernizing the federal structure – a move that eventually resulted in a deal that saw the *Länder* get the right to determine more at local level (particularly on education) in return for a reduction in the proportion of bills (from 60 to 35 per cent) that could be blocked by the *Bundesrat.*

Hiring is indeed crucial, as we have suggested when looking at government formation. But it normally pits one party or collection of parties against another rather than the legislature as a whole against the executive. Moreover, once the task is complete, the power is essentially 'used up' until next time. Similarly, the power granted by the right to fire the executive lies more in the threat to use it than its actual use. The fact that it is a 'nuclear option' probably explains why, although the right of dismissal exists, it is surprisingly rarely used. Few European governments are actually brought down by votes of no confidence: indeed, a recent study shows that only 5 per cent of such votes result in the government falling (Williams, 2011). This is partly, of course, because some governments choose to jump before they are formally pushed. Others are sufficiently adaptable to avoid the kind of policies that would offend the MPs that originally supported their formation. Still others, when this cannot be

done, are sufficiently prescient to have arranged alternative sources of support.

In a handful of cases, institutional rules make votes of no confidence, once a government has formed, even more unlikely. In the Czech Republic, for instance, for a government to form takes only the votes of a majority of the MPs in the chamber at the time the vote is held. But to remove a government it takes a majority of all MPs (i.e. 101 out of 200) whether or not they are all present. In Germany, Spain and Poland, as we have seen, they go even further: a government can be defeated only by a 'constructive' vote of no confidence, which demands that the opposition already has an alternative government ready to take over immediately. In many countries, a government defeat in the house can – although it does not always – lead to new elections that can come as a merciful release after a period of political crisis or legislative gridlock. But in Norway, where elections can be held only every four years, this option is unavailable. This makes motions of no confidence motions a less attractive way of 'solving' a supposedly intractable parliamentary problem. The fact that a government defeat on a motion of confidence can lead to fresh elections in other countries points to the fact that parliament's right to defeat the executive is, in any case, normally balanced by the executive's right to dissolve (or request the head of state to dissolve) parliament – a right that exists in all European democracies outside Norway, Switzerland and Finland. If, as an MP, your party is not likely to do well in a snap election, you are unlikely, however dissatisfied you are with the government, to stage a vote of no confidence and thereby risk cutting off your nose to spite your face.

Parliaments – the production of law

Parliament's other important function is the making (or at least the production) of law – the consideration and passing of legislation. There is provision in most countries for so-called 'private members bills'. But by far the bulk of the proposals (and certainly the bulk of proposals that stand an earthly chance of actually ending up on the statute book) will come from governments. International Parliamentary Union (IPU) data from the 1990s showed not only that six out of ten bills originated in government (a figure rising to nine out of ten in countries like the UK, the Netherlands and Sweden), but also that over eight of ten of those bills made it on to the statute book. Moreover, although recent research suggests there are big differences in how long it takes for legislation to go through each parliament (see Box 4.6), these differences are generally due to inefficiencies in parliamentary process rather than government control. Most governments, especially those which control the agenda of the house, get their legislation through – particularly if it refers to a policy settled on in their coalition agreement (De Winter, 2004). Consequently, it is all too easy to buy into the caricature of European legislatures as merely 'rubber stamps' or 'talking shops' – or, worse, 'sausage machines' into which the executive shoves its bills, cranks the handle, makes mincemeat out of the opposition, and smiles as its statutes pop, out at the other end. Without going too far the other way, it is

---

BOX 4.6

How long does law-making take?

In a comparative study of almost 600 bills across 17 parliaments in Europe, Becker and Saalfeld (2004) found that having more parties in a coalition did not slow legislation down, even if they were ideologically quite far apart. By the time a bill is introduced, the partners in a coalition will normally have made the necessary compromises and, particularly if they operate with a majority that gives them the right to control the agenda of the house, can get their legislation through, although considerable time (an average of nearly 80 hours out of 128 hours) is lost in many countries by delays between the various stages – and it is this that accounts for the differences that are superficially so apparent (Table 4.4)

Table 4.4 Hours to pass a bill through parliament

Country	Hours
Sweden	101
Germany	127
17-country average	128
UK	219
Spain	228
Netherlands	378
Italy	620

Becker and Saalfeld found that 75 per cent of bills passed, and that just under 10 per cent of bills fail at each stage (pre-committee, committee and post committee). Interestingly, only 5 per cent of the bills that reached the second chamber (where one existed) failed.

---

fair to suggest that such metaphors can be misleading. For one thing, opposition parties (and, indeed, government backbenchers) continue in most parliaments to make some attempt to set the agenda by introducing legislation of their own, even if only to signal that they have an alternative programme and/or to raise their profile (see Bräuninger

---

BOX 4.7

France's feeble parliament

Most observers agree that the *Assemblée Nationale* is one of Europe's weakest legislatures, and, judging from recent research, few of its members are under any illusions about how much influence they have over the executive (Costa and Kerrouche, 2009). This makes what some would see as their retreat into constituency work understandable, but critics would argue that they do themselves no favours by often staying away in order to attend to the affairs of local government, in which many continue to hold elected office and have their main power-base. The government controls parliament's agenda. It can insist on it taking a yes/no 'package vote' on a bill in its unamended state. It has nothing to fear from committees which are unwieldy and oversized. And it has at its disposal a host of procedural techniques to overcome any residual power of delay. Parliament, constitutionally, can legislate only in certain prescribed areas outside of which government can issue what amount to decrees. The censure motion necessary to oust any government determined to insist on treating a particular bill as a matter of confidence is difficult to employ. Moreover, parliament is constitutionally unable to pass a nongovernmental bill or amendment that would involve lowering state revenues or increasing expenditure.

Fortunately, France's Constitutional Court (see Chapter 3) has now made decree laws subject to much greater constraint. In addition, regulations can be amended by the Assembly. Theoretically, it also gets to subject all bills to committee scrutiny before the plenary session and now even gets to meet all year round, not just the six months initially allotted to it. But the picture painted is, nonetheless, one of weakness – one which, critics suggest, was not much altered in the wake of a committee, headed by former Prime Minister Édouard Balladur, which reported in October 2007 on the modernization and re-balancing of France's governing institutions.

---

and Debus, 2009). For another, such metaphors disguise a good deal of variation. Once again, however, it is patterned variation.

Broadly, one can divide parliaments in western Europe into two groups that correspond to the distinction between 'majoritarian' and 'consensus' democracies made by Dutch political scientist, Arend Lijphart (1999). In the majoritarian group, one would include the UK, along with Ireland, Greece and France. In these countries, the government pursues its agenda with little regard for the input of other parties, which are more often than not clearly regarded as the opposition. This opposition knows that government is almost guaranteed to get its way. And anyway, it is likely to be sympathetic to the theory that its winning of the election gives it a mandate to do so. Therefore, opposition parties can do little more than offer the kind of criticism that (a) will allow them to say 'I told you so' at the next election, at which, hopefully, the mandate will pass to them; and (b), hopefully, undermine the government's popularity in the meantime. It is

unlikely to be able to use the upper house to block the government's programme because in majoritarian systems the lower house enjoys clear superiority. Parliament as a whole is an 'arena' rather than a truly 'transformative' institution – and one that reacts to, and can do little or nothing to stop, or even seriously slow up, government initiatives (see Box 4.7).

The same can be said of parliaments in consensus democracies like Germany, the Netherlands (and Belgium), Sweden (and other Scandinavian coun-

KEY POINT

Governments set the agenda on legislation and get most of what they want through. The pace of that legislation, and the extent to which it is modifiable by parliaments varies considerably. Some parliaments – notably those in 'consensus' systems – are stronger than others; namely, those that operate in more 'majoritarian' cultures. The committee system is a key variable.

tries) and Italy, but not without some qualification. While they are still essentially 'reactive' (at least when compared to the US Congress) parliaments in these countries tend to feature more constructive criticism and operate at least sometimes in 'cross-party' rather than always 'inter-party' mode (King, 1976). These tendencies are, or have become, culturally ingrained, though they may be institutionally supported. At the macro-level, consensus democracies tend towards highly proportional electoral systems and multiparty politics that make coalition inevitable; they also tend to accord interest groups an important consultative role (see Chapter 9). At the micro-level, parliament's agenda might, for instance, require the unanimous (or near-unanimous) consent of all parties (as in Scandinavia, and the Germanic and Low Countries, as well as Spain and Italy) rather than being decided by the government majority (as in the United Kingdom, Ireland, France, Greece and Portugal). No doubt, ministers who operate in a 'Westminster' system, where their government has all sorts of procedures it can resort to in order to curtail debate, would be horrified to learn that in countries like the Netherlands and Sweden such manipulation is virtually impossible.

While, as some analysts are right to warn us, the differences between consensual and majoritarian democracies can be overstated (see Arter, 2006), they are nonetheless significant when it comes to parliaments. And they are visual as well as rule-based. Some countries even have seating systems designed to take some of the heat out of the more adversarial aspects of parliamentary politics. Sweden, for example, makes its MPs sit in regional blocs rather than according to party, and many parliaments in Europe avoid the adversarial layout of the British House of Commons (see Andeweg and Mijzink's chapter in Döring, 1995, for the layout of European legislatures).

Perhaps most important, however, both for the facilitation of cross-party activity and the overall power of parliament, is the existence of powerful legislative committees. These are especially prevalent in Scandinavian parliaments (see Box 4.8), in Germany and in some of the newer democracies in central and eastern Europe, especially Poland. In many countries in those regions, such committees get to make amendments to (and in some cases

redraft) bills before they are debated on the floor of the house by all interested MPs in what is known as 'plenary session'. In majoritarian systems, committees usually get to go over the bill only once it has received at least one, and possibly two, readings in plenary, by which time party positions have already hardened up and legislation is more 'set in stone'. Contrary to the position in their consensual counterparts, committee membership in these systems might not even be distributed according to each party's share of seats. In more consensual systems, proportionality is taken as given and (especially where there are minority governments) increases the chances of committees taking an independent line. As a result – and because what they do actually matters – committees in consensual systems are often quite conflictual (see Damgaard and Mattson, 2004). A very valuable table covering the composition, autonomy and powers of committees in west European parliaments provided by Mattson and Strøm (2004: 100–101) makes it clear, however, that such conflict does not undermine their importance compared with their counterparts in more majoritarian parliaments.

These committees, according to most scholars both reflect and explain the differences in the power enjoyed by parliaments across Europe. In a recent book – one that stands out because there is so little genuinely cross-national comparative research on legislatures (see Martin, 2008) – the political scientists Lanny Martin and Georg Vanberg (2011), assemble a series of indicators of the 'policing powers' of Western European parliaments. They summarize them as follows:

[L]egislatures with strong policing powers have a relatively large number of specialized committees, small in size, which correspond to government ministries, that they have the authority to rewrite bills and to demand outside information, and are not bound by previous debates of the plenary body....[M]inisters in such legislatures do not have tools at their disposal to curtail deliberation or to curb the passage of amendments. In contrast,...legislatures with weak policing powers have a small number of specialized committees that are unwieldy in size, have little jurisdictional correspondence to ministries, have no authority to demand supplementary information or rewrite

BOX 4.8

Power outside the plenary – Danish parliamentary committees

Although other Scandinavian parliaments – and Germany and Poland – boast influential committees, and although some Italian committees traditionally had the right of final assent on some minor legislation, experts agree that the Danish *Folketing* possesses Europe's most powerful parliamentary committees. It has 24 standing (i.e. permanent) committees, each with 17 members, with membership roughly proportional to the party distribution of seats in parliament. Most committees cover the work of one particular ministry. When a minister proposes a bill, he or she can expect a flood of written questions by committee members and could well be asked to appear in person, too. Delay is not advisable because any bill that does not make it through all its stages in the parliamentary session in which it is introduced will have to start all over again. The committee's report on the bill outlines the parties' positions and amendments that they hope to see adopted in the second reading. In many parliaments that would be it, but in Denmark an MP can demand that the bill go back to committee after the second reading for a supplementary report.

All *Folketing* committees are potentially powerful because, as in other Scandinavian countries, minority government is so common, meaning that the executive will rarely have a majority in committee. But the two most powerful are, without doubt, the Finance Committee, whose say on the budget is much greater than its counterparts in other legislatures, and the European Affairs Committee, which is able to dictate to the country's ministers the stand they must take on certain issues when voting in Brussels. Ministers are first answerable to the Committee, and only then to their colleagues for their EU-related actions. This loss of executive autonomy – albeit one which may not be as great in practice as on paper because Committee solidarity is balanced by party loyalties (Damgaard and Jensen, 2005) – is seen as a price worth paying by governments keen to ensure that rows over 'Europe' do not break them apart or cause other parties to withdraw their support.

government bills, and are restricted to making incremental amendments to bills previously agreed to at the plenary stage….[Moreover, m]inisters operating in weak legislatures have tools such as the urgency procedure and the guillotine that allow them to run roughshod over legislators opposing their policies.

This then allows them to score the parliaments according to their power (see Table 4.5).

Of course, this particular method of ranking Europe's legislatures is not the only one available – a more recent attempt, for instance, scores them on more dimensions and, in doing so, makes the point that parliaments which are strong in one area may well be weak in another and vice versa (see Sieberer, 2011). Even if we could agree on a method, however, there would still be arguments about some of the individual rankings: few experts, for instance, would place the Spanish *Cortes* above the Norwegian *Storting*. Moreover, many would claim that it is still

difficult to fit central and eastern European parliaments into any schema. At first, a combination of volatile party systems, arguments between presidents and prime ministers, and weak bureaucratic support for the executive seemed to suggest that postcommunist parliaments had, if not the upper hand, then rather more power than in the more established democracies (see Kopecký, 2007). Certainly, the Polish *Sejm* (which, it must be said, has a proud history stretching back over centuries) could claim to be one of Europe's more independent legislatures: it has a powerful committee system (a generally accepted indicator of strength, as we see below) whose members can initiate legislation, up to half of which (a very high proportion in relative terms) passes (see Zubek, 2006: 89–90). Moreover, 'the government possesses weak agenda control and few formal means of defending its legislation against rival bills and amendments' (Goetz and Zubek, 2007). Yet it is hard to know how much of this parliamentary strength and executive weakness is insti-

Table 4.5 European parliaments – the strong and the weak

Stronger parliaments (Policing strength above zero)	Weaker parliaments (Policing strength below zero)
1 Netherlands	12 Greece
2 Austria	13 France
3 Luxembourg	14 Ireland
4 Germany	15 UK
5 Denmark	
6 Sweden	
7 Finland	
8 Spain	
9 Norway	
10 Italy	
11 Portugal	

Source: Martin and Vanberg (2011).

tutional and how much derives from the difficulties faced by Polish governments because of what was an unusually large number of parties and degree of 'party-hopping' by Polish MPs. Governments in Lithuania, where the first two years of the parliament elected in 2004 saw over one-third of MPs change their affiliations, were similarly afflicted.

Across the region as a whole, however, decreasing turnover among, and increasing professionalization of, MPs and the declining number of parties in most of its parliaments (including Poland), have made them easier to manage (Kopecký, 2007, though see also Mansfeldova, 2011). But it would be wrong to imply uniformity. Recent research, which focuses on the ability of the executive to block opposition attempts to set the agenda in parliament concludes that it finds it much easier to do so in Hungary, Poland and Slovenia than in the Czech Republic, Estonia and Slovakia – but that much of the explanation lies in the fact that the opposition is generally stronger in parliaments with more parties (Zubek, 2011). Also important in strengthening governments' hands have been the fast-track procedures brought in to ensure that parliaments could get through the huge body of legislation needed to meet the requirements of accession to the EU (Kopecký, 2007).

Parliaments – scrutiny and oversight

MPs, and therefore parliaments, can exercise the crucial role of scrutiny and oversight over the executive (see Pelizzo and Stapenhurst, 2011) via parliamentary questions, written or oral. The use of this technique (once a hallmark of 'Westminster', majoritarian systems) is now ubiquitous and rising throughout Europe, not least because of the realization, particularly by opposition parties, that hard-hitting questions and possibly inadequate replies are eagerly picked up on by the media and can therefore set the political agenda (Green-Pedersen, 2010; see also Martin, 2011). The latter (as we shall see in Chapter 7) is always looking to focus on the controversial and the dramatic in order to hold consumers' interest in a subject that they fear might otherwise cause them to change channels or switch papers. In many countries, questions can lead direct to a special debate on the reply. These so-called 'interpellation' debates serve to keep the spotlight on the government for even longer, even if, critics argue, they tend (like many of the goings-on in parliament) to generate more heat than light.

KEY POINT

Europe's highly partisan parliaments are neither programmed nor resourced to do as good a job as their US counterpart in keeping an eye on governments. The situation is probably even worse when it comes to policing the EU.

The main way, however, that Europe's parliaments perform scrutiny and oversight on the executive is via the committee system. Interestingly, in some countries where committees play a relatively weak role in legislation, they play a much bigger role in holding ministers to account for the work of their departments. For instance, the UK parliament's 'select committees' are more specialized, have long-term membership and can instigate and take evidence in their own enquiries. They therefore offer far more of a challenge to the executive than the much larger, ad hoc 'standing committees' that are charged in the UK with examining legislation. Conversely, committees in Sweden are less active in this respect than they are in law-making, where they frequently (and successfully) make changes to legislation. The committee system of the *Riksdag* also helps ensure that it ranks (alongside the Hungarian parliament) at the most powerful European legislature when it comes to 'the power of the purse' (Wehner, 2006) – financial scrutiny over the government's budget (see Figure 4.7).

It is unusual, though not altogether unknown, for Europe's legislators to carve out a powerful niche for themselves as committee specialists in the manner of their US counterparts. But being seen to do a good job in this area can boost the chances of promotion into the ranks of government, although whether, as a government backbencher, 'a good job' means giving ministers a hard or an easy time is a moot point! Committee work also gives MPs a chance to bring to bear their own professional experience on questions of national importance: those with, say, a military or a medical background might be valuable on the Defence or Health Committee. But such work does more than merely pad out MPs' résumés. It can throw the spotlight on issues the executive would rather remain obscure.

Moreover, with the increasing impact of EU legislation on domestic affairs, committees can arguably go some way to closing the so-called **democratic deficit**. Germany's constitution, the Basic Law, for instance, obliges its government to inform the

The EU's **democratic deficit** is the gap between the powers and competences assumed by the EU and the ability of European citizens to determine the make-up of its institutions and oversee the exercise of those powers and competences. It arises from the tendency of member states, via treaty or treaty-based legal decisions, to cede legislative and executive functions that would hitherto have been the preserve of elected parliaments and governments to unelected bodies (such as the Council of Ministers and the Commission) that the EP cannot effectively hold to account Some argue that the problem that it is overstated and that what the EU should focus on is 'output legitimacy' – gaining tacit consent by producing tangible benefits for voters who supposedly don't care too much about how the EU is run as long as it delivers. The problem is: what will see the EU through if, as in the current economic crisis, it not only doesn't deliver but, in its insistence that some countries pursue austerity, it actually makes ordinary people's lives even more difficult?

Figure 4.7 The power of the purse – how much influence European parliaments have over government budgets

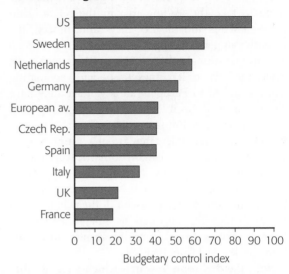

Source: Data from Wehner (2006: 781); Wehner's index (which includes nineteen European countries but not Poland) covers a range of parliamentary powers over the government budget.

Bundestag's EU Affairs Committee (attended by both MPs and MEPs) of impending European legislation before it becomes too late to change it. Indeed, national parliaments all over Europe – though not necessarily at the same pace – are waking up to the fact that, in order to have any influence at all on European legislation, they have to assert a right to examine and express their opinions on proposed EU law much sooner than governments would otherwise like them to. Indeed, they can now invoke what are now treaty rights to be warned of proposals for legislation in sufficient time to allow them to do something about them, reinforcing the 'gatekeeping' role that national parliaments (effectively or not) seem to have taken on with respect to EU matters (see Raunio, 2011; see also Cooper, 2012)

On the other hand, the time thus granted is often insufficient in practice if not on paper, and partisan considerations, like protecting or damaging the government, are often only just below the surface in the work of European affairs committees, which continue to vary a good deal in both their readiness and their capacity to assert themselves (see Stephenson, 2009). In any case, paying them too much attention can distract us from an arguably much more profound truth, albeit one that, as some experts note, is easily exaggerated (see O'Brennan and Raunio, 2007: 2–8). This is the fact that, because governments continue to take the leading role in the relationship between states and the EU, they (and, indeed, the executive in general) enjoy a profound institutional and informational advantage over their legislative 'colleagues' when it comes to policies emanating from or linked to Europe – an advantage they have always enjoyed with regard to diplomacy and foreign policy (see Putnam, 1988). They also benefit from the fact that, unless they are in a minority, governments – just as they can on domestic legislation – can normally rely on the fact that the majority of MPs want them to succeed. As a result, they are highly unlikely to want to bind their hands too tightly before EU negotiations nor to embarrass them by trying to overturn the results once they bring back a deal from Brussels.

Now, there is some research which suggests that this apparently effortless superiority is mitigated if the issues involved attract media attention (de Wilde, 2011), reminding us that one of the reasons why MPs haven't rushed to assert their rights in this area is that EU matters are regarded as insufficiently 'political' to merit their attention. Moreover, we cannot always assume that scrutiny runs along lines dictated by formal rules: as recent research on parliaments in central and eastern Europe (generally regarded as having lost out to governments during the accession process) shows, informal norms and routines are also important (Knutelská, 2011). Meanwhile, a recent comparison of the French and German parliaments finds that the key to effective scrutiny may well be the use of the mechanisms already established to scrutinize 'domestic' legislation and the willingness of government MPs to act in such cases almost as if they were in opposition (Sprungk, 2010). Nor can we assume that scrutiny of EU legislation is necessarily better in supposedly stronger than it is in apparently weaker parliaments (Neuhold and de Ruiter, 2010).

Generally, however, as long as the EU continues to rest, ultimately, on intergovernmental bargaining and to exclude national legislatures from that part of its governance which can be called 'supranational' (see Chapter 2), Europe's parliaments can hardly look to 'Brussels' to strengthen their position against their respective executives. As a fascinating case study of the Austrian parliament shows (Falkner, 2000a), even those parliaments that thought they had negotiated extra safeguards against marginalization prior to their country joining the EU were disappointed. Even parliaments in those European countries that are not EU member states have lost out. A study of Switzerland, for instance, illustrates that when (as often happens) the country has to undertake legislative change so as to ensure that it remains roughly in line with what is going on within the EU itself, the executive wields more power than it would do on purely domestic legislation (see Sciarini *et al.*, 2004). On the other hand, we need to avoid overstating the case: Europe's legislatures may, indeed, play something of 'a bit part' in the EU policy process (Ladrech, 2010: 74) but Europeanization has not left them totally powerless in the face of their executives, not least (but not only) because they were never that powerful in the first place (O'Brennan and Raunio, 2007).

Parliament and government – the European level

It is perfectly possible to slot into our discussion of the functions and strengths of parliaments, and their relationships with governments, mention of the institution that, more than national legislatures, is supposed to help close the 'democratic deficit' – the European Parliament (EP). At first glance, this may not seem obvious: the EU, after all, can be portrayed as an 'upside-down polity' wherein jobs at what could be seen as the 'lower' (national) level are generally more sought-after by politicians than jobs at the 'higher' (EU) level, hence the number of Commissioners who jump at the chance of a return to a cabinet post back home and the fact a seat in the national legislature is often seen as a better start to a political career than a seat in the EP – this in spite of the fact that ordinary MEPs (if they want it) generally have far more chance of influencing legislation than do MPs, who more often than not have to bow to the will of their government (see Hix, 2008). However, many now argue that the EP (and, in fact, the EU in general) should nevertheless be analysed, not as *sui generis* (constituting a unique class of its own), but using the same tools of analysis (coalition theory, disaggregating the various roles and functions of different parts of the system, etc.) that comparative politics uses to examine other political institutions (Hix *et al.*, 2007). This is not merely an analytical imperative, but a normative one, too. As we have suggested above, national parliaments find it hard to play much of a role in European law-making, while links with each other and with the EP through bodies such as COSAC (the Conference of Community and European Affairs Committees) seem unlikely to lend them that much leverage (though see Neunreither, 2005). This makes it all the more vital for democracy in Europe that we understand the workings of the EP, using what we already know about legislatures more generally to help us.

KEY POINT

The EP can be analysed as a legislature like any other: it has, for example, a party system that most Europeans, if they knew about it, would recognize. However, there is a disconnect between the ideological composition of the parliament and the political direction of the EU, which therefore, neither voters nor their elected representatives seem to control.

For instance, one can argue that the EU has what amounts to a bicameral legislature along the lines of some federal parliaments. The increasing use of the co-decision procedure (see Chapter 2), for instance, gives equal power on some legislation to what are effectively two houses or chambers, the EP and the Council of Ministers. This is particularly the case now that the two have to resolve their differences in a conciliation committee (not unlike the German parliament's *Vermittlungsausschuß* mentioned in Box 4.5) in order for legislation not to fail. On the other hand, at least until co-decision becomes the norm for every piece of EU legislation, one can argue that there remains a big difference in that, in the EU, the chamber representing the people (the EP) is weaker than the one representing the states or regions (the Council). And the dissimilarities do not, of course, end there. For instance, the Council of Ministers, despite its reputation as a 'bastion of intergovernmentalism' (see Chapter 2), often cooperates with the supposedly 'supranational' Commission (in its role as the 'executive' of the EU) on the rejection of amendments by the EP (see Tsebelis *et al.*, 2001); and, unlike any other legislative chamber in Europe, the Council gets to hold its debates in secret! The other big difference between the EU and its member states is that, in the EU, the 'executive' or 'government' (such as it is) is not formed by a majority in the legislature. Instead, it is divided between the Commission and the European Council, made up by the heads of government of the member states.

This means that there is a relatively (indeed, a very) indistinct relationship between the results of elections to the EP (see Chapter 6) and the political direction of the EU. Even if one side of the political spectrum, can occasionally claim what amounts to a 'majority' in the Commission, the Council of Ministers and the EP, it rarely lasts long. And it may not be that significant: national governments change, and there is no hard and fast relationship between commissioners' and ministers' party affiliations and the policy line they take (see Hagemann and Hoyland, 2008; Wonka, 2008). Moreover, while the EP can withhold its approval of the president and the Commission and can (and has on rare occasions, such as 1999) help to effect their removal, its role in 'hiring and firing' the executive is, again, rather less direct than its counterparts in member states.

Another key difference between many national parliaments and the EP is that voting in the latter often proceeds along cross-party lines. Often this is because, in order to realize its potential legislative strength vis-à-vis the Council of Ministers, the EP needs to cobble together an absolute majority of all members, notwithstanding the fact that, as members of national parties, nearly all of them belong to increasingly consolidated European parliamentary groups, stretching from the far left GUE-NGL to the far-right EFD. This kind of majority is difficult, even impossible, to achieve unless the two biggest parties, the social democratic S&D and the Christian democratic/conservative EPP, vote together. Given they are often joined by the relatively large liberal grouping, the ALDE, this means that the EP is often dominated by a kind of 'grand coalition' that marginalizes the smaller, less centrist groups (which include not just the GUE-NGL and EFD but also the Greens and the ECR, which is dominated by the

British Conservative Party). The party line-up might, then, resemble that of, say, the Netherlands or Germany (see Chapter 5), but unlike those countries (and others) it shows little sign of moving from cosy centrism to more bipartisan competition between right and left (see Chapter 9). Of course, we should not forget that cross-party voting also goes on in some of Europe's more consensual parliaments, such as the Swedish *Riksdag*. There, it is largely the product of a law-making process in which parliamentary committees play an important role. Given that committees also play a similarly vital role in the life of the EP, this is one way in which it can be said to demonstrate significant similarities with national parliaments. Another is the ongoing attempt by the EP to improve its scrutiny and oversight of the Commission (see Corbett *et al.*, 2011).

Arguably, in fact, MEPs have more incentives than MPs to play the scrutineer and the overseer. Unlike at least some of their national counterparts (and even US Congressmen to some extent), they have no partisan interest in protecting the executive, which allows them more freedom to range across party lines in their criticisms. That said, we need to be very careful not to think that parties (or, technically, party groups) are not that important in the EP. If anything, they are becoming increasingly important. True, national parties, where issues are thought to be sufficiently important, can occasionally request (and normally rely on) their MEPs to vote differently to the EP group to which the party belongs (see Hix, 2002). But the extent to which MEPs now vote along party group lines (called 'cohesion' in the jargon) is higher than ever, and at nearly 90 per cent is much closer to European than to US levels. Meanwhile the bigger groups appear to be competing more often along predicable ideological lines (see Hix *et al.*, 2007 and follow the action at http://www.votewatch.eu).

Parliament, power and parties

Talk of cohesion and voting along party lines brings us back to the reasons why legislatures in Europe are generally relatively weak. While the patterned variation that emerges between consensual and majoritarian democracies can be summed up graphically (as in Figure 4.7), we should be careful not to think things are that simple. Because government in Europe is parliamentary and party government, there is no clear, US-style separation between the executive and the legislature. This means that the conflicts between the two branches are likely to pale into insignificance alongside conflicts between the government majority and the 'opposition'. Moreover, the power of parliament is as contingent on parliamentary arithmetic (and therefore electoral fortunes) as it is on constitutional conventions or internal organization. Even in consensual countries, an executive made up of a majority coalition or single-party majority will encounter fewer problems with the legislature than a minority government. In any case, schemas of strong and weak parliaments risk relying too much on comparisons of formal powers when, in fact, the strength or weakness of the institutions may lie elsewhere. A clue to where this 'elsewhere' might be comes in the observation made about the UK by French political scientist Maurice Duverger (see Duverger, 1954: 46): 'Parliament and Government,' he noted, 'are like two machines driven by the same motor – the party.'

KEY POINT

The majority of MPs (who are not, incidentally, descriptively very representative of most of the citizens who elected them) are committed to parties that support the government or, at least, do not wish to bring it down. Essentially, then, Europe's parliaments are relatively weak institutions because they contain strong parties.

How hard do most European governments have to work to command the votes of their MPs? In most countries, the answer – normally, anyway – is not terribly hard at all. Levels of party discipline are very high in most of Europe's parliaments (see Depauw and Martin, 2009). Parliaments in the newer democracies of central and eastern Europe initially experienced higher turnover of MPs and more party splits – something that, along with their role as constitutional founders and executives that initially suffered from divisions between presidents and prime ministers, made them appear rather stronger than they really were, constitutionally speaking (Kopecký, 2007). But turnover and defections – labelled 'party tourism' (see Millard, 2004: Chapter 6) – have, in general, dropped. Nowadays, all over Europe, most members in most parliaments stay loyal. They have more in common ideologically with their own party than with others and, even in CEE, they are becoming ever more professionalized, full-time politicians. As such, they are ever more dependent on the party to whom they owe their (re-)election, their salary, their staff (such as it is: US congressmen are far better resourced), their privileges, and their chance of executive office. Although their effectiveness varies, parties can sanction their members, but for the most part they can rely on ambition and on internalized norms of loyalty and solidarity to maintain discipline (see Kam, 2009).

Europe's MPs may have some vestigial loyalty to their home base or perhaps the profession or pressure group with whom they were associated before they came into parliament. But, in general, it will weigh relatively lightly with them compared with, say, their counterparts in the US Congress. The same is even true for members of the EP, for whom domestic concerns, while still important, are giving way more and more to loyalty to what appear to be increasingly competitive party groups. Moreover, inasmuch as the links between national parliaments and the EP have increased over the years – and it is easy to overplay the extent to which even timetabled joint sessions of committees constitutes significant growth – any meaningful coordination in the future will probably need to take place at the intraparty as much as at the interparliamentary level (see Messmer, 2003).

All this means that the key to the executive dominance demonstrated in both the consensual and majoritarian democracies of Europe, is to be found inside parties – forums that, sadly, political scientists, although they can make educated guesses (see Heidar and Koole, 2000), are almost never allowed into. But it also means that the power of the executive can at least potentially vary over time according to the hold it has on its own 'backbenchers'. This might depend, say, on the selection processes of the parties that form the government, as well as on what those backbenchers think are its chances of re-election. Put bluntly, a government that (a) looks likely to suffer at the next election, and (b) is made up of one or more parties that can do little to stop the reselection of recalcitrant MPs, is probably going to

have to pay attention to those MPs (and therefore parliament). One that is polling well, and maintains firm and centralized control over who gets to go where on the party list next time around, is likely to have fewer problems.

Europe's unrepresentative representatives?

We should, of course, avoid allowing the question of who is weaker and who is stronger, the government or parliament, to completely overshadow our thinking on these 'branches of government'. After all, although politics is about power, it is also about function. Parliaments hire and fire, produce laws, scrutinize the activities of the executive and its bureaucracy, but they also play a vital role in legitimizing (if not necessarily popularizing!) rule by a necessarily smaller set of people over a much larger group of us. Moreover, they perform a recruitment role by launching the political careers of that smaller set of people. Whether they do it very well (at least when it comes to being representative) is another matter.

The political theorist (and sometime politician) Edmund Burke famously insisted (to his voters, no less) that parliamentarians are not delegates but representatives. As a result, their job is not simply to parrot the views of their parties, but to exercise their judgement in the best interests of their constituents and the country as a whole. Should they therefore be literally representative of its population? If 5 per cent of citizens, for instance, are of Arab descent, should 5 per cent of MPs also be Arabs? If 40 per cent are working-class, should parliament reflect the same proportion? And given that women make up at least half the population, then should not every other MP be female? Anyone answering 'yes' to all these questions is likely to be disappointed. And any change, if it occurs, is likely to take place only very slowly: recent cross-national research confirms that turnover in a typical (west) European parliament is low (Cotta and Best, 2007: 424; 476).

Legislatures in Europe are notoriously unrepresentative of racial minorities. They are also becoming ever more middle-class and professionalized (Cotta and Best, 2007; Millard, 2004: 156–83). Today's politicians are drawn from a narrow (and some would say – rightly or wrongly – narrowing)

DEBATE 4.1

Are parliamentary systems better than presidential systems?

YES

- Parliamentary systems, particularly if they routinely lead to coalition governments, avoid the winner-takes-all logic of presidential systems, ensuring that the executive takes account of more shades of public opinion and making it more likely that minorities in deeply divided societies will have an influence.

- Most governments will have the support of a majority in the legislature, meaning that laws can be more quickly made, while there is a more direct relationship between what is promised at elections and what is then delivered.

- Wisdom is more likely to reside in collective actors with more voices, like a political party or parties, than in one individual with the sole power of decision elected in what amounts to a beauty contest. Parliamentary government puts a premium on leaders who are good brokers and compromisers.

NO

- The winner-takes-all logic of presidential systems is overstated: the whole point of divided government is that the president cannot pass laws without the legislature, which may well be more representative of the population. Other members of his administration may be, too.

- Since most governments are coalitions anyway, party's policy promises are inevitably diluted. And do we want laws to be made quickly? After all, one person's 'time-wasting' and 'gridlock' are another's 'checks and balances'.

- While presidents may be individuals, they, too, have advisors and a cabinet around them. In any case, many prime ministers are key to their party's election prospects and are effectively as powerful (or if they have a majority in parliament) more powerful than the average president. Nor is every prime minister a 'healer' rather than a 'warrior'.

---

section of society. After reaching something of a peak in the late 1940s, for example, the number of working-class MPs and those with only basic education plateaued and then began to decline, and whereas the decades following democratization were something of a golden age for those coming from the 'free' professions such as law, they have gradually been replaced in recent years by people who have spent their entire career since gaining a university degree (now virtually a necessity) in politics working for, say, lobbyists, political parties, think-tanks, pressure groups and trade unions – a process that began first in Germany, the Netherlands and Italy with the UK and France catching up later (*ibid.*: 426–9).

As for gender, as Table 4.6 shows, there is huge variation across the continent, with the latest figures from some central and eastern European countries (for instance, Hungary as well as the Czech Republic) appearing to dash hopes that female rep-

resentation may at least return to the relatively impressive levels achieved under communism (see Forest, 2011; Rueschemeyer and Wolchik, 2009). It also shows that women lose out at cabinet level, too, although the fact that, at least in some countries, the proportion of women in cabinet exceeds that in parliament might mean that not only is affirmative action being taken at this level but that it is effective (see Franceschet *et al.*, 2012). It is of course possible to qualify the advancement of women into the very top-rank of politicians by pointing out that they are often left to languish in less prestigious portfolios in which 'their responsibilities replicate a gendered division of labour arising from stereotypical sex role expectations' (Buckley and Galligan, 2011: 150), thereby locking them out of, for instance, foreign and finance ministries and of course the very top job of Prime Minister. On the other hand, we should remember simply being in cabinet affords a politician a degree of veto-power in collective decisions.

Table 4.6 Women losing out?

	Percentage of women in:	
	Parliament	**Cabinet**
Sweden	45	50
Spain	36	29
Netherlands	31	33
Germany	33	31
France	19	27
UK	22	22
Poland	24	20
Italy	22	17
Czech Rep.	22	0

Source: Caramani *et al.*, 2011.

One can also argue that it is inherently sexist to regard, for example, the foreign or defence ministries as more important than health and education, which almost certainly have bigger budgets and impact more on ordinary people's lives. Moreover, recent research (Krook and O'Brien, 2012) suggests things are improving, even if it demonstrates, once again, significant differences between countries (Figure 4.8)

There may be a link between proportional representation (see Chapter 6) and greater representativeness, but it seems to depend on the precise method employed, and in any case the electoral system may well be less important than (a) the tendency of left-wing parties (an example would be the Spanish socialists elected to government in 2004) to promote women more heavily, and (b) the eventual adoption of quotas and affirmative action (see Buckley and Galligan, 2011, Christmas-Best and Kjær, 2007, Krook, 2009, and Praud, 2012). For all this, the trend toward parliamentary gender equality is hardly impressive across the continent. Apart from the odd earthquake election, turnover among MPs (at least outside the more volatile party systems of CEE) is not that great even if it is higher than in the USA (see Matland and Studlar, 2004). So men have a built-in incumbency advantage that may well take time to overcome (see Schwindt-Bayer, 2005).

Generally, women are best represented in those countries where they can expect to enjoy greater equality (in practice as well as in theory) in other areas of life. Rules to encourage 'parity' do not always work. A one-in-three quota was in operation for local elections in Slovenia in 2010, for instance, but parties almost always put female candidates in third, sixth and ninth spots, almost guaranteeing, because few parties gained three or more seats in any council, that few women would actually get elected. The Polish election of 2011 was fought under new rules which insisted that each party must include at least 35 per cent of each gender, but it failed to deliver a huge increase in female MPs. Quotas were introduced for the 2002 elections in France, but many parties simply paid the fines involved rather than change the habits of a lifetime (see Murray, 2007). The parties in question, one supposes, can always argue that at least they are not in the same league as the Dutch orthodox protestant party, *Staatkundig Gereformeerde Partij*, which normally wins at least a couple of seats in the *Tweede Kamer* (the Dutch parliament), but has never yet fielded a female candidate since it does not believe that women should play such a role – a stance that, despite recent legal challenges, has not yet rendered

Figure 4.8 Female leverage in cabinet

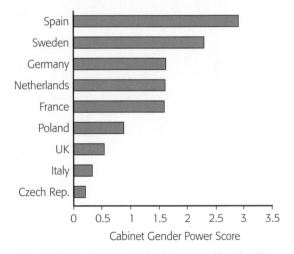

Note: Gender Power Score is calculated for 2009 and based on 'the proportion of female cabinet ministers, as well as the gender and prestige of their positions, with greater weight given to nominations that break most with traditional distributions. This measure explicitly recognizes that the overall numbers of women may not necessarily match the gender and prestige of the portfolios to which they are assigned.'

Source: Data from Krook and O'Brien, 2012.

it ineligible for state subsidies to the tune of some half a million euros every year!

Whether having more women in the legislature makes a difference, however, is of course the proverbial 64,000-dollar question. The answer would seem to be yes. For instance, a recent study concludes that 'adequate female representation fosters political involvement of women. Female MPs seem to function as role models, inspiring other women to be politically motivated and active themselves' (Bühlmann and Schädel, 2012: 109). When it comes to policy, too, there is evidence that the parliamentary presence of women does influence social spending (see Bolzendahl, 2009) and particular policies, such as parental leave (Koole and Vis, 2012). There is also evidence that governments with female cabinet ministers pursue more 'female-friendly' policies (Atchison and Down, 2009; see also Bergqvist, 2011: 167–9). But, as we have learned, not all cabinet ministers have to be members of parliament.

In the end, however, the fact that female cabinet ministers push for, or vote down, particular policies may well have less to do with the fact that they are women and more to do with the fact that they, like their male colleagues, are ultimately political partisans. Indeed, one of the main messages of this chapter is that anyone searching for evidence of the power of parliaments and governments in Europe probably needs to look behind closed doors. They will not find it by focusing on the kind of open confrontation that sometimes occurred between, say, kings and queens and their parliaments in times past, or that still occurs between executive presidents and their legislatures outside Europe. Instead, they will find it, as Duverger implies, in institutions that, while they attract their fair share of criticism these days, nevertheless continue to play a crucial part in politics in Europe. It is to these institutions – the political parties – that we now turn.

Learning Resources for Chapter 4

Further reading

On the political executive, see Helms (2005), *Presidents, Prime Ministers and Chancellors,* and the collection edited by Poguntke and Webb (2004), *The Presidentialization of Politics.* For an overview of cabinet structures and norms, see the edited collection by Blondel and Müller-Rommel (1997), *Cabinets in Western Europe,* and Blondel *et al.* (2007), *Governing New European Democracies.* The obvious starting-points on parliamentary coalition governments is Müller and Strøm (2000), *Coalition Governments in Western Europe* and Strøm, *et al.* (2008), *Cabinets and Coalition Bargaining.* For parliaments, see the contributions to the collections edited by Döring (1995), *Parliaments and Majority Rule in Western Europe,* by Norton (1999), *Parliaments and Governments in Western Europe,* and by Döring and Hallerberg (2004), *Patterns of Parliamentary Behaviour.* For a more unusual take, see Ilie (2010), *European Parliaments under Scrutiny* or Rai (2010), *Ceremony and Ritual in Parliament.* The ultimate reference work on parliaments not just in Europe but the world over is Fish and Kroenig (2011), *The Handbook of National Legislatures.* For an invaluable attempt to get at what goes on behind dosed doors in Europe, see Heidar and Koole (2000), *Parliamentary Party Groups in European Democracies.* Also useful is the collection edited by Müller and Saalfield (1997), *Members of Parliament in Western Europe.* For CEE, see the chapter by Kopecký in the collection edited by White *et al.* (2007), *Developments in Central and East European Politics* and the special issue on 'Post-Communist Parliaments: Change and Stability in the Second Decade' of the *Journal of Legislative Studies* edited by Olson & Ilonszki (2011). On the EP, an accessible yet sophisticated read – one that will also point to other useful sources – is provided by Hix *et al.* (2007), *Democratic Politics in the European Parliament.* On the distinctions between 'consensual' and 'majoritarian' democracies, see the incomparable Lijphart (1999), *Patterns of Democracy.* Millard (2004), *Elections, Parties and Representation in Post-Communist Europe,* not only provides, among other things, an account of the situation of women in that region's parliaments, but a good introduction to the issue of female representation more generally. The 'must-reads' on this topic, though, are Kittilson (2006) *Challenging Parties,* Mateo-Diaz (2005), *Representing Women?,* and Franceschet *et al.* (2012) *The Impact of Gender Quotas.*

On the web

https://www.cia.gov/library/publications/world-leaders-1/index.html – current PMs and cabinets
www.europarl.europa.eu – EP
www.rulers.org – heads of state and government
www.ipu.org – research and statistics on parliaments throughout the world
http://www.cosac.eu/en/links/parliaments/ – links to national parliaments in Europe

Discussion questions

1   Europe's presidents, and especially its kings and queens, are often seen as simply symbolic figure-heads. Do you agree?

2   Some of Europe's prime ministers seem to be more powerful in relation to their cabinet colleagues than others. Why do you think that is?

3   Why would you expect most European governments to be 'minimal winning coalitions'? But why and how do some administrations govern without controlling a majority in parliament?

4   Why do some European governments last longer than others?

5   How is it decided which ministers get which jobs? What do ministers actually do, and how (well) do they all pull together as a cabinet?

6   Do the 'upper houses' of Europe's parliaments have much influence?

7   Some parliaments are more powerful than others: which are they, and how and why do they have more influence than their counterparts in other countries?

8   Has European integration undermined the power of national parliaments? And what about the EU's own parliament: what, in your opinion, most distinguishes it from its national counterparts?

9   Some of Europe's parliaments seem more representative of its citizens than others: do you think that they should all be striving to contain MPs who are more like those who elect them?

10 Most observers agree that, for all the variation between them, Europe's legislatures are not much of a check on its executives: why do you think that might be?

ONLINE RESOURCES AVAILABLE

Visit the companion site at **www.palgrave.com/politics/bale** to access additional learning resources.

Chapter 5

Parties – how the past affects the present, and an uncertain future

In Chapter 4 we suggested that parties are the key to understanding how the executive in Europe dominates the legislature – how the government, in other words, controls parliament. In fact, parties are crucial to the government and politics of European countries more generally. Without them representative democracy could not function. And yet Europeans seem not to trust them very much (see Figure 5.1). In this chapter we explain what parties are, and how they came to be. We also look at the ways they organize, and at the way political scientists have tried, by looking at their ideas and their origins, to sort them into meaningful categories that they call **party families**, most of which are represented in almost every individual country's **party system**. We go on to look at these systems and at how political science tries to classify them, and ask whether, why, how and how much they are changing. Finally, we touch on debates on how parties should be funded and explore the popular notion that parties – unpopular with the public and struggling for members – are on the way out.

What are parties, and what are they for?

Countries with something in common tend to contain similar parties, even if those parties tend to call themselves by different names. Political scientists interested in comparison and generalization often group these parties into a **party family** (see Mair and Mudde, 1998), on the basis that, while some national variation is inevitable, what each party stands for and how it organizes itself tends (historically, at least) to 'run in the family' – all of which means it makes sense to talk about, say, conservative (or social democratic or green or liberal) parties in general.

Although they have been around for some 200 years, political parties still sometimes seem easier to recognize than to pin down. We have made an attempt to come to a workable definition, but it is necessarily qualified. The qualification 'for the most part' is necessary because there are parties, for instance, that refuse either to contest elections at all or, if they do, make it clear that their eventual aim is not to work within the system but to dismantle it. Others exist only for their own (and hopefully others') amusement. 'More often than not' is also a necessary caveat because there may be no clear link between a party's ideas and certain interests and/or values. Its ideas might reflect the personal predilections of a charismatic leader. A party's ideas might also owe more to historical hangovers than current concerns.

As far as functions go, a hypothetical job description for parties would include, at a minimum, the following:

A country's **party system** is the more or less stable configuration of political parties which normally compete in national elections. It is normally characterized by how many parties there are, what they stand for and their relative strengths. Alternatively (see Mair, 1996) it can be characterized by the extent to which competition between parties is predictable or unpredictable, and post-election changes in government tend to be marginal or wholesale.

- ◆ representing socially or culturally significant interests at the same time as 'aggregating' (lumping together and packaging) their sometimes contradictory preferences;
- ◆ recruiting, selecting, socializing and providing material and ideological support to candidates and elected politicians who will do the representing, often at both national and sub-national level;
- ◆ structuring an otherwise bewildering array of choices available to voters at parliamentary and local elections, which, by their very presence, they render competitive;
- ◆ facilitating the formation of governments that produce relatively coordinated and coherent policy responses to perceived and real problems
- ◆ effectively mediating between millions of citizens and a state that otherwise might act exclusively in the interest of those it employs and those whose economic clout could give them a disproportionate say in its direction.

Like most job descriptions, however, this list fails to cover some of the less formal – and possibly less admirable – functions fulfilled by parties. One that has attracted some interesting cross-national research in recent years, for example, is the way parties are used as generators and distributors of 'jobs for the boys' – employment in or contracts with either parties themselves or the governments (central, regional and local) they help control (see Kopecký *et al.*, 2012). Not surprisingly there is a fine line – one which varies considerably between countries – between this 'patronage' and outright political corruption (Hough, 2013). But wherever that line is drawn, there is no doubt in some instances that an appreciation of the way in which leaders and internal factions supply often quite tangible benefits to their supporters is vital to an understanding of the way many parties are organized.

> **Political parties** are organizations that, for the most part, recruit candidates to contest elections in the hope that they can then participate in government, or at least push it in the direction of their own ideas – ideas that, more often than not, reflect the socio-economic interests and/or moral values of those who support them.

KEY POINT

Parties perform a range of crucial tasks in all European democracies: representing and packaging interests and values so that alternatives are simplified and meaningful; recruiting and supporting candidates; and forming governments with coherent programmes.

Organization

The way political parties organize themselves, as well as being influenced by both electoral competition and the political philosophy the party claims to represent, is heavily constrained, if not wholly determined, by their history and by changes in their environment – an environment they can only do a little to help shape (see Box 5.1). All this matters not simply for our understanding of the parties per se, but because how they organize themselves impacts on, say, their willingness and capacity to serve in governments: parties in which parliamentary representatives are forced to vie for control with a powerful non-parliamentary executive, for example, not only tend to oblige those representatives to give up some of their salary to help fund the party (see Bolleyer, 2012) but, more importantly, may not find it quite so easy to sign a coalition deal (see Pedersen, 2010b). Organization may also impact on ideology (and vice versa): the tendency of mainstream parties to appeal to as many voters as possible is likely to increase the influence of those in their ranks who believe in political marketing – in other words the idea that there has to be an interaction between product and consumers that goes beyond merely selling the former to the latter; should that occur, then fewer and fewer principles are likely to be regarded as non-negotiable, whether or not that is seen as good or bad for democracy (see Lees-Marshment *et al.*, 2011).

On a superficial level, accounts of modern party organization do not depart much from the common wisdom found in the media. This portrays most mainstream parties as in the hands of leaders determined not to allow their more zealous supporters to scupper their electoral chances by remaining true to whatever cause the party was set up to promote or defend. In fact, however, when we look more closely, that portrait – and, therefore, the common wisdom

BOX 5.1

The evolution of political party organization

Cadre parties (Duverger, 1954) were clearly controlled by an elite *caucus* (or small group) commonly consisting of parliamentarians and local notables, with the addition later on of a national organization to deal with members who were expected not so much to decide policy but simply to contribute funds and campaign at elections. Examples include **nineteenth-century liberal and conservative parties**.

Mass parties (Duverger, 1954) were founded by those who did not enjoy political power (at least to begin with) and tended to adopt a 'branch' structure in which members, as well as providing financial and campaign resources, could hope to contribute to policy. This meant that party leaders enjoyed rather less autonomy from the centre than their counterparts in the cadre parties. Examples include **early twentieth-century socialist parties**.

Catch-all parties (Kirchheimer, 1966) seek to broaden their base beyond their traditional support and attract the 'floating voter' and interest group backing. Such parties downplay ideology in favour of pragmatism, and cede considerable autonomy and control to the leadership over the active membership. In the age of mass media, such parties could become **electoral professional parties** (Panebianco, 1988) – dominated by career politicians employing experts (see Webb and Kolodny, 2006) to track public opinion and market the party accordingly via resources derived not from membership subscriptions but from interest groups and the public purse. Examples include **mid- to late-twentieth-century social democratic and Christian democratic parties**.

Cartel parties (Katz and Mair, 1995) arguably become so reliant on public subsidies and so distant from their largely symbolic membership that they have become not so much brokers between society and the state as components of the latter. Organizationally, such parties shift or maintain the balance of power away from parts of the party that might be captured by activist members, such as the national, extra-parliamentary, organization (*the party in central office*) towards the parliamentary wing (*the party in public office*). The latter is controlled by the leadership, which communicates over the heads of activists with the rest of the largely passive membership (*the party on the ground*) and potential voters via direct mail and the mass media. Survival is their main goal and the existing 'winners' collude with each other over electoral and funding rules to exclude newcomers. Examples suggested include **most twenty-first-century mainstream parties**, in both western and postcommunist Europe (Krašovec and Haughton, 2011). Some political scientists, however, reject or at least qualify the thesis, citing a lack of hard empirical evidence: parties, they suggest, still maintain links with organized interests, seek members, and compete rather than collude (see Allern and Bale, 2012; Detterbeck, 2005; Kitschelt, 2000).

Anti-system or anti-political establishment or 'challenger' parties (see Abedi, 2009; Hino, 2012) are a reaction to the collusive consensus which arguably results when established parties join a cosy, only superficially competitive, cartel. Examples often cited include **1980s Green Parties** and **1990s far-right parties**.

For a constructively critical discussion of all the models and their evolution, see Krouwel (2006).

– is far from describing the reality for many, if not most, parties. Repeated investigation by political scientists of what is sometimes called the 'law of curvilinear disparity' (the idea that leaders and voters are routinely less 'extreme' and more electorally minded than activists) suggests that it is no more a law – or

at least a universally applicable one – than is Michels' so called 'iron law of oligarchy' (see Box 5.2). Party supporters and members are just as interested in winning elections as leaders, while the latter care deeply about values and policy. Research also suggests that present-day forms of party organiza-

KEY POINT

The way parties organize themselves varies over time and, to some extent, according to ideology.

tion do not necessarily mean decreased internal democracy (see Allern and Pedersen, 2007).

There is a tendency for parties in European democracies to conform to 'common-sense', essentially hierarchical, norms of organization that apply across a variety of social, government and commercial sectors. Whether or not this so-called 'isomorphism' (or fit) obeys the 'iron law' outlined in Box 5.2 is, however, a moot point. After all, the extent to which they conform to those norms varies considerably. For instance, the Italian party *Forza Italia* was founded in the early 1990s by continental media magnate and later Italian Prime Minister Silvio Berlusconi (see Chapter 7). But it began very differently from traditional parties, being arguably little more than a hollow holding company and marketing organization for the ideas and interests of its charismatic leader (see Hopkin and Paolucci, 1999). Some would argue that the 'business firm model' represented by *Forza Italia* is, in fact, only the ultimate extension of a wider European (or possibly

Figure 5.1 (Lack of) trust in political parties

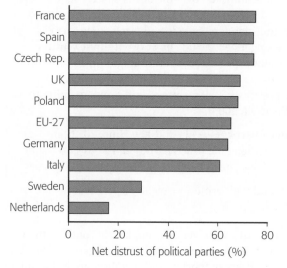

Note: Net distrust figure obtained by subtracting the percentage of those who say they trust political parties from the percentage of those who don't.

Source: Eurobarometer, 74 (2011).

BOX 5.2

Michels' iron law of oligarchy

To an early theorist of party organization, Robert Michels, the adoption by mass, left-wing parties of elitist or cadre-style organization (and the concomitant watering down of their radicalism) was wholly predictable. According to his 'iron law of oligarchy', a combination of bureaucratic necessity, the inevitability of specialization, the trappings of office and the submissiveness of supporters would eventually ensure that power would pass from the membership to a leadership more interested in survival than social change (Michels, 1962). A later theorist like Angelo Panebianco might qualify the extent to which this necessarily implies a decline of ideological distinctiveness and question the existence of a truly cohesive leadership (Panebianco, 1988). But he, too, notes that party survival rather than the implementation of its founding philosophy becomes the name of the game.

---

global) trend toward presidentialization (see Chapter 4), which sees parties, even in parliamentary systems, play little more than a supporting role to the celebrity policiticians (see Chapter 7) who are their leaders.

In fact, we are a long way off from that situation. Research suggests that presidentialization (some prefer to call it personalization) is nowhere near as pervasive as the common wisdom suggests (see Karvonen, 2010; also Blondel *et al.*, 2009). And even if one reduces parties to brands (Snyder and Ting, 2002), it is clear that the majority of them existed before and will survive the passing of the current 'face' of the brand. And they are often quick – though not always quick enough – to replace that face if he or she doesn't manage to attract customers. The idea that leaders will prove all-conquering also ignores the link that political scientists continue to observe between party ideologies and the way they go about organizing themselves (see, for example, Pedersen, 2010a). Left-wing parties, for instance, still tend to give members a greater say than their more conservative counterparts. But the paradigmatic example of this link is provided by green parties. Despite modifying the 'flat' (i.e. non-hierarchical), ultra-participative values and structures that they brought with them from their beginnings in social movements (see Chapter 8), green parties still stress membership consultation, consensus, and limitations on leadership (see Frankland *et al.*, 2008). This is a big contrast, for instance, with far-right parties at the other end of the spectrum, which tend to afford their leaders a great deal of discretion and control. Openness to gender quotas is another characteristic that seems broadly (if not solely) to vary according to party family (see Murray, 2010) Recent research which looks at parliamentary elites across decades also suggests that party families tend to have distinct patterns of recruitment, so that, generally speaking, MPs representing conservative parties look different from those representing, for instance, green or social democratic parties (Cotta and Best, 2007: 480–81). It must be said, however, that the distinctions fade a little over time as new parties are incorporated into the system. Moreover, in Europe's younger democracies there is less likely to be a match – even an inexact one – between ideology and organization more generally. With the exception of communist parties and their successors, parties began with comparatively little infrastructure or grass-roots, and many have found it difficult or unnecessary to do anything about it (van Biezen, 2003).

Ideology, then, might be a guide to understanding the distribution of power within different parties, but it is by no means a complete explanation. This becomes obvious if one looks at how they go about selecting their candidates (see Hazan and Rahat, 2010). For one thing, there are some states where the process is subject to legal obligations – Finland, for example, insists that all its parties give their members a vote. Another obvious institutional factor is the electoral system (see Chapter 6): in most European states, parties fight elections in multi-member constituencies or districts so need lists, chosen either at the national or the regional level; a few continue with the single-member constituencies associated with British- or US-style 'first-past-the-post' elections, so the choice needs to be much more local. Even then, however, there may well be intervention (or attempted intervention) from the national head-quarters in order to prevent the adoption of an unsuitable candidate or parachute in a favourite of the leadership. In Germany, however, such intervention would be not just controversial – as it often is in the UK (and can be in Spain despite a tradition of central control) – but actually illegal. The law has also been enlisted to block or to allow gender quotas – an increasingly important institutional effect on the process (see Krook, 2009; Norris, 2006).

When it comes to candidate selection (see Hazan and Rahat, 2010), size also matters – generally speaking, the larger the party, the more central control over the process – and it also seems different parts of Europe have different preferences on the subject. Nordic countries tend towards local autonomy, whereas southern European countries go for central control (Lundell, 2004). Finally, practices vary not just between countries and between parties in the same country, but over time and with political fortunes as well. For instance, not many European countries or parties have followed the USA and held 'primaries' where (virtually) anyone can turn up to select a party's candidates, although this may just be beginning to change, at least when it comes to electing leaders (see Kenig, 2009). The fact that the idea seems to have caught on quickest in English-speaking countries perhaps explains why it was the world's oldest political party, the British Conservatives, which was one of the first in Europe to choose to experiment with the idea – something few would have predicted. But then few would have predicted that the party would suffer three consecutive landslide defeats between 1997 and 2005 which eventually ushered in a 'modernizing' leadership keen to encourage (although wary of obliging) local branches to choose a more diverse range of candidates (see Bale, 2011; Childs and Webb, 2011). The Conservatives' journey into the wilderness – albeit temporary – also illustrates, incidentally, one of the perennial problems of party organization, namely the need to allow a degree of diversity without the internal factions that can sometimes develop as a result damaging the party's electoral competitiveness – something to which not just small radical parties but also large, temporarily dominant parties (like the Conservatives or DC, the Italian Christian democrats) are prone (see Boucek, 2012).

Party systems and party families

When it comes to parties, history matters, often far more so than the media's treatment of day-to-day political events would sometimes have us believe. It certainly influences what political scientists refer to as the party system. Most political scientists employ a dual approach to classifying party systems. Following the Italian political scientist Giovanni Sartori, who pioneered work in this area, they give equal weight to the degree of 'fragmentation', essentially the number of parties present in the system (often calculated using a weighted system known as the **effective number of parties**) and the ideological distance between them (referred to as the degree of 'polarization'). Both of these can be seen as dimensions that can be plotted against each other on a graph. Countries can then be located on the graph according to how they score on each dimension (see Figure 5.2). Doing this reveals similarities and differences between countries. Taking our core countries, we find only one – the UK – that has few parties and (relatively) little distance between significant parties on the left and the right – a situation we call 'moderate two-partyism'. There are rather more countries (Germany, Sweden, and probably the Czech Republic, Poland and Spain) where the distance between right- and left-wing parties might not be that great, but where there are more of them – a situation we know as 'moderate multipartyism'. The rest (France, Netherlands, Italy) are illustrations of 'polarized multipartyism' – lots

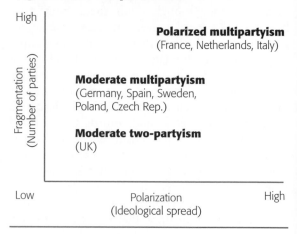

Figure 5.2 Party system classification, by fragmentation and polarization

High

Fragmentation (Number of parties)

Polarized multipartyism
(France, Netherlands, Italy)

Moderate multipartyism
(Germany, Spain, Sweden, Poland, Czech Rep.)

Moderate two-partyism
(UK)

Low   Polarization   High
          (Ideological spread)

of parties and a big difference between the most left- and right-wing parties.

The late Peter Mair, who was one of Europe's finest scholars of party politics, suggested that we employ a different method of classifying party systems on the grounds that nowadays so many party systems fall into the 'moderate multipartyism' category that it has become somewhat meaningless, and that any increase or decrease in the number of parties at the margins doesn't necessarily tell us much about the core or essence of a system. Mair (2006a), suggested a more discriminating measure could be based on competition for government. The latter can be 'closed' or 'open'. Closed systems are those in which: (a) alternation in government tends to be wholesale (all the parties in office lose power after an election) rather than partial; (b) the combinations of parties that form governments are familiar rather than innovative (parties on the right govern together, as do parties on the left, for example); and (c) a narrow range of (mainstream) parties tends to govern. An example would be the UK. Open systems are more opaque, fluid, innovative, inclusive and rather less predictable. Outside the newer democracies of Europe, an example might be the Netherlands. This new means of classification would also have implications for how we measure change (see below) but, at the moment, it looks as if it will simply supplement rather than replace the Sartori-style schema which has become common currency among political scientists interested in parties.

When comparing countries' party systems it would be misleading simply to count the number of parties in each without taking some account of significance: as in the UK, for example, there might be lots of parties with seats in parliament but few of them really count. Political scientists have therefore devised a system of weighting parties for their significance and then calculating an **'effective number of parties'** that can be compared. A recent international comparison (Carter and Farrell, 2010) for instance, puts the figure for the UK (which then had ten parties in parliament) at 2.32 and in Germany (which had four) at 3.72. The effective number in Sweden (seven parties in parliament) was put at 4.19 and in France (where there were twelve parliamentary parties) 2.38.

KEY POINT

Countries' party systems – and the parties themselves – can usefully be categorized into 'ideal types' to facilitate comparison and contrast: systems vary in the extent to which they are fragmented and polarized, or open to innovation; parties vary according to ideology and organization.

These classifications are interesting because they provoke predictions and hypotheses that can be tested. One obvious hypothesis involves the relationship between party systems and the kind of party competition that occurs within them. For example, in a system with few parties and a narrow range of ideological difference (i.e. one that exhibits moderate multipartism or two-partyism), we might predict that parties will tend to campaign in the centre ground rather than emphasizing their left and right credentials. Party competition will, in other words, be 'centripetal' (tending toward the centre) rather than 'centrifugal' (tending toward the extreme). This is the case, for instance, in the UK. Under conditions of polarized multipartyism, we are likely to see more centrifugal competition as a number of parties aim to occupy niches along the entire political spectrum, just as they do, for example, in the Netherlands.

These classifications of party systems, however, in some ways beg the question. How did countries' systems come to be the way they are in the first place? Many political scientists believe that party systems are rooted in social (or, increasingly, values-based) conflicts, which they call cleavages (see the definition given on p. 8). Most of these were those already in place at the end of the nineteenth century and the beginning of the twentieth century, when democracy (or at least the vote for all adult males) was introduced. Indeed, one of the most famous theses in comparative politics holds that, as a result, they helped to structure – or even freeze – Europe's party system for decades to come (see Lipset and Rokkan, 1967). Some, of course, have developed since, while others have declined in salience or, as in CEE, supposedly had their development arrested, either temporarily or permanently (Toole, 2007; Zielinski, 2002). The extent to which a cleavage was more or less important in a particular country helped to determine which parties (or, compara-

tively speaking, representatives of the various party families) were present, as well as which were stronger or weaker. So, too, did the extent to which existing parties were able to adapt in order to mobilize on that cleavage as well as the one that gave birth to them. Figure 5.3 shows the evolution of a hypothetical party system containing all the main cleavages and, therefore, all the party families we will go on to discuss. But clearly, not all countries will have been affected by all cleavages and so most will contain representatives of only some, rather than all, the party families.

We can go through Figure 5.3 (which is, of course, a stylized diagram) from the top down. The different interests of landowners and those who were beginning to make money from industry or the professions had led, around the middle of the nineteenth century, to the foundation of, on the one hand, *conservative* parties and, on the other, *liberal* or *radical* parties. These parties stood on either side of the *land–industry* cleavage. The increased need and willingness among wage-earners to express their own interests gave rise, as the nineteenth century drew to a close, to *socialist* or *social democratic* parties, which then spawned *communist* parties that believed in a more revolutionary route to power. These mobilized one side of the *owner–worker* cleavage and reinforced the basic division between what we have come to call 'right' and 'left'. The rise of the city (especially in Scandinavia) saw the creation of *agrarian* parties dedicated to defending the interests of farmers (the *urban–rural* cleavage). Another conflict that influenced politics was the *church–state* or religious cleavage (see Ertman, 2009) that, in time, saw the creation of conservative *Christian democratic* parties opposed to the secularism, as well as the progressive social and economic policies, of the left in particular. Meanwhile, the *centre–periphery* cleavage encouraged, in some countries, the formation of *regionalist* parties which defended the autonomy of communities with separate identities (and possibly languages) against state centralization. More recently, agrarian parties have become *centre* parties, and (with the end of the Cold War) some communist parties have become *left parties*. Even more recently, cleavages seem to have opened up around more values-based *postmaterialism* (see Chapter 6 for a full definition) and responses to globalization.

Figure 5.3 The evolution of Europe's party families, from the nineteenth to the twenty-first century

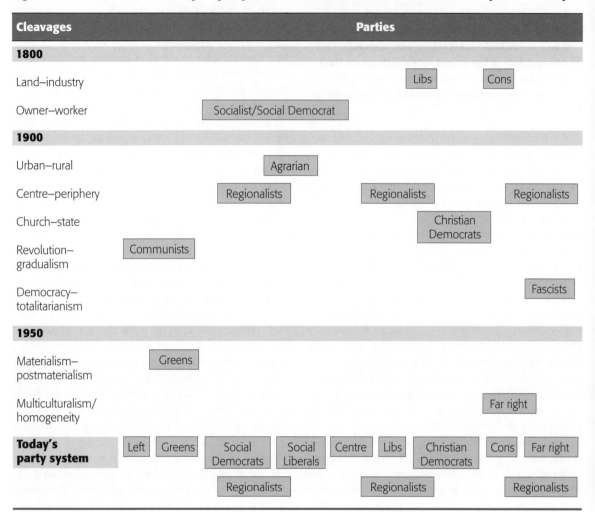

These focus on matters such as the environment and multiculturalism, giving rise to *green* parties and helping to give a new lease of life to *far-right* parties. Indeed, many political scientists nowadays believe it is possible to collapse party competition into two dimensions, namely left–right (originating in the owner–worker cleavage and tapping into attitudes to the state vs the market) and authoritarian–libertarian – a cultural rather than an economic dimension (see Kriesi *et al.*, 2008) that has been labelled by some as GALTAN after its two poles: Green/Alternative/Libertarian and Traditionalism/Authority/Nationalism (Hooghe and Marks, 2009). In some states (for instance, the UK and most Nordic countries) parties and voters, while they

care about cultural questions, care more about economic disputes. In others – notably those where differences on economic and social policy between the mainstream right and left are relatively muted (those with the conservative/corporatist welfare states we talked about in Chapter 1), cultural questions arguably seem to matter even more (see Henjak, 2010).

The relationship between cleavages (or, more precisely, the conflictual 'issue dimensions' they give rise to) and parties can, incidentally, be used to predict the number of parties in a system. This is done with a simple formula produced by influential Dutch political scientist Arendt Lijphart (whose distinction between 'majoritarian' and 'consensual' systems we have already referred to in Chapter 4). More often than not, there is a relationship between the number of issue dimensions and the number of parties. This can be expressed as $N = I + 1$; namely; the number of parties will equal the number of issue dimensions, plus one. So, for example, in the Netherlands, the issue conflicts are religious, socio-economic and postmaterialist, which means (at least) four parties. Of course, this does not always hold exactly, and requires that one ignore very small parties that might well be influential at certain times or on certain issues – as the UK's and Spain's regional parties are, for instance. The number of parties might also change as issue dimensions become more or less important. Nevertheless, it is probably one of the more robust formulas in political science.

Whether this formula and the issue dimensions it relies upon – or, indeed, the notion that cleavages structure party systems – can be applied to Europe's newest democracies is open to argument. Many observers routinely assume, for instance, either that the transition from communism is still so recent that it would be foolish at this stage in the game to expect to find such deeply embedded conflicts or that, even if they are emerging, they will be very different from those that structure party competition in the established democracies. Recent research using large surveys of European voters, however, suggests that – due in no small part to the efforts of parties themselves to politicize them – 'the pattern of social cleavages and their political consequences is similar between the established and emerging democracies, with religion and the owner–worker cleavage dominating political conflict' (McAllister and White, 2007: 211–12; see also Casal Bértoa, 2013).

If this turns out to be right, it could help explain why parties in many postcommunist European countries look not unlike their 'western' counterparts, and now of course associate formally with them in European party federations and parliamentary groups (see below). Scepticism as to whether parties in postcommunist countries can be fitted into the same families is understandable: might political scientists be rushing – not for the first time – to employ off-the-peg schemas and frameworks when they should instead be going for tailor-made explanations? However, recent research suggests that, by and large such scepticism is unwarranted

(see Hloušek and Kope ek, 2010) even if (as is true, after all, in western Europe) the dimensions of party-political competition vary between states, with Rovny and Edwards (2012), for instance, identifying the following five clusters:

In the first group (Czech Republic and Slovakia), competition occurs mostly along the left–right dimension. In the second group (Hungary, Poland and Lithuania), competition occurs primarily along the socio-cultural dimension, [where] the right-wing combines social conservatism with left-leaning populism. In group three (Estonia and Latvia), competition is mostly along the economic dimension, but a number of parties champion left-liberal positions. In group four (Bosnia, Croatia, Macedonia and Slovenia) competition occurs almost solely along the socio-cultural dimension, with distinctive social liberal and social conservative party clusters, however the major left-wing parties always belong to the liberal cluster. The final group (Bulgaria, Romania, Serbia) is the only group that exhibits the [supposedly] typical eastern European competition pattern proposed by earlier research. The left is a remnant of communist left-wing authoritarianism, while the right forms a liberal, market-oriented opposition. Strikingly, … these competition patterns do not coincide with different communist regime types or transition paths.

We now look at each party family in turn, not in order of foundation (as in Figure 5.3) but instead in broad order of contemporary political importance. We also provide examples of each, partly to show that, although generalizations are useful, membership of the family does not always involve direct lineage.

Socialist and social democratic parties

These parties first began to emerge in the last quarter of the nineteenth century as those on one side of the owner–worker cleavage began to agitate not merely for political rights, such as the vote, but also for an economy and a society run in the interests of the many rather than the few. Such demands were obviously anathema to conservatives. But liberals were divided into those who wanted to work with (and ideally retain control of) any progressive forces in politics and those who regarded socialism as a threat to private property and individual freedom. Many socialist parties allied with the increasingly powerful trade union movements. Partly as a result, and partly because many radicals departed to form communist parties following the Russian revolution (1917), it became clear that these parties aimed not to overthrow capitalism but to mitigate and even dynamize it. This they hoped to do by using the state: through the ownership (or at least the regulation) of key industries and utilities, the use of progressive taxation and redistributionary government spending, governments would cooperate with trade unions (and hopefully employers, too) to deliver full employment and social security, health and education for all (see Box 5.3).

The postwar period saw the implementation of key planks of the social democratic programme across western Europe. This was initially by social democrats themselves, but then also by parties of the centre-right which believed, rightly or wrongly, that outright opposition to such measures would be electorally damaging. During this period, social democrats had the support of at least a third (and in the UK, Sweden and Austria considerably more) of the electorate. When the postwar boom came to an abrupt end in the mid-1970s (see Chapter 1), social democratic parties with the misfortune to be in government – whether or not they or their policies were to blame (and with the exception of Austria and Sweden) – bore the brunt of public displeasure. Conversely, the social democratic success stories of the 1980s were in Spain, Portugal and Greece, where socialist parties turned out to be the main beneficiaries of the collapse of dictatorships (Merkel, 1992). The French *Parti Socialiste,* having won a historic victory in 1981, however, ran into far greater difficulties when, unlike its Mediterranean counterparts, it attempted to buck, rather than adapt to, the trend toward economic liberalism. Its radical programme of nationalizations and public spending quickly ran into trouble (not least with the financial markets) and it was forced to execute a U-turn toward austerity (see Ross *et al.,* 1987). This trauma, and ongoing defeats of sister parties in the UK and Germany, led some commentators to predict 'the death of social democracy', its ideology outdated and its core support (the manual working class and trade unions) shrinking. A process of policy renewal and

reaching out to middle-class voters, plus a series of electoral comebacks in the late 1990s seemed to have put paid to such pessimism for a while. But elections in twenty-first century have not been so positive, not even when the relatively unfettered capitalism which social democrats were traditionally wary of seemed to implode in the global financial crisis which began in 2007 (see Chapter 9).

In the postcommunist democracies of central and eastern Europe, the performance of, and prospects for, social democratic parties are better than some might have predicted – particularly when one considers that for the most part they began as the means by which Cold War communist parties attempted, almost overnight, to establish their newly moderate, democratic, credentials. In many states in central and eastern Europe, social democratic parties have already made it into government on one or more occasions and regularly garner a substantial share of the vote: the Czech Republic being a good example. Although recent years have seen spectacular (and possibly terminal) electoral reverses in countries like Hungary and Poland, social democrats in other countries – Slovakia in 2012 being the most obvious example – have enjoyed big comebacks.

While the likeness may not be exact, the newest members of the social democratic family, then, bear some resemblance to those in the west that have been around much longer. New or old, most social democrats, as we argue in Chapter 9, continue to believe in using the power of public initiative and the public purse to (at the very least) protect the less fortunate and, in the long term, reduce their numbers via strategies promoting equality of opportunity. All, however, realize that this power is constrained by what is deemed prudent by international financial markets and reasonable, taxwise, by their electorates. To them, the state still has an economic as well as a welfare role, but it is as a regulator or framework-setter as opposed to an owner or driver. And while not immune to both differences of emphasis and internal division on the issue, all are basically in favour of an EU that aims to liberalize and increase trade – though not at the expense of social provision or labour standards, commitment to which is reinforced in some cases by continuing close links with the union movement. On issues of morality, conscience and sexuality, social democratic parties are firmly in the secular liberal tradition.

BOX 5.3

Modernization over Marxism – two social democratic parties

It is often said that the British Labour Party originated 'from the bowels of the trade union movement' rather than the philosophical beliefs of impractical ideologues. Its original purpose was to ensure that laws passed by parliament did not unfairly hinder unions in their role as protectors and promoters of the interests of ordinary working people. Once the bulk of those people became entitled to vote, it quickly became clear that Labour would become one of the UK's two main parties. Despite *Clause IV* of its constitution – committing it, in theory, to extending public ownership of the economy – Labour in practice came to be associated not so much with the more radical Marxist diagnosis and prescriptions that characterized continental social democratic parties but, rather, with redistribution via progressive taxation, the welfare state and the sort of 'nationalization' of key industries that made sense in the 1930s and 1940s but was seen by many as outdated by the 1950s. The very vagueness of Clause IV, and fear of the infighting that would greet any attempt to replace it, meant that it was only in the 1990s that the party finally equipped itself with what its leadership argued was a more relevant, realistic 'mission statement'.

All this is in marked contrast with other European social democratic parties. Despite close relationships with the trade unions (particularly in Scandinavia), these parties were not so financially or so organizationally dependent on them. Neither were they so uninterested in ideological direction and debate. In their early years, they were heavily influenced by the writings of Marx and his followers. Initially, indeed, the really significant difference between them and the more radical *communists* (many of whom started out as social democrats) was their commitment to a peaceful and parliamentary road to socialism – even if the plan originally was to refuse (unlike the British Labour Party) to get involved in government until an electoral majority for their cause had been won. Ironically, it was their stress on social analysis – and frustration with ruling themselves out of government despite their relative electoral strength – that made these parties more open to change in order to adapt to new circumstances. One of the best examples is the German SPD, originally founded in 1875. At its famous *Bad Godesburg* congress in 1959, the party announced its abandonment of old-style, Marxist, socialism and its embrace of the 'social market economy', setting itself on a path toward both catch-all party status (see Box 5.1) and, quite soon afterwards, coalition government.

For all these reasons, and because in northern if not in southern Europe (see Allern *et al.*, 2007; Astudillo Ruiz, 2002) they continue to be linked (although not necessarily institutionally) to trade unions, Europe's social democrats might perhaps be more comparable than ever with the US Democrats. Those looking for a single 'European equivalent' of the Republican Party, however, will have a harder time. In their enthusiasm for a strong defence of the nation, no-nonsense policies on crime and punishment, and a low-tax, no-meddling government, the Republicans share much in common with Europe's conservative parties. But in their rhetorical commitment to 'compassionate conservatism' and their anti-permissive stance on family values and personal (and especially sexual) morality, they have strong affinities with Europe's Christian Democrats.

These are the party families we go on to look at next.

Conservative parties

Europe's conservative parties were formed in order to coordinate the defence of the socio-economic privileges of the traditional, mainly landed, hierarchy against what were seen as the pretensions of the rising liberal middle class. Where liberals were supposedly motivated by theory, enthused by international free trade, obsessed with the individual and possessed of an off-putting earnestness, conservatives declared themselves to be more pragmatic, more patriotic, more paternalistic and yet also more fun! In the UK, for instance, they were backed by brewing and agricultural interests, as well as a moderate church. They were able to survive the granting of universal suffrage – first, by poaching middle-class voters who were put off by liberalism's identification with sectarian, urban and (increasingly) radical politics and, second, by appealing to the nationalism, the traditionalism and the respectable aspirations of newly enfranchised working-class voters.

The second challenge for conservative parties was the advent of the welfare state. Although conservative parties were paternalistic, they argued that the less well-off were best protected by a thriving private sector and a mixture of self-help and charity. State intervention should be limited largely to policing law and order and providing for the defence of the realm. However, the obvious popularity of increased social provision and what, at the time, seemed the inevitability of public involvement in key sectors such as transport and energy, meant they concentrated their efforts for most of the postwar period on limiting rather than 'rolling back' state spending and activity. Following the economic difficulties encountered by European nations in the 1970s, when countries such as Germany and the UK were governed by the centre-left, the opportunity arose to pursue a more aggressive attack on the state (see Chapters 1 and 9). This was taken furthest in the UK, where the emphasis was on cutting state subsidies to industry, reducing the role of the trade unions and selling off state assets. Although welfare provision suffered, there were electoral constraints on how much could be cut.

This was in keeping with the fact that Europe's conservative parties have historically been careful not to allow their ideological instincts to sway them too far away from the centre of the political spectrum (Box 5.4). This might well be due to the fact that they are strongest in countries that display two characteristics. The first is the tendency among the country's voters, irrespective of the electoral system, to give power to one of two main parties (or blocs): traditionally this would include countries like the UK, Greece, and, since the fall of the wall, Hungary. The second is the weakness or absence of a traditionally more centrist *Christian democracy* (see below) in that country; instances include the UK, Malta, Spain, Greece and, since the 1990s, Italy and postcommunist countries. Notable exceptions to the 'Conservative or Christian Democrats, but not both' rule, however, include Sweden and – at least until the 2010 election – the Czech Republic. In the latter,

in fact, voters had two ostensibly conservative parties to choose between: ODS, which has become increasingly Eurosceptic and another, newer party, TOP09, whose more positive attitude to European integration means it may well have as much in common with Christian Democrats as conservatives. Meanwhile in Hungary, the conservative party, *Fidesz*, is considerably less liberal on the economy than many of its supposed sister parties both west and east.

Christian democratic parties

These parties, especially those of Roman Catholic origin, were around in various forms by the beginning of the twentieth century (Box 5.5). But representatives of this centre-right party family really came into their own following the end of the Second World War (see Kselman and Buttigieg, 2003). While clearly opposed to the collectivist, class-based ethos of the left (and in particular the communists), Christian democratic parties were markedly more positive about state and trade union involvement than some of their conservative counterparts (see Hanley, 1994; van Kersbergen, 1995). Prizing social harmony above individualism and unfettered free markets, Christian democratic parties were instrumental in the development of 'corporatism' (see Chapter 8) in Austria, and to a lesser extent Germany, in the second half of the twentieth century. The stress was on 'capitalism with a conscience' and on a role for the state in facilitating long-term, mutually beneficial and institutionally supported relationships between business and unions. But the collective good wasn't everything, as it supposedly was to parties on the left: individuals mattered, too. Yet they had to be seen not as the autonomous, primarily self-interested actors beloved of economic liberals, but as socially embedded contributors and beneficiaries of an organic whole (an idea known as 'personalism'). The stress was also on support for the family – especially the traditional family that was seen as the embodiment and transmission belt for Christian moral values. But while compassion and help for the less fortunate was important, tolerance and compromise had their limits when it came to issues such as abortion and divorce.

Although strong feelings on those issues are most associated with Roman Catholicism, it is important

BOX 5.4

Fighting in the centre ground? – three conservative parties

The Spanish *Partido Popular* (PP) began life in 1976 as the *Alianza Popular* (AP), a home for members of the Franco dictatorship who wished to pursue their conservative politics in the new, democratic Spain. Finally, in 1990, the centre-right, at the same time as reforming under the single banner, *Partido Popular* (PP), found a leader from a new generation too young to be tainted by the past. José María Aznar was able to exploit his image as a reliable, pragmatic, centrist – and, above all, clean – politician to his advantage. In 1996, PP assumed office as a minority government with the support of smaller regionalist parties. Centrist policies, and the support of young people for whom the socialist opposition now meant monolithic, old-fashioned, corrupt politics, helped PP win itself an overall majority (in a PR system) in the general election of 2000. It seemed about to win again in 2004 when the Madrid train bombings propelled a renewed Socialist Party (PSOE) into office. The booming economy, plus measures to counter discrimination on the grounds of gender and sexual orientation (see Chapters 1 and 8), as well as the PSOE's apparently more successful (because more flexible) stance towards demands for greater regional autonomy (see Chapter 2), made things uncomfortable for PP, and its new leader Mariano Rajoy. Under pressure from, for example, the Catholic church, victims groups and Spanish nationalists, the party risked a return to the kind of (moral) conservatism that put it at odds with more moderate voters and in 2008 it suffered its second election defeat in a row. By 2012, however, the Spanish economy was in deep trouble and so was the socialist government, setting the stage for a big election win for PP.

For most of its life, the Conservative Party in the UK was a pragmatic operator, using its claim to be 'the natural party of government' and its unashamed nationalism to ensure that any concessions to social democracy (such as public ownership and the welfare state) were kept within limits. It was not until 1979, with the coming to power of Margaret Thatcher, that the Conservatives attempted – with some success – to roll back these concessions in pursuit of a more ideological free-market approach. Helped by the weakness of its Labour opponent, the party stayed in power for eighteen years, but the price of longevity proved high: by 1997 it was faction-ridden, sleazy, and had even managed to blow the reputation for economic competence that had allowed it to overcome suspicions about its supposed lack of social compassion. Its increasingly hostile attitude to the EU, and its traditionally tough line on immigration and law and order appealed to large numbers of voters, but nowhere near enough to win a general election against a rejuvenated Labour Party which appeared to combine economic efficiency with social justice. Seen as old, out of touch, and (ironically) too ideological, the party lost a second and third election before it finally turned to a leader, David Cameron, who in opposition committed his party to 'fighting on the centre ground' but who, once he became leader of the country's first coalition government since 1945, produced economic and social policies that recalled Thatcher (see Bale, 2011 and 2012).

Whether Cameron's strategy pays off remains to be seen. He appeared, though, to have taken some heart from Sweden where, at a general election at the end of 2006, a centre-right (or *bourgeois*) alliance led by the Swedish conservatives, the *Moderata samlingspartiet* (the Moderates) was elected to office. Their leader, Fredrik Reinfeldt, had been something of a neoliberal but, soon after taking on the job in 2003, he did everything he could to suggest the party would move to the centre: the country's generous welfare state and (in his view) overregulated labour market needed only adjustment not tearing apart; tax cuts, yes, but only for the lower paid. For a while, he even went so far as to ape Tony Blair by rebranding his party as *De Nya Moderaterna* – the New Moderates. Opponents suggested this was merely a marketing tactic. In fact, two consecutive terms in government, during which some liberalization has occurred but not to the extent feared by some on the left, suggest that Sweden's conservative party is, by its very nature, more moderate than its sister party in the UK (Lindbom, 2008).

to emphasize the fact that, outside traditional strongholds like Austria, Belgium and (until the early 1990s) Italy, some Christian democratic parties (for example, in Germany and the Netherlands) came to appeal to Protestants as well. In fact, in almost uniformly Protestant Scandinavia, they could do little else. Ecumenical appeals, however, cannot completely insulate the Christian democrats from the decline in the number of western Europeans who are practising Christians (see Chapter 1). On the other hand, Christian democrats outside Scandinavia (where they continue to concentrate

their appeal to people of faith) have, since the Second World War pursued a 'catch-all' strategy (see Box 5.1). Their centrist, pragmatic policies consciously appeal to as wide an audience as possible even as they begin to adapt slightly more 'neoliberal' economic policies and, in so doing, start to look increasingly like secular conservative parties (see van Hecke and Gerard, 2004). Outside of Germany, this does not seem to be working particularly well electorally, although a declining vote share has not necessarily denied Christian democratic parties the chance to govern, at least in coalition (see Bale and

---

BOX 5.5

Crossing classes and denominations – Christian democratic parties

Germany's *Christlich-Demokratische Union* (CDU) traces its roots back to the predominantly Catholic Centre Party of the interwar years. Indeed, Christian democracy in Germany still attracts disproportionate support from Catholics, especially in Bavaria, the stronghold of the CDU's sister-party, the *Christian Social Union* (CSU). But its appeal in the postwar period has been non-denominational and to a great extent non-religious in character. It became, in effect, one of Europe's archetypal 'catch-all' parties (see Box 5.1 and Green and Turner, 2013). Unlike its Bavarian sister-party, the CDU is not overtly nationalistic, nor morally or socially very conservative. Although in recent years it has been influenced – just like its similarly 'cross-confessional' Dutch counterpart, the *Christen Democratisch Appèl* (CDA) – by economic liberalism, it continues to see a place for government intervention, for consultation with trade unions and for a strong, insurance-based, welfare state (see Chapter 1). After dominating German politics in the 1980s and 1990s, the CDU then enjoyed rather less luck until it narrowly 'won' the 2005 general election under its new (and first) female leader Angela Merkel, who was, however, forced to form a 'grand coalition' with bitter rivals, the SPD. After the next election in 2009, Merkel, who exudes calm and competence rather than charisma, was able to form a centre-right coalition with the market liberal FDP instead and was widely seen (with the help of economic reforms pushed through by the SDP in previous years) to have steered the country through economically choppy waters. Her insistence that those Eurozone countries that ran into trouble after 2008 impose harsh measures in order to rebalance their books should not, however, fool anyone into thinking she is some sort of neoliberal – the German Maggie Thatcher: she has made clear her support for the introduction of a minimum wage and even expressed interest in a European financial transaction tax.

Norway's *Kristelig Folkeparti* – the model for the Christian democratic parties of Scandinavia – might be a member of the same party family as the CDU, but is different in many ways that may even challenge the notion that there is such a thing as a pan-European party family. Far from being a catch-all party (see Box 5.1), it relies on a core support of Lutherans, many of whom feel very strongly (and conservatively) on social issues (particularly on their opposition to alcohol and to abortion) and/or their right to hang on to their particular Norwegian dialect (*Nynorsk*). The party, which was founded in 1933, is also geographically highly concentrated, and attracts nowhere near the catch-all cross-class vote of the CDU. For a while, its loyal support, plus the charismatic leadership of Kjell Magne Bondevik (who could claim the prime minister's post in centre-right governments even though his party was by no means the biggest in the coalition) managed to prevent it from dropping too far below 10 per cent. But, in 2005, it took less than 7 per cent and in 2009 dropped to just over 5 per cent – a share that may represent its core support.

Krouwel, 2013). The situation in the new postcommunist democracies is less positive, however. With the exception of Slovenia, Christian democratic parties either never got off the ground or, where they did, are no longer doing particularly well (Bale and Szczerbiak, 2008; Grzymala-Busse, 2013).

Liberal parties

These parties were first set up to promote the interests of people who earned their living from commerce and the professions, and lived in the towns and cities that grew quickly in the Industrial Revolution of the nineteenth century (Box 5.6). Early on, they promoted the legal, property, political and religious rights of the individual, in contrast to the arbitrary rule of a traditional, landed interest that was happy to see the state identify with a particular church. In the twentieth century, however, liberal parties seem to have gone one of two ways. The first, sometimes called 'neoliberalism', prioritizes a commitment to the free market and opposition to state interference in the economy as well as in matters of morality – all of which distinguish it from centre-right parties belonging to the Christian democratic family. In very recent years, however, this brand of liberalism has been concerned not to appear too 'soft' (i.e. libertarian) on issues such as drugs and civil liberties issues, and has begun to incorporate a hard line on immigration into its platform. The second strand of liberalism, sometimes labelled 'social liberalism', has generally not abandoned its reputation for tolerance and the promotion of civil liberties. It is generally more sympathetic than the first strand toward government intervention in the economy and welfare policy, believing that it helps to ensure that people can actually benefit from the freedoms they should enjoy.

The UK Liberal Democrats are an example of a liberal party in which these two strands co-exist – with the tension between them becoming more visible once the party, for the first time for nearly a century, entered government in 2010. Elsewhere in Europe, of course, liberal parties, whether on the neoliberal right or in the more 'progressive' centre, have been involved in government far more frequently. Sometimes this has been as part of a so-called 'bourgeois bloc' against social democracy (as in Sweden). At other times, they have been 'third

parties' able to join either a right- or a left-wing government (as in Germany) or a wider 'rainbow coalition' (as in Belgium and the Netherlands). In western Europe, they now poll on average around 10 per cent, though the range is large: from around half of the average in Scandinavia to two or three times the average in the Benelux countries, Switzerland and, recently, the UK. The liberal party family is also represented in some of Europe's newer democracies, even if, outside Romania and Estonia (where the liberal Reform Party is particularly strong), it hasn't performed particularly well in recent elections.

Green parties

In Europe, the Greens began to take shape in the 1970s and 1980s when 'new social movements' (which are defined in Chapter 8) campaigning against the supposed unsustainability and exploitative nature of growth-oriented economic development sought parliamentary representation (Box 5.7). Their appeal was said to be 'postmaterialist' (about quality of life rather than standard of living) or even anti-materialist: although the environment remains the primary focus, the green agenda also encompasses anti-militarism and anti-discrimination, solidarity with the developing world, social justice, and liberal tolerance of alternative life-styles – the kind of thing which (judged by their voters) appeals in particular to young, highly educated, non-churchgoing, city-dwellers (see Dolezal, 2010). Greens also differentiated themselves from so-called conventional, 'grey' parties by their continued (if, over time, slightly diluted) commitment to participatory democracy and local autonomy – a commitment which typically saw them adopt much flatter organizational structures than other, generally hierarchically organized, parties.

Although not as successful as the far right, the Greens are clearly one of the 'success stories' of politics since the 1970s, having found what seems to be a secure footing in several major European countries. And they have been in coalition government (see Rihoux and Rüdig, 2006) – not just in Germany, where the high-profile and popular Joschka Fischer became foreign minister, but also in Ireland, Finland, Belgium, Slovakia and the Czech Republic, and in France and Italy, despite their electoral performance in the last two countries being poorer than it is in, say, Sweden, Austria and Switzerland.

BOX 5.6

Two liberal parties; one country

The *Volkspartij voor Vrijheid en Democratie* (People's Party for Freedom and Democracy, VVD) may have been founded in 1948, but it benefited from a long list of liberal predecessors stretching back into the nineteenth century. During that time, politicians objecting both to the religious influences of Dutch conservatives and the statist inclinations of Dutch workers' parties were instrumental in progressive social reform and the expansion of civil and political rights. In the postwar period, the VVD grew to become the Netherlands' third-largest political party and in recent years has commonly formed part of the government, usually in coalition with the Christian Democrats, but also with the Labour Party. Their focus was on tax reductions and on decentralization, and, in the 1990s under their leader Frits Bolkestein (later appointed EU commissioner for the internal market and tax reform), on the dangers of immigration and multiculturalism. This potentially potent combination of liberal economics and populist calls for restriction and integration has caused internal tensions between members prone to division over the issues (see van Kersbergen and Krouwel, 2008). However, after a very difficult few years, its leader, Mark Rutte became, after the 2010 general election, the Netherlands' first liberal prime minister since the First World War, albeit at the head of a minority government supported by the votes of the even more populist (some would say far-right), PVV (see van Kessel, 2011). In 2012, he was re-elected, the VVD having confirmed its new-found status as the dominant party on the centre-right.

D66 (*Democraten 66*) is the Netherlands' other liberal party. It is much closer than VVD to the Labour Party on welfare and economic policy, and in recent years has stressed the need for investment in education and the environment. It has distinctive stances on constitutional reform (it believes in 'bottom-up' and direct democracy) and is very committed to the freedom of the individual above and beyond the market place. It traces its roots back to the *Freethinking Democratic League* founded at the beginning of the nineteenth century. But it really got going in the late 1960s as a reaction to the seeming impasse between liberals and social democrats – an impasse that was allowing the Christian Democrats to rule yet ignore the need to modernize the country. D66's stress was on the need to bypass class and religious loyalties in favour of participatory democracy wherein all express their personal values – so much so that some see it shading into the 'postmaterialism' exemplified by the Greens. D66 has tended to support governments of the left but, in 2003, entered a centre right-coalition – along with VVD! This did not prove an easy experience, especially when controversial support for conservative policies did not achieve the expected pay-off in terms of electoral reform, and internal splits began to occur. Finally, disagreement with VVD's hard-line Minister for Integration and Immigration caused D66 to pull the plug on its coalition partners, although it performed abysmally at the ensuing election, taking just 2 per cent. Fortunately, the unusually low threshold employed by the Dutch electoral system (see Chapter 6) saved it from a parliamentary wipe-out and in 2010 it won nearly 7 per cent of the vote, upping its share of seats from just three to a more respectable ten – a haul it improved on slightly at the general election of 2012.

The relatively poor performance in France and Italy is probably explained in part by their more majoritarian electoral systems (see Chapter 6). But it may also reflect the fact that Green parties have found it hard to progress in southern Europe generally: their strength in Spain, Portugal and Greece is negligible. It is not much better, interestingly, in Norway or Denmark. There, the lack of Green success may be due to the fact that the general level of environmental consciousness is so high that mainstream parties factored it in to their own platforms at a very early stage. In Denmark, however, there is (as there is in the Netherlands) a small 'Red–Green' party – one which joined a centre-left coalition that came to power after the 2011 general election. The appearance of such parties, plus the fact that Green parties

The difficult art of compromise – two Green parties

The first Green Party to make it into government in western Europe was the Finnish *Vihreä Liitto*, whose 6.4 per cent of the vote in 1995 was enough to earn them a cabinet seat in a so-called 'rainbow coalition' stretching all the way from the Left Alliance to the Conservatives. This was only eight years after the formation of the party in 1988, though Greens had been elected as MPs in 1983 and 1987. The coalition was returned to power, with the Greens improving their vote to 7.3 per cent and retaining the Ministry of the Environment. During their time in government, the Greens scored notable successes in extending conservation land and introducing more sophisticated environmental taxes. They were unable, however, to prevent a majority of MPs (most other parties were split on the issue) voting to begin work on a fifth nuclear reactor. In May 2002, the party met and decided to leave the government in protest. They made a point of saying, however, that they would be willing to enter coalition negotiations following the next elections in 2003. This offer was, not surprisingly, turned down by other parties. But the party's tactics did it no harm at the ballot box and the party increased its vote slightly. The upward trend was continued in 2007, when the party took 8.5 per cent – enough to take it once again into a coalition government – and, although it lost some support in 2011, it was nonetheless invited to continue in office after the election

Ireland's Green Party arrived in government for the first time in 2007 and, although in Ireland it has never been quite so easy as it is in most European countries to analyse politics using left–right categories, it was difficult to argue that the coalition it joined was particularly progressive. The Greens had made their big breakthrough in parliament at the general election of 2002, and managed to match that performance five years later. When the prime minister came calling, and after tough negotiations which netted them a few bankable policy wins and a couple of significant portfolios (Environment and Energy), the increasingly pragmatic Green leadership decided it was now or never – and just as importantly managed to convince their membership, who had to vote on the deal before it could go ahead. The experience of other Green parties suggested that government might well be a rough ride, and so it proved: the party's last-gasp abandonment of a coalition widely blamed for the country's dire economic problems could not save it from a total wipe-out at the 2011 general election – a result which also meant that the Greens lost their state funding. Whether this means they will, like other minor parties before them (see O'Malley, 2010), effectively disappear from Ireland's political landscape remains to be seen.

have taken on more and more issues traditionally associated with the left-libertarianism, means that, although one can still argue that left–right values and environmentalism are not one and the same thing (not least because many traditional left of centre parties do not buy wholesale into the Green agenda), there is a strong tendency for them to go together (see Dalton, 2009).

As in southern Europe, the level of environmental consciousness in the postcommunist democracies, where material necessities are still very much the issue for the vast majority of the population, is very low. Consequently, the Greens are virtually non-existent in electoral terms in central and eastern Europe (see Hloušek and Kopeček, 2010: 73–85).

Virtually, however, does not mean totally. Greens entered government in the Czech Republic in 2006, although (as in Ireland: see Box 5.7) participation was followed by oblivion at the following election. Generally, of course, this kind of total wipe-out is by no means inevitable – the Greens in Finland have been in power, then out of it, and then back in it again, for instance. Moreover, the problems thrown up by government participation should not be allowed to obscure the other challenges faced by the Greens, not least their need, like other parties, to ensure that they move on and innovate in order to adapt to social and economic shifts and to changes in the composition and demands of their voters (see Blühdorn, 2009). In Germany, in particular, some see their now-traditional role as the 'anti-party' force in the country passing to the web-based Pirate Party (*Piraten Partei*) with its enthusiasm for 'liquid feedback' from online members and its mixed feelings about leadership and conventional forms of organization – an ambivalence which (along with their tendency to attract more men than women) has not prevented them from taking seats in a number of *landtage* (Germany's state parliaments).

Far-right parties

Far-right parties were first founded as highly nationalist, conservative and militaristic responses to the communist revolution in Russia and the economic difficulties that followed the end of the First World War (Box 5.8). After that war, they seized power – sometimes after being elected to it – in several European nations including, most notoriously, Italy and Germany (see Chapter 1). The aggressively expansionist policies of those regimes, their blatant disregard for democracy and human rights, and their ultimately genocidal theories of racial superiority, were largely discredited following their defeat in the Second World War. But this did not mean that some of the tendencies they managed to mobilize disappeared completely.

While few far-right parties in the West actively celebrated their connection with the fascist past, some were still willing to play on similar themes in the postwar period. At first, they enjoyed little success. But more recently – as hostility to immigration has risen among Europeans (see Chapter 10) – this has changed. Along with its xenophobic (anti-foreigner) thrust, contemporary far-right rhetoric is characterized by populism (see Albertazzi and McDonnell, 2007; Mudde and Rovira Kaltwasser, 2012). Although by no means the preserve of the right, especially recently (see Box 5.8), populism targets supposedly corrupt 'politics as usual', which, it claims, is conducted by cosy cartel of mainstream politicians more interested in their own survival than in the real needs or views of 'ordinary people'. Ideally led by a charismatic leader who promises to clean up the mess at a stroke, many far-right parties began the 1980s and 1990s by offering potential voters a mix of strong support for a low-tax, low-interference, free-market economy, and conservative social values – all of which appealed most to middle-class ('petit bourgeois') voters. Recently, however,

---

BOX 5.8

Populism: purely a right-wing phenomenon? You must be joking...

Italy now has something of a reputation for populist politics – but not only of the far-right variety. Many forget that former Prime Minister Silvio Berlusconi began his political career in the early 1990s by promising to come in as an outsider and clean up Italian politics – and to do so from the centre-right rather than the far right. The fact that, instead, he left it in even more of a mess has, together with the failure of the Italian centre-left to provide a convincing alternative, opened up space for another (and possibly even more unlikely) political entrepreneur. Frustrated with the failure of the existing political class, satirical comedian Beppe Grillo had already displayed his power to mobilize people back in 2007 when he used his web presence and social media to bring well over a million Italians on to the streets for his *Vaffanculo* ('Go Fuck Yourself') day of protest. In 2009 he launched MoVimento 5 Stelle (M5S), which, by deliberately eschewing formal organization and opting for a virtual rather than a physical infrastructure, soon began not only to mount demonstrations but field candidates at elections. It won a notable victory in the Italian city of Parma – long a stronghold of the right – in May 2012, at which point it began to register around 15 per cent in national opinion polls. The movement's platform could fairly be described as eclectic, but on the face of it looks more left-wing than right-wing, stressing as it does, not only euroscepticism (and of course anti-corruption and direct democracy) but also environmentalism, anti-austerity and anti-globalization. While it may be tempting to throw up one's hands and say 'Only in Italy!', it would be a mistake. After elections in 2010, political control of Reykjavik, the capital city of Iceland, passed to a new party (the Best Party) led by another comedian, Jón Gnarr. Its main promise – hopefully tongue-in-cheek – was to break all its promises once in power.

BOX 5.9

Different, but all here to stay? Three far-right parties

Jean-Marie Le Pen – a charismatic former soldier, active in extreme politics for decades and even willing to flirt with Holocaust denial took his *Front National* (FN) from relative obscurity to a seemingly permanent place on the French political scene, where it can claim to enjoy around 10–15 per cent support nationwide – and much higher in certain regions in the east and the south of the country. But there are limits to the FN's success. First and foremost, it tends to be more pronounced in presidential than parliamentary contests, which are fought under an electoral system which severely handicaps smaller parties who might do better under PR (see Chapter 6). Moreover, the FN's favourite themes of immigration and law and order are also grist to the mill of the centre-right *Union pour un Mouvement Populaire* (UMP) party (see Marthaler, 2008; see also Chapters 9 and 10). That said, Le Pen's successor, his daughter Marine Le Pen, who lacks some of her father's ideological baggage, performed very well at the 2012 Presidential election, where she took just under 18 per cent of the vote. And in the parliamentary elections which followed soon after, the FN won two seats – quite an achievement under France's first-past-the-post system.

In other European countries, the far right is led by rather younger leaders who, unlike the Le Pen family, enjoy the advantage of operating under PR and have worked hard to render themselves more acceptable to potential allies on the centre-right, in the hope that they will one day share in (or at least influence) government. A good example is Pia Kjaersgaard, whose *Dansk Folkeparti* (DF) has, since 2001, regularly taken between 10 and 15 per cent of the vote. For a decade until 2011, Danish elections led to the formation of a centre-right minority coalition which required the votes of MPs from the DF to keep it in power, giving the party considerable sway over immigration policy (see Chapter 10) without it suffering the fate suffered the Austrian Freedom Party (FPÖ) led by the late Jörg Haider. In 1999, FPÖ could claim to be the continent's most successful party of its kind, winning 27 per cent of the vote at that year's general election, after which it became a full coalition partner with the Austrian Christian Democrats, the Austrian People's Party (the ÖVP). But being in power proved rather more difficult than carping from the sidelines and, at the end of its second consecutive term in office, the party split in two, with Haider forming the Alliance for the Future of Austria (BZÖ) which only just squeaked back into parliament, along with the FPÖ, in 2006. But by 2008, the combined vote for the two parties stood at just over 28 per cent, suggesting that in Austria, as in many countries in Europe, the far right seems likely to be a fact of political life for some time to come.

they have made big inroads into the working-class vote, focusing more on promises to cut immigration in order to cut crime and to ensure that the traditional welfare entitlements of the native-born are not compromised by allowing in foreigners with unrestricted access to them (an appeal known in the jargon as 'welfare chauvinism'). Many are also proudly Eurosceptic (Vasilopoulou, 2011). Meanwhile, their economic policies, such as they are, are, if anything, rather centrist (see de Lange, 2007). Generally, while there are of course differences between individual far-right parties in different countries, those differences are no greater than those which characterize, say, individual

Christian Democratic or conservative parties (see Ennser, 2012).

It is the so-called 'populist radical right parties' (see Mudde, 2007) which have gained ground recently in Italy, in Switzerland, Denmark, Norway and Austria (see Chapters 9 and 10). In central and eastern Europe, however, the issues of national minorities (see Chapter 1) and the Roma are more salient than immigration and multiculturalism (see Chapter 10). Consequently, the far right in the region tends toward the older model of ultra-conservative nationalism – perhaps mixed with religion, as in the case of the *Liga Polskich Rodzin* or League of Polish Families that was wiped out in the election of 2007 (see Pankowski, 2011) and/or barely concealed racism of the kind that characterizes, say, the extreme right in Germany or the BNP in the UK: for example, the Bulgarian *Ataka* or 'Attack' Party which won just under 10 per cent of the vote in both 2005 and 2009. Whether extremism – perceived or real – presents less of a barrier to office than before is a moot point: in Italy, the anti-immigrant Lega Nord was ensconced in the Berlusconi governments (Fella and Ruzza, 2011) and in Slovakia, a government put together by the self-styled social democratic party, *Smer,* in the summer of 2006 included *Slovenská národná strana* (SNS) – a party that seemed to specialize in demonizing the country's Hungarian, homosexual and Roma minorities; on the other hand, *Vlaams Belang* continues to be subject to a *cordon sanitaire* agreed on by Belgium's mainstream parties (see Box 5.10), while the Austrian ÖVP (Christian democrats) are clearly not overly keen on repeating the experiment they carried out between 2000 and 2005 when they invited the far-right FPÖ to govern alongside them (see Box 5.9).

Communist and Left parties

Communism provided an expression for those dissatisfied with the gradualism of social democracy and who believed that the replacement of capitalism by a collectivized, classless society could be achieved by rapid, revolutionary means (Box 5.10). In those countries that found themselves within the sphere of influence of the old Soviet Union, communist parties were able to seize control in the fledgling democracies that briefly replaced the defeated dictatorships after the Second World War. The regimes they established resembled the Soviet Union's in that they were essentially party dictatorships that replaced the market with state planning, trading off political freedom and private property rights for near-universal (though low-level) economic and social security (see Chapter 1). In the West, however, the prospect of communist parties winning power looked increasingly unlikely as the Cold War wore on. In Sweden and France, admittedly, the Communist Party supported social-democratic administrations on more than one occasion. But in Italy, where the communists (the PCI) received significant electoral support, they were largely kept out of formal participation in government by an American-backed agreement on the part of other parties to form whatever coalitions were necessary to keep them out. This was in spite of their fairly flexible, forward-looking, democratic and less state-centric 'Eurocommunist' stance.

The end of the Cold War, however, has presented the radical left with a new opportunity. So, too, has the tendency of social democratic parties to back away, in word if not necessarily in deed (see Chapter 9), from state ownership, high taxation and generous social spending. Former communists, now calling themselves *Left* parties, consciously provide a home for those dissatisfied with social democrats' defence of the welfare state and labour market protection (see March, 2011). But they also stress so-called 'new politics' (or postmaterialist) issues, such as anti-discrimination, aid to the developing world, environmental awareness, anti-militarism and, increasingly, anti-globalization, as well as opposition to what they claim is the neoliberal agenda of the EU (see Heine, 2010). These new-politics values mean that many (Western) former communist parties now have a lot in common with parties first set up in places such as Denmark and Norway in the 1960s to offer a radical alternative to both communism and social democracy.

Some left parties, however, have not adapted, neither have they fared so well. The French PCF, for example, is a shadow of its former self, and in Spain, the path toward modernization has been an uneven and slow one, perhaps because, for some time, the Communists were keener on using *Izquierda Unida* (United Left) as a front organization they could control rather than a genuinely new formation. In Germany, the PDS – formerly the Communist Party that ran East Germany in the days of the Soviet bloc (see Chapter 1) – initially drew nearly all its strength from that part of the country and therefore seemed doomed to limited success. However, it then formed an electoral alliance with a breakaway party from the social democratic SPD and in June 2007 the two organizations merged to form *Die Linke* (see Hough *et al.,* 2007). Since then, however, it has been prone to political and personal splits, and – on the federal level at least – continues to be shunned as a coalition option by the SPD despite the fact that, in other European countries (Denmark is one recent example), left parties have entered government (see Bale and Dunphy, 2011; Dunphy and Bale, 2011; Olsen *et al.,* 2010,). Meanwhile, it was recently

Making the best of a bad job? Three 'former' communist parties

The Swedish Left Party had its roots in the break-away from the social democrat SAP by hopeful revolutionaries in 1917. The party remained loyal to the Soviet Union from the 1920s until the 1960s, when a newly independent stance led to a partial name change. The 'Communist' label was finally dropped in the 1990s since when it has spent time acting as a support party for minority SAP governments (see Chapter 4). This role, in the halfway house between government and opposition (see Bale and Bergman, 2006), resulted in some concrete achievements on the issues it has made its own – gender equality and resolute defence of the welfare state. However, it ate away at its support, which dropped from 12 per cent in 1998 to 8 per cent in 2002 and then just under 6 per cent in 2006. Back in outright opposition it continued to find it difficult to negotiate a compromise between, on the one hand, a 'new left' agenda built around issues like civil liberties, anti-discrimination and environmentalism and, on the other, the old-style 'class politics' of its leader Lars Ohly, who quickly ran into trouble for declaring himself a communist, thereby allowing the media to rake up old allegations about the party's past involvement with the Soviet bloc. Ohly stepped down in 2011 after the party lost even more seats at the general election the previous year, to be replaced by Jonas Sjöstedt, a former union activist and MEP who took time out of politics between 2006 and 2010 when his wife, a diplomat, was posted to New York.

But 'keeping the faith' – choosing 'leftist-retreat' over 'pragmatic reform' (Hough, 2005) – need not necessarily mean electoral decline, at least in the short term. In the Czech Republic, the existence of the social democratic ČSSD effectively closed off the latter option for the KSČM. Instead, it stuck to its traditional ideas about state ownership and opposed market reforms and membership of NATO and the EU. It also tapped into nationalist fears about the reclaiming of Czech lands by dispossessed foreigners (especially Germans) and antipathy to economic restructuring on the part of those who had lost their industrial jobs as a consequence. The party made the most of its relatively large, disciplined membership to maintain a healthy share of the vote, particularly among older people. In 2002, these strengths, along with widespread dissatisfaction with the social democrats, the collapse of a nationalist alternative on the far right, and an eye-catching campaign involving topless models, delivered the Communists 18.5 per cent of the vote. Although things didn't go quite so well in 2006, they didn't get any worse in 2010 – but maybe only because the party's ability to attract disillusioned social democrats served to mask what many predict will be a slow, demographically-driven decline (see Hloušek and Kopeček, 2010: 54–6).

The one relic of the past the KSČM did ditch was the Soviet-style hammer and sickle on its logo (now a rather jaunty couple of cherries). Even this concession to modernity, however, has so far proved too much (but also it would seem unnecessary) for Europe's most successful left party. AKEL of Cyprus, for the moment at least, seems to have found (and retained) the secret of combining ideological and policy modernization with a nostalgic attachment to its traditional communist logo and subculture (see Dunphy and Bale, 2007). Its leader became Cypriot President in 2008, although he came under intense political pressure after a huge (and wholly avoidable) explosion at a naval base killed a dozen people and knocked out one of the island's most important power stations. Cyprus's need for an EU bail-out to cope with its banking system's difficulties may also affect his popularity.

revealed that many of its representatives are still being monitored by the security services: some commentators expressed surprise and sympathy; others thought 'quite right too', given that some members of the party seem unable or unwilling to distance themselves from the past

In the former communist countries of eastern Europe, communist parties – as we note above –

BOX 5.11

Insiders and outsiders – two successful regionalist parties

Europe's regionalist parties come in all ideological shapes and sizes. Among the most powerful is the *Convergència Democràtica de Catalunya* (CDC), the biggest partner in the Catalan nationalist union or CiU (see Chapter 2). Formed at the end of the Franco regime, it dominated politics in the province of Catalunya throughout the 1980s and 1990s, under its leader (and five-term head of the Catalan government, the *Generalitat*), Jordi Pujol. It also vies with *Izquierda Unida* (an alliance that, after all, covered the whole of Spain) for the position of third party behind PSOE and PP in the national parliament – a position it used to support the former and then the latter in government in 1993 and 1996, with ever more autonomy for Catalunya as its price (see Chapter 2). It is able to do this partly because it is courted by the other parties but also because the size of the Catalonian population means it can win 3–5 per cent of the nationwide vote just by fighting there. The politics of the CiU have been described as slightly to the right of centre, but above all pragmatic.

In Belgium, the *Vlaams Belang* (formerly *Vlaams Blok, VB*) campaigns not only for a fully independent Dutch-speaking Flanders (see Chapter 2) but also for the barring and even the repatriation of immigrants. Founded in 1977 by radicals impatient with the gradualist nationalism of other Flemish parties, it has a solid base in the biggest Dutch-speaking city of Antwerp and took 12 per cent of the vote in the 2007 general election, despite (or perhaps because of) the decision of Belgium's other parties to treat it as an extremist 'pariah' with whom they would have no dealings. Although this 'cordon sanitaire' continues, they clearly have to pay attention to the support VB gathers on issues such as crime and immigration, while fear of increasing its support has undoubtedly led to further concessions to Flemish demands for more autonomy. Attempts to ban the party – at least indirectly – may not have proved as counterproductive as many predicted and may (along with the name change from *Blok* to *Belang*) even have accelerated a move away from the overt racism that alienated some potential voters (see Bale, 2007) – but neither, it seems, have they done it much harm.

---

have generally transformed themselves into social democratic parties. As in Italy, however, where the once-mighty PCI became the (much less mighty) Left Democrats (DS), a minority of supporters who see this tendency as a sell-out have remained 'true to the faith', albeit with a now avowedly democratic stance. Support for these 'hardliner' parties is generally small. It has some similarities with the support base of the more traditionally inclined former communist parties of the West but it contrasts with that of the Scandinavian Left parties, which appeal to younger, more middle-class, urban and educated voters, as well as to the trade unionists that both kinds of former Communist Party try to target.

Regional and ethnic parties

Some parties exist to promote the cause of those who argue (see Chapters 1–3) that their group and/or region merits autonomy or even complete independence from the state (Box 5.11). In some western European countries they play an important role in sub-national, and sometimes national, coalition governments (see Elias and Tronconi, 2011). Most important are those in Belgium, where all party families that are active are also regional, representing either Dutch-speaking Flanders or French-speaking Wallonia. Most numerous are those in Spain. The views of such parties on economic or social and moral issues vary considerably from left, through centrist to far right. Regionalist parties also exist in the postcommunist democracies, where they sometimes represent national minorities who identify with another country, perhaps one just across the border. In Romania and Slovakia, Hungarian minorities (and in Romania plenty of other minorities) are represented in parliament, and indeed in government, by their own parties; so, too, is the Turkish minority in Bulgaria. In Latvia, the

Harmony Centre party, which draws its strength mainly from ethnic Russians, was the biggest party in parliament, controlling nearly one-third of the seats, after the general election of September 2011. Indeed, one of the successes of the transition from communism in such countries is the extent to which such parties have been included in coalition politics for reasons of both political necessity and ethnic stability (see Millard, 2004: Chapter 9).

Agrarian and Centre parties

Some parties were originally set up to defend and promote the interests of farmers – often small-scale producers and peasants – especially in Scandinavia (Box 5.12). This is still part of their identity but, as the decline in the number of people employed in agriculture has eroded their core support, agrarian parties have repositioned (and often renamed) themselves as *Centre* parties, moving, as it were, 'from farmyard to city square' (see Arter, 2001). Currently the most successful example is the Finnish *Keskusta* (KESK) which has proved capable of garnering up to a quarter of the national vote. Centre parties target middle-class, often small-town, voters looking for a party that will moderate both the left and the right. Perhaps as a consequence, they cannot easily be pigeonholed ideologically. Private enterprise and traditional morality is important, but so, too, is generous welfare, agricultural support and in some cases environmental conservation. In post-communist Europe – including Hungary where there was some early success – such parties barely exist, the one significant exception being Poland. There, agrarian parties reflect the suspicions of the still extensive (but often small-scale) agricultural sector that the larger, urban-based parties will sell out small producers to multinationals and the European Union.

The bases of party systems – social and institutional; luck and skill

Acknowledging that historical cleavages help structure present-day party systems need not blind us to the way parties may develop away from their original intentions and support. Neither does it mean

downplaying the extent to which parties either enjoy or make their own luck. Often, a cleavage can be given political expression by a party founded on one side of another cleavage but sufficiently flexible to incorporate other concerns as well. From very early on, for instance, the British Labour Party managed to express the interests not just of the working-class (owner–worker cleavage) but also those of Wales (centre–periphery). But, by the same token, parties cannot rest assured that they have one or other side of a cleavage 'sewn up'. To take the same example, Labour 'inherited' Wales from the Liberal Party, but now faces a serious threat to its virtual monopoly from *Plaid Cymru,* the Welsh Nationalists – just as it does (even more so perhaps) from the Scottish National Party, the SNP, in Scotland. Similarly, some argue (see below) the conflict over the reach and power of the EU will become a new cleavage in many European countries – especially, though not solely (see Verney, 2011) in the EU's more northerly states, which generally speaking contribute more to its budget than their southern counterparts. For instance, there is a British party devoted to Euroscepticism (the United Kingdom Independence Party or UKIP). Yet it faces stiff competition on that score from the much older, much bigger, Conservative Party; whether it is wise for the latter to focus too much on the issue, especially at the expense of more traditional 'bread and butter' topics, is debateable (see Bale, 2006) but it will undoubtedly pick up more voters on the issue than UKIP – as long, that is, as the country's electoral system (see Chapter 6) continues to favour larger parties.

KEY POINT

A country's party system is influenced not only on historical and contemporary social and value conflicts, but also by institutions like the electoral system.

This brings us neatly to the fact that, as well as the skill shown or the luck enjoyed by particular parties, their relative strength (or even their very presence) – especially at a parliamentary level – is explained not just by social conflicts but also by man-made, constitutional arrangements. Academic observers who take an 'institutionalist' (as opposed to a sociological) approach argue that the political 'rules of the

---

BOX 5.12

Two farmers' parties – 'ecohumanists' and populists

The Swedish *Centerpartiet* was founded in the second decade of the twentieth century as the Farmers' Federation, and functioned essentially as a parliamentary pressure group until the 1930s, after which it worked closely with the social democratic SAP. Cooperation continued until the late 1950s when the federation, sensing it no longer had a future if it continued to appeal purely to its rural constituency and to cosy up too closely to the SAP, changed its name to the Centre Party and began to take a more independent stance. This strategy proved highly successful for a while: in 1956 it had polled under 10 per cent, but by the end of the 1960s, the *Centerpartiet* could claim to be the biggest non-socialist party in the country. In 1976, it took almost 25 per cent of the vote and its leader became the first non-social democrat prime minister in forty years. It was not, however, the best time to be in office (the world economy was in a mess) and the party arguably became distracted by its strong opposition to nuclear power. It was not in office again until 1991, but by then only as the smallest party (scoring only 8.5 per cent) in a four-way non-socialist coalition that lasted only three years. Following that unhappy period, it helped keep the minority SAP government in power between 1995 and 1998. At the 2002 election, fighting on what it called an 'ecohumanist' platform, mixing social liberalism with environmentalism, it took just 6.2 per cent of the vote. In 2006, however, it threw in its lot with Sweden's centre-right parties and, not only raised its vote-share to 7.9 per cent but became a partner in the ensuing government – a position it maintained despite losing a few seats in 2010. The next year it elected a young leader, 28-year old Annie Lööf, suggesting it was moving further than ever from its agrarian roots towards an economically liberal and individualist appeal to voters.

Self-Defence (*Samoobrona*) started life as a Polish farmers' union in the early 1990s but – under the leadership of the charismatic populist, the late Andrezj Lepper – soon turned itself into a political party and, in 2001, overtook the hundred-year-old Polish Peasants' Party (PSL) with 10 per cent of the vote. Where the PSL, as a member of several coalition governments, had headed toward the mainstream, *Samoobrona* put itself at the head of demonstrations and protests by Poland's large agricultural sector. But, by calling for greater government intervention in the economy, it also broadened out beyond its agricultural base to express the concerns of the many Poles for whom the transition to capitalism has not been easy – the 'transition losers' (see Szczerbiak, 2003). It combined this 'economic populism' with calls to get tough on crime and corruption and, unlike most of Europe's centre and agrarian parties (see Batory and Sitter, 2004), did not reconcile itself to the EU. After the 2005 election (which saw it marginally increase its support), Self-Defence swapped its role as the quintessential outsider for membership of the right-wing coalition government, but found the transition from sloganeering to sitting around the cabinet table a difficult one. The coalition fell apart and some of the party's MPs began to desert it. At early elections, held in the autumn of 2007, *Samoobrona's* vote collapsed from 11.4 per cent to just 1.5 per cent, a loss of 1.1 million votes which resulted in it losing its place in parliament. It never recovered and in 2011, Lepper, who had earlier been convicted of using his position to obtain sexual favours from female party members, was found dead.

---

game' shape party systems just as much as cleavages, and neither rules nor systems should be seen as mere reflections of socio-economic 'reality'.

The most obvious institutional influence on party politics is the electoral system used in a particular country. These systems are examined in more detail in Chapter 6, so here we will limit ourselves to just a few key observations about their potential effects. Parties from some of the smaller or more extreme party families (such as the agrarians or the far right or the communists) could find it harder to win parliamentary seats in a country such as the UK. There, as in France, the electoral system does not award parties seats according to the proportion of votes received, unlike countries such as Norway or Austria. On the other hand, a 'plurality' system with plenty of small constituencies, such as the UK's, might well make it easier for regionalist parties, whose share of the overall national vote would see them failing to make it into parliament but for the fact that their support is concentrated in particular parts of the country. However, this effect, in turn, depends on the extent to which a proportional system has large or small constituencies or districts. The Netherlands' system treats the whole country as one district, offering little hope for regional parties. The Spanish system divides the country into regions, which makes it more likely that they will be represented at a national level. In other words, the size of a country's party system is – though not always in the most obvious way – influenced by its electoral system (Best, 2012).

Once again, however, it is important to stress that party systems are the product of both institutional arrangements *and* social forces – and that neither of these will necessarily prevent the emergence of a skilful or a lucky party nor guarantee the survival of a short-sighted or unlucky one. Things are doubly complicated because parties are themselves involved in setting and changing the institutional framework in which they operate. All this is most obvious early in the life of the new democracies of postcommunist Europe. There, at a time when it was difficult to predict which social cleavages would become important or salient, those political parties which enjoyed initial success tinkered with thresholds and district magnitudes in order to ensure such success continued (see Bale and Kopecký, 1998). For some it did, but some have declined or even disappeared as they were rendered less relevant by more pressing social conflicts and outmanoeuvred by other 'political entrepreneurs' (see Millard, 2004). As the Spanish UCD, which disappeared almost overnight after seeing the country safely into the democratic era, could have told them, voters are not necessarily grateful once the job is done (see Hopkin, 1999).

And while postcommunist party systems still tend to be more fragmented, polarized and fluid (Lithuania is a good example) than those of their 'never-communist' counterparts, in some countries (notably the Czech Republic, Hungary and Slovenia)

Figure 5.4 The German party system after 2009

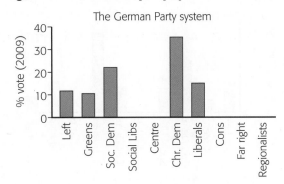

Note:
Left: *Die Linke*. (11.9%)
Greens: *Die Grünen* (10.7%)
Social Democrats SPD (23.0%)
Christian Democrats: CDU-CSU (27.3% + 6.5%)
Liberals: FDP (14.6%)

Source: Data from Parties and Elections in Europe, www.parties-and-elections.eu

they are now presenting voters with a familiar set of options and issues rather than a bewildering array of choices (see Casal Bértoa, 2013; Rohrschneider and Whitefield 2009; see also, for a useful single-country case study, Gwiazda, 2009). In many of Europe's new democracies (even those where party competition remains unsettled), a sizeable social democratic party, sometimes flanked on its left by a smaller socialist or communist party, competes against a more or less fluid right, though there are still centrist (e.g. liberal) parties that may be willing to play a role in governments of either bloc. This pattern would, for instance, be readily recognizable to Scandinavian voters long used to this kind of basically *bipolar, two-bloc* competition. French (and, more recently, Italian and German) voters would recognize the pattern, too (see below).

Figure 5.4 illustrates the relative strength of the parties in the German party system, mapping the actual parties' share of the vote in 2009 on to a graph of support for party families. Figure 5.5 performs a similar mapping exercise for our eight other 'core countries' at the most recent available elections. There is always room for disagreement about which party belongs to which family, of course, but it emphasizes once again that, although not every party family is represented in every country, a good many of them are. This makes generalizations about

Figure 5.5 Eight contemporary European party systems

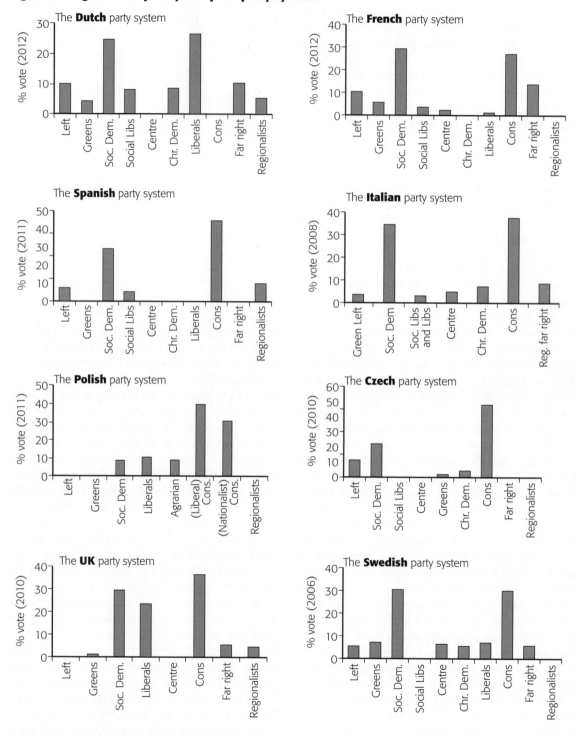

Note: See Figure 5.4 for the German party system after 2009.

Source: Data from Parties and Elections in Europe, www.parties-and-elections.eu

European party systems more feasible and credible even if (a) there is still room for argument as to whether systems in Central and Eastern Europe can really be described as fully **institutionalized**, and (b) it sometimes seems harder to convincingly collapse the various dimensions of postcommunist politics into an encompassing, conventional left–right dimension, making it more difficult to line up parties along it or to pigeonhole them.

> When political scientists speak of party systems as being more or less **institutionalized** they are not talking about the number of politicians in each country who deserve to be locked up in a lunatic asylum. Instead they talking, among other things, about its predictability, its stability, its legitmacy – the extent to which, if you like, it is taken as a given by those who stand for office and those who elect them (see Scarrow, 2010). Systems which have such characteristics are labelled strongly institutionalized. Those which do not – where loyalties are fluid and shifting, where parties break up, where no one can be sure from one election to another quite what's what – are seen as weakly institutionalized.

Party system change?

Interestingly, however, if the party systems of the continent's older and newer democracies are beginning to look more like each other, it may not simply be a matter of the former East 'catching-up' with the West – arguably a rather patronizing way of seeing things anyway. It could also be that politics in the latter is in flux – possibly, some would argue, because it is becoming detached from its historical roots. In other words, it could be that the Europeanization of party systems from west to east and north to south might be a two-way process. Voters and parties in the newer democracies might be taking time to discover where they stand. Meanwhile, in the older democracies both voters and parties are less and less likely to think, do or say things just because political custom and tradition dictates it.

This has led some political scientists to argue that, after years in which they were in effect 'frozen', party systems in western Europe since the 1970s are undergoing profound and accelerating change. The central features of this are an increase in fragmenta-tion (the number of parties in the system), accompanied and in part explained by two things: **electoral volatility** and **dealignment**.

As we show in Chapter 6, the evidence that cleavage-driven voting has disappeared completely is weak: it might not necessarily be foolish, even now, to think we could predict a person's voting behaviour from his or her occupation or religion. However, we would, indeed, be less likely to make a correct prediction than we would have been 30, 40 or 50 years ago. It also seems, as we show in Chapter 6, that predicting how a person will vote based on how they voted last time is less easy than it was. In the 1990s, every west European country saw volatility rise compared to the 1980s – in many cases, to levels never reached before (see Chapter 6). The most comprehensive recent survey (Drummond, 2006) paints a picture of relative consolidation between 1945 and 1970 giving way to one clearly characterized by 'increasingly erratic party fortunes' thereafter – a trend evident not only in the new parties (where we might expect instability) but (more significantly) in the older, established parties. Scandinavia in particular, has not only experienced high volatility, but has seen the newcomers gain at the expense of the old-timers.

> **Electoral volatility** occurs when voters switch their votes between parties from one election to another. **Dealignment** describes the way in which people's political preferences seem to be becoming less related to their location on one or other side of certain key cleavages than they used to be – preferences, in other words, seem to be increasingly individual and diminishingly collective, less fixed and more floating.

Postcommunist democracies experienced high levels of volatility in the first decade and a half after the fall of the wall (Epperly, 2011). Indeed, volatility remains relatively high and may well stay that way (see Millard, 2004: Chapter 5). Some analysts detect a certain amount of consolidation in eastern and central Europe as voters learn both where there interests are and which parties are likely to best serve them (see Dawisha and Deets, 2006; Tavits, 2005). Others, though, maintain that the stabilization of political competition does not automatically occur after a few years of flux (see Mainwaring and Zoco,

KEY POINT

Party systems are changing: in the west there are more new parties and the fortunes of (and the alliances put together by) parties fluctuate more than they used to; further east, things will not necessarily 'settle down'. But change should be expected and is rarely wholesale: left and right score about the same as they ever did.

2007) and note that the citizens of postcommunist states came to politics after, not before, the advent of mass education and media systems, meaning they might never take on the partisan loyalties associated with the earlier era (see Enyedi, 2006: 228). Certainly they have so far been less likely, on average, than voters in the West to stick with mainstream parties of left and right if they feel let down by them – and consequently more willing to give 'unorthodox' alternatives a try (see Pop-Eleches, 2010). Change, then, may become the rule and not the exception right across Europe.

What about *fragmentation*? Has all this switching of votes led to more parties? And are some of them new parties? Our answer – even if we exclude Italy, whose party system underwent an unusually complete transformation in the early 1990s once the corrupt Christian democratic DC could no longer frighten voters with the spectre of a communist takeover (see Newell, 2000) – has to be 'yes', especially in Scandinavia (see Drummond, 2006). But it should be a qualified 'yes'. There is no doubt that in many west European countries there has been a rise in the number of parties capable of making it into parliament. The increase, however, is by no means large and, according to recent research (Tavits, 2006) would seem to depend (a) on how long the country has been democratic (older systems have fewer new entrants); (b) on an electoral system that is not stacked against small parties (see Chapter 6); and (c) on the extent to which parliament (as opposed to major interest groups brought together by the government – see Chapter 8) has much purchase on policy. In addition, there have indeed been many new parties, but also many (such as the pensioners' party, AOV, which suddenly made it into the Dutch parliament in 1994) that have proved to be what political scientists sometimes call 'flash parties', disappearing into obscurity as quickly as they

Table 5.1 Party family and bloc performance across 16 West European democracies since 1950

	1950s	1960s	1970s	1980s	1990s	2000–9
Left	7.9	8.4	9.1	8.0	5.3	4.9
Green	n/a	n/a	n/a	2.3	4.8	6.1
Soc. Dem.	33.6	32.1	31.8	30.7	29.9	28.2
Left bloc	**41.5**	**40.5**	**40.9**	**41.0**	**40.0**	**39.2**
Liberal	8.7	9.8	9.6	10.3	10.1	9.9
Centre	6.6	6.9	6.7	5.4	6.4	5.8
Ch. Dem.	22.9	23.4	22.1	21.5	17.6	17.8
Cons.	15.4	15.8	15.2	16.3	15	15.3
Far right	1.0	0.5	1.6	2.2	6.3	7.8
Right bloc	**54.6**	**56.4**	**55.2**	**55.7**	**55.4**	**56.6**

Note: n/a = Not applicable.

Source: Data from Gallagher *et al.* (2011: chapter 8).

appeared. Of course, the green, far-right and regionalist parties that first emerged in the 1970s have not only gatecrashed their way into the politics of many countries, but also look set, eventually, to become 'old' parties themselves.

Yet even the impact of these successful new parties can be overstated. This is not because, as is commonly assumed, they cannot cope if and when their success thrusts them into government: they may pay a price at the ballot box for incumbency (see Chapter 6) but it may only be temporary; nor do they necessarily fall apart as organizations (see Bolleyer *et al.*, 2012). However, their disruptive impact (positive or negative) often fades over time because, for the most part, and sometimes in spite of their own efforts to retain their 'anti-system' or 'anti-party' reputation, they often become identified with one side or other of the familiar left and right blocs. The far-right parties have ended up either joining (as in Italy) or effectively supporting (as in Denmark) coalitions led by more moderate conservatives. The Greens may have argued that they were 'neither left nor right but out in front', but few voters buy this line and most green parties have gradually accepted their fate as part of the left – although recent developments in the Czech Republic, Finland and Ireland suggest this is not the case everywhere. Regionalist parties, it must be said, have always been harder to pigeonhole, but even this can be exaggerated. Few were surprised, for instance, when the Catalonian nationalists (CiU) supported the then minority government of the conservative *Partido Popular* (PP) in Spain between 1996 and 2000.

In fact, if we look at the support for the two blocs, left and right, across western Europe it has remained remarkably consistent since the 1950s (see Table 5.1). If we include in the left bloc socialists (including former communists), greens and social democrats, it still commands around 40 per cent of the vote across Europe. The right, if we include not only conservatives, Christian democrats and the far right, but also liberals and agrarians, continues to poll around 55 per cent – a margin, over the left bloc, incidentally, that, while impressive, is lower than the one that exists in central and eastern Europe, where, after 2000, it has averaged around 25 rather than 15 percentage points (see Hloušek and Kopeček, 2010: 216). Some have even suggested that, even if it is popularly believed that there is little policy difference between the two blocs or 'poles' in many European countries (see Chapter 9), they are attracting smaller parties from both the centre and the flanks, thereby 'bipolarizing' political competition (see Bale 2003; Krouwel, 2012; Mair, 2001). On the other hand, one can make the argument that recent trends in both voting (see Chapter 6) and government formation (see Chapter 4), suggest that parties and voters may well be becoming more adventurous or 'promiscuous' (i.e. increasingly willing to give new parties a try) and thereby encouraging parties to be just as innovative when it comes to putting together coalitions – innovation that, in turn, may encourage voters to embrace novelty still further. It is noticeable that the years since the end of the Cold War have seen governments in many west European countries joined or supported by parties that previously might have been considered beyond the pale (see Table 5.2). Although, such innovation may (at least for the moment) go on within rather than between left and right blocs, these are exactly the kind of trends that may move some party systems from what Mair (see above) called 'closed' to 'open'.

Should we, then, conclude that western European party systems are no longer 'frozen' but thawing fast? Rather than being 'caught up' by (unevenly) consolidating east European party systems, will they not instead meet them coming the other way? Quite possibly, yes. However, three points need to be made.

First, the apparently sharp increase in the pace of change in party systems should not blind us to long-term, albeit previously imperceptible, causes. These may well be sociological. The structural shifts in occupational, migration and family patterns discussed in Chapter 1 have almost certainly produced in every country a more heterogeneous and less tradition-bound electorate, for instance. But there will also be institutional causes. Mainstream centre-left and centre-right parties, for instance, might well have contributed to the partial 'de-coupling' of social class and voting (see Chapter 6) by their attempts to broaden their 'catch-all' appeal by stressing pragmatism and competence over ideology and particular interests (see Chapter 9).

Second, it is possible that, in focusing on what, some argue, is (so far at least) only relatively small changes to party systems, we may in fact be peering down the wrong end of the telescope. Perhaps, given the huge changes to European societies over the 50 years since the end of the Second World War, it is the lack of any correspondingly huge change in the continent's party systems that needs explaining! And here again, the danger of putting things down to *either* sociology *or* institutions becomes obvious. The lack of change in party systems might indicate, for example, that political scientists have always tended to overstate the links between those systems and social realities. Perhaps parties – and especially old parties – have found it easier to adapt to (and maybe even help shape) those realities that they are sometimes given credit for. Or perhaps the constitutional and electoral arrangements which they had a hand in designing have served to constrain the kinds of party system change that a more sociological approach might have predicted.

Third, the fact that, arguably, such change does now seem to be gathering pace does not necessarily mean that Europe's party systems will for ever more be subject to such volatility, fragmentation and dealignment that we may as well abandon the search for patterns and predictions and, indeed, kiss goodbye to the whole notion of party systems and even to parties themselves. If the twentieth century is anything to go by, change is a constant but often a gradual process, and by no means always in the same direction. Even so-called 'earthquake elections' (contests which see many of the old parties

Table 5.2 **No longer beyond the pale – west European radical parties in or supporting governments after 1989**

	Left parties	Green parties	Far-right parties
Austria			Government (1999–2006)
Belgium		Government (1999–2003)	
Cyprus	Government (2003–)		
Denmark	Support party (1993–2001) Government (2010–)		Support party (2001–)
Finland	Government (1995–2003)	Government (1995–2002) Government (2007–)	
France	Support party (1989–1993) Government (1997–2002) Government (2012–)	Government (1997–2002) Government (2012–)	
Germany		Government (1998–2005)	
Greece	Government (1989–90)		Government (2011–12)
Ireland	Government (1994–7)	Government (2007–11)	
Italy	Support party (1996–8) Government (1998–2001) Government (2006–08)	Government (1996–2001) Government (2006–8)	Government (1994–5) Government (2001–06) Government (2008–11
NL			Government (2002) Support party (2010–12)
Norway	Support party (1994) Government (2005–)		Support party (2001–05)
Spain	Support party (2004–11)		
Sweden	Support party (1998–2006)	Support party (1998–2006)	Support party (1991–4)

losing seats to new competitors appearing out of nowhere) rarely end up rendering the political landscape utterly unrecognizable – especially a couple of elections down the line. Party systems of the future will probably end up looking different from how they look today, but rarely completely so – just as how they look today strongly resembles how they looked three or four decades ago. Then, just as now, they will be the product of a subtle and reciprocal interaction of institutional arrangements and sociological realities, both of which will influence and be influenced by the behaviour of parties themselves.

Are parties in decline?

Whether party systems change profoundly or stay more or less the same, will many Europeans even care? Certainly few of them – particularly in bigger countries (see Weldon, 2006) and especially in east central Europe but also in the west – join parties nowadays (see Table 5.3). Even in those states where there is a clear link between party membership and jobs in the public sector (most obviously Austria and Cyprus) have experienced declines in recent years, the only significant exception to the rule being Spain where membership has continued to grow from the very low base established in the years of dictatorship. And, from what we know from various surveys, the vast majority of party members are inactive. They are also socially unrepresentative, being better-off, better-educated and older than most voters. Membership is heavily skewed toward men rather than women, although there is good evidence to suggest that if women join parties and rise through the ranks into parliament, they can make a significant difference to the platform of the party (Kittilson, 2011). Some young people – male and female – still join parties, but nowadays it is often because they themselves have ambitions to become professional politicians (see Bruter and Harrison, 2009). Interestingly, however, there is no evidence to suggest that declining membership has left parties with only their most ideological partisans: recent research shows that parties' members are generally more zealous than their voters but that, as ever, the difference is much, much smaller than is often imagined and that it is not getting any wider – all of which means that, even if their memberships are a diminishing resource, parties are no more likely nowadays than they were before to be pushed towards greater radicalism by grassroots extremists (Scarrow and Gezgor, 2010).

Still, if ever there was a golden age for parties in the postwar period, it is over now. There are many other things that people with more leisure and money can now do with their time, and, for the politically inclined, there are many single-issue groups that seem to offer a more direct (and possibly more enjoyable) way to get what you want (see Chapter 8). Members are still useful to parties, in terms of finance or legitimacy or campaigning (see Scarrow, 1994) – and parties may be responding to the lack of supply by making themselves more democratic (Scarrow and Kittilson, 2003). However, it would seem they are able to cope without too many people on the ground – especially if it means they will be free of the damaging impression that internal wrangling can cause in the media.

KEY POINT

Parties may not be popular but there is no better alternative: partly because of this they are increasingly publicly funded and are likely to be with us for the foreseeable future.

To many media pundits, and quite a few political scientists, high levels of anti-party sentiment and electoral apathy across the developed world indicate something of a crisis – one which might mean the long-term, even terminal, decline of parties as genuinely representative institutions linking citizens to governments (see Dalton and Weldon, 2005; Mair, 2006b). There might be some truth in these predictions of party 'failure', but we should not expect wholesale change – at least, not too quickly (see Debate 5.1). There is a great deal of inertia around, and parties are adept at adapting. For instance, in the face of reduced (or never very significant) membership income and of donations that cannot always be relied upon (or relied upon to be strictly legal!), parties in almost every country, especially in central and eastern Europe (see Smilov and Toplak, 2007) seem to have persuaded the states they help to run that they are worth subsidizing, although, in many cases this has meant them having to accept limits on contributions from other sources and limits on what they themselves can spend – limits which could be seen by some as an infringement of both of their liberties as private associations and, indeed, of free speech itself (see Scarrow, 2007; van Biezen, 2010a).

This so-called 'rent-seeking' has fuelled allegations that parties are indeed operating as cartels (see Box 5.1), although the latest comparative research shows that, in fact, state funding regimes – which often, incidentally, go hand in hand with increased state regulation of parties (see van Biezen and Kopecký, 2007; van Biezen, 2008) – do not seem systematically to tilt the playing field in favour of existing outfits and against would-be challengers, as suggested by the cartel party model (see Nassmacher, 2009). Nor, incidentally, does the same research support the common wisdom that politics has become exponentially more expensive these days, even if it does seem to show that parties will happily spend money if they can get access to it. All of this suggests that state funding is (a) unlikely to completely remove the

Table 5.3 Party membership: now and then

	Total number of members	Percentage of electorate belonging to parties	Percentage change over time
Italy (2007)	2,623,000	5.6	−36 (since 1980)
Spain (2008)	1,530,803	4.4	+375 (since 1980)
Sweden (2008)	267,000	3.9	−47 (since 1980)
Netherlands (2009)	304,000	2.5	−29 (since 1980)
Germany (2007)	1,423,000	2.3	−27 (since 1980)
Czech Rep. (2008)	165,000	2.0	−70 (since 1993)
France (2009)	814,000	1.9	−53 (since 1978)
UK (2008)	535,000	1.2	−68 (since 1980)
Poland (2009)	304,000	1.0	−7 (since 2000)

Source: Data from van Biezen *et al.* (2012).

temptation to seek out illicit sources of finance, and (b) may keep spending artificially high. Certainly, small donations from private individuals are much less important in Europe than they are in the USA, even though research suggests there may be considerable scope to narrow the gap, which should perhaps prompt us to ask why it is that parties do not do as much as they might to tap into an obvious source of funding – especially when it would help them reconnect with their supporters (something they always claim they want to do) as well as boost their resources (see Ponce and Scarrow, 2011). Corporate funding of political parties, on the other hand, seems subject to more variation – quite important (although skewed heavily in favour of the Conservative Party) in the UK, where pragmatic businesses seem to see it as a combination of insurance and lobbying, but less so in Germany, whose more coordinated form of capitalism (see Chapter 1) sees firms preferring to use collective interest groups to help persuade governments of their case (see McMenamin, 2011).

In fact, there are plenty of arguments which supporters of state funding can point to. Parties are the least bad option when it comes to ensuring competitive elections and contestable national governance. This is because they are, at base, information-economizing devices, providing distinctive but manageably-packaged alternatives (see Budge and McDonald, 2006) for voters who would otherwise be confronted with a chaotic choice of alternatives and

agents whom they could neither conceivably hope to know nor to trust. This is even the case in some of Europe's newer democracies where politicians swap party labels, and parties come and go, with astonishing speed (see Zielinski *et al.*, 2005). Parties – especially established ones – offer a reasonably predictable set of diagnostically-based responses to both novel and perennial problems. They also offer – in extreme cases – some hope of bridging the gap between the majority and minorities who feel strongly enough to pursue armed struggle. They possess sufficient democratic credentials – often exemplified in their own internal practices – to spare citizens the worry that those whom they choose to govern will turn around and deprive them of that choice next time around. Finally, they make it easier for those who did not get the government they wanted: if your team did not finish top, then at least it was beaten by an outfit or outfits playing roughly the same game under the same rules, and who you might hope to beat in the future. Parties, in other words, are worth funding because they are, in a sense, public utilities – something we need but which, left to our own devices, we might be incapable of raising sufficient resources to obtain and supply, meaning that the state has to step in so as to prevent a 'market failure' and underwrite political competition (see van Biezen, 2004).

That said, there is (as Table 5.4 shows) widespread variation in the regulation and the scope of funding across Europe, although the reasons for that varia-

	Parties obliged to disclose donations?	Limit per donor?	Ban on foreign donations?	Ban on corporate donations?	Tax privileges for parties?	Parties obliged to disclose spending?	Limit imposed on spending?	Direct public funding?	Public funding based on?	Free media access at election?	Media access based on?
Czech Rep.	Yes: all	No	Yes	Yes	Yes	Yes	No	Yes	Votes at current election + parliamentary seats held	Yes	Number of candidates
France	Yes: all	Yes: c. €5,000 per election cycle	Yes	Yes	No	Yes	Yes	Yes	Votes at current election + candidates + gender equality	Yes	Parliamentary seats held
Germany	Yes: all	No	No (but limited to EU)	No	Yes	Yes	No	Yes	Votes at previous election and membership dues	Yes	Mix of factors
Italy	Yes: above c. €6,000.	Yes: c. €10,000 per election cycle	No	No (unless they do work for government)	Yes	Yes	Yes	Yes	Votes at current election	Yes	Equal time
NL	Yes: corporate donations over c. €3,000	No	No	No	No	No	No	Yes	Parliamentary seats held	Yes	Parliamentary seats held (but also for new parties)
Poland	Yes	Yes: fifteen times minimum wage p.a.	Yes	Yes	No	Yes	Yes	Yes	Votes at current + previous election	Yes	Number of candidates
Spain	Yes: all	Yes: c. €60,000 p.a.	No	No (unless they do work for government)	Yes	Yes	Yes	Yes	Votes at current election	Yes	Votes at previous election
Sweden	No	No	No	No	No	Yes (but not public)	No	Yes	Votes at previous election + parliamentary seats held	Yes	Equal time
UK	Yes: above c. €7,000 (& €1220 in constituencies)	No	Yes	No	No	Yes	Yes	Yes	Parliamentary seats held	Yes	Number of candidates

Source: Data from http://www.idea.int/political-finance/index.cfm.

tion – which, not surprisingly, are intimately connected to parties' self-interest and discourses around corruption – are debateable (see Koß, 2010). Still, breaking down the data collected by van Biezen (2010b), there are some things that most states do. True, only half of them (40 per cent in the west and 67 per cent in the east) impose a ceiling on contributions on parties made by individuals, groups and companies. And even fewer – one-third (in both Eastern and Western Europe) – impose a ceiling on election spending. However, most (60 per cent in the West, 90 per cent in the East) ban certain types of donations. Eight out of ten (nine out of ten in the East) oblige disclosure of donations above a certain amount. Meanwhile, there are only two states (out of a total of 24 examined) where parties do not receive significant direct public funding – Latvia and Switzerland – even if some of the others (the UK, for instance) like to pretend to themselves (and to the public) that they do not.

Supporters of the role of parties in a democracy also deny that other groups can fulfil a governing function because governing involves balancing various social claims for resources. By definition, pressure groups and protest movements – which may indeed be better at expressing the direct material or identity needs of their participants, but which also promote one interest or cause to the exclusion of most or all others – are unable to do this, at least with any degree of efficiency and legitimacy (see Chapter 8). The idea that neutral, non-political state managers would be able to help them do so is patently false, since (as we note in Chapter 8) state bureaucracies sometimes fall victim to 'producer-capture' by well-funded and well-organized interests – even when overseen by parties with different concerns and constituencies. How much more likely and worse would this be without those parties around at all?

This is not to say that Europe's parties are by any means perfect. There is evidence to suggest that they still do a pretty good job of reflecting citizens' preferences and translating them into government (see Dalton *et al.*, 2011). But that hardly gives them the right to talk as if they have a monopoly on good ideas, especially when they know that they are heavily reliant on input from other players, including other parties – something which proportional systems that help facilitate coalitions implic-

itly acknowledge. This, and other elements of their gamesmanship (and their salesmanship), can drive some citizens either to despair, or away, or both, as evidenced in recent British and EP elections, for example. But a great many others enjoy politics at least a little, even if only as a spectator sport. There is little evidence that those who stay at home would be any more actively involved by some other means of legitimately organizing the periodic, and at least semi-public, surrender of collective sovereignty to a handful of individuals. Parties might well be no more popular than (and just as stuck in the past as) other despised professions such as used-car salesman, but people will almost certainly continue to use them both for a very long time to come – something citizens themselves seem to recognize (Table 5.5).

Whether tomorrow's parties will look exactly like yesterday's, however, is another matter. So is the more normative question of whether government by organizations which survive for want of anything better, rather than because they are truly representa-

Table 5.5 Feelings towards political parties – not close but necessary

	Feeling close to a political party (%)	Agreeing parties are necessary (%)	Identifying a party that represents their views (%)
Sweden	63	78	78
Spain	56	81	74
NL	55	85	n/a
Czech Rep.	53	73	78
France	51	n/a	59
Italy	48	n/a	n/a
UK	46	77	n/a
Germany	45	82	58
Poland	40	61	40
'Western' average	52	75	66
Postcommunist average	44	60	59

Note: n/a = not available.

Source: Data from Tóka (2006: 123, data covers 1996–2004).

Table 5.6 Transnational party federations

Party family	Federation	Website
Left	European Left Party	http://www.european-left.org
Greens	European Green Party	http://europeangreens.eu
Soc. Democrat	Party of European Socialists	http://www.pes.org
Liberal	European Liberal Democrats	http://www.eldr.eu
Christian Democrat	European People's Party	http://www.epp.eu
Conservative	European Conservatives and Reformists	http://ecrgroup.eu/

tive, can be said to constitute democracy. In order to cope with lower levels of partisanship and commitment, for instance, parties might well evolve into more 'open source', networked organizations with a much more shifting, less tightly-defined membership. Conversely (and rather more pessimistically), they might become even more like hollowed-out brands – still useful to those with the resources and skills to exploit them but increasingly intangible.

The Europeanization of parties and party systems?

Primarily because they contest national elections, we tend to think of parties as national bodies. However, in many cases – in response to the trends identified in Chapter 2 – they are multilevel organizations, operating and constituting themselves in both sub-national (see Deschouwer, 2006) and, as we now go on to discuss, transnational arenas. Sheer proximity aside, the EU provides not only opportunities to persuade and learn from other parties of like mind but also a whole new electoral battleground and set of issues (organizational and ideological) with which to contend (see Hanley, 2007; Ladrech, 2002; Mair, 2000; Marks and Hooghe, 2009). Nor should we discount completely the idea that, although they do not directly control, say, the European Commission, parties do have some traction in the EU and possibly some indirect influence on its policy outputs (see Lindberg et al., 2008). It is no surprise then, that political scientists have begun to look at the effect on parties and party systems of Europeanization – the potential we identified in the Introduction for European integration to impact on the constraints, incentives, resources

and influences experienced by hitherto 'domestic' political actors.

The impact on organization is immediately apparent. For instance, representatives of national parties elected to the EP need to work together, which they do by forming party groups in the EP (see Chapter 4). They may also be members of transnational federations outside the EP (see Table 5.6 and Johansson and Zervakis, 2002). Clearly, this transnational activity could lead to coordinated campaigning at EP elections – indeed, it has already done so in the case of the Greens in 2004. The tendency for the various national leaders of the party families to caucus together before European summits might also both build on and facilitate transnational relationships that might have a policy impact at the European level, to the extent perhaps that centre-right leaders might, say, agree to coordinate a push for business deregulation.

> **KEY POINT**
>
> Parties are adapting to European integration but it has not undermined their primary 'domestic focus', although its indirect effects may pose problems as time goes on.

But there is an awful lot of 'could' and 'might' about all this when, in practice, domestic politics and ideological differences between national parties belonging to the same federation often get in the way (see Lightfoot, 2005). Party politicians attend the European Council as heads of government and tend to push their national interests as much as their ideological positions. For example, centre-left leaders in Sweden, the UK and the Netherlands from 1997 onwards might have been interested in reforming the CAP, but their counterparts in France and Germany did not stand shoulder-to-shoulder with them; and on liberalization of the European economy during the same period, the agenda was driven by an alliance between a centre-left prime minister in the UK (Blair) and a centre-right prime minister in Spain (Aznar).

It is also doubtful in the near or medium term whether the increasing power of the EP will change the incentives parties have to keep their activities largely national. For one thing, organizational change not only disrupts vested intra-party interests (Panebianco, 1988), it also presents coordination problems at a time when many parties already have enough on their plates adjusting to the moves toward multi-level governance, regionalization and devolution discussed in previous chapters (see Hopkin and van Houten, 2009; Swenden and Maddens, 2009; see also Hepburn, 2010). For another, parties are not so rich that they can devote significant resources to relationships between national parties, transnational federations and EP party groups (EU funding for which cannot legally be filtered back to the national party). In addition, we should note that the propensity to get involved in transnational activity may well vary according to ideology, with radical right-wing populist parties (often nationalistic and preternaturally suspicious of supposedly elite projects like European integration) least likely to cooperate in this way (see Almeida, 2010). Notwithstanding all this, we should remember that parties are, above all, adaptive organizations, and it could be that in future they will adopt a kind of 'franchising' model, whereby (like many fast-food chains) the component parts of the organization will be allowed a good deal of autonomy as long as they use and promote the basic brand (Carty, 2004). This less hierarchical structure might facilitate within parties the kind of multilevel governance they are having to adjust to both at home and in Europe.

On the other hand, political cycles in European countries show little sign as yet of synchronizing and are unlikely to, given different constitutional arrangements. This makes working together across national borders difficult. And, as we saw once again in 2009, the EP elections themselves are still fought largely on national issues under national systems and are not seen to impact that strongly on the policy direction of the EU, either by parties or by voters (see Hertner, 2011). They also tend to see incumbent parties suffer, irrespective of the party family they represent, making coordination between the levels (for example, between parties in national government and EP groups) difficult and, arguably, pointless. A party may have sent a lot of MEPs to Strasbourg at the last election but, if it is in opposition at home, its MPs could well be less enthusiastic than those MEPs are about European legislation, seeing it more as the product of a government they object to than the result of the hard work of their Euro-colleagues. Moreover, there have been very few major changes in party practices to allow those colleagues a greater say in the running of national parties. The latter have adapted, recognizing that they need to operate in a multilevel environment, but the shift in resources and control has hardly been huge (for more detail, see Poguntke et al., 2006). Finally, the influence of party federations and EP party groups on the policy and organization of the national political parties that belong to them appears to be minimal – and that is the case even when we look at central and eastern Europe, where we might have expected, say, the Party of European Socialists to have helped sponsor and shape nascent social democratic parties (see Holmes and Lightfoot, 2011; though see also Johansson, 2008).

None of this, however, should allow us to think that the structures and issues that form the environment in which parties have to operate (either as governments or in terms of electoral competition) are somehow unaffected by European integration. A major development since the 1980s, for example, is the extent to which social democratic parties – albeit at a different pace and with varying degrees of enthusiasm (see Dimitrakopoulos, 2010) – have reoriented themselves towards a more 'pro-European' position as they recognize, first, that coordinated continental action may make more sense than the pursuit of the same goals at a purely national level and, second, that the latter is no longer clearly demarcated from the transnational anyway. Whether, of course, this turn to Europe can continue quite so smoothly in the face of the stringent Fiscal Compact first proposed by the EU at the end of 2011 is debateable. The same caveat applies to Left parties, which have also had to come to terms with Europe, recognizing that, unless they engage positively in transnational politics in

DEBATE 5.1
Are political parties doomed to extinction?

YES

- Parties used to fulfil a social and a patronage function. Nowadays, there are more and better places to meet people and patronage tends to be seen as corrupt.
- They are losing members, especially active members: they are hollow shells.
- Fewer people identify with one party rather than another: football teams invoke more loyalty.
- The differences between them are less obvious now: it's all managerialism, not passion and ideology.
- Fewer people are bothering to vote for them: if votes are like purchases, they are losing customers.
- According to opinion polls, they are some of the least trusted institutions in present-day society, and people don't believe parties care what they think and that they are only interested in power.
- Parties are closed, secretive institutions that call for discipline and dedication from their members. This puts them out of step with a wider trend toward transparency, autonomy and more instant gratification.
- They can't survive without state subsidies, which they don't deserve but still get, thereby increasing cynicism.
- People nowadays – especially the young – are more likely to get involved in pressure groups than parties.
- Developments in IT and telecoms will soon allow us all to vote on every issue in instant referendums, just like we do for television talent shows, rendering parliament (and therefore parties) redundant.
- The media does just as good a job of exposing government wrongdoing and thus ensuring accountability.
- The media is, anyway, what counts when it comes to appealing to voters: parties (at least, as they are traditionally organized) are relatively inefficient vehicles for tomorrow's aspirant politicians.
- Politics and governance is becoming more transnational or even supranational. Parties are irredeemably national institutions that will find it hard to adjust to this new era.

NO

- They have never had as many members as some like to think. And, in any case, the boundaries between membership and non-membership are now quite blurred.
- Loss of party identification is no bad thing: we shouldn't expect better educated, better-off people to maintain the old tribal loyalties.
- Turnout in elections can go up as well as down, and the media tends to pay more attention to low rather than high turnout. In any case, turnout varies a great deal between countries.
- It's hardly surprising that people don't think much of political parties and politicians given the way the media portrays them; when people do have direct contact with them they tend to feel more favourably. Anyway, you don't have to like someone or something to realize that they have a job to do: polls show that people still think that parties are necessary.
- State funding of parties varies considerably, but if we want representative democracy then we have to pay for it somehow. It's like any public good – left to the market it will be subject to undersupply.
- Pressure groups push only their point of view and their issue to the exclusion of all others – parties try to produce balanced programmes that will appeal to a wider audience. Pressure groups are rarely internally democratic and are often financed by special interests.
- Anyone who thinks that there is enough time in the day for all sorts of often very complicated issues to be debated and then voted on by people who are understandably not interested in everything is living in cloud-cuckoo land!
- The media doesn't actually do that much investigative reporting. It largely relies on parties to structure and inform coverage of political issues, and to blow the whistle on government.
- Even those entrepreneurs (be they individuals or cause groups) who make most use of the media find it necessary, if they want to get into government, to capture or create a party as well.

general and with the EU in particular, their fears about the latter locking-in neoliberalism (see Chapter 9) are more likely than ever to be realized (see Dunphy, 2004; see also Charalambous, 2011). Green parties, too, like other parties that think of themselves as progressive, have learned to live with, if not completely overcome, their ambivalence (see Holmes and Lightfoot, 2007): in particular, success at EP elections has given the Greens extra exposure, while perceived failure has helped speed up organizational reform (Bomberg, 2002; see also Bomberg and Carter, 2006). All of this indicates (Bomberg, 2002: 46) that 'Parties need not simply lie back and "let Europe happen to them": they can (and often do) actively engage and exploit European structures for their own party political gain.'

In keeping with this, we should reflect on other recent research which suggests that, despite the potential for 'Europe' to provoke internal tensions in some parties, most parties can, by and large, incorporate 'Europe' into existing and familiar modes of competition. Party (family) stances, and voter preferences, on European issues might well be consistent with, rather than cutting across, their left–right (and their postmaterialist–materialist) positions (see Marks and Steenbergen, 2004). For instance, social democratic parties tend to favour a 'social Europe' that helps to correct market failures, while conservatives tend to favour a Europe that promotes the cause of economic liberalization and business deregulation – something that really worries left parties. Meanwhile, green parties appreciate the opportunities provided by the EU for environmental regulation. Far-right parties fear a loss of national sovereignty will undermine their ability to keep out immigrants and maintain a home-grown culture and welfare state. Partly as a result, and partly because left parties (at least before the Eurozone crisis struck) began to wake up to the need for transnational action, the far right would now seem to be the most determinedly Eurosceptic of all the party families (see Conti and Memoli, 2012). We should also note, however, that in recent years the mainstream right has found it more difficult than before to present a united front in Europe (see Wagner, 2011), with the British Conservative Party leaving the EPP-ED and setting up (with Czech and Polish conservatives) a new Eurosceptic formation,

the European Conservatives and Reformists (Bale *et al.*, 2010b)

Partly because of all this and partly because of strategic and tactical imperatives, the pace, direction and extent of European integration is itself becoming an issue for voters in national elections: voters can see for themselves how the EU impacts on their daily lives (especially in the wake of the Eurozone crisis) and, if they can't, there are plenty of Eurosceptic parties to draw their attention to the situation (see Szczerbiak and Taggart, 2008). Accordingly, 'Europe' is now a potentially potent war-cry – and some would argue even a new political cleavage (see Kriesi, 2007) not just in the UK and Scandinavia, where it has played a part in partisan competition for some time, but in elections all over the continent. It is these contests that are the focus of Chapter 6.

Before moving on, however, it is worth pausing, firstly, to remind ourselves that, with the exception, say, of the UK, the Czech Republic and Switzerland, mainstream parties of government in Europe have not been tempted to adopt the significantly more sceptical stances that characterize parties that are unlikely to make it into office and/or that represent specifically regional interests (see Statham and Koopmans, 2009; see also Elias, 2009). Secondly, we should ask whether, in all this talk of 'Europe' affecting (or not affecting) party organization and political competition, we might be ignoring more indirect effects – and more normative questions – that are just as, or perhaps even more, important. Research on these might be at an early stage, but it might well be the case that, as Peter Mair (2006a) suggested, any flow of policy competence to the European from the national level (inasmuch as the two remain separate) will (a) mean that, because so many previously available policy instruments (such as protecting certain sectors from competition) are no longer available, domestic political competition has to be carried out on an attenuated or at least altered agenda; and (b) weaken parties even further by making it obvious that the real power lies elsewhere (for instance, with unelected EU institutions and/or the interest groups that seek to influence them). This, combined with a lack of interest and respect for the EP that might spill over into views on national legislatures and elections, could lead to a crisis of representation (see also Bartolini, 2007) that cannot help but damage parties, except perhaps those that – in predictable populist fashion – jump on the bandwagon in order to exploit it.

Parties as doers, not simply done to

We should note, however, that parties – populist or otherwise – do not simply jump on bandwagons. They also build them. In other words, they do not have to accept the economy, the society, the voters, and the institutions they inherit: as 'agents' they can and do take steps to alter them to their advantage and/or in line with their ideologies (Deegan-Krause and Enyedi, 2010). The list is endless but would include the following: establishing new alliances (or even new parties) to fight elections and/or form coalitions; pursuing policies which target particular voters in the hope that they shift their allegiances; abandoning, strengthening or setting up links with interest and cause groups; making appeals which deliberately divide and polarize citizens; and changing the constitution and/or the system under which elections are fought. It is to those contests – to those who take participate in them and to the means by which their preference are translated into parliamentary seats – that we now turn.

Learning Resources for Chapter 5

Further reading

Katz and Crotty (2006), *Handbook of Party Politics,* is a great place to start. So too are Lawson (2010), *Political Parties and Democracy* and Krouwel (2012), *Party Transformations in European Democracies.* The case for party system change is most easily grasped by reading Drummond (2006) in the journal *Political Studies.* Most of the 'classic' readings are helpfully collected in Wolinetz (1997), *Party Systems* and (1998), *Political Parties.* Anyone particularly interested in parties should consult the following collections: Webb *et al.* (2002), *Political Parties in Advanced Industrial Democracies;* Dalton and Wattenberg (2002), *Parties Without Partisans;* Gunther *et al.* (2002), *Political Parties;* Luther and Müller-Rommel (2002), *Political Parties in the New Europe;* Mair *et al.* (2004), *Political Parties and Electoral Change; and* Dalton *et al.* (2011) *Political Parties and Democratic Linkage.* For stimulating reads on decline, resilience and Europeanization, respectively, see the articles by van Biezen *et al.* (2012), Yanai (1999) and the book edited by Külachi (2012), *Europeanisation and Party Politics.* Also recommended is the collection edited by Lawson and Merkl (2007), *When Political Parties Prosper.* For postcommunist states in particular, see Hloušek and Kopeček (2010), and Bakke and Peters (2011), *20 Years since the Fall of the Berlin Wall.* See also Spirova (2008) *Political Parties in Post-Communist Societies* and the collections edited by Lewis and Mansfeldova (2007), *The European Union and Party Politics in Central and Eastern Europe* and by Webb and White (2007), *Party Politics in New Democracies.* On party members, the must-read is the collection edited by van Haute (2011), *Party Membership in Europe.*

On the web

www.wikipedia.org – type in 'politics' plus the name of the country for links to parties

http://www.partylaw.leidenuniv.nl/ – guide to, and database on, the legal regulation of parties and political funding throughout Europe

http://www.europarl.europa.eu/aboutparliament/en/007f2537e0/Political-groups.html – European party groups

www.idea.int – party funding plus more besides

Discussion questions

1   What roles are political parties supposed to play in Europe's representative democracies? In your opinion, are there any conflicts and contradictions between those roles?

2   How has the way parties organize varied over time? Should we expect a party's ideology to relate to the way it organizes itself?

3   Why do you think some countries' party systems are more fragmented and/or more polarized than others'?

4   Do you think the 'party families' dreamed up by political scientists are useful guides to understanding European parties? What do you see as the pros and cons of categorizing parties in this way?

5   Why are there not representatives of each and every 'party family' in each and every European country? What is the relative importance of sociology, on the one hand, and institutions, on the other, when it comes to party systems?

6   What are the symptoms and causes of party system change in Europe?

7   Are there any arguments and evidence that suggest to you that some observers might be overstating the degree of change in Europe's party systems?

8   Do you think that parties are dinosaurs on their way to extinction or are they destined to be around for some time still to come? If so, why?

9   Why is it easy to play down the impact of European integration on parties and party systems, and would be right to do so?

ONLINE RESOURCES AVAILABLE

Visit the companion site at www.palgrave.com/politics/bale to access additional learning resources.

Chapter 6

Elections, voting and referendums – systems, turnout, preferences and unpredictability

The term 'democracy', like the term 'Europe', disguises a wealth of variation. Representative democracy, at a minimum, implies the chance for every adult to vote periodically (see Box 6.1) in order to help choose and hold accountable those who legislate and govern on their behalf. Democracy came to Europe in the late nineteenth and early twentieth centuries. But the process was far from complete even before it was set back for decades, first, by authoritarian dictatorships which began in the 1930s and, second, by the forty years of communist rule in east-central Europe which followed the Second World War. In France, Italy, Belgium and Greece, for instance, women won the vote only in the wake of that conflict; in most parts of Europe, they won it just before or not long after the First World War, although in Switzerland they had to wait – almost unbelievably – until 1971. On the other hand, in all European countries, the age at which people become entitled to vote (though not to stand as candidates) now matches the age at which they legally become adults, with the sole exception of Austria which, after passing legislation in 2007, now allows people to vote from the age of sixteen – an experiment that seems not to have produced spectacular or surprising results (Wagner *et al.*, 2012). There is more variation, however, surrounding the participation of citizens living overseas. Most states allow them, after jumping through a few hoops, to cast a vote in their former home district and to participate in referendums – something which has caused considerable trouble when their votes seem to have made a difference to electoral outcomes in places like Romania, whose diaspora can be pretty much guaranteed to support the centre-right against anything that smacks of socialism. Some countries, like France, Croatia, Portugal and Italy, however, have gone even further and set aside seats in parliament for overseas electors.

This chapter begins by looking at different electoral systems and their effects, including their interaction with the party systems we described in Chapter 5. It then goes on to examine the decline in turnout that some believe is coming to afflict all liberal democracies. Is it happening, and if so, why? It also asks whether voters are becoming more footloose. Next, it tackles the thorny issue of electoral behaviour. Why do people vote the way they do? Have party identification, class, and religion given way to values as a source of preferences? Are elections, instead, being determined by more short-term considerations? Finally, the chapter looks at so-called 'direct democracy' – referendums and the like – which is touted as one solution to disaffection and disillusion with politics-as-usual. Is it a viable substitute for the representative democracy that all European states, if not all those who live in them, still seem to prefer?

BOX 6.1

The timing of elections

In most European countries, there is considerable flexibility with regard to when elections are held. Naturally, all have a maximum (generally four years, though five in France, Ireland and the UK). Only Norway (where elections can only be held every four years) has a minimum time between national contests. The UK now has a fixed term of five years but this can be overridden if the government is unable to reverse a vote of no confidence in the lower house within a fortnight or if there is enough parliamentary support for a motion triggering an early dissolution. Sweden is also unusual in that it is committed to holding a general election every fourth September, irrespective of whether an early election has been held in between. Elsewhere, convention mostly has it that the government can decide when it wants to call an election providing that it is within the maximum permitted. Even in countries where this kind of 'cutting and running' is frowned upon and unusual, it is sometimes inevitable – as the Netherlands (in 2012) and Germany (in 2005) have both discovered in recent years.

Europe's myriad electoral systems

In all European democracies, the physical process of voting is still simple and similar and increasingly overseen by independent or semi-independent Election Management Bodies or EMBs (see Carter and Farrell, 2010: 41–3). Notwithstanding some isolated (though interesting) developments in electronic voting (see Box 6.2), most voters still enact the same ritual. They enter a private space with a ballot paper, mark it in some way to record a preference and then deposit it in a ballot box for counting later. Only then do things get complicated. The number and percentage of votes each party gets has to be translated into a number and percentage of parliamentary seats. The match between votes and seats is rarely exact in any country, but in some it is more exact than in others. The crucial mechanism is the electoral system.

BOX 6.2

'I-voting' in Estonia

The Estonian general election of March 2007 was the first in the world to allow voting over the internet. On two days in the run-up to polling day, voters could use their chip-enabled national ID card to vote from the comfort of their home computer. If they changed their mind, they were able to annul that vote and vote physically, though very few did. By no means everyone took advantage of this opportunity: over one million people have ID cards but there were just over 30,000 'i-votes' out of a total of just over 550,000 votes cast – around 5.5 per cent – with younger people slightly more likely to vote this way than their older compatriots. On the other hand, this was the launch of the process and it was one that went very smoothly – not surprising perhaps in a country that prides itself on how wired-up it is. E-Estonia, as it's sometimes called, has carried on with i-voting but it hasn't been followed by any other country in Europe, although Switzerland has made moves to allowing its citizens living overseas to participate virtually. This may be because of concerns about the technology and the costs. But it may also be because i-voting does not seem to have given a big boost to turnout since those who do it may well have voted anyway (see Trechsel and Vassil, 2011). That said, in the 2011 general election just under 141,000 people out of 580,000 who voted did so online – a huge rise to just over 24 per cent (see NEC Estonia, 2012).

Europe's electoral systems can be split into two main groups: **plurality/majority**, on the one hand, and **proportional**, on the other. One can then split

Plurality/majority systems use single-member constituencies or districts, with the candidate who gets a *majority* (more than half the votes cast) or a *plurality* (more votes than any other candidate) getting elected. **Proportional systems** – often known collectively as PR or proportional representation systems – make use of multimember constituencies or districts so that the seats a party gets in the legislature more accurately reflects its share of the vote.

Table 6.1 Who uses which electoral system?

Plurality	(List) PR	Mixed
UK, France (majority required to win on first of what will otherwise be two ballots)	Czech Republic, Italy, Netherlands, Poland, Spain, and Sweden.	Germany

the first group into two – plurality and then majority – and the second group into three – list PR, mixed systems, and single transferable vote or STV (which is used by only two countries, Ireland and Malta). Each of the systems is explained in more detail below. Table 6.1, indicates which system each of our common core countries uses for its general elections. Research suggests that both the original decisions on which system should be adopted and the tinkering with those systems that follows are often (though not exclusively) the result of parties pursuing their own best interests (see Gallagher and Mitchell, 2005: 539–40). Experience suggests, however, that parties – perhaps fortunately – don't always get what they bargained for.

Plurality and majority systems

Europe's simplest electoral systems are those that employ plurality and majority rules. These were also initially the most widely used systems, but they are now employed by so few countries that they may be more familiar to Americans than most Europeans. A 'plurality system', often called 'first-past-the-post' (FPP), is one in which the candidate who gets the most votes is elected. It is the system employed in the UK, with the exception of elections in Northern Ireland and elections to the Welsh Assembly, and the Scottish and European Parliaments (for details see Mitchell, 2005). A 'majority system' is slightly different. It requires that the winning candidate get over half the votes, with the most common way of ensuring such an outcome being a second, 'run-off' election between the top two (or more) candidates. This method is employed in presidential but not parliamentary contests in Austria, Finland and Portugal.

France, like the UK, conducts its legislative elections in hundreds of single-member constituencies (also known by electoral systems experts as 'dis-

tricts'). But there the similarities end. In France, there are two rounds of voting, the second held a week after the first. A candidate who wins over 50 per cent in the first ballot is elected but those who only win a plurality (i.e. the most votes of all those standing but not an overall majority) must contest a second ballot a week later against all of his or her opponents who won 12.5 per cent or more in the first ballot. In the second ballot, the winner is the candidate who wins the most votes (i.e. a plurality), although often (because many second-ballot contests turn into two-horse races) he or she will actually win a full-blown majority. France's president is also elected under a two-ballot majority system, with only the top two candidates going through to the second round. This system seems to encourage voters to 'vote with their hearts' first time around, spreading their votes around a diverse variety of candidates from extreme left to extreme right, and finally 'with their heads', eliminating the candidate furthest from their own stance – often at the request of the defeated candidate for whom they voted in round one (see Blais and Loewen, 2009).

Plurality systems can produce very disproportionate results, although the extent of the disproportionality can vary considerably from election to election. In France, for example, the centre-right UMP won 62 per cent of the seats with just 33.3 per cent of the vote in 2002; in 2006, however, while its vote share improved to 39.5 per cent, its haul of seats (while still disproportionate) dropped to 54 per cent. In 2012 its 27.1 per cent of the vote netted it 'only' 34 per cent of the seats in comparison to the 48 per cent of the seats which the Socialists won with 29.4 per cent of the vote. It all depends, in essence, on where a party wins its votes – a point well illustrated by the UK. On the one hand, a party doesn't want to spread its vote too thinly across the country. The Liberal Democrats may have won 22 per cent nationwide at the 2005 election but that netted them under 10 per cent of the seats in parliament because it was insufficiently concentrated to allow many Lib Dem candidates to win a plurality in individual constituencies – one of the reasons why the Lib Dems insisted on a referendum on changing the voting system (a referendum they eventually lost) as the price of coalition with the Conservatives after the 2010 election (at which they took just under 9 per cent of the seats with 23 per cent of the vote). On the other hand, it doesn't do simply to pile up votes in so-called 'safe seats'. The Conservatives only lost out to Labour by 2.9 per cent of the national vote in 2005 but they were trounced in terms of seats by 55 per cent to 31 per cent because Labour's votes were more efficiently distributed in the hundred or so 'marginal constituencies' whose results, in practice, decide British general elections. Even when Labour suffered a catastrophic loss of support in 2010, its 29 per cent vote share still netted it 40 per cent of the seats in parliament, ensuring that the Conservatives, even with a seven percentage point lead over Labour, had no hope of forming a majority government.

In fact, it is possible (although it has happened only twice since 1945: once in 1951 and once in 1974) that the party which wins most votes in the UK will win fewer seats than its main rival and therefore lose office. This risk, however, is by no means confined to plurality systems. Indeed, with the exception of Malta (which now has a rule declaring that whichever of its two largest parties wins the most votes must also win the most seats) and Italy and Greece (which both award a majority bonus to the winning party or electoral alliance to try to ensure that it has a majority in parliament), it is a fairly common occurrence in more proportional systems where coalition government is the norm.

PR systems

In fact, by far the majority of European countries use electoral systems that attempt to ensure that the share of seats a party has in parliament more or less reflects the (nationwide) share of the vote it received at the election, accepting that this more often than not means multiparty politics and coalition government. However, there are many subtle variations in the systems used by each country, all of which affect just how accurately votes are converted into seats. Although the advocates of PR emphasize its 'fairness' when compared to FPP systems, most are aware that what are all too easily dismissed as dull, technical differences between proportional systems are actually crucially important in determining which parties are likely to do well, or at least better than their competitors.

That this is the case is not surprising, given PR's history. It did not replace FPP as the system used by most countries (beginning with Belgium in 1899 and Sweden in 1907) because it was universally acknowledged to be fairer or more rational. Some even argue that it started out – at least in part – as the means by which the various parties representing the privileged and the propertied hoped to survive the coming of universal suffrage, and thus the enfranchisement of the working class (see Boix, 1999; see also Kreuzer, 2010). It was widely assumed that such parties would suffer if they stood in individual constituencies because their better-off voters would always be in the minority. The only way this could be avoided without a shift to PR was if constituency boundaries were drawn so as to make some of them middle-class strongholds and/or just one party could be pretty confident of mopping up the anti-socialist vote – both of which applied in the UK, which stuck to FPP. Other analysts argue that the choice of electoral system depended more on the type or style of capitalism that operated in a country (see Chapter 1): liberal capitalist countries like the UK chose FPP; but 'protocorporatist' countries, where parties across the spectrum were already tied more closely to organized economic interests (business, unions, farmers etc.) used to bargaining with each other, chose PR – largely because it precluded parties having to appeal too far beyond the niches that that they had established (see Cusack *et al.*, 2010).

Whatever the explanation, it is undoubtedly true that, since these first changes, parties of all stripes have continued to play a major role in determining the 'rules of the game' and, unsurprisingly, have done their best to ensure that they are helped (or at least not harmed) by the sophistication and the subtleties of those rules. However, their thinking on such things tends to be pretty short-term, and their best-laid plans to protect and promote their own interests often prove futile and even counterproductive (see Andrews and Jackman, 2005). This is one reason, perhaps, why – outside of ongoing or recently completed transitions to democracy – major electoral reform is not actually that frequent (see Renwick, 2011; see also Leyenaar and Hazan, 2011). Knowing how uncertain outcomes can be, parties in mature democracies who do reasonably well out of the status quo are risk-averse, rejecting changes even when, on the face of it, they would seem set to benefit from them – in marked contrast to parties that are disadvantaged by the electoral system currently in place, who are understandably more prepared to try something new (see Pilet and Bol, 2011).

Interestingly, though, parties are finding it slightly harder than before to keep the question of reform, minor or major, to themselves, with the public exerting more pressure on them from, as it were, the outside – something which, the research suggests, may make moves toward more proportionality (which is what elite bargaining tends to produce) less likely but moves towards personalization (the ability of voters to express a preference for particular people and not just parties) more likely (Renwick, 2011). That said, a recent study of abortive attempts in three postcommunist countries to move away from PR towards majoritarian systems is a useful reminder that the cooperation and coalitions it is intended to facilitate make it all the more unlikely that first-past-the-post will make a comeback any time soon (Nikolenyi, 2011).

Before going on to look at some of the subtleties and sophistications of PR systems that either facilitate such things or else render them more difficult, we should first understand the basic differences between them. They can be conveniently divided (following Lijphart, 1999) into three: list PR systems, mixed systems and STV systems.

List PR systems involve voters voting in multimember constituencies or districts for lists of candidates provided by political parties or alliances of political parties. When the votes are counted, each list is awarded seats in proportion to the votes cast for it. In the Netherlands there is only one national constituency, which guarantees a proportional result overall. In other countries, however, regional variations could produce an overall result that is disproportionate. While some (like Spain and the Czech Republic) are prepared to live with such an outcome, others are not. A number of countries (mainly Scandinavian states, including Sweden) reserve a certain proportion of seats (normally 10–20 per cent) in order to correct any such imbalance – the so-called 'higher-tier' seats.

There is one more important difference between countries employing list PR. Some (e.g. Spain, Portugal and now Italy) employ 'closed' lists, in the sense that the party (or parties if they are fighting as an electoral alliance) determines the rank order of the candidates on the list: those voting for the list can do nothing to change that order. Others (such as Finland, Estonia, Switzerland and Poland) employ 'open list PR', where the candidates who make it into parliament off the list are determined by the voters who rank order or actually simply vote for the names on the list. Still others employ hybrids, whereby voters can express a preference within a party's list. In some (e.g. Sweden and the Czech Republic, as well as Cyprus and Greece), their preference can and does make a difference (see Karvonen, 2004). Popular candidates can leapfrog into parliament over those placed higher on the list by their parties, although the proportion of MPs thus elected is often only around 5 per cent. In others (e.g. Norway and the Netherlands), the rank order provided by the party nearly always determines things. Clearly, 'closed list' PR makes it more difficult for candidates who make themselves unpopular with their parties and therefore end up with a low list position, and thus strengthens the disciplinary capacity of party managers.

Mixed systems give voters two votes. They use one to vote for a candidate in their local constituency or district. They use the other to vote for a list in a multimember constituency (often covering a particular region). The list is 'compensatory': it is used to ensure that, whatever the results of the constituency contests, the overall result of the election is more or less proportional. Its ability to do this, however, is to some extent dependent on how many seats in parliament are constituency seats and how many are party or list seats. In Germany, about half of all parliamentary seats are non-constituency seats, a number adequate to produce a pretty proportional result: this is why its system, still sometimes called AMS (additional member system), is increasingly labelled MMP (mixed member proportional). In Lithuania, however, the number of party or list seats is insufficient to compensate fully for a disproportionate result in the constituencies, so its system can be labelled 'mixed-parallel'. Hungary's hybrid system is, broadly speaking, a variant of MMP, though its subtle contortions mean that, strictly speaking, it is 'a mixed-linked, majoritarian-proportional, two-vote system, with two-round majority-plurality and regional PR list elements and a compensatory national list' (Birch *et al.*, 2002: 60)!

The advantage of mixed systems is that they supposedly give voters 'the best of both worlds' – a link with a constituency-focused MP but also a parliament which accurately represents the spread of opinion throughout the country. Recent research suggests, however, that like any electoral system, it fails to live up fully to the expectations of its advocates and brings with it downsides as well as upsides (Doorenspleet, 2010). Recognizing these trade offs, however, is one way of coming up with a system that maximizes advantages and minimizes disadvantages (see Carey and Hix, 2011 for an interesting recent attempt).

In STV systems, voters in multimember constituencies or districts, are presented not with lists but with names of individual candidates (along with their party affiliations) which they are then invited to rank order. Candidates receiving a certain quota of first-preference votes are deemed elected, after which any of their votes over and above the quota are transferred (as if they were first preferences) in proportion to that candidate's voters' second choices. The same thing happens to the second-preference votes on the ballots of the weakest candidate. The transfer process continues until all the seats allocated to the constituency are filled by candidates reaching the quota (for a full description of this process, see Farrell, 2011). It may sound complicated to the uninitiated, but Irish and Maltese voters seem to cope perfectly well. To many, STV has the considerable advantage of ensuring reasonable proportionality at the same time as maintaining a strong link between individual legislators and voters, who will often pay as much, if not more, attention to the candidate than to the party he or she represents (see Marsh, 2007). To critics, STV weakens parties by heightening competition between its members standing in the same constituency when they should be focusing their fire on the opposition. They also

claim that it encourages MPs to take constituency service so seriously that they spend more time delivering benefits to and solving the problems of local voters than they do thinking about national issues. Interestingly, however, cross-national research suggests that how much contact MPs have with their voters does not vary that much between electoral systems (Curtice and Shiveley, 2009).

PR's subtleties and sophistications

The subtleties and sophistications mentioned above are myriad, but only two or three of them are worth focusing on here. The first two are features that impact on the proportionality of PR systems; namely, 'thresholds' and 'district magnitude'. The third is the mathematical formula adopted to working out the allocation of seats. All three can negatively impact on the proportionality of PR systems (see Anckar, 1997).

A threshold is a percentage figure of the vote that a party (or electoral alliance) has to score before it is awarded a share of seats in parliament or, if a higher-tier exists, a share of those seats. Thresholds exist in almost every country that employs PR, normally because of a desire to limit fragmentation (i.e. a large number of parties in parliament) for fear that this would threaten stable government – and, of course, the position of existing parties. Thresholds vary between a low of 0.67 per cent in the Netherlands and a high of 5 per cent in the Czech Republic, Poland and Germany, where avoiding a return to the extreme multipartism of the interwar years was uppermost in the minds of those who designed its electoral system. Basically, the higher the threshold, the higher the hurdle and the harder it is for small parties to make it into parliament. Given this, it is not entirely surprising that thresholds have been tinkered with in many European countries by those parties with a vested interest in preventing competition. This was a lesson quickly learned by the parties that initially did well in elections in the postcommunist democracies (Bale and Kopecký, 1998). After the 'velvet divorce' that saw Czechoslovakia split into two countries, for example, both new republics raised thresholds, particularly for parties that formed alliances to fight elections, and in 1999 the Romanian parliament voted to increase its threshold from 3 to 5 per cent, with electoral alliances needing to obtain an additional 3 per cent of the vote for every party

---

BOX 6.3

The uncertain science of electoral engineering – Italy and Poland

In 1993, Italians voted in a referendum to abandon their country's relatively 'pure' form of list PR in favour of a mixed system, combining party lists and first-past-the-post contests in individual constituencies (see Baldini, 2011). This, they hoped, would bring political stability by making it harder for small parties to gain parliamentary representation. But a fantastically intricate rule (the *scorporo*) brought in to buy off the resistance of smaller parties to the change, plus the willingness of parties to form electoral alliances meant the number of parties in parliament has not decreased anywhere near as much as many people expected. As the 2006 election approached, however, the then prime minister, Silvio Berlusconi (see Chapter 8), attempted to stave off defeat by passing a new electoral law which returned the country back to list PR. However, the new system (see Massetti, 2006 for details) differed from its pre-1993 counterpart by establishing higher thresholds (10 per cent for a coalition; 4 per cent for a party not in a coalition; and a minimum of 2 per cent for each coalition party), the intention being to encourage broad left-wing and right-wing coalitions. More unusually, the new system also featured a majority bonus: a coalition with the most votes but which wins under 340 seats in the 630-seat parliament is awarded that number of seats (i.e. 55 per cent of the total), thereby ensuring that one or other coalition will be able to govern. Berlusconi's gamble backfired: the election was incredibly close, with the left-wing coalition beating his right-wing alliance by 49.8 to 49.7 per cent (around 25,000 votes out of 38 million) and, with the winner's bonus, ousting him (albeit temporarily) from office. Although no parties outside the two pre-electoral coalitions made it into parliament, the latter still contained nineteen parties – so much, perhaps, for consolidation.

This would come as no surprise to Poles. Poland undertook a number of changes to its electoral system in its first few years as a democracy, with larger parties insisting that a reduction in fragmentation – the number of parties in parliament – would be good for stability and good government (as well as, of course, reducing the competition). Many casual observers noted that these seemed to work: the number of parties in parliament reduced quite markedly. After the 1991 election, the *Sejm* contained 18 parties (though, significantly, the Senate, elected by plurality, afforded representation to 31). In 1993, with the introduction of thresholds of 5 per cent for single parties and 8 per cent for alliances, the number declined to just six. However, the extent to which this reduction was directly due to rule changes, rather than a more general 'learning curve' that saw central and east European voters avoid wasting their votes on tiny parties with poor prospects (see Tavits and Annus, 2006), is debatable.

---

belonging to it. In fact, such manipulative measures are rarely foolproof (Andrews and Jackman, 2005), as the smaller parties in Poland quickly discovered (see Box 6.3). But they are by no means confined to Europe's newer democracies: Belgium, for instance, upped its threshold to 5 per cent in time for the 2003 elections (see Hooghe *et al.*, 2006), although, as often seems to happen, the goal of reducing the number of parties does not seem to have been realized.

The number of MPs allocated to each constituency – known in the jargon as 'district magnitude' – can make a significant difference to the proportionality of a PR system, especially where there is no second tier of seats to correct any disproportionality at the regional level. Basically, the lower the district magnitude (i.e. the lower the number of MPs allocated to each constituency), the lower the proportionality of the overall result. This arithmetical relationship results from the fact that, as some of us may remember from primary school, dividing a relatively small number by a relatively large number entails a greater likelihood of a remainder. Proportionality is therefore pretty easy to achieve in the Netherlands where (like Slovakia since 1998) the whole country is treated as one constituency with 150 MPs. But it is much less likely in Spain. There, in addition to having

Table 6.2 PR electoral formulas and the parties they favour

Formula	Largest remainders	Modified Sainte-Lagüe	D'Hondt
Formula favours	Smaller parties		Larger parties
Countries using formula for constituency seat (first-tier) allocation	Italy	Sweden, Poland	Netherlands, Spain, Czech Rep.
Countries using formula for list seat (higher-tier) allocation	Germany	Sweden	

Sources: Data from Birch *et al.* (2002: 27, 86), and Gallagher *et al.* (2011: 378-9).

strong regional differences, the country is split into fifty-two constituencies with an average of seven MPs per constituency. At the general election of 2011, this allowed the centre-right *Partido Popular* (PP) to form a single-party majority because its 45 per cent of the vote afforded it 53 per cent of the seats. The opposition PSOE could hardly complain, however, because it had taken advantage of the same sort of disproportionality in earlier elections. Almost invariably, such disproportionality favours larger over smaller parties: at the Czech elections of 2006, for instance, the Greens won over 6 per cent of the vote but only 3 per cent of the seats, whereas the Civic Democrats (whom they eventually joined in government) won 40 per cent of the seats with 35 per cent of the vote.

An electoral system can be made to work to the marginal advantage of larger parties according to the mathematical formula used to allocate seats to parties in PR systems. Table 6.2 deliberately eschews a detailed discussion of the mathematical merits of each formula (on which, see Farrell, 2001), but summarizes their effects. Some countries use one formula for allocating constituency seats and another for the compensatory higher tier of list seats. This combination can cancel out the bias toward larger or smaller parties. Others, which generally employ a formula that favours larger parties, do not have a higher tier and therefore the bias goes uncorrected: Spain is an obvious example. While these matters can seem awfully abstruse to some of us, they matter a lot to parties. For instance, in Poland, prior to the election of 2001, right-wing parliamentary parties, fearing (correctly) that the more unified social democrats were about to win a big victory, got together to change the electoral

formula from d'Hondt in favour of St-Lagüe, which is thought to favour smaller parties. It might well be that the change did enough to deny the social democrats an outright victory that year. Not surprisingly, the new government, led by the social democrats, changed back to d'Hondt in time for the 2005 election – although its move did little to save it from near-meltdown in that contest, illustrating once again that institutions aren't everything in politics.

Generally, we can say that the Netherlands (and Denmark) have the most proportional PR systems, with most others somewhere in the middle. The exceptions are Spain and Greece (and to some extent Portugal) where larger parties do better than, strictly speaking, they should. On the other hand, levels of disproportionality are still under half of that experienced by the UK and under one-third of that experienced by France. This is what we would expect: political scientists have constructed what they call an index of disproportionality (the higher the figure, the less proportional the system); worldwide, plurality and majority systems score 12 to 15, while List PR and MMP systems score 4 and STV systems, at 5, only marginally more (see Farrell, 2011). Table 6.3 illustrates the scores for our core countries.

Electoral systems and party systems

We noted in Chapter 5 that political scientists have constructed another kind of index to ensure that they don't overestimate the amount of party system change. The effective number of parliamentary

Table 6.3 The mismatch between votes and seats at the most recent election – and the effective number of parliamentary parties (ENPP) after it

	System	Disproportionality	ENPP
Netherlands	List PR	0.81	6.7
Sweden	List PR	1.25	4.5
Germany	MMP	3.4	4.8
European average	Various	4.5	4.3
Italy	List PR	5.73	3.1
Poland	List PR	5.95	3.0
Spain	List PR	6.93	2.6
Czech Rep	List PR	8.76	4.5
France	Plurality	17.66	2.8
UK	Plurality	15.1	2.6

Note: The higher the score for disproportionality the greater the mismatch, zero being a perfect match. Italy uses list PR but there is a winners' bonus for the biggest party or alliance. European average covers west and east and is for 2000s as a whole

Sources: Data from Gallagher (2012) and Hopkin (2011: 84).

parties (ENPP) combines a simple count of political parties in a system with a sense of their strength, ensuring that the presence of one or two very small parties won't lead us to record a big change. They have also used this to see whether the type of electoral system is associated with a country having more or less parties. Looking again on a worldwide scale and using the ENPP rather than simply the absolute number of parties in a system, there does, indeed, seem to be a relationship. Again, it is in the expected direction: plurality and majority systems tend to have two or three significant parties, STV systems three, and List PR and MMP systems four or five (see Farrell, 2011). Table 6.3 gives the figures for the effective number of parliamentary parties for our core countries and displays them alongside those for disproportionality, allowing us to see that there is an obvious (though not always exact) correlation between the two: although it's worth noting (once again) that List PR can produce quite different outcomes in different countries, generally speaking it would appear that, over time, countries with the most proportional systems also have more parties of some significance in parliament, with lower thresh-

olds in particular making a big difference (see Best, 2012). The ideological dispersion of the parties in those systems also seems to be greater: in other words, more proportional systems tend to support more extreme parties, while less proportional systems tend to promote clustering nearer the centre (Dow, 2011).

However, one of the biggest mistakes we can make is to assume correlation (some kind of relationship between two factors) means causation (suggesting that one causes the other). Doing so would lead us to think that, because countries with proportional electoral systems tend to have multiparty systems, the latter must be the result of the former, or that two-party systems are all down to FPP – views sometimes associated with Maurice Duverger, one of the 'founding fathers' of comparative politics. There are two problems with such reasoning. First, it does not quite fit contemporary and historical reality. For instance, the most solid two-party system in Europe is in Malta, but Malta uses STV. Historically, most of the countries that moved to PR just before or just after the First World War already had multiparty systems even under plurality rules – even if some of those parties did not get their fair share of parliamentary seats. And the move toward multiparty politics in, say, Austria and Ireland, occurred only recently despite decades of using PR systems. Italy's (as it turned out, temporary) move towards a less pure proportional system did not, as people hoped, cut down on the number of parties in parliament – something Poles could have told them (see Box 6.3). Secondly, as we have already suggested in Chapter 5, treating the electoral system as the prime cause of party systems would be to place too great a weight on institutional factors and too little weight on the social factors that also help to shape things.

Obviously the electoral system plays a role, but it is not necessarily the be-all and the end-all. As Carter and Farrell (2010: 36) note, 'the relationship between electoral systems and the number of parties gaining representation in parliament is a *probabilistic* one rather than a deterministic one'. If plurality systems really did create two-party politics and PR multiparty politics, how would we explain either the duopoly that exists in Malta, which operates STV, or the range of parties (albeit some of them relatively insignificant) on offer to French voters under their plurality system? Giovanni Sartori (whose work on party systems we referred to in Chapter 5) has persuasively argued (Sartori, 1997) that a plurality system cannot in and of itself produce a two-party system. This is because the existence of the latter also depends on limited polarization and on the absence of geographically concentrated minorities that are unwilling to be represented by either of two big parties (and therefore elect MPs from regionalist parties instead). On the other hand, Sartori suggests, if two-party competition does take hold, a plurality system will exert 'a brakelike influence' and 'a freezing effect'. By the same token, moving to PR (or a more 'pure' form of PR) will, of course, remove obstacles to new entrants. It may also encourage the splitting of old parties whose two wings previously had to put up with each other in order to avoid the electoral wilderness. But Sartori argues that this simply gives institutional expression to what was going on anyway – 'freedom to increase [the number of parties]', he writes, 'is no more the cause of increasing than freedom to eat is the cause of eating'. Given the epidemic of obesity now plaguing the developed world, however, one might be forgiven for wondering whether his argument holds water. Knowing you can walk out of the party taking some of your colleagues with you and/or start up a new party and still stand a chance at the next election surely might cause political actors to do something they otherwise might not even contemplate. Likewise, the consequent expansion of the alternatives on offer may well also encourage voters to vote in a way that would otherwise never have occurred to them. This goes beyond even the 'psychological effect' posited by Duverger (1954), who concentrated on the tendency of voters under FPP not to bother voting for smaller parties that (because of the 'mechanical effect' occasioned by their failure to win their fair share of seats) have no chance. Still, that psychological effect is important. It is neatly illustrated in the UK where, even discounting for their offering a chance to register a protest vote, European Parliament elections fought under PR produce much better results for smaller parties – notably the Eurosceptic UKIP – that rarely get much of a look in when it comes to general elections fought under plurality rules.

Academic disputes over the causal relationship (or lack of it) between electoral and party systems, however, pale in comparison to wider arguments about the relative merits of proportional and plurality systems. These are summarized in Box 6.4. Understandably, given the perceived political effect of different systems, there is considerable passion on either side. It is possible that we might be dealing here with what philosophers call 'an essentially contested question' – one involving so many underlying assumptions and motivations that it is unlikely ever to be satisfactorily answered.

Rather more practically, however, we can follow political scientist Michael Gallagher (see Gallagher and Mitchell, 2005: 571). He synthesizes a set of eight qualities that the ideal electoral system would deliver: (1) 'accuracy of representation of voters' preferences'; (2) 'socio-demographic representation in parliament'; (3) 'personal accountability of MPs to constituents'; (4) 'maximization of participation opportunities for voters'; (5) 'cohesive and disciplined parties'; (6) 'stable effective government'; (7) 'identifiability of government options'; (8) 'opportunity for voters to eject governments from office'. Different electoral systems score high or low on each of these desired qualities. Which one you prefer will depend on how you rank those qualities. In short, the choice of electoral system is like any other political choice: as well as depending a great deal on where you are starting from (since the past determines the present and the present constrains the future), there are always trade-offs involved, ensuring that there is no such thing as a perfect or one-size-fits-all solution.

Turnout – decline and variation

The fact that people bother to vote, even though the chances that an individual ballot paper will change the result are minuscule, has always preoccupied those who see politics as rational choice (see Dowding, 2005). Recent elections throughout the democratic world, however, have given cause for concern among pundits and politicians because the number of voters appears to be dropping – in some cases, like a stone (see Table 6.4). Some political scientists like Mark Franklin (2002) argue that the decline, while not insignificant (just compare some recent elections against long-term averages), is not

BOX 6.4

PR or plurality – for and against

The case for plurality

Voters vote directly for governments and MPs: less horse-trading by parties forced to water down their election promises in order to become part of a winning coalition; better chance of calling to account or completely getting rid of governments and MPs, forcing the latter to take account of local feeling rather than simply toeing the party line.

Stronger, and very often single-party, governments: administrations can pursue mandated programmes instead of delaying or rendering them incoherent through compromise; this allows them to tackle problems properly rather than waste time on searching for a consensus; governments more stable and durable; not prone to being blackmailed into unpopular policies by small, fringe parties.

Although some argue that such governments aren't as likely to provide as accurate a match with overall voter preferences, research suggests that any lack of 'congruence' depends on how polarized the party system is: in countries where the mainstream alternatives tend to compete with each other on the centre ground, governments formed by one or other of them can often be quite close to the so-called median voter (see Kim *et al.*, 2010, Golder and Stramski, 2010; McDonald *et al.* 2012).

The case for PR

Fewer 'wasted votes' on the part of people who vote for parties or candidates that do not go on to get into parliament.

More representative parliaments: MPs come from right across the political spectrum in line with voter preferences, providing them with a real choice; more women and ethnic minority MPs are chosen because parties do not need to worry about the risk of putting up a female and/or an ethnic candidate in an FPP constituency when voters are assumed (rightly or wrongly) still to prefer white men.

More coalition governments: legislation and policy theoretically has the support of a majority of voters and not just a majority of MPs; the need to balance the interests of various parties necessitates and promotes consensus politics – and prevents an essentially unrepresentative executive inflicting its programme on the country even though a majority of voters did not vote for it; the increased likelihood of having to take account of ethnic parties promotes consensual solutions to ethnic conflicts.

Little or no opportunity for parties to tinker with electorate boundaries (redistricting) in the hope of giving themselves an advantage – something that occurs frequently in the USA, and has occurred occasionally in the UK and Ireland.

Boosts electoral turnout – the proportion of people who actually go to the polls at a general election tends to be measurably higher under PR, not so much because there is a wider selection of parties on offer but because, unlike plurality systems which contain large numbers of safe seats that in effect belong to one party or another, most districts (constituencies) are, to a greater of lesser extent, competitive, thus making voting seem worth the trouble (see Selb, 2009).

Enhances female representation, although the impact can be overstated (see Salmond, 2006).

Table 6.4 Turnout in selected European countries from the 1950s onwards – long-term decline?

	Italy	NL	Sweden	Germany	Czech Rep.	UK	France	Spain	Poland
1950s	94	95	79	87	n/a	80	80	n/a	n/a
1960s	93	95	86	87	n/a	77	77	n/a	n/a
1970s	93	84	90	91	n/a	75	82	n/a	n/a
1980s	89	84	89	87	n/a	74	72	74	n/a
1990s	85	76	85	80	78	75	69	78	46
2000–09	82	79	81	76	61	63	62	73	47
Average	91	84	86	87	66	75	75	74	47
Latest	81	75	85	71	63	65	57	72	49

Note: n/a means not applicable. Italy has (barely enforced) compulsory voting – something the Netherlands dropped in 1971.

Source: Data from Gallagher *et al.* (2011: 306, 318) and http://www.parties-and-elections.eu/

as large as is often thought. Franklin also suggests that we need to start taking the levels achieved in the 1950s as an unusual high point rather than as a norm from which we have now sadly departed. Nowadays, for better or worse, he argues, there may be fewer 'great causes' and profound disputes. And we need to remember that a handful of high-profile cases of low turnout (most notably perhaps the UK election of 2001) do not necessarily constitute a trend. Rather they point to the importance of contingency in explaining variation over time within one country – something that is also stressed in explorations of turnout in CEE (Millard, 2004: 75–81; see also Kostadinova, 2003) and is, of course, obvious at particular elections, such as the presidential contest in France in 2007 which saw 84 per cent turn out compared with 72 per cent five years before and 80 per cent in 2012.

Franklin's analyses suggest that a shorter than usual period between elections, for instance and, more significantly still, a highly predictable result, both tend to depress turnout. So, too, does a feeling on the part of the electorate that, first, the differences between the alternatives on offer and, second, the connection between who is in power and the

KEY POINT

Turnout seems to be declining but still varies – between people, between countries and regions, and between elections – in ways that we can predict.

policies pursued, is vague. These factors can sometimes work in opposite directions: for example, the German election of 2005 looked like it would be desperately close, which should have encouraged turnout, but in the end voters' scepticism about the actual effect that a change of government would have on policy seems to have trumped everything, producing the lowest turnout in Germany since the war. What also depresses turnout (especially among worse-off voters) is inequality (Anderson and Beramendi, 2012). This is particularly worrying because it appears to be increasing (see Chapter 1) and because it may mean the needs of poorer people are ignored by politicians, even by those on the left, especially when (as in the UK) they have no serious competitor on that side of the political spectrum.

Such a result points to the fact that talk of fluctuation and only marginal change in turnout might, however, be masking the beginning of a trend downwards. Political scientist Peter Mair (2006b) drew a helpful analogy with climate change – one that anyone who has seen Al Gore's environmentalist film, *An Inconvenient Truth,* will readily appreciate. Of course, Mair conceded, there has been fluctuation before, just as previous decades have seen ups and downs in temperature and carbon dioxide. But, just as when we look at, say, temperature and notice that a disproportionate number of record highs seem to have occurred in the 1990s, so too have record lows in turnout.

Just as interesting as the apparent decline in turnout are the variations in turnout between

Table 6.5 The European turnout league table, 1961–99

85% +	80–84%	75–79%	70–74%	65–69%	45–60%
Malta, Belgium, Italy, Austria, Iceland, Luxembourg, Sweden, Denmark	Germany, Greece, Netherlands, Norway	Portugal, Romania, Finland, UK, France	Spain, Bulgaria, Ireland	Estonia	Hungary, Switzerland, Poland, Lithuania

Source: Adapted (and updated) from Franklin (2002).

European countries (see Tables 6.4 and 6.5). We know that the richer and/or more educated and/or more interested in politics a person is, the more likely he or she is to vote. Belonging to a trade union also increases the chances that someone will turn out (Flavin and Radcliff, 2011). And, in most countries, older people are more likely to vote than younger people, although one can debate whether this is inevitable due to a natural 'life-cycle effect' (see Goerres, 2007) or whether it is the product of a media environment hostile to politics that is affecting young people first but will eventually have consequences right the way through the age-range (see Wattenberg, 2011). Arguably, however, none of this demographic variation really matters as much as the fact that a voter is from, say, Sweden (where turnout is generally high) or from Poland (where it is much lower) – or indeed from Switzerland, which has a very well-off and well-educated population but consistently records some of the lowest turnouts at general elections in Europe.

There seem to be several reasons behind these geographical variations. One may well be inequality (Anderson and Beramendi, 2012). But, as Franklin's work shows, there are others. Compulsory voting, postal voting and weekend voting, and proportionality itself, are significant, as is the extent to which one party or another is close to getting an overall majority. But by far the most important factor is 'electoral salience' (the extent to which elections are seen actually to impact on the complexion and conduct of government). Countries in which elections are seen to mean something boast turnouts up to 30 per cent greater than countries such as Switzerland, in which 'whoever you vote for the government still gets in'. Compulsory, postal and weekend voting seem to increase turnout by just over 5 per cent each, while every percentage point closer to perfect proportionality a country gets is apparently worth around half a per cent in additional turnout – presumably because the greater number (and ideological spread) of parties with a genuine chance of making it into parliament increases the chances that a voter will perceive differences between parties, that he or she will find one to his or her liking, and that he or she won't abstain on the grounds that to vote for it might result in a 'wasted vote'. Countries that present voters with the possibility of voting for or against a party that is close (but only close) to getting an overall majority seem to have turnouts around 5 per cent higher than those that do not. Smaller countries have higher turnouts, but the difference turns out to be minimal.

Clearly, then, things need not be set in stone, but turnout does seem to be something of a long-term cultural phenomenon, albeit one that might also be affected by institutional arrangements. Fluctuation will occur over time, but even a record turnout in some countries may never come close to matching what would be a record low in others. Variation occurs between countries but there are also obvious regional differences. Within 'western Europe', Scandinavians – perhaps because they continue to display a stronger all-round sense of civic literacy (see Milner, 2002) and see voting as a duty – are the champion voters. Meanwhile the postcommunist democracies of CEE seem unlikely to reach the comparatively low levels seen in non-Nordic European states, although there is variation within the region. As Figure 6.1 shows, Poland seems to suffer from persistent low turnout in parliamentary elections – a die that also seems to have been cast in the Baltic republics of Lithuania and Estonia (but not Latvia). However, Slovenia, Slovakia and Hungary (apart from a blip downward in 1998) seem to have relatively 'healthy' levels of turnout, with around seven or even eight out of ten people voting. Meanwhile, the Czech Republic is a good illustration that what goes down can come up. There (as Figure 6.1 shows) turnout seemed to be trending downward after an initial burst of enthusiasm, and dropped alarmingly in 2002. Yet at the next election (which promised – and turned out – to be close), turnout ticked up again, although it dropped slightly four years later in 2010. Interestingly, turnout rose markedly (albeit from a very low base) in Poland in 2007 – an election widely portrayed as a close clash between two visions of the country, one outward-looking and the other traditional and nationalistic. That voters were more interested than they had been two years earlier when the parties promoting those visions were at the time seen to be basically on the same side and supposedly on course to form a coalition supports the idea that citizens in postcommunist countries are just as 'rational' as those in other European democracies – when more is at stake they vote in greater numbers (Pacek *et al.*, 2007).

A recent 'meta-analysis' (a study of other studies) on turnout comes to some pretty clear conclusions on what makes for higher turnout (see Geys, 2006). Turnout is higher in countries with historically higher turnouts, in countries with smaller populations (presumably because there is an increased chance that a handful of votes can make a difference to the result), where (for the same reason) the result is forecast to be close, where parties spend more on campaigns, where PR is used, where voter registration is easy, and where a number of elections are run concurrently. The most robust finding, however, is something of a no-brainer: compulsory voting ensures higher turnout. To some, we should ignore this: the right not to vote is as important as the right to do so, and there are (as yet seemingly unfounded) fears that obliging people to turn out will lead to frivolous or protest voting. Others, however, are much more worried about low turnout. There comes a point, they claim, where so few people vote that the legitimacy of the polity is called into question. They also worry about the fact that rational politicians are bound to pander to those who do vote (the better off and the elderly) and ignore those that do not (the poorer, the less educated and the young). Indeed, so worried are they that they now advocate the extension of compulsory voting to all mature democracies (see, for example, Wattenberg, 2011).

Volatile voting

We touched on volatility (the extent to which people switch their vote from one election to another) when discussing party system change in Chapter 5. In fact, even though we should stress again that much of it involves voters transferring their votes within rather than between left and right blocs, volatility may be even more of a phenomenon than the headline figures suggest, because it might well be increasing over time. This isn't immediately apparent from the long-run averages. These (if we calculate electoral

Figure 6.1 Turnout in two postcommunist democracies, 1990–2011

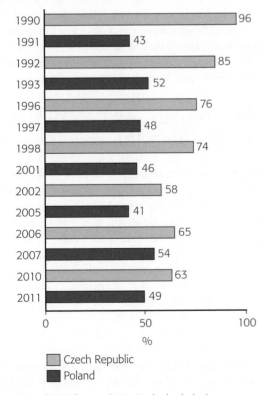

- 1990: 96 (Czech Republic)
- 1991: 43 (Poland)
- 1992: 85 (Czech Republic)
- 1993: 52 (Poland)
- 1996: 76 (Czech Republic)
- 1997: 48 (Poland)
- 1998: 74 (Czech Republic)
- 2001: 46 (Poland)
- 2002: 58 (Czech Republic)
- 2005: 41 (Poland)
- 2006: 65 (Czech Republic)
- 2007: 54 (Poland)
- 2010: 63 (Czech Republic)
- 2011: 49 (Poland)

%

Czech Republic
Poland

Note: 1990 and 1992 figures relate to Czechoslovak elections.

volatility as the sum of losses and gains of the various parties divided by two) suggest seemingly trendless fluctuation, with volatility rising and then falling as one moves through the decades from 1950 to 2010. But Peter Mair (2006b) again drew an analogy with climate change, noting that 'the more recent the election, the less likely it is to yield a predictable outcome'. Only eleven elections since 1945 that have recorded over 20 per cent volatility – namely, Italy (1948, 1994, 2001), the Netherlands (1994, 2002, 2010), Austria (2002), Denmark (1973), France (1958), Germany (1953), and Ireland, where in 2011, the governing Fianna Fáil party, which had won 42 per cent of the vote in 2007 was reduced to just 17 per cent in the wake of Ireland's financial and fiscal crisis and a corruption scandal (see Gallagher and Marsh, 2011). Seven of those eleven elections took place in the last two decades. It is also worth pointing out that electoral volatility in central and eastern Europe, while it seems to be dropping slightly as the region moves out of the transition phase and gradually (but only gradually) leaves behind its Soviet legacy (see Epperly, 2011), is still significantly higher than it is in the west of the continent. For instance, in the latter average volatility was 11.3 per cent in the 1990s and 10.5 per cent in the following decade; the figures for postcommunist Europe were 27.9 and 25.7, respectively (see Gallagher *et al.*, 2011: 310, 318).

That said, we could be understating the true extent of volatility, even in the West, if use figures based on aggregates calculated from election results rather than figures based on survey research that actually asks people how they voted. Research suggests that aggregate figures disguise, first, the extent of switching (between parties and between voting and non-voting) that goes on between one election and the next at the individual (or 'micro') level and, second, the extent to which such switching has risen (though not always in strictly linear fashion) from the late 1960s/early 1970s onwards. For instance, in 1960 only 7 per cent of those surveyed by the Swedish election study said that they had changed their vote from four years previously; in 1998 the figure was 31 per cent – an increase seemingly replicated in other European countries where the question was asked (see Dalton *et al.*, 2002).

This picture of flux fits with figures from the same surveys which seem to indicate that voters are

KEY POINT

Voters switch parties more, and make up their minds later, than they used to. Votes seem to switch within left and right blocs more than they switch between them.

increasingly leaving their decision about which way to vote until nearer polling day. To use the Swedish example again, only 18 per cent made up their minds during the campaign in 1964; 34 years later, in 1998, the figure was 57 per cent. This might, of course, have been particularly high in the latter year because many social democrats defected (temporarily) to the Left Party in protest at the government's welfare squeeze (which may also explain the high level of volatility in that year). But compiling an average which 'smooths out' peaks and troughs in the data across a number of countries suggests that there has been an increase over time – and not just in Sweden (Dalton *et al.*, 2002). To some analysts, this increase – the growing instability of political choice, if you like – is a symptom of a developing crisis in trust between voters and parties which is not only fragmenting party systems but rendering electoral systems that were constructed in very different circumstances operationally dysfunctional (see Baldini and Pappalardo, 2008).

Preferences – what makes people vote the way they do?

Despite the increasing sophistication of the research tools employed by political scientists, explaining why people vote the way they do has always been much harder than we would like. The reason is that there are so many possible factors that go into such a decision that it is impossible to control for all of them – certainly at the individual level. This does not mean, however, that we cannot make educated guesses based on aggregate data – in other words, by using survey research to see if there is a correlation between certain characteristics (which become the 'independent variable', the thing doing the influencing) and voting for one party or another (the 'dependent variable', the thing being influenced). Decades of research in this area has traditionally accorded particular significance to three things: class and religion (both of which fitted quite neatly with Lipset and Rokkan's (1967) idea of 'cleavages' discussed in Chapter 5) and 'party identification' (the extent to which someone feels 'close to' a particular party). The problem is that the same research now suggests that the effect (or at least the predictive power) of all three has not necessarily disappeared, but has almost certainly declined. Indeed, so much so, some argue, that we would have just as good a chance of predicting which party someone is going to vote for if we were to flip a coin instead of bothering to ask them which party they identify with or about their social background and religious beliefs.

Left–right and Party ID

We routinely talk of voters and parties as being on the left or the right, and there is a good deal of evidence to suggest that this makes sense inasmuch as the vast majority of voters when asked by survey researchers will locate both themselves and political parties on this spectrum, although there is some variation across countries (see Dalton *et al.*, 2011: chapters 4 and 5): in the Netherlands, France, Sweden, Germany and the Czech Republic, over 90 per cent of respondents are willing to do this; in Spain and Italy well over 80 per cent are; and in Poland and the UK the proportion drops to around 75 per cent. We also know that there is a correlation between left–right attitudes and left–right voting (see Dalton, 2010: 147, 161–2 and Dalton *et al.*, 2011: chapter 6). Party identification (often referred to simply as 'party ID'), however, refers to something more specific and is often associated with the 'Michigan model' of voting (so-called because it was pioneered at the University of Michigan in the USA). This model held that the majority of people were socialized into feeling closer to one party rather than another. Although this did not necessarily mean they would always vote for it – judgements

about economic conditions or particular issues or candidates could play a part as well – normally they would. This 'homing instinct' made party identification a powerful predictor. Many political scientists in Europe question whether survey respondents are able to disentangle their current political preference from any long-term identification they might or might not have, but others argue the concept is useful outside the USA (see Evans, 2004).

Many analysts remain unconvinced that there is a clear-cut answer to the question of whether there has been a Europe-wide decline in party ID over time (see Schmitt and Holmberg, 1995). Individual countries aside, by no means all cross-national studies suggest there has been any overall decline in party identification (van Deth and Janssen, 1994). On the other hand, some researchers are now convinced that the evidence both for decline of party ID and a declining relationship between party ID and party choice at elections is there (see Dalton, 2000), even if it does vary between countries (see Figure 6.2) and is sometimes pretty marginal (Thomassen, 2005). If they are right, this will of course leave political scientists with another challenge – not simply showing that people are less attached to parties than previously and that remaining attachments count for less, but explaining why that has happened.

Two possibilities spring to mind in this respect. One is to suggest that the decline in (and the decline

Figure 6.2 Proportion of population feeling close to a political party in the twenty-first century

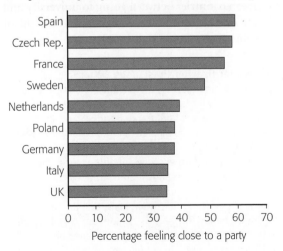

Percentage feeling close to a party

Source: from Scarrow (2012: 59–60).

in the predictive power of) party ID is linked to public dissatisfaction beginning in the 1970s with the relatively unimpressive performance of their countries' economies. This was transferred to the parties, which seemed to be incapable of doing much to make things better and which more recently have had their reputations badly damaged by scandals, financial and otherwise. The evidence for this is not particularly impressive, however. Those who are least partisan are not necessarily those who are most dissatisfied, and vice versa. The other explanation for a decline in party identification links it to the increased educational capacity of most electors and the greater access they have to information supplied by the media rather than by parties (see Chapter 7). Taken together, these mean that people have less need to rely on instinct and loyalty and, instead, can make the kind of consumerist, individual choice they are increasingly used to in other areas of life – an idea sometimes labelled the **modernization thesis**. This will almost certainly sound plausible to readers of this book, but there is a problem: comparative research suggests that the relationship between more education and less partisanship is non-existent in some countries (e.g. Netherlands and Germany) and declining over time in others (e.g. the UK and Sweden) as people (especially younger people) with little education also appear to be turning their backs on parties as much as those who have, say, been to university (see Thomassen, 2005: Chapter 5). That said, it is interesting to note that there is a clear correlation in most European countries between going to university and placing oneself on the left rather than the right of the political spectrum (Dalton, 2010: 154–6).

The **modernization thesis** (see Dalton 2002) holds that economic progress, mass education and media penetration will create new citizens who are more knowledgeable, confident and autonomous, and because they are 'cognitively mobilized' – are more willing and able to make up their own minds about politics and try different ways of getting what they want. They will be less inclined to develop or rely on old loyalties, and more sceptical about what parties and elections can offer them. Many will be attracted by 'new politics', driven less by concerns over the distribution of economic gains than by issues like the environment and multiculturalism.

A second, simpler but perhaps more robust explanation is that party ID was associated with the very social characteristics that we go on to explore below; namely, class and religion. As their hold on people has waned so, too, has the tendency to feel closer to the parties most associated with such collective identities (like the social and the Christian democrats), while newer (and often smaller) parties have not made up for the decline by generating similar loyalties. This certainly seems to be the case in Germany, where partisanship has been gradually declining over at least thirty years (see Arzheimer, 2006) – a fact that may help explain why, at the election of 2005, the country's biggest parties the CDU–CSU and the SPD achieved their lowest combined share of the vote for fifty years. And, of course, any decline in party identification will feed on itself: there is less loyalty to pass down to the next generation of voters, ensuring that more and more young people never develop identifications (strong ones anyway) in the first place. This possibility calls to mind the postcommunist democracies. There, partisan identification was weak to start with and, in the opinion of some analysts, is by no means logically bound to develop at all (see Vlachová, 2001). Even if it does, it may well be the case – as some analysts are now arguing is the case in more mature democracies – that there is nothing to stop people developing meaningful (if not necessarily particularly strong) attachments to more than one party (Mughan, 2009).

The 'end of class voting' and the rise of values?

As Chapter 1 suggested, class has not disappeared, either as a useful categorization or as an identity that means something to many, perhaps even most, people. So we should be careful before we rush to write its obituary as an influence on voting – something that many commentators have been accused of doing (see Franklin et al., 1992). On the other hand, there is some truth in the suggestion that, for too long, researchers tended to let class overshadow other cleavages, such as religion, language and ethnicity, that are more cultural than economic, social or geographical (see Dogan, 2001). Perhaps we should ask first whether class is as important in some countries as it is in others, and then whether there is evidence that it has declined as an influence over time. On the first question, there is reasonably broad agreement that class voting (the extent to

Table 6.6 The historical importance of class voting

Low	Relatively low	More significant	Relatively high
US, Postcommunist countries	France, Ireland, Italy, Netherlands, Portugal, Spain, Switzerland	Austria, Belgium, Germany	Denmark, Finland, Norway, Sweden, UK

Source: Data from Nieuwbeerta and De Graaf (1999).

which, put at its most basic, the working class votes left and the middle class votes right) varies considerably across countries (see Table 6.6).

The second question – the decline (or not) of the influence of class on voting – is rather more controversial. What is *not* at issue is that, however measured, the proportion of the population that can be categorized (or thinks of itself) as working class has shrunk by around one-third in the postwar period (see Chapter 1) – this is sometimes labelled the 'composition effect.' What *is* at issue is the extent to which people vote in a certain way because they belong to (or at least can be labelled as) a certain class – the so-called 'correlation effect.' There are, of course, plenty of country studies that do support such an effect: for example, work on the French party system (see Evans, 2002) shows very convincingly that the left-wing parties have lost whatever claim they had to be the party of the working class. It also suggests that many blue-collar workers (as in Austria, too) now vote for the far right (see Chapter 9) – evidence of both 'dealignment' (see Chapter 5) and a certain degree of 'realignment' (i.e. groups of voters not so much losing their loyalty as taking it elsewhere).

All this certainly fits nicely with the tale told by most media commentators and one often repeated in academic texts. Actually, however, there is considerable debate about its truth. For one thing, research suggests that even if socio-economic conflict is not the only dimension that matters, and that potentially cross-cutting, cultural issues around ethnicity and national sovereignty are increasingly important (Kriesi *et al.*, 2008), it remains the dominant dimen-

sion as far as parties are concerned – all of which casts considerable doubt on notions of de-alignment and re-alignment (Stoll, 2010). For another, some country-level and cross national studies on voters would appear to contradict, or at least severely qualify, this conventional wisdom (see Brooks *et al.*, 2006; Evans, 1999). On balance, recent research suggests that, while overall there has been a significant decline in class voting from the late 1960s and early 1970s (see Knutsen, 2006), it is more pronounced (and the trend more linear) in some countries than others (see for example Thomassen, 2005: Chapter 4; see also Achterberg, 2006). For instance, Ireland and the Netherlands do not appear to have experienced a decline; Austria, Belgium, France and Italy have experienced a decline, but not as pronounced as that in Britain, Germany and above all Scandinavia, especially Norway and Sweden. This variation, it is argued, puts paid to the modernization thesis, which would surely apply to all advanced industrial or postindustrial countries at pretty much the same time.

And even if we do accept the dealignment thesis, of course, we are still left with the task of explaining *why* class is now a less reliable predictor of vote. This is not an easy one, and explanations so far are more deductive (based on theoretical speculation which might or might not fit data from a process that is still unfolding over time) than inductive (emerging from a clear body of evidence). These (largely sociological) explanations are summarized in Box 6.5 (see Evans, 1999: 6–7).

It is, of course, possible to argue that class was, and is, a relatively vague way of categorizing voters and thereby explaining their political choices. Much better, perhaps, to employ more precise distinctions based not just on what they do for a living but also the sector – private or public – they work in. Quantitative cross-national research by political scientist Oddbjørn Knutsen (2005) does just this.

Knutsen finds that there is a relationship between the sector worked in and party support but that its strength varies considerably between countries, being strongest in a Scandinavian welfare state like Denmark, moderate in France, Italy and the UK, small in Germany and the Netherlands, and insignificant in a country with a comparatively underdeveloped welfare state like Ireland. Interestingly, the strongest relationship between sector and party choice is not just between those who work in the

BOX 6.5

Why people's class might no longer predict their vote

1 As services supersede industry, creating so-called 'postindustrial societies' (see Chapter 1), other cleavages (such as gender, nationality, ethnicity) could be superseding class which, after all, had its roots in industrialization.

2 As suggested by the modernization thesis, the growth of education and an emphasis on individual over collective identities has increased people's ability to think for themselves and make more rational, calculating and issue-based political decisions.

3 As most people now have met their basic material needs, some experts argue that they tend to think more in terms of values rather than interests: this **postmaterialism** cuts across class voting, encouraging, for example, many middle-class salary earners to vote for social liberal, new-left and green parties, while many workers gravitate toward the far right.

4 As the manual working class has declined as a proportion of the population (something not even those who are sceptical about the decline of class voting dispute), mainstream social democratic parties have had to – or at least convinced themselves that they have had to – extend their appeal to the middle classes. This 'catch-all strategy' has met with some success, but the downside is (supposedly) a loss of some disillusioned working-class supporters.

5 European societies may not be becoming 'classless' in the sense that life-chances are no longer influenced by social background (see Chapter 1). But class has never been an objective category; it is a cleavage and an identity that is latent and dormant unless (explicitly) mobilized by political actors: if parties choose not to appeal to such antagonisms and to pick policies that polarize debate, then it is hardly surprising that they cease to drive people's voting behaviour.

private sector and conservative parties (which tend to be in favour of a smaller state and lower taxation) but also between those in the private sector and populist radical right parties, which are not necessarily keen on shrinking the state (see Chapter 5). There is (perhaps more predictably given their vested interest in the election of a government committed to upholding the welfare state rather than trimming it to cut taxes) a relationship between being employed in the public sector and voting for parties on the left. However, there is considerable variation between countries when it comes to which parties benefit most from this relationship: in Britain and France, for example, it seems to be the social democrats (Labour and the *Parti Socialiste*), while in Germany and the Netherlands it seems to be green and/or left parties. Finally, the political impact of working in the public or private sector tends to be greater if you work in services.

Both class and occupational or sectoral explanations were focused on western European countries. As such, they could be of limited use in helping us to understand the links between social structure and voting in CEE. One could argue that in postcommunist countries, such as Poland and the Czech Republic, class will in fact increase its influence on voting, as 'marketization' since the early 1990s makes it clearer to people with which side of the left–right divide their material interests (perceived as much collectively as individually) lie, although this may be counteracted by an observable trend for younger people (unlike their elders) to feel they have gained from the transition to the market (see Whitefield, 2002; see also Evans, 2006 and Horvat and Evans, 2011). In any case, not all analysts agree that class, any more than party identification, will necessarily come to take its 'proper place' as a cue for voters in CEE countries such as Poland and the Czech Republic (see Zielinski, 2002). Instead, it can be

Postmaterialism refers to the supposed trend in advanced countries, once the basic needs of the educated and reasonably well-off have been met, for such people to eschew political beliefs and behaviour based on the defence or promotion of material interest in favour of an interest in 'quality-of-life' issues, self-expression and ensuring the rights and well-being of minorities and/or the less fortunate (see Inglehart and Rabier, 1986).

argued that a voter's self-placement on a left–right scale – one that is often more rooted in historical understanding and moral values rather than socio-economic issues – may continue to be a much better predictor of political preferences than, say, occupation (see Gijsberts and Nieuwbeerta, 2000, Jasiewicz, 2009; Mateju and Vlachová, 1998; Szczerbiak, 2003).

Interestingly, a stress on the electoral importance of the values held by voters rather than their class position is by no means limited to those interested in east-central Europe. Not everyone agrees that older cleavages such as class and religion (see below) are paling into insignificance beside something we touched on in Chapter 5 in the context of green parties and go on to talk about in Chapter 8 namely, postmaterialism. Although the existence of such a trend is often taken for granted, and has even been used to help explain not just the rise of the Greens but also that of the far right (see Ignazi, 2003: Chapter 12), there are those who are highly sceptical (see, for instance, Wilensky, 2002: 191–207). Yet many analysts argue that 'values voting' is at least as important as 'cleavage' or 'structural' voting (see Knutsen and Scarbrough, 1995), although they might, of course, be connected (see Kriesi, 1998).

Yet many of those who support the idea of 'values voting' (the tendency to cast one's vote according to a conception of 'the good life' held irrespective of one's occupation, religion, etc.) are by no means sure that it began in the 1970s. It may, they note, have been important (but unmeasured) in the 1950s and 1960s, helping to explain in part why party systems have not undergone the kind of change we might have expected given the huge changes in society in the postwar period (see Chapters 1 and 5). In other words, 'values', even if they weren't 'new politics' values have always informed people's voting decisions. Obvious candidates here would be where people placed themselves (or could be placed by their answers to certain survey questions) on a 'left–right' or an 'authoritarian–libertarian' dimension – a location which, interestingly, appears to have little to do with their social class (Thomassen, 2005: 260). Thomassen suggests, in fact, that, as with class, the impact of all these value orientations is not determined by an inevitable modernization process – one that would predict either the rise of new politics and the decline of more traditional orientations or the declining impact of all value orientations as voters become more and more individualized and therefore idiosyncratic. Rather their impact depends, once again, on the extent to which political actors effectively mobilize them: if parties choose (or manage) not to frame their disagreements in terms of a left–right or authoritarian–libertarian conflict, then voters are less likely to bring such value orientations to bear on their choice of party or candidate.

Religion – another death announced prematurely?

Just as some political scientists are beginning to challenge the common wisdom on the putative end of class voting in an era where individual values are supposedly coming to the fore, others are warning that, likewise, we write off religion (see Chapter 1) at our peril. Similarly, their criticisms do not involve an attempt to refute the obvious. Just as those who see a continuing link between class and voting do not try to argue, for instance, that there are just as many manual workers as ever there were, those who still see religion influencing votes do not contest the fact that fewer and fewer people go to church these days – a 'composition effect' which means religion, like class, is having less and less of an impact on voting as well as shrinking what used to be thought of as the 'natural constituency' of certain parties (see Best, 2011). What they argue, however, is that a 'correlation effect' still exists; namely, that for those who are religious, religion remains a strong a predictor of their vote. Specifically, they maintain that (a) religion impacts most on the voting behaviour of those who attend regularly; and (b) even many non-attenders still consider themselves to be believers/members of churches and that this continues to have at least some influence on their vote. This influence may be direct, in that they vote for, say, a Christian democratic party. Or it may be indirect, in the sense that it encourages them to support a certain party because of the stances it takes on issues on which their opinions are in part shaped by their religious convictions.

So what about the evidence (see Broughton and Ten Napel, 2000; Dalton, 2010: 151 –153; Esmer and Pettersson, 2007; Knutsen, 2004; Minkenberg, 2010; Norris and Inglehart, 2011; van der Brug et al., 2009)? Certainly, there does seem to be evidence that, in some countries, differences between Christian denominations might matter less than differences between those who go to church and those who just

Italy (Italia)

History: Italy was, for centuries, a collection of sometimes foreign-ruled city-states. In the nineteenth century, however, nationalists led by Garibaldi built on the achievements in the north by Cavour and, by 1861, had succeeded in unifying the country under a constitutional monarch. Italy held its first mass elections on the eve of the First World War, a conflict from which Italy emerged on the winning side.

From the 1920s onwards, Italy, like Germany, collapsed into authoritarian dictatorship (in its case under the fascist leader Benito Mussolini). Following its defeat in the Second World War, in which it allied itself with Germany, Italy became a republic. Its politics were dominated by the centre-right DC (Christian democratic party), which benefited from an unwritten pact between most political parties to keep the powerful communist party (PCI) out of office at the national level. The DC's constant presence in every postwar administration until the early 1990s provided a kind of disguised stability for a system that saw

47 governments between 1947 and 1992. But it also relied on clientelistic corruption, as well as links with organized crime. With the collapse of communism, Italians were finally able to express their discontent, and the early 1990s saw the end of the DC. The electorate divides between a left-wing bloc based around the former PCI, and a right-wing bloc originally composed of a former fascist party (the now conservative National Alliance), a xenophobic regionalist party (the Northern League) and the dominant partner, *Forza Italia,* led by media mogul Silvio Berlusconi. The Right narrowly lost the election of 2006 to the Left, led by former Prime Minister and President of the European Commission, Romano Prodi. But Berlusconi soon returned to power where he remained – fighting off court proceedings against him – until 2011 when the dire state of the Italian economy, plus numerous scandals, finally caught up with him and he stood down in favour of non-party prime minister, Mario Monti.

Economy and society: Traditionally, Italy's superficially chaotic politics did little to harm its postwar economic revival, and the country retains its reputation for producing stylish, high-quality goods in demand all over the world. Its population, however, enjoys a *per capita* GDP which is close to the EU average. This is because there is a big gap between the rich industrialized and service-oriented north and the poorer, more agricultural south (or *Mezzogiorno*) that also includes the islands of Sicily and Sardinia. This has led to tensions, with people in

Area: 294,000 km² (7.0% of EU-27)
Population: 60.8 million (12.1% of EU-27)
Religious heritage: Roman Catholic
GDP (2010): € 1,549 billion (12.4% of EU-27)
GDP *per capita* as percentage of EU-27 average: 101
Female representation in parliament and cabinet (end 2011): 22% and 17%
Joined EU: founder member, 1957
Top 3 cities: Rome – capital city (2.8 million), Milan (1.3 million), Naples (1.0 million).

the north feeling resentment at having, as they see it, to subsidize the south. Partly because there is a relatively low level of identification with the nation state, Italians have been very pro-EU but have become increasingly antagonistic towards migrants in recent years, even though the country may well need more of them to offset its rapidly ageing population: projections suggest that by 2030 there may be only two Italians of working age for every retiree. Italians nevertheless worry about the fact that the proportion of foreign-born residents increased from just under 1 per cent in 1990 to 7 per cent in 2010, by which time there were nearly a 900,000 Romanians living in the country.

WHAT'S IN AN ANTHEM?

Il Canto degli Italiani was written and popularized in the middle of the nineteenth century during the ultimately successful campaign for a free and united Italy. But it did not become the country's anthem until the founding of the Italian Republic in 1946. The first verse (the only one that is really sung) dips a toe into classical imperial glory, with Italy wearing the helmet of Roman general Scipio and God having apparently made the goddess Victory 'Rome's slave'. Italy, goes the chorus that winds up the anthem, has called and 'we are ready to die'. And just to leave no one in any doubt that they are, the very last word is a resounding 'Yes!'

Governance: Italy is a parliamentary democracy elected, between 1994 and 2001, under a mixed system that failed in its intention to reduce the number of parties. Very unusually, both houses of the legislature have practically equal power. Also, in recent times, Italian presidents, elected by parliament and supposedly with little more than ceremonial power, have shown themselves more willing than their counterparts in other European countries to criticize the government of the day. Italy's judiciary is also renowned for its willingness to investigate its politicians and their actions. Relations became even more strained during Silvio Berlusconi's second period of office, although he largely managed to stave off his legal pursuers. These high-profile spats, should not, however, obscure other fundamental developments in the governance of Italy, not least the move toward granting its regions much greater autonomy, although this is has not gone as far as some northerners would like.

Foreign policy: Italy, like Germany, spent most of the latter half of the twentieth century atoning for its over-assertiveness before 1945. A staunch member of the EU and NATO, it has, however, often been accused of not living up to the commitments it often seems to observe more in word than in deed. In recent years, Italy has modified its knee-jerk enthusiasm for European integration and, with the UK and Spain, its right-wing government (in contrast to its population) was a strong supporter of the Iraq war. The country was instrumental in putting together an EU peacekeeping mission after the Lebanon War of 2006. However, it had to work hard to adjust to the Arab Spring of 2011 in the wake of its earlier attempts to forge good relations with

A KEY CONTEMPORARY CHALLENGE
BALANCING COMPETENCE AND DEMOCRACY

Technocratic governments are nothing new in Italy: non-party administrations led and largely staffed by experts were established under Carlo Azeglio Ciampi in 1993 and Lamberto Dini in 1995. The latest to form took shape in November 2011 after even those Italian politicians who had hitherto supported the country's controversial prime minister, Silvio Berlusconi, finally realized that he would have to go. This was after his failure to provide sufficient reassurance to the financial markets and other governments that he had the support and the will to bring in the spending cuts, tax rises and liberalization measures that were widely agreed to be necessary if Italy was to carry on being able to borrow at reasonable cost in order to service its debt and cover its budget deficit without a bail-out from the EU that many worried might be unaffordable. In came a 'technocratic' government, headed by the academic economist and former European Commissioner Mario Monti and supported by most of the parties in parliament (including Berlusconi's). Offered the premiership until 2013, Monti began with considerable public goodwill. Not surprisingly this lasted only until he began to actually take the tough decisions his predecessor had avoided: his package to free up the Italian economy (and the country's consumers) from vested interests, announced in January 2012, brought strikes and protests from, among others, previously cosseted taxi-drivers, pharmacists, and lorry-drivers. Previous attempts to reform labour laws in the late 1990s and early 2000s resulted in the assassination of the ministers responsible. It was therefore all the more worrying when the government's simultaneous clamp-down on tax evasion triggered bomb attacks on the offices of the revenue service, Equitalia. Berlusconi withdrew his support and Monti resigned, triggering an election in February 2013.

North African dictators, such as Muammar Gaddafi, in the hope that they would provide help in stemming the flow of migrants across the Mediterranean.

Contemporary challenges
- Balancing competence and democracy: technocratic government in an age of austerity.
- Getting growth into an economy that averaged only 0.25% growth per annum in the decade after 2000: only Haiti and Zimbabwe performed more poorly.

- Bringing in, in a climate of fear, sufficient migrant labour to fill vacancies and offset the shrinking population so that future pension commitments can be met.
- The persistent disparity between the rich north and the poor south.
- Rooting out organized crime from government and business.
- Reforming education and the labour market so as to counteract the brain drain of talented but frustrated young Italians.

Learning resources. There are a number of books that serve as useful primers to the colourful politics of recent years, while trying to give a journalistic/historical insight into Italian society more generally. The most recent is Emmott (2012), *Good Italy, Bad Italy*. For something more academic, try the collection edited by Guiliani and Jones (2010), *Italian Politics* and the approachable textbook by Newell (2010), *Politics of Italy*. Keep up with the news at http://www.ansa.it/web/notizie/rubriche/english/english.shtml.

think of themselves as members of one. In Germany, for instance, people are more likely to vote for the CDU–CSU if they are regular churchgoers, be they Protestant or Catholic. But things are complex. In a country such as France, for example, there is still a difference between denominations (Catholics still tend to vote for right-wing parties), though one reinforced by regular attendance (at least on the Catholic side) and, significantly, by higher social status – a warning to us of the risks of dismissing either class or religion simply because, investigated in isolation, they do not seem to make much of a difference. They also seem to be linked in Scotland (and to a lesser extent) England, where Catholicism is – very unusually – associated with centre-left rather than centre-right voting. In the Netherlands, active Protestants vote disproportionately for explicitly religious – Protestant – parties and practising Catholics are most likely to vote for the CDA. Interestingly, however, research lends little support to the suggestion that there might exist widespread indirectly religious voting for particular parties owing to their stances on 'moral issues' such as abortion or marriage and the family, although, rather intriguingly, it does suggest that those who vote for religious parties and those who vote for secular parties have very different ways of rating the alternatives on offer (Pellikaan, 2010). Research also suggests that if right-wing parties have traditionally benefited more than the left from the impact of faith on voting, there is a flip side. People who consciously reject religion tend to vote for left-wing parties – either for social democrats or (especially if there is a parliamentary left or green alternative) for smaller parties on their flank.

So, religion remains a better predictor of voting than other social characteristics, including class, even if the extent to which religious belief predicts one's political stance might (according to Norris and Inglehart's massive cross-national study) gradually be weakening over time. But we should not let this lack of dealignment on the part of those who have faith obscure the possibly more important fact that (as we saw in Chapter 1) fewer and fewer people are going to church regularly (if at all) nowadays. Hence, the value of this relationship (especially to the right side of the political spectrum) would appear to be a wasting asset – much as the decline in trade union density we consider in Chapter 8 may well harm the left. Accordingly, mainstream centre-

right parties all over Europe have been attempting to reduce any reliance they may have had on religious voters, just as their social democratic counterparts have been scrambling to ensure they can cope with the decline of the 'traditional working class.'

Secularization, in other words, might not make things easy (see Duncan, 2006, 2007), but it need not spell the death of parties whose appeal may have begun as religious – as long as that appeal is leavened or tempered by a show of concern with other issues. True, Christian democrats have struggled in, say, France (where they were never strong), in Belgium (where the French-speaking Christian democrats re-labelled themselves as the 'Humanist Centre Democrats') and Italy (where voters deserted the party in droves for more secular right wing parties when the extent of the party's corruption became clear after the end of the Cold War). In the Netherlands, too, the Christian democrats are a shadow of their former selves, although there are smaller Christian parties which are surviving if not exactly thriving in a permissive electoral system that means they can continue to zero in on what some would see as fundamentalist voters. In Austria, things have also been difficult for the Christian democratic ÖVP in recent years. In Germany, however, support for the Christian democratic CDU–CSU has remained relatively steady, notwithstanding unification with the former East Germany, where levels of religious belief (and, of course, church attendance) are very low. Whether, however, this has much to do with the continuing power of religion to structure the vote or because the CDU–CSU has simply been better led, delivered better government, and been quicker to divest itself of its Catholic identity than its counterparts is a moot point (see Bale and Krouwel, 2013).

In CEE countries, many of which were (officially anyway) atheist under communism, religion is likely to be less of an influence on voters. There are, however, exceptions (see Whitefield, 2002), to this rule. A big one is Poland, where Roman Catholicism, and the extent to which it is actually practised rather than simply adhered to, continues not just to influence voting but (along with attitudes to the communist past) actually structures popular conceptions of what is and is not right- or left-wing (see Szczerbiak, 2003). Many parties on the right make a specific pitch for the country's most religious voters, combining a scathing attitude to the supposedly aggressive (but, in practice, very tame) secularism of the left with an assertive nationalism that means they have little in common with the larger, more moderate, Christian democratic parties of the west (Bale and Szczerbiak, 2008).

Few other countries in Europe, however, can come anywhere near matching the USA in terms of religiosity and, therefore, the potential impact of religion on politics. However, once again, we should stress that (as with class) any such impact depends not just on the voters themselves – the 'demand side' of the equation, if you like – but also on the supply side, namely the parties that compete for their votes (and to some extent the interest groups they listen to). If parties choose, or feel obliged, to mobilize on the church–state cleavage (see Chapter 5), then what are otherwise dormant religious attitudes among voters can begin to seem more relevant when choosing between parties. For instance, having won the election of 2000, the PASOK socialist government in Greece decided to remove religious affiliation from some state-held identity data, thereby provoking a huge row with the powerful Orthodox Church. Its campaign to stymie the move was publicly backed by the opposition conservative party, which moved ahead in the polls and won a convincing victory at the next election. The fight with the church was by no means the only reason that saw voters turn away from PASOK, but it might well think twice before picking one again. Its counterpart in Spain, however, seemed to many to be determined to do just that after unexpectedly winning the 2004 election. Prime Minster Zapatero's PSOE government quickly began passing all sorts of liberal legislation, provoking the Catholic church to urge its most devoted adherents onto the streets to protest and also call on the conservative opposition, the PP, to join it. Aside from the fact that the socialists clearly believed in what they were doing, the calculation might have been that identifying PP with values that fewer and fewer Spaniards now seem to share would allow PSOE to paint its main opponent, once again, as the party of the past. That said, the power of religion to polarize, particularly in divided and, in an age of immigration, increasingly diverse societies, may well mean that its role in helping people decide how to vote may remain stronger than many of us once assumed (see van der Brug *et al.*, 2009: 1280 and Minkenberg, 2010: 405–8).

Other social characteristics – ethnicity, gender, and geographic location

The fact that, as we noted above, Catholics in England tend to vote Labour, can be explained by the fact that Catholicism was the religion of (poorer) Irish immigrants. But this begs questions about whether the relationship in question is actually to do with religion or with ethnicity. The same goes for the fact that Britain's black and minority ethnic (BME) population continues to vote overwhelmingly for Labour. Is it because some of them are non-Christian (a problematic explanation because Afro-Caribbeans, for example, are relatively observant Christians)? Or is it because they are non-white and therefore suffer disproportionately from discrimination, are more likely to be in lower-paid occupations, and less likely to favour a party (the Conservatives) that (rightly or wrongly) has been perceived as tougher on immigration? Admittedly, the UK is unusual: as in the USA, there is only one party (Labour in Britain, the Democrats in the USA) that picks up the majority of the 'multicultural' vote. But not that unusual: recent research from Norway, for example suggests that ethnic minority voters tend to favour left-of-centre parties, irrespective of their socio-economic position or indeed their ideology (Bergh and Bjørklund, 2011). There is also research (Sprague-Jones, 2011) which suggests that the presence of a significant far-right party (see Chapter 10) may heighten minorities' sense of their own ethnicity and their support for multiculturalism, which may reinforce this tendency More generally, there is surprisingly little research published (at least in English) on the voting patterns and political participation of ethnic (and particularly immigrant) minorities in Europe, especially outside of the UK (for which see Dancygier and Saunders, 2006; Garbaye, 2005; Saggar, 2000) – although we do, of course, know much more about the more obvious link between minority nationalism (which relies in part on ethnic if not racial identity) and the success of regionalist parties (De Winter *et al.*, 2006).

This gap in our knowledge is serious, especially given the growing presence of such minorities all over Europe and the distinct possibility that a backlash against immigration is helping to create a new ethnic cleavage (see Chapter 10 and Dogan, 2001). Until it is remedied, however, we are fortunate enough to have most of what we do know ably summarized by Anthony Messina (2007: Chapter 7). First, although immigrants who hold citizenship participate more than those who do not, they still tend to vote in lower numbers than the native-born, although the longer someone is resident the more they vote. This is partly because it takes time to build up an interest (material and otherwise) in political outcomes in the new country, especially when one retains an interest in these matters in one's country of origin. It is also because some immigrant groups (particularly those who do not do well or who feel especially discriminated against) are clearly prone to alienation and apathy. Second, where immigrants do vote, however, there is a clear tendency across Europe for them to support parties of the left: this is as obvious in, say, Germany (where parties on the left receive between two-thirds and three-quarters of the votes of naturalized Turks) and the Netherlands, as it is in the UK. And this appears to occur irrespective of class: parties on the left, even though they have in recent years moved to change the perception that they are 'soft' on immigration (see Bale *et al.*, 2010b), are seen to be more immigrant-friendly; their interest in promoting equality and support for a welfare state also seems to resonate with migrant voters. Third, there are significant differences between participation rates not just between different immigrant groups in the same country but between the same immigrant group in different countries – differences that we lack the research to explain.

The relationship between gender and voting is also relatively under-researched especially at cross-national, comparative level. This is not because of small sample sizes (women, after all, constitute the majority of the adult population) but possibly because in most countries there appeared to be little difference between the voting behaviour of men and women – although in the UK, for instance, it is well-known that the Conservatives would have lost almost every general election in the postwar period had only men been entitled to vote. Inglehart and Norris (2000), however, suggest that things may be changing throughout the advanced industrial world and, therefore, in Europe. Women used to be more conservative than men, at least insofar as surveys were able to determine their position on a left–right scale. However, with the exception of the French presidential election in 2012 (when the numbers voting for the *Front National*'s Marine Le Pen were exception-

ally high), they have so far remained far less persuaded of the charms of the far right than their male counterparts. Moreover, outside of postcommunist democracies, they appear to have moved more generally to the left of men (see Dalton, 2010: 154–6). Whether this development is as significant as some suggest, and whether gender differences in ideological self-placement has (or will) influence voting, remains open to debate (see Brooks *et al.*, 2006: 110). We have some interesting country studies (e.g. Campbell, 2004 and Johns and Shephard, 2007). What we need is more comparative work.

Finally, although it is easier theoretically and practically to do more about where one lives than about one's gender or ethnicity, we have already seen in Chapter 2 that there are good reasons to think that geographical location is an important part of people's identity all over Europe. To some extent this has always been recognized by social scientists interested in parties and voting: what, after all, is the centre–periphery cleavage that we referred to in Chapter 5 if not a political expression of this geographical identity? We also know that, traditionally, this cleavage and the parties it helped give rise to was interwoven with economic structures and grievances. Recent research suggests that, in fact, this is still the case: a good deal of often stark regional differences in voting patterns can be explained by socio-economic difference and consequent conflicts on the left–right dimension (Knutsen, 2010). Interestingly, however, the same research suggests that in countries where regional tensions spill over into minority nationalism – most obviously in Belgium and Spain but also in Italy – then values and territorial identities exert an additional influence on voters.

Issue-voting, retrospective judgements and leadership

If long-term factors like class and religion seem to matter less, if values haven't taken their place as determinants of party choice, and if voters are more footloose, then perhaps we should look for an increased impact on voting of more short-term factors. Perhaps contemporary, 'cognitively mobilized' voters, knowing their own preferences on a range of concerns, now vote for those parties whose policies most closely match those preferences: has 'issue voting' increased? Or perhaps, just as rationally, they now place more emphasis on whether the parties (or party) in power have (or has) delivered on promises made, especially, say, on the economy. It would appear that these 'retrospective judgements' have more impact on voting in some countries rather than others, with the rank order (the UK, Sweden, Spain, Germany, France, Italy and finally the Netherlands) appearing to vary according to the extent to which parties (or predictable coalitions) can reasonably be blamed (or given credit for) economic policy (see Duch and Stevenson, 2006) – a blame game which voters maybe less and less willing to indulge in as they realize (or at least believe) that a more globalized world weakens the ability of their politicians to control the country's destiny in this respect . In central and eastern Europe, voters punishing incumbent governments on economic grounds seems to be quite common – possibly too common, say some analysts: voters are so much more inclined to punish than they are to reward that this 'hyperaccountability' could end up persuading parties that they may as well do what they want in office because whatever they do they will soon be returned to opposition (Roberts, 2008). This would be interesting because it cuts across the argument that, given economic perceptions seem to have an impact (although not necessarily an overwhelming one) on voting, parties in government can actually do quite a lot to manipulate those perceptions, for example by timing elections to their advantage, or by creating some sort of 'feel-good factor', or, if things go wrong, by blaming external circumstances – something which it would appear it is significantly easier to do in liberal economies (see Hellwig, 2010).

There are good reasons – not least the decline of partisanship in the electorate – to think that the state of the economy now looms larger than ever in people's decision on which way to vote, and indeed some cross national research on European countries seems to support that theory (see Kayser and Wlezien, 2011). But the economy is by no means the be-all and end-all. What about the leaders that, especially in the contemporary media (see Chapter 7), now loom so large in political life (see Blondel *et al.*, 2010)? Are voters – not altogether irrationally – more swayed than they were by personality? If we wrap all these questions up together, is it the case that European voters have grown out of their tribal instincts, care more now about competence and delivery than ideology (see Clark, 2009), about

valence rather than **position issues**? Do they then believe that one of the best ways of getting what they want is to elect individuals rather than worry overly much about parties, whose claims to **issue ownership** seem meaningless given the fact that (a) virtually all of them believe in more or less liberal capitalism; and (b) globalization means their policy options are severely narrowed?

Leaving aside objections, or at least qualifications, to the idea that parties are all the same and globalization means they cannot make a difference anyway, which are dealt with in Chapter 9, the answer (for the moment at least) would seem to be no. Issues, retrospective judgements and leaders are undoubtedly important, although we need to exercise considerable caution when it comes to the latter (see Barisione, 2009). Most of the latest research finds that, generally, individual leaders may not be as important to voters is commonly assumed (King, 2002; see also Aarts *et al.*, 2011; Brettschneider *et al.*, 2006; Schulz *et al.*, 2005; see also Mughan, 2009). Not surprisingly, perhaps, there is some indication that the influence leaders have on voters could vary with how high-profile those leaders are (see Schoen, 2007) or between parties (see Costa Lobo, 2006). Researchers also make the point that, from the voter's point of view at least, leader images and party images are inextricably bound up with each other so that what counts is how well they complement each other (Wagner and Weßels, 2012; see also Garzia, 2012). That said, whatever the common wisdom concerning the 'presidentialization' of politics, the latest comparative research suggests that – at elections anyway – media coverage is no more focused on particular politicians than it was three decades ago: where leaders play a big part in the

> **Position issues** are those on which people tend to take sides (e.g. more or less tax and spending), whereas **valence issues** are those on which most people want basically the same thing (e.g. sustainable economic growth or safer streets) and, as a result, judge politicians according to their competence in achieving more or less rather than either/or. **Issue ownership** refers to the tact that certain parties are seen by the majority to have consistently better policies and/or to care more about certain issues than their opponents; this leads parties during elections to try to ensure that 'their' issues dominate the news agenda (see Chapter 7).

system (as in France), or where the electoral system means it is easy to portray the campaign as a two-way contest (as in the UK), or when particularly charismatic or effective communicators are around (be they on the flanks, like Blocher in Switzerland or in the centre, like Blair, in the UK), then there is more concentration on them; if not, not (Kriesi, 2012).

Moreover there is, in fact, little evidence to suggest that leader images (nor indeed retrospective judgements or issues) drive voters' decisions more than they used to (Aarts *et al.*, 2011). A recent cross-national study looking at six European democracies since the 1960s (Thomassen, 2005) found that:

▶ Although there was evidence voters preferred parties that 'owned' the issues they thought were important (or 'salient' – see Chapter 7), there was no increase in 'issue voting' over time. In fact, issues have always played a role in voters' choices but that part hasn't grown.

▶ Although voters tend to punish the parties they perceive as responsible for their own and the country's economic difficulties, they don't do so now any more than they have always done

▶ The importance of leadership evaluations to voting differs between countries – leaders (of large parties) are more important in countries in which they are seen to be serious prime ministerial contenders (as in the UK). But it doesn't differ significantly over time.

Of course, it might be that we are just at the beginning of a era in which these short term factors come to trump 'cleavage' or 'values' voting. After all, it seems to make so much sense. As we saw in Chapter 5, Europe's parties (especially mainstream parties) can no longer rely on large numbers of members either to reflect back the views of the electorate to them or to spread their message to the electorate and keep some of it loyal. Acting increasingly on the basis of opinion polls and focus groups, and having to rely more and more on a media they cannot control (see Chapter 7), parties descend (as some would see it) into political marketing (see Savigny, 2008). They stress their 'catch-all' centrist pragmatism and emphasize their leaders and their stances on valence issues – the things that every government is expected to deliver – rather than on the issues they traditionally (and generally still) 'own'.

For instance, parties of the mainstream left and right will make more of their ability competently to run a stable and growing economy than they will of their intentions – albeit ones they still profess and even act on (see Chapter 9) – to, say, decrease taxation (the centre-right) or defend the welfare state (the centre-left). Europe's voters, taking their cues from the parties, begin to vote on the basis of the content and the credibility of the more specific offers being made to them by the salesmen (or women) concerned – in other words, they vote ever more instrumentally than ideologically. The parties pick up on this consumerist response and adapt their appeals accordingly. And so on and so on.

But just because this is intuitively plausible – and has even taken on the guise of common wisdom in some quarters – doesn't mean that it's right, at least as far as the available evidence goes. Even where 'valence' considerations do seem to be important to voters, this is not necessarily associated with a convergence between right and left (Pardos-Prado, 2012). Moreover, voters are (still) driven by a mix of class, religion, values and shorter-term factors, with the political impact of all of these varying according to what parties in different countries are willing and able to make of them (Elff, 2007). And, as the evidence from postcommunist countries suggests, voters also learn over time, taking previous results into consideration during any current election (see Dawisha and Deets, 2006). The importance of each factor varies between elections, but we are a long way yet from explaining – let alone predicting – how and why. That does not of course mean we should stop trying. One potentially fruitful avenue of research, for instance, focuses on differences between voters according to age, and in particular the age at which they are 'socialized' into politics: it may be that older voters are just as tribal as they always were and that middle-aged voters just as ideological, but their influence is waning as more and more young people with less fixed loyalties and attitudes enter the electorate (van der Brug, 2010; van der Brug and Kritzinger, 2012; see also Walczak *et al.*, 2012). And perhaps individual psychology, political interest and knowledge, and intellectual capacity also play a bigger part than traditionally more sociological approaches have acknowledged. Different people, for instance, will use different 'heuristics' (short-cuts) to make their decision on which party to vote for – or, indeed, whether to bother voting at all (see Baldassarri and Schadee, 2006). And a psychological predisposition to traditionalism and security, and acceptance of inequality, is associated with support for the right of the political spectrum, whereas openness to new experiences and a preference for equality is associated with support for the left – at least in western Europe. In the east, individuals with a strong psychological need for security favoured the left (which under communism had provided it), whereas those who were most open to new experiences tended towards the right of the political spectrum, presumably because it was associated with capitalist risk-taking, all of which suggests an interaction between individual character traits and collective history (see Thorisdottir *et al.*, 2007).

The fact that political scientists are beginning to acknowledge this kind of complexity – and, incidentally, to take seriously the idea that parties which look incompetent or split get punished by voters (see Clark, 2009) – doesn't make their task any easier, but it at least brings us closer to the real world. It's also worth noting that even the most partisan and/or ideological of voters live in that real world too. Because of that, they are more than capable of tactical or strategic rather than 'sincere' voting – in other words, lending their support to parties which they like as much as or perhaps a little less than their habitual favourite in order either to get rid of a government they dislike or install one that, on balance, they'd prefer. What is interesting is that recent research

(and, some would say, common sense) suggests that it is not just voters in plurality systems (where voting for one's favourite party can often be a complete waste of time if you live in the wrong constituency) who do this: even in the highly proportional Dutch system, where one would be hard-pressed to waste one's vote, people think about the impact of their vote on coalition outcomes and may change it accordingly (Irwin and van Holsteyn, 2012; see also Duch *et al.*, 2010; Karp and Hobolt, 2010).

EP elections

Elections to the EP take place every five years. Notwithstanding the increasing power of the EP in the EU's law-making system, turnout at the elections (which, note, are fought as simultaneous national contests not as one pan-European election) has dropped across the continent in recent years (see Table 6.7). True, a modest recovery in some countries can be hidden by the average figure, which now includes very low turnout countries in CEE. And, over the years, the average has also dropped with the inclusion of other less 'Europhile' countries, the position of the elections in national election cycles, the reduction in compulsory voting – and, of course, the trend toward turnout decline discussed above (see also Franklin, 2001a, 2001b). But the turnout difference between national and European elections is marked.

Table 6.7 Turnout in EP elections, 1979–2009 – and the contrast with general elections

	1979	1984	1989	1994	1999	2004	2009	Closest general election
Italy	85.65	82.47	81.07	73.60	69.76	71.72	65.05	80.5
Germany	65.73	56.76	62.28	60.02	45.19	43.00	43.30	70.8
EU av	61.99	58.98	58.41	56.67	49.51	45.47	43.00	n/a
Spain	–	–	54.71	59.14	63.05	45.14	44.90	73.9
France	60.71	56.72	48.80	52.71	46.76	42.76	40.63	60.2
Netherlands	58.12	50.88	47.48	35.69	30.02	39.26	36.75	74.7
Sweden	–	–	–	–	38.84	37.85	45.53	84.6
UK	32.35	32.57	36.37	36.43	24.00	38.52	34.70	65.1
Czech Rep.	–	–	–	–	–	28.30	28.20	62.6
Poland	–	–	–	–	–	20.87	24.53	53.8

Source: Data from http://www.europarl.europa.eu/aboutparliament/en/000cdcd9d4/Turnout-(1979-2009).html and http://www.parties-and-elections.eu

Political scientists are divided on the extent to which voters currently (or could potentially) fit EU issues into their existing left–right and materialist–postmaterialist orientations (see Gabel and Anderson, 2002; Marks and Steenbergen, 2004). There is considerably more agreement on the point that EP elections are still what political scientists call 'second-order' contests (though see Blondel *et al.*, 1998). Like local and regional elections, they are often used by voters to send a message (often one of dissatisfaction conveyed by voting for small and/or opposition parties) to the national government of the day (see van der Eijk and Franklin, 1996). This means that EP elections seem unlikely, at least for now, to contribute much to the creation of a European identity among the citizens of the member states. Whether, though, this is because those citizens are irretrievably nationally focused or whether they are encouraged to be so by parties who are neither ready nor willing to supranationalize their appeals or their focus, is a moot point (see van der Eijk and Franklin, 1996: 364–5). As we noted at the end of Chapter 5, many political scientists argue that it may only be a matter of time before 'Europe' becomes a key political cleavage – something that will depend not only on how voters are affected by EU policies but also on whether and how parties choose to mobilize on the European issue and thus provide 'cues' for those voters (Hooghe, 2007; Down and Wilson, 2010). Certainly 'Europe', in some countries at least, now a sufficiently big issue for enough voters to make it a vote-winner at national elections for parties which choose to take a sceptical position, particularly if they are in opposition (de Vries, 2010). Presumably this will only increase when and where the EU is seen to be associated with unpopular austerity measures designed to counteract a crisis in the Eurozone (see Chapter 9). And if this is true for national elections, how much truer is it likely to be for elections which impact directly on the EU itself?

Of course, the last question assumes that EP elections are, for most voters, about Europe. In fact, this is a highly questionable assumption since EP elections are 'second order' contests and as such often used by voters (particularly when national elections are a long way off) to punish incumbents by protest voting. Partly as a result, there are always likely to be 'mismatches' between member state governments (and maybe the commissioners they nominate) and the EP. These mismatches, given a legislative process relying on 'co-decision' between the EP and the Council of Ministers (representing national governments), could make European law-making more conflictual, especially if the EP begins – as it seems to be doing (see Chapter 2) – to vote more on left–right (or at least party-bloc) lines. Whether this will mean that at least some national governments will be faced with more European legislation of which they do not approve, however, is another moot point. Hypothetically, a government which loses out in the Council of Ministers under QMV (see Chapter 2) might be able to rely on MEPs on its end of the political spectrum to make the kinds of changes it desires at a later stage of the legislative process. If this proves difficult, however, we could see more and more instances of governments having to answer at general elections for policies not of their own making. They could always blame 'Europe' but then this might increase the salience of the European issue – something most mainstream parties on both the left and the right would almost certainly rather not do for fear that voters might defect to more populist alternatives on their respec-

KEY POINT

The EP has become more powerful, but voters – even if their preferences on European integration may dovetail with their views on other issues – still accord it relatively little importance. EP elections can be (and are) used, though, as a useful test of opinion and tactics in domestic politics.

tive flanks.

Irrespective of these unintended consequences of EP elections, the latter play an important part in the domestic politics of member states (see Gabel, 2000). Both parties and voters use them (and their results) as signals and portents, which may then affect their subsequent behaviour. A party may finally realize, for instance, that it has to dump its underperforming leader, while a protest vote allows voters to register their dislike of the direction in which a particular party is travelling and/or provides an opportunity for catharsis, after which they return to the fold by the next general election. Or the effect of that vote is perhaps to allow a new entrant onto the political scene who then stays around for good. For instance, EP elections – fought as they are under

PR even in countries that ordinarily use majoritarian systems – gave the far-right *Front National* and the Greens an early boost. Similarly, EP elections have finally given voters in Europe's other majoritarian system, the UK, the chance to cast a vote for a small party count. Conceivably this may make them more willing to vote for smaller parties in other elections – a logic that also applies, incidentally, to the use of PR for elections to the Scottish Parliament and the Welsh Assembly, and could well spill over into increasing support to change the system at national level. These possibilities, however, probably pale into insignificance alongside the more immediate fact that European integration more generally (rather than the EP in particular) is increasingly part of domestic political disputes, either on its own or because hostility to it is becoming a now familiar favourite for populist politicians all over the continent (see Szczerbiak and Taggart, 2008).

Direct democracy – useful tool or dangerous panacea?

Representative democracy is not the only form of democracy in Europe: all of the continent's states, including all our core countries apart from Germany (see Table 6.8), also have experience of **direct democracy** at the national level – most famously in Switzerland (see Box 6.6). The referendums used in the latter take various particular forms (see Table 6.9). But the issue is worth studying for anyone interested in European politics. For one thing, direct democracy has played and could well continue to play a role in European integration (see Hobolt, 2009), notwithstanding the fact that referendums (in France and the Netherlands) famously scuppered the EU's Constitutional Treaty in the spring of 2005 (see Chapter 2). Just as importantly, direct democracy is also put forward as an alternative, or a cure, for the supposedly moribund state of party-driven

> **Representative democracy** is the election of parties and candidates to parliament where they then form governments and pass legislation on the people's behalf. By **direct democracy**, we mean the holding of referendums in order to decide policy and/or constitutional changes.

KEY POINT

Many European countries use referendums, but their purposes and powers vary considerably. Direct democracy comes with risks but can be a useful adjunct to representative politics.

politics in Europe. Direct democracy would also seem to be particularly attractive to younger people (see Donovan and Karp, 2006).

Supporters of direct democracy, like its opponents, put forward a whole host of arguments (see Debate 6.1). At the more fundamentalist or populist end of the spectrum lie claims that referendums have the potential to save democracy from parties that are portrayed as distant from the people and a distortion of, or even as parasites on, democracy. In the middle are claims, first, that referendums encourage participation and informed voting on crucial issues that would otherwise be subsumed in the packages of policies on offer at elections and, second, that parliaments make better laws if they know they risk being overturned. At the minimalist or pragmatic end of the spectrum lies the argument that they provide, first, a useful safeguard, particularly on constitutional issues that affect the political 'rules of the game' (be they domestic or European or the interaction between the two) and, second, that they prevent particular issues paralysing the system.

This pragmatic argument for direct democracy

Table 6.8 Number of referendums held in selected European countries, 1945–2011

Switzerland	430
Italy	72
Poland	12
France	11
Sweden	5
Spain	4
UK	2
Czech Rep.	1
Netherlands	1
Germany	0

Note: Total given for Sweden counts referendums on several options on the same subject held on the same day as one vote.

Source: Data from http://www.c2d.ch

DEBATE 6.1

Should we have more referendums?

YES

- Direct democracy bypasses an unpopular and disconnected political class which is either too ideologically blinkered or too 'politically correct' to deliver commonsense solutions in accordance with the views of ordinary people.
- Referendums can encourage lively debate and informed decisions on an issue which may not only cut across party lines but are also too important to be decided at general elections when voters have to take into account a whole host of topics.
- Direct democracy can help decide questions that would otherwise cause ongoing division and distract the country from other important matters.
- Referendums ensure that constitutional issues that will affect the political 'rules of the game' are not decided by those who play – and, indeed, only temporarily play – it.
- Governments and parliaments that know any legislation they produce may be overturned by a referendum will tend to ensure that such legislation is in accord with the will of the people. And – in the case of citizens' initiatives – allowing the people to recommend or even compel politicians to act on certain issues means they can never drift too far out of touch or close their eyes to a vital matter of public concern.
- Improving technology will allow us to vote instantly – think of TV's *Big Brother*.

NO

- Boiling down a complex issue into a straightforward question that everyone can understand will encourage dangerous oversimplification; it also rips particular issues out of context. People may end up voting for something that, for instance, will impact negatively on other programmes that they value or for policy that, given wider constraints, can be neither implemented nor afforded.
- Turning issues into either/or questions provides a field day for populists and a dumbed-down media – forces that will encourage voters to make irrational and prejudiced decisions when they might be better off leaving things to politicians who, when all is said and done, have been elected to do just that job and have more time and resources to do it properly.
- Low turnout is a problem: getting less than, say, half of the electorate to vote will throw the legitimacy of a referendum result into question and can even mean the result is not binding; this can encourage campaigners for the status quo to call for mass abstention – not what we need in a democracy.
- Even a 'respectable' turnout will be unrepresentative, given that older, better-off and better-educated people are more likely to vote.
- Referendums don't always bring closure – what is to stop the losing side calling for another vote on the same question at a later date?

certainly seems to reflect reality. In western Europe, the most widely used type is the ad hoc referendum and most referendums (of whatever type) have been used in order to decide questions that are considered too difficult (perhaps because they involve moral judgements on such things as abortion or divorce) or too crucial (normally because they touch on the constitution or on matters of sovereignty, particularly with regard to the EU, see Chapter 2) for parliament to decide for itself. This has been the case especially when an issue looks like splitting parties and/or when governments are hoping to insulate themselves from negative electoral effects it might have on them. The UK government's surprise announcement in 2004 that it would hold a refer-

endum on the EU's Constitutional Treaty is typical: in light of the Treaty's rejection by Dutch and French voters, no referendum was held, but the promise of one was enough to get Labour safely through the 2005 general election.

Referendums on social or economic policy are not uncommon in the 24 US states which have citizen-initiated referendums. But (outside Switzerland) they are very unusual in Europe, one recent exception being Iceland where in 2010 and 2011 outraged citizens voted to stop the government doing a deal to compensate UK and Dutch victims of the collapse of a big Icelandic bank. Votes on moral issues – despite media interest in them – are also quite uncommon, especially outside Italy and Ireland. Three European

Table 6.9 Types of referendums and where they can be used

Called by	'Law-controlling'	'Law-promoting'
Constitutional requirement	*Mandatory* (law in this area – normally constitutional) requires a referendum before coming into force) **Austria, Denmark, Estonia, Ireland, Latvia, Lithuania, Romania, Slovakia, Spain, Switzerland**	
Elected representatives	*Abrogative* (overturns laws already in force). **Italy, Switzerland**	*Ad hoc/optional* (called on a particular issue and may or may not be declared binding) **Austria, Belgium, Denmark, Finland, France, Greece, Hungary, Norway, Portugal, Slovenia, Sweden, UK**
	Rejective (overturns – normally constitutional – laws passed but not yet in force) **Austria, Bulgaria, Czech Rep., Denmark, Estonia, Greece, Ireland, Italy, Lithuania, Poland, Romania, Slovakia, Slovenia, Spain, Sweden, Switzerland**	
Citizens	*Abrogative* **Italy, Switzerland**	*Popular initiative* (draft law proposed by citizens which becomes binding if passed) **Hungary, Latvia, Lithuania, Poland, Romania, Slovenia, Switzerland**
	Rejective **Switzerland**	

Source: Adapted from Setälä (1999); entries for postcommunist states from Auer and Bützer (2001).

countries have resorted to referendums on the divisive – and possibly postmaterialist – issue of nuclear power (Austria, 1978, Sweden, 1980 and Italy, 1987). All rejected it (the Italians voting to ban their country's activity in projects outside of Italy). Spain's socialist government in the 1980s used a referendum to legitimize its decision to remain in NATO, and Hungary held a referendum in 1997 before joining it – unlike Poland and the Czech Republic, neither of whom felt in necessary to hold one before doing the same thing. Referendums have also been held in southern and east-central European states during their transition to democracy, not least as a way of gaining legitimacy for new constitutions. Latvia's constitution is unusual in that, since 2009, it also allows for a popular vote, by referendum, on the calling of extraordinary parliamentary elections: if two-thirds or more of the number of voters who turned out to vote at the previous general election approve, then an early general election is triggered.

In fact, constitutional referendums are the biggest single group, closely followed now by EU referendums, not least because so many CEE states held referendums for both purposes (see Szczerbiak and Taggart, 2004). Some (the Baltic states and Slovenia) used referendums to declare themselves independent; significantly this was an option denied to the Czech and Slovak people by their politicians, who feared their plans for a 'velvet divorce' might be vetoed. With the odd exception, referendums on new constitutions have resulted in 'yes' votes. This stands in marked contrast to referendums on constitutional amendments that have sought to extend the power of one branch of government, normally the executive, or somehow seem to advantage the ruling party and do not have cross-party support (as was the case in Ireland in 1959 and 1968 when the Fianna Fáil party tried unsuccessfully to introduce FPP). The exception to the rule is provided by France, where Charles de Gaulle persuaded the people to back the creation of a directly elected president in 1962. But even this is only a partial exception: when de Gaulle tried to limit the powers of the Senate in 1969, his plans were rejected in a referendum and he resigned.

Most states limit such votes to those proposed by the legislature or the executive, though interestingly there are some grounds to think that they propose them more often in states where the judiciary may be called on to oblige them to do so (as has happened in Ireland on three occasions in the postwar period; see Qvortrup, 2002: 105–7). However, two states – Switzerland and Italy – allow citizens themselves to call a vote on a particular question, requiring only that they gather sufficient signatures to show that such a vote would be worthwhile holding. The relative ease with which this can be done, however, is balanced in both countries by safeguards designed to reduce the risk to minority rights by requiring that any vote be passed by a 'double majority'. In Switzerland, this involves the cantons (see Box 6.6).

In Italy (where referendums can only repeal an existing law and where 500,000 signatures or five regional councils' support must be obtained first) they require at least 50 per cent of the country to actually turn up and vote, and the repeal option has to gain majority support among those who do. After a golden period in the early 1990s, when voters used referendums practically to oblige politicians to overhaul the electoral system, Italian referendums failed to attract sufficient people to turn out and vote, rendering them – in the eyes of critics, anyway – an expensive waste of time. This verdict was premature, however. In June 2011 Italians voted on four questions arising from citizens' initiatives – two on water privatization, one on nuclear power and another on whether those holding high office should be exempt from appearing in court. All surpassed the threshold and produced clear victories for those who had cam-

---

BOX 6.6

The home of direct democracy

The Swiss confederation is famous for a century or more of referendums. Nationally, it takes just 50,000 of the country's 7.3 million citizens who so object to a law or policy that they want to see it struck down to sign a petition to force a binding referendum. To win, they need to muster 'a double majority': Switzerland is made up of *cantons* (mini-states that enjoy a great deal of independence from the federal government at the centre); in order to pass at the national level, a referendum proposal has to win not only a majority of all those voting but also has to pass in a majority of cantons. Switzerland is also one of the few places in Europe to allow its citizens the right of initiative. As in California, they can propose a new law and, if passed, it becomes binding on parliament. Getting a vote on a proposal, however, is more demanding than getting one that seeks to strike something down; 100,000 citizens must sign and, more often than not, their proposal will be rejected. Frequently, though, the campaign (perhaps even before it has achieved all the signatures needed) will prompt the government into a counterproposal. Indeed, research suggests that the Swiss political class have become increasingly adept at doing deals in order to head off, or at least control, the effects of referendums (Papadopoulos, 2001). Whether this means that, ultimately, no one can beat politics-behind-closed-doors, or that those who conduct such politics are nonetheless more responsive to those outside the room, is a moot point.

---

paigned to get the questions asked.

Turnout in referendums has been an issue in other countries, such as Lithuania, which holds the record (19 since 1990) for the most referendums in CEE. In Slovakia in September 2010 voters were asked to decide on six questions in the one referendum, most of them (apart from the abolition of compulsory television licences) involving a reduction in the privileges of politicians: each question was given a positive response which varied between 70 and 95 per cent; the strength of feeling, however, made no difference because only 23 per cent of voters actually turned out, making it the seventh referendum in a row to be invalidated because it failed to attract 50 per cent of voters to come to the polls. In Poland, the referendum turnouts have been even lower than at elections: in 1996 just 32 per cent turned out to vote on privatization, in 1997 only 43 per cent bothered on the constitution. However, turnout on EU accession improved to 59 per cent, higher than in other 'candidate countries, although generally turnouts in the referendums they held before joining could have been predicted by their levels of turnout in other contests (see Szczerbiak and Taggart, 2004). Even countries where referendums are used sparingly can have trouble with turnout, The Portuguese government abandoned plans to liberalize abortion laws when the restrictionist case 'won' a referendum on the issue with a 1 per cent majority in 1998 but on a turnout of only 32 per cent despite weeks of high-intensity media coverage. When the same subject was put to a vote in February 2007, turnout (at almost 40 per cent) fell short of the 50 per cent required, although this time the government made it clear that it would regard the 59 per cent vote for liberalization as a mandate to legislate.

This falling-off of interest is not, of course, the only argument against direct democracy. Another is that, owing to the correlation between political participation and both affluence and education, those voting in referendums will be particularly unrepresentative of the electorate as a whole. Some critics also hold that they they risk the basest instincts and blinkered prejudice of the majority being whipped up by populist politicians who want to override the law and the rights of ethnic and other minorities – just as they were used by fascist regimes in the 1930s. Others believe that they discourage compromise, oversimplify complex matters and can produce contradictory laws and policies which are popular only because their wider context is not considered.

However, outside of Switzerland (where there is some evidence to suggest that poorer, less-educated voters are disproportionately less likely to vote in referendums) opponents of direct democracy have, as yet produced no evidence to show that this is the case in other European countries or, if it is the case, that this under-representation is any worse than it is in parliamentary elections. The same goes for the suggestion that voters in referendums are ill-informed.

Again, this is unproven and, even if it were, the situation would probably be just as bad in parliamentary elections where some voters' knowledge of party and candidate positions (and names) is woefully poor. Advocates of referendums can point to evidence from Denmark and Switzerland that they actually help improve citizen understanding of the issues under consideration. This could affect not just the result of the referendum, but opinion on the wider issue of which it might be just one facet. For instance, those who know more about the EU tend to be more supportive of it: holding relatively frequent referendums on EU matters could then affect levels of support for the EU more generally, even perhaps if the referendum in question is 'lost'. That they are sometimes (though rarely) lost reflects a problem to which EU referendums are said – incorrectly the latest research suggests (Hobolt, 2009) – to be particularly (but not exclusively) prone, namely, that they become party political popularity contests and/or protest votes against the government rather than a carefully considered answer to a specific question. This is even more likely if the politicians that order them are obliged neither to obey the result nor to hold them in the first place (see Hug, 2002; see also Qvortrup, 2002: 76).

This raises another common criticism of referendums; namely, that governments more often than not pull the strings, holding them only if and when they think they can win. However, the accusation is not borne out by the record, which suggests that over three-quarters of referendums held in Europe between 1945 and 1997 were not within their control. It also shows that just over one-third did not turn out to be supportive of the government's stance on the issue in hand (see Qvortrup, 2002). Neither is there much evidence that national-level referendums in Europe have oppressed minorities, although one could make a claim that this was exactly what happened in a Swiss referendum in November 2009 in which just under 60 per cent voted to ban the building of minarets even though the country's 400,000 Muslims had by then only built four in the entire country. On the other hand, we need to be careful not to paint the Swiss people in too illiberal a light: for instance, they supported what was clearly the long overdue decriminalization of homosexuality back in 1992. Often, indeed, voters turn out to be surprisingly liberal. Referendums on moral issues are very rare outside Italy (where divorce was controversially permitted in 1974) and Ireland (which has had long debates on both divorce and abortion). But voters in these two Catholic countries have on several occasions surprised commentators by voting for the more liberal option – though in Ireland, it took a second referendum on both issues (abortion in 1992 and divorce in 1995) before this result was achieved.

Yet referendums rarely resolve an issue if it reflects deep-seated divisions within a society. For instance, in 1950 a majority of Belgians voted for the restoration of the monarchy, but only because of such strong support for the idea from the Flemish community; riots ensued (mainly involving French speakers from Wallonia) which forced the king to abdicate in order for the monarchy to survive. More recently, the British government's ability to garner referendum backing for the Northern Ireland peace process in 1998 may well have helped prevent things slipping back into chaos, but it took longer to bring a lasting settlement appreciably closer. Meanwhile, the recent history of referendums in the Republic of Ireland shows that those on the losing side of the argument (whether they be citizens or the government) do not necessarily give up; instead they go for another referendum. This happened on abortion in the 1990s and, more recently, the ratification of the EU's Treaty of Nice.

Demands for direct democracy are often a function of disenchantment with and distrust of 'politics as usual' and, as such, we might expect them to increase. But, going on the evidence, referendums are not a 'silver bullet' that can revivify ailing democracies. Indeed, evidence suggests that they are just as (or more) likely to mobilize those who are already sufficiently interested to participate as they are to encourage those who are turned off politics to join in (see Donovan and Karp, 2006: 683–4). On the other hand, 50 years of experience suggest that they no longer need be tarred by association with the rigged 'plebiscites' of Fascist and Communist dictatorships. Instead the evidence suggests that, used sparingly, referendums can help democracy function more efficiently and, in some cases, provide a valuable reminder to politicians that getting elected every four or five years does not give them licence to ignore voters' views, particularly on issues of fundamental concern.

There is, however, one caveat, relating to a common criticism of direct democracy. The argument that money can buy, or that 'special interests'

can manipulate, referendums can in part be dismissed by noting that it applies with equal force to parliamentary elections. Indeed, one could argue that it is much easier for a wealthy interest group to 'buy' a small group of legislators than it is for them to 'purchase' the votes of millions of citizens. We also know that the overwhelming imbalance of financial resources in favour of the 'yes' campaigns in recent EU accession referendums was nowhere near reflected in the results, with substantial minorities voting 'no' in many countries. Those contests, like the one that resulted in the Swedes rejecting a switch to the euro, showed that 'it is possible to run an amateurish but populist and effective campaign against a much more glossy but off-putting one' (see Szczerbiak and Taggart, 2004: 767).

But the argument that the media might sometimes play a part in swinging the result one way or another could have some force, notwithstanding the fact that referendum results (as they did when voters in Sweden and Denmark rejected the euro) have often gone against the media consensus. As we go on to suggest in Chapter 7, fears of media influence on voting (if not on politics more generally) are often overplayed, yet they are not totally groundless, particularly when it comes to very close results. In most proportional systems, such marginal 'distortions' will be spread across the parties. But in referendums, just as in two-horse races in FPP systems, media influence on just a few thousand voters can – just occasionally – mean the difference between winning and losing (see Siune *et al.*, 1994). On the other hand, analysis of the EU accession referendums (see Szczerbiak and Taggart, 2004) strongly suggests that voters – who also, of course, have their own opinions and knowledge-base – are not influenced simply by the media per se but also by the cues they receive in (and not exclusively in) the media by parties and politicians, as well as by other, sometimes more credible actors, up to and including formally non-partisan presidents and even popes! In short, and once again, while it may be fashionable in these populist times to claim that referendums should replace representative democracy or to insist on separating voters from politicians, in fact they each have an impact on the other (see Setälä and Schiller, 2009). This is also the case when we come to examine the relationship between politics and the media, the subject of Chapter 7.

Learning Resources for Chapter 6

Further reading

For amazingly accessible yet erudite and informative coverage of the electoral systems debate in Europe and elsewhere, see the collection edited by Gallagher and Mitchell (2005), *The Politics of Electoral Systems.* Farrell (2011), *Electoral Systems: A Comparative Introduction* is also highly-recommended, managing to make potentially difficult material both intelligible and interesting. Anyone really fascinated in voting and elections should also check out the journal *Electoral Studies.* For the more academic arguments about the relationship between electoral and party systems and political and electoral behaviour, see Norris (2004b), *Electoral Engineering,* Sartori (1997), *Comparative Constitutional Engineering,* and Klingemann (2009), *The Comparative Study of Electoral* Systems, which focuses on the (apparently somewhat limited) impact of the rules of the game on individuals' voting behaviour. Franklin (2004), *Voter Turnout and the Dynamics of Electoral Competition in Established Democracies since 1945,* discusses turnout and plenty more of interest besides. Electoral behaviour in (western) Europe, and particularly the decline (or not) of class voting, is discussed in the collections edited by Evans (1999), *The End of Class Politics?,* and by Thomassen (2005), *The European Voter.* A useful introduction to political science's attempts to understand voting behaviour is Evans (2003), *Voters and Voting* (Sage). A stimulating discussion of some of the issues raised here is the chapter by Pennings in the collection edited by Keman (2002b), *Comparative Democratic Politics.* On referendums, the first port of call should be LeDuc (2003), *The Politics of Direct Democracy*; but see also Kaufman and Waters (2004), *Direct Democracy in Europe.* Also useful are two books by Qvortrup (2005), *A Comparative Study of Referendums,* and (2007), *The Politics of Participation.*

On the web

http://aceproject.org/regions-en/regions/europe – all things electoral
http://www.sussex.ac.uk/sei/publications – election and EU referendum reports online
www.parties-and-elections.de, http://psephos.adam-carr.net/ and wikipedia.org – election results
www.unc.edu/~asreynol/ballots.html – examples of ballot papers
www.idea.int/vt – electoral turnout
www.c2d.ch and www.iri-europe.org – news, data and research on referendums

Discussion questions

1   There is more than one type of proportional representation or PR electoral system used in Europe and they all have their strengths and weaknesses. Which do you prefer, and why?

2   What sort of rules can affect, and even undermine, the proportionality of PR systems? Can you give some examples of where these things have had an impact?

3   A handful of European countries employ 'plurality' or 'majority' systems: what do you see as the pros and cons of such systems?

4   Many people assume that a particular electoral system automatically leads to a particular party system: are they right to do so?

5   What causes variations in turnout at elections, and how seriously should we take concerns about turnout dropping right across Europe?

6   Voters seem to be less loyal to parties than they once were: how would you go about explaining this?

7   Do you think class and/or religion make much difference to the way people vote any more?

8   If you were asked to sum up the differences between today's European voters and those of 30 or 40 years ago, what would you say?

9   Do people vote differently in EP elections?

10 Referendums are distrusted, even disdained, by their critics: do you think they have some justification for their dislike of direct democracy or are you a fan of 'letting the people decide' as often as possible?

ONLINE
RESOURCES
AVAILABLE

Visit the companion site at www.palgrave.com/politics/bale to access additional learning resources.

Chapter 7

The media – player and recorder

In a representative democracy made up of millions of people, politicians need to communicate with those whose votes they rely on and whose welfare should be their main concern. To do so, they rely on the media – so much so, in fact, that some analysts talk about the 'mediatization' of politics (see Schulz, 2004 and Strömbäck, 2008). Inasmuch as politics and the media operate as separate institutions – and the media is best seen as an institution since it persists over time with norms and rules that impact systematically on those who work in and deal with it (see Ryfe and Blach-Ørsten, 2011) – the membrane that separates them is highly permeable. The media in Europe does not simply observe political activity but also helps to drive, structure and police it – so much so that it is increasingly difficult to distinguish where politics ends and media begins, and vice versa. The media is a source (and, on many matters, for most citizens practically the only source) of information and of interpretation. And it is a source of power (Street, 2011: 283–289), whether that power be *discursive* (lying in its capacity to construct reality), or to do with *access* (the ability to marginalize or promote certain points of view) or *resources* (which can be brought to bear on governments).

The media thereby both produces and reflects what (admittedly rather loosely) we call 'public opinion'. It also acts as a 'watchdog', not necessarily doing good or behaving admirably but exposing and preventing abuses, keeping politicians on their toes for the rest of us who are too poor or too busy to do so ourselves (see Schudson, 2008). It provides what those who conceive of it as a kind of 'fourth estate' see as a pseudo-constitutional check and balance – particularly in countries where, for instance, parliament (and therefore political opposition between elections) is weak. This so-called 'monitory democracy' (Keane, 2009) is not just theoretical: extensive cross-national empirical research strongly suggests a positive association between good governance and human development, on the one hand, and media freedom and accessibility, on the other (see Norris, 2004a).

Partly because it is recognized that the market might fail to perform these valuable functions, the state in most European countries continues to own, or at least subsidize, public broadcasting. Rather less obviously (via lower rates of sales tax or postal/telecommunication rates), it also subsidizes the press – particularly in Scandinavia (see De Bens, 2007: 164–166; see also Ots, 2009 and Kleis Nielsen with Linnebank, 2011). State 'interference', however, does not stop there: the state – at both national and local level – regulates the media in myriad ways, from the granting of broadcast licences to the imposition of obligations towards political impartiality and the setting up of more or less arm's-length press councils (see Fielden, 2012). In

Table 7.1 Press freedom rankings

World ranking		Score
3	Netherlands	−9.00
12	Sweden	−5.50
14	Czech Rep.	−5.00
16	Germany	−3.00
24	Poland	−0.67
28	UK	2.00
38	France	9.50
39	Spain	9.75
47	USA	14.00
61	Italy	19.67

Note: for a useful critique of the methodologies of freedom surveys like these see Behmer, (2009).

Source: Reporters without Borders http://en.rsf.org/press-freedom-index-2011-2012,1043.html

some countries, it goes even further, with the government of the day exerting a degree of control over output, or even indulging in plain old censorship that in others would be regarded as an insidious and ultimately dangerous infringement of press freedom (see Newton and Artingstall, 1994; Czepek, Hellwig and Nowak, 2009; and Bajomi-Lázár, 2008; see also Table 7.1). The government of Estonia, for instance, drew widespread criticism – not just at home (where newspapers printed blank front pages) but also from abroad – when, in 2010, it passed a media law supposedly intended to crack down on breaches of privacy but which many saw as an attempt to stymie investigative reporting by obliging journalists to reveal their sources. The same happened to the Hungarian government after it pushed what many regarded as a highly illiberal reform to its system of media regulation which was henceforth to be supervised by a figure appointed (on an extraordinarily long contract) by the Prime Minister.

Given the state's concern to maintain a degree of control of the media – and we should never forget that in most countries broadcasting in was originally monopolized by states lest this frighteningly powerful new technology fall into the 'wrong' hands – it is hardly surprising that the Europeanization of media regimes has been slow. This does not mean that there are no similarities in the political role and impact of the media in individual countries. Indeed, it could be that the media – especially television – varies less across Europe than do many of the other institutions (governance, parliaments, parties, etc.) we have examined in previous chapters. There is of course some patterned variation, and this chapter begins by providing some general and country-specific material on media use which suggests significant regional differences. It then goes on to look at the structure of the media and the regulatory and ownership environment in which it operates across Europe, with a particular focus on the implications for government control and for the coverage of politics. It then looks at possible connections between states' media systems and their political systems. Next, it explores how that coverage has changed in recent years, particularly with regard to the media's increased focus on personality-driven and 'presidential' coverage even in parliamentary systems and its move toward a less deferential style. It then deals with the difficult question of the media's effect on politics: is it overblown, can we measure it, and is it more about agenda-setting than directly influencing either voters or those for whom they vote? It goes on to explore the contribution of the media to the visibility and success of pressure groups and populist politicians. It moves on to examine the impact of new information and communication technology (ICT) on European politics and the contribution of the media, old and new, to European identity and integration. It ends with a brief look at the way the media in Europe covers foreign (including other European) countries.

Variations in usage and style

Broadly speaking, the further south and east you go in Europe, the less people read newspapers and the

KEY POINT

Television is far and away the most important medium. Newspaper-reading is more important in northern than in southern and central and eastern Europe, but is on the decline everywhere, especially among young people.

less time people who buy them spend time reading them (Table 7.2). This is probably because mass education and democracies with entrenched freedom of the press came later to Mediterranean countries and eastern and central Europe. Certainly, as Hallin and Mancini (2004: 64) show, there is (with the exception of France) a striking correlation between a country's newspaper circulation today and its adult literacy rate at the end of the nineteenth century – an example, if ever there was one, of the 'dead hand of history'. Conversely, the further south (and possibly east) you go, the more television people watch, the big exception to the rule being the UK. There adults watch three and three-quarter hours a day, which puts them on a par with people in Spain but ahead of people in Italy who (like the Czechs and the Dutch) watch only just over three hours – slightly less than the French and the Germans who watch around three-and-a-half hours. Scandinavians (although not the Danish) watch considerably less than three hours a day. At the other end of the scale, the Poles, watch four hours a day but, like everyone else, are beaten by the Greeks who watch nearly four and a half hours. Still, Europeans have some serious watching to do before they catch up with the Americans who watch over eight hours a day (OECD Communications Outlook, 2011).

Precisely how all these differences in media use feed into variations in political participation, whether it be voting (Chapter 6) or other forms of activity (Chapter 8), is an interesting debate. On balance, the evidence suggests that paying attention to political news seems to increase participation, although the effect is stronger for newspapers than it is for television (Shehata, 2010). There is less research – and less research than there should be – on radio (see Box 7.1).

These regional variations also apply to media styles: for instance, the Scandinavian media, despite its mass reach, takes its mission to inform and educate more seriously than most and, especially when it comes to local newspapers, is financially supported by the state for so doing (De Bens and Østbye, 1998: 14). This does not mean, however, that Nordic necessarily means high-minded. True, the UK tabloid press is even more heavily focused on entertainment than its equivalents elsewhere in Europe. But Sweden has its *Aftonbladet* just as Germany, where the 'tabloidization' of news has

Table 7.2 Newspaper reading in Europe

	Mins per day reading newspaper	% not reading newspaper
Sweden	37	8
Netherlands	35	20
Germany	33	19
UK	38	26
Czech Rep.	32	22
Poland	26	31
France	23	39
Spain	18	49
Greece	16	66

Source: Data from Elvestad and Blekesaune, 2008

arguably proceeded at a slower pace than in, say, the UK, has its *Bild*. In central and eastern Europe, tabloids quickly took hold: Poland's bestselling paper, *Fakt*, is essentially a *Bild*-clone, owned by the same (German) publisher (Downey, 2012: 124–8). Interestingly, it is newspapers in southern Europe that are, by and large, relatively serious affairs bought by relatively few people, with most going to weekly magazines (the *prensa del corazón* most famously exemplified perhaps by *¡Hola!* in Spain) for the celebrity gossip that the British (and the Germans and the Swedes) get every day.

We should also note the rise and rise of so-called 'free-sheets' – newspapers that can be picked up at no cost at, for example, railway stations and which often contain reworked content from the same day's paid-for papers (see De Bens, 2007: 158–60). Those tempted to scoff that such outlets are either irrelevant to, or bad for, democracy because they contain little political content need to be careful: in fact, they vary considerably. Viennese commuters, for example, can indeed pick up *Heute*, whose 'lite' political coverage is on a par with what Londoners expect from, say, *Metro* or Parisians from *20 Minutes*; but, if they were to plump instead for *Österreich*, they would be getting more politics for free than, say, British tabloid readers pay for when they read the *Mirror* or the *Sun*. That this is the case reflects a clear trend over time in most (though not

---

BOX 7.1

The agenda-setting Cinderella – radio and politics

Writing on Spain, Sanders (with Canel, 2004: 200–201) observes that radio is both 'a key source of political news' and 'the most unconstrained medium for the discussion of politics', it is also, she notes, an important agenda-setter, whose journalists are trusted more than their counterparts in TV and in the newspapers (an assumption confirmed in Figure 7.3). Generally, however, there is little mention of radio in work on the media and politics in Europe, even though many governments subsidize both local and national radio, even though audience figures are actually quite high, and even though the medium's possibilities are still as endless as they ever were, especially given the rise of digital and internet platforms (see Hendricks, 2012). Most of those listening to music hear news bulletins on-the-hour-every-hour, and talk radio, (particularly the 'flagship' programmes made by public broadcasters that feature news and interviews with major political figures), often plays an important role in setting the day's news agenda. Appearing on those programmes is also a means by which those figures signal their positions and intentions to each other, as well as the audience. Since the advent of television, governments have paid rather less attention to radio. However, in a 24/7 news culture that continually seeks new angles in order to refresh and move a story on – and where there is considerable cross-ownership of radio, TV and print media – a radio story is more than capable of causing politicians headaches. In addition, radio, more than television perhaps (see McNair *et al.*, 2002), can be a genuine public-access medium allowing people to break through into what they – rather than the media or the politicians – want to talk about (see Ross, 2004). The phone-in 'talk-back' show is nowhere near as developed or significant a format in Europe as it is in the USA, but politicians ignore the medium at their peril, even if research suggests that their appearances on it are unlikely to improve their image much.

---

all) countries for popular (i.e. non-broadsheet) paid-for papers to feature less and less hard news (see Table 7.3). What this has not done, however, is to arrest the decline in readership, especially among the young – something that some political scientists (see Wattenberg, 2011) connect, first, to surveys showing decreasing interest in and knowledge of politics and, second, to the worrying decline in turnout mentioned in Chapter 6.

One aspect of the media in Europe that is seemingly universal is 'news values' – the criteria that determine whether editors include or reject a story (see Brighton and Foy, 2007 and Palmer, 2002). All over the continent, stories have much more chance of seeing the light if they are visual, emotive, conflictual, intense, unambiguous, of majority relevance, unpredictable and apparently capable of some kind of 'commonsense' solution. Nevertheless, one can detect subtle national variations in journalistic methods, ethics and notions of objectivity and, more generally, style (Hanitzsch *et al.*, 2011). A fascinating comparative study (Donsbach and Patterson, 2004) of journalists in Germany, Italy, Sweden and the USA, reveals all sorts of significant differences. German journalists, for example, are quite happy to provide both reportage and commentary on events, whereas, at the other extreme, US journalists tended to do either one or the other, not both. The Italians, like the Germans, were much less concerned with what their counterparts in other countries would think of as objectivity; Swedish journalists were much more likely than their counterparts in the UK and Italy to seek out their own information rather than more passively relying on the cues of parties, interest groups and government. When it comes to broadcast news styles, there are also variations. Programmes in Italy, Spain and France, for instance, tend to carry more domestic news, longer items with fewer contributors and more studio-based content, whereas more 'Germanic' (as opposed to 'Romantic') news cultures, such as the UK and the Netherlands, go for short, sober, location-based reports (see Heinderyckx, 1993).

Interestingly, there is little hard evidence that increasing commercial competition in broadcasting, as opposed to the print media, has led to an

Table 7.3 Changes in space devoted to hard news, sport and TV/radio in popular newspapers

	News		Sport		TV/radio	
Year	1960	2000	1960	2000	1960	2000
Poland	57	23	15	19	3	8
Italy	53	72	12	10	0	2
France	50	30	15	25	3	11
UK	48	26	20	24	4	6
Czech Rep.	47	36	25	18	0	3
Germany	43	42	14	28	0	7
Sweden	41	27	20	37	2	6

Note: Neither the Netherlands nor Spain were included in the original research.

Source: Data from Weibull and Nilsson, 2010: 62.

unequivocal 'dumbing down' of news provision, either when it comes to the privately owned channels themselves or to public broadcasters (though see Gunther and Mughan, 2000). Some detect 'divergence' – public broadcasting stays, or gets even more, 'serious' – while others observe 'convergence' – news on public channels becomes less 'serious' but commercial stations raise their game away from mere 'infotainment' in order to compete (see Pfetsch, 1996, for a fascinating case study). More controversially, it is perfectly possible to make an argument that it is about time that coverage was 'dumbed down', if by that we mean the employment of less precious and self-consciously high-minded formats which help to make politics more accessible for the many citizens who have, at best, only a passing interest in the subject (Temple, 2006).

Structure and regulation

The extent to which media is national or more regionally based varies considerably in Europe, particularly when it comes to the press. We would be hard pushed in some countries to assert the existence of a national newspaper market. The latter might exist in the UK, with the main division between downmarket 'tabloids' and upmarket 'broadsheets'. But regional titles continue to play a big, indeed bigger, part elsewhere. This is perhaps to be expected in a federal republic such as Germany, where many of the titles routinely cited in overseas press reviews (such as the *Frankfurter Allgemeine Zeitung* and the *Süddeutsche Zeitung*) are regional newspapers, albeit nationally distributed. Nor is it surprising in 'asymmetrically federal' Spain (see Chapter 2), where the combined circulation of the four top-selling national dailies is only a quarter of that of the regional press (Sanders with Canel, 2004: 199). Yet the same is true of supposedly centralized France where daily titles that are well known abroad (*Le Monde, Le Figaro* and *Libération*) sell predominantly in Paris; elsewhere regional papers rule the roost, to the extent that 'three out of four French citizens never read a daily national paper' (Kuhn, 2004b: 26). The regional daily, *Ouest France,* for instance, has a higher circulation (800,000) than any of its 'national' competitors, none of which sells more much than 300,000 per day, although national weekly news magazines (like magazines in general) seem still to be popular (Jouët, 2010: 159).

While regional titles do cover national news, there is clearly less room for it, meaning that citizens in those countries where they predominate might be, first, more likely to think that what goes on in regional and local politics counts for something and, second, even more likely to turn to television for national-level political information. This serves to reinforce television's dominant role as most people's main source of political information, and hence the tendency of government and politicians to focus on broadcast rather than print media. The latter still has a place, though – both as a forum for elite-level, in-depth debate and, paradoxically, as creator of and conduit for populist opinion and political pressure. Unfortunately, the range of opinion and the direction of that pressure is not as diverse as it might be: the newspaper market in all European countries, with the partial exception of Scandinavia, has seen a fall in the number of titles – one which is likely to continue as advertising migrates to the internet – as well as increasing concentration of ownership (see Meier, 2007 and De Bens, 2007) of those that survive; the huge entry costs into the market also make it very difficult for newcomers to make it (De Bens and Østbye, 1998: 11). For many, a worrying aspect of the capital required to run a media outlet

---

BOX 7.2

Defending whose interests? Ownership and the French press

In 2004, the centre-right supporting daily, *Le Figaro,* was bought by Serge Dassault, ex-boss (and still honorary chairman) of the Dassault group which, among other activities, produces military equipment, including the famous Mirage and Rafael jets. By 2005, he was reported as telling his senior editors that 'you have to take a lot of care with the news. Some of it does more harm than good', while later reports hinted at suppression of articles on the company's products and associates. *Le Figaro,* however, is not the only paper to have connections with the defence industry. In early 2005, Lagardère, which has interests in aviation as well as media, and supposedly began its media investment as a platform to oppose suggestions that it be nationalized, took a stake in the more liberal *Le Monde.* But it's not only defence companies who are involved in the media in France: so, too, are utility and public works companies like Bouygues, Suez-Lyonnaise, and Vivendi; they depend on government contracts and are naturally concerned about government regulation. And, of course, these companies' interests are by no means limited to France: Lagardère and Vivendi own publishing and broadcast assets in a range of European countries – something which is also true of all the other big groups operating across the continent, including News Corporation, Bertelsmann-RTL, Mediaset, ProSieben Sat, Modern Times Group, and CME. Whether ownership by these companies makes a difference to how particular outlets cover politics is predictably hard, however, to prove: partisanship is easier to spot in newspapers (especially those owned by News Corp) than in television where (outside of Italy anyway) news programmes in particular try hard to retain a reputation for balance and objectivity.

Sources: Harcourt (2005), Lloyd (2005)

---

is the tendency in some countries for them to be owned by companies with outside, non-media interests which may (directly or indirectly) bias the editorial line. France is just one example (see Box 7.2).

Owning newspapers is now a rich man's sport and rich men are not generally noted for their left-wing views. This does not, of course, mean that all Europe's newspapers are conservative or neoliberal in persuasion. The logic of the market dictates that there is money to be made from papers that cater to the tastes of the millions of potential readers with a rather different outlook on life, and it is possible to argue that a decline in the number of titles will actually result in a decrease in 'political parallelism' (outlets being closely linked to one 'side' or other), which may in turn reinforce the 'catch-all' tenden-

cies of parties we discussed in Chapter 5 (see Hallin and Mancini, 2004: 267ff.). But it does mean that those newspapers are unlikely to put themselves at the head of campaigns for, say, root and branch redistribution of wealth or a tax on international financial transactions.

Television may be dominant in Europe, but it has undergone considerable changes in recent years as technological progress (not least the arrival of digital and satellite) and free-market ideas have combined to turn what was once the fiefdom of a few (often state-run) terrestrial providers into a fragmented multichannel world of round-the-clock choice. This poses major challenges for democracies and for the politicians and governments trying to run them. Deregulation of the broadcasting environment has, if anything, multiplied the tasks and the complexity of those charged with its oversight, albeit increasingly at arm's-length through 'independent' bodies that in a number of European countries (Germany and the Netherlands, for instance) contain representatives from supposedly important social interests, making regulation these days more a matter of *gov-*

KEY POINT

The media is subject to country-specific regulation and restrictions on ownership, but these are being undermined by EU law and a tendency toward commercial concentration and cooperation.

BOX 7.3

Witch-hunt or welcome change? Rupert Murdoch and the politicians

Rupert Murdoch is one of the most powerful 'media moguls' on the planet, with newspaper titles and broadcast channels that give him a reach into many of the world's democracies, large and small. He began in Australia but began to make his global reputation in the UK, where he started out by buying two very different national dailies, the upmarket 'paper of record', *The Times*, and the popular tabloid, the *Sun*, which he took decidedly downmarket and in so doing turned into Britain's bestselling title, with a readership – at its pre-internet peak – of over five million people. His company, News International, also bought the salacious Sunday paper, the *News of the World*. The money he made from these operations helped to bankroll the extremely expensive set-up of the satellite television broadcaster Sky – and helped him move into the American market, where he is best known for owning Fox TV, as well as the *New York Post*.

Right from the outset, Murdoch was known as a hands-on proprietor, influencing (and in the case of the *Sun* and the *News of the World*, sometimes virtually dictating) the political line taken by his editors. It was not entirely surprising, then, that British politicians sought to keep on the right side of him – a trend hastened by the apparent association between the support given by his newspapers to the Conservative Party under Margaret Thatcher and later on to the Labour Party under Tony Blair. The latter, convinced like many of his colleagues that he would find it very difficult to win an election against a hostile *Sun*, went out of his way to court Murdoch's good opinion, famously flying half way around the world to address News International executives when he was in opposition and, in government, qualifying (though never quite abandoning) his early enthusiasm for the European Union – a particular bugbear of Murdoch, who sees it as something of a Trojan horse for socialism and, more directly, a regulatory threat to his business interests.

Hoping for the supposedly all-important endorsement from Murdoch, David Cameron, who took over as Conservative leader in 2005, recruited Andy Coulson, a former editor of the *News of the World*, despite the fact that Coulson had been forced to step down from that post after it was discovered the paper had been hacking into private voicemails in order to generate stories about the British Royal family. The claim at the time that it had all been the work of one 'rogue reporter', however, was blown apart in July 2011 when it became clear that the practice had been far more widespread than acknowledged and that it not only involved celebrities but the victims of crime. Coulson was forced to resign from his post as the Prime Minister's Director of Communications and the Chief Executive of News International (another former editor and, it transpired, a personal friend of Cameron), Rebekah Wade, also stepped down; both later faced criminal charges. Allegations also arose about corrupt payments by journalists to police officers, and the Commissioner of the Metropolitan Police had to go too. Meanwhile as a gesture of contrition, Murdoch announced the closure of the *News of the World*. Even worse for him than the loss of that cash cow, the government, which seemed all set to give a green-light to his News Corporation's takeover of Sky then went cold on the idea. The government, however, did not escape scot-free. Not only was Cameron criticized for his poor judgement in appointing Coulson, but his Culture Secretary, Jeremy Hunt, was widely suspected of having favoured the Newscorp takeover for political reasons. Just as damagingly, the Prime Minister was practically forced into holding a full-scale judicial enquiry in the media, headed by Lord Justice Leveson, which demanded much stricter regulation – something that was bound to alarm Murdoch and other proprietors and make them less well disposed to any politician or party prepared to, as they saw it, muzzle free speech.

ernance than *government* (see Chapter 3 and Meier, 2011).

States have to reconcile the demand for free speech with the fact that the market can potentially lead to monopolistic (and perhaps foreign-owned) media empires narrowing rather than widening the range of opinions on offer. This requires them to maintain regulatory regimes and pass media laws that are often controversial, either because they are said to be overly restrictive or too lax – or sometimes because they attract accusations of political interference (see Box 7.3). But, once these bodies are established and the laws are passed, this simply means an unending series of decisions to be taken on, say, awarding licences and on preventing or allowing takeovers. These decisions, rightly or wrongly, often draw flak from those who believe that they are influenced by the promise of political favours. Successive Spanish governments of both left and right have been attacked, and even successfully challenged in both domestic and European Courts, by opponents for allowing sales to go through in contravention of rules on concentration (see Sanders with Canel, 2004: 201).

In most west European countries, some foreign ownership of newspaper titles occurs. In Spain, for instance, the campaigning daily *El Mundo* is Italian-owned, while in the UK US-based News International owns a number of British titles. But it is actually still quite uncommon (see De Bens and Østbye, 1998: 12). In postcommunist countries, however, it is by no means so unusual, not least because overseas interests were often able to buy into print media markets relatively cheaply; they also had more money to do so than domestic concerns. In Poland, for example, German publisher Axel Springer has just over 40 per cent of the newspaper market, while another German company, WAZ, has a near-monopoly position in Bulgaria (Downey, 2012: 124–8). Foreign ownership, however, is less of a concern to most governments than cross-ownership, where one firm has, say, newspaper and television holdings, and overconcentration, where a few firms own most of the outlets (see Meier, 2007 and Baker, 2007). But they might be fighting a losing battle as technological advances and free-speech arguments, plus the logic of the market – and, in particular, the single European market (SEM) – begin to overwhelm them. Europe's increasingly corporate (as opposed to individually or family-owned) media groups are cooperating with each other more and more, which arguably promotes efficiency (if not genuine competition) and possibly reduces political partisanship. It does, however, risk reducing diversity, not least because the need to deliver shareholder value might drive out relatively expensive home-grown production in favour of imported (which means American) content (see Harcourt, 2005: 117–57).

True, states still have their own rules – dictating, for instance, the number of titles and channels in which a single firm is allowed to have a stake based on proportions of shares owned and/or audience share (see Meier, 2007 for details). Some even give this responsibility to lower tiers of government: public broadcasting in Germany may be controlled by a supposedly socially representative Federal Broadcasting Council, but most media regulation is done at the *Land* level. Yet as Harcourt (2005) points out, EU member states have had to accept the principle, laid down by the ECJ (see Chapter 2), that broadcasting is not simply a cultural matter, and therefore under national control, but a tradeable service and therefore subject to European competition law. The ECJ also prevented states from blocking broadcasts from abroad into its domestic market, and, as Harcourt shows, has been a lever for liberalization. It has obliged governments in the Netherlands, Greece and Belgium to abandon legislative attempts to restrict competition. It has also limited the privileges of state-owned or subsidized public service broadcasting, even though the continued role of the latter received a vote of confidence and a measure of protection in an important protocol to the Amsterdam Treaty of 1997 (see Box 7.4).

Meanwhile, the Commission, in its role as regulator of the internal market, has had to get involved in the policing (and – especially in Germany and also in Spain – the prevention) of mergers and takeovers of media firms, many of which now have holdings in a number of European countries. Some governments have objected to such interference. But, interestingly, some have been grateful to Brussels, even if only privately: they find it very difficult to take on media empires for fear of alienating a potentially powerful political opponent (see Harcourt, 2003: 196) – a good example of a hard task being contracted out to the EU. On the other hand, there

The EU as (a partial) protector of public service broadcasting

Governments and public service broadcasters were concerned that commercial concerns should not use EU competition law to try to undermine them completely on the grounds, say, that such broadcasting was an example of illegal state aids. They therefore inserted a protocol into the EU's Treaty of Amsterdam. This notes that 'the system of public broadcasting in the Member States is directly related to the democratic, social and cultural needs of each society and to the need to preserve media pluralism'. It goes on to note that nothing in the Treaty should be allowed to infringe on 'the competence of Member States to provide for the funding of public service broadcasting', although, it also observes, only 'insofar ... as such funding does not affect trading conditions and competition in the Community to an extent which would be contrary to the common interest'. The tension between cultural and economic logic, therefore, has not entirely disappeared (see Wheeler, 2009) and, given continuing pressure from powerful commercial enterprises on issues like state-subsidized broadcasters maintaining powerful web presences, it is unlikely to do so (see Donders, 2011; Harcourt, 2005; see also Humphreys, 2009; Klimkiewicz, 2009: 56–8).

evidence of Europeanization, then media regulation (although not, as we shall see, output) is a very good example. Recent media legislation in the member states (including those who joined in 2004), and even in Switzerland, shows significant signs of having been influenced by and redrawn to take account of the EU's 1989 and 1997 *Television Without Frontiers* and 2007 Audiovisual Media Services Directives, which (notwithstanding general moves toward liberalization) attempt to limit advertising and boost European content (see Wheeler, 2009). The latter aim does not go down well with the USA, but the EU (especially under French pressure) has tried to hold the pass on the issue at international trade forums like the General Agreement on Tariffs and Trade (GATT) and the World Trade Organization (WTO). Whether resistance is ultimately futile – as US companies buy into European media firms and satellite broadcasters really do create television without borders by only having to comply with media legislation pertaining where they are headquartered rather than where they transmit to (see Czepek, Hellwig and Nowak, 2009: 15) – remains to be seen. What we may see more of is a gap opening up – as it has already opened up in central and eastern Europe (see Harcourt, 2012) – between a rhetorical commitment to a 'European' model and what actually happens on the ground, namely a move towards a more American, market liberal model.

State and public service broadcasting

In 1980, television in every European country, apart from Britain, Luxembourg and Italy, was public television, but by 2000 every country had allowed commercial competition (Semetko *et al.*, 2000: 123). But while public broadcasters might be under pressure, they have not disappeared. Outside Luxembourg, there is no European country without a state-funded or, if commercial revenue-raising is permitted (see Figure 7.1), at least a state-subsidized public broadcaster existing alongside commercial stations. True, the daily audience share of public broadcasters in postcommunist countries can be very low (ranging from around a third in the Czech Republic and Poland to well under a fifth in Hungary according to

is, of course, a tension – as there always is – between allowing a degree of concentration in order to create European businesses which can compete effectively with large overseas conglomerates (one of the main drivers of the single market project, after all) and preventing monopoly at home. It is also increasingly difficult in such a fast-moving environment to use audience share (which changes all the time) or share ownership (which can be hidden by complex inter-business networks) as measures of market dominance.

That said, the EU is clearly a force, not just in terms of legal and competition decisions but also in terms of setting the agenda for, and promoting the convergence of, national regimes (see Harcourt, 2005 and Humphreys, 2009). If one is looking for

http://mde.politics.ox.ac.uk) and some commentators question whether they can ever really emulate their western counterparts. The latter were not faced with the same legacy of distrust of state television as a provider of propaganda; they also had years to establish themselves (in terms of ethos and audience) before facing commercial competition (see Jakubowicz, 2004 and EUMAP, 2009). In western Europe (including Norway, Sweden and the UK, where they are advert-free and rely largely on the licence fee), relatively embedded public broadcasters are not without their own troubles. But they can still boast considerable audience share, as well as the support of politicians who may be groping around for a new media policy paradigm but have not (yet) abandoned the public service model completely (see van Cuilenburg and McQuail, 2003; also Thompson, 2006).

European governments' support for public broadcasting – symbolized both by funding and by the common insistence that cable or digital services must include public channels in their subscriber packages – is driven by genuine concern to preserve national culture and a well-informed civil society, as well as by a suspicion that, without a mix of public and private, the technologically-driven expansion of

> **KEY POINT**
>
> **Television in Europe has changed considerably since the 1980s towards a more commercial and multi-channel environment, but public broadcasting is still important – and, in some countries, still not entirely free from government interference.**

choice will lead not to diversity but to dumbing down. But it also stems from the belief – strengthened by fears of commercial concentration – that democratically elected politicians, and those who vote for them, should have access to at least one source of information and opinion that is insulated from the interests of this or that entrepreneur or enterprise, as well as bound by codes (some of them statutory) promoting political impartiality or, at least, 'balance'.

Most (if not all) politicians in Europe are now used to the fact that state ownership (or rather funding) no longer provides them with direct access to quiescent cronies dedicated to serving the needs of the government of the day. But it has taken rather a long time (as well as professional codes of conduct among journalists and legal constraints on politicians) to get some governments to recognize the fact, meaning that the degree of independence of public broadcasters does vary significantly between countries (see Hanretty, 2011 and Table 7.4). Ongoing attempts at political interference are not confined only to Europe's newest democracies, such as Hungary, the Czech Republic and Poland, where state control, even if it was never as absolute or uniform as we might think (see Sparks, 2000: 37–40), was considerable. They also occur in countries that emerged from dictatorship over quarter of a century ago, such as Greece and Spain (see Box 7.5). And even when state interference, as such, is no longer an issue, governments are inevitably keen on trying to manage the media so that it presents them in the best light: erstwhile French president, Nicolas Sarkozy, was a case in point (Kuhn, 2010), although, in the end, his efforts were of little practical (or at least electoral) use.

In fact, broadcast journalists have been moaning for some time about the way in which their bosses seem to indulge in anticipatory self-censorship. During the suburban riots that shook France in

Figure 7.1 How public broadcasting is funded

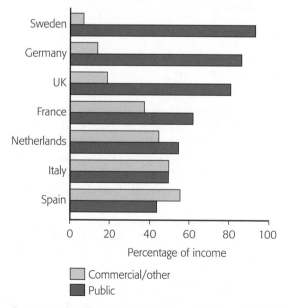

Percentage of income

☐ Commercial/other
■ Public

Source: Data from d'Haenens *et al.*, (2011) covering the years 2006–8

Table 7.4 How independent from political interference are Europe's public broadcasters?

Germany	0.91
UK	0.89
Sweden	0.86
Italy	0.81
Poland	0.75
France	0.72
Czech Rep.	0.64
Spain	0.56

Notes: Index, in which a score of 1 would indicate complete independence is calculated using the relationship between turnover of those in charge of public broadcasting and government change. No figure available for Netherlands.

Source: Data from Hantretty, 2011: 16.

November 2005, broadcasters around the world eagerly transmitted vivid images (and even a nightly tally) of burning cars; their French counterparts, however, were much more cagey about showing such graphic pictures (and keeping a tally), apparently because they believed their duty not to inflame the situation further (and possibly boost support for the far right) came before their duty to show what was going on. We should be careful before condemning their attitude as pompous and spineless, however: many media outlets (print and broadcast) in Europe and elsewhere took a similarly 'responsible' stance when it came to publishing (or rather not publishing) the 'Danish cartoons' of the Prophet Muhammed that caused such a furore at the end of 2005 and beginning of 2006 (see Ryan, 2008; see also Eide *et al.*, 2008). We should also note that in the last five years websites like http://www.mediapart.fr/, by being more open and offering an alternative, have in effect forced the mainstream media in France to tackle issues (not least the private lives and corruption of some of the country's senior politicians) that for years went unreported.

Most other states in Europe (with the partial exception of France) try to avoid these problems by eschewing this 'politics-over-broadcasting systems' mode of governance. Instead, they operate the kind of 'formally autonomous systems' which exist in, say, the UK and Sweden, or the 'politics-in-broadcasting

BOX 7.5

Spain – a return to government control?

In 2006, the Socialist administration then running Spain responded to persistent criticism that it exercised too much control of the public broadcaster RTVE, whose news programmes have long been widely criticized for favouring the government of the day – not only by the public but even by journalists who work there. RTVE's board was made more representative and, while it was still possible for an incoming administration in Madrid to appoint a new RTVE President, the appointment would require the approval of a two-thirds majority in parliament, virtually ensuring that some sort of consensus candidate would win through. The Act which brought in the changes, however, was simply amended by the conservative government which took over in late 2011. New Prime Minister Mariano Rajoy proceeded to appoint Leopoldo González-Echenique, who had previously worked for a conservative government (Harrison, 2012). The new President then set about recruiting what some saw as conservatively-inclined heads of news, while journalists previously accused of being especially combative and/or left-leaning then found themselves moved around or dropped from the schedules. Whether all this would have a marked impact on coverage of the government's austerity programme – so severe that by the autumn of 2012 it was beginning to provoke violent street demonstrations – remained uncertain: the proof of the pudding will be in the eating (or rather the viewing and listening). Watch this space.

systems' (where governing bodies include representatives of political parties and interest groups) that still characterize Germany and the Netherlands (see Brants and Siune, 1998: 129). In the latter, this mode of media governance has led, following the introduction of commercial television in the late 1980s, to a system of three public service channels (one serving up supposedly family fare, one sports and entertainment and the third more 'cultural' and informative material). On each channel, time is allocated (partly in accordance with their membership numbers) to eight not-for-profit associations of social and religious groups which make programmes reflecting their interests and points of view – a system that promotes considerable diversity (see Wurff, 2004). In Italy, the 'politics-in-broadcasting' mode was taken to its logical extent by giving control of each state channel to one of the main political parties. Recently, however, elite agreement on this *lottizzazione* system has broken down, with accusations from the left that the right-wing government of media magnate Silvio Berlusconi was not playing fair (see Box 7.10), all of which persuades some analysts that Italy should now be categorized alongside Greece as a 'politics-over-broadcasting' system (see Hardy, 2008).

The connection between media systems and political systems

What we observe, then, notwithstanding the possibility that journalism in Europe has enough in common to distinguish it from its counterpart in the USA (see K. Williams, 2006), is considerable variation in the way media works and is regulated and consumed. But our task should also be to look for patterns in and essay an explanation of that variation – ideally, one that connects the political systems of states and the media systems they help structure but which in turn help shape them. Until recently, academics had avoided such a daunting comparative enterprise. In 2004, however, Daniel Hallin and Paolo Mancini published what must rank as one of the most important books in the field of media in politics. In it, they argue that it is possible and useful to categorize Europe's media systems and link them to types of political systems that rest on the distinctions familiar to comparative politics. Three distinctions are particularly important to their schema. The first is the distinction between polarized and moderate systems, as suggested by Sartori for party systems (see Chapter 5). The second is the distinction between majoritarian and consensual systems developed by Arend Lijphart, which we mentioned when dealing with governments and parliaments in

Chapter 4. The third is a distinction, which we go on to explore in more detail in Chapter 8 but which we touched on in Chapter 1 when talking about different types of welfare states. This is the distinction between more 'corporatist' systems (where governments tend to take a hands-on role, working alongside powerful economic interest groups, and where the welfare state is comprehensive, if not necessarily delivered by the public sector) and more liberal 'pluralist' systems (where the government tends to take less of a role and interest groups tend to be more fragmented and competitive, and where the welfare state is not quite so comprehensive).

KEY POINT

Research into how variations in countries' media systems may be connected to their differences in their political systems is at an early – but fruitful – stage.

Hallin and Mancini argue that it is feasible and fruitful to think of European countries as members of one of three 'media systems': (i) the *Mediterranean* or *Polarized Pluralist model* (e.g. France, Greece, Italy, Portugal and Spain); (ii) the *North European* or *Democratic Corporatist model* (Benelux, Scandinavia, Germany, Austria and Switzerland); and (iii) the *North Atlantic* or *Liberal model* (UK and Ireland), which also includes the USA and Canada. Each of these is associated with – and influenced (though not absolutely determined) by different types of political systems. In each media system there will be, among other things, a characteristic level of circulation, a characteristic degree of linkage between the media and parties and/or interest groups, a tendency toward advocacy or 'objectivity' among journalists, a characteristic regulatory regime, and a different role for the state. Naturally, they expand on these system characteristics, and the links between them and political factors, in a book which relies on sophisticated historical reasoning and lots of empirical evidence, but they can be summed up as follows:

▶ Polarized pluralist model. State and parties involved in many aspects of life, including the media, and adherence to widely differing ideologies is strong, both among the general public and journalists, meaning that there is relatively little sense of an objective common good or, for journalists, professional norms which trump ideology. Politically active minority consumes heavily-slanted, comment-heavy output of predominantly serious newspapers, while less-interested majority sticks more to television.

▶ **Democratic corporatist model.** Extensive state intervention in the market – including the media market – to facilitate (and subsidize) the representation and reconciliation of different interests and viewpoints, as well as transparency and local autonomy, for the common good. The value placed on the latter ensures that while journalists may advocate for one side or other, they do so within a framework of shared professional norms. Serious news is produced for and consumed by a mass as well as an elite audience.

▶ **Liberal model.** State not so involved, especially when it comes to the print media. Journalists (with a strong rhetorical commitment to objectivity and independence) are less concerned with representing interest groups and/or ideologies than with playing a watchdog role on behalf of citizen-consumers. Many still read papers but rely more on television for news.

Of course, there are all sorts of criticisms to be made and debates to be had about Hallin and Mancini's schema. For one thing, one can argue that it captures traditions very well but that these traditions (while still important) are being bypassed as media systems – no longer as insulated as they once were – converge (in part because of technology) on more globalized, homogenized or at least hybrid practices (see Nord, 2006 and Petersson *et al.*, 2006 on Swedish election coverage, for example). For another, one can argue that the systems of Ireland and the UK, where there is, first, still a very strong assertion of the importance and subsidy of public broadcasting and, second, a highly partisan print media, simply don't belong in the same category as the overwhelmingly private broadcasting and non-partisan system of the USA. In addition, their speculation that the media systems of east central Europe will fit into the democratic corporatist model seems highly questionable. The polarization and partisanship that characterized the region's media in the early 1990s might have been dampened by commercial concerns, but has by no means withered away,

while public service broadcasting is finding it difficult to compete against commercial stations with little interest (but considerable bias) in politics; the arbitrary interpretation of media of law and the lack of an institutionalized professional ethos among journalists also stand out (see Gross, 2004). All of this is surely more reminiscent of the Mediterranean or polarized pluralist model than any of the others. Yet most of these are issues which Hallin and Mancini themselves wrestle with and invite further discussion on. This, after all, is how comparative study progresses: models are proposed, criticized, qualified and adjusted, the better to resemble (and to explain) reality.

The changing coverage of politics

Fragmentation

Just as Europe's politicians – or, at least, most of them – can no longer guarantee that state broadcasters will do their bidding, they can no longer rely on the fact that by speaking on two or three television channels they will get their message across to the majority of citizens. Admittedly, some futurologists oversell the pace of fragmentation. But it is happening. Sheer habit means that most Europeans – especially the middle-aged and elderly for whom choice used to be fairly limited – may well continue to rely on three or four channels for the bulk of their viewing even after analogue services are switched off. For younger viewers growing up with digital TV, however, this will not be the case.

The advent of on-demand services and 'narrowcasting' – the arrival of specialist channels providing an exclusive diet of, say, sport or music or wildlife or celebrity or life-style programmes – means that many people will be able to do what they have

> **KEY POINT**
>
> **Media coverage of politics is more fragmented across a bigger range of outlets, possibly more personalized, and certainly less respectful towards politicians. Whether, though, this has led to increasing cynicism on the part of voters, or a serious loss of agenda-control by parties (especially at elections), is debatable.**

always wanted; namely, tune out politics and current affairs altogether. Political junkies, however, will increasingly have to search for what they crave (and perhaps pay for it via a subscription to a specialist channel) rather than being spoonfed for free. Given that the linkage between the public and parties has come to rely so much on mass rather than face-to-face communication, this development threatens to erode what is already a rather tenuous link even further. One can argue already that a market-driven media is unlikely to provide the kind of 'public sphere' or forum that is supposedly necessary for informed, democratic and hopefully rational politics and decision-making (see Habermas, 1989). Whether any such space can be meaningfully said to exist when so many can contract out of it altogether is, anyway, questionable. In fact, contracting out is a feature of the non-digital environment, too, given the increased provision in recent years of regional and minority-language stations – something digitization will only make easier. It may be no accident, for example, that the difficulty countries such as Belgium and Spain – and possibly now the UK – have in holding themselves together has been accelerated by the opening up of 'sub-spheres' that allow minorities to cut themselves off from the rest of the state.

From 'party logic' to 'media logic'

Many European media outlets are cutting down on – or at least changing – their coverage of politics and current affairs, not just in between elections but also during them. For commercial newspapers and broadcasters, this is largely on the grounds that elections, and politics more generally, do not deliver audiences and, therefore, advertising revenue. But even public service broadcasters are seen to be backing away from what used to be thought of as a responsibility to inform and educate voters, irrespective of whether the low turnout at elections which they use as justification for their shrinking coverage could conceivably also be a function of that shrinking (Semetko *et al.*, 2000: 127–8).

Certainly programmers and editors are less and less willing to allow politics and politicians to operate in some kind of 'reserved area' in which normal news values are suspended at crucial times (such as elections) in order to give people what they supposedly need as citizens rather than what they

---

BOX 7.6

Ads

European political parties spend much less on political advertising than their US counterparts. But that is partly because they are less well-resourced and partly because many countries prohibit paid spots (see Table 7.5), although this may not last forever. In Norway, the right was keen to open things up but lost power to a left-wing government that halted the plan. At the end of 2008, however, the European Court of Human Rights held that a fine on a Norwegian television station for airing a party advertisement violated Article 10 of the European Convention, which defends freedom of expression – a decision which the centre-left government responded to by boosting the free airtime afforded to small parties. Most European states, however, allow parties a limited number of party election broadcasts (PEBs) funded by the tax-payer (see Chapter 6). Research (see Kaid and Holtz-Bacha, 2006) reveals that advertising does have an effect – although it may not always be in the direction the candidate or party intends! Interestingly, it also reveals that, unlike their US counterparts, Europe's parties produce overwhelmingly positive rather than negative advertising; this is possibly because many of them know they have to work with other parties in coalitions.

---

apparently want as consumers. Kuhn (2004: 35) notes, for example, that in the 2002 French presidential election, not only the commercial brand leader TF1, but also the main public service broadcaster, France 2, 'devoted significantly less time to election news and debates than in the previous presidential contest' and that 'frequently the election was not the lead story on television news'.

But this is not simply a question of a decrease in the time allotted to politics, but also the way in which it – and hard news in general – is treated. It now has to interest and entertain as well as inform – an imperative that used to be stronger in 'liberal systems' (see Donsbach, 1995) but has now spread to others. As one very prescient study of Italian elec-

Table 7.5 What the media provide at elections

	Paid election ads?	Free time on public TV	Leaders' debates?
Czech Rep.	Yes	Yes	Yes
France	No	Yes	Usually
Germany	Yes	Yes	Yes
Italy	Yes	No (but on private TV)	Yes
Netherlands	Yes	Yes	Yes
Poland	Yes	Yes	Usually
Spain	No	Yes	Usually
Sweden	Yes	Yes	Yes
UK	No	Yes	Recently, yes
US	Yes	No	Yes

tion-time broadcasting put it, coverage has moved from 'party logic', where political institutions' right to set the agenda and occupy a prominent place in the schedules went unquestioned, towards 'media logic', where neither can be taken for granted (see Mazzoleni, 1987). There has for some time been a 'struggle for the agenda' between the media and politicians (see, for example, Asp, 1983, on its manifestation in Sweden in the 1970s). But, increasingly, normal news values – presumed topicality, obvious visuality, surprise and drama, easy intelligibility, personalization and negativity – are now applied to political stories. This means politics either falls out of favour or it becomes more entertaining – either by being more gimmicky or gladiatorial or, more subtly, by associating itself with the media's celebrity and lifestyle focus.

Gimmicks there are aplenty; but it is hard to identify a trend. Perhaps fortunately, few European politicians followed a spate of Italian politicians who, in the early 1990s, appeared naked or semi-naked in order to court publicity and earn a reputation for liking a bit of good, clean fun (see Roncarolo, 2004: 113). As for gladiatorial contests, more and more parliamentary democracies seem to be going in for televised candidate debates (see Boxes 7.6 and 7.7), although holding one at the previous election is no guarantee that one will be held

at the next, often because the frontrunner (seeking to minimize risk) successfully resists taking part. This happened in Spain in 2004, where, despite polls showing that 75 per cent of the public wanted a debate, the man who expected to win the election, PP's Mariano Rajoy, refused to 'get into the ring' with the man who actually won it, Jose Luis Rodriguez Zapatero, around whom PSOE conducted a notably 'presidential' campaign. In most countries, however, weaker performers effectively have no choice and in any case it is not always clear before the debates take place who will and won't do well. At the Dutch election in 2012, for example, there was all to play for since opinion polls suggested that many voters hadn't made up their minds who to vote for before the campaign began: in the event, in spite of many pundits forecasting success for more radical alternatives, the mainstream centre-left and centre-right saw their support rise – something that many put down to stronger than expected performances by their leaders (particular the Labour Party's Jan Samsom) during the televised encounters.

Leader's debates would seem to reinforce the trend that many political scientists claim to have identified toward the 'presidentialization' of not just campaigning (Mughan, 2000) but also European politics more generally (see Poguntke and Webb, 2004; see also Fabbrini, 2011). Moreover, in the face of the common wisdom (see Chapter 9) concerning the ideological convergence of mainstream left and right (summed up nicely during the 2002 presidential election in France by *L'Express* publishing a despairing article entitled *A la recherche du clivage perdu*: 'In search of the lost cleavage'), parties feel they must seek new ways to demonstrate that they are different. Given that politics, some claim, is no longer about big ideas but about competent and credible management, it makes sense for parties to try to embody their claim to such qualities by increasing the focus on their leaders. Ironically, however, as leaders become more important to party campaigns, it is not only competence and credibility that count: all-round personality could become more important, creating a premium on candidates who can project personal warmth and charm irrespective of worthiness. Perhaps, as some seriously suggest they should (see Coleman, 2003), both those who do politics and those who cover it are learning

---

BOX 7.7

Mars or Venus? Head-to-head debates in France and Germany

In 2002, some forty-two years after they began in the USA, German TV held its first head-to-head debates – watched by almost half of the voters – between the 'Chancellor Candidates' of the two leading parties. The reporting of them may have been predictably dominated by boxing metaphors, but academic research suggests that they made a difference: exposure to them seems to have increased turnout and believing one candidate to have won the debate increased the chances of voting for him – effects that were magnified among voters without strong party identification (see Faas and Maier, 2004). The 2005 election represented another first in that one of the televised contenders was a woman. Angela Merkel was widely judged to have been bested by the media-savvy incumbent, Gerhard Schröder, during the single head-to-head debate to which she agreed. After it, her party's ratings began to slide badly, although not enough to prevent her becoming Chancellor after the election. By the next election, which kept her in office Frau Merkel had found her stride.

A couple of years later, another male–female pairing took place in France, as the favourite Nicolas Sarkozy took on the less-fancied (but, as the media typically never tired of mentioning, supposedly highly fanciable) Ségolène Royal. As in other countries, the instantaneous judgements provided by pundits, pollsters and party PR flaks were probably as important as the debates themselves – which was why, for instance, the Royal camp was incensed by the release of what it saw as a dubious post-debate poll that saw Sarkozy as the clear winner despite the fact that the balance of opinion among 'commentators' and 'analysts' called the two-and-a-half hour marathon, watched by 23.1 million people, a score-draw. Whether Royal's decision – after the confrontation was billed as 'Action Man vs Mrs Nice' – to put in a highly combative performance was a wise one, however, was debatable: a display that might have been seen as simply robust had it been given by a man was condescendingly dismissed as hysterical by opponents. Interestingly, Sarkozy's opponent in 2012, the relatively mild-mannered François Hollande (who, until their relationship ended after her presidential bid, had been Royal's partner for thirty years) agreed, as frontrunner, to only one head-to-head debate, which seemed to have little influence on the election result – a useful reminder, especially to the British (see Bailey, 2011), that the format, frequency and impact of debates can change from one election to another.

---

from TV shows such as *Big Brother*. The obvious risk – one that is theoretically greater in countries (such as the UK) where ministers are normally elected representatives and not prime ministerial (or presidential) appointees from outside of parliament – is that voters end up with politicians who come over well on television but can't do the very serious job they are elected to do.

What certainly seems to be embedding itself in political coverage, irrespective of gimmickry and gladiatorialism, is what Kuhn (2004: 34) calls 'the mediatization of intimacy' – the deliberate courting by politicians of appearances by themselves and often their wives (less commonly their husbands) in supposedly non-political formats. These – the chat-show or the magazine portrait are the arche-

types – purport to concentrate on the 'real' man or woman behind the public persona in the knowledge that in so doing they are (a) likely to reach voters who might otherwise be turning off and tuning out of politics; and (b) avoid hard questions by experienced and knowledgeable specialist journalists.

Even if one believes – and not everybody does (see Street, 2011: 250 ff) – that 'celebrity politics' and the 'personalization of politics' (Adam and Maier, 2010; Karvonen, 2009; Langer, 2012), is a bad thing, either because it may unduly favour charismatic populists (see Takens *et al.*, 2011) or simply encourage mainstream politicians to focus on building up ultimately fragile 'media capital' (Davis, 2010: 82–97; see also Helms, 2012), there may still be an upside to these attempts at 'political impression management' (Landtsheer *et al.*, 2008). Since politicians have allowed the cameras into their lives in order to film friendly stories about just how like the rest of us they are, they are finding it increasingly difficult to prevent the media from exposing sides of them that might not go down so well. In many European countries there are strong privacy laws: France, where stories about the state of the main presidential contenders' relationships with their spouse/partner were suppressed during the election of 2007, is a good example. But even that suppression was far from complete, suggesting that protection of privacy is gradually being eroded as politicians who decide to live by the sword are deemed liable to die by it too (see Stanyer and Wring, 2004). And even if domestic law or journalistic custom is still strong enough to prevent the emergence into the public domain of matters that many would regard as essentially private, the availability of many foreign newspaper titles on the internet and the advent of cross-border satellite broadcasting mean that it is almost impossible to keep things from anybody interested enough to find out.

We need, however, to bear two or three points in mind. First, it is still possible for politicians, particularly if they live fairly conventional lives and are determined not to become celebrities, not to be treated as such – and perhaps to benefit from such distance (see Zoonen, 2006). Second, even if their private lives are paraded all over the papers, voters may well (as they famously did in the USA with Bill Clinton) separate the politician from the person. For instance, in 2006 and 2007 the leaders of the Czech Republic's two biggest parties (both of whom have now served as prime minister) had to endure titillating press-coverage of their personal lives, but it made little dent in either's support.

Third, we should be wary of thinking that packaging politics and politicians is a recent phenomenon in Europe. Kuhn (2004: 31) reminds us that, before he won the 1981 French presidential election, Francois Mitterrand underwent an 'image makeover'. So, too, did his British counterpart Margaret Thatcher before becoming Prime Minister in 1979, and she famously eschewed inquisitions by trained interrogators from the ranks of political journalism in favour of rather more cosy chats with sympathetic radio presenters. Even in the 1974 French election,

Kuhn reminds us, 'the youthful Valery Giscard d'Estaing presented himself as a man of the people by being photographed in a football strip and playing the accordion (though not both simultaneously)'. Holtz-Bacha (2004: 48–9) reminds us that a 1960s TV-ad for former Chancellor Willy Brandt sought to portray him as a man of the people by showing him driving himself to work through west Berlin, where he was mayor. Indeed, 'personalization' seems to have been part of election campaigning and coverage in Germany as far back as 1949 and, rather than there being an overall trend towards an increase, it tends to vary from election to election, often depending on the charisma of the candidates involved (Wilke and Reinemann, 2001: 301–2). We should also note that, in the UK, a *Times* newspaper editorial was already lamenting as far back as 1970 that people were being asked 'to vote not for a Member of Parliament, but for a Party; not for a Party but for its Leader; and not for its Leader but for a pre-packaged television presentation of what Market Research suggests the Leader should be'.

This is not to say that there is nothing new under the sun: simply that some developments we see as recent have being going on rather longer than we think. In any case, there are some changes in the media's coverage of politics that do stand out as genuinely novel – if not always welcome – developments. For instance, media providers throughout Europe are, especially during elections, crowding out their already limited discussion of policy issues and party programmes with a focus on speculation on who is winning (poll reporting and the 'horse race' aspect). Analyzing Germany between 1980 and 1994, for instance, Brettschneider (1997) recorded a big increase (from 65 to 168) in the number of polls reported in the German media in the twelve weeks before federal elections. Broadcasters also seem to be 'dumbing-down' their coverage by forcing politicians into ever shrinking soundbites, although we need to remember that there is still variation across nations in this respect (Esser, 2008; see also Schulz *et al.*, 2005: 74–5). That said, politicians themselves are moving away at election time from old-style party political broadcasts (a 5–10 minute lecturette from a talking head) to 2-minute spots that resemble the US-style adverts that many European countries now allow them to pay for in addition to publicly funded airtime.

Spain (España)

Area: 499,500 km² (11.9% of EU-27)
Population: 46.2 million (9.2% of EU-27)
Religious heritage: Roman Catholic
GDP (2010): €1063 billion (8.5% of EU-27)
GDP *per capita* as percentage of EU average: 99
Female representation in parliament and cabinet (end 2011): 36% and 29%
Joined EU: 1986
Top 3 cities: Madrid – capital city (3.3 million), Barcelona (1.6 million), Valencia (0.8 million).

History: Modern Spain was created in 1479 by dynastic intermarriage. After defeating and expelling the last remnants of the Arab kingdom of Andalusia in the south in the name of Catholicism, its monarchs led the Counter-Reformation against Protestantism in Europe. Further intermarriage joined them to the Habsburg dynasty. As a result, Spanish monarchs ruled not just Spain, but also Austria and what were to become Belgium and the Netherlands, as well as parts of modern-day Italy, France and Germany. Meanwhile, the discovery of America gave Spain an empire (Florida, Mexico, part of the Caribbean and Latin America) and, of course, gold and silver.

By the eighteenth century, however, imperial decay had set in. Spain became a backwater, ruled by a conservative aristocracy determined to preserve its own privileges, as well as Madrid's control of industrially and commercially more advanced regions such as the Basque Country and Catalunya. The nineteenth century saw Spain consumed by a series of wars between liberals and monarchists who were supported by the still-powerful church. This conflict witnessed the brief flowering of a federal republic before the return of the monarchy and a level of repression which radicalized both peasants and the growing urban working class into anarchism and communism. Following a short-lived dictatorship in the 1920s, free elections ushered in a republic and then a left-wing government that threatened not just the privileges of the church and the propertied, but the very existence of the nation state. A military *coup* in 1936 led to three years of civil war that also served as a proxy conflict between Fascist Germany and Italy and Communist Russia.

The victor in the civil war, Francisco Franco, established an authoritarian dictatorship, backed by the Catholic Church, that lasted from 1939 till his death in 1975. The early years saw thousands of opponents put to death, diplomatic isolation (notwithstanding Spain's neutrality during the Second World War), and the country's economic and social development all but arrested. In later years, Franco bought his country a place in the 'west' by allowing US air bases on Spanish soil. He also allowed millions of Spaniards to work abroad in northern Europe and eventually millions of tourists to make the trip south. This assisted economic development but also helped open up the country to foreign influences and the possibility of change. Following Franco's death, his anointed successor, King Juan Carlos, combined with reformists within the regime to restore democracy. After a failed army *coup,* the Socialist Party (PSOE) assumed office and held on to it from 1982 to 1996, until it was finally overhauled by the centre-right Popular Party (PP). The latter won a bigger majority in 2000 and was forecast to win again in 2004 until, just days before the election, Islamic terrorists exploded bombs in Madrid, and the Socialists snatched a narrow victory. They defended it successfully in 2008 but, widely blamed for Spain's severe economic difficulties, they lost badly to PP in November 2011.

Economy and society: Prior to the economic crash in 2008, Spain's inhabitants saw their standard of living increase

WHAT'S IN AN ANTHEM?

The answer, in the case of *La Marcha Real*, has been absolutely nothing as far as the words go – at least, since the death of Franco, under whom the lyrics were (predictably enough) about Spain triumphing, the 'hymn of the faith' and 'Glory to the Fatherland'. With the coming of democracy, clerico-fascism was no longer in fashion and coming up with something that might prove acceptable to the Basques and the Catalans was always going to be difficult. A competition was held to find a new set of lyrics that everyone could feel comfortable with but the winning entry has not so far caught on.

markedly after the end of the Franco era as the economy became integrated into Europe and was boosted by EU funding. Agriculture and fishing (Spain has easily the largest fleet in Europe) has become less important as the economy has diversified, particularly in the more industrial and commercial north. Annual per capita income essentially matches the EU average. Other big changes since the advent of democracy include a steep decline in the influence of the church, vast improvements in health, welfare and education and in the position of women, who now have one of world's lowest birth rates. Perhaps the most visible change of the last few years, however, has been brought about by the influx of immigrants, both from sub-Saharan Africa and from Spain's former colonies in Latin America – an influx due in part to the tendency of successive Spanish governments to grant amnesties to hundreds of thousands of formerly illegal immigrants but also to the uncontrolled boom in property and construction for which the country is now paying dearly. In the four years from January 2008, nearly three million jobs were lost, at the end of which period nearly a quarter of the labour force was unemployed – and over half of those under 25.

Governance: Spain is now a solid parliamentary democracy, with both houses of parliament elected by a PR system that favours the two largest parties and parties from the country's regions. Under the 1978 constitution these 'autonomous communities' have been granted so much power that the country now resembles a federal state. This has not been enough, however, to end calls for independence from some regions, especially the Basque country and Catalunya. Fortunately, however, it looks as if those who were willing to pursue violence to

A KEY CONTEMPORARY CHALLENGE
AVOIDING DEFAULT AND EXIT FROM THE EUROZONE WITHOUT STRANGLING THE ECONOMY IN THE PROCESS

The overall majority won by the centre-right Partido Popular in November 2011 ensured that Spain would not take the supposedly easy way out of its economic troubles and instead commit itself to even more austerity than the outgoing Socialist government, which, albeit belatedly, had impressed ratings agencies with its commitment to reduce the government's deficit. While welcomed by the markets and other EU governments, which were worried about some sort of default and even an exit from the Eurozone, this was not such good news for the nearly quarter of Spanish adults (and nearly half of those under 25) who were out of work: any austerity programme, at least in the short term, would not only fail to stimulate the economy but could actually make the situation worse by slowing economic growth, thereby reducing revenue and increasing the amount needed to support even more people losing their jobs. It was not altogether surprising, then, when the PP and its prime minister, Mariano Rajoy, decided to inform the EU in 2012 that the government would have no alternative but to miss its targets in the first year. Nor, after that, was it any surprise that Spain's powerful regions then told the central government that they would be doing the same. Before leaving office, PSOE, with PP's cooperation, had amended the Spanish constitution in order to enshrine within it – and in such a way as to ensure that it applied both to regional as well as national governments – EU rules on budget deficits and debts. In the light of Rajoy's decision not to try and deliver what perhaps he should never have promised, and given that the amendment to the constitution predictably contained a get-out clause that could be activated in an emergency situation, critics were entitled to wonder whether it was really worth the paper it was written on.

achieve their aim have finally given up the bullet in favour of the ballot box.

Foreign policy: Spain, initially concentrated on 're-joining' western Europe, via NATO (1982) and the EU (1986). Since then, it has tried to persuade its fellow member states to take Europe's relations with North Africa more seriously and, before it pulled its troops out after the Madrid bombings, angered many of them with its pro-American stance over Iraq.

Contemporary challenges
- Avoiding default and exit from the Eurozone without strangling the economy in the process (see box above)
- Managing separatist feeling
- Coping with the legacy of a civil war that for years was never really talked about
- Controlling immigration
- Living with reduced EU funding as a consequence of eastern enlargements, 2004–7.

Learning resources. For a good all-round textbook, see Magone (2008), *Contemporary. Spanish Politics* and Gunther and Montero (2009), *The Politics of Spain*. For those wanting to understand the full enormity of what the so-called *pacto de olvido* hid away for decades after Franco's death, Preston (2013) *The Spanish Holocaust* is highly recommended. Keep up to date on the news at http://www.expatica.com/es/main.html

It is also argued across Europe that the media is allowing prediction, punditry (including journalists interviewing other journalists) and 'the ranters, columnists with little knowledge but strong opinions' (Riddell, 2006: 77) to crowd out the space and time devoted to the 'straight reporting' of political events, especially if those events are routine, complex and parliamentary (see Negrine, 1998). Research has even noted a trend towards the media reporting not simply on politics but also on how it (the media) reports on politics (Esser *et al.*, 2001). We need to be careful, however. The media in European countries might be spending less time on reporting parliament (and/or reporting only those parts of it that are dramatic and conflictual, such as question times), but they are still fairly reliant on familiar political institutions to provide a steady stream of the raw material for much of what still passes for news (policy conflicts, calls for legislation, airing of issues and the like). What in the UK is called the 'silly season' – that period where news organizations struggle for stories as parliamentarians go on their long summer break – is testament to the ongoing (if uncomfortable) mutual dependency between politics and the media, between journalists and their sources (see Ericson *et al.*, 1989).

'Disdaining the news', or at least the parties

In the face of this ongoing dependency, there is a tendency by journalists in many European countries to assert their autonomy from politicians in the face of increasingly intense efforts on the part of the latter to control the news agenda and the way they are presented within it. Political parties all over the continent have professionalized their political communication or at the very least adapted their practice (rarely as 'amateurish' as is often rather patronizingly suggested) to changing media technologies and the more commercial, fragmented landscape in which they are employed (Negrine *et al.*, 2007). At election time this has seen them seeking, first, to bully journalists into their version of what is and is not important and fair and, second, to spoonfeed them with neatly prepackaged stories based on stage-managed 'pseudo-events' from the so-called 'campaign trail'. Notwithstanding a putative move towards stressing 'valence issues' such as economic competence over more ideological 'position' issues, parties still aim, broadly speaking, to keep the focus of the campaign on the issues they 'own' or are associated with – for instance, health and welfare for social democrats or smaller government for conservative parties (see Chapters 5 and 6).

To maintain control and cope with media change, parties (and governments) in Europe are engaging in what one critic calls 'institutionalized political impression management' (Louw, 2005: 26) – the agenda setting and celebrity-handling that we now routinely associate with so-called 'spin doctors'. Although there are some exceptions, notably in the postcommunist democracies in Europe, where politics is still party-centred rather than candidate-centred, these almost iconic figures are rarely roving consultants-for-hire or 'parajournalists' (see Schudson, 2003: 3) in the American mould (see Plasser and Plasser, 2002). Instead, they are partisans with considerable experience in the media who are either explicitly employed or simply relied on to get the party's message across (see Esser *et al.*, 2000, for a comparative study of the UK and Germany).

As a response, European journalists have taken, like their American colleagues, to 'disdaining the news' (Levy, 1981). They were already just as (if not more) prone to a much-criticized tendency to use 'strategic or game frames in political reporting, which focus on the strategies of political elites and their success or failure in playing the political game, at the expense of the policy concerns that motivate ordinary citizens' (Hallin and Mancini, 2004: 141). But they began to go even further, undermining the efforts of politicians by pointing out to viewers the spinning and the strategic intent behind their statements and pseudo-events, and by revealing the tensions beneath the shows of unity and the fluster and flap beneath the calm and collected exterior (see de Vreese, 2001: 170).

Journalists have also become less deferential and even aggressive, moving from the 'watchdog journalism' of earlier decades to the so-called 'attack-dog journalism' that seems to assume that all politicians are in it for themselves and out to put one over on the people (see Barnett, 2002). These developments have not, however, proceeded at the same pace throughout the continent. The populist 'disdaining', 'attack-dog' stance was first evident in the USA and it is, therefore, no surprise that it spread first to the UK. Other media cultures have been slower to adopt

BOX 7.8

Making and faking the news: political satire

For a long time, French journalists have been dismissed as unduly deferential. However, France also has a long tradition of biting satire, both in magazines like *Le canard enchaîné* and in television programmes like the puppet show, *Les guignols de l'info*. Indeed, all around Europe politicians are routinely lampooned – increasingly in 'fake-news' programmes taking their inspiration from programmes like *The Daily Show* and *The Colbert Report* in the USA. Examples include *Striscia la Notizia* in Italy and *heute show* in Germany. The UK has experimented with the format with the *10 O'Clock Live Show* but viewers seem to prefer panel shows where comedians (and the occasional journalist and politician) get to take the mickey out of the political class and celebrities, the most popular being *Have I got news for you* and *Mock the week*. The Dutch have *Dit Was Het Nieuws* (see Coleman *et al.*, 2009). It is easy to dismiss these shows as mere entertainment, but they have big audiences – and they could well be the only vaguely political output to which young people in particular are actually exposed. Views about their influence, presuming they have any, are divided. To some they perform a necessary function by subverting power and puncturing pomposity. To others they contribute to undermining the credibility of representative democracy. A useful discussion and survey of this phenomenon is provided by Sandvoss *et al.* (2012).

it – at least wholesale. A recent study of election coverage in (admittedly quality) newspapers in Germany from 1949 onwards did find that journalists tended to do more of their own interpreting rather than simply reporting what politicians said and did – a trend also identified in the Netherlands (see de Vreese, 2001: 172). But its authors could find 'no overall trend toward negativism' (Wilke and Reinemann, 2001: 291; see also Schulz *et al.*, 2005: 75). Nor, apparently, are German journalists as interested as their British colleagues in 'exposing' the black arts of the spin doctors, possibly because they are less subject to direct pressure from them, which might in turn be because German parties (whose chancellor candidates are not always the undisputed leaders of their parties) have neither centralized their media operations to quite the same extent nor spent so much money on them (see Esser *et al.*, 2000).

It could be, of course, that academic studies are simply lagging behind a reality that British commentators (see Lloyd, 2004) were the first to pick up on but which is now spreading. In the marathon back-to-back interviews with all the candidates who took part in the first round of the French presidential election in 2012, for instance, there was little sign of the traditional deference shown to politicians – at least by journalists (see Box 7.8). In postcommunist

polities like Poland and the Czech Republic, too, politicians now get a far less easy ride than they used to as some of the 'disrespect' shown to them by commercial broadcasters began to rub off on their public service counterparts. Whether this is a good thing, of course, is debateable. Some commentators, especially in the USA where it has gone furthest, think that this style of journalism is contributing to falling trust and rising cynicism among voters. Others rebut or at least qualify this idea. Media consumption can have a positive effect on political knowledge, participation and trust – and anyway the putative decline in the latter, even when it is not overstated (which it often is), may have other, more convincing explanations: for example, rising expectations (Norris, 2000, 2011a; see also de Vreese, 2005). Things might also depend on which side you're watching: Aarts and Semetko (2003) found that, in the Netherlands, the effects were positive for those who got their news from public service broadcasters but negative for those who watched the news on commercial television. If more and more people switch from one to the other, perhaps we will indeed witness the 'spiral of cynicism' and apathy that some critics are worried about.

Yet for all this talk of a struggle for control between politicians and journalists, they are still playing what is essentially a collusive, albeit edgy, game with each other – one shot through with resigned cynicism on both sides (Brants *et al.*, 2010; see also Davis, 2010 and Gulbrandsen, 2010). One of the fascinating things about the UK's Leveson Inquiry was the way that what started out as an investigation of the press's excesses turned into a daily exposé of the close, yet simultaneously uneasy, relationship between politicians and journalists. Arguably, indeed, the symbiosis has grown so strong that in many ways it excludes the very public both sets of players claim to represent. This is most obvious at elections. These events, as demonstrated by the frequent disjuncture between what opinion polls show are the issues that most matter to voters and the subjects actually covered in the media during the campaign, are still largely 'about what politicians talk about rather than what the public want them to talk about' (Brookes *et al.*, 2004; see also Brandenburg, 2002). Polling data is used by the media not to help set the agenda but largely as a supposedly real-time measure of how each party is doing, with the results used both to predict outcomes and to challenge politicians about their 'performance' so far. If, say critics, those same polls suggest alienation and/or apathy (findings which are, somewhat ironically, then used by both media and politicians as a stick with which to beat one another) why would we be surprised?

Bias and its effects

Most politicians at election time, however, are less worried about supposedly media-fuelled cynicism than they are about whether they are getting a fair deal on TV and in the press compared with their opponents. So aware are they of the importance of media coverage, that they are acutely sensitive to, and often complain about, bias. It would be easy, but not entirely correct, to dismiss these complaints as predictable paranoia. This is especially the case when they come from smaller parties. These parties, sometimes on the extreme of the political spectrum, claim – with some justification – that they are squeezed out of mass coverage by their larger and possibly more mainstream competitors: the *Front National* in France, *Izquierda Unida* in Spain and the Czech Communists, for instance, routinely (if not always rightly) make this point. Mainstream parties,

of course, will reply that coverage should be based on support and the likelihood of getting into government, not on some abstract idea of giving all voices an equal say. This might make sense between elections, but less so, perhaps, during election campaigns that should presumably be about everyone getting the chance to put their point across. Nevertheless, in many countries free election broadcasts are allocated according to party support: in Spain, for example, parties are allocated between 10 and 45 minutes in total, though they can divide this up between however many individual spots they like (see Sanders with Canel, 2004: 197). Interestingly, however, the media in general does devote more news time to so-called minor parties at election time, which conceivably could have the effect of boosting their vote by improving their visibility.

KEY POINT

The ability of the media to influence both voters and politicians, even indirectly, is easier to assume than to prove, not least because there are so many other influences at work.

But smaller and/or extreme parties are not the only ones complaining. Larger, mainstream parties are also acutely concerned. We have already seen that public broadcasters in those states that have not created an arm's-length relationship between government and broadcasters are accused of bias (normally, in their case, in favour of the government of the day). But so, too, are privately owned media outlets – particularly those whose owners are said to exert undue influence on coverage, either directly or via the anticipated reactions of their journalists or even politicians themselves. Accusations of bias and improper influence were levelled at Rupert Murdoch in the UK long before they were laid bare by the Leveson Inquiry in 2012 and, before his empire went bust, Leo Kirch in Germany. Both were accused of editorial interference and for allegedly using their large share of media markets to 'bully' politicians afraid of their influence on voters into granting them policy concessions and regulatory exemptions. And then, of course, there was Europe's one-man media-minefield, Silvio Berlusconi (see Box 7.9).

But is the influence of these 'moguls' – and the media in general – on voters really as great as it seems? Even assuming that biases exist, do they really matter? Certainly, at first glance, it is logical to think that since (as we suggested in Chapter 6) people are becoming less attached to particular parties and more volatile in their voting behaviour, their political choices at election time might be more and more open to influence through and by the media. But being convinced, for instance, that 'campaigns make a difference' is one thing (see Farrell and Schmitt-Beck, 2002); being able actually to prove 'media effects' on political behaviour is another. One noted expert on politics and the media (Mughan, 2000: 76), for instance, warned not so long ago that 'It must be remembered that a great deal of myth and hyperbole suffuses discussion of the political role of television. In truth, much remains shrouded in mystery' – so much so, in fact, that he quotes another authority to the effect that: 'The state of research on media effects is one of the most notable embarrassments of modern social science ... [T]he scholarly literature has been much better at refuting, qualifying, and circumscribing the thesis of media impact than supporting it.'

In short, while the common wisdom nowadays may be that 'people vote the way they do because they believe what they read in the papers' or, because television is where most people get their political news from (see Figure 7.2), that 'elections are won and lost on TV', we are a long way from knowing whether this is indeed the case. Such sentiments are common wisdom among political elites as well as the rest of us: in one case, Latvia in 2010, it apparently drove politicians from one new party (PLL) to attempt to help buy the daily newspaper, *Diena*, in order to gain its endorsement at the upcoming election; in Portugal, in the same year, the governing socialist party was accused of encouraging the part-state-owned Telecoms company to acquire a television station, TV1, in order to clamp down on its critical journalists. As such, the belief, whether or not it is well-founded, might be helping to drive the continuing mediatization of politics throughout Europe. But the evidence is very thin – especially for some kind of 'direct' effect like the conversion of what would have been, for example, a Socialist vote to a Conservative one. Against this scepticism, it must be said that the absence of proof for such effects might be down to the inability of political scientists to find convincing ways of measuring

Figure 7.2 The main sources of political news

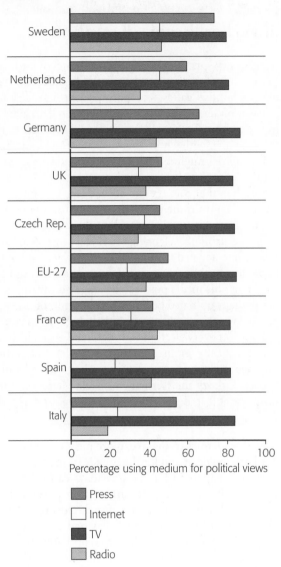

Source: Data from *Standard Eurobarometer*, 76 (2012).

them and isolating them from all the other impacts on vote choice. There are so many factors and influences that intervene between us receiving a message from the media and our making political decisions, many of which could well be far more powerful and persuasive than anything we have read or seen (see Newton, 2006 and Box 7.10). Moreover, media messages often cancel each other out (see de Vreese and Boomgaarden, 2006a). This has not, however,

BOX 7.9

Silvio Berlusconi – *il cavaliere*

Acres of newsprint and thousands of hours of air time throughout Europe have been devoted to Silvio Berlusconi. This is not just because of his allegedly dubious business dealings. Nor was it simply because of his infamous 'gaffes' (comparing a German MEP to a concentration camp commandant, claiming that 'the war on terrorism' was a clash between Christian civilization and the rest, and suggesting that he might introduce the photogenic Danish Prime Minister to his wife on the grounds that he was better-looking than the man with whom she was rumoured to be involved). It is also because of concerns that his way of doing politics might be the start of a trend which spreads beyond Italy (Mancini, 2011) and because the conflict of interest inherent in his dual role as Prime Minister of Italy and owner of multiple media interests both in that country and abroad (see Ginsborg, 2004). He was accused by opponents of using his position in government to protect and promote his business interests (including opening up the possibilities for cross ownership), of politically interfering (even more than they did!) in RAI's affairs by fixing its board, securing the silencing of critical journalists and the appointment of toadies, measurably reducing the airtime devoted to opposition politicians on both RAI and his own channels, and of using the latter to drive the supposed 'dumbing down' of political and other coverage. All this, plus the way Berlusconi was able to use his media power to leverage his overnight entry into politics in 1993, challenges comforting but perhaps outdated beliefs in a separation of powers between those who do politics and those who supposedly watch over them on our behalf. Sceptics could point out that, for all Berlusconi's media power, he did not win every election he fought and could ultimately do nothing to prevent Italy's economic problems practically forcing him from office in 2011. Rather deliciously, it was widely acknowledged that *il cavaliere*'s exit was hastened by what became an iconic camera shot of fellow European leaders, France's Nicolas Sarkozy and Germany's Angela Merkel, smiling ironically together at the idea that Mr Berlusconi would be able to deliver the budgetary rigour demanded of Italy by the EU.

stopped academics trying to explore media influence – for both the print and for the broadcast media.

Few newspapers in Europe nowadays can be dismissed as no more than mouthpieces for particular parties. Although many have faced closure (the Italian Communist daily, *Unità*, has had a number of near-death experiences but has probably been saved by the web), a few party organs (normally on the far left) still exist (such as the French Communist *l'Humanité*), but they sell very few copies. This is not to suggest, however, that European newspapers do not have their biases, even if those in the UK tend to be very much more strident about their partisan loyalties than most of their continental equivalents. But just because they are not diehard supporters of one party, and almost never 'announce for' one candidate or party in the way that British papers are expected to, does not mean that in France and Germany, for example, both regional and national newspapers do not lean fairly obviously to the left or to the right. And

because the bias is obvious, it is to some extent self-selected: a right-wing reader may choose a right-wing paper rather than the paper making her right-wing. Moreover, the extent to which readers appear to agree with the editorial line of their newspaper (something which, some argue, may encourage them to go out and vote for their favourite party) varies considerably between country, while the relationship between viewers' political preferences and those of television stations is (rather predictably given that the latter tend to be more balanced than newspapers) much weaker (see Table 7.6). The impact of bias is also discounted by some observers, not least because trust in newspapers – indeed journalists in general, some would say (Coleman *et al.*, 2009a) – is not high (see Figure 7.3).

This scepticism notwithstanding, there is some recent research from the UK which suggests, first, that newspapers may influence our outlook on the economy which might then feed through to voting

Other influences

One obvious, but easily overlooked, example of non-media influence is talking to family and close friends. German political scientist Rüdiger Schmitt-Beck is by no means a sceptic when it comes to the possibility of media and campaign influence: his comparative study of the UK, Germany, Spain and the USA (Schmitt-Beck, 2004) suggests that knowing the extent to which voters were exposed to the media added to our ability to predict their vote, especially in the more volatile Spain and the USA. However, the very same research showed him that – outside Germany – 'the informal political exchange between voters in their everyday life world has a higher capacity to influence their votes than the mass media'. Interestingly, but perhaps not surprisingly to people who are married, 'spousal relationships stand out as particularly conducive to interpersonal influence'. Given this, it might be more fruitful for researchers to worry less about what people are reading or listening or watching as they eat their breakfast and pay more attention to who they are eating it with (see Coffé and Need, 2010). On the other hand, detailed audience research suggests that there is at least some crossover between media consumption and people's everyday talk about issues of public concern, even if few of us (at least according to the research) move from talk to action; it also suggests incidentally, that people are more than capable of realizing the distinction between what passes for news and what really matters (see Couldry *et al.*, 2010).

(see Gavin and Sanders, 2003) and, secondly, that newspaper bias might have more electoral effect than we were previously able to detect, though only sufficient to make a difference in very close contests (see Newton and Brynin, 2001). Yet even one of the researchers who argues for this possibility, Ken Newton, also emphasizes that it is severely limited by the considerable distrust many people display towards newspapers (see Figure 7.3) and by the fact that they filter what they read through their own upbringing, experience, values, social contacts and

Table 7.6 Press- and television-'party parallelism' in Europe

	Press	Television
Italy	7.2	8.0
Spain	8.0	3.5
France	5.4	3.2
UK	6.9	0.5
West European average	5.2	2.2
Sweden	6.0	0.6
Netherlands	5.2	0.8
Germany	0.7	0.2

Notes: 'Parallelism' is a measure of the extent of agreement between the partisan preferences of the reader/viewer and their favourite newspapers and television stations; it runs from 0 (no agreement) to 100 (full agreement).

Source: Data from van Kempen (2007: 310).

maybe even their husband's or wife's take on matters political (for which see Coffé and Need, 2010). In short, 'people do not so much believe what they read in the newspapers, but read what they believe' (Newton, 2006: 217).

Partly because of this, and partly of course because it is usually the most important and most trusted source, television is seen as more of a problem by many of those worried about the impact of bias. Certainly, there is some limited research evidence of what are called 'indirect effects'. Most of the time, TV seems to reinforce partisanship (in short, the viewer has her prejudices confirmed whatever she watches), but might have a stronger, short-term effect on the politically undecided and inattentive (for a summary of this more qualified position, see Curran, 2002: 133). Given the fact, (as we saw in Chapter 6) that more and more people could be said to fit into these categories, this short-term effect on elections could become more and more important. Against this, however, we have to weigh the fact that if 'those who are least interested, involved and knowledgeable about politics are the most susceptible to media influence' they are also the least likely to be watching and reading anything remotely political (Newton, 2006: 225).

It is also possible to argue, though not without qualification (e.g. Semetko, 2000: 362–3), that the

Figure 7.3 Trust in the media

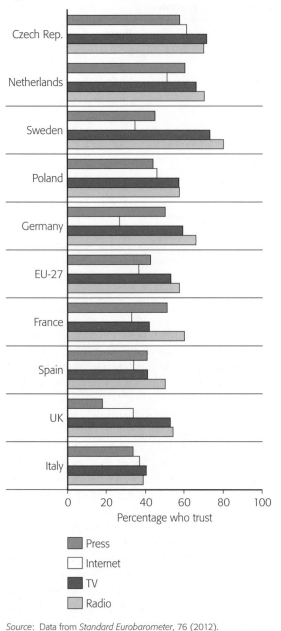

Percentage who trust

■ Press
□ Internet
■ TV
▨ Radio

Source: Data from *Standard Eurobarometer*, 76 (2012).

Media **priming** occurs when emphasis on a particular issue makes it more salient, makes it seem, in other words, more important to us than perhaps it might be otherwise, opening up the possibility that we can be persuaded to change our political decisions and judgements according to what the media is or isn't talking about. Priming is an 'indirect effect' – the media doesn't so much tell people what to think as tell them what to think about.

ularly, some claim that TV debates (and, importantly, media reporting of who won and who lost) can help shift votes if held sufficiently close to election day so that their effect does not wear off (see Denmark, 2002; see also Gunther *et al.*, 2000 and Pattie and Johnston, 2011).

What about the agenda-setting power of the media when it comes to politicians themselves? Again, there is more common wisdom than there is hard evidence. According to many liberals in the UK, for instance, politicians are increasingly driven by the press into populist stances that they otherwise might eschew, particularly on immigration (see Chapter 10). The problem for political scientists, of course, is that, however well connected or persuasive they are, they are unlikely to tempt politicians into admitting that this or that policy was pursued (or such and such a minister was dismissed) because of a press or television campaign (see Kepplinger, 2007). But because it is difficult to measure or prove media influence, does that mean it is unimportant? True, the current state of our empirical knowledge is limited. However, we have a study which clearly shows that the media seem to exert a significant (and, what's more, growing) impact on parliamentary agendas in the UK, the Netherlands and Belgium (van Noije *et al.*, 2008; Vliegenthart and Walgrave, 2011). A degree of agenda setting, then, would seem plausible, Walgrave and van Aelst (2006) observe: politicians are avid consumers of the media; they use it to signal to each other and to the public, and they are – even if research on effects presents a mixed picture – convinced that the media plays a huge role in determining public opinion and setting the agenda (see also Walgrave, 2008 and van Aelst and Walgrave, 2011). Perhaps, as they suggest, the first task is to assume that the media's influence on political actors varies and to think about when it is more, and when it is less, likely to count. For

media already has considerable 'agenda-setting power'. This power derives from **priming** voters' sense of what is and is not important to think about when casting their votes – all the more important if 'issue voting' (see Chapter 6) as well as personality preferences are indeed becoming more crucial to results (see Kleinnijenhuis *et al.*, 2001). More partic-

instance, research into the so-called 'CNN effect' (the idea that coverage of foreign news, particularly when it centres on humanitarian issues, influences public policy) finds that it may be stronger when politicians are divided and uncertain and when the coverage is critical (Robinson, cited in Street, 2011: 118–20); other research also notes that international NGOs may have an important influence if and when they are seen as authoritative by journalists (see Ecker-Ehrhardt, 2010). Meanwhile, the latest research into the media's impact on political parties' agendas, reminds us that attention to an issue attracts attention from political parties when the issue is one that political parties would have an interest in politicizing in the first place (Green-Pedersen and Stubage, 2010).

Researchers – sometimes but not always from a Marxist and/or cultural studies perspective – would also suggest that the effect of the media simply cannot be traced over a short period, like an election. For them, the political power of the media has much more to do with the general legitimation of governments sitting atop (and doing very little about) pervasive structural inequalities. We might, the argument goes, struggle against some of these if our attention were not so distracted and our aspirations so limited by the 'non-political' product served up to us nightly by a corporate oligopolists, as well as by the public broadcasters increasingly forced to compete with them on their terms (see Curran, 2002). We might also profitably turn to examine the political effects of supposedly non-political programmes: research suggests, for example, that regular viewing of cop-shows increases concern about crime and that such concern influences opinions about politicians (see Holbrook and Hill, 2005); it has also shown (this time using the environmental issue) that people draw on a blend of fictional and non-fictional television in the construction of their views (Delli Carpini and Williams, 1994).

These warnings are important. For one thing, some argue (though not uncontroversially) that television militates against active involvement in society, political and otherwise (see Putnam, 2000; see also Hooghe, 2002). For another, it is hardly the stuff of crude conspiracy theory to suggest that the media, particularly the privately-owned media, is unlikely to produce shows of any genre (current affairs or soaps) that routinely question and undermine the

idea that liberal capitalism is the inevitable and best system, especially with advertisers breathing down their necks – evidence for which is plentiful in the USA (see Campbell, 2004: 62–3) even if the topic is under-researched in Europe. Even if the media avoid systematically (though perhaps unconsciously) excluding those who question the consensus completely, it may well be **framing** them negatively. It is not hard for journalists, either consciously or unconsciously, to present people as extreme (far-right or far-left organizations), disruptive (unions in industrial disputes or environmentalists taking direct action) or possibly violent (animal rights and anti-globalization protest groups).

> **Framing** is an 'indirect effect' of the media, which decides on the way stories are packaged so as to highlight (often subconsciously) who should take credit and blame, or who are the good guys and who we should trust less or take less seriously.

On the other hand, none of this is going to make much difference if those watching the broadcast know from their own experience that things are not as they seem, or if they share the concern of those who are demonized. An obvious example of this is strikers and demonstrators disrupting daily life; if they are expressing a cause for which there is sympathy, then they will be supported by many of those watching at home, whether the media or politicians like it or not – something to which numerous French presidents and prime ministers, who have been forced to back down in the face of street demonstrations and (more recently) so-called 'boss-nappings' (Parsons, 2013), can attest (see Chapter 8).

When it comes to agenda-setting and effects, then, it is worth repeating the disarmingly honest conclusion from a recent piece of research looking into the impact of government efforts to spin economic news to its advantage (Gavin, 2010a: 80)

> The picture … is exasperatingly complex, and the processes dynamic and interactive … [W]hen it comes to the relationship between the media, the political agenda and the policy process, we certainly ought to be sceptical of one-dimensional models of cause-and-effect that run in uniform directions.

Pressure groups and populists

This might explain why, if all this partial exclusion and negative framing is going on, it does not seem to have completely marginalized those trying to change the status quo. Indeed, as we shall see in Chapter 8, a number of them seem to be flourishing – something that is often put down (not least by their corporate opponents and by governments) to their skill in exploiting, of all things, the media! Rather than being a target for the media or running the risk of being ignored or sidelined by it, many pressure groups are an ideal source of stories and have almost certainly begun to take up a bigger share of media time and space than they used to – mainly at the cost, it would seem, of organized interests that used to command far more respect (see Chapter 8) and claim more clout than they do now, most obviously business and trade unions (see Binderkrantz, 2012). As a result, they can claim to play an important part in the agenda-setting 'issue-attention cycle' (see Downs, 1972) that politicians and governments might try to manipulate but – given the disdaining attitudes and the acceleration of news delivery – are possibly less and less able to control.

KEY POINT

Changes in the way politics is covered arguably advantage media-savvy pressure groups and populist politicians at the expense of more conventional actors.

On a practical level, the groups' now-professionalized media staff do a lot of the investigative work news organizations cannot themselves afford to do, and go on to reproduce it in effective, easily digested formats that the organizations can rapidly turn into finished product. Their sometimes conflictual and often highly visual modes of engagement – mass protests, daring stunts, and so on – dovetail well with conventional news values, especially those of television. They also provide journalists with an alternative to more conventional news sources, such as governments, parties and corporations, to whom the public and journalists alike seem to afford less and less trust and respect. This is particularly the case where groups appear to be taking 'the public's' side against those

other institutions in situations where the latter seem intent on ignoring popular feeling: hence the media 'sexiness' of protests against genetically modified (GM) crops. Groups are also finding that the Internet helps them mobilize and aggregate otherwise passive and fragmented audiences whose feelings and/or purchasing power (see Bennie, 1998) can then be used to outflank companies and, indeed, states (see Rodgers, 2003: Chapters 4 and 5). Certainly the sheer wealth of material out there on social and economic issues and on the doings of both firms and governments – some of it helpfully made available and neatly packaged by conventional news organizations as part of their commitment to so-called 'data journalism' (see http://www.guardian.co.uk/news/datablog and http://datajournalismhandbook.org/) – can be used both to raise awareness and (theoretically anyway) level the playing field between ordinary people and vested interests, be it on the global scale favoured by sites like gapminder.org and wikileaks.org, or on the domestic level, typified perhaps by http://parliament.telegraph.co.uk/mpsexpenses/home.

All this brings some comfort to those on the progressive end of the political spectrum, seeming as it does to bear out Habermas's reformulation of the public sphere as a much more contested, congested and potentially transnational space in which civil society can use the media to transmit concerns to the political core and which thus acts as a countervailing power (see Curran, 2002: 135–6). But this also has what some would see as a darker side. Supposedly liberal and progressive 'media-savvy' cause groups are undeniably attractive to a media keen to put itself onside with the public against a 'political class' that increasingly has to justify inclusion in coverage on news values alone. But so, too, are charismatic populists from the other end of the political spectrum – particularly (because the media tends to pay attention to political actors who might make or unmake governments) if they lead parties which slowly or suddenly become relevant to coalition formation after an upcoming election (see Hopmann et al., 2012). Prepared to say what 'everyone' is thinking in terms that anyone can understand, and launching attacks on 'the establishment' that 'no-one' likes or trusts, in a style that resonates with almost universally-held news values, men like Jörg Heider in Austria, Jean-Marie Le Pen in France and the late Pim Fortuyn in Holland are (or were) a news editor's dream. Recent research certainly seems to suggest that the media was an important resource for the radical right wing populist parties we discuss in Chapters 5, 9 and 10, their task made all the easier because their colourful and controversial stances make for good stories which help sell newspapers (see Art, 2007, Ellinas, 2010 and Mazzoleni *et al.*, 2003; see also Jagers and Walgrave, 2007). They also benefit from broadcasters' belief that they have a duty to protect free speech and represent a variety of opinions, especially if those opinions attract votes – one reason why the BBC followed the lead of other countries by deciding in October 2009 to allow the leader of a far right party which had just won seats in the European Parliament to guest on its flagship *Question Time* programme.

Little wonder that, in a public sphere increasingly dominated by media logic, their more mainstream opponents, constrained by the compromises inherent in responsible politics but condemned for 'spin' if they try to compete, are finding life harder and harder. It is not only their fault. If the populism we discussed in Chapter 5 is, indeed, the spirit of the age (see Mudde, 2004) – a *Zeitgeist* that fashionably sees politics as a problem rather than a solution – then what some see as the media's 'culture of contempt' (see Lloyd, 2004) should perhaps shoulder some of the blame as well. As one respected foreign correspondent from Germany (Krönig, 2006) notes, 'politics is more often than not undramatic, complex, not easy to understand and therefore ... difficult and boring to report'; worse still, its results take a long time in coming. If the typical response on the part of journalists, who still feel obliged to cover some (if less) politics but despair of making it sufficiently attention-grabbing, is 'permanent linguistic overkill' (billing every critical report as 'damning', 'devastating' or 'scathing', all internal disagreements as 'dramatic splits', all warnings 'stark' and all developments 'alarming') then it is hardly surprising, say some critics, that so many sensible people are turned off the whole business.

A brave new digital world?

It is not just trends in the conventional, 'mass' media that play into the hands of populists and promotional groups. By speeding up communication (including communication with the mass media), digital technology has significantly cut the cost of starting from scratch. It also has the advantage of appealing to some who might otherwise bypass politics, particularly the young who are especially attracted by what Castells (2009) calls 'mass self-communication' – a form that is 'self generated in content, self-directed in emission, and self-selected in reception by many that communicate with many'. Theoretically anyway, this new form allows non-conventional political actors rapidly to network their way to prominence, and perhaps success (see Donk *et al.*, 2003). It is also encouraging more conventional political actors across Europe – such as parties (see Gibson, Nixon and Ward, 2003; Gibson, Römmele and Ward, 2003; Pedersen and Saglie, 2005) and trade unions (see Ward and Lusoli, 2003) – to try and pull off the same trick, even if they are still at the stage of using the new technology simply to speed and spruce up what they do already, thereby ensuring that their 'e-campaigning' is merely an extension of their conventional (journalist-oriented) campaigning rather than anything more novel or transformative (see Schweitzer, 2012).

KEY POINT

The Internet may really change and open up politics, but it has yet to realize that potential – and, because of inequalities of access and its capacity to insulate users, it may not be an unalloyed benefit if it does. At the moment, mobile telephones and consumer databases are having just as big an impact.

But academic research on all this is still in its infancy (though see Chadwick and Howard, 2009) and the extent to which the web has blown (or will blow) 'politics-as-usual' out of the water can be overdone according to 'cyber-sceptics' (see Zittel, 2004) and even those who simply want to make the point that new technologies shape existing political and media cultures but are inevitably shaped by them in turn (Street, 2011: 277). There is a great deal of as-yet unfounded speculation concerning the impact of new technology on how people use the media and how the media will interact with politics. Anyone, then, who assumes – or at least hopes (see Coleman and Blumler, 2009; see also Dahlgren, 2009) – that the potential proliferation of spaces for political expression and genuinely two-way exchange offered by new technology will result in a more egalitarian, reinvigorated 'digital democracy' might be fooling themselves. There is no reason to assume that the web will always be as unregulated as it is currently. Moreover, one can argue that even now our use of it is to some extent determined by search engines that do little more than reproduce the existing distribution of power and create overlapping commercial networks, meaning we now live in a *Googlearchy* rather than a *Googlocracy* (see Hindman, 2008 and Castells, 2009). This is especially when one considers, first, the uses (largely passive and commercial/'leisure' oriented) to which the web is currently put by most citizens and, second, the extent to which politicians current use of the same medium 'has more to do with adaptive self-preservation' and self-presentation than a desire to move beyond conventional ideas about representation (Coleman, 2005).

It is also worth pointing out that any expansion of ideological diversity brought about by the web will provide opportunities, too, for extremists whom many would regard as beyond the pale, especially when it comes to race and religion (see, for example, Caiani and Parenti, 2009; see also Bartlett *et al.*, 2011). Meanwhile, the extent to which that expansion will be meaningful (in the sense of altering policy outcomes, for instance) is equally open to doubt. For example, 'e-petitions' (see http://epetitions.direct.gov.uk/) might have given the UK government pause for thought on the subject of, say, road pricing; but the web coverage gained by an environmentalist direct-action group like 'Plane Stupid' in the same country was (a) no less critical than the coverage the group's supposedly 'selfish antics' attracted in the mainstream media and (b) seems – partly as a result perhaps – to have little or no impact on government policy (see Gavin, 2010b).

This is not to say that things will not change significantly. Generally, it seems clear that the web is becoming an ever more interactive (and less male) medium, with social networking sites like Facebook, along with micro-blogging tools like Twitter and video-sharing sites like YouTube attracting more and more users, especially among the young (see Figure 7.4) – even though over three times as many Europeans (according to the same survey used in that table) say they would get political information from media organizations' websites than from social

Figure 7.4 Internet and social networking by age

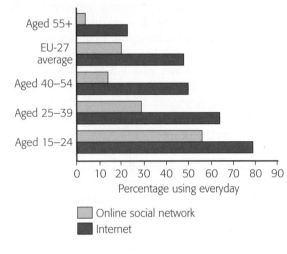

Source: Data from from *Eurobarometer*, 76 (2012).

networks, let alone blogs. Nor should we assume that styles of political communication that are now relatively peripheral will never catch on in ways that profoundly alter, say, the relationship between electors and elected, and between leaders and led. Blogging by (strangely enough) journalists, politicians, party activists – self-confessed political anoraks – is one potentially fruitful example (see Coleman, 2005; Ferguson and Howell, 2004). But of course blogs can also have much less benign effects: the destructive November 2005 riots in France were in part fuelled by bloggers (some of them later arrested) on sites like skyblog.com (now skyrock.com/blog/) who were accused of urging other young people to burn cars and attack the police. After similarly destructive riots in the UK in 2011, a number of people were convicted and imprisoned for inciting violence (even where none actually occurred) via Facebook and Twitter – the very same media that, earlier in the year, had been credited with helping to facilitate a more noble cause, namely the so-called 'Arab Spring'.

At the moment, however, it is, to coin a cliché, too soon to tell whether the web will transform politics and/or the coverage of politics on a more prosaic, day-to-day level. Future works may well describe a politics and a media that are unrecognizable and even unimaginable from those described here. Yet inertia is a powerful force, and Europeans are just as likely as anyone else to adapt to novelty rather than adopt it wholesale, using the Internet to complement rather than necessarily replace existing information sources (see Gaskins and Jerit, 2012). There will also be considerable cultural (albeit institutionally-influenced) differences in uptake and use (see Box 7.11 and Table 7.7) – and, indeed, in production: many of the best-read blogs, for example, are those which make up part of the online presence of existing news organizations, many of which will simply hire rather than crush talented individuals who emerge 'from nowhere' online. And it remains the case that when Europeans go online for news, they go most often to sites run by existing news organizations: in 2012 the top two general news sites in France were run by newspapers *Le Monde* and *Le Figaro*; in Germany by news magazine, *Der Spiegel*, and the tabloid, *Bild*; in Italy by newspapers *La Repubblica* and *Il Corriere della Sera*; in Spain by newspapers *El País* and *El Mundo*; in Sweden by tabloids *Aftonbladet* and *Expressen*; and in the UK by public broadcaster, the BBC, and by newspapers the *Daily Mail* and the *Guardian* which vie for second place; the only exception is the Netherlands – there the second most visited news site is run by top-selling newspaper *De Telegraaf* but the most popular is nu.nl, started from scratch in 1997 (see http://www.alexa.com/topsites/countries; see also Trappel and Enli, 2011)

To some, the fact that the impact of the Internet on politics is perhaps oversold might not be such a bad thing. To them, the **digital divide** seems likely to perpetuate existing political inequalities and participation rates. Interestingly, however, one thing that

---

To talk of a **digital divide** is to remind ourselves that access (and willingness to use) to the Internet is not equal (see Norris, 2001; see also Zillien and Hargittai, 2009). It varies between countries and between people within countries (Fuchs, 2009) – men, the better off and the young, for instance, are generally more likely to make use of the Internet but also to use it in different ways. Variations between countries are largely determined by their wealth, the extent of democratic freedom and the extent to which they are plugged into the global political economy. But, they also depend on government policies: privatization and telecommunications deregulation and competition tend to boost the introduction, take up and usage of the Internet (see Guillén and Suárez, 2005).

BOX 7.11

Legislators 2.0?

Thomas Zittel (2004) carried out an interesting project to compare legislators' use of the web in the USA, Germany and Sweden. US congressmen were much quicker to set up personal websites than their counterparts in the *Bundestag* and *Riksdag*, but few of the sites were very impressive, used not so much to enhance two-way communication but as a place for press releases, a bit of biography and some basic contact details. The Swedes, like the Germans, were not just limited by resource constraints (whereas US representatives employ about eighteen staffers, German MPs get three staffers and Swedish members barely one each); they also had concerns about individualized communication undermining the importance of the party-voter relationship. On the other hand, the Europeans were less concerned about discussion fora than the Americans, who were much more concerned about their inability to moderate or control disruptive or embarrassing contributions due to the strong tradition of free speech.

Table 7.7 indicates is that use of the Internet (and social networking) seems to vary as much across European nations as it probably does across social classes. Much less variation, however, is detectable in mobile phone penetration which is at or over 100 per cent in most European countries. This means that mobile telephony may have a far bigger (or at least more immediate) impact than the Internet.

The political impact of the mobile phone is becoming apparent in the activity of some of the protest groups we look at in Chapter 8. Both fuel protesters and environmental activists – and, indeed, those who have helped kick off violence at recent EU and G8 summits, as well as rioting in the French suburbs – use mobiles to organize and to send pictures which undermine attempts at government censorship or spin. So, too, did hundreds of thousands of Spaniards who came onto the streets to protest the then government's attempt to blame ETA for the Madrid bombings of 2004 and who could well have changed the result of the subsequent general election as a result. At the other extreme, those Islamists

Table 7.7 Internet and social networking in Europe

	Internet Users, 31/12/2011	Penetration: % population	Facebook Subscribers, 31/12/2011	Penetration: % population
Sweden	8,441,718	93	4,519,780	50
Netherlands	15,071,191	90	5,759,840	34
UK	52,731,209	84	30,470,400	49
Germany	67,364,898	83	22,123,660	27
France	50,290,226	77	23,544,460	38
EU	359,530,110	72	171,305,880	34
Czech Rep.	7,220,732	71	3,502,420	34
Spain	30,654,678	66	15,682,800	34
Poland	23,852,486	62	7,524,220	20
Italy	35,800,000	59	20,889,260	34

Source: Data from Internet World Stats http://www.internetworldstats.com

who committed the atrocities used mobiles to detonate their explosives and Islamist use of the Internet to recruit and organize is also a cause for concern (see Ryan, 2007). European parties have already made huge advances in campaigning not via the Internet, but via call centres. Now, they are beginning to use text messaging on election day in order to get their known supporters out to vote. In some cases, governments have woken up to the potential, too. Predictably, perhaps, it was the Italian government run by Silvio Berlusconi which sent a text message to all Italians with mobiles reminding them to vote in the European elections of 12 and 13 June 2004. Unfortunately, it was a course of action that landed him in hot water with political opponents and those who wondered who had paid the estimated €3 million cost: if it was the government, was it a waste of money and a breach of privacy; if it was *Forza Italia*, why did the message go through the government? Leaving aside these questions, however, it is perhaps significant that turnout in Italy (always high) was actually up in 2004 (73 per cent compared to 71 per cent in 1999), when across many other countries the decline was steep.

On the other hand, getting the same text message as millions of other people is unlikely to impress many of us these days. It may well be the case that personalization is the way ahead for the media as it is

for other goods and services: futurologists, for instance, have predicted generic news sources will be replaced by 'The Daily Me' which electronically delivers us only the kind of news we are interested in from multiple sources. Leaving aside the potential downsides for democracy of people being able to insulate themselves from inconvenient truths and the potential withering of collective concerns (Sunstein, 2007), parties operating in such an environment will have to work harder to produced customized appeals. One way they are already doing this is via the most understudied (because it seems so boring) yet most heavily exploited uses of digital technology – direct mail based on sophisticated consumer intelligence (garnered from shop loyalty cards, magazine subscriptions, official censuses and credit records, for example) that allows marketers to predict preferences and target people accordingly (Gertner, 2004).

'Overseas' news

The transfer of campaign technology between the UK and the USA is facilitated, of course, by a shared language, but it also has to do with the (not unrelated) fact that US politics takes an arguably disproportionate share of the British media's overseas news coverage – just compare the amount of airtime and column inches devoted to American elections (including the presidential primaries) compared to contests in major European countries like Germany, France and Italy, even if the balance shifted slightly in recent years owing to the obvious importance of the Eurozone crisis. Given challenges presented by the latter, the extent to which, and the manner in which, the European media covers other countries (both inside and outside Europe) is a vital question. The answers may not appear particularly encouraging.

While it almost certainly remains the case that, irrespective of exposure to media, Europeans remain

---

KEY POINT

Although there are some differences between countries, the European media as a whole is not very different from, say, its US counterpart in providing only a very limited window on a world that is supposedly more interconnected and interdependent than ever.

---

more aware of things going on beyond their countries' borders than Americans, their media is no less prone to the hierarchy of coverage that applies elsewhere (see Rössler, 2006: 275). This hierarchy, because it is shot through with historical variation, ensures that for the most part the foreign news watched by one country's viewers will not bear much resemblance to that watched by another's, even on the same night. First, come the 'news centres' that gain consistent coverage (the country itself plus, in most cases, the USA). Second, come the 'news neighbours' that appear reasonably often (important – but not necessarily geographically or linguistically proximate – countries). Then come the 'topical news neighbours' that are covered because they are important to ongoing stories (Iraq and Afghanistan were obvious examples, especially for those countries who had troops there). And finally, a long way back, comes the 'news periphery' made up of countries that feature occasionally, perhaps because of some kind of disaster or human interest story, and then disappear.

Neither is the media in Europe much less prone than its US counterpart to 'domesticate' foreign news by pointing out not just the relevance of a story for domestic affairs but the similarities with events at home and, of course, the actual or possible involvement of nationals. Interestingly, however, there may be

slight variations in the time devoted to foreign stories by television news in different countries: Rössler (2006) reports on his own research which showed that Spanish and Italian TV news programmes are even more likely to stick to events at home than their US counterparts (73 per cent and 67 per cent compared to 64 per cent), while in France, Denmark and Norway over half of their time was devoted to domestic news. Only in Germany, Switzerland and Austria did foreign news seem to have the edge, and they were also more likely to bring in the periphery than simply concentrate, like the Spanish and the Italians, on the USA. Interestingly, European countries' television news was far more likely than its US counterpart to include other nations' political leaders. There were some commonly featured stories, but not enough for researchers to spot any trend toward convergence of coverage – in other words, as Rössler (2006) puts it, we may all be part of one world but each nation is getting different pictures.

Whether this is depressing depends, in part, on one's point of view. Those who routinely complain about globalization could take some comfort from this continued heterogeneity. Those who believe we should be all be focusing on common problems, or who believe that it is possible to identify objectively what does and doesn't matter, might be disappointed. On the other hand, an encouraging finding from Rössler's research (as well as more recent research on British coverage of overseas countries by Dover and Barnett (2004) which shows trendless fluctuation in time devoted year-on-year) is that it seems to be driven by events rather than – as some pessimists claim – by an editorial desire to cut down on foreign news. We should also remember that, even if recent research suggests that time and space devoted to foreign stories does seem to be dropping, it was never that big in the first place (see Biltereyst and Desmet, 2010). Moreover, the huge range of channels available on digital and satellite now mean people can access different perspectives on foreign stories and, if they can cope with the language, even watch them as 'domestic' news – sometimes to the extent that it allows them to stay so wedded to their country of origin and/or their religion (see Ibrahim, 2009) that it increases concerns about immigrant integration and even national security.

On the other hand, much of the above may be false comfort. One former BBC producer, now an academic, focuses on the combination of costcutting and technology that can satisfy the demand for instant pictures in advance of coherent journalism to run alongside them – all of which means a future of foreign coverage as 'a series of disassociated disasters' fronted by globetrotting 'dish-monkeys' who, tethered to their satellite phones in order to service 24-hour rolling news, are unable to gain or communicate any real understanding of context (Franks, 2006: 94; but see also Sambrook, 2010). More systematic, comparative research also suggests that coverage of the 'outside world' varies considerably, not just between countries (with the UK, for example, beginning to follow the USA towards fewer foreign stories, unlike, say, Finland and Denmark) but between commercial and public service outlets, with the latter continuing to cast their nets wider than the former and, in so doing, helping the public to be much better informed as a result (Curran *et al.*, 2009). That said, of course, the insulating effects of any decrease in the quantity or quality of media coverage of foreign countries could, in theory, be offset by the massive increase in foreign travel enjoyed by Europeans as the result of increasing wealth and ever-cheaper flights, especially within Europe itself. On the other hand, it is interesting to note that the British, who have taken particular advantage of these trends and are regular (and, at least in economic terms, welcome) visitors to cities all over the continent, remain as firmly Eurosceptic as ever.

The media and 'Europe'

A certain amount of scepticism is warranted when it comes to considering the extent to which the media has affected politics in Europe by helping to construct a 'European' identity (see Chapter 1) or promote a greater understanding of either other countries or the EU among its citizens. It is difficult to see its impact in these areas as much more than minimal, not least because there is as yet no genuinely pan-European media presence on the continent. There is, as we have seen, a degree of Europeanization at the level of regulation and ownership. And there are clearly a handful of countries that have so much in common with their neighbours, not least linguistically, that they are happy to, say, watch their television and even read their news –

even if the flow tends to be one- rather than two-way (see Collins and Butler, 2004 on Ireland, for instance). The Internet, too, theoretically makes a nonsense of borders, although the extent to which most people actually view non-entertainment content from other countries, particularly those with which they have nothing in common linguistically, is more limited than 'the world's informationized networking elite' who look forward to everyone sharing their own 'cosmopolitan globalism' might have us believe (see Louw, 2005: 133–8).

There is, then, as yet, no genuinely European media market at the level of product. This is in spite of it being over a decade since the EU's 1991 *Television Without Frontiers* Directive came into effect (pre-

KEY POINT

The media may be Europeanizing when it comes to regulation and ownership, but not when it comes to content. Coverage of the EU varies according to country and issue, but is generally very low.

venting member states from placing restrictions on the transmission of broadcasting from other member states) and despite the growth of cable and satellite television, to which getting on for a half of households in the Union now subscribe. Ultimately, European media integration faces a huge hurdle; namely, the cultural and language barriers that do so much to make the continent the diverse place it is. Attempts to create genuinely 'Euro-TV' have so far proved difficult: the audience share of pan-European channels 'rarely passes the 1 per cent mark' (Chalaby, 2002: 189), although there is a potentially lucrative market for transnational news channels which appeal to the same wealthy elites who consume papers like the *FT*, the *IHT* and the *Economist* and whose knowledge of the world may, therefore, be wide but ideologically rather circumscribed (see Chalaby, 2009 and Kantola, 2006). Pan-European satellite services' most popular offerings would appear to be shopping, fashion and porn (Harcourt, 2005: 121). Programming like this, which like sport, has obvious crosscultural appeal, has achieved limited success. But even this – like the 'reality TV' concepts that turn into quite different shows when they are exported into foreign markets – has required skilful (and expensive) 'localization' or tailoring to different national audiences; on balance, they prefer domestically oriented (even if foreign-inspired) programming, although clearly the ability of a country to deliver domestic content depends in part on its GDP (see Chalaby, 2002; see also Štětka, 2012).

This preference, moreover, is supported by governments and parliaments who routinely insist on broadcasters showing a prescribed quota of domestically produced material as a condition of their licences. This insistence (mirrored by the EU Directives that insist on quotas for European programmes, apparently in order to stave off American hegemony) characterizes not just western but also central and eastern Europe. There, an acute awareness of the importance of the media in 'nation-building' (maintaining a sense of identity and community) has, in combination with the still widespread belief among elites that the media should reflect the views of the government, often trumped enthusiasm for market liberalization (see Sparks, 1997: 112–14). All of this means that, with the possible exception of a few transnational 'top people in the Brussels micropolity' of the EU and their interlocutors in government and business circles in Europe's capitals, there is as yet no genuinely 'European public sphere'. Apart from the *Financial Times* and a handful of upmarket satellite news broadcasters, there is little or no media space in which 'European citizenship' (see Meehan, 1993) can fully develop, certainly not without major inequalities in access and information (Schlesinger and Kevin, 2000).

On the other hand, these kinds of analyses might be unduly pessimistic. For one thing, the conception of a 'European public sphere' that they employ is arguably too ambitious. To pass their test, such a sphere would need to be truly supranational rather than (less ambitiously) simply multidimensional, encompassing multilevel linkages in mediated political coverage between the national and the European. In fact, with the exception of the UK (where the focus remains heavily internalized) these multilevel communication linkages are becoming more common. It is possible, for instance, to point to a handful of EU stories that gain Europe-wide coverage that differ systematically from the coverage of the same story in, say, the US media (see Steeg, 2006). And while political stories covered by the 'continental' media are still predominantly national, they can also involve national figures commenting or 'making claims' about other European countries or the EU – especially where these 'European' actors can reasonably be expected to have an impact on policy (for instance, monetary policy and currency matters, rather than, say, pensions). As a result (with the exception of the UK) 'we can speak of a Europeanized public sphere to the extent that a substantial – and over time increasing – part of public contestation neither stays confined to its own national political space …, nor extends beyond Europe without referring to it' (Koopmans, 2004; see also Risse, 2010).

This qualification notwithstanding, it remains true that a media beginning to Europeanize at the level of ownership and regulation seems unable to do much to Europeanize its product and, by implication, those who consume it. But can it at least improve their knowledge and their goodwill concerning the European Union itself? With the possible exception of attitudes towards EU enlargement where media coverage may have made a difference (see de Vreese and Boomgaarden, 2006b), the answer seems to be 'no' – for several reasons. One former EU Commissioner, the UK's Chris Patten, probably put his finger on one of the key, but possibly intractable, problems at a conference held in London in February 2002 to discuss the British media's ignorance and negative treatment of European affairs: 'So much of what the EU does is, frankly, boring and technocratic. It does not lend itself to simple or attractive reporting.' Although there is evidence to suggest that European elections, for instance, do spark at least a modicum of interest in and information gathering on the EU by ordinary people, the effect very soon wears off – and it seems to be decreasing (along with turnout!) with each election (see Lord, 2004: 60–1). But the media also share some of the burden of responsibility: people cannot be expected to take much of an interest if the media simply takes that lack of interest as a given and reacts accordingly – sometimes in spite of the fact it complains in the same breath that 'Brussels' is controlling more and more aspects of Europeans' lives.

This should come as no surprise, however, given what research has revealed about media coverage – research summarized as part of Christopher Lord's admirable (and surely timely) 'democratic audit' of the EU (see Lord, 2004: 62–4). First, media coverage is 'sporadic' and 'events-based', often concentrating (unsurprisingly) on personalized conflict and bad news. It also varies across countries with regard to the amount of time and space devoted to EU matters, though there is no simple connection between lots of attention and enthusiasm in that member state for the EU. Second, while we should be careful not to forget that different media outlets in the same country will place their own meanings on the same piece of EU/European news (Triandafyllidou, 2003, ter Wal *et al.*, 2009 and Eide *et al.*, 2008), the EU is nonetheless presented largely through national frames and filters. In other words, the focus is often on what 'it' (an external actor) is doing for or to 'us'. Not only is each nation therefore supplied with a different take on the same issue, but each is presented with a different notion of what the EU is about. For instance, if one compares German and British media coverage, the latter tends to present the EU as all of a piece whereas the former more often breaks it down into its component institutions. When the UK media does that, however, supranational institutions (the ones 'we cannot control' like the Commission) are four times more likely to be mentioned than the (arguably more powerful) intergovernmental ones. Lastly, the coverage of EP elections differs between countries, but only to the extent that some countries' media provide their publics with the most basic coverage while others fail to do even that.

Interestingly, however, if one compares the EP election years of 1999 and 2004, there does (outside of France, Italy, Austria and Portugal) seem to have been a significant increase in television coverage of EU news right across Europe, although perhaps unsurprisingly, given they were experiencing their first ever EP elections, the media in the new member states (at least outside the Czech Republic) was generally much more interested (see de Vreese *et al.*, 2006). The same research, however, noted that the visibility of the EU was greater in public service broadcasting than on commercial stations, and in 'quality' as opposed to 'tabloid' newspapers. Perhaps surprisingly, the tone of coverage, when it was evaluative, was largely negative – particularly in the older member states. But, for the most part, coverage everywhere could be described as neutral. Of course, this increased visibility did nothing to boost turnout at the elections – another illustration, some might argue, of weak media effects.

Outside of elections, as a summary of recent research (Machill *et al.*, 2006) puts it, 'EU topics account for an extremely small proportion of reporting' while 'the players at EU level also only

feature in minor roles' even in EU stories, while coverage of fellow member states is skewed towards the most economically powerful. On the other hand, it does suggest that there are significant differences between countries, with media in Germany, Denmark and the Netherlands paying most attention to 'Europe'. The other Scandinavian countries come next, followed by France, Spain and Austria, with Italy, Ireland and (perhaps surprisingly) Belgium giving the topic relatively little space. The UK is in the last group, although discussion there, when it occurs, can be very intense and heated, not least because journalists (as much as proprietors) often feel just as strongly about the issues as their audiences (see Firmstone, 2009). Other research (Koopmans and Erbe, 2004) suggests – very plausibly – that the amount of attention paid in the media to 'Europe' varies according to the extent to which the EU has policy competence in the matter being discussed: on agriculture, for instance, Europe will be brought up; on taxation or health, it won't.

Hardly surprising, then, that few people throughout Europe think of themselves as well-informed about European affairs, although there are variations according to country, gender, class and attitudes. On average, a third of people living in the EU see themselves as well-informed about European affairs, according to the 76th *Eurobarometer* survey, published in 2012. The proportion hovers just above and just below 40 per cent in the Netherlands, Poland, Sweden, the UK and Germany. Italians are close to the average, with the Czechs just below it. However only one in four French people and only one in five Spaniards claim to be well-informed. Generally (and not unusually when it comes to perceived political knowledge), more men (39 per cent) than women (27 per cent) put themselves in that category. More people working in managerial (50 per cent) than manual occupations (28 per cent) think of themselves as well-informed, with a similar difference (48 percent to 26 per cent) between those who have a positive attitude to the EU and those who have a negative attitude. Generally, however, people feel that media coverage of the EU is sufficient and reasonably objective, although, interestingly, far more people (32 per cent) in the UK than elsewhere (the EU average is just 14 per cent) seem to think that press coverage in their own country is too negative, which suggests that the rabid Euroscepticism of some British newspapers does not go unnoticed even if its effects are possibly exaggerated (see de Vreese, 2007; see also Leconte, 2010).

Overall, one gets a strong sense that Europeans really aren't very interested in the EU and, even while they may express a vague desire to be better informed by the media, aren't exactly desperate to see that happen. This could have implications, however – practical as well as normative. While the 'general public' of European countries is looking elsewhere, organized groups who, by definition, do not necessarily have 'the general interest' at heart are busy making their presence and their pressure felt in the EU. We turn to these groups in the next chapter, but not before dealing with an ongoing issue that relates back to concerns raised in previous chapters.

Women and the media in Europe

There is no doubt that women are underrepresented in news and current affairs in Europe, both as producers and (much more so) as subjects. But things are gradually changing. On the production side, this is less evident: when we look at the percentage of stories in European newspapers and on radio and television which are reported or presented by women the figure was the about the same (41 per cent) in 2010 as when the figures were first compiled ten years before. Moreover, women are still far more likely to be employed in media roles where visual and verbal impact count: there are significantly more women employed as reporters on European television and radio than in newspapers, and there are significantly more women employed in broadcast media as presenters rather than reporters. But when we look at women as subjects there has been a striking rise: in 1995 just 16 per cent of news subjects were women; fifteen years later in 2010 it was 26 per cent. On the other hand, women feature much less frequently than they should do, given changes in employment in many of the professions, for instance, in an expert capacity. They are also far more commonly portrayed as victims than are men – and far more likely to find that their family status (wife, mother, etc.) is mentioned. And they feature much less frequently in stories about, say, the

Table 7.8 Male domination of the media: percentage of men presenting, reporting and featuring in the news, 2010

	Presenter %	Reporter %	Subject %
Czech Rep.	43	51	82
Italy	31	57	82
Europe average	57	62	78
France	50	53	74
Germany	66	71	74
Netherlands	73	78	73
Poland	67	72	72
Spain	36	56	71
UK	49	68	70
Sweden	53	48	68

Note: European average calculated from the 20 EU countries studied.

Source: Data from Global Media Monitoring Project (2010).

economy and foreign or domestic politics than they do in those involving social, legal and family issues and especially arts and entertainment. (All this information comes from http://whomakesthenews.org/.)

Of course, to some extent, this reflects the extent to which women, as we have seen, are underrepresented in politics and business. However, if this were the only explanation we might expect the variation between countries to be more evident and consistent with the differences seen in female representation in previous chapters. Table 7.8 (as well as making it obvious that the Italian media likes women to present the news but not to make it) suggests that there is some relationship there but it is not as powerful as one might expect. There is also, of course, a chicken-and-egg problem here. Are women not seen, read and heard as much as men because they are underrepresented in politics, government and business? Or are they underrepresented in those places, at least in part, because they are given less exposure in the media?

Learning Resources for Chapter 7

Further reading

The literature on politics and the media is massive, partly because – as Street (2011), *Mass Media, Politics and Democracy* notes – it deals with both power *over* the media and the power *of* the media. A good place to start is Sanders (2009), *Communicating Politics in the Twenty First Century* and the bumper collection edited by Semetko and Scammell (2012), *The SAGE Handbook of Political Communication*. Anyone wanting a widely comparative study should consult Hallin and Mancini (2004), *Comparing Media Systems*. Also useful are the collection edited by Esser and Pfetsch (2004), *Comparing Political Communication*, a collection comparing the Netherlands and the UK edited by Brants and Voltmer (2011), *Political Communication in Postmodern* Democracy, and the collection edited by Strömbäck and Kiousis (2011), *Political Public Relations*. There are also very useful case studies of the media landscape in thirteen countries in the collection edited by Czepek, Hellwig and Nowak (2009), *Press Freedom and Pluralism in Europe*. Anyone interested in political advertising should read the collection edited by Kaid and Holz-Bacha (2006), *The Sage Handbook of Political Advertising*, while those interested in how the news media covers election should consult the collection edited by Strömbäck and Kaid (2008), *The Handbook of Election News Coverage around the World*. The most comprehensive coverage of the media policies of European polities is Psychogiopoulou (2012), *Understanding Media Policies: a European Perspective*. Books on the political potential of the internet include the controversial Sunstein (2007), *Republic.com 2.0.*, the suggestive Castells (2009), *Communication Power*, and the exhaustive survey edited by Dutton (2013). Finally, for a devastating critique of modern 'churnalism' (not least its over-reliance in straightened times on press releases) by the journalist who helped expose the phone-hacking carried out by News International's UK titles, see Davies (2008), *Flat Earth News*.

On the web

www.thesun.co.uk, www.bild.t-online.de and www.aftonbladet.se – tabloids

www.ketupa.net and www.pressreference.com – media facts and history

http://mde.politics.ox.ac.uk – country reports and research on media and democracy in central and eastern Europe

http://www.soros.org/issues/media_arts – debates on free expression

http://drseansdiary.wordpress.com/ – quirky academic take on Czech (and European) politics

http://blogs.lse.ac.uk/europpblog/ – more short accessible academic blogging on European and EU politics

www.order-order.com, http://www.spectator.co.uk/coffeehouse/, http://ukpollingreport.co.uk/ and http://www.hopisen.com/ – UK political blogs

http://www.bbc.co.uk/news/correspondents/gavinhewitt/ – BBC Europe Editor's blog

http://en.rsf.org/ – reports on media freedom

http://www.comparativeagendas.org/ – research on agenda-setting

http://www.levesoninquiry.org.uk/ – the relationship between press and politicians (and police!) laid bare

http://www.ejc.net/ and http://mediastandardstrust.org/ – non-profit bodies dedicated to raising standards in journalism

http://www.indymedia.org/en/index.shtml – alternative, anti-corporate, DIY media outlets

Discussion questions

1   There are some very obvious regional variations in media use in Europe: how would you sum them up?

2   How do governments in Europe attempt to regulate the media, and how has European integration impacted on those attempts?

3   What is public service broadcasting? Despite its problems, do you think it still has a future in Europe?

4   What do people mean when they suggest that political coverage now conforms to media rather than party logic – and what are the implications for politicians?

5   Do you have any sympathy with the view that the media are actually undermining democracy by the way they report it?

6   Are European politicians right to pay so much attention to, and get so worked up about, bias in and the influence of the media?

7   Why might trends in media coverage benefit pressure groups and populists rather than more mainstream, conventional political actors?

8   Do you think new information and communications technology (ICT) will have a fundamental impact on politics in Europe?

9   How well do the European media cover 'Europe' and foreign news?

ONLINE RESOURCES AVAILABLE

Visit the companion site at **www.palgrave.com/politics/bale** to access additional learning resources.

Chapter 8

Participation and pressure politics – civil society, organized interests and social movements

The idea at the heart of representative democracy in Europe (see Chapter 6) is that citizens play a role in their own governance via the election of parliaments (and possibly presidents). It is also generally accepted that, like it or not, parties play a mediating role, helping to structure choices and aggregate interests, be they economic or cultural or religious (see Chapter 5). At the very least, according to the Austrian economist and political analyst Joseph Schumpeter – a man who thought too much citizen participation would be unworkable – parties provide competing teams of managers that we can choose between at the ballot box (see Best and Higley, 2010). But it would be a very 'thin' conception of democracy indeed that supposed citizens would – or, indeed, should – limit their participation to joining parties and voting or, between elections, be content simply to leave the politicians and the bureaucrats to get on with it. After all, the policies initiated and implemented between those elections will rarely suit everyone and may even be seen as unfair by some people. Unless of course they happen to own a huge media empire, individuals are rarely so powerful that they can hope to influence policy on their own. They also recognize that voting and political parties are not the only way to exercise that influence or simply to get involved. They are, therefore, likely to engage in other forms of political participation. And they might well band together in order to secure the introduction, prevention, continuation or abolition of whatever measures they feel are important to them – a tendency that, ever since de Tocqueville (a famous nineteenth-century French analyst of politics and society) wrote his comparative work on America, has been celebrated as one of the indicators and bastions of a healthy democracy.

Forms of political participation other than voting or joining a political party can be relatively low cost and episodic – signing a petition is a good (and, as we shall see, increasingly common) example. But they also include the collaborative or 'associative' activity that creates **pressure groups** which, no less than parties, mediate between the state and the individual,

Pressure groups are more or less organized collections of people who aim, if they feel their interests or their ideals are at stake, to influence (but not to get elected to) government. This influence may be pursued directly, through access to politicians or bureaucrats, and/or indirectly – for instance, through the media or perhaps the legal system. Groups can be highly institutionalized or very informal. They can be permanent (and possibly well-funded) fixtures in the political landscape, involved in a wide range of policy debates, or organizations that come and go according to whether their particular issue preoccupies (or can be made to preoccupy) people.

expressing the demands and preferences of citizens and helping government to formulate, and sometimes even to deliver, the policies that meet them. Such activity and such groups constitute what is now routinely referred to as 'civil society' (see Box 8.1) – something that, it is claimed, not only minimizes the risk of an over-mighty and unresponsive state, but also helps create (at the same time as it draws on) the '**social capital**' that some see as essential for a genuinely participatory democracy and a healthy economy (see Hooghe and Stolle, 2003; Putnam *et al.*, 2000; van Deth *et al.*, 2007). It is this kind of collective participation and action, and the political response to it, which this chapter explores.

In the words of its most prominent promoter (Putnam 2000: 19):

Whereas physical capital refers to physical objects and human capital refers to the properties of individuals, **social capital** refers to connections among individuals – social networks and the norms of reciprocity and trustworthiness that arise from them.

The chapter begins by looking at forms of political participation other than voting or joining political parties. It goes on to focus on pressure groups, the ways they have been classified and variations in the way they work and in their relative success. It then moves on to look at two classic categories in which European states have been placed in relation to the role of organized interests – pluralism and corporatism – to see to what extent these 'ideal types' (used by social scientists to simplify analysis) tell us anything useful about the real world. It focuses in particular on two key real-world examples: first, a group that is often said to be very close to government and successful all over Europe – the agricultural lobby – and, next, one that many casual observers believe, we argue mistakenly, has been frozen out – the trade unions. It then looks, conversely, at business and notes that, although powerful, it does not always 'win'.

Both of these groups can be defined as 'interest groups' in the sense that they have something material to offer their members. To some theorists, this explains their success despite being outnumbered, if you like, by the general public. We question this idea by pointing to big national variations in the willingness of different nations to join groups and by looking at one of the most significant developments in Europe over the last three decades – the mobilization of so-called *new social movements* (NSMs). These groups offer people the chance to support a cause and, in so doing, express themselves and their values. We should not, though, be too naive. Many such groups have turned into 'protest businesses'. Others are testament to the fact that the comfortable distinction between civil society (supposedly good) and direct action (widely regarded as questionable) is not necessarily hard and fast. Finally, we look at the extent to which all the groups previously examined are operating at the European, transnational level.

Participation – the expanding but not necessarily alternative repertoire

In Europe's liberal democracies there are many more ways of being involved in politics than simply voting. People might, for example, confine them-

The label *new social movement* (NSM) is applied to pressure groups, many of which began to emerge in the 1960s, expressing a radical critique of mainstream societies, cultures and institutions for ignoring people and issues that did not fit conveniently or inexpensively into 'politics-as-usual'. Characteristic concerns include equality for women and for racial, ethnic and sexual minorities, the environment and animal rights, international peace and, more recently, globalization. Many observers see such concerns as typical of 'postmaterialism' and/or 'identity politics', wherein solidarity with a cause not directly associated with one's self-interest combines with a need for self-expression and self-realization to mean that 'the personal is political'. NSMs are also distinguished (at least, initially) by their commitment to more general anti-authoritarian and pro-egalitarian values. This commitment also underpins the way they (supposedly but not, in fact, in all cases) work: informal and fairly pluralistic networks, non-hierarchical structures and (what used to be thought of anyway as) non-conventional forms of protest, often involving (normally) non-violent direct action, such as marches, demos, sit-ins and boycotts.

BOX 8.1

What is civil society, is it a good thing, and how much does each country have?

Civil society is a term more often bandied about than defined. The best short definition is probably by the political theorist David Held (1987: 281), who sees it consisting of 'areas of social life – the domestic world, the economic sphere, cultural activities and political interaction – which are organized by private or voluntary arrangements between individuals and groups outside the direct control of the state'. A good longer definition is the one used by the now-defunct London School of Economics' Centre for Civil Society. According to the CCS (2004), civil society is:

> *the arena of uncoerced collective action around shared interests, purposes and values. In theory, its institutional forms are distinct from those of the state, family and market, though in practice, the boundaries between state, civil society, family and market are often complex, blurred and negotiated. Civil society commonly embraces a diversity of spaces, actors and institutional forms, varying in their degree of formality, autonomy and power. Civil societies are often populated by organizations such as registered charities, development non-governmental organizations, community groups, women's organizations, faith-based organizations, professional associations, trades unions, self-help groups, social movements, business associations, coalitions and advocacy groups.*

The common wisdom is that not only is all this is a terribly good thing in itself, but also that being involved in such activity breeds social trust and confidence in political institutions. Recent research across twelve European countries, however, provides little or no support for this claim (see Zmerli *et al.*, 2007). And although some research reveals even apparently non-political groups have 'a remarkably high level of ... contacts' with local politicians, parties, and bureaucrats (Lelieveldt and Caiani, 2007), it also finds that the vast majority of groups focus on leisure pursuits, with ostensibly 'political' groups in a small minority that contains more passive than active members (Maloney and Roßteutscher, 2007a). Wider survey research also reveals that people are much more involved in groups of any kind in the established democracies of northern and central Europe than they are in the south and, especially, the newer democracies of eastern Europe (see Figure 8.1).

---

selves to casting a ballot every four or five years or signing a petition on the street or the Internet. They might take the next step by demonstrating against a law or a proposal that they don't agree with, realizing perhaps that they might end up breaking the law, or at least confronting those charged with upholding it, as a result. Or they might go so far as to join a political party or a group concerned with a particular issue or set of issues and end up being the kind of person who seeks the votes, the signatures and the attendance of others. In the most extreme circumstances, the group they join may even be clandestine, like an animal rights group prepared to countenance illegal and even violent action to stop what it regards as unwarranted cruelty. The opportunities, in other words, range from very 'low cost' to

'high-intensity' activities that suck up an individual's time and possibly his or her money too. And some of the more 'unconventional' types cross (or at least come close to crossing) the line between what is within and what is outside the law: the entire 'repertoire', however – even those which involve violence – can claim to count as political participation (see Dalton, 2002: 61).

Participation – especially when it is peaceful and legal – is generally seen as a good thing, although there is a long-running argument among political scientists about whether, like all good things, you can have too much of it. For example, in what is now regarded as one of the 'classics' of comparative politics, Almond and Verba (1963) promoted the 'civic culture' they claimed to have identified in the

Figure 8.1 Variations in associative activity in selected European countries

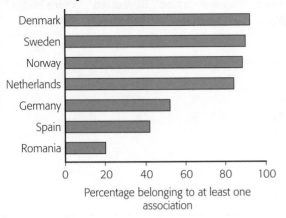

Percentage belonging to at least one association

Source: Data from Morales and Geurts (2007: 138).

UK as the best compromise between 'subject cultures', where the government was accorded possibly too much respect and autonomy, and 'participant cultures', where citizens were so active and demanding that they made it difficult for representative politicians to get on with their job. This argument, however, seems to have faded as observers have become increasingly worried about a supposed decline in political participation in Europe, as well as other advanced liberal democracies – worries we have already touched on in Chapter 6 when we discussed turnout at elections.

Survey evidence clearly suggests, however, that 'petitions, boycotts, and other forms of elite-challenging activities are no longer unconventional, but have become more or less normal actions for a substantial part of the citizenry of postindustrial nations' and that '[a]lthough passive and elite-directed forms of public participation, such as

KEY POINT

There are plenty of other (normally complementary rather than alternative) ways of participating in politics beyond parties and voting. But those that have increased most in recent years tend to be more ad hoc and require little ongoing commitment, while the likelihood of engaging in them varies considerably according to where in Europe people live and their demographic and socio-economic profile.

voting and church attendance, have stagnated or declined ... these newer forms of public participation have become increasingly widespread' (Inglehart and Catterberg, 2002: 302). In other words, if one looks at new forms of political action, the oft-voiced fears that Europe (and other advanced nations) have over the last two or three decades been experiencing worrying levels of 'civic disengagement' are unfounded. For the former communist countries, research covers a rather shorter period, but suggests a different pattern. There seems to have been a 'post-honeymoon' dip in 'elite-challenging action' as the inflated expectations surrounding the transition to capitalist democracy were punctured by a rather grimmer reality (see Bernhagen and Marsh, 2007; Inglehart and Catterberg, 2002). However, generally speaking, this dip either did not take place at all or was much less significant in central Europe, especially where people-power played a part in bringing down the former regime (for instance, in the Czech Republic and Poland) than it was in those states that were part of the former Soviet Union and where transition was elite-dominated (for instance Latvia, Lithuania and Estonia).

The other, normative concern about participation is that it is socially skewed, thereby disadvantaging the already disadvantaged. Essentially, participation in all its forms tends to be positively associated with socio-economic status and education, although clearly it is also driven by party and union membership, by an interest in politics, by individual psychology (see Bekkers, 2005) and by family traditions. Classing yourself as left-wing also counts for a lot – although interestingly, being right-wing, which in western Europe tends to make you less likely to participate in 'elite-challenging' or 'uninstitutionalized' activity, is positively correlated with such activity in central and eastern Europe. On the other hand, being environmentally aware in that region seems to make no difference but it is associated with such activity in the west (see Bernhagen and Marsh, 2007: 61, 64). Age makes a difference in the west as well, with middle-aged people (often with more secure jobs and an interest in the system because they have children in education and parents receiving healthcare and welfare/insurance benefits) more inclined to participate. So, too, does length (and indeed security) of residency, which means

Table 8.1 Patterns of political action in Europe

	Contacted an official	Worked in an organization	Signed a petition	Demonstrated lawfully	Boycotted products	Wore badge/ sticker
Sweden	15	25	44	6	33	13
France	16	16	33	15	27	12
UK	17	9	39	4	23	9
Germany	12	20	30	9	24	5
Spain	12	16	24	23	11	10
European average	15	15	23	7	15	8
Netherlands	14	22	22	3	9	4
Italy	13	8	15	11	7	8
Czech Rep.	19	10	14	4	8	5
Poland	8	5	7	1	4	3

Source: Data from Norris (2011b) based on European Social Survey.

that it generally takes time, for instance, for immigrants to participate as much as the native population, although this might be offset by their very strong interest in securing policy that benefits or does not discriminate against their compatriots. Many of the factors that predispose an individual to involve themselves in these kinds of activity are, incidentally, the same as those that make them more likely to join a group of any kind, be it purely social, sporting or cultural, or political, although group membership is even more skewed towards men (see Armingeon, 2007; Badescu and Neller, 2007; Zmerli *et al.*, 2007).

That said, just as with voting (see Chapter 6) and media use (Chapter 7), these individual-level drivers of activity might ultimately be less important than the region and the particular country a person comes from. As Table 8.1 shows, there are (not for the first time) big and apparently systematic differences between north and south and between post-communist democracies and the rest, even if not every country (as the relative position of, say, Spain and Italy shows) fits the pattern precisely. Moreover people from different countries might well see things in very different ways even when they are ostensibly campaigning on the same side and on the same issue (see Box 8.2).

The rise of political activities like petition signing, consumer boycotts, and demonstrations potentially increases the range of people who will get involved

in politics. The fact that they are more sporadic, take up less time and are less hierarchical might make these new forms of participation more attractive to, say, young people and women. Fascinating research by Stolle and Hooghe (2005) suggests that the latter is indeed the case, although the closing of the gender gap (see also Marien *et al.*, 2010) is more significant than the closing of the age gap: it seems that increasing numbers of people are carrying the protest 'habit' of their youth into middle age (see van Aelst and Walgrave, 2001), while it may be the case that younger people – but not of course only younger people (see Pickerill, 2010) – are finding newer, digital ways of protesting.

But the same research also shows that, while these forms of participation are no more likely than 'old-style' political activities to attract and favour people who are comparatively well-educated, well-to-do, and politically interested and driven, they are nevertheless still engaged in disproportionately by those groups (see Marien *et al.*, 2010). To take just one example of the 'emerging action repertoires', the consumer boycott, the most highly educated are three-and-a-half times more likely to engage in such action than the least educated. In other words, the sort of people who are more likely to vote, join parties and pressure groups, and contact MPs and officials (see Aars and Strømsnes, 2007) are also more likely to sign petitions, attend demos, and support consumer boycotts and 'buycotts' – the pur-

BOX 8.2

The F-15 anti-war demo, 2003

February 15 2003 saw what was the largest transnational protest event the world has ever seen. Millions of Europeans – among others – marched in opposition to the upcoming US-led invasion of Iraq. Luckily for those interested in comparative politics, a team of academics was there distributing surveys in order to find out who they were and what they thought they were doing. It turns out that there was a fairly even mix of men and women, but that most were young to middle-aged, disproportionately highly educated (in most countries researched, over half had been to university). They were also much more interested in politics than most people and overwhelmingly left-wing (60 per cent putting themselves on the left and over 20 per cent on the far left), with a large minority working in the caring professions. Seven out of ten were active members of a group or association. So far, so postmaterialist, some would say. Interestingly, however, there were significant variations when it came to what protesters from each country actually wanted – beyond, of course, preventing war. There was consensus on the war being really about oil, while nearly half the protesters in every country believed the Americans were conducting some kind of crusade against Islam. But when it came, for example, to believing that war was always wrong, protesters in the UK (and the USA) were much less likely to agree that this was the case than their counterparts in Spain, Italy, the Netherlands, Sweden, Belgium and Germany – and were much more focused on getting a diplomatic solution to the conflict as opposed to simply stopping any invasion. Even transnational protest, then, seems to be shaped by national concerns and traditions.

Source: Verhulst and Walgrave (2007).

chase of goods which, for example, promote 'fair trade' (see Stolle *et al.,* 2005). 'Elite-challenging' participation, then, is not so much an alternative but a complement to 'conventional' participation (see Norris, 2002): the same researchers, indeed, found that only 1 per cent of Europeans surveyed had engaged only in the former and not in the latter.

Should we, however, equate the relatively brief and episodic participation required by signing petitions, going on demos and boycotting certain goods with the more high-intensity participation required by, say, active (not simply passive) engagement in a political party or pressure group? It seems absolutely right to argue that 'elite-challenging' activity, even if it is relatively 'non-institutionalized', should be seen as just as important to civil society and to building social capital as, for example, membership of voluntary associations (see Welzel *et al.,* 2005). Yet it is difficult to escape the feeling that there is an important difference in the character and quality, if not the quantity, of participation involved (see Bale *et al.,* 2006). The most recent research also suggests that, whereas people who volunteer for any kind of political group are significantly more likely to volunteer for another such group, involvement in one form low-intensity participation (say, signing a petition) is much more likely to lead someone into participating in another (say, boycotting certain goods) than it is to lead them into getting involved in something more time-consuming (see de Rooij, 2012).

On the other hand, we should note that relatively low-intensity protest activity is not the only participatory indicator on the up. So, too, at least in some countries, is membership – including membership by young people under the age of 25 – in 'sociotropic' associations (as opposed to religious or 'utilitarian' associations like political parties, trade unions or professional organizations), such as community, charity, environmental, international or cultural groups (see Welzel *et al.,* 2005: 127–8; see also Dekker and van den Broek, 2005; Norris, 2002). We should also note, in all fairness, that research on the less institutionalized protest activity referred to above (petitions, boycotts, demos, etc.) suggests that the level of such activity is strongly correlated with open, accountable and efficient government rather than with the membership of groups, which those interested in social capital tend to concentrate on (Welzel *et al.,* 2005).

In fact, recent cross-national research casts doubt on the 'neo-Tocquevillian' argument, associated with Putnam and others who stress the importance of social capital, that active participation, even in non-political, associations makes for a healthier, more vibrant democracy. True, the research identifies 'a strong, positive correlation between associational involvement and political action'. However, that correlation is 'stronger for interest and activist organisations than for leisure organisations.' Interestingly, it looks as if simply belonging to an organization rather than necessarily being active makes it more likely that one will get involved in political action. But it also seems clear that the latter has little to do with belonging; it is simply that the type of people who choose to join organizations also choose to get involved politically – all of which suggests that voluntary associations are not so much 'schools of democracy' as 'pools of democracy' (van der Meer and van Ingen, 2009: 281; but see also Howard and Gilbert, 2008). Consequently, because the link between being well-heeled and well-educated, on the one hand, and participation, on the other, is so strong (except perhaps for immigrants: see de Rooij, 2012), policy makers who are genuinely interested in boosting involvement, especially among those who currently do not get involved, should probably concentrate on building a welfare system that reduces inequality (van Ingen and van der Meer, 2011). They should at least think about whether the higher levels of activism in Nordic countries might be related to the sorts of societies that decades of wrap-around welfare have helped to create.

Pressure groups – different types, different opportunities

Any organized attempt politically to promote a particular course of action or way of life which falls short of founding a party to contest elections can be labelled a pressure group. But such groups take on many forms in twenty-first-century Europe. Some will clearly be based on self-interest on the part of those involved, most of whom will be tied to the group through their occupation: these are sometimes labelled 'sectional' or even simply 'interest' groups since their core function is the protecting the interests of a section of society. Others may well be less self-regarding (at least in theory), and are known as 'cause' or 'promotional groups', though recently they may choose to call themselves NGOs.

Analysts have for some time found it useful to distinguish between what British political scientist Wyn Grant labelled 'insider' and 'outsider' groups. The former had cosy, private and possibly more influential relationships with those in power, while the latter were excluded and therefore obliged to take a different, more public route that involved trying to shame rather than inveigle the government into action. More often than not, sectional interest groups were seen as insiders, providing the state with the information and the implementation infrastructure that otherwise it might have lacked in exchange for a degree of influence on policy. Cause groups, on the other hand, were seen as outsiders.

> **KEY POINT**
>
> **Pressure groups may be in the business of defending a tangible (often economic or 'sectional') interest, or they may promote a cause or ideal. There are now no hard and fast distinctions between the tactics both types use, their choice (and to some extent their success) being based on the political environment (or 'opportunity structure') they have to work in.**

These distinctions, which were never hard and fast (see Box 8.3), might, however, be proving increasingly redundant. Governments have tried, in the spirit of 'the new public management' (NPM) that we spoke about in Chapter 4, to insulate themselves from the 'producer capture' (control of policy by insider groups) that too cosy a relationship with a pressure group may engender. And, as the structure of the economy has changed and economic growth weakened, they have also been less and less keen to provide the kind of pay-offs that some of those groups might traditionally have expected. Conversely, the success of increasingly professional outsider groups at getting their issues on to the agenda has forced governments to take them more seriously and suggested to insider groups that they may have something to learn, particularly when it comes to using the media (see Chapter 7).

Nowadays, then, instead of particular strategies being associated with particular groups, they are best seen as a range of options which any group may exploit as it sees fit – bearing in mind, of course, that there may be a trade-off between, for example, a group embarrassing the government and how keen

BOX 8.3

The church – sectional or cause group, insider or outsider?

One of the most successful pressure groups in many European countries – even if it is not thought of as such – is the church. Given the precipitate decline in the number of devotees, the traditional religions have managed to retain many of their privileges and to maintain a possibly disproportionate influence on national life (see Madeley, 2011). Churches in Scandinavia and Germany for instance, still collect revenues, albeit on a voluntary basis, through the tax system. In Scandinavia, they have been instrumental in dissuading governments from liberalizing laws on alcohol consumption and opening hours. Meanwhile, in other countries, including Ireland and especially Poland, they have managed not only to protect vast financial assets but also to exert a brake-like effect on political responses to social change – most obviously when it comes to education and, in particular, the abortion law. But churches' influence as 'societal veto players' varies (see Fink, 2009) and might not last forever. In 2005, Spain became only the second country in Europe (after the Netherlands) to put same-sex marriage on exactly the same legal basis as conventional marriage; a determined centre-left government – boosted by opinion poll findings that it was reflecting majority opinion – drove through the measure notwithstanding the Roman Catholic Church organizing counter-demonstrations and encouraging legal challenges. Meanwhile in Ireland, child-abuse scandals have seen the same church lose so much public support that in July 2011 the Irish prime minister, Enda Kenny, felt able to lay into the Vatican for its 'dysfunction, disconnection and elitism' and to declare that the historically close relationship between church and state in Ireland could never be the same again – something none of his predecessors as *Taoiseach* would never have dared to do.

the government is to keep it in the loop. Often, the decision of which path to pursue will be determined by circumstances or by what is sometimes referred to as the **political opportunity structure** prevailing not just in each state but also, given the importance of the EU for some policy domains, Europe as a whole.

The idea of a **political opportunity structure** originates from research into social movements (see McAdam *et al.*, 1996). The strategies and the success of groups, while obviously dependent on contingency and on factors such as effective leadership or resources, also depend on more consistent institutional and even cultural factors: Is there a supranational authority above the nation state? Who are the 'veto-players'? Is the party system fragmented and polarized, or restricted to just a few relatively centrist parties? Are the media centralized and are they independent? Do people regard all or only some forms of direct action as acceptable in a democratic, civilized society?

A good illustration of the point is provided by the extent to which (and the ways in which) pressure groups in different countries bother with parliament. In CEE, where communist states would have nothing to do with anything remotely resembling a pressure group and where even now governments remain ambivalent and unsure about such groups' legitimacy and rationale, the regions' fledgling interest groups are more likely to lobby parliament than lobby government direct (see Pérez-Solórzano Borragán, 2006). The studies of western European countries gathered together by Philip Norton (1999) suggest that for most of them, however, government is the main focus. However, they also suggest that the more chance the parliament has to modify and even make policy, the more effort groups put in to influencing it. Accordingly, the Italian parliament is seen not just as a channel to get to where the real power lies, but a target in itself. Generally, pressure groups focused on committees, not only because they regarded this as the best way of getting their views on record – a particular attraction for 'outsider' groups – but also because this was where small, but perhaps significant, changes could be made. The country studies also suggested a significant difference in the relationships between groups and parliamentarians. In Germany and the

Netherlands, the relationship is both formalized and in some ways incestuous: many MPs started off in pressure groups and maintain strong links with them, although, interestingly, this is now declining with the rise of the 'career politician'. Such a decline will make those countries rather more like the UK, where the relationship between pressure groups and parliamentarians has always been rather more indirect.

This parliamentary manoeuvring serves to emphasize that the relationship between pressure groups and political parties is not a zero-sum game. In other words, rather than being self contained, alternative ways of doing politics, they continue to need and to use each other. This is a very important point – particularly in the context of the common wisdom surrounding the so-called 'cartel party', referred to in Chapter 5, that political parties have lost their links to interest groups and are consequently less embedded in civil society. Contemporary studies of these links – the most obvious are between social democratic parties and trade unions, business groups and parties on the centre right (including liberals, Christian Democrats and conservatives), and environmental groups and the Greens – are few and far between. However, they suggest that these links are still strong, even if they take different, less institutionalized forms (see Allern and Bale, 2012). In short, representative politics and pressure group politics are part of the same game: the latter is not replacing the former.

Pluralism, corporatism, and policy networks

Underpinning the political opportunity structure in each state are national traditions – not immovable, but nonetheless influential – concerning the extent to which groups, particularly groups representing employers and employees, are expected (and expect) to play a role in governance alongside the state. Some European states can be said to have a tradition of pluralism, while others are traditionally corporatist (see Figure 8.2). In pluralist countries, the government might, of course, take advice from and occasionally rely on groups, especially for

Figure 8.2 Scoring corporatist and pluralist countries in Western Europe and beyond

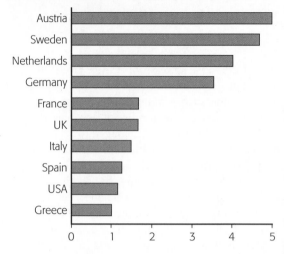

Note: Scores running from 1 to 5 are based on work by Alan Siaroff: the higher the score, the more corporatist the country; the lower the score, the more pluralist it is.

Source: Gallagher, Laver and Mair (2011: 461)

implementation of its policies; generally, however, groups are supposedly kept at arm's length, granted access to make their case but given no special favours. Countries with a corporatist tradition, on the other hand, are those in which so-called 'peak organizations' (such as the national federations of trade unions and employers) have an institutionalized role in the planning and the implementation of certain key state policies, notably on the economy and social policy. Traditionally, meeting with each other and with the government in so-called 'tripartite' bodies, groups make (and, crucially, stick to) trade-offs which are supposedly in the best interests of the whole country: a typical example would be unions agreeing to wage restraint in return for employers' efforts to maintain employment, with both trusting the government to do its best to maintain a stable and benign economic environment.

However, as is often the case in political analysis, these are ideal types. Even supposedly corporatist European states have been wary of the degree of compulsion, monopoly, and (some would argue) economic sclerosis that full-blown corporatism might potentially entail; they can at best be labelled

BOX 8.4

Sweden – the coexistence of corporatism and parliamentary democracy

Sweden has in place all the ingredients associated with classic corporatism: long periods of government by social democrats and an economy relying on trade with other countries. The trade unions, via two federations – the massive LO (*Landsorganisationen*) and the smaller, more white-collar, TCO (*Tjänstemännens Centralorganisation*) – have an institutionalized place at all levels of Swedish governance. They have places on the boards of many of the agencies that play such an important part in the running of the country (see Chapter 3). The employers, via their organization Swedish Commerce (*Svenskt Näringsliv*) used to enjoy the same rights, but in the early 1990s argued that such bodies should be left to politicians alone. Despite this, and despite their criticisms of labour law and national wage bargaining, however, they continue to work with the unions and the government to maintain an 'active labour market policy', aimed less at creating employment and more at maintaining and improving 'employability' by facilitating training and mobility (geographical and between benefits and work). This helps to ensure that the economy, which is heavily export-oriented, retains its flexibility and capacity for low-inflationary growth despite the relatively high wages, taxes and benefits that are associated with what is sometimes called the 'Swedish model' (see Chapter 9). Yet none of this means there is no place for parliament. Indeed, the *Riksdag* is acknowledged to be one of Europe's most powerful legislatures (see Chapter 4). In fact, there is no 'zero-sum game' between corporatist-style concertation and parliamentary democracy. The *Riksdag's remiss* system illustrates this nicely: each piece of proposed legislation is sent out to pressure groups (and to the wider public, if they wish) for comment before being formally introduced as a bill before the country's MPs.

'neocorporatist'. In these countries there is, in certain sectors, a degree of 'concertation' between government and groups that other countries (and certainly neoliberal right-wingers) might frown on. Indeed, as we suggest later, such concertation, far from disappearing, has made something of a comeback in recent years, even if (as we shall see) commitment to it (particularly in some former communist countries) is more rhetorical than real. But, even where it is meaningful, such concertation comes nowhere near undermining or replacing democratic government, as some critics of corporatism allege. Some of the countries in which this kind of sectorally specific 'liberal corporatism' and 'tripartism' is especially strong also have strong parliaments: Germany is one, Sweden another (see Box 8.4). In any case, by no means all pressure groups or sectors are involved in, or benefit from, what tend to be framework agreements between what are routinely called in Europe (and in EU jargon) 'the social partners' (i.e. unions and employers or their 'peak – sometimes called 'umbrella' – associations'). Equally, as we shall see, there is no European state (and whatever its zealous advocates in the USA might maintain, probably no state in the world) where pluralism is so pure that it does not systematically advantage some groups over others.

KEY POINT

Some countries institutionalize the relationship between powerful interest groups, especially business and labour – a system labelled corporatism. Others see more advantage in a more arm's length and ad hoc relationship with groups, all of which have to compete with each other for access and attention – a system labelled pluralism. Most policy areas attract what are known as policy networks of interested groups – networks that are more or less insulated from outside interference. Insulation and influence, however, is not necessarily permanent, as the case of agriculture suggests. Nor is the power of business relative to, say, the trade unions necessarily a done deal.

The way in which a group tries to exert influence depends on the political opportunity structure of the state or states in which it operates, but in all cases its success is likely to be based on its ability and willingness to:

- recruit all, or at least a very high proportion, of those people who have a stake in a particular issue;
- bring to bear significant economic resources and/or connections;
- provide the state with something it needs but cannot or is unwilling to provide for itself in sufficient measure to allow it complete autonomy: financial/human capital; information/ expertise/knowledge;
- seriously put at risk the popularity either of the parties in government, or those that hope to be when that government is brought down.

To the extent that a group meets these criteria, and also to the extent that it is pressing a case to which there is little or only diffuse (rather than organized) opposition, it will tend to have a cosier relationship with those charged with the executive. Political scientists, as we saw in Chapter 3, label the cosiest of these institutionalized relationships (or policy networks) 'policy communities', while at the other end of the spectrum are what they call 'issue networks'. Once again, of course, we have moved into the realm of the ideal type. In real-world Europe things are rather more messy and, indeed, changing over time, as we can see when we look, for example, at agricultural policy.

Farming – a real-world example of power under pressure

The archetypal policy community in many European states is often said to be agriculture. As we saw in Chapter 1, farming contributes less and less to European economies relative to other sectors. Yet it continues to attract vast subsidies from all European states, the bulk of which are now disbursed through the EU's Common Agricultural Policy (CAP) – a mechanism which, critics argue, allows the cost of subsidizing the sector to be hidden from voters at the domestic level. That might be true, but there are good reasons to suppose that even if it were not the case, agriculture would be relatively insulated from interference. For one thing, while European consumers do pay more for food than

they need to, food nevertheless takes up a steadily declining proportion of family expenditure as increases in real wages have, over decades, outstripped increases in prices. Traditional notions about the rejuvenating simplicity, beauty and tradition of rural ways of life also continue to occupy an important place in our conceptions of what it means to be, say, French, or Danish, or Polish.

Taken together, this means that there is little opposition to what, if it were applied to industry, for example, might be seen as 'featherbedding' (making life so easy for producers, often via subsidies or protective measures, that they have no incentive to remain competitive). This makes for what political scientists refer to as an 'asymmetry of interests'. You have, on the one hand, a group of individual or family consumers who are not particularly bothered by subsidies just as long as food is reasonably cheap and plentiful. On the other, you have a highly organized group of farmers for whom the continuation of subsidies is a matter of the utmost importance, as well as politicians and bureaucrats who rely on them for their expert knowledge and their help in policy implementation. Given this asymmetry, the power of farming groups in every state – and, just as importantly, at the EU level, where they operate effectively under the umbrella of the the Committee of Agricultural Organizations (COPA) – to extract money from governments with almost no questions asked by taxpayers is hardly surprising. Neither, of course, is it unique to Europe (see Smith, 1993).

Yet the politics of agriculture also suggest that not even the tightest policy community can insulate itself entirely or forever. First, this is because one sector invariably impinges on others. Second, once we dig a little deeper, we find that even the most well-organized pressure group contains within it a number of potentially conflicting interests. An illustration of the first point is the way in which the rather cosy relationship between farmers and governments has been disrupted in recent years by a number of food-scares (over BSE or 'mad cow disease' and dioxin contamination, for instance) whose trans-European implications are testimony to the extent of integration and interdependence. In such cases, the fear that practices in one sector, agriculture, might have negatively impacted on another (namely, health) meant that the policy community lost control over policy to the extent that political (though, interestingly, not agricultural) heads rolled. Common wisdom suggests that it sacrificed some long-term trust and legitimacy by being less than open about the issues involved. This can be overdone, however. In fact, levels of trust in food and farming in individual European countries seem to be related more to levels of general political and personal trust than to whether or not a country has experienced food-scares or not. For example, the Italians, who have little experience of food-scares, are not very trusting compared with the British or even the Germans, who have had more than their fair share but appear to have been reassured somewhat by government reforms (see Poppe and Kjærnes, 2003).

Second, we need to realize that even the so-called 'agricultural lobby' is made up of many potentially conflicting parts. 'Feisty French farmers' are a common media stereotype across Europe, and especially in the UK, where their theatrical forms of protest – blocking roads, dumping manure, and so on – are guaranteed a place in the news. Interestingly, such antics are by no means an indicator that agriculture is an outsider group in a country that is still one of the largest exporters of food in the world. Indeed, they are testament to a political culture in which direct action has long been an acceptable (and effective) way of getting what you want and to the willingness – perhaps increasing willingness – of even well-connected pressure groups to pursue tactics that belie their categorization as 'insiders' Yet insiders is very much what they are. FNSEA (the French Farmers' Federation) for example, sends representatives to sit on state commissions responsible for setting both policies and prices, on ministerial advisory councils and on regional economic development bodies. Its former leaders have even held prominent political posts, particularly in administrations formed by the centre-right, which is particularly strong in the rural districts that some would say get a disproportionate number of seats in the National Assembly. In 1986, for instance, former FNSEA leader, Francois Guillaume was made agriculture minister in the Chirac government.

To some French farmers, however, 'insider' status has compromised their representatives, encouraging them into even more radical action: José Bové, who grabbed world headlines (and plenty of support) for an attack on a McDonald's franchise to protest at the plight of small farms in an increasingly globalized market, is one example, although he has since pursued a more conventional approach, getting himself elected to the European Parliament in 2009. Similar protests about the agribusiness domination of the National Farmers' Union (NFU) are occasionally heard in the UK, especially when times are tough (as they were, for example, in the foot and mouth outbreak in 2001). In Italy, the split is institutionalized: large- and small-scale farmers have traditionally organized in different groups, with the former's group, *Confagricoltura*, traditionally being less powerful than the latter's, *Coldiretti*, which historically controlled the parapublic body, *Federconsorzi*, responsible (with the Agriculture Ministry) for overseeing the sector. More generally, however, it has to be understood that farmers are but one part of a wider 'agro-industry', in which food-processing firms are increasingly important; as a result, while they (and the organizations which represent them) are still powerful and both the domestic and the European level, and while their clout may increase again as food becomes an increasingly scarce commodity in a heavily-populated global market, the farming lobby isn't quite what it once was (Grant and Stocker, 2009).

There is (still) power in a union

Interestingly, Italy's farmers, whether large- or small-scale, are not as powerful as their counterparts in France (or Britain, via the NFU, or Germany, via the *Deutscher Bauernverband*), which would seem to indicate that 'unity (especially when combined with the ability to recruit a majority of the potential members of a group) is strength'. The old adage certainly seems to hold good for one of the potentially most important pressure groups in any European country; namely, the trade unions.

Although set up, at least in theory, to defend the interests of ordinary people, the vast majority of whom earn salaries and wages, unions are not universally popular or trusted (see Figure 8.3 below). Unions have also suffered significant declines in membership over the last three decades (see Sano

Table 8.2 Trade union density (and hours worked)

	Percentage belonging to a trade union	Average hours worked per year
Sweden	68	1624
Italy	35	1778
UK	27	1647
Netherlands	19	1377
Germany	19	1408
OECD av	18	1718
Czech Rep	17	1795
Spain	16	1674
Poland	15	1939
USA	11	1695
France	8	1439

Note: Union density at latest year (2010, 2009 and 2008).

Source: Data from OECD.stat

and Williamson, 2008) – a decline most obvious and rapid in the former communist countries, where unions that had recruited around nine out of ten workers could count only two or three out of ten within a decade of the end of the Cold War. Indeed, the proportion of the total workforce who are union members – known as 'trade union density' in the jargon (see Table 8.2) – is lower now than in 1970 in almost every European country, with the picture becoming worse for the unions in each successive decade – and younger people are these days considerably less likely to join a union. The exceptions to the general decline over time (eg Finland, Sweden, Denmark and Belgium) were countries where the unions managed to secure themselves a big role in the delivery of unemployment insurance and/or where, crucially, unions have managed to maintain wage bargaining processes at the national or at least the sectoral or industry level (see Scheuer, 2011), rather than at the level of the firm, which theoretically allows employers (to use a slightly pejorative phrase) to divide and rule (see Table 8.3). In all countries, however, union membership has held up much better in the public than in the (more internationally competitive) private sector (Visser, 2006): in

the UK, the proportions are 59 : 17, in France 15 : 5, Germany, 56 : 22, Spain, 32 : 15, and the Netherlands, 39 : 22; in Sweden, the gap (at 93 : 77) is much smaller, but still significant. The union movement, therefore, has a considerable vested interest in the survival of a welfare state (see Chapter 9).

However, rather like the welfare state itself, trade unions might be in trouble but they are not about to disappear, in part because they are (in some cases anyway) capable of adapting to changing circumstances (see Phelan, 2007, and also Upchurch *et al.*, 2009). Moreover, there is a great deal of variation in their size and strength, with some countries (mainly in Scandinavia) displaying density rates around five times those in the USA, while others (notably in CEE, as well as in France) dipping below even that figure. Of course, as Tables 8.2 and 8.3 suggest, density isn't destiny as far as hours worked or workers being covered by collective bargaining agreements is concerned. However, in countries like Sweden (and other Nordic nations), Germany and (especially) Austria, where most unions are concentrated or at least willing to subordinate themselves to one 'peak' federation, labour can expect to have its views taken into account. Often, indeed, it will be institutionally involved in neocorporatist economic and social management.

Not for the first time, geography is less useful as an indicator than is history. True, Scandinavian unions (dense and concentrated) are powerful, but there is no typically 'Southern European' case. For instance, Italian unions might be fragmented but, even discounting for the large number of retired employees they continue to represent, they have far more members than unions in, say, France or Spain, where the importance of employee-elected works councils entering into binding deals with firms means that there is little incentive for workers thus represented (and bound) to join a union. Elsewhere in southern Europe, Cyprus and Malta have density levels approaching those of Scandinavia, and Greece (although only if we presume the economic crisis there has made no difference) falls between the UK and the Netherlands and Germany on the other, where density levels match those of Portugal. Density varies considerably in CEE, too: Slovenia is on a par with the UK but Slovakia and Hungary look more like the Czech Republic and Poland (see Box 8.5) meanwhile Estonia ranks alongside France.

Table 8.3 **Which wage deals are done where?**

	National level	Sector/ industry level	Firm/ company level	Workers covered by collective agreements (%)
Czech Rep.		•	•••	21–30
France		•	•••	91–100
Germany		•••	•	61–70
Italy		•••	••	61–70
Netherlands	•	•••	•	81–90
Poland		•	•••	41–50
Spain	••	••	••	81–90
Sweden		•••	•	91–100
UK			•••	31–40

Notes: ••• main level; •• important; • some bargaining done at this level.

Source: Adapted from Avdagic and Crouch (2006: 209).

Clearly, unions are not perceived as worthwhile by most postcommunist workers, particularly younger people and those who work in the private sector. They were tainted by association with the 'official trade unions' of the Communist era and possibly suffered from what some see as a more general retreat into private life once 'people power' brought that era to an end. That said, this 'legacy effect' may not be permanent: now that most of the older, inessential workers have been shaken out of the system leaving behind their skilled (and sometimes younger, more ambitious) brethren, and now that unions in eastern and central Europe become part of the EU's trade union network, there are at least possibilities for renewal (see Ost, 2009).

Again, then, we should be careful, however, not to equate low union density and high fragmentation with powerlessness on the part of workers. Just like their (rather more numerous but equally divided) Italian counterparts, France's trade unions have on several occasions since the mid-1980s (most famously in 1995), employed direct action (strategic strikes and demonstrations) to derail plans by centre-right governments to make what they argued were much-needed labour market and pension reforms. And notwithstanding this kind of action

BOX 8.5

Poland's trade union movement – defeat from the jaws of victory

Poland's overthrow of Communist dictatorship was a triumph for the independent trade union, Solidarity (*Solidarność*), to whom some 60 per cent of Polish workers had belonged in the early 1980s and whose leader, Lech Wałesa, went on to be elected President of the newly created democratic republic. But any euphoria was short-lived. In contrast to its willingness to stand up to the old regime, Solidarity – legal, once again – became an avid political sponsor of governments whose 'shock therapy' liberalization of the economy disadvantaged (at least, in the short term) many ordinary people. As a consequence, it never recovered its prestige – or, indeed, its membership. Taking into account the membership of Solidarity's rival, the OPZZ, which has close affiliations with the social democrats, and a few much smaller unions, only around 15 per cent of eligible Poles are union members, which is lower than in most European countries. As for those who do join, they tend to be older, poorer and much less likely to be employed in the go-ahead sectors of the economy that attract foreign capital, and whose owners seem determined to keep unions out. Such low density and fragmentation explains why most observers (not altogether fairly, suggests Iankova, 2002) see Poland's 'Tripartite Commission on Socio-economic Issues' not as an indicator of incipient corporatism, but as a toothless 'talking shop' whose union delegates cannot possibly hope to deliver the cooperation of the Polish workforce – even if government and business organizations were of a mind to seek it. Perhaps it is not surprising, then, that a Eurobarometer survey in 2006, suggested that only 27 per cent of Poles trusted trade unions, although we should be careful not to assume that the outlook is entirely bleak (Mrozowicki, and van Hootegem, 2008).

(and the widespread belief that it is the only way to make France's supposedly aloof and elitist state listen), French unions are by no means absent from the dense undergrowth of advisory councils attached to all levels of the country's government. Some even accuse them of being powerful enough to be responsible, like their counterparts in other continental European countries like Spain and Germany, for the difficulties experienced by young people in getting a job, or at least a permanent contract, from employers who find it practically impossible to fire or lay-off older workers who are protected either by unions directly or by the labour market regulations to which they have obliged governments to adhere.

Conversely, we should remember that much of the power of big recruiting unions and (in the jargon 'encompassing') trade union movements is perhaps more contingent than we think. True, their power is to some extent institutionalized through government consultation and (as in Sweden and Germany) membership of agencies and para-public bodies that help make and deliver welfare and labour market policies (see Chapter 3). But it also relies on their close relationship with social democratic parties. If the latter either lose office or, in office, are pushed by economic difficulties into taking 'tough decisions', then their trade unions allies might not appear quite so strong after all – especially if they simultaneously face rising unemployment. True, British trade unions were never able to embed corporatism in the same way as some of their continental and Scandinavian counterparts; but their swift marginalization in the 1980s, after two decades or more of influence (beer and sandwiches at Number Ten, etc.) is a case in point. So too is the way that Germany's supposedly much more powerful trade union movement was unable to stop the SPD pushing through its liberalizing 'Agenda 2010' and 'Hartz IV' reform packages in the early 2000s.

That said, corporatism – or at least government-facilitated 'concertation' between employer organizations and trade unions – has not gone away (see Jensen, 2011a; Woldendorp, 2011). If anything it has made a comeback recently – sometimes in the most unlikely places (supposedly liberal and pluralist Ireland being the most obvious example). Partly, this has been a response to exceptional circumstances. In the Netherlands, whose so-called 'polder model' (named after cooperative efforts needed to create and maintain land reclaimed from the sea) in some ways pioneered this new style of corporatism, cooperation between government, workers and

employers came about in the 1980s in order to deal with fast-rising unemployment. In the 1990s, elsewhere in Europe, cooperation seemed to originate in the economic stability (and in some cases belt-tightening) that was required to ensure qualification for the single currency (see Chapters 1 and 9). However, the reasons why some countries have gone down that route – or at least part of the way down that route – are more complex than often suggested: institutional factors like the type of government (i.e. minority or majority, Chapter 4) and the extent of trade union centralization interact with more contingent problems like electoral concerns and joblessness, inflation and deficits (Avdagic et al., 2011; Hamann and Kelly, 2010; see also Hassel, 2009; Menz, 2011). As a result it may be less easy than some imagine to predict whether and where more pacts will (successfully or otherwise) be negotiated in order to deal with the ongoing financial and fiscal crisis in Europe.

This kind of 'post-corporatist concertation' (O'Donnell, 2001), then, is more than a matter of cultural tradition: it is an instrumental and slightly more (party) political affair (see Hamann and Kelly, 2007). Rather than creating obstacles to the growth that hopefully gets parties re-elected, government-enabled pacts between 'the social partners' have the potential to ensure that wage inflation does not undermine it. Getting unions on board also makes it easier for governments to promote active labour market strategies that enhance a country's human capital and workers' flexibility – both key factors in competitiveness and productivity. Unions are also the key in many countries to governments pushing through pension reforms (see Anderson, 2001; Baccaro, 2002) although, again, this is more likely to happen under centre-left governments (with whom the unions are more willing to work) than centre-right governments (whom they trust even less). Agreement between the social partners also helps to 'proof' policies against attempts to undo them by governments that might be composed of their opponents.

That said, as the example of Sweden suggests, the support of the social partners, particularly the employers, is far more contingent than in the so-called 'golden age' of corporatism in the first three decades after the Second World War. And often – as in Italy – negotiating and announcing a *patto* (pact) is one thing – delivering it and it making a difference is quite another (Molina and Rhodes, 2007). We should also sound a note of caution about CEE. There, early moves towards setting up corporatist-style consultation between government, business and workers – the Polish 'Tripartite Commission on Socio-economic Issues' is a good example – produced, with the exception of Slovenia, what have been labelled little more than time-wasting talking-shops as the market liberalism favoured by transnational corporations triumphed and home-grown business organizations preferred to go their own way (see Bohle and Greskovits, 2007; Crowley and Stanojevi , 2011; Duvanova, 2009).

Taking care of business

The power of farmers or unions in Europe, then, cannot be directly 'read off' from the quality or the extent or the coherence of their organizations. And the same goes for the power of business. Take, for instance, the Spanish Employers' Association, the CEOE (*Confederación Española de Organizaciones Empresoriales*). The federation represents an impressive nine out of ten Spanish employers across a range of sectors. Yet in the democratic era, and facing an ostensibly fragmented union movement with few members, it has been unable to stave off labour market regulation which, while light compared to more corporatist countries, looks heavy compared to the regime in, say, Poland.

There, in common with most CEE countries, civil society, at least as measured by ordinary people's associative activity, can hardly be described as burgeoning: one survey for example, concludes that the average citizen of the European Union belongs to 1.05 groups, a figure which drops to 0.58 in central and eastern European member states, and to 0.4 in Poland – relatively unimpressive even if we observe that the total in many large western states (e.g. Germany, the UK and Italy) is only around 0.75 and that Sweden (at 3.22) is, along with the Netherlands (at 3.09) very much an outlier (see Sissenich, 2010; see also Howard, 2003). This is partly because many of those who might have taken an active leadership role were attracted instead by parliamentary politics. It is also because those who took over the old state enterprises stuck with the personal and clientelistic

nomenklatura (communist bureaucratic elite) networks they already knew. The fact that many new businesses were run by self-employed people or were very small also militated against associative activity (see Padgett, 2000). So, too (and this applies to pressure groups in general), did the desire of postcommunist governments of all stripes to avoid the creation of groups that could exercise countervailing power at a time when they were already concerned about their states' capacities to implement transitional reforms – concerns that probably led the EU to do little or nothing to prod them into filling this 'institutional void' (see Bruszt, 2002), although this may be changing (see Börzel, 2010). Over time, however, business associations are showing signs of institutionalizing and potentially becoming more influential, though often (and perhaps unfortunately) more through reputational and informal contacts than as-of-right formal processes (McMenamin, 2002). In the meantime, it must be said that Polish employers, relatively unencumbered as they are by government regulation, hardly seem to have been handicapped by the absence of powerful organized pressure groups fighting on their behalf.

Conversely, the vast majority of France's employers, accounting for some 800,000 firms, are represented by MEDEF (*Mouvement des Entreprises de France*), which, especially under the leadership of the combative Ernest-Antoine Seillière between 1997 and 2005, called for economic liberalization. It has not been entirely unsuccessful, but its influence can easily be overstated. For instance, France's centre-left government, elected in 1997, controversially introduced a maximum 35-hour week in order to 'share out' jobs. MEDEF managed to bring 30,000 businessmen out onto the streets to protest, but in vain, in 1999. Indeed, the 'failure' of successive French governments (including that of Nicolas Sarkozy who won the presidency in 2007 with a mandate for change) to make it easier for bosses to hire and fire and to grasp the nettle on pensions and health costs belies MEDEF's claims to have put 'l'entrepreneur au cœur de la société française' – 'the entrepreneur at the heart of French society' (see Woll, 2006). Similarly in Italy, the employers' organization, *Confindustria,* after a period of drift in the 1960s and 1970s (when individual firms such as Fiat exercised far more influence over policy than *Confindustria* ever could) has emerged as a dynamic advocate for liberal reforms. Indeed, much was made of its partisan support for Silvio Berlusconi's *Forza Italia* party at the general election of 2001, particularly by Berlusconi himself. Yet the resulting centre-right government failed to deliver the pension reforms, tax cuts and labour market deregulation that the pressure group had demanded.

To some on the right of the political spectrum, the failure of business in some European countries to get government to deliver on its neoliberal agenda is illustrative of the vestigial but nonetheless damaging influence of quasi-corporatist or statist arrangements – or of a residual anti-business culture which, especially in the current economic difficulties, means that even in a country like Germany, which is famed for its cooperative industrial relations and industrial might, big firms are less trusted than trade unions (see Figure 8.3). On the other hand, the fact that 'capital' in European countries cannot always get what it wants can be seen in positive terms. Perhaps it reflects the vitality and value of pluralism in the face of criticisms from so-called 'neopluralists' (see Lindblom, 1977) that business is inevitably at a huge advantage, given the structural dependence of politicians on it to provide the economic growth that is normally vital to their re-election (see also Bernhagen, 2007; Przeworski and Wallerstein, 1988). Of course, the fact that so many groups (unions being only the most obvious example) have a vested interest in a status quo that some regard as ultimately self-defeating can also be taken to illustrate the tendency of pluralism towards 'hyperpluralism' or 'overload' – a situation in which the sheer weight of groups forces governments to take on more than they can handle and makes them unable to tackle serious problems (King 1975; see also Olson, 1982). This is precisely the interpretation that lent momentum to the 'new public management' (NPM) discussed in Chapter 3.

Of course, it is easy to fall into the habit of talking about 'business' as it if were one undifferentiated mass or unitary actor. However, this is far from true. Different companies in different sectors have different interests, and matters seen as crucial by small firms (for example the cost of complying with government regulations) may be no more than a small blip on the radar screens of global concerns. Differences in scale may also have major implications for corporatism itself. The system depends not

Figure 8.3 Public trust in big companies and trade unions

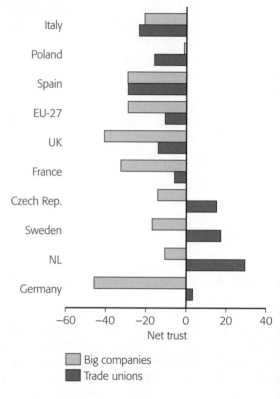

Source: *Eurobarometer* 74.2 (2011).

just on government enthusiasm but on the ability of, say, employers' associations to capture and therefore represent the majority of businesses in the same way as unions have to recruit as many workers as they can. If that is no longer the case – and research suggests that it might not be as large transnational firms get used to taking a more direct route to influence – then the game, for governments and unions as well as other firms, may no longer be worth playing: as the twenty-first century progresses, in other words, corporatism – or what is left of it – may well fragment organizationally as well as ideationally (see Traxler, 2010). Whether this will necessarily boost the power of business is arguable: probably it will be good for those firms big enough to look after themselves and be bad for those for whom joining an association was a way of punching above their weight. In any case, some would argue – quite persuasively – that, in looking at how business people ineract with government in the open, we are looking in the wrong place since the key to their power is their ability to use their more private interactions to ensure that most issues are effectively dealt with before they ever become public (Culpepper, 2011).

Rebels with a cause? NGOs and (new) social movements

It was once assumed the prominence of business and unions, however qualified, proved that 'sectional' pressure groups which defend and promote the collective material interests of their members were likely to exert more influence in society than those that tried to do the same for so-called 'diffuse interests' (such as those of consumers) or for causes (such as 'the environment', 'peace' or 'developing countries'). This consensus was based on a theoretically persuasive explanation from what is labelled the *rational choice* school of political science (Box 8.6).

Sectional groups, the argument goes, tend to possess more of what government wants (in terms of resources, information and implementation). And, because they are more likely actually to pick up potential recruits in whichever sector they represent, they make it difficult for governments to appeal 'over their heads'. They recruit so well by offering what political scientists, following economists, call 'selective incentives' – largely material rewards that benefit only that group. Cause and even consumer groups, face a 'collective action problem' in that they have no significant selective incentives to offer a set of potential recruits. Even if material benefits exist, as they might for consumers if, say, price-fixing by a cartel of companies could be brought to a halt, recipients of those benefits are so numerous that any gain would be thinly spread and would be tiny compared to the gains of those doing the fixing – this is the 'asymmetry of interests' we referred to when discussing farmers. Additionally, if peace, an end to world poverty and sustainability are achieved through the efforts of a cause group, then everybody (aside, perhaps, from arms manufacturers and producers of pollutants!) will benefit. The fact that they can't be excluded from those benefits makes it

KEY POINT

While 'rational choice explanations would lead one to expect people not to participate in groups that give them nothing tangible that they could not otherwise get, this is clearly not the case. Social movements that see often relatively privileged people mobilizing on behalf of entities that cannot protect or promote themselves have been a persistent, and even growing, feature of European politics – although there are considerable regional variations in the willingness to get involved. We should not, however, draw too big a distinction between such movements, and more conventional political actors, nor between the strategies and tactics both employ, especially as movement organizations are often highly professional operations.

rational for people to 'free-ride' on the efforts of a few activists.

That, of course, is the theory, but the reality – at least, in many European countries – is rather different. Domestic consumers, it has to be said, are still hard to organize, and pressure on prices and cartels tends to come from those businesses disadvantaged by them, rather than from the small consumer associations that do exist in Europe. The pressure also comes (as we shall see below) from the EU. However, the theory does little or nothing to explain why it is that the willingness to join groups – be they pressure groups or any of the other myriad social and cultural groups that make up civil society – is so different across Europe. As we noted when talking about civil society at the beginning of the chapter, study after study has found that people in Scandinavian countries (and the Netherlands, possibly because of the tradition of church-based activity) are much more willing to join (and join several) groups than are southern Europeans, particularly those in Greece, Portugal, Spain, Italy (as a whole) and France, where activity is often more family- and friendship-based. Countries such as the UK, Germany, Belgium and Ireland sit somewhere in the middle. Eastern Europeans (see Sissenich, 2010) are very much in with their southern counterparts. In other words, while individual characteristics (gender, age, income, education, political interest, etc.) make a difference, it is often easier to make a prediction about how likely someone is to be a joiner by knowing which country or region they are from than from their personal characteristics. Associative activity would seem to be related, then, to the length of time the country in which you live has been a democracy and perhaps even to the extent to which the dictatorship that formerly ruled allowed non-party or state groups to exist.

These regional differences are not the only reason to cast doubt on the rational choice approach. Notwithstanding the variation just mentioned, one of the major developments in Europe in the second half of the twentieth century was the growth of new social movements (see p. 267 and also Kriesi et al., 1995) which some see as outgrowths of the postmaterialism fuelled by the spread of education and the comparative wealth that freed up so many Europeans (at least in the more prosperous west and north of the continent) to think beyond themselves and their bread and butter concerns. Those very same developments have also given them the capacity to voice their concerns effectively and to put their money where their mouths are. They have also driven a concern with self-identity and the (emotive) expression of that identity not just in consumption but also in politics (see Goodwin et al., 2001).

The spread of education and the comparative wealth that seem to have freed up so many Europeans (at least in the more prosperous west and north of the continent) to think about such issues have also given them the capacity to voice their concerns and to put their money where their mouths are. They also seem to have fuelled a concern with self-identity and the (emotive) expression of that identity not just in consumption but also in politics (see Goodwin et al., 2001). Simultaneously, the postwar growth of the electronic mass media (see Chapter 7) provided a platform for the increasingly well-funded cause groups and non-governmental organizations (NGOs) to promote their ideals and exert pressure on both business and government.

That is not to say that the task of social movements is an easy one. They have, after all, to balance a number of sometimes competing or even contradictory means and ends: as one observer (Rochon, cited in della Porta and Diani, 2005: 179) notes 'the ideal movement strategy is one that is convincing with respect to political authorities, legitimate with

---

BOX 8.6

Rational choice and political participation

Rational choice is the name given to the idea, borrowed by political science from economics, that political phenomena can be explained by remembering that all actions are purposive, goal-oriented and 'utility-maximizing' within given constraints (see Elster, 1986 and Hargreaves Heap *et al.*, 1992). This allows the construction of formal models – often using 'game theory' – that enhance the study of politics' claim to be a science rather than a humanities subject, such as history. This has its downsides: in the wrong hands, it is capable of rendering the interesting uninteresting and the intelligible unintelligible; more profoundly, it relies on unrealistic assumptions about human behaviour and motivations, and can often be stronger theoretically than it is empirically (see Green and Shapiro, 1994). But it also has its upsides: in the right hands, it can cut through the detail to provide generalizations; in addition, proving why its hypotheses do not hold (or at least modifying them so that they accord with more realistic assumptions) can be an enormous boost to creative thinking and empirical research (see Dunleavy, 1991; Friedman, 1996). Work on coalitions (i.e. why are there so many minority governments when a slim majority is surely the most rational option?) is one example (see Chapter 4). Work on those who join and do not join groups is another: Jordan and Maloney (2006), for instance, show that non-joiners are not simply 'free-riders' as rational choice analysis would suggest; instead they are very doubtful about the efficacy of groups (and, for that matter, personal sacrifices); nor do they have the kinds of skills and resources that would lead others to ask them to join or that would make joining (or even knowing about the organizations in question) easy for them.

respect to potential supporters, rewarding with respect to those already active in the movement, and novel in the eyes of the mass media. These are not entirely compatible demands.' Indeed, the mainstream media can be particularly hard to please: as we noted in Chapter 7, it craves and rewards the providers of novel and innovative action but, at the same time, is conventionally censorious about anything too 'radical' or 'extreme'.

That said, social movements have clearly been helped by, and might have done something to drive, something we have already discussed; namely, the increased willingness, especially in western Europe, to take political action that was previously seen as unconventional, if not illegitimate. However, we need to be careful about drawing too strong a distinction between both the tactics and the concerns of materialists and postmaterialists. When it comes to the tactics, groups of both types often use similar techniques (see Box 8.7). Moreover, research shows that environmental groups, for instance, especially the moderate ones, tend to lay off the direct action and focus instead on media work, on lobbying and participation in government consultation when that government (perhaps simply because of its platform, perhaps because it is an administration which is broadly on the left and/or contains Green parties) is seen as relatively eco-friendly (Poloni-Staudinger, 2009). When it comes to concerns, solidarity with (for example) the oppressed and exploited peoples of the developing world can be accompanied by anxiety and anger about the supposed impact of globalization on the domestic front. This fusion, after all, is partly what the global justice movement is all about, bringing together a diverse coalition or network of groups under the banner of opposition to what it insists is neoliberal globalization – an agenda apparently pursued by transnational corporations, international organizations (the IMF, the World Bank being the chief culprits) and supposedly spinelessly compliant governments (see della Porta and Diani, 2005; see also Diani and McAdam, 2003).

When dealing with social movements, we also need – once again – to stress (see della Porta and Diani, 2005: 210–18) that many, even most of them, inhabit the same universe and often overlap with more conventional interest groups (most often trade unions) and political actors (almost inevitably left-wing political parties). The need to transcend this 'normalization' of mass action may go some way to explaining the ratcheting up of those protests and groups that attract young people in particular. Certainly, it seemed for a while as if riots were going

Different aims, similar tactics – direct action, old and new, in Germany

German 'postmaterialist' anti-nuclear activists pioneered direct action tactics in the 1970s, so there was little that was new about the social movement-style protests that attempted to block the passage of a train carrying nuclear waste from France to a storage site in Gorleben in north-western Germany in November 2001. Thousands of police officers, with dogs and helicopters and hundreds of metres of barbed wire, kept 1,000 protesters from disrupting unloading. Earlier, they had been forced to remove protesters who had chained themselves to railway tracks. The shipment and the unloading went ahead, notwithstanding the government's commitment, long-term, to phase out nuclear power.

Just over a year before, in September 2000, Germany (as France, Italy, Spain and the UK) was hit by blockades mounted by lorry drivers, farmers and taxi drivers protesting against what they saw as unreasonably high petrol prices. Even though there were protests across Europe, they were not 'European' in the sense of being coordinated or targeted against the EU – in fact, their targets (and, in the end, the solutions they accepted) were domestic (see Imig, 2002: 917–18). In Berlin, more than 7,000 truck drivers brought the city centre to a standstill. This form of direct action had more effect, with the government (like other governments in Europe) announcing tax concessions to fuel users, notwithstanding its commitment to hiking eco-taxes.

to become an inevitable accompaniment to meetings of the G8 industrialized countries and, since 2001 when it met in Gothenburg, Sweden, the EU's European Council. On the other hand, it is easy to forget that European protest activity has often sparked violence in the past: the scenes in Gothenburg and in Genoa were as nothing, for instance, to the demonstrations in Paris in 1968. It is also easy to dismiss violence as ultimately counter-

Poland (Polska)

Area: 304,500 km² (7.3% of EU-27)	
Population: 38.2 million (7.6% of EU-27)	
Religious heritage: Roman Catholic	
GDP (2006): €354 billion (2.8% of EU-27)	
GDP *per capita* as percentage of EU-27 average: 65	
Female representation in parliament and cabinet (end 2007): 24% and 20%	
Joined EU: 2004	
Top 3 cities: Warsaw – capital city (1.7 million), Łódź (0.8 million), Kraków (0.8 million).	

History: Poland, which between the fourteenth and eighteenth centuries was part of a Commonwealth with Lithuania which also stretched into what is now Belarus, Latvia and the Ukraine, was for centuries one of Europe's most disputed territories. Its borders shifted time and time again as it fell victim to German and Russian imperial ambitions. For a time in the seventeenth century, it was one of the continent's largest states. Yet between the end of the eighteenth century and the end of the First World War, Poland officially ceased to exist. It regained its independence in 1918 but democracy collapsed in 1926. Soon after 1939, Poland had once again ceased to exist, initially carved up between Nazi Germany and Soviet Russia, and then occupied solely by the former.

During the war, Poland lost about one fifth of its population, with half the victims Jews who perished in the Holocaust. Most, of course, were killed by the Germans. But the Russians, too, were brutal, massacring Poland's military and civil elite at Katyn and other sites and sending hundreds of thousands more Poles into exile in Siberia and Central Asia. And by failing to come to the aid of the Warsaw uprising in 1944, the Russians effectively allowed the Germans to kill hundreds of thousands of the city's population.

In the elections that followed the end of the war, the Russian-backed Communists took power and immediately began the process of dismantling democracy. Both anti-Russian feeling and the Roman Catholic church remained strong, however. In 1978, Polish cardinal Karol Wojtyła was chosen as Pope Jean Paul II. His visit to Poland a year later, combined with industrial unrest in the country's important ship-building industry, saw the birth of the *Solidarność* (Solidarity) trade union, led by Lech Wałesa. Faced with the threat of a Russian invasion, the Communist authorities banned the union and imposed martial law in 1981. When, however, it became apparent some eight years later that the threat from the east no longer existed, the authorities began the round-table process that led to the end of the Communist regime and the election of Wałesa as president. In the following decade and a half, Poland was governed by coalitions led either by a fragmented centre-right or by the former communists now standing as social democrats. After a catastrophic election defeat in 2005, however, the latter have lost credibility, with over two-thirds of voters plumping instead for one of the two centre-right parties: Law and Justice (PiS), which caters for more rural, less well-educated voters, and Civic Platform (PO), which is strongest among those who live in urban areas and have more education. At the 2011, the coalition government led by Civic Platform was re-elected for a second consecutive term – a first for postcommunist Poland.

Economy and society: Initially touted as a shining example of 'shock therapy' (deregulation, currency reform and price liberalization). Unemployment and state finances remain chronic problems but Poland's large domestic market and its reasonably efficient use of EU cohesion funds helped sustain uninterrupted economic growth throughout the economic

WHAT'S IN AN ANTHEM?

Mazurek D browskiego, which was penned at the end of the eighteenth century, was officially adapted as the country's anthem in the late 1920s. Perhaps predictably, given that it was written as a call to resist one of the numerous foreign occupations that Poles have had to endure over the years, it begins with the stirring first line 'Poland has not yet perished'. 'Sword in hand', it claims, we will seize back what the foreign foe has taken and save our country, taking (possibly a little naively in hindsight) Napoleon Bonaparte as an inspiration. Fortunately, perhaps, especially in view of recent diplomatic spats, the verses that mention resisting Germans and Russians with sabres and scythes are not part of the official version.

downturn that hit the rest of Europe after 2008. The Poles also stand out on account of the strength of their religious faith: Roman Catholic churches are well attended and remain an important influence on education, the media, and social mores and policy.

Governance: After flirting with the idea of a powerful president, Poland came down on the side of parliamentary democracy in its 1997 constitution, although even now the president (like the Senate in the country's bicameral legislature) has a veto over legislation. The veto can be overridden if the lower house (the *Sejm*) can muster a three-fifths majority. There is a constitutional court, but only recently, with its striking down of the government's lustration (or vetting) law in May 2007, can it be said to have made a major intervention in Polish politics. As for pressure groups, neither the trade unions (including the once-popular *Solidarność*), nor business associations are particularly powerful. Government in the country's sixteen regions (*województwo*), however, is becoming more significant.

Foreign policy: The Poles have succeeded in achieving their two main priorities – protecting themselves from Russia and locking themselves into the European economy – by joining NATO (in 1999) and the EU (in 2004). Cordial relations with Germany were accorded a particularly high priority by both countries but (hopefully temporarily) came under severe strain while a strongly nationalist government held power between 2005 and 2007. That government also presided over a further deterioration of relations with Russia – a situation that any new government is going to find difficult to improve, even presuming it wants to. Relations with

A KEY CONTEMPORARY CHALLENGE
TO JOIN OR NOT TO JOIN THE EURO

Compared to many European countries, Poland got off comparatively lightly when it came to feeling the effects of the global financial and economic crisis. In part this was because (outside the biggest cities) the country, whose banks and central banks were conservative and cautious, did not experience a boom in property prices. A generous share of EU structural and agricultural funding helped, as did the money injected into the economy by those Poles working abroad sending back money to their families. But Poland also performed relatively well because, in the wake of the crisis, its currency, the *zloty*, was able to take some of the strain of economic adjustment while the government, because it did not have to impose austerity in order to prove to markets that it should stay in the single currency (see Chapter 9), could afford to maintain public spending at the cost of running temporary deficits. For all that, Poland is still, theoretically anyway, committed to joining the single currency as soon as it qualifies for membership. Fears that, in doing so, it will be locking in the inflexibility that has caused and continues to cause a number of Eurozone countries so many problems are widespread. On the other hand, Poland is acutely concerned that if, as a response to the Eurozone crisis, its members move further and faster towards closer political as well as economic integration then it will be somehow be seen as outside the European core. For a country that sees Europe as its safe haven against the former Soviet Union, this is a worrying possibility. It may have been this that prompted Radosław Sikorski, Poland's British-educated Minister of Foreign Affairs, to make a speech in Berlin in November 2011 that was regarded as so federalist as to prompt the increasingly Eurosceptic main opposition party, Law and Justice, to lay down a parliamentary motion of no confidence in him. It may also explain why, when at the end of 2011 the UK had a big bust-up with other member states over the economic governance of the EU, Warsaw – often portrayed as thinking along the same lines as London – made it clear it stood with the majority.

the USA, however, are generally very good: nearly 9 million Americans have Polish ancestry and many Poles remain grateful for the role the USA played in defeating Communism in eastern Europe.

Contemporary challenges
- Whether or not to join the euro when Poland qualifies for membership.
- Continuing rationalization of the economy, moving out of low-value

heavy industry and agriculture, and establishing a stronger but affordable welfare state.
- Refusing to be bullied by Russia without causing a complete breakdown in relations or being seen as a US government stooge.
- Finishing the big infrastructure projects initiated but not completed before the successful co-hosting of the 2012 European Football Championships.

Learning resources. Start with Lukowski and Zawadzki (2006), *A Concise History of Poland.* Then go on to Sanford (2002), *Democratic Government in Poland,* Szczerbiak (2012), *Poles Together?* and (2011), *Poland within the European Union.* Also very useful is the article by Jasiewicz (2009) on Polish voters. Keep up with the news at http://www.thenews.pl and http://www.warsawvoice.pl.

productive: a study of Germany (see Rucht, 2003) suggests it has to be seen, along with other unconventional 'social movement' tactics, as helping to provoke change and an increased sensitivity among conventional politicians towards the concerns of the less conventional. In other words, we might not like it but (in central and eastern Europe as well as in western Europe) it may be wrong to draw too hard and fast a distinction between civil society and what has been termed 'uncivil society': they are part of a continuum (see Kopecký and Mudde, 2002). On the other hand, it would be wrong to suggest that violence predominates in the 'anti-globalization' movement, which is not only extremely diverse but something that social and political scientists are only just beginning to get to grips with (see Poitras, 2003).

Just as it would be wrong to tar all 'internationalist' activism with the same brush, it would be wrong to fall too easily into the idea that it is detached from 'real' problems at home which might benefit from all the energy 'wasted' on its rather diffuse targets. Sidney Tarrow, one of the world's foremost experts on 'contentious politics' makes a very persuasive case that 'transnational' activists often embody (as well as help forge) the link between the local and the global: the most effective – those, in other words, who get things done as well as protest – are '"rooted cosmopolitans" – people who grow up in and remain closely linked to domestic networks and opportunities' (Tarrow, 2005: xiii). He also reminds us that we need to be careful not to categorize all protest activity, especially among 'young people' as 'a reflex against globalization' that, given both the vague nature of the latter and the absence of a genuinely transnational government, is unlikely to achieve much: a great deal of protest activity is still targeted, just as it was in the 1950s, 1960s and the decades that followed, against an institution that continues to count; namely, the state.

Despite its darker side, then, all this might give heart to those who believe that democracy is ultimately about 'the people' triumphing, or at least controlling 'the interests'. But digging a little deeper suggests that this view might be a little naive. This is because it fails to come to terms with the fact that groups like Greenpeace, Friends of the Earth, the Worldwide Fund for Nature or even Amnesty International, which are active in virtually every European country, and even some of the larger domestic cause groups, have so institutionalized their operations that they are not by any stretch of the imagination 'bottom-up' organizations which are inevitably more democratic than interest-based outfits (see Binderkrantz, 2009). Rather, they are professional movement organizations (McCarthy and Zald, 1977) or even 'protest businesses' (see Jordan and Maloney, 1997) or 'transnational social movement organizations' (TSMOs) (see della Porta and Diani, 2005: 146–7). Even groups that do not qualify as such now tend to join European or, very often in fact, worldwide federations in order to boost their presence – and, hopefully, their clout. For example (see Table 8.4), Birdlife International, a worldwide partnership of groups dedicated to the

Table 8.4 Bird protection societies

Country	Society	Members	Staff
Czech Rep.	Česká spolecnost ornitologická (ČSO)	2,100	7
France	Ligue Pour La Protection des Oiseaux (LPO)	35,000	127
Germany	Naturschutzbund Deutschland (NABU)	405,000	90
Italy	Lego Italiana Protezione Uccelli (LIPU)	42,000	95
Netherlands	Vogelbescherming Nederland (VBN)	125,000	153
Poland	Ogólnopolskie Towarzystwo Ochrony Ptaków (OTOP)	2,000	12
Spain	Sociedad Española de Ornitologfa (SEO)	8,000	50
Sweden	Sveriges Ornitologiska Förening (SOF)	11,000	24
UK	Royal Society for the Protection of Birds (RSPB)	1,049,000	1,440

Source: Data from Birdlife International (2007).

BOX 8.8

Greenpeace: not a grassroots organization but still seen as a threat

With headquarters in Amsterdam and offices in 40 countries worldwide, Greenpeace is, according to some, the ultimate 'protest business' – no more accountable (and maybe even less so) to its nearly three million donors than many of the businesses that it campaigns against are to their shareholders. That said, it has lost none of its capacity to scare some of the corporations that are in its firing line. In November 2011, a French court fined Energy giant, EDF, some € 1.5 million and handed out custodial sentences to the Head and Deputy Head of its nuclear security operation for instructing a private security firm (two of whose operatives also received jail terms) for spying on the environmental charity. Greenpeace was also awarded half a million euros in damages. The fact that the security firm involved was associated with former employees of the French secret services dredged up memories of the incident in 1985 when agents working for the country's *Direction Générale de la Sécurité Extérieure* planted explosives in order to sink Greenpeace's flagship, *Rainbow Warrior*, in Auckland, New Zealand. The operation killed a man and sparked a huge diplomatic incident which ended in the conviction of some of those involved and big compensation payouts.

promotion and protection of birds and their habitats, provides a home for small groups that are little more than promoters of an interest in birds and birdwatching (such as the Swedish society), as well as groups which are quasi-commercial concerns (such as the Royal Society for the Protection of Birds (RSPB) in the UK). Even accounting for population differences, the latter has fifteen times as many members, as well as a much bigger profile and a larger role in actually managing projects in lieu of government – an 'insider' role, incidentally, which, critics suggest, prevents it from taking an effective (or, at least, publicly aggressive) stand against detrimental environmental practices.

Much of the activity of traditionally 'outsider' transnational protest businesses such as Greenpeace is capital-intensive (as opposed to labour-intensive) and media-intensive. So, while membership is important for providing them with legitimacy, it is most important for providing them with the finance to carry on campaigns – many of them so successful (see Bennie, 1998) that they clearly cause the corporate world huge anxiety (see Box 8.8). Nor is there much evidence that the internet is making much difference in this respect (Kavada, 2005). Most people who join groups – whether they be 'real' or the kind that appear (sometimes only very briefly) on Facebook – do so for short periods and without expecting or desiring to participate actively beyond perhaps signing a petition, possibly joining a march and/or giving the account details or credit card number that constitutes their donation to the cause. Some of this activity is counted by some political scientists as 'participation', but whether all such activities, simply because they go beyond turning up to vote every so often, really deserve to be included under the umbrella term of 'collective', let alone 'unconventional', action is a moot point. It is easy to overstate popular involvement in groups and other forms of pressure politics. When it comes to politics (and, indeed, the non-political group activity that some political scientists believe may facilitate involvement in politics; see Bowler *et al.*, 2003), 'low-intensity participation' and a move away from membership of traditional groups towards more flexible activity (see Inglehart and Welzel, 2005: 295) are the keynotes for most Europeans at the beginning of the twenty-first century. The web and mobile telephony clearly lower the barriers to participation, but they are unlikely to change this. Indeed, particularly when we factor in Facebook and Twitter, which allow users simply to 'like' a page or retweet a tweet, they might make it almost too easy to get involved on the casual and ultimately meaningless basis that (in the USA especially) has been dismissed as 'slacktivism'.

The fact that groups campaigning for supposedly postmaterialist causes, such as human rights and the environment, do not necessarily have more spontaneous or 'flatter' structures than traditional sectional or interest groups does not, of course, mean that they play exactly the same role. Some of the functions of a campaigning environmental group outlined by a director of such a group (Box 8.9) would presumably not sit well with an 'insider' interest intent on maintaining the convenient insulation of its 'policy community'. 'Outsider' groups, of course, have to weigh up whether some of these functions are worth trading off in return for being kept in the loop by government. Conversely, they have to consider whether incorporation may also mean neutralization. Nowadays, more traditional, sectional interest groups simultaneously (and not just as a fall-back option) pursue 'indirect strategies', such as media campaigns, as well as 'insider access'. By the same token, so-called 'outsiders' ('cause groups' and the like) pursue more traditional forms of direct contact with the government, the bureaucracy and with legislators at the same time as acting in the media and on the streets – not just because the latter strategy, while sometimes counterproductive (see Gavin, 2010b), can pay off in terms of influence but because, even if it didn't, groups have to compete with rivals for members and public attention: they must therefore do everything they can to show they are active (Binderkrantz, 2005; see also Binderkrantz, 2012; Gamson, 2004; Kriesi *et al.*, 2007).

Media presence is, of course, one of the keys to social movement influence, much of which rests on the ability to put new problems and possible solutions on the agenda of makers of public policy and, even, if they are very lucky, to exercise 'normative power' by helping to define what is or is not politically acceptable or urgent – as groups campaigning on, say, genetic modification in food and agriculture or on climate change have been able to do (see van der Heijden, 2010) This is not, however, the only way that influence occurs or can be measured (see della Porta and Diani, 2005). Even if it is hard, using another traditional measure, to say this or that piece of legislation would not have been passed (or, indeed, properly implemented) without them, we can trace their involvement across a range of government responses that once were novel but are now fairly standard. These include referendums, the setting up of expert commissions, arm's length regulatory and consultative bodies (that might well employ former representatives of social movements), and participative fora (citizens' juries, etc.). Social movements could also be involved in information exchange and other activities conducted

---

BOX 8.9

Functions of a campaigning group

Broker: carrying information between parties and actors

Demonstrator: demonstrating new responses and solutions

Educator: education of specialists, concerned parties and the public

Ferret: digging for information and conducting investigations

Innovator: developing new responses, solutions and policies

Orchestrator: engineering and manipulating events

Scout: scanning for future problems

Watchdog: monitoring legal processes and agreements

Whistle blower: alerting the public, the government and other groups.

Source: Burke, cited in Rawcliffe (1998: 20–21).

---

under the auspices of the EU (see Lahusen, 2004), although some radicals write off such developments as nothing more than window-dressing and/or capture.

'Venue shopping' and the Europeanization of pressure politics

Traditionally, the activity of pressure groups in Europe went on at or below the level of the state. With the increasing importance of the EU, however, the activity of some groups has taken on an additional 'European' dimension. Business interests, for instance, have had to adjust to the fact that the regulatory environment in which they operate – one which may well have a fairly direct impact on their 'bottom line', their investment decisions and their

DEBATE 8.1

Are pressure groups good for democracy?

YES

- Despite the criticisms, as long as groups operate in a competitive and transparent environment and governments are strong, savvy (and rich) enough to stand up to them, then they perform valuable functions; members who want them to be more democratic are free to leave or to agitate for better representation; people who don't join groups only have themselves to blame if those who do get what they want.

- Without pressure groups, citizens would, between one election and another, have to rely on politicians and possibly the media to hold the government to account: this would be particularly problematic where parliament and the press are relatively weak.

- Government can neither know nor do everything: groups provide expert, on-the-ground information to policy makers and often ensure effective implementation of the policy they make. The work of groups does not therefore reduce efficiency, it increases it. The interchange of personnel adds to the knowledge and capacity of groups and politicians.

- Participating in groups teaches people about the importance of working together, encourages them to think about and come to workable solutions, and promotes the trust and the networks that hold society together. The alternative would be a 'mass society' of individuals incapable of pursuing the collective good and at risk from a consequently more powerful state.

NO

- Groups only think of their own interests or ideals, which they pursue to the exclusion of the collective good, and often sell easy, quick-fix solutions when real life is more complicated.

- Some groups are more powerful than others: policy should depend on what works or what is right, not on who can mobilize the most money or members.

- Pressure groups and lobbyists may make sophisticated use of the media, but much of their contact with politicians and decision makers is inherently 'off-the-record'. This lack of transparency damages the political process and its reputation.

- The growth of groups has created a multi-million dollar, euro, and pound industry that is essentially parasitic on democracy, wasting resources that would be better ploughed into more productive economic and social activity.

- The world of pressure groups and representative politics is now so closely intertwined that it contributes to the formation of a hermetically sealed 'political class'.

- Pressure groups – even those that sell themselves as the defenders of the environment or the oppressed and disadvantaged – are not themselves very democratic or very socially representative organizations. Those who join them can become even more zealous and unwilling to listen to alternatives.

ability or willingness to compete in certain markets – is, depending on the sector, increasingly subject to European rather than simply domestic rules (see Majone, 1996; Young and Wallace, 2000).

Take competition policy, and mergers and acquisitions (M&As). This issue is attracting ever-more attention from a European Commission determined to make a reality of the single or internal market. This clearly poses a threat to both firms and sectors that previously relied upon domestic rules to help maintain what some would argue are restrictive practices and/or cosy cartels – notorious examples would include the airline industry and (often highly subsidized) national carriers, or the automotive

industry and its ability to restrict the sales of its products to franchised dealers. Since the Single European Act (SEA), the Commission has made efforts to liberalize such sectors. Trying to limit the damage, the big players in both sectors sought to lobby national governments, but also found it necessary to take their case direct to the Commission. The effect may have been to slow down the reforms, at the very least buying time either to work out an exit strategy or how to compete in the new environment. But liberalization, since it is part of the logic of the EU's single market and is backed up by European law (see Chapter 2), cannot be held off forever, particularly if and when, for some countries at least, it becomes part of any EU rescue package for its ailing economy.

In any case, other groups that stand to benefit from entering the market or from the lowering of costs – and, indeed, governments who see liberalization as the key to faster growth through a more dynamic economy – will be lobbying in its favour. They might also, as a result of a better 'fit' between their domestic traditions and the EU's way of working, be better lobbyists. The inability in recent years, for instance, of state-owned companies and their government sponsors to prevent an EU-assisted attack on what were, in many mainland European countries, their virtual monopolies, might well be a case in point. Schmidt (1999: 164) notes more generally, the UK's 'larger, more fluid, more fragmented, horizontally integrated policy networks' do better at promoting domestic interests 'in the multi-polar, competitive decision-making structure of the EU' than, for example, what she calls 'France's smaller, tighter, more cohesive, vertical, state dominated networks' or Italy's traditionally 'under-the-table' mode of business influence. Realizing this perhaps, French governments, far from being concerned at being outflanked abroad by groups it can more easily control at home, have, since the beginning of the 1990s, been encouraging France's domestic interest groups to get active and involved at the European level (Szukala, 2003: 230) – something they have found more difficult than their German counterparts, for whom the EU system is in some ways simply an extension of the multi-level game they already have to play in the Federal Republic (Quittkat, 2009).

Liberalization, however, is not inevitable across all sectors once responsibility for their regulation no longer resides solely with the state and takes on a supranational element. We shall discuss this further in Chapter 9. But, for the moment, one has only to think of the continuing support for agriculture as testimony to the capacity of some groups to maintain their grip even after the national state has lost (or voluntarily surrendered) its own. This is not surprising. Pluralism is no more 'pure' at the European than at the domestic level. Just as national governments are vulnerable to pressure because they rely on groups to provide them with information and help with implementation, so too are European institutions – perhaps even more so. Most obviously, the Commission – for all the talk of 'armies of Brussels bureaucrats' – has very few staff relative to its very large and very varied responsibilities. Even at the policy initiation stage, Directorate Generals (DGs) rely heavily on pressure groups to give them a sense of both what is needed and what is feasible. Given the limited time and resources available, the 'one-stop shops' provided by so-called 'Euro-groups' – groups often composed of the various national federations in a particular sector – are an attractive option. Bringing them on board, or at least getting them on-side, boosts the chances of an initiative being taken seriously and, if adopted, actually being implemented.

Implementation and enforcement is something which the Commission has great difficulty in ensuring, given its reliance on the member states. The fuss made (and law suits begun) by businesses and pressure groups (and individuals) whose interests or ideals are adversely affected by non-compliance on the part of member states (see Falkner *et al.,* 2004) are a good example of and a vital part of what have been called the 'horizontal enforcement' mechanisms (Neyer and Wolf, 2003) of the EU – an entity that ultimately depends not simply on rules but on the political willingness of states to follow them. Consulting with groups also provides a way – if not an entirely convincing one – round the so-called 'democratic deficit'. Even if the Commission cannot claim that its policies are subject to the will of the populace, the fact that some of the most well-informed and potentially vocal sections of it have been involved in the process provides them with at least some legitimacy.

So, whether pressure groups are campaigning to stimulate or to stave off change, the EU is now an

Figure 8.4 Organizations registered to lobby in the EU

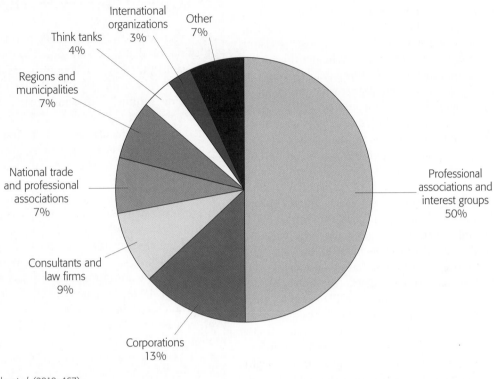

Source: Wonka *et al.* (2010: 467).

important part of the political opportunity structure in which they operate. This explains why there are around 4000 organizations of various different types lobbying in Brussels (see Figure 8.4) – and why, under pressure from critics, the Commission in June 2011 announced a (still voluntary and some therefore argue pointless) *Transparency Register* (see Marziali, 2009 for background). In some ways, 'Europe' has obvious potential advantages over the state level for pressure groups. For a start, it affords the possibility of obliging (or at least giving an excuse to) domestic governments to make changes that might otherwise be difficult, either for electoral reasons or because there are plenty of institutions (corporatist structures, strong parliaments, active courts, etc.) that might combine to block reforms. The transnational firms that were active in lobbying the Commission to come up with the SEA (see Chapter 2) were certainly aware that it would be one way of getting governments and states that were

reluctant (or, at least, claimed they were reluctant) to deregulate and privatize eventually to do just that once it came into effect in the early 1990s.

Likewise, for some interest groups, in marked contrast to cause groups, success depends in part on their ability to insulate their sector from the cut and thrust of mediatized and party politics. The EU theoretically provides a relatively benign environment where agendas can be set and deals cut in even more privacy than they are used to domestically. Depending on your point of view, what some have termed the 'network' governance of the EU (see Eising and Kohler-Koch, 1999) – multilevel and transnational 'problem-solving' between interested parties – either brings with it a much-needed maturity and flexibility to policy making or effectively depoliticizes it, putting it even further beyond the reach of democratic control. The chemical and pharmaceutical industries are often cited as examples of sectors that are prepared to swap the supposed limitations imposed by banding together as a 'Euro-group' (the European Chemical Industry Council (cefic) and the European Federation of Pharmaceutical Industries and Associations (EFPIA) respectively) in return for a fairly cosy relationship with the European institutions whose decisions could impact on their business. Whether this means, of course, that they, or any other interest group with similarly good access, actually get what they want – a charge frequently made not just by anti-globalization protesters but also by cause groups with objections to specific policies – is another matter.

In any case, some would say, cause groups can hardly complain about the 'business-friendly' nature or 'corporate domination' of EU policy making because many of them, too, have found 'Europe' conducive to pursuing their goals (see Ruzza, 2004). For one thing, getting changes made to EU rules and standards sometimes allows them to 'outflank' governments (and otherwise more powerful rival groups) at the domestic level (see Fairbrass and Jordan, 2001). For another, the EU provides them with considerable subsidies. For instance, it provides environmental groups with information via the European Environmental Agency (EEA) – information that can be used in campaigns, and the legitimacy of which is hard for opponents to question and for which otherwise campaigners would have to pay themselves. The EU also tried hard to help energize civil society in central and eastern Europe during the enlargement process by making expertise available, facilitating links with counterparts in western Europe, and obliging governments working towards accession to consult groups and grant them legal rights. It has to be said, however, that such efforts met with mixed success – in part because the groups it wanted to help were in some cases prevented from making the most of its assistance because they lacked the resources to do so, in part because they were wary of being seen to be too close to state bureaucracies (see Börzel, 2010: 4).

The Commission also makes a point of consulting groups – east and west – at all stages of the policy-making process as a counterweight to the commercial interests (national and European) whose resources routinely buy them access if not necessarily success (Quittkat, 2009). And environmental groups, too, can provide the Commission with information (for example, on implementation fail-

BOX 8.10

REACH and the Services Directive

December 2006 saw the EU finally pass two pieces of legislation that were so disputed by those for and against that they took literally years to get onto the statute book. REACH (the Registration, Evaluation, Authorization and Restriction of Chemicals) was fought tooth and nail by a sustained lobby and media campaign by industry bodies and individual firms, which insisted health and safety concerns were exaggerated and the new regime would render them uncompetitive. On the other hand, the eventual compromise they agreed to left some environmental campaigners furious that the EU had watered down what they believed were essential safeguards. The so-called 'Services Directive', which aimed to make the single market a reality for the non-manufacturing sector that (as we saw in Chapter 1) is increasingly the most important sector in contemporary Europe, also roused passions. Thousands of (mainly trade union) demonstrators came out onto the streets in 2005 to protest against what they saw as a neoliberal threat to their jobs. After various amendments were made, particularly on areas (mainly in the public sector) that could be excluded from the requirement to open up competition, the unions – still quite influential, especially when it comes to centre-left and left-wing parties in the European Parliament (see Chapter 2 and 4) – calmed down and the legislation was passed. Some business representatives, and economists, claimed victory, but some believed that the directive had been essentially neutered, ending up as a codification of existing law rather than a genuinely liberal development. It also, incidentally, accelerated a trend toward cooperation and lobbying among groups concerned with both welfare advocacy and delivery (see Toens, 2009).

ures by member states) and nudge it into action. Certainly, the Commission is already aware that environmental policy is one of the few areas where there is majority public support (even in supposedly 'Eurosceptic' countries) for a greater EU role. Moreover, some member states (e.g. in Scandinavia)

Table 8.5 Who they like to see most – EU institutions and corporate lobbying

Commission	Council of Ministers	Parliament
(1) Individual large firms	(1) National associations	(1) European associations
(2) European associations	(2) European associations	(2) National associations
(3) National associations	(3) Individual large firms	(3) Individual large firms

Source: Adapted from Bouwen (2002: 383).

are concerned lest those that have lower environmental standards (in southern and central and eastern Europe), for example, exploit them 'unfairly' to attract more foreign direct investment (FDI). Hence, there has been a perceptible increase since the 1990s in environmental legislation and action plans on matters such as air and water quality, and waste. Again, though, no one should come away with the impression that means, motive and opportunity necessarily add up to overwhelming influence for pressure groups, at least when it comes to environmental policy (see Jordan and Adelle, 2012): their efforts, after all, are balanced by those on the opposite side (see Box 8.10)

'Europe' also provides pressure groups with other opportunities to influence policy. Given the 'judicialization' of politics referred to in Chapter 3 and the potential power of the ECJ as well as the Court of Human Rights, it is hardly surprising that even supposedly 'counter-cultural' movements, such as those set up to promote gay and lesbian rights, have pursued a legal route to getting what they want. It is important, however, to realize that recourse to the courts often occurs alongside (rather than going on instead of) the strategies more commonly associated with NSM pressure groups, such as media campaigns or some kind of direct action – or, of course, more discrete lobbying. There is no necessary 'zero-sum' game between the various strategies on offer (see Hilson, 2002). Similarly, many of the large firms that are represented by sectoral interest groups and associations are increasingly willing to lobby simultaneously on their own behalf at both domestic and European levels (see Coen and Richardson, 2009: chapter 8). Indeed, they are encouraged to do so by the Commission if not all the EU institutions (see Table 8.5). Meanwhile, as we have seen, national associations are often members of European associations (the so-called 'Euro-groups' referred to above),

but this does not stop them lobbying EU institutions directly.

More generally, one would be mistaken to think that pressure groups, whether they represent causes or interests, have to choose between the domestic or the European stage. Many of them, just like businesses and trade unions (Erne, 2008), pursue their aims at both levels simultaneously, which is one reason why by no means the majority of the organizations lobbying in Brussels operate only at the EU-level. And being well or poorly connected at the level of the state does not mean pressure groups tend, in turn, to ignore or stress the EU level (see Beyers, 2002). In short, in an era of multilevel governance, pressure groups and their individual or corporate members – especially if they are well resourced – are happy to be 'promiscuous'. As Richardson (2001) points out, with the possible exception of Germany, 'the EC/EU as a polity presents an American-style plethora of opportunity structures for interest groups, which respond accordingly by "venue shopping"' (see Richardson, 2001: 105–6). In other words, they will work both domestically and transnationally, and tolerate a fair amount of duplication on the grounds that, on balance, it is better to risk wasting one's time and money (especially when it constitutes a tiny fraction of an annual turnover that may run into millions of euros) than miss a potential opportunity (see Figure 8.5).

By the same token, it is clear from research (Beyers, 2004) that, as at the 'domestic' level, pressure groups operating at the European level do not (at least nowadays) need to choose between 'voice' and 'access', between more public 'outsider' strategies and more private 'insider' routes to influence – a finding that holds good not just for 'interest' groups like business sector associations and trade unions, but also for more 'diffuse' and 'cause' groups, such as consumer groups and environmental and other

Figure 8.5 Where are organizations registered to lobby in the EU based?

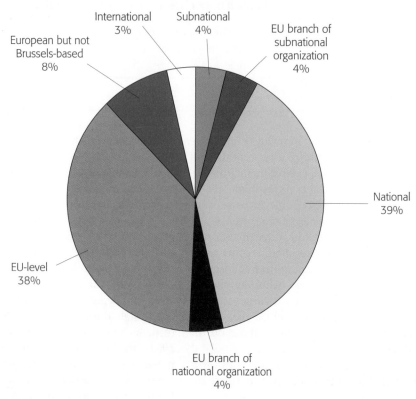

Source: Wonka *et al.* (2010: 469).

NGOs. That said, the same research does suggest that groups tend to vary their strategies according to which EU institution they are trying to influence: interest groups getting access to the relatively technocratic DGs of the European Commission tend to tone down public pressure. Interestingly, though, it also suggests that groups representing causes and diffuse (as opposed to sectional) interests do not find that their very public activities put off Commission officials from dealing with them. Given this, and given the Commission and the rest of the EU is concerned to counter accusations of a lack of transparency and a democratic deficit, there is no reason to expect that the process by which pressure groups seek influence will become as depoliticized as some who are sceptical or worried about European integration's impact on democracy suggest.

Groups are also, of course, involved in lobbying the most obviously politicized of all the EU institu-

tions – namely, the EP, not least because it has gained more legislative power and can therefore help or hurt them more than ever before (see Earnshaw and Judge, 2002 for a useful summary of this activity and an interesting case study involving tobacco). It certainly appears that groups will try the more political, lobbying route first before they resort to (more expensive!) litigation at, say, the 'non-political' European Court of Justice (see Bouwen and McCown, 2007). But even when it comes to the influence process that characterizes the supposedly 'de-politicized' and technocratic realm of the Commission, recent research reveals, first, that 'the policy networks [involved] reflect a basic cleavage between a progrowth and a prosustainability coalition' and, second, that 'the granting of access by public officials is not predominantly a matter of functional resources' like expertise and information. These things are not unimportant but access is also based on 'the perceived capability of interests to mobilize public support or to deal with issues on which the public may be easily mobilized, all of which means that policy networks 'are not reducible to functional information exchange processes' but remain 'channels through which principled political debates are triggered and public concerns are represented' (Beyers and Kerremans, 2004: 1147). Recent research into successful EU-level lobbying also suggests that the resources available to a particular group, while not irrelevant, are ultimately not as important as whether, on the particular issue in question, the group is part of a coalition of groups that, in the end, is simply bigger than the coalition of groups on the losing side (Klüver, 2011).

Given the activity of business interest groups at the European as well as at the state level, it may be hard to understand why some critics, especially in the UK, accuse the EU of introducing what former British Prime Minister Margaret Thatcher termed 'socialism by the back door'. What they really object to, however, is what they see as the institutionalization of corporatism in the EU system, symbolized by the so-called 'Social Chapter' of the Maastricht Treaty. Under the procedure it lays out, it is possible for legislation affecting the labour market – for example, the equal treatment of part-time workers or rules governing maximum working hours – to be agreed on by the so-called 'social partners' and then be simply rubber-stamped by the EU's normal legislative bodies, the Council and the EP (for full details see Falkner, 2009). To (mainly British) critics of limitations on business, this is 'Europe' handing back unwarranted power to the trade unions just as they have been finally 'conquered' at home.

Many politicians in countries without a strong tradition of social partnership might have some sympathy. Governments in CEE, for instance, will be hoping that accession to the EU does not provide the region's fragmented unions (or, indeed, its similarly poorly organized, if not utterly uninfluential, business groups) an opportunity to make up for their domestic weakness, although there is some evidence that interest groups are beginning to take advantage of their enhanced ability to network with and learn from their 'western' counterparts (see Pérez-Solórzano Borragán, 2006). Some observers, however, would point out that because the EU's policy making process is so dependent on interest

groups, such an attitude is naive: as a member state, better to risk having groups that can constrain you at the domestic level if it means they are also capable of exerting some influence on the country's behalf in Brussels (see Bruszt, 2002). In any case, there are politicians, even right-wing politicians, from more long-standing member states where 'concertation' between the government and economic interest groups is par for the course, and who therefore have few qualms about at least a limited reproduction of the process at the European level.

In fact, social partner agreements are not that common, nor are they exactly rushed into. Indeed, the ETUC (the trade union federation), and particularly *BusinessEurope* and CEEP (the private and public sector employers) are often persuaded to take such a route only in order to stave off what might be even less welcome legislation made in the normal way (see Falkner, 2000b). *BusinessEurope* in particular should not be caricatured as some sort of inveterately corporatist soft-touch, even if it is willing to engage with the other social partners on concepts like 'flexicurity' (combining, in Scandinavian style, liberal and active labour market policies with top-drawer social security). That said, institutions such as the Social Chapter, and the embedded respect for trade unions it seems to symbolize, help in part to explain why the latter have reconciled themselves to Europe (see Visser, 1998) – even in the UK, where Euroscepticism was and is unusually strong (Strange, 2002). In short, the EU has provided trade unions with a way of putting the brakes on, and even reversing labour market deregulation and 'anti-trade union legislation' at the domestic level.

When it comes to social movements, however, the evidence for Europeanization is, so far, quite limited, although this could be a case of academic research catching up with the reality on the ground (see della Porta and Caiani, 2007). At the moment, it seems as if the existence of European federations to which national groups belong (environmental groups are a good example) can give a misleading impression of the extent to which they actually cooperate and/or work at the European level (see Rootes, 2004). This is partly a matter of resources. Even the larger environmental organizations, for instance, are nowhere near as well staffed as some of their corporate counterparts: for instance, Birdlife International has only three permanent staff in Brussels and fewer than ten at its European headquarters in the Netherlands. Campaigning organizations out of the mainstream, who may object, even violently, to some of what is done in their name (and in the name of the EU), are even less able to afford to 'venue shop'.

But this is also about focus. For instance, notwithstanding the increased competence of the EU in environmental policy, study of environmental protest in western Europe stresses 'the extent to which both issues and forms of protests reflected the distinctive concerns and idiosyncratic dynamics of politics within each of the several states' it looked at (Rootes, 2004: 255). Other researchers have also found that most attention and direct action is directed at the domestic level, even when the target might (directly or indirectly) be the EU. And while demonstrations against EU-imposed austerity packages in countries like Greece and Spain may be the start of a new trend, the day-to-day reality for many of groups is less transnational, while many of the protests against the EU are carried out not by NSMs but by occupational interest groups, especially farmers and fishermen (see Imig, 2002), whose livelihoods are, of course, directly affected by its policies. Some research suggests that social movements are indeed beginning

to act more frequently at a European level and against European targets (see della Porta and Caiani, 2007; see also Balme and Chabanet, 2008), but others are more sceptical, producing figures which indicate not so much a rising trend as the fact that EU-directed protests seem to be connected to 'the occurrence of central events in the development of the Union' (Uba and Uggla, 2011: 387). On the other hand, given the recent crisis in the Eurozone, and the fact that any assistance to those countries most effected is almost always accompanied by demands that it cut spending, liberalize its economy and boost revenue – all of which are liable to make large numbers of people unhappy – then this could mean we should see a spike in such protests.

Nevertheless, it will undoubtedly take time before most Europeans – if they ever do – stop thinking of home not just as where the heart is but also where power lies. The most pressing problem, many of them argue, is not so much Europeanization but that it no longer makes much difference which set of politicians, left or right, holds that power. This, and the common wisdom that surrounds it, especially in the light of responses to the recent economic crisis, is the focus of Chapter 9.

Learning Resources for Chapter 8

Further reading

On political participation in Europe, see the book edited by van Deth *et al.* (2007), *Citizenship and Involvement in European Democracies,* and on associative activity in Europe, see the volume edited by Maloney and Roßteutscher (2007a), *Social Capital and Associations in European Democracies.* The collection edited by Morales and Giugni (2010), *Social Capital, Political Participation and Migration in Europe* highlights an important new dimension. On social capital more generally see the various contributions to the comprehensive collection edited by Castiglione *et al.* (2008), *The Handbook of Social Capital.* Anyone interested in social movements should begin with della Porta and Diani (2005), *Social Movements,* and Snow *et al.* (2004), *The Blackwell Companion to Social Movements.* They should then move on to the collection edited by della Porta and Tarrow (2005), *Transnational Protest and Global Activism.* Rootes (2007), *Environmental Protest in Western Europe* is also very useful, while Tilly (2004), *Social Movements, 1768–2004,* provides plenty of historical (and contemporary) food for thought. On pressure group activity at the European (as well as the domestic) level, see the authoritative Greenwood (2011), *Interest Representation in the European Union,* the collection edited by Coen and Richardson (2009), *Lobbying the European Union: Institutions, Actors, and Issues,* and the special issue of *West European Politics* on 'The Politics of Organised Interests in Europe', edited by Beyers *et al.* (2008).

On the web

www.etuc.org – trade unions in Europe
www.eurochambres.be and www.businesseurope.eu – European business groups
http://ec.europa.eu/social/main.jsp?catId=329&langId=en – EU-facilitated 'social dialogue' and industrial relations in Europe
http://ec.europa.eu/transparency/civil_society/index_en.htm and
http://www.act4europe.org/code/en/default.asp – pressure groups and civil society in Europe
http://www.alter-eu.org/ – Alliance for Lobbying Transparency and Ethics Regulation
www.sociosite.net/topics/activism.php – social movements
http://www.greenpeace.org/eu-unit/en/ – the 'Brussels branch' of a global 'protest business'

Discussion questions

1   Do you think a country needs a healthy civil society and, if so, why? How and why does the level of popular participation in non-party political activity vary across Europe?

2   What role do you think cultural and institutional factors play in how a pressure group goes about trying to gain influence?

3   How can we explain the power of the agricultural lobby in European countries? Do you think it will last?

4   Have trade unions all over Europe lost their influence?

5   Does the power of business in European countries depend simply on its importance to the economy?

6   Do you have any sympathy with, or are you actually involved in, the activities of new social movements? If so, why? If not, why not?

7   Do you think that big NGOs with their roots in new social movements remain true to their ethos, or have they become part of the mainstream and even the establishment?

8   Why has lobbying at the EU level become an integral part of most interest groups' strategies, and why might groups from some countries be more successful at it than others?

9   Do you think Europeanization poses a threat or an opportunity to groups whose aims do not dovetail neatly with liberal capitalism?

ONLINE
RESOURCES
AVAILABLE

Visit the companion site at **www.palgrave.com/politics/bale** to access additional learning resources.

Chapter 9

Politics over markets: does politics – and left and right – still matter?

Social democracy – the ideology associated with the centre-left – advocates the promotion of equality and well-being via universal welfare provision that ensures the cross-class support necessary for its continuation. It also involves state intervention in the economy to ensure the stability and growth that supposedly creates jobs, helps pay for welfare, and shifts power from the market to politicians who, in theory, are more accountable to ordinary people.

In 2009, Iceland, one of the European countries worst hit by the world financial crisis, experienced something akin to a revolution – or at least a demonstration that 'people power' still counts. The country's right-wing government, which many ordinary Icelanders felt – with some justification – had let the country's investment and banking sectors run out of control during the boom years, was refusing to acknowledge responsibility and clinging onto power. In January 2009, when parliament (the *Althingi*) assembled after the Christmas break, thousands came out on to the surrounding streets, many banging together pots and pans and a few throwing missiles of other descriptions at the parliament buildings. Eventually, one of the government parties, the Social Democrats, cracked and pulled the plug on its coalition with the ruling Independence Party, leading to the formation, just prior to and then after a general election of the country's first socialist-green party government and its first female prime minister, Jóhanna Sigurðardóttir, who was, incidentally, also Europe's first openly lesbian head of government. Her administration then set about big policy changes, not the least of which was to maintain welfare and other spending in order to avoid the kind of austerity that, it believed, would choke off growth. Since then, as many other European countries have chosen to make cuts and risk recession, Iceland's economy has recovered.

In spite of this, many people now regard 'left' and 'right' as increasingly meaningless labels as governments and parties from both sides of a political divide that used to be organized around more or less state intervention, spending and taxation are obliged to follow the same policies in order to cope with globalization, Europeanization, and now an 'age of austerity' brought on by the near-collapse of the world's financial system, the ensuing slow-down in the economy and the debt and deficit crises into which a range of governments found themselves plunged. Centre-left parties in particular, the common wisdom runs, have retreated from **social democracy** and embraced **neoliberalism**, having finally realised that 'Anglo-Saxon' or 'American-style' capitalism (with its labour-market flexibility, private ownership and a limited, low-spending role for the state) is the way of the future,

Neoliberalism advocates 'shrinking' the state by lowering taxation and privatizing its assets, opening up the economy to free-trade, de-regulating the labour market, keeping inflation low and rewarding and encouraging individual responsibility and achievement – in other words, the kind of policies that conservative and market liberal parties (see Chapter 5) have long stood for and which, sceptics argue, continue (not coincidentally) to serve the interests of large, global corporations (see Crouch 2011).

anything else being seen as recipe for continued debt and deficit and for low growth, high unemployment, uncompetitiveness and international decline. Many who share this view also argue that the absence of such an alternative is leading either to political apathy, reflected in ever-decreasing electoral turnout (see Chapter 6), or, especially, in those countries worst affected by the current crisis (Greece being the most obvious example) to the rise of populist politics which offers radical but ultimately illusory solutions to the nation's problems (see Crouch, 2004).

The problem with this common wisdom is that research suggests that it is wrong or at the very least overblown. For one thing, although there is some evidence – mainly gleaned from looking at their manifestos (see Chapter 5) – to suggest that, especially in government (see Warwick, 2011), social democratic parties have (in common with many other parties, in fact) moved towards the centre of the left–right spectrum and (to a lesser extent) away from their traditional positions on welfare, it also reveals (a) a good deal of variety, and (b) that, 'to a large extent, the position of many social democratic parties still tends to be "leftist" in the traditional sense' (Keman, 2011: 677). For another, Europe is not becoming inevitably ever more like the USA – or at least like the neoliberal nightmare vision of the latter which left-wingers like to conjure up even if it bears little resemblance to the variegated reality of a nation composed of 50 often very different states (Baldwin, 2009). In fact, Europe's traditions of social welfare and state intervention remain strong. They have never, however, precluded political differences between right and left, and those differences remain relevant today, even if their specifics have inevitably changed over time. The supposed triumph of neoliberal globalization is in reality severely constrained by (a) the fact that the left of the political spectrum does not want it to triumph and many on the right are either ambivalent about such a triumph or worried about the electoral consequences of being seen to pursue it too vigorously; (b) the fact that the welfare and regulatory state is path-dependent and supported by key constituencies, which means that it is unlikely simply be rolled back at will even under pressure from a combination of markets, credit ratings agencies, the IMF and the EU; and (c) the fact that the political-cum-institutional arrangements of many countries would make change difficult even if (a) and (b) did not apply.

This chapter, then, looks at whether 'politics matters': first, in the sense of being an activity that counteracts, mitigates and channels (global) market outcomes and, second, in the sense of those effects being dependent on which side of the political spectrum controls the government. It suggests that, even if we acknowledge and engage with the complexity of the challenges European states face, especially in today's highly troubled times, right and left are still meaningful concepts, especially if we don't insist on defining them in absolute, unchanging terms.

The chapter begins by tackling one of the most exhaustively researched questions begged by the idea that European politics has moved 'beyond left and right': has politics ever really mattered that much, or have 'left' and 'right' never been much more than interchangeable management teams? It then goes on to explore the extent to which 'politics matters' in key areas such as welfare spending and taxation, privatization, and labour market policy. Each of these areas also allows us to look at the collapse or persistence of national regimes that seem to stand out against the supposedly uniform trend toward liberal capitalism. And it allows us to evaluate the common wisdom that many countries in eastern and central Europe have gone all the way from full-blown communism to capitalism 'red in tooth and claw', by-passing the 'kinder, gentler' version often associated with their western counterparts. The chapter continues by examining how European integration and the multi-level governance it entails, especially in the wake of the so-called Eurozone crisis, both hinders and hastens what neoliberals would like to claim is a necessary drive toward liberalization, deregulation and 'sound' policies. It goes on to suggest that, once we separate the facts from the hype about the triumph of liberal capitalism and the decline of left and right, differences between ideologies, as well as nations, persist – and that politics continues to provide a means by which people can mitigate the sometimes damaging consequences of market forces.

Has politics ever really mattered?

Representative democracy in Europe assumes, and even relies on, political parties standing for a set of ideas-based policies rather than simply competing for the spoils of office. We should expect, then, that who governs (and, therefore, politics as a whole) matters. In other words, there should be some observable link between, on the one hand, a particular party or set of parties being put into power and, on the other, public policy. In fact, the impact of parties is harder to measure than might be imagined: even the smallest 'ship of state' resembles a supertanker rather than a speedboat – a small touch on the tiller or turn of the wheel takes a long time to register as a change of course, by which time the party or parties in question may be out of office. Nevertheless, political scientists have made some effort to make such measurements – and in a variety of ways. Few of those studies, of course, are without problems (see Pétry and Collette, 2009). But their conclusions are fairly clear and (for those who want to believe that politics matters) fairly positive, even if they are unlikely to have much impact on ordinary people, since, as recent research reveals, most of us are so convinced that politicians never keep their promises that we are all but immune to evidence to the contrary (see Naurin, 2011).

One way of trying to find out whether parties make a difference is to see to what extent parties' manifesto promises (the promises that they make in writing at election time) are translated into the formally announced programme of the governments they form or help to form. But this means of measurement is only talking about the translation of one form of words into another, not the translation of words into action. For this, we have to look at studies examining the extent to which governments actually redeem the pledges made in their programmes. Unfortunately, these studies are surprisingly rare, not as rigorous as some would like, and tend to be confined to countries such as the UK and Greece (see Bara, 2005; Bevan *et al.*, 2011; Kalogeropoulou, 1989; Rallings, 1987), which are unusual in that they normally have one-party majority governments (see Chapter 4), although more recently there have also been studies of Sweden and Ireland (see Naurin, 2011 and Mansergh and Thomson, 2007), which do not. The fact that this research seems to show that around two-thirds of promises are kept (Pétry and Collette, 2009) – quite a high figure, given the contingencies of office – does seem to support the case for parties

making a difference. However, most European democracies are run by multiparty majority coalitions or either multiparty or single-party minority governments, making it much harder for a single party to see its ideas translated into deeds (see Colomer, 2011). This assumption was confirmed by one of the first comparative studies in this area involving the Netherlands and the UK (see Thomson, 2001), although the study, by showing that governing parties did most of what they said they would, also gave us some grounds for optimism that parties (and, by extension, politics) do make a difference.

The latest comparative study in this vein (Thomson *et al.*, 2012) does the same. It detects considerable variation between countries in the extent to which governing parties fully fulfil their election pledges: for instance, this occurs around 80 per cent of the time in Sweden and the UK, and around 70 per cent in Portugal, but only half of the time in Germany and the Netherlands and one-third of the time in Ireland. The variation, as expected, is largely explicable by differences in the extent to which each country experiences single-party and coalition government. Parties in single-party governments (irrespective, interestingly, of whether they are majority or minority governments – see Chapter 4) are most likely to fulfil their election pledges, while those in coalition governments (particularly minority coalition governments) are least likely to do so. As might be expected, and in some ways proving that parties are right to negotiate hard when governments are being formed, controlling the premiership and/or particular ministries makes pledge fulfilment more likely. On the other hand, it is not simply down to parties: pledges are more easily fulfilled when the economy is growing rather than shrinking and (perhaps not surprisingly) if they promise to keep things as they are rather than change things.

Other studies aim to answer the question by looking at public spending – mainly on the grounds

KEY POINT

Historically, at least in the latter half of the twentieth century, there does seem to be a relationship between which parties were in office and government policy.

that left-wing parties (historically supportive of the welfare state and improved access to education) would be expected to spend more than right-wing parties (which historically have tended to worry more about, say, defence, and also where the money is going to come from). Again, taking these studies as a whole (see Alvarez *et al.*, 1991; Blais *et al.*, 1996; Hicks, 1999; Imbeau *et al.*, 2001; Schmidt, 1996, 2002) the verdict would seem to be a cautious 'yes' – in eastern as well as western Europe (see Careja and Emmenegger, 2009) though it is important to note that some scholars would argue that 'politics hasn't mattered – much' (Caul and Gray, 2000: 234).

Taking cross-national studies first, states that have experienced left-wing government for a considerable time (in Scandinavia and Austria) seem to have a bigger public sector than those for which the opposite is the case (most obviously, Ireland and Switzerland). There also seems to be a link over time between left-wing government and more spending on education and welfare, though not health. Within-country studies (which can, of course, be added together to produce a cross-national conclusion) also seem to show a relationship between left-wing governments and higher spending and conservative governments and lower spending, even if the effect (a) is confined to majority as opposed to minority governments; (b) is influenced by the size and strength of the opposition (as well as the existence of a strong trade union movement); and (c) can vary according to which area of spending is looked at: since most of those who take advantage of subsidized higher education come from relatively well-off backgrounds, it isn't perhaps surprising that this is one area seemingly favoured by right-wing governments (see Rauh *et al.*, 2011; and see Ansell, 2010) – a stance that makes all the more sense when one remembers they face competition on the issue from left-wing governments looking to boost their own middle-class support (Busemeyer, 2009a). On economic policy, there also appears to be a historical tendency for governments of the right to prefer lower inflation at the cost of higher unemployment, and governments of the left to prefer the opposite. Income inequality also seems to be affected – going up when there are right-wing parties in government and down when their counterparts on the left are in charge, although more recent research which takes a much longer time frame suggests that that, in fact,

neither left-wing government nor the more centralized bargaining systems that have traditionally been associated with more egalitarian income distributions made much difference in this respect (see Scheve and Stasavage, 2009).

This last finding notwithstanding, there still seems to be some truth, then, in the argument that 'politics matters' or 'makes a difference'. Parties and governments of the left and right do different things and have different priorities – even if, as we shall see, many assume that the differences have narrowed (see Huber and Stephens, 2001). Indeed, politics might even make more difference than studies involving large-scale averages suggest. Such indicators cannot possibly hope to capture the myriad policy acts by an individual government that even the casual observer of politics would say were unimaginable under a government run by another party or set of parties. We can all cite examples from countries we know well. Would a Conservative government in the UK have announced a national minimum wage as its Labour counterpart did in 1997? Would the Popular Party in Spain have withdrawn Spanish troops from Iraq had it, rather than PSOE, been elected in the wake of the Madrid bombings in 2004? And would it have gone on to legislate for same sex marriage in 2005? In the unlikely event that the former communist social democratic party had been re-elected in Poland that same year, would it have attempted, like the administration led by Law and Justice, and headed by the Kaczynski twins, to once again re-open the files in order to discover and sanction people who collaborated with the Communist regime? And was it really such a surprise that, having defeated Law and Justice at the next election, the Civic Platform party, rather than pursuing those collaborators with the same vigour, instead concentrated more on mending fences with (some of) Poland's neighbours (see Chapter 11)? These, however, are individual acts. They do not necessarily constitute long-term trends.

Drifting to the right? The centre-left in Europe

One such trend – or supposed trend – has become something of a commonplace these days. It is that

Europe's centre-left parties have moved away from a traditionally social democratic emphasis on government intervention, welfare spending and prioritizing full employment. The charge does not come solely from crowing conservatives. But neither is it simply the catch-call of left-wingers torn between despair and trying to capitalize on the ensuing discontent of social democratic traditionalists (see Callaghan, 2000; Callinicos, 2001). In fact, the abandonment of old-style socialism has been reflected in the rhetoric of some of social democracy's most prominent leaders, particularly in the UK and in Germany. In the mid-1990s, while seeking (successfully) to win office from centre-right parties which had been in power for over fifteen years, both Tony Blair and Gerhard Schröder insisted they were pragmatic centrists. Their so-called 'Third Way' or *Neue Mitte* sought not to expand or to 'shrink' the state, but to reconstruct it in order better to equip ordinary people to cope and compete in an increasingly global economy (see Green-Pedersen *et al.*, 2001).

KEY POINT

Social democratic parties have updated, but have not necessarily abandoned, their traditional goals and even the traditional means of achieving them. They are, however, being more honest with themselves and with electors about what they want to (and are able to) achieve.

To devotees of the Third Way, globalization, voter resistance to tax rises and inflation, and market antipathy to profligate spending, were – rightly or wrongly – to be treated as givens. The state, whatever the evidence to the contrary (see Weiss, 1998), was no longer so powerful. The majority had a stake in the health rather than in the hounding of capitalism. Governments of the left therefore had to work with, not against, the grain of what was a 'post-ideological' age – an era where (see Green, 2007) 'valence politics' (the question of who can best deliver progress toward broadly accepted goals) had replaced 'position politics' (the clash of opposing worldviews). They had to admit that they had no monopoly on good policies, and that some of what their opponents stood for made sense: unions were important but they could not be allowed to run the show; welfare benefits should provide 'a hand-up not a handout'; sometimes the market did know

better than the state, the consumer better than the civil servant. Dogma, they claimed, had to take a back seat: 'What counts is what works.'

But was all this really such a quantum leap from the past? Common wisdom relies on the assumption of some kind of postwar 'golden era' during which ideologically committed social democratic parties in Europe were conquering capitalism, building welfare states and economies safe from the depredations of international markets. But the reality was rather more prosaic. The European centre-left spent most of the twentieth century trying not just to tame and humanize capitalism, but also to make it work better, all the time operating within constraints imposed by both moderate voters and powerful international markets (see Pierson, 2001; Sassoon, 1997). Recent developments are part of an ongoing story. Of course, one can compare contemporary and 'classic' social democracy 'now' and 'then', and find the latter wanting (see Thomson, 2000). Yet such comparisons not only risk caricaturing both periods but also downplaying the fact that social democracy has always been a particularly plastic ideology which varies over space as well as time (see Stammers, 2001).

This plasticity has, it would seem, allowed social democrats in Europe to internalize the 'common sense' surrounding the advisability of, say, low inflation, balanced budgets and (to a much lesser extent) the new public management (or NPM) (see Chapter 3). Moreover, they know that pursuing such policies earns them valuable credibility with finance markets. No doubt, some are also privately relieved that, when their political opponents carry out painful reforms, they could be doing social democracy a favour by doing what it would find difficult to do itself in the face of opposition from its own supporters. But none of this learning and adapting necessarily means that Europe's social democrats threw the baby out with the bathwater (see Green-Pedersen *et al.*, 2001; Martell, 2001). Part of the claim of 'Third Way' social democrats like Schröder and Blair, after all, was that means can be de-coupled from ends, that values such as fairness and equality of opportunity (if not outcome) are best realized in up-to-date ways (Blair and Schröder, 1999). Utilitarianism and pragmatism has always been a strong streak in European social democracy: if the old ways of achieving the greatest

Manifesto tracking

One of the longest continuous research projects in political science is the collection and coding of the manifestos of (western) Europe's political parties. One piece of analysis from the project (Volkens, 2004; see also Volkens and Klingemann, 2002) explores the extent to which parties of the mainstream right and left have converged over time. Its findings are clear: in the 1940s–1960s, most centre-left parties moved to the left; but it also finds that they were followed in the same direction by almost all their centre-right opponents. From the 1970s onwards, the move was in the opposite direction: the centre-right moved right, and the centre-left, needing to keep in touch with the electorate, followed. Volkens' study cautions us, however, against exaggerating the extent of these shifts. Contrary to other scholars who use similar data (see Caul and Gray, 2000), Volkens also argues strongly against the idea of convergence: parties continued to maintain, at least, a semantic distance from each other. Interestingly, she also concludes that the 'policy shift to new Third Way issues ... is no recent development, but started as early as the 1950s'. Other analysts of the manifesto project data, including those, such as Caul and Gray, who do see more convergence, also make the point that it has been going on for four or five decades, rather than being a knee-jerk response to resurgent neoliberalism.

good for the greatest number 'cannot be successfully implemented in the socio-economic and cultural environment of advanced capitalism' then they 'ought no longer be pursued' and, instead, be swapped for something that might work better (Kitschelt, 1994: 7).

Neither should we forget that the sheer size and inertia of polities and economies has meant – and will mean – that the differences between right- and left-wing governments (if not parties) tend to be ones of degree rather than kind. It will also mean – especially given that a measure initiated by one government might end up coming into effect under a successor from the other side of the political spectrum – that partisan differences in policy outputs might be difficult to pick up, making it difficult for us to see if they are still relevant. Nevertheless, it is important to make the effort to do so. In politics, discourse and rhetoric are undoubtedly important and arguably revealing (see Schmidt, 2001). But much of it – including the manifestos that political scientists have spent so much time studying (see Box 9.1) – is designed to reassure and reposition, rather than provide a blueprint for action. It might be fashionable to say there is no longer much difference between left and right, but it might not be true, or at least not wholly so. This can be illustrated by looking at parties' records on what has long been a key battleground in European politics – the welfare state.

Party positions on the welfare state – words and deeds

The extent and form of the welfare state has traditionally been a matter of ideological and partisan contention between left (basically pro) and right (either anti or, at least, anti overly generous welfare provision). It is often suggested, however, that this is no longer the case, that there is a 'new politics of welfare' marked by retrenchment and austerity (see Pierson, 1996) in the midst of which the left in particular has given up its values and its fight to maintain, let alone extend, welfare. Is this really the case?

One way of answering that question is, of course, to look at every European country and check out the debate in each one. However, this would be a highly intensive exercise and, because they vary so much on so many different dimensions, coming to a con-

KEY POINT

When it comes to welfare spending, redistribution and taxation, there has been no big roll-back of the state. Moreover, left-wing and right-wing governments still seem to behave in a manner consistent with their ideologies. The differences might have narrowed in the 1990s but, if they have, this is due to the centre-right, as well as the centre-left, moderating its policies.

vincing conclusion either way might be difficult. One more practical way of trying to find out whether the left has collapsed in the face of neoliberalism – or, for that matter, whether the right is too comfortable or too scared to fight for it – is to restrict the analysis to a group of countries that are not only broadly similar, and therefore more comparable, but also well known as strong welfare states. If the left has moved away from its commitment there, the argument runs, then it will almost certainly have done the same in countries where that commitment is less strong.

A relevant attempt to pursue this more focused strategy used party manifestos to explore the changing positions of political parties on the welfare state in four Nordic (or Scandinavian) countries – Denmark, Finland, Norway and Sweden – between 1970 and 2003 (Nygård, 2006). Each has seen (in the light of shared concerns about competitiveness, spending and employment) retrenchment and reform – sometimes carried out by the left and sometimes the right. But all continue with a level and a style of welfare that continues to ensure that the region stands out as a beacon (at least for those of a left-wing persuasion) of equality and universal provision. The findings of the study make for interesting reading, not least because, once again, they question and qualify the common wisdom.

First, although there was more interest in market-based solutions to social problems expressed as time went on, there was no overall decline in partisan support for welfare state expansion; if anything, support increased towards the end of the period. True, there were calls for cutbacks, but these tended to be made during economic recessions. Second, the clear trend was for parties on the left to continue to be staunch promoters of the welfare state, even though they had at times to recognize that reform and retrenchment might be necessary, whereas parties on the right were more likely to be the ones calling for limits and more market-based solutions, although this instinct was often muted (possibly by electoral concerns, possibly because of genuine attachment to the Nordic model). In the words of the author of the study, 'the left–right axis still plays a significant role' and 'parties still matter' (Nygård, 2006: 376–7). This conclusion would seem to be borne out by developments since then in Denmark at least. True, there has over time been a shift from the ideal-type universalist, social democratic model to a multi-tiered welfare system in which access to benefits is tied more closely to labour market participation (Kvist and Greve, 2011). However, the programmes offered to the electorate by the right-wing and left-wing alliances vying for government in 2011 were markedly different, with the right offering spending cuts and a squeeze on benefits while the left (the eventual winner) offered tax increases on higher earners and banks and much milder pension reforms.

Focused studies like this are useful, especially where they can be cross-checked and fleshed out by other similarly focused research. For instance, as well as research that points out that Scandinavian democracies were always likely to reform welfare sooner rather than later owing to the advanced nature of their economies (Bonoli, 2007), there is work which suggests that their social democratic parties not only undertook those reforms because they were under pressure but also because they were (and remain) well aware that the welfare state is a political asset that must be maintained and therefore kept up-to-date (see Klitgaard, 2007). On the other hand, focused studies have their limitations. They don't tell us about all the countries we are interested in and – especially if they analyse manifesto promises rather than government actions – they may tell us more about rhetoric than reality. This is why it makes sense to complement them with cross-national studies, often of a more quantitative type.

Two such studies – contributions to a branch of political science known as 'comparative political economy' – have been carried out by Allan and Scruggs (2004) and Korpi and Palme (2003). Both make a strong case for the continued importance of class-based political differences when it comes to welfare. Looking at the value of benefits paid to those who do not or cannot work, they find, admittedly, that – if only on this crucial dimension – the welfare state is not as generous as it once was, although they do not put the retrenchment of the 1990s down to 'globalization'. Yet they also have no doubt that politics still matters: right-wing governments, especially when the economy is in poor shape, are more willing to make cuts in benefit entitlements and levels – things which really do make a difference to rates of both relative and absolute poverty (Scruggs and Allan, 2006b; see also Brady,

2003). Support for the idea that parties and politics matter also comes from economists: a study of eighteen countries between 1981 and 1999 found a very clear effect – 'left-wing governments reacted to shocks not with cutbacks [as did right-wing administrations, even if few could match the stringency of Margaret Thatcher's in the UK], but with a rise in welfare-state generosity in order to cushion the effects of structural changes' (Amable *et al.*, 2006: 437). This finding, especially as it applies to right-wing parties, suggests that if (as we go on to discuss) the latter have reconciled themselves to the welfare state, then that reconciliation is either merely rhetorical or else comparatively recent.

The direction of these findings is reinforced by studies which look not just at the welfare state but at what, for those on the left anyway, was traditionally one of its key rationales; namely, its ability to redistribute income not just between different age groups or between, for example, the well and the unwell, but also between the better and the less well-off. In short, if parties and politics matter, we would expect to see a relationship between the redistributionary effect of welfare states and who governs. In countries where the centre-left has been in power more, we should see more redistribution between rich and poor compared with those where the centre-right is strong. Bradley *et al.*, (2003) explore this question and set up a particularly hard test by comparing (Scandinavian) social democratic states not just with Anglo-Saxon or liberal welfare states (such as the UK and the USA) but also with states like Germany and the Netherlands where Christian democrats, who are traditionally less hostile to generous welfare provision than their conservative and market liberal counterparts, dominate the centre right. Their findings (see Bradley *et al.*, 2003: 225–6) are unequivocal:

> leftist government very strongly drives the redistributive process directly by shaping the distributive contours of taxes and transfers and indirectly by increasing the proportion of GDP devoted to taxes and transfers. By contrast, if we add the direct and indirect effects of Christian democratic government, the net result is actually negative though not strongly so ... [If] Christian democratic welfare states have slightly more egalitarian effects than liberal welfare states, our analysis

shows that this is the case because they spend more and they have stronger unions or longer periods of left government, and not because of Christian democratic governance.

Inevitably, given the room for argument over how to measure it, there are quantitative studies which are more sceptical about the impact of 'partisan politics' on the welfare state. For instance, Kittel and Obinger (2003) clearly reject the suggestion that there has been some kind of 'race to the bottom' wherein governments have made swingeing cuts to welfare entitlements and provision in order to cope with globalization. But they note that the 1990s was a fairly difficult time for many governments when it came to social spending and argue that, during the last couple of decades, parties have made less of a difference on that score than they did in the past – certainly when compared with more structural drivers like ageing populations and unemployment. Indeed, which party or parties were in power mattered less than how many of them were in power, since larger coalitions made compromises on welfare reform difficult.

If Kittel and Obinger are right, and differences in welfare spending from the 1990s onwards were not influenced by parties quite as much as they were before, then this would, indeed, fit with the idea that the centre-left has recently begun to re-think welfare, at least at the margins – perhaps because they are re-assessing their ideas; perhaps because they realize that a tougher line might appeal to voters and to other parties with whom they hope to govern (see Schumacher, 2011). But their findings – especially their insistence that reforms might have meant retrenchment but never 'roll-back' – could also accord with criticisms coming from neoliberals that the right in Europe is no longer (and perhaps never was) as convinced as it should have been that, to quote former American President Ronald Reagan, 'Government is not a solution to our problem, government *is* the problem'.

In fact, there is research which suggests that, at least before the onset of the global financial and economic crisis, some of Europe's mainstream (centre) right parties (like the conservative *Moderaterna* in Sweden) toned down any enthusiasm for liberalizing reforms because they have concluded that it makes more sense to patch up the welfare state rather than put it to the sword (see Lindbom, 2008). One can also point out that the centre-right in Europe was never wholly committed to neoliberalism in the first place – particularly not the continent's Christian democrats. In Austria, for example, the Christian democratic ÖVP did, once in office after the 1999 elections, at least try to make good on its promise of *weniger Staat, mehr privat* (less state, more private), but the leadership of its German counterpart, the CDU–CSU, encountered more internal opposition to its policy of *mehr Markt, weniger Staat* (more market, less state) – a policy that also frightened voters so much that the party ended up having to govern with the social democrats after the 2005 election (Haupt, 2007). Recent research covering thirteen European countries between 1980 and 2000 also makes it clear that, although right-wing governments in general spend less on social policy, this is not the case in countries which are more often run by left-wing than right-wing parties; indeed, in those countries, right-wing governments – quite possibly because they are concerned about the negative electoral consequences of voters' lack of trust in them when it comes to the welfare state – sometimes spend more than their left-wing counterparts, who in turn worry about being seen as profligate soft-touches (Jensen, 2010). Other research shows that, while right-wing governments may try, and sometimes succeed in, cutting back, they, in common with other governments, often attempt to achieve savings in other parts of the budget before taking an axe (and even then only a small one) to the welfare state (see Keman, 2010).

We should be careful, however, before leaping to the conclusion that the centre-right more generally has really reconciled itself to 'tax and spend'. Even if the caution exercised by Christian democratic, conservative and market-liberal parties in 'left-wing countries' survives the economic downturn, there is no reason to think it will be replicated in countries where the left and the trade unions do not traditionally exercise a great deal of power. Take the UK, for example: notwithstanding media stories in the run up to the 2010 election about David Cameron learning all he could from the Swedish Moderate Rally Party's modernizing leader (and Prime Minister) Fredrik Reinfeldt, the British Conservative Party insisted that this was 'an age of austerity' and that it would be cutting back and reforming the

country's already relatively residual welfare state accordingly. This almost certainly cost the Tories the chance of an overall majority in 2010, although it may not – given what research shows are often reasonably effective 'blame avoidance' strategies which governments embarking on retrenchment can employ (see Box 9.2) – necessarily condemn it to failure at the following general election, even though its deficit-reduction and welfare-reform programme (endorsed by its coalition partner, the Liberal Democrats, but condemned by the opposition Labour Party as going 'too far, too fast') is in some ways more radical than the one pursued by Margaret Thatcher in the 1980s (see Taylor-Gooby and Stoker, 2011).

On the other hand, a recent survey of responses to economic crises from the 1970s onwards, by stressing both the lack of any uniform response and the mediating influence of multiparty government and welfare state size (Starke *et al.*, 2011), serves to remind us that not every centre-right party in Europe will necessarily follow the orthodox path blazed by the British. Take Hungary, where the supposedly conservative *Fidesz* government's response to economic and financial crisis included, for example, not only moves which looked radically neoliberal, like writing a flat-tax and a cap on public debt into the constitution, but also measures which would frighten right-wing economists, such as increasing political control of (and even levying a transaction tax on) the central bank and passing legislation to oblige commercial banks to accept that the many Hungarians with mortgages taken out in foreign currency will be paying them back at an exchange rate set by the government rather by the market. That said, the British example reminds us that not every coalition government conforms to the norm found by recent research covering 33 parliamentary democracies over a period of 28 years, namely that governments made up of more than one party find it much more difficult to agree on cutting spending in bad times (and, just as interestingly, on raising spending in good times) than single-party administrations (Blais *et al.*, 2010).

Returning again to the left, if there is a 'new macroeconomic consensus: fiscal stabilization = reduction in government debt burden = lower interest rates = more investment = increased economic growth = lower unemployment and stable

BOX 9.2

Avoiding the blame for imposing cuts

It is commonly thought that cutting back on welfare is a difficult and risky business for political parties: any programmes which are well established not only have a momentum of their own but have beneficiaries who can kick up the kind of fuss that may cost votes. But retrenchment does sometimes occur, and parties are not automatically punished since they can often rely on some tried and trusted 'blame avoidance strategies' – all of which we have witnessed being put into operation during the economic crisis which began in late 2007, the consequences of which continue to rumble on. For instance, governments – a body which includes not just politicians but also their partisan political advisors (see Dahlström, 2011) – can pick on programmes which are less visible than others (sometimes labelled obfuscation). They can try to restrict cuts to programmes whose beneficiaries lacking public sympathy and/or voting muscle ('division'). Or they can provide alternative benefits ('compensation') to at least some of those who will lose out. Governments can also make cuts at arm's length, hoping that the agency or perhaps the local or regional authority which has to implement the policy on the ground will take most of the flak ('delegation'). And they can suggest that those who are going to lose out fully merit their fate and have only themselves to blame ('scapegoating'). They can also, of course, insist that cuts and reforms are rendered inevitable by economic hardship.

How well these strategies work, of course, depends in part on political skill and in part on just how many people will be directly affected and what kind of a protest they are able to mount: it is much easier to cut payments, for instance, to 'excessively' large and workless (some even say 'workshy') families living on nothing but 'handouts' than it is to hit old age pensioners or a health system that everybody uses. The extent to which parties can cut welfare and 'get away with it' also, research suggests, (see Giger and Nelson, 2010), depends on voters' pre-existing perceptions of the parties themselves. Some parties seem not only to be able to pursue cutbacks without losing votes but may even gain them as well – possibly because they are still trusted to do the right thing – although this finding is disputed by other research which suggests that parties seen as pro-welfare risk a particularly harsh voter backlash if they fail to live up to their image, with those voters defecting to parties who remain committed, albeit from the easy vantage point of opposition, to defending the welfare state (Schumacher *et al.*, 2013). On the other hand, researchers seem to agree that parties which enjoy a reputation for trying to keep costs down may benefit from doing so when in power (*ibid.*) – which may explain why some of Europe's conservative and market liberal parties will stick to their austerity programmes even when the political going gets really tough. This is even more likely if they have carefully targeted their cuts. A recent study (De Vries and Hobolt 2012) finds that people who are adversely affected by spending cuts are, indeed, less likely to approve of the government. However, it also notes that the extent to which this occurs varies with the political sophistication of the voter. Highly sophisticated voters are more able to make the link between the policy, its authors and the impact on them and therefore change their party preference (and perhaps their vote) accordingly.

inflation' (Teague and Donaghey, 2003: 110), this does not necessarily mean that, when they can, Europe's social democrats have given up spending. In Spain, for instance, PSOE may have been accused of selling out to market liberalism throughout the 1980s, but public expenditure, especially on health and education, climbed relentlessly as the party, in power for the first time in over forty years, attempted to make up for decades of neglect under a right-wing dictatorship (see Astudillo Ruiz, 2002: 16–19; Boix, 1998). More recently, the UK Labour government, supposedly keener than most to surrender social democracy to the market and the middle classes, presided from the late 1990s onwards over unprecedented rises in spending, particularly on youth unemployment, family support, education and (above all) on health (Mullard and Swaray, 2010). Moreover, it did not pay for this largesse simply via economic growth and a decline in unemployment (which have always been social democrats' favourite sources). It also did it through tax rises – primarily via an early hit on the excess profits of privatized utilities and pension funds, and then via so-called 'stealth taxes' on the middle classes and taking a share of the huge profits made in the boom years by Britain's burgeoning financial services sector (see Corry *et al.*, 2012) – one reason, some argue, that Labour politicians were far more relaxed than they should have been about regulating banks and other institutions.

Little surprise, then, that, at the same time as left-wing critics in Spain, the UK and elsewhere have been hounding social democrats for not doing enough, the centre-right in Europe continues to accuse them of doing both far too much and the same old thing. According to conservatives, centre-left politicians remain addicted to spendthrift policies that promote inefficiencies, stifle initiative and swallow up resources that would be better employed in the private sector. Yet when these criticisms hit home and the right is re-elected, it finds it difficult to throw things into reverse, possibly increasing voters' cynicism and their inability – much, if not all, of the time – to see the differences between the parties that, objectively speaking, do still seem to be there.

In fact, both politicians and voters are to blame, if 'blame' is the right word. Historical evidence suggests that, notwithstanding promises of (and worries about) austerity during the current crisis, levels of taxation and public spending, while not utterly impervious to government action, are very 'sticky', making it difficult even for supposedly right-wing (let alone supposedly left-wing) administrations to do much 'dismantling of the welfare state' (see Green-Pedersen, 1999). This is partly, as we have suggested above, because programmes create powerful constituencies with large numbers of votes. It is also because a great deal of public spending (and therefore taxation) is devoted to items which have been seen by most west Europeans – for good or ill – as rights rather than privileges. These include (above all) pensions, education, health care and social security in the event of illness, accident, or unemployment. Many people also expect the state to supplement wages that no one can realistically live on, although there is more ambivalence throughout western Europe about helping the supposedly 'undeserving poor' who could do more to help themselves (see Wilensky, 2002: Chapter 10) and are therefore likely to be the first target of welfare cutbacks in tough times. In short, the extent to which welfare states can be cut back by governments of whatever ideological stripe – and indeed the variation between welfare states in different countries – depends upon underlying public preferences as well as institutions and parties, none of which change that swiftly (see Brooks and Manza, 2007).

There is little to suggest that central and eastern Europeans (many of whom were, after all, brought up to believe that state provision of these things was automatic) view things very differently to their counterparts in the west. Certainly, their political representatives seem to reflect those preferences, notwithstanding some initially radical rhetoric from right-wing parties, reinforced by the recommendations of international bodies such as the IMF and the World Bank (see Ferge, 2001), about moving toward a more 'residual' or 'Anglo-Saxon' welfare state (see Box 9.3). Looking at social policy broadly defined, the picture is mixed, but to label it neoliberal would be a caricature (see Fuchs and Offe, 2008). Take healthcare, for instance. Reforms in most postcommunist states 'have not been noteworthy for their emphasis on market competition or privatization' but were instead 'geared to securing universal access to health-care funded out of compulsory public or state-owned insurance schemes' and payroll taxes (Deacon, 2000: 155).

In many of the areas just mentioned, in fact, there is an almost inbuilt pressure for spending increases right across Europe. Some of this pressure of course, is cyclical (or rather counter-cyclical), with economic downturn giving rise to higher spending as 'automatic stabilisers' like benefits kick in as a consequence. Some of the pressure, however, is structural. Countries' government spending on education, for instance, varies between 4 and 8 per cent of GDP, with an average of around 5 per cent; but it is generally recognized that in order not to get left behind economically, a country's 'human capital' has to be constantly improved. Sweden and the UK, for instance, upped the numbers going into higher education between 1991 and 2001 by 85 per

---

BOX 9.3

East is east? Left and right in the Czech Republic

It has become commonplace – and probably sensible – for most analysts of CEE party politics to warn readers unfamiliar with the region that definitions of left and right derived from western Europe do not necessarily apply. And there are plenty of examples of former communist parties that repackaged themselves as social democrats after the fall of the Berlin Wall appearing, for instance, to espouse the cause of socio-economic and cultural modernization (often via European integration) more loudly than some of their right-wing opponents, even if that meant painful – and electorally costly – welfare reforms and, in some cases, conservative politicians spending more than their centre-left rivals on public services and the alleviation of poverty (see Tavits and Letki, 2009).

Arguably, however, the differences between right and left in postcommunist Europe will, in the long term, come to resemble those elsewhere. In some countries, the similarities have long been apparent. One such is the Czech Republic, whose president, Václav Klaus, during his time as prime minister in the 1990s, was already being called a Thatcherite. It should have come as no surprise, then, that the coalition government dominated by Klaus' own party, the conservative ODS, announced in April 2007 a package that combined cuts in income and corporation taxes with reductions in entitlements to benefits, increases in VAT (sales tax) on many staple consumer goods and a hike in healthcare charges.

By the same token, the promise to fight the package on the part of the opposition social democrats and the smaller Communist Party (notwithstanding the fact that it was partly justified on the grounds of helping the Czech Republic to prepare to join the Eurozone) was also very much in line with what anyone familiar with left–right politics in 'the West' would have predicted. The same held true when, in 2011, the centre-right coalition government introduced an element of workfare into the unemployment benefits system and private provision into the pension system. In short, as party systems institutionalize (see Chapter 5) they begin to reproduce familiar left–right divisions and differences in policy and policy implementation, although more so, it seems, in economic policy than elsewhere (see Jahn and Müller-Rommel, 2010: 38). This may explains why the 'tough decisions' associated with austerity seem to have been easier to make in post-communist countries (for example in the Baltic region) whose party systems have not settled down so quickly (see O'Dwyer and Kovalčik, 2007).

---

cent and 64 per cent, respectively. In health (see Figure 9.1), improvements in medical technology mean that people expect to be treated for conditions that previously would have been ignored and that might have served (as Charles Dickens' Mr Scrooge once put it) to 'decrease the surplus population'. As regards social security, there are several reasons why the state is more likely to spend in the future rather than save. These include the end of the concept of a 'family wage' (i.e. one big enough to support a non-working wife bringing up children) brought about by the entry of women into the labour force (see Chapter 1), the inability (or unwillingness) of governments to ensure full employment and the low wages paid to many in the (largely non-unionized) service sector economy –

all situations that the state often ends up subsidizing through income support.

The other 'big-ticket item' – in some countries, the biggest ticket item – is old age pensions, spending on which by the state, according to Eurostat, accounts on average for around 13 per cent of GDP in EU member-states. We noted in Chapter 1 that Europe's ageing population was one of the biggest challenges facing its politicians. But, outside the UK (where governments of both right and left have made use of the highly majoritarian system to force through pension reform with little consultation) many have ducked it, or at least had to take things very slowly (see Schludi, 2005). Here is one issue on which there does seem to be a consensus among political elites, be they on the right or the left. Unfortunately,

Figure 9.1 Average annual growth in real health expenditure *per capita* 1998–2008

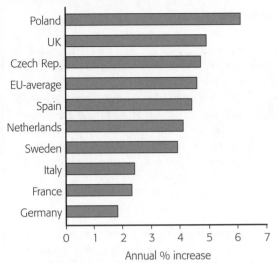

Annual % increase

Source: Data from OECD, Health at a Glance: Europe 2010, available at http://www.oecd-ilibrary.org/social-issues-migration-health/health-at-a-glance-europe-2010_health_glance-2010-en

however, the consensus often seems to unite those that are in government rather than in opposition.

An obvious exception to this rule has been Sweden, where a commission involving stakeholders and five political parties in the 1990s managed to produce a package which essentially supplemented the state earnings-related scheme with private provision and went some way to means-testing the basic pension. Something similar was agreed in Denmark in 2006. Elsewhere, however, the situation has, sadly, been very different. In office, most governments in Europe have at least attempted to tackle the problem by a combination of the following: by reining back entitlements, most obviously by indexing to inflation rather than average wages; by raising the retirement age; by de-privileging public sector employees on particularly generous schemes (a real problem in France and Italy); and by encouraging or mandating private provision. In opposition, however, many parties have opportunistically supported (or, at least, declined to criticize) protests even when, had they been in government, they might well have been taking the same action.

In many European countries, the lack of explicit (as opposed to tacit) consensus, especially when

combined with popular protest, makes it difficult, and even impossible, for those supposedly in power to act decisively. Of course, this is not always the case. Austria's right-wing government faced mass protests and strikes over its planned pension reforms in the summer of 2003, but promised to soldier on – partly perhaps because the country has no recent history of such events bringing down governments. Elsewhere, however, things are different. The right-wing Italian government of Silvio Berlusconi, for instance, almost forfeited office in the summer of 2004 when – in the face of mass public protests reminiscent of those that had brought it down in the mid-1990s – it just managed to pass relatively minor changes to a pension system that swallows up a large proportion of GDP and current spending by the state. Similarly, until President Sarkozy, who promised big changes in 2007 (see Box 9.4) but subsequently crashed to defeat in 2012, drove through reductions in pension entitlements in 2010, French governments had pursued only piecemeal reform. And even that they did almost by stealth lest they spark a repeat of the 1995 demonstrations that effectively brought down one of the few administrations (a socialist one) apparently willing to face the situation (and the trade unions) head-on. This is a serious problem because both countries operate what are effectively 'pay-as-you-go' systems, where pensions – be they state earnings-related schemes or occupational schemes – are paid by contributions from those currently working: since the size of that group is going to shrink relative to pensioners (see Chapter 1), those countries will face an increasing (and perhaps politically intolerable) tax burden unless something is done. And this is before one even gets into the argument that European societies (with Italy being the most egregious example) actually devote far too much of their welfare spending to the elderly when they should – on both efficiency and equity grounds – be directing it toward children and young families (Esping-Andersen, 2009) and ongoing skills training for the many young adults finding it difficult to get a job, especially in a country like Spain, where unemployment among 16–24-year-olds touched 53.3 per cent in July 2012.

It is clear from these examples that the capacity or willingness of parties and governments to make these 'hard choices' (Pierson, 2001) does not necessarily vary according to whether they can be described as

---

BOX 9.4

A clear choice – recent elections in France

It has become something of a truism that voters these days aren't offered a clear alternative. But no-one who had to choose between Nicolas Sarkozy or Ségolène Royal at the French presidential elections in the spring of 2007 could have argued they couldn't tell the difference. Royal's 'Compact with France' was, to some, a real blast from the socialist past, although, in part, one foisted on her by her less centrist party. It proposed, among other measures, raising pensions, disability and housing benefits, and the minimum wage. The programme – costed at anything between € 35 to € 50 billion – also guaranteed jobs or training for young people, and promised to abolish a government scheme that made it easier for small businesses to hire and fire workers. Sarkozy, on the other hand, made no bones about his admiration for the world's more flexible economies: he promised to cut red-tape and taxes, especially for higher income earners, and get around the country's 35-hour week by making overtime easier and more profitable. All this, in order to liberate France's entrepreneurial spirit.

The obvious difference between the candidates probably helped produce a high turnout (85 per cent) and saw a comfortable 53–47 win for Sarkozy, who thereby claimed a mandate to change France (forgetting perhaps that his party and its predecessor had held the presidency for the previous twelve years). Once in power, however, he proved more wary of change and rather keener on less 'Anglo-Saxon' forms of capitalism than his critics feared and his supporters hoped. By the time the next presidential election came round in 2012, he was fighting the election less on the economy and more on law and order and immigration. There was, however, still a clear choice for French voters because his Socialist opponent, François Holland (Royal's ex-partner and the father of her children), nonetheless tried to portray the incumbent as a neoliberal fan of austerity and produced a left-wing programme whose economic and social policies which were every bit as radical (if not more so) than Royal's.

'left' and 'right'. This is just as true in central and eastern Europe, where governments have taken the opportunity offered by majority acceptance that there needed to be at least some reform to put in place multi-tiered (Swedish-style) pension systems that many of their western counterparts are struggling to implement (see Keune, 2006). In Hungary, for instance, it was the ex-communist Socialist Party which, in the mid-1990s, radically reformed the country's pension system, introducing mandatory second-tier private provision (see Deacon, 2000).

Again, this does not necessarily mean that 'right' and 'left' have no meaning. But because Europe's voters seem to want to have it all (for instance, low taxes and early retirement on generous pensions) they have helped create a new division that does, indeed, threaten to go 'beyond left and right'. This is the division between parties and politicians who, however reluctantly, force voters to face up to the impossibility of 'having it all' and those who are prepared to pretend for the sake of office that 'hard choices' can be

avoided (see Box 9.5). Unless voters change, it may be facile (even if very fashionable) to put all the blame for 'the state we're in' on politicians. After all, they are simply trying to make the 'least worst' trade-offs they can between what Europeans want and what they need (see Kitschelt, 2000: 160–66). What Europe's politicians are not doing, however, is taxing much less (see Table 9.1) or spending much less either, whether it be generally (see Table 9.2) or on social protection for their citizens (see Table 9.3, which, note, uses figures – the latest available – which apply to the period before the current economic crisis).

Of course, one can argue that overall tax take is not what is important. What really matters politically is where (or rather who) it is coming from. Perhaps supposedly spineless social democrats are sneakily shifting the overall tax burden away from the forces they were traditionally supposed to be trying to control and on to those who they claimed to be protecting, in other words from capital to labour? In fact, there is little evidence for this: although in most

BOX 9.5

Finally, an honest politician? Who's to blame in Hungary?

In September 2006, Hungary was thrown into turmoil when a radio station played a recording of a speech – made behind closed doors – by Prime Minister, Ferenc Gyurcsany, to his Socialist Party MPs a month or so after his government was re-elected in the spring (for a transcript, see BBC, 2006). In it he admitted, at times in very strong language, that they had spent most of the previous term lying to the electorate about the dire state of the country, afraid to take vital but painful reform measures lest they were thrown out of office. Now, he pleaded with them, they had to get real, tell the truth and implement the programme they'd been preparing in private.

Violent demonstrations against the government erupted in Budapest, spurred on by condemnation from the centre-right opposition, which made the most of the situation in the local elections that followed. The incident seemed to confirm people's worst suspicions of politicians as cheats. But was Mr Gyurcsany really such a villain? Both main parties had promised way more than they could possibly deliver at the general election a few months previously. Nor was it entirely surprising that *Magyar Szocialista Párt* (the Socialist party) had been cagey about pushing through painful measures in the run up to the election, even though it believed they were necessary: in previous spells in office it had done the right thing by the country only to find itself voted out by a population convinced it could have its cake and eat it, too. Indeed, from the first free elections of the early 1990s right up until the election of 2006, no Hungarian government had been able to win itself two consecutive terms. In 2010, however, the Socialists were routed, losing more than half of the 40 per cent vote share they won four years previously – a result which saw them reduced to just under 60 seats and their main opponent, Fidesz able to govern with a majority so big that it could change the country's constitution and other rules of the game almost at will.

The whole affair suggests that the head of the EUs so-called 'Euro-group', ex-prime minister of Luxembourg Jean-Claude Junker was right when he observed, at the height of the continent's economic crisis, that governments normally know what has to be done, but what they don't know is how to get re-elected once they have done it.

Table 9.1 Total tax revenue as a percentage of GDP, 1973–2010

	1973	1981	1986	1995	2004	2010
Sweden	38.8	47.4	49.3	48.5	50.4	45.8
Italy	24.4	31.6	35.9	41.2	41.1	43
France	34	40.9	43.4	44	43.4	42.9
Netherlands	39.8	43	43.4	41.9	37.5	38.2
Germany	33	34.2	34	38.2	34.7	36.3
UK	31.4	36.7	38.2	34.8	36	35
Czech Rep.	n/a	n/a	n/a	40.1	38.4	34.9
Poland	n/a	n/a	n/a	39.6	34.4	31.8
Spain	18	24.3	29.6	32.8	34.8	31.7
Average	31.3	36.9	30.4	40.1	39.0	37.7

Note: Earlier years chosen coincide with EU enlargements. Average is for these core countries.

Source: Data from OECD Revenue Statistics.

Table 9.2 Annual average government expenditure as a percentage of GDP, 1961–2011

	1961–73	1974–85	1986–90	1991–95	1996–2006	2007–2011
France	36.7	n/a	51.4	54	53	55
Sweden	n/a	57.5	57.9	63.8	58.8	52.3
Italy	32.3	43.9	52.2	55.6	48.7	49.7
Netherlands	37.1	53.2	54.9	54.3	46.3	48.9
UK	35.7	49.2	42.5	44.9	41.9	48.5
Germany	n/a	46.6	45	48.6	47.5	45.8
Poland	n/a	n/a	n/a	49.8	44.3	43.8
Spain	n/a	31	41	45.4	39.6	43.2
Czech Rep.	n/a	n/a	n/a	61	43.7	42.9
Average	35.5	46.9	49.3	53.0	47.1	47.8

Note: Average is for these core countries.

Source: Data for 1961–95 from European Commission, DG Economic and Financial Affairs, *European Economy, Statistical Annexe* (Spring 2004). Data for 1996–2011 from *Eurostat*.

Table 9.3 Expenditure on social protection, 1998 and 2008 compared

	1998		2008	
	€ per capita	% of GDP	€ per capita	% of GDP
Sweden	8171	31	8705	30
France	6711	30	8312	31
Germany	6981	29	8101	27
Netherlands	6740	28	9199	28
Italy	4945	25	6102	28
UK	5985	26	6082	26
Spain	2895	20	4412	22
Poland	949	20	1278	19
Czech Rep.	1052	18	2294	18

Notes: No data available for Poland in 1998; figure is for 2000.

Source: Eurostat, http://epp.eurostat.ec.europa.eu/portal/page/portal/social_protection/data/main_tables

European countries revenues from taxing labour have increased from 1970 onwards (from just over 15 per cent of GDP then to around 20 per cent now), mainly in order to pay for welfare expansion, revenue from taxing capital remains pretty much the same (between 5 and 7 per cent of GDP) as it was nearly forty years ago (see Genschel, 2004) – a useful reminder that, sadly (at least for radicals on the left), social democratic governments seeking to build and then maintain welfare states have always preferred, or at least found it easier, to tax ordinary people than large accumulations of wealth, meaning that (see Cusack and Beramendi, 2006). That said, it is true that corporate tax rates (as opposed to revenues) have fallen in Europe (and all over the world) in the last two decades, and research strongly suggests, as globalization theorists argue (see Box 9.6), that these falls were down to governments keen to ensure that their countries were seen by companies as good places in which to do business – a concern shared just as much by left-wing as right-wing governments (Ganghof, 2006). On the other hand, the same research shows that, when it comes to top rates of income tax, which are more obvious to electors and which apply to individual actors who are not always as internationally mobile as is sometimes reported, left-wing parties consistently preferred higher and more progressive taxes than their right wing counterparts.

Privatization

Of course, progressive taxation and support for (as opposed to scepticism towards) the welfare state were not the only touchstones for the centre left:

BOX 9.6

Does globalization render politics powerless and pointless?

Political Scientist Philipp Genschel (2004) observes that 'there are basically three stories about the global-ization-welfare state nexus'.

Globalization theorists assert that globalization opens up economies to the international market and forces them to be more competitive. In order to ensure that their nation can compete, and in order to be able both to attract investment and to borrow money on international markets, governments lose their autonomy and power: they are, in effect, obliged to reduce the tax burden and spend sensibly, meaning that costly welfare programmes have to be cut or, at least, cut back.

Globalization sceptics claim there is precious little evidence of any relationship between increasing inter-national interdependence and welfare strain. In fact, the welfare state has not shrunk, there remain big dif-ferences in welfare spending and delivery between countries that have supposedly been subjected to the same all-consuming pressures and, in many countries, governments are still playing a very active role. Globalization may indeed be going on, but that shouldn't scare governments and voters into thinking pol-itics is powerless or pointless.

Revisionists argue that globalization is real enough, but that it is not the main threat to welfare states. That comes from structural problems caused by, for example, demographic trends and cumbersome and self-defeating government intervention. The ironic – but good – thing about the crisis rhetoric sur-rounding the impact of globalization on the welfare state is that it encourages governments and voters to think that something must be done to tackle the underlying structural problems that are the real issue.

---

there are other indicators we can use to answer the question as to whether politics makes a difference. State involvement in, or even public ownership of, certain key sectors of the economy, for example, was seen by many to be the *sine qua non* of socialism and, therefore, parties on the left. Of course, the extent of state involvement varied not just according to government ideology but also national tradition and each country's 'variety of capitalism' (see Chapter 1) – a variety often bolstered by its legal system: historically, state involvement has tended to be higher in France and in other continental European countries (e.g. Germany) where codified civil law is more important than common law (see Chapter 4 for more on this distinction; see also Bortolotti and Siniscalco, 2004: 49–50). In addition, the capacity to change things (i.e. to 'roll back the state') varies across countries: it might (as in Portugal, France and Germany) necessitate constitu-tional change or involve getting agreement among institutions (second chambers, powerful regional governments, presidents, the public through referen-dums) that in some countries (Italy, Germany,

France, and Switzerland, for example) are powerful 'veto players' but in others (the UK, for instance) either don't exist or don't matter. However, there are good reasons to think that more right-wing political parties would favour reducing state involvement and therefore be keen on privatization (the transfer of state assets into private hands most commonly achieved by selling shares in those assets with the proceeds going to the government). Parties of the right believe, after all, in the market as the most effi-cient way of providing for people's needs and wants,

KEY POINT

Left and right can at times do things that look very similar but that does not mean that they are the same and that it makes no difference which side is in power. The selling-off of state-owned enter-prises is another case in point. Left wing govern-ments have privatized not so much because (like right-wing governments) they were ideologically committed to the policy but rather because they needed the money.

and they were in part created to defend the sanctity of private property. It is also possible that, by creating a 'share-owning democracy' or 'popular capitalism' via selling off state-owned enterprises (SOEs) to the general public, they might boost support for their values in the electorate.

In the postcommunist countries of course, as we suggested in Chapter 1, privatization was a crucial part of the move away from the party-state past: outside Romania and Bulgaria (though they are now 'catching up') most governments (even those run by communist successor parties) showed themselves to be reasonably keen 'systemic' privatizers (see Box 9.7). In the West, public ownership was clearly far less important than it was in the Soviet bloc, but the decision on whether to reduce or maintain it was theoretically no less political: the left should, on the face of it, have tried to block privatization and the right should have been associated with promoting it. Given, then, that privatization, after being pioneered in the 1980s by the UK's Conservative government, supposedly took off all over Europe, we would seem to have a *prima facie* case not so much for convergence between right and left but at least for the ideological dilution of the latter. So what is the evidence? Is there a clear correlation between a country being run by right-wing governments and it 'selling off the family silver' (see Boix, 1998) – a correlation that would suggest that partisan differences are still meaningful? Or is privatization a game that all governments play irrespective of which parties are in power, indicating that rhetorical differences between left and right matter very little in practice?

Sophisticated statistical analysis by Zohlnhöfer and Obinger (2006) suggests that in the countries that made up the EU before the 2004 and 2007 enlargements, privatization receipts between 1990 and 2000 were – perhaps unsurprisingly – largest in those countries where the state sector (and economic regulation more generally) had initially been most significant. Institutions also mattered: receipts were lower where there were more 'veto players'; namely, in countries with an important upper house of parliament and in federal countries. Interestingly, however, neither trade union density nor constitutional constraints appeared to exert much of a restraining effect. In addition, the findings suggested that budget deficits – especially at a time when the

pressure to get them down in order to qualify for the single currency was intense – were an important driver of privatization (Clifton *et al.,* 2006; Parker, 1998). They are likely to be all the more important now: indeed, it is noticeable that the reform programmes agreed by troubled European countries with institutions like the EU and the IMF almost always include a commitment to sell off underperforming (or simply revenue-raising) state assets.

On the question of whether privatization was more associated with right-wing than with left-wing governments, however, the results of research have been less clear – at least for the EU countries. In the OECD as a whole, there was a statistically significant relationship between the ideological complexion of governments and the amount of privatization business countries did. In the EU, it was only towards the end of the period – specifically once the decision had been made that every member state that wanted to adopt the euro had brought its deficit sufficiently under control to allow it to do so – that the association between centre-right government and privatization receipts was unambiguous. This led the researchers to conclude in a manner that supports the idea that left and right – and, indeed, politics and political institutions in general – still matter. Social democratic parties, they note, 'are indeed ready to sell off SOE[s] when under intense fiscal strain, but ... they – in contrast to bourgeois [i.e. centre-right] parties – do not regard this policy as an effective instrument to enhance economic growth and thus abstain from using it in the absence of fiscal problems'. In short, selling off state assets 'was not caused by a fundamental change of the ideological positions concerning privatization on the part of left parties'. And both the extent to which it was done and the extent to which it could be done did, indeed, depend not just on economic pressures but also on countries' arrangements – no one should expect a country like Germany, for instance, whose federal system means power (and, indeed, ownership) is shared between the centre and the regions, and between the executive and the legislature, to be the world's biggest privatizer.

Given the obstacles – ideological and institutional – it is not surprising, then, that privatization has not proceeded quite as rapidly as some would like and has often taken place in stages rather than as a 'big bang'. On the other hand, it has happened. For

---

BOX 9.7

Privatization as politics

Privatization can be motivated by politics rather than pure economic theory. These political motives are often mixed, but can be analytically separated as follows.

Systemic privatization hopes to alter a country's socio-economic and political environment fundamentally by reducing the state's role (and people's expectations of the state's role) in it. The privatization programmes of CEE and, to a lesser extent, those of southern Europe before it, could be labelled 'systemic'. So, too, could those pursued towards the end of the 1980s and the early 1990s by the Thatcher and Major governments of the UK; they also aimed at the reduction of the power of organized labour, which is often at its strongest in the public sector.

Tactical privatization, by contrast, is mainly about achieving the short-term, often electoral, goals of parties, politicians and the interest groups that support them. The adoption of privatization by centre-right politicians in France during the late 1980s was driven by a desire to distinguish themselves from their Socialist opponents, as well as the need to reward key supporters. The revenue thus gained, however, allowed the government to finance measures to combat unemployment (and, ironically, to keep afloat other state-owned holdings) that otherwise it would have had trouble affording.

Pragmatic privatization is even more ad hoc and often crisis-driven: governments simply need the money to offset debt or public spending and are prepared to override even their own reservations in order to get it, especially because selling off SOEs can be politically easier than raising taxes or restraining public sector pay. The privatization that went on in European countries in the late 1990s was one way of ensuring that countries such as Italy qualified for entry into the single currency – a process that required them to bring their budget deficits, their debt and their current spending into line with agreed norms. Privatizations carried out by centre-left governments in France and Germany also qualify as pragmatic.

Source: Based on discussion in Feigenbaum *et al.* (1998).

---

instance, the nominally socialist government of France in the late 1990s introduced the 35-hour-week, spent millions on public schemes to reduce unemployment, upped welfare benefits, and was distinctly lukewarm about the 'Third Way' touted by its British and German counterparts (Clift, 2001, 2002). But, as it worked hard to qualify for the euro, it chose (rather than, say, raising taxes on the middle classes) to preside over what was the biggest sell-off of state assets in the country's history. Even though many of them were only part-sales (the state continued to hold majority stakes in France Télécom and Air France, for instance, and still owned a quarter of well-known car-maker, Renault), the Jospin government raised over €30 billion between 1997 and 2002. The left-wing government in Italy, at the same time, also sold off state assets in a desperate, and ultimately successful (if not entirely convincing),

attempt to bring down its budget deficit in order to squeak into the single currency.

Those who are sceptical about the continued difference between left and right also point out that, even if the economy forced social democrats into something they would not otherwise have done, they have done nothing to reverse the trend once those pressures have come off. Others would see this criticism as unfair and unrealistic. Compensating shareholders would cost a fortune. And international financial markets seem to take a dim view of any government going against neoliberal orthodoxy, even if there is evidence that organizations such as the World Bank, IMF and the OECD were beginning to question some of that orthodoxy's component parts even before the current crisis (see Deacon, 2005) – a crisis that has resulted, too, in some questioning whether that orthodoxy is inimical to the resumption of growth. Attempting, therefore, to turn back the clock would be insane. Neither, it has to be said, is there any evidence that private business provides any worse a service than the state for consumers, and therefore voters, some of whom (though often fewer than is imagined and certainly fewer than in the USA) now hold shares.

In other words, one does not need to posit some sort of damascene conversion to gung-ho neoliberalism on the part of the mainstream left in Europe to understand privatization (and the unwillingness to reverse it) was driven by instrumental rather than ideological motives (see Box 9.7) – not least the desire to join the euro. Indeed, there was another EU motive, too. This was the need to respond to demands (expressed through the European Commission, but coming from corporations in countries that had already privatized such sectors) that states open up their telecoms and energy markets to competition. Such demands were designed to kick-start the so-called 'Lisbon process' by which European leaders – left and right – rather ambitiously promised at a summit in Portugal in March 2001 to make the EU economy the world's most competitive and dynamic economy by 2010 (see Wincott, 2003).

In fact, privatization is rarely so thoroughgoing as media headlines might suggest or true believers might want. We noted in Chapter 1 that, even in the keenest postcommunist states, sell-offs, irrespective of whether they are ultimately beneficial (see Gould, 2011), are still by no means always complete and often proceed in stages. The same is true for countries in western Europe. For instance, Norway seemed to stand out among Scandinavian countries as a keen privatizer, raising approximately €1.5 billion from the sale of shares in its fantastically wealthy Statoil company and almost €500 million from a massively oversubscribed sale of shares in Den Norske Bank in 2001. But, even after the latter sale, the state continued to own 47 per cent of the shares and, in the case of the former, still controlled a full 80 per cent. The centre-right government that took over from the Labour government that sold those assets did not, in fact, go much further because both right- and left-wing politicians are sensitive to voter opposition to the foreign takeover of domestic firms – something a continuing controlling share on the part of the state can prevent.

This kind of 'economic nationalism' is still important in other European countries, notably France. But in other countries, too, governments supposedly keen to privatize surreptitiously left the state in *de facto* control by awarding it a 'golden share' that allowed it to intervene, for example, to block a takeover bid. Indeed, the technique originated in the 'home' of privatization, the UK, in the 1980s. Recently, however, the British government, and governments in Germany, Italy, the Netherlands and Spain, have been taken to task over the practice by the European Commission. In May 2003, the ECJ ruled that both the UK and Spain, which had owned 'golden shares' in numerous companies that had supposedly been set free by privatization, would have to give them up. The only justification for such shares will henceforth be confined to enterprises involving national security considerations – a definition which, judging by experience, will probably be stretched to the limit.

We should also note that there has been a considerable slowdown in privatization since the peak of the process in the late 1990s, both in the number of sales taking place and in terms of value. This is due, in part, to the economic slowdown that struck large parts of the world's economy (i.e. Asia and the USA, as well as Europe) and sent share markets downwards. Sensible governments postponed asset sales in the hope that they would find a better price in the future. The slowdown in privatization in Europe is also due to the rather prosaic fact that much of what can easily be sold has, in many countries, already been offloaded. To coin a phrase, many of the 'cash cows' have gone and only the 'lame ducks' remain.

European governments are also having to face the fact that some sectors might simply be too risky (strategically or financially) to privatize – at least, to privatize fully. True, this does not mean a complete halt to private-sector involvement in previously state-run areas. For instance, the UK Labour government elected in 1997 initially disappointed those observers who hoped it would carry on where its pro-privatization Conservative predecessor had left off: the not-very-successful part-privatization of the air-traffic control system was about as far as it went. However, it also angered left-wing critics with its enthusiasm for 'public–private' financing (PFI, the Private Finance Initiative), whereby the private sector builds roads, transport systems, prisons and (increasingly) hospitals which are then leased back to the state. Yet even under that government, one can argue that things went backwards. In 2001, for example, the UK government had to re-establish state ownership (albeit via a not-for-profit company) of the railway track operations that a Conservative government had privatized in the early 1990s. Interestingly, nobody suggested that this *de facto* 'renationalization' was a sign that 'New' Labour was returning to its socialist roots. It might not be any more accurate, then, to see its plans to involve the private sector in public projects as proof that it has sold its soul to neoliberalism.

By the same token, it is easy to pick up on headlines that seem to suggest that, 'at last', privatization is embedding itself in countries that have a tradition of what neoliberals would see as 'state meddling' in the business sector. Thus, much is made of Germany's grand coalition's apparent desire to float Deutsche Bahn, which is now not just a railway but also a highly profitable logistics and freight business. But the culture of state involvement is very strong in many countries, especially in France, despite the liberal hopes that the EU will undermine it in the long term (see Cole, 1999; Cole and Drake, 2000). Nicolas Sarkozy might have won the French presidency in 2007 by promising to liberalize the economy (see Box 9.3), but only a few years before, as Finance Minister, he famously prevented the Swiss pharmaceuticals giant Novartis from gatecrashing a merger between Aventis and Sanofi, two French firms that together could create a French 'national champion' to compete on the global stage. Sarkozy also bailed out Alstom (the trains, turbines and ship maker) by converting an €800 million loan it had been granted into a government shareholding worth just over 30 per cent.

In fact, what in EU jargon is called 'state aid' is not confined to France, even though, on balance, it has declined in the last decade. That said, a study completed before the recent downturn (Curzon Price, 2004) noted while it was 'gradually being brought under control ... most governments find it difficult to relinquish this instrument of policy'. It also noted that the European Commission 'still has problems enforcing discipline on member states' and predicted – very presciently given what some would regard as the inordinate bail-outs and guarantees provided to banks by governments (see Box 9.8) –

that that any decline could still be put at risk in an economic downturn.

Flexible labour markets?

One of the other key shifts in economic and social policy since the 1970s has been a de-emphasis of 'demand-side' solutions to unemployment towards 'supply-side' measures and 'smart' welfare states that help people into, rather than holding them back from, employment. The former attempted to use Keynesian government spending to smooth out the business cycle and offset recessions (see Chapter 1). Supply-side solutions, however, concentrate on removing rigidities in the labour market. These rigidities include 'excessive' worker protection or bureaucratic benefits systems that put people off taking up offers of work. Supply-side measures also focus on providing education and skills training the better to equip firms and people to adjust to economic change. Generally, it is governments of the right that are most associated with a desire to move towards more 'flexible labour markets'. For example, despite the general strike staged by Italian unions against such policies in April 2002, Silvio Berlusconi's centre-right administration could claim a mandate for trying to untangle the mass of laws and regulations that some would argue protect the rights of those with a job at the cost of those trying to get one. It was also a centre-right government in France that tried to do something about the country's high rate of unemployment among the under-25s (one in five of whom are jobless) by introducing the CPE (*le contrat de première embauche* or first employment contract). This was designed to make it easier for companies to hire (because they knew they could also more easily fire) workers, albeit one that was strangled at birth by street demonstrations and sit-ins by the very young people it was apparently supposed to help.

KEY POINT

The embrace by social democrats of the idea of flexible labour markets as a sensible supply-side response to unemployment and the need for a competitive economy is not necessarily a new departure in a right-wing direction.

BOX 9.8

Ireland: not so much the government as the banks – and perhaps the people too

Apart from Greece and Spain, the two European countries worst affected by the global financial meltdown were Iceland and Ireland, which was awarded a bail-out of €85 billion from the Eurozone. The contrast between them is instructive. Iceland essentially bit the bullet and allowed its banks to crash, doing little more than guaranteeing the savings of ordinary people and trying, not altogether satisfactorily, to help out those in other countries (notably the UK and the Netherlands) into which its banks had expanded – a decision which led to considerable political turmoil but seems to have worked out much better than many expected economically (for the background, see Tranøy, 2011). In Ireland, things were very different.

It is important to realize that the Irish government (like the government of Spain, another country in a lot of trouble) did not get into difficulties because, like Greece, it had been living beyond its means. Ireland, like Spain, had a healthy public debt-to-GDP ratio and was not routinely running deficits. When the financial crisis began in 2007, Ireland's debt was running at 28 per cent of GDP and its deficit was less than half of one per cent; Spain was likewise well within the 60 per cent and 3 per cent ceiling set by EU rules, its debt coming in at 42 per cent and its deficit at just under 2 per cent; the figures for Greece were 104 per cent and 4 per cent. Instead, the Irish government's problems stem, firstly, from its failure (one shared with its Spanish counterpart) to do anything about the property bubble and the related private sector debt that had built up and, secondly (and even more catastrophically), its decision to guarantee the deposits of Irish banks which, as the economy headed south, were left holding billions of euros' worth of loans that would almost certainly never be repaid and themselves owing some €500 billion to other European banks, especially in Germany and the UK. It was this, and the money pumped into the banks and used to set up the state's National Asset Management Agency to buy all their bad loans, that blew a massive hole in the government's finances and forced it to request EU help, in turn resulting in the requirement to make huge cuts in public spending and some increases in taxation to repair the damage. Put bluntly, Ireland is in trouble because its politicians, fearing a run on the country's banks, turned private sector liabilities into public liabilities. However, those who complain that it is the taxpayer who is left to pick up the tab conveniently forget that many (though by no means all) of those taxpayers played a part – albeit as individuals a small one – in creating the speculative, credit-driven boom which helped cause the country's problems in the first place. The same is true in Spain, although few believe that that they, any more than ordinary Irish people, deserved the austerity programme foisted on them by a government which decided that prolonged and painful recession was ultimately preferable to the country defaulting on its debts.

There is no doubt, however, that some social democratic parties, though not all of them, have been part of this shift, or that much has been made (by both critics and fans) of their going with the flow instead of trying to stem the tide. Much to the chagrin of its union backers, for instance, the UK's Labour government made it clear on assuming office in 1997 that, like its Conservative predecessor, it would not allow the EU to re-regulate the country's comparatively unregulated labour market. Meanwhile, the SPD–Green government in Germany tinkered with that country's heavily bureaucratic and heavily taxed labour market. Its *Agenda 2010* package, announced in the spring of 2003, was designed to make it more tempting for small and medium-sized enterprises (SMEs) to take on workers and to ease rules on collective bargaining. These changes (plus following the UK down the road of making it harder for unemployed people repeatedly to refuse offers of work) seem, along with wage restraint and an economic upturn, to have begun to make a dent in the country's high unemployment rate. That lesson, plus the fact that most central and eastern European countries which joined the EU in 2004 tend (at least on balance) to line up with countries that prefer the more liberal version of capitalism favoured by the UK to the more regulated version traditionally associated with more corporatist countries (see Copeland, 2012), means that supply-side measures may well become increasingly popular across the continent – and of course that attempts to provide, say, greater protection to workers at the European level are less likely to succeed.

The adoption of supply-side measures, however, should not be taken as proof that differences between right and left have disappeared. The evidence suggests that the social democratic version of supply-side policies – which some see as the essence of the 'Third Way' (see Green-Pedersen *et al.*, 2001) – can be quite different to the version preferred by the right. Unlike the centre-left, the centre-right has tended not to balance deregulation with more spending on human capital (see Boix, 1998). Social democrats in countries such as the Netherlands might not grab the headlines like their counterparts in the UK or Germany, but they have long demonstrated there is nothing inherently 'right-wing' about a shift to supply-side policies (see Hemerijck and Visser, 2001). If there were, then we would have to re-write the record on what is widely acknowledged to be Europe's (not to say the world's) most persistently 'social democratic country' (Box 9.9).

In any case, even if we look at (say) Labour, in the UK, which has gone further than many of its centre-left counterparts in embracing deregulation, we see a government that extended trade union recognition, a government that for the first time ever brought in a minimum wage and a government that was regularly attacked by employers' organizations for introducing too much worker protection. We also see a government that signed up to the EU's 'Social Chapter' – a measure that allows some EU labour law (examples so far include maximum working hours and rights for part-time workers) to be made by union–employer agreement (see Chapter 8). On the other hand, as if determined to make itself difficult to pigeonhole, the Labour government, since signing, did its best to limit 'European interference' in labour market matters, claiming that light-touch' regulation is one of the keys to the UK's relatively

---

> ## BOX 9.9
>
> ## Supply-side social democracy in Sweden
>
> Social democratic Sweden's relative economic success has long been underpinned by supply-side policies and, in particular, an 'active labour market policy' through which the state provided a safety net, social services and skills development that would allow people and firms to adjust swiftly to changes in the international markets. This also had the considerable economic advantage of maximizing women's employability. In recent years, Sweden has looked less immune than previously to recession, and social democratic led governments have had little compunction in slowing the growth of welfare spending, not least on pensions. They have also, like Labour in the UK, granted independence to the central bank to set interest rates. Indeed, they have gone further than their UK counterparts by cutting income tax and privatizing the Swedish postal service in order to allow it to compete more efficiently in Europe. The so-called 'people's home' might not be quite what it used to be, but few accuse Sweden, or the party that has run it for so long (the SAP), of a comprehensive betrayal of the ideals of social democracy. None of this, of course, is any guarantee of continued support for the SAP. Indeed, its failure, notwithstanding the above, to make more of a dent in unemployment, combined with the centre-right parties' decision to publish a joint manifesto which made clear they were not intending to undermine the welfare state, turned the general election of 2006 into that rare thing – a defeat for the Swedish social democrats.

---

low unemployment. It has also attempted to 'upload' its ideas into EU discourse by encouraging other countries to follow its liberalizing lead. The relatively residual nature (see Chapter 1) of the British welfare state, however, means that fellow EU members with more generous systems seem likely to look more favourably at the 'flexicurity' – the use of a comprehensive welfare state combined with liberal labour laws to promote a responsive economy pioneered by Denmark and the Netherlands (European Commission, 2007; see also Campbell and Pedersen, 2007; Gualmini and Rhodes, 2011: 185–6).

Interestingly, just as not every centre-left government in Europe resists labour market liberalization, especially when they are worried about economic growth, some centre-right governments actually end up legislating for greater regulation – at least at the margin, and most labour market reform actually does turn out to be a marginal affair rather than some sort of slash and burn exercise (see Avdagic, 2013). On the face of it, this 'role reversal' suggests that traditional ideas about what left and right do are, indeed, outmoded. Indeed, one can become even more cynical when one realizes that, although this happens when the two sides are in government, in opposition the left protests against liberalization while the right is all for it! Examined more closely, however, the picture is (as usual) a little more complicated. True, as we have already noted, there is something of a consensus that overly-protected labour markets can damage an economy and increase unemployment. But left-wing parties in government, it seems, are rather more likely to do deals with trade unions on the issue so that a reduction in employment protection is balanced by, say, a

---

BOX 9.10

It takes two to tangle: Greece (and Germany)

When the global financial crisis first began to unfold in 2007 and 2008, a number of commentators and politicians put the blame on the 'casino capitalism' which they believed was characteristic of the United States and the United Kingdom. Continental European countries, whose financial and banking systems were supposedly better regulated and inherently more conservative, would, they believed, prove more resilient. With the odd exception – Finland, for instance – they were wrong. In some countries – Ireland being the most obvious (see Box 9.8) – banks had been instrumental in creating a property boom that rapidly turned into a bust, leaving them massively exposed to debt that would never be repaid. In others, they had been lending to companies, individuals, banks and governments in other member states, many of whom were now going to find it difficult if not impossible to keep up their payments. The Greek government in particular had (along with banks in Spain, Portugal, and Ireland) used cheap money provided by German, French and other banks to make up for its failure either to collect sufficient tax revenue or to cut public sector wage costs. Until the economic crisis began to hit home in 2008, this arrangement had suited everyone: banks all over Europe had money to lend; Greece wanted to borrow it; and financial markets assumed that, in the supposedly unlikely event that it ran into trouble, it would somehow be bailed out by the European Union; after all, the most powerful country in the EU, Germany, knew full well that its banks were amongst the most at risk were Greece or any other country to default on their loans (see Jones, 2011).

In fact, the markets had long suspected that the Greece had hidden the true size of its deficit and were not entirely surprised when the country's new centre-left PASOK government, upon winning the election in October 2009, announced that the figure was much higher than its centre-right predecessor had admitted. What began to worry them, however, was that Germany and other creditor nations, rather than providing the kind of reassurances that they had always issued before, chose instead to criticize the new Greek government, warning that it could not simply rely on foreign assistance in order to avoid painful structural adjustment and the possibility of IMF supervision. Suddenly, the interest rates paid by Greece to borrow more money on the markets increased, and the prospect of a Greek default began to be seriously discussed. In spite of this, German politicians carried on criticizing, hoping perhaps to placate an electorate whipped up by tabloid tales of lazy Greeks living beyond their means and off the backs of hard working northern Europeans – tales which conveniently forgot the fact that Greeks on average work longer than Germans and that Germany had been happy enough to set aside Eurozone rules when it had suited it to do so (see Box 9.12).

compensatory increase in unemployment benefits. Meanwhile the enactment of greater regulation by right-wing parties in government comes about, at least in part, because they are complying with EU regulations.

The EU to the rescue?

In fact, the EU is a key factor in any discussion of the triumph (or otherwise) of liberal capitalism and the constraints it imposes on supposedly sovereign governments – all the more so in the wake of bail-outs for certain countries (most obviously Greece: see Box 9.10) being made conditional on them following a prescribed programme of reforms, repayments and reductions in spending. Even before that, the EU helped provide a framework of binding legislation and decision rules within which both economic and political activity in European countries must take place, as well as an arena in which politicians and the representatives of interest groups articulate their views and attempt to move that framework in their desired direction. It also – and this should never be forgotten amid all the talk of globalization – helps constitute what for all

Questioned by YouGov at the end of June 2012 just 11 per cent thought 'Germany should be as generous as possible, to help countries in difficulty, as the collapse of the euro would be bad for Germany and bad for Europe.' Some 44 per cent thought 'Germany should support other countries but impose strict conditions, and accept that if these conditions are not met, the Eurozone might break up.' Even more ominously, 37 per cent thought 'Germany has done enough; we should not spend more money to help countries in difficulty and instead allow the Eurozone to break up'. Hardly surprising, then, that Chancellor Merkel, the German prime minister, talked tough. And she was not just concerned about domestic public opinion and the bad example Greece might set to other, much bigger, debtor nations who might conclude that they could get away without reforms because, ultimately, Germany would prefer to see European debt 'mutualized' than the Eurozone break up. Just as worrying was the fact that bail-outs triggered a challenge – although in the end an unsuccessful one – in the Federal Republic's powerful Constitutional Court (see Chapter 3).

As the situation worsened through 2010, it became obvious that some form of assistance would be needed if Greece were to be saved from default and exit from the Eurozone, after which, it was feared, the markets would turn their attention to countries like Spain and even Italy – countries whose private and public sector debts to German and other banks were so vast that they were simply 'too big to fail'. That assistance was eventually forthcoming in a bail-out package worth € 110 billion for Greece, but came with crucial strings attached, namely the insistence that the Greek government, policed by both the EU and the IMF, put together (and, worse, show signs of actually implementing) an austerity package that would inevitably plunge the country even deeper into recession. However, even this proved insufficient to completely calm the markets – in part because they doubted the ability of Greek politicians to persuade their voters (some of whom were already protesting on the streets) to accept such a package, in part because politicians in other countries (most obviously Germany) clearly thought that a Greek exit from the Eurozone (quickly dubbed 'Grexit') might be both possible and desirable, and in part because it looked as if there might be a limit to the willingness of taxpayers to carry the losses of bondholders and banks. A second bail-out (worth € 109 billion) was agreed in July 2011. After two knife-edge general elections held in Greece in quick succession in 2012, Greek politicians put together a coalition between the centre-right New Democracy, the ailing, centre-left Pasok, and the more radical (but not populist) Democratic Left. Whether this would be able to take sufficiently strong measures to persuade the markets of their intent was debated all over Europe.

European countries has become by far their biggest market (see Chapter 1).

The EU seems to get it in the neck from both sides of the left–right divide. On the one hand, neoliberals characterize it as a self-delusionary refuge from the bracing winds of globalization – a supplier of subsidies to sectors and states that should have woken up and smelled the coffee ages ago, and which would be in less trouble now if they had done. Seeing the EU's commitment to enforcing fair competition (Box 9.11) as a mere sideshow, they also see it as a bastion of 'continental corporatism' (see Chapter 8), whose support for labour and environmental standards and excessive product regulation risks clogging up still further the arteries of an already ailing European economy, even if carefully targeted 'structural funding' to economically backward regions may just about make sense if it focuses on improving infrastructure and human capital.

On the other hand, their left-wing opponents see the EU as a potentially anti-democratic (and anti-social democratic) attempt to embed or institutionalize neoliberalism that has taken on its own momentum – a momentum that the largely domestic focus of Europe's centre-left, which actually encompasses a variety of views on the role and future of the EU (see Dimitrakopoulos, 2010) is likely to prevent it doing much about, even assuming it wanted to (see McGowan, 2001). To these radical critics, the EU is the creation of politicians who are convinced that there is no alternative, yet sceptical about their own ability (or the ability of their counterparts in other countries) to persuade their voters of the case. The key to this project, the argument runs, is a single market that encourages capital, among other things, to relocate to where labour is cheapest, regulation is lightest and taxes are lowest, in so doing forcing governments to 'shrink' the state in order to ensure that their country remains an attractive place in which to do business (see Box 9.11). Also vital to any such project is the single currency.

The run-up to joining the euro was supposed to oblige Europe's overspending governments to tighten their belts by forcing them to meet 'convergence criteria' (set levels of debt, deficit and inflation) in order to qualify. And, when the single currency was adopted, it meant governments surrendering control of interest rates to the European Central Bank (ECB) (see Chapter 2), thus depriving them of an important tool of economic policy and control. At the same time, their new-found inability to devalue their currencies in order to adjust to balance of payments problems was designed to force them into structural measures (such as squeezing real wages and taxes, and introducing supply-side measures) to regain international competitiveness. Moreover, in order to ensure that all countries in the 'Eurozone' (the name given to the collection of states that have adopted the euro) played the game and preserved the credibility of the new currency, they had to sign up to the Stability and Growth Pact (SGP), policed by the Commission (see Box 9.12; Heipertz and Verdun, 2003; Howarth, 2004). This was supposed to stop them building up debts and deficits by, for example, countercyclical spending to offset a Eurozone ('one-size-fits-all') interest rate that might be set so high that it risked choking off their economic growth. In the event, although there is some evidence that EMU may have exerted some downward pressure on spending (see Keman, 2010), the pact was never properly enforced (see Box 9.12), and there were more instances of interest rates being too low than too high, therefore encouraging excessive borrowing (sometimes by the private sector, sometimes by high spending governments and sometimes by both) and, especially in countries like Ireland and Spain, a speculative property boom that eventually turned into a bust.

At the beginning of the global financial crisis in 2007 the coordination between the ECB, member states and their central banks was actually quite impressive: along with the Commission dropping its normal objections to state aid, it proved sufficient to stave off what might otherwise have been a continent-wide banking collapse. The real problem came when an already difficult situation developed into a sovereign debt crisis as the cost to states of bank bail-outs and decreasing economic activity became ever-more apparent. Those countries less directly affected, especially Germany, seemed determined to

BOX 9.11

EU competition and deregulation – just good for business or good for people, too?

The European Commission is committed to opening up competition in sectors where, traditionally, firms (and governments) have hidden behind national barriers in order to keep competitors out and prices up. Very often it will give a sector a chance to dismantle those barriers itself. But, if necessary, it will legislate them away. Recent years have seen the EU taking action to cap and reduce roaming charges that meant excessively expensive international calls, after the mobile operators in question dragged their feet on a voluntary agreement. European legislation, too, has been brought in (albeit with national governments – even Eurosceptic governments like the British – claiming the credit) to protect online consumers against websites which were obliging customers to untick (rather than tick) boxes offering expensive, additional services – a practice much favoured by budget airlines. The EU has also gone into battle against the software behemoth, Microsoft, fining and forcing it unbundle its offer to consumers.

So, is this neoliberalism in action or unwarranted interference in the affairs of legitimate businesses? If it is the former, it is difficult to see how it harms the people who opponents of the free-market claim to be trying to protect, most of whom presumably benefit from not being ripped off. And what of left and right in all this? Clearly, the willingness and ability of the Commission to take action is an example of politics winning out over the market. But it is also operating on an essentially pro-market agenda – the same one that drove the Commission's desire to open up Europe's hugely important service sector to the same kind of cross-border competition that manufacturing has had to get used to. Trade unions worried about companies based in other European countries that would, under the Commission's proposals, only have to meet the standards imposed in those countries rather than the one they were operating in, forcing down pay and conditions – or simply taking the jobs to countries where they were already lower. There were also concerns that workers in the service sector would be undercut by migrants from the new member states – concerns that crystallized around *le plombier polonais* (Polish plumber) who EU commissioner Frits Bolkestein, in charge of the Commission's Services Directive, said he'd like to hire to help out at his second home in France!

Some on the left took the trade unions' side and, as we saw in Chapter 8, the directive was diluted so as to exclude certain key publicly provided services. Others, however, made the point that inefficient and overly expensive services – whether public or private – were of no great benefit to the ordinary people social democrats were supposed to represent: moreover, it was better that over-protected and over-paid workers be encouraged to do deals to prevent their employers moving production to other EU countries rather than, in the long-run, see their jobs simply exported to other parts of the globe. And, they argued, denying the chance of earning better salaries and working in better conditions to hundreds of thousands of poor people in CEE was hardly progressive either. Interestingly, many supposedly Eurosceptic politicians of a conservative persuasion didn't seem too exercised about this particular piece of Brussels 'interference' in domestic affairs and, indeed, complained when the directive was watered down. National sovereignty, it seems, doesn't always trump ideology.

make an example of those countries – most obviously, Greece (see Box 9.10) – that had run into trouble rather than making clear right at the start that they would be helped. As a result, the 'contagion' (namely, market anxieties about government default, which then pushed up the cost of funding debt and deficits) spread to other countries, most obviously Portugal and Ireland (which, as a result, both introduced swingeing austerity programmes) but also – and more dangerously because because

BOX 9.12

Big stick or big joke? The EU's SGP

Under the terms of the Stability and Growth Pact, Eurozone countries are not supposed to run budget deficits of more than 3 per cent of GDP. If they do, they are eventually liable to fines payable to the European Commission. However, it is not the Commission but the other member states, acting through the Council of Ministers, that decide on punishment. So far, they have proved reluctant to allow the Commission to do anything other than issue warnings and reprimands. One of these, issued in 2001, was enough to make Portugal cut spending in order to keep below the ceiling in 2002. Since then, however, the failure to take action against Germany and France, the most persistent offender, has rendered the Pact something of a laughing stock – so much so that, in 2004, six of the twelve Eurozone countries (France, Germany, Greece, Italy, the Netherlands and a rather bitter Portugal!) looked set to breach the rules. The Commission responded by taking the Council of Finance Ministers to the ECJ for failure to act. In July 2004, the ECJ found in favour of the Commission, although this 'moral victory' became something of a pyrrhic one when it was rendered partially redundant by a review of the pact in the spring of 2005 that made it easier for countries to claim temporary exemptions from the 3 per cent rule. Given all this, it is understandable why some of the Eurozone states in so much trouble after 2010 found being lectured on sticking to the rules by Germany and France somewhat difficult to swallow. Arguably, however, the SGP lives on – as part of the Fiscal Compact to which the majority of member states (with the notable exception of the UK) signed up in December 2011, those countries are now committed to sign the EU's debt and deficit ceilings into domestic law. Whether that will ensure that this time they are not breached is anyone's guess.

sequences of which would be catastrophic even for countries which themselves were not in danger of default.

As the risk of one or more of the kind of defaults whose consequences no member state (even those outside of the Eurozone) could escape became greater and greater, the political leaders of Europe began – too slowly some would say – to respond more robustly. The first substantial measure was the announcement in May 2010 of the European Financial Stability Facility (EFSF) as a temporary arrangement outside the Treaties to provide billions of euros of loan finance (€440bn from EU countries, €250bn from the IMF) to countries unable to raise it on the markets sufficiently cheaply via bonds guaranteed by Eurozone members (though not, as some argued would simply have to happen in the end by the EU as a whole). This, and some rather vague promises of greater fiscal coordination between Eurozone countries, was then followed in March 2011 by a supposedly permanent European Stability Mechanism (ESM). Next came a Fiscal Compact (not, because of UK objections, a treaty) negotiated in December 2011 establishing greater EU surveillance of members' budgetary plans (see Box 9.12). This appealed not just in Germany but also smaller, poorer member states which understandably chafed at having to help out Greece when the latter was clearly unwilling or unable to take the medicine that they themselves had swallowed in order to survive the global financial crisis: Slovakia and the Baltic states (all three of which slashed jobs and welfare benefits in order to remain competitive) are obvious cases in point. Doubtless some countries signed up simply because they could see little alternative: indeed in its final shape the agreement came into force when 12 of the 17 Eurozone countries ratified, while it was made clear that any country who chose not to ratify would not be receiving any new bail-outs.

Meanwhile, the ECB began, effectively, to provide a measure of so-called quantitative easing in order to increase liquidity, although the scope of its intervention plus the lack of a massive fiscal stimulus package, meant efforts to jump-start the continent's economy were as nothing to those made by the supposedly 'neoliberal' US federal government, notwithstanding the fact that (partly as a consequence) its fiscal position grew worse than that of

their economies are so much bigger – Spain and Italy. Fears then mounted that this might lead not only to Greece leaving the Eurozone but to the breakup of the zone altogether, the immediate con-

many European countries. The ECB also began in the summer of 2011 to intervene in the bond markets to try to reduce Spanish and Italian borrowing costs and from the beginning of 2012 began making trillions of euros worth of low-interest loans to banks all over Europe. In September, its governer, Mario Draghi, went even further, announcing a new programme (called 'outright monetary transactions' or OMTs) of supposedly unlimited buying of short-term bonds from governments (like Spain's) which were currently paying over the odds to service their debts and which were prepared to apply for a bail-out to which 'strict and effective' conditions would be attached. In so doing, the ECB effectively declared itself a credible 'lender of last resort' – about the only thing capable of calming markets.

The EU (or at least the Eurozone) has also taken a serious step toward a banking union, first, by allowing European money to go directly to banks in difficulty rather than insisting it go first through member-state governments and, second, by declaring that the ECB should become the single supervisor for banking across the 17 member states which use the euro. Moreover, the Europeanization of financial market regulation did get under way, albeit without attracting much attention, and subject to national derogations, with the setting up of the European Securities and Markets Authority, the European Banking Authority and the European Insurance and Occupational Pensions Authority, with an overarching European Systemic Risk Board, chaired by the ECB – none of which is a bad idea given the role that private-sector, as opposed to public-sector, debt played in the economic difficulties suffered by so many European countries. At the same time, the Commission and the European Council have cobbled together a new growth strategy, 'EU2020', which stresses the need for coordinated supply-side reforms (for which read deregulation as well as an emphasis on education and R&D).

While it is hard, therefore, to argue that the member states of the EU took sufficiently swift and decisive action, we must not run away with the idea that they did nothing. We also need to be aware of the huge constraints they faced, not least the difficulty (especially in Germany) not just of selling the idea of helping out other countries in the face of media stories that suggested that those countries only had themselves to blame, but also in ensuring that nothing they did fell foul of their own constitutions. It is easy to point to the need for greater harmonization of tax and spending but much more arduous to achieve it, even though, in fact, the EU already has more regulatory say over taxation (especially indirect taxation) in member states than many people realise (see Genschel and Jachtenfuchs, 2011; see also Kemmerling, 2010). The idea of 'tax harmonization' – the bringing into line of all member states' tax rates and policies –actually pre-dates the latest crisis and can be argued for on two grounds. First, from a neoliberal point of view, national differences in tax regimes and rates represent inefficient and trade-distorting barriers to genuine competition. Second, there are those who believe there must be European control of tax and fiscal policy in order to offset the ECB's control of interest rates and monetary policy – something that some neoliberals might support if they could believe (which, interestingly, few can) that tax rates would, as a result, be lower rather than higher. But while the current crisis has prompted some politicians to rethink the issues there is no sign that their voters – many of whom continue to think (wrongly) that by preventing any further moves towards integration they can somehow insulate themselves from the fires raging in other countries – are listening yet.

That said, the fact that the Eurozone's supposedly sovereign nations have agreed – albeit incrementally and as a result of ad hoc 'muddling through' – to permanent surveillance (and potential sanctioning) of their governments' spending and borrowing by a supranational institution represents a major development in the political economy of Europe and European integration. In some ways we should expect the sovereign debt and banking crises to end up pushing and pulling the EU, or more precisely its member states, towards more coordinated fiscal policy and market regulation. After all, integration has often been driven forward by 'external shock' (see Diedrichs et al., 2011). Ultimately, however, it would be surprising if that coordination translates into fully-fledged harmonization of tax and spending across the board. Thus far, the EU's competence over the details of 'social policy' (see Hantrais, 2007), for instance, has, at the behest of the member states, been limited so as not to impact too directly on what most people would consider to

The Netherlands (Nederland)

Area: 33,900 km² (0.8% of EU-27)	
Population: 16.7 million (3.3% of EU-27)	
Religious heritage: Roman Catholic and Protestant	
GDP (2010): €591 billion (4.7% of EU-27)	
GDP *per capita* as percentage of EU-27 average: 131	
Female representation in parliament and cabinet (end 2011): 31% and 33%	
Joined EU: founder member, 1957	
Top 3 cities: Amsterdam – capital city (0.8 million), Rotterdam (0.6 million), The Hague (0.5 million).	

History: After breaking free from Habsburg and Spanish rule by the mid-seventeenth century and French rule by the beginning of the nineteenth, the Netherlands assumed its present status as a constitutional monarchy in 1848. Even though much of its Roman Catholic-dominated south became part of Belgium in 1839, the Netherlands remained a religiously divided society, with profound cultural differences not just between Catholics and Protestants but also between different branches of the latter. These differences were both maintained and contained by the *verzuiling* ('pillar') system: social groups marked off from each other by their denomination or ideological affiliation led largely separate existences, with their own welfare services, unions, business groups, political parties and media. From 1958 to 1973, all coalition governments were dominated by the centrist Christian democrats. After a period of 'grand coalitions' with the Christian democrats, the social democratic Labour Party finally got together with the

economically liberal VVD and the more centrist D66 party to form what became known as 'the purple coalition'.

The Christian democrats finally made it back into office in 2002, but not without the help of the far-right *Lijst Pim Fortuyn* (LPF) – a collection of political novices put together by a media-savvy maverick who was assassinated by an animal rights activist just before the election. After it, the LPF – and, consequently the government – fell apart. Since then, the country has seen the founding of a new populist radical right party, PVV, by Geert Wilders, a former VVD MP whose controversial views on Islam have seen him face death threats and court cases. After a strong performance in 2010, the party then supported a centre-right minority government. However, after it withdrew its support and caused that government to collapse, the PVV paid the price at the election of 2102, which confirmed the VVD's displacement of the once powerful Christian democrats as the main choice for centre-right voters and saw Labour perform much more strongly than many had expected.

Economy and society: The Dutch economy is one of the strongest in Europe. Rotterdam, half of whose population are said to be immigrants or from immigrant families, is the continent's biggest port, but the country as a whole is strong in, petrochemicals, consumer electronics and banking. It also has a highly efficient agricultural sector. This export-oriented economy may be vulnerable to downturns in big

markets such as Germany, but it has helped the Dutch build one of the world's most developed welfare states; indeed, the supposedly successful combination of the two became known as the 'Dutch miracle'. While the Netherlands' (or at least its cities') famously tolerant attitude to drugs and alternative life-styles continues, its embrace of multiculturalism has come under severe strain in recent years especially after episodes of religiously motivated violence. This may make life more difficult for the country's substantial Muslim population.

Governance: The Netherlands is a parliamentary democracy, elected under a

WHAT'S IN AN ANTHEM?

Popular from the end of the sixteenth century, *Het Wilhelmus* is the oldest song in the world to be used as a national anthem, although it was only sanctioned as such in 1932. At fifteen verses (the first letters of which combine acrostically to spell the name of its hero, William of Orange) it is also one of the longest, although (not uncommonly) only the first verse (sometimes along with the sixth) is usually sung. Written (unusually) in the first person, it's an account of a 'free and fearless' prince's struggle for the 'Fatherland' against Spanish 'tyranny'.

PR system with a low threshold that facilitates a large number and spread of parties in the more powerful, popularly elected *Tweede Kamer* (Second Chamber). The less powerful First Chamber is chosen by the councils of the country's twelve provinces. Majority coalitions are very much the norm, even if their formation takes two or three months of hard bargaining. Notwithstanding this preference for majorities, the policy process is typically consensual – indeed, some say getting *anything* done takes too long (the so-called 'Dutch disease').

Foreign policy: The Second World War put paid to the Netherlands' century-old policy of trade-boosting neutrality, as well as to its empire in South America and the Dutch East Indies (most of which is now Indonesia). It was a founding member of NATO, and worked hard to maintain a good relationship with the USA, as well as the UK. This traditionally 'Atlanticist' outlook came under fire in the 1980s, with huge public protests against the siting of US nuclear missiles in the country. Some also argue that the Netherlands, one of the biggest net financial contributors to the EU, is also cooling in its enthusiasm for further European integration.

Contemporary challenges

- Coping with growing Euroscepticism (see box).
- Defending the Dutch tradition of toleration in an era of mass immigration and concerns about Islam, even if – as the economy dominates debate – they have receded a little.
- Responding the extraordinarily high levels of volatility displayed by Dutch voters in recent years

A KEY CONTEMPORARY CHALLENGE
COPING WITH GROWING EUROSCEPTICISM

It is often assumed that, as founder members of the EU, the Dutch have been uncritical fans of European integration. In fact, the Dutch were cagey right from the start about the supranational aspects of the project, consenting to them mainly because they saw no other way of ensuring that their bigger partners, France and Germany, played fair and didn't dominate. There were also real concerns about the country being absorbed into what the country's many Protestants saw as a continental Catholic union. More generally, the Netherlands has long prided itself on its independence (hard-won from imperial Spain) and on its outward-facing commercial culture, both of which might be compromised by the loss of sovereignty and possible move towards protectionism entailed by EU membership. By the early 1990s, Dutch voters and politicians began to chafe at what they saw – not unreasonably – as the comparatively hefty contribution they were making to the EU's coffers.

The country's rejection of the proposed EU constitution in 2005, therefore, may have surprised mainstream politicians whose complacency led to a woeful Yes campaign, but it should not have come as a complete bolt from the blue. It may, though, have been a critical juncture, allowing concerns that until then had been expressed only occasionally to become more mainstream – a process enhanced by the increasing support given by voters to parties on the ends of the political spectrum (like the PVV on the right and the SP on the left) that made Euroscepticism an integral part of their appeal to the electorate. Also significant was the generally more 'Europhile' Christian democrats' displacement as the country's main centre right party by the free-market-friendly VVD. The latter was careful to talk tough enough on the EU so as to avoid any loss of vote share to the PVV on its right flank. By the same token, the social democratic PvdA had to adopt a position on Europe which was sufficiently sceptical to stave off defections to the more left-wing SP. VVD's leader, Mark Rutte, noted at one point that 'I am "Mr No" when it comes to a Brussels that's expanding more and more.' Research suggests that people often follow the cues of their preferred parties on issues like Europe. So if Dutch politicians find that their voters are increasingly sceptical, and if that scepticism ends up causing them problems, then they may have no-one to blame but themselves.

- Acting to do something serious about global warming which, given that half of the country lies below sea level, is a real threat – yet not one that looms large in political discussion.

Learning resources

An excellent overview is provided by Andeweg and Irwin (2009), *Governance and Politics of the Netherlands.* For incisive treatments of the dilemmas posed by immigrant integration, try Baruma (2007), *Murder in Amsterdam* and Sniderman and Hagendoorn (2007), *When Ways of Life Collide.* For more on the role of Europe in Dutch politics in recent times see van Kessel and Hollander (2012). Keep up to date with the news at http://www.rnw.nl/english.

be core areas of welfare, such as social security and healthcare provision. Although the ECJ (to take just one institution) has forced changes at the margins on, for example, the retirement age and the eligibility of EU citizens for benefits in other member states, the latter continue to remain 'highly reluctant to shed their national welfare-state obligations in favour of pan-European solutions' (Hemerijck *et al.*, 2006: 276). As a consequence, the EU has not yet been able to enforce 'European' models of welfare (see Chapter 1) on the region, nor, conversely, to prevent its governments adopting them, albeit in hybrid fashion (see Cerami, 2010; Cook, 2010; Keune, 2006). Even as it helps to impose austerity programmes in exchange for assisting those countries worst-hit by the economic crisis, it seems unlikely that it will get into the business of telling member states exactly how they should run their welfare states – in part because it has no one model in mind, in part because it is already worried enough about its democratic legitimacy with European citizens to want to be too prescriptive.

The end of the welfare and regulatory state? Separating the facts from the hype

Comparative scholar Martin Rhodes has the happy knack of providing brief but authoritative overviews of welfare state developments in Europe (see Rhodes, 2002) which separate the fact from the hype about the triumph of neoliberalism and the market over politics generally and the state in particular (see Ohmae, 1996 for an example). In a recent contribution (Gualmini and Rhodes, 2011), he and his co-author, provide us with a useful reminder that, while both the 'external shock' of economic crisis and underlying social change are bound to impact on the scale and orientation of social spending, reform is usually incremental rather than immediate. Reforms like the 'shift of emphasis from passive income support to a proactive employment policy that seeks to "activate" benefit claimants in more flexible labour markets', or like 'a higher individualization of risk' – particularly when it comes to pensions (see Bridgen and Meyer, 2009) – are occurring everywhere (albeit not at the same pace nor with the

KEY POINT

The welfare state is not dead, nor is it in imminent danger: the economic crisis has increased calls on the right for its scaling back but it is proving both its worth (in affording some protection to those out of work and therefore preventing demand dropping still further) and its persistence. That said – and even before the crisis – it was undergoing reform, some of it much needed. But that reform is unlikely in the short term to erode the long-term cultural and institutional differences between easily identifiable types of welfare states.

same sophistication or results). However, they have barely impacted on the lasting distinctions between the Nordic states (and the Netherlands) that combine efficiency and equality, more liberal states (residual welfare systems, often plagued by poverty and inequality) and conservative and southern European countries, which, despite differences that (in the former) make it easier for those out of work, have a tendency to privilege labour market insiders over outsiders (see Sapir, 1996).

Welfare states, Rhodes points out (see also van Kersbergen, 2000), have continued to grow even in an era of supposed globalization, but their ongoing sustainability is a serious issue. Meanwhile underlying national differences (see Swank, 2005: 187 and 184), most of which continue to correspond to Esping-Anderson's (1990) regime types outlined in Chapter 1, persist. The conclusion that markets do not simply crush everything in their way is backed up not just by the findings of large quantitative projects (see Stephens *et al.*, 1999) but by country studies and cross-national studies of particular policy areas (see Henderson and White, 2004; Mahler, 2004; Timonen, 2003). It is not altogether surprising, then, that the authors of one comprehensive review (Starke *et al.*, 2008) conclude as follows:

Contrary to what one might expect from much of the theoretical literature, we find that, although there is evidence of moderate welfare state convergence, it is limited in magnitude, various in directionality and contingent upon the indicator under examination. Overall, our findings do not provide any strong evidence either for a race to the bottom or for the Americanization of social policy, the two most common convergence scenarios encountered in supposedly informed public policy commentary.

Clearly, we will need to see how austerity affects things in the long term: it could be that, just as war has a habit of ratcheting up public spending on welfare, the current crisis turns out to be so serious and prolonged that it will take it back down a notch or two. It could even be the case that the need to compete in an increasingly global economy was already putting pressure on governments to cut spending and make their welfare states more like all the others, but the consequences of that pressure have only just begun to show up in long-run statistical analyses (Busemeyer, 2009b; see also Jensen, 2011b). For the moment, however, it seems reasonable to agree that politics still matters (and matters as much, if not, more than markets) and that, because of that, Europe's welfare states remain distinctive and, though not unchanged or unchallenged, relatively intact.

Beyond welfare – and left and right

Much of the discussion on the persistence of differences between political parties focuses on the left and right and touchstone issues like the welfare state and privatization. But these are clearly not the only party divisions nor the only issues in which we might be able to trace the impact of politics and the capacity of human agency to tame so-called 'market forces'. One obvious case in point is immigration, which, if it were left completely up to workers and businesses, would presumably generate a free-for-all but, which because of political decisions, is not only heavily controlled by states (as we note in the next chapter) but seems to vary according to the partisan composition of the governments which run them (see Gudbrandsen, 2010). Another obvious – and given its intrinsic importance to future generations highly relevant – alternative is to look at the extent to which parties can and do make a difference to environmental policy. This is just what a recent study, which focuses mainly on the period between 1970 and 2000, does (Knill *et al.*, 2010). Perhaps unsurprisingly given all the above, it clearly demonstrates that the more parties go into government professing to want to protect the environment, the more those governments produce policies which aim to do just that. It also seems to be the case, rather more surprisingly perhaps to those who argue that green views now cut across the supposedly old-fashioned left–right divide, that left-wing governments tend to adopt more environmentally-friendly policies than their right-wing equivalents. Other things tend to prompt more environmental policy, too: countries which have open and advanced economies tend to legislate to protect the environment more than those which do not, for example. It is also worth noting that EU-member states adopt more environmental policies than those outside the EU – *prima facie* evidence for Europeanization on that score.

Why it still makes sense to be different

Returning, however, to our main theme, it would seem to be the case that, just as Europe's welfare states are still welfare states, its social democrats can still claim, with some justification, to be social democrats, though not perhaps without qualifications. The biggest of these is that they have largely abandoned their goal of a more equal society – a goal that survived (at least as rhetoric) even long after most social democrats had embraced (more or less grudgingly) a role for the market as well as the state. This does not necessarily mean they are happy to let the poor get poorer – certainly in absolute terms – although both the persistence and the continued redistributionary effects of welfare mean that there is (reassuringly perhaps) little danger of that happening (Kenworthy and Pontusson, 2005; Scruggs and Allan, 2006b). But it does mean that they are less concerned than previously about the gap between rich and poor which, as we saw in Chapter 1, has got wider all over Europe (largely as a result of the rich being allowed to get richer). Instead, they seem more willing to admit that their primary concern has always been with *horizontal redistribution* (between old and young, sick and healthy, employed and unemployed) rather than *vertical redistribution* (between rich and poor) (see Bonoli, 2004).

KEY POINT

It makes political and economic sense for parties to continue to differentiate themselves from their main opponents. This is especially the case in PR systems, but differences are still evident in countries operating FPP.

Europe's social democrats have also admitted the difficulty of maintaining full employment via demand management. Some have therefore shifted their focus (at least in terms of rhetoric if not resources) on to maximizing employment via 'active labour market policies'. Such policies are favoured by governments of both right and left, although more so (because they do not come cheap) when times are good than when times are bad (see Vis, 2012) and have proved particularly successful in the Netherlands and the Nordic countries. And social democrats have adopted them, even though they involve a level of obligation to retrain and seek work that some see as draconian and an easing of regulations on hiring and firing that some on the left will regard as a sell-out. They also risk provoking tension with trade unions (and their supporters within parties in question) who are seemingly more interested in protecting labour market 'insiders' already in work than assisting 'outsiders', who are not – a position which may explain why so many of those who are poor and marginalized no longer have much faith in centre-left parties (see Rueda, 2007), making it, in turn, even less likely that their views will be reflected in government policy (see Giger *et al.*, 2012).

Enlightened social democrats have also gone beyond the idea that 'more is (necessarily) better' when it comes to state involvement and public spending, and admitted the private sector into areas that previously might have been thought to be public sector preserves. Such an agenda might not be what some radical critics want; but it may be sensible (even superior) in the light of increasing evidence that, in the real world, individuals slip in and out of need over their lifetimes far more than we previously imagined – and far more than media-sexy terms like 'underclass' or 'middle-England' (and their European equivalents) imply (see Goodin *et al.*, 1999). But simply because social democracy is not what it was (what political ideology or institu-

tion or policy regime is?) need not mean that it is no longer social democracy. There is nothing particularly admirable, many centre-left leaders at least would argue, in remaining pure and refusing to acknowledge the possibility that reforms might actually grow the economy and thereby help people whose every day lives are a struggle – all the more so if failure to do so costs you more votes than does your supposed sell-out to neoliberalism (Marx and Schumacher, 2013). Social democracy, at least since the end of the Second World War (see Chapter 5) has never been interested in being a prophet crying in the wilderness. Indeed, it has left that role to Europe's left parties, many of whom, incidentally, are in the forefront of opposition to the supposedly 'neoliberal' side of the EU (see Dunphy, 2004).

In fact, these left parties are far from impotent or unimportant (see March, 2011), not least because most European countries operate proportional representation systems (which interesting research – see Iversen and Soskice, 2006 – suggests are themselves associated with more left-leaning government and redistribution). PR makes it all the more unlikely that social democrats will ever take what their critics call 'betrayal' too far: if they did, then many of the votes of the disillusioned and the disadvantaged might accrue to more radical alternatives that stand a chance of gaining seats at their expense, which would in time probably swing the centre-left back to the left in order to win them back. This happened at the 1998 election in Sweden, when the social democratic SAP lost significant support to the Left Party and was henceforth distinctly cagier about rationalizing the welfare state. Likewise, the existence of the Greens (and more liberal or libertarian variants of the left) relies on social democrats failing – at least, in the eyes of their critics – to defend core values (in this case, civil liberties and the interests of developing countries). But the presence of alternative parties on the social democrats' left flank – Germany's SPD, Sweden's SAP, and the Dutch Labour Party, for instance, all face completion both from more socialist and greener alternatives – also ensures that, looking over their shoulders, they do not completely forget such things. The same of course applies to conservatives and Christian democrats, who cannot afford to completely ignore, the completion which they face from parties which support either more neoliberal reforms or more authoritarian and restrictive policies than they themselves are strictly comfortable with. Moreover, there is little chance, least in the short-term, of these more radical alternatives disappearing or, indeed, moderating their stances – indeed, recent research strongly suggests that these smaller parties are actually more likely to win votes if they stress their extreme 'unique selling points' than try to play them down (see Wagner, 2012).

Of course, any 'anchoring' effect of Green and Left potential on social democratic policy depends in part on the extent to which this potential is likely to cause serious damage to the capacity of the social democrats to get into and dominate government. This depends in part on those citizens who support redistributive social and economic policy: if they react to, say, increasing inequality by defecting from the centre-left to the left, then this may well alarm the centre-left sufficiently to see it return (at least rhetorically) to more traditional policies. If, as seems to be happening more and more, they react instead by not bothering to vote and not protesting in some other way, then the centre-left will be under less pressure to make a more egalitarian pitch to the electorate (see Pontusson and Rueda, 2010). But even if those voters do defect, social democrats have in the past been able to bank on the fact that the parties they defect to will probably join them in a progressive bloc that should prove capable of amassing more parliamentary seats than the bloc on the other side. The Swedish SAP, for about ten years after the mid-1990s, could count not only on the Greens, but also on the Left Party, notwithstanding its concern not to cede it too many of its voters. The German SPD, however, was stuck with the Greens alone, since it refused to work with the former communist (and largely East German) PDS or its successor (the more all-German party) the Left (see Hough *et al.*, 2007). Indeed, concern about losing too much support to the latter (as well as dissent in its own ranks over negotiations with the centre-right Christian Democrats) meant that, although Chancellor Schröder, labelled as the *Genosse der Bosse* (the bosses' best-mate) by left-wingers, managed to steer his '*Agenda 2010*' and Hartz welfare and labour market reforms through the notoriously cumbersome German system (see Chapter 4), he was forced into an early election and, eventually, early retirement (see Saalfeld, 2006).

In other countries, the centre-left has to be even more careful about not allowing too much space to open up on its left flank. France, Italy and the Netherlands all have party and electoral systems that consistently deliver up small, radical parties to whom unwary 'centrists' can lose votes if they stray too far and then find difficult to corral into coalitions. The French socialists' candidate for the presidency in 2002, Prime Minister Lionel Jospin, for example, is widely thought to have blown his chances by taking too centrist a stance, leading some on the left either to abstain or vote for no-hopers who wore their radical hearts on their sleeves. But perhaps he was in a no-win situation: when the party's candidate at the next election, Ségolène Royale, presented a more left-wing programme which contributed what some radicals (on both sides) regarded as a healthy contest between an advocate of state intervention and (in Sarkozy) a supposed champion of liberal reform, it looked outmoded and jarred with her own image as something of a 'Blairite' modernizer. Her successor (and former partner) François Hollande, however, got the balance about right, managing to pick up in the second round of voting enough of those who in the first round had voted for the more populist left-winger, Jean-Luc Mélenchon. On the other hand, this did mean promising to tax incomes over €1m at a marginal rate of 75 per cent, to cap the salaries of companies where the state owns a majority stake to roughly 20 times the rate of the lowest paid worker, to return the retirement age (at least for those who began their working lives early) from 62 to 60, to rapidly create an extra 60,000 teaching jobs, and to prevent the closure of French factories. These are not policies that one can imagine many other social democrats, let alone conservative politicians, committing to – and it wasn't long before Holland, now President, began to change his tune, admitting there were some closures he couldn't stop, some services and business taxes he might have to cut, and some labour market reforms that could not be put off any longer.

But France, which operates a variant of FPP (see Chapter 6), suggests that keeping a respectable (if not respectful) distance from the other side of the political spectrum is not merely an artefact of the electoral system. So, too, does the UK, where, as we have already suggested, facile clichés about a move to the right under Blair and Brown obscure more than they illuminate. Indeed, defenders of Labour's continued centre-left credentials cannot only point to the huge rises in health and education spending already mentioned. They can also argue that, by focusing on (and delivering) economic growth and employment, and concentrating government help on working families, the 1997–2010 Labour government pursued a 'classic postwar' social democratic strategy – even if, by 'talking right and acting left', it did it by stealth. In any case, the radical rhetoric that characterized Labour before the party began its 'modernization' in the mid-1980s was always rather unconvincing, given what (with the exception of 1945–8) was its very modest style of socialism in government. More generally, research (and to some extent common sense and observation) suggests that there is no contradiction between the opening up of the economy and continued or even increased support by centre-left parties for the welfare state (see Burgoon, 2012): Nordic countries have long known that an extensive welfare state can help a country both compete in a globalized world and protect its citizens from the ups and downs that exposure brings.

European social democracy, then, has always been accommodating and has always operated in diverse institutional, cultural and competitive settings. These have, of course, increased as the end of communism in central and eastern Europe has produced a new bunch of parties that have adopted – some would say simply pasted on – the 'social democratic' label. This is problematic because, as we suggested in Chapter 5, the differences between left and right do not map precisely on to traditional western distinctions (see Sitter, 2003; see also Rovny and Edwards, 2012). The latter are rooted in the extent of state involvement in the economy and welfare provision. Distinctions in some postcommunist democracies have more to do with attitudes to the communist past, moral and family values and, indeed, to European integration, with 'social democrats' in central and eastern Europe being generally more favourable to the EU than their slightly more 'sceptic' right-wing opponents. These different bases for distinguishing the two sides are particularly the case in Poland, although the left and right in the Czech Republic (see Box 9.3) and Hungary could possibly claim to be more like their western counterparts (see Millard, 2004). They, too, hope to make moderate use of the power of the state to enhance citizens' quality of life and to maximize their equality of opportunity and their access to decent and hopefully helpful support whenever markets fail. As a result, they tend to spend more than their right-wing counterparts (Careja and Emmenegger, 2009). That said, they, too, have stopped trying to pretend that they have either the will or the means to prevent those markets failing in the first place.

So, the supposed collapse in the distinction between right and left, and the concomitant weakening of the welfare state, is, to say the least, an idea in need of severe qualification. It is also one that offers us little purchase on one of the defining features of party politics since the 1990s and perhaps longer. This is the 'bipolarization' of politics we referred to in Chapter 5 – the fact that many of Europe's party systems appear to be structured by competition between blocs of parties, cleaving to either the left or the right, even if (as in Germany in 2005 or the Netherlands in 2006 and 2012) the electoral arithmetic (and the unwillingness of one of the mainstream players to govern either as a minority or alongside more radical alternatives) can still effectively oblige the formation of a 'grand coalition' across the blocs. The left bloc generally contains left parties, Greens, social democrats and some progressive or social liberals. Its counterpart on the right includes Christian democrats, conservatives and market liberals. It also includes, increasingly, the far right – a force whose rise is sometimes blamed (rather simplistically) on the supposed decline of difference between right and left, as well as (and rather more convincingly) on anxieties about migration and multiculturalism. It is to these issues that we now turn.

Learning Resources for Chapter 9

Further reading

For a spirited and highly sophisticated defence of the power of party politics to produce policies that, over time, effectively represent the preferences of citizens, see Budge *et al.* (2012), *Organizing Democratic Choice*. Roberts (2009), *The Quality of Democracy* is likewise upbeat about central and eastern Europe. Soroka and Wlezien (2010), *Degrees of Democracy: Politics, Public Opinion, and Policy*, which is similarly sanguine – both about the responsiveness of policy makers to the public and the responsiveness of the public to policy changes – is also highly recommended: the only European country covered is the UK but its method will no doubt be applied to Europe more generally in the future. On the survival of the welfare state and the continuing power of politics, see Geoffrey Garrett's article in the journal (Garrett, 1998); Francis Castles (2004), *The Future of the Welfare State*; and the collection edited by Peter Taylor-Gooby (2004), *New Risks, New Welfare*. Starke (2007), *Radical Welfare State Retrenchment*, is also helpful, even though it, too, was written before the economic downturn. The collection edited by Palier (2010), *A Long Goodbye to Bismarck*, which details and discusses the politics of welfare reform in Europe, is also highly recommended, as is the admirably succinct summary of recent developments across the continent by Gualmini and Rhodes (2011). On the centre-left, the volumes edited by Bonoli and Powell (2004), *Social Democratic Party Politics in Contemporary Europe*, Oliver Schmidtke (2002), *The Third Way Transformation of Social Democracy*, and Merkel *et al.* (2008) *Social Democracy in Power* are still useful, but more up to date are the collections edited by Cronin *et al.* (2011) *What's Left of the Left?*, by Cramme and Diamond (2012) *After the Third Way*, and by IPG (2010) *The Future of Social Democracy*. For a more radical take, see Bailey (2009), *The Political Economy of European Social Democracy*. Anyone interested in a long-term comparative political economy and its links to politics should also dip into Wilensky (2002), *Rich Democracies*. Anyone interested in how markets react to (and try to predict) political outcomes like changes of government, see Bernhard and Leblang (2006), *Democratic Processes and Financial Markets: Pricing Politics*. Finally, for a stimulating read on whether governments should provide adequate welfare to their citizens in order to avoid an economically-damaging backlash against globalization, see Hays (2009), *Globalization and the New Politics of Embedded Liberalism*.

On the web

www.tni.org – left wing takes on neoliberalism
www.stockholm-network.org – neoliberal enthusiasts
http://www.policy-network.net/ – debate on social democracy

Discussion questions

1   How might we tell whether having a left- or right-wing government makes any difference to a country? Going on the evidence, does it make a difference?

2   Why did some on the centre-left of politics in Europe think social democratic and labour parties needed to 'modernize' and follow a 'Third Way'?

3   Privatization may still be fashionable – in some parts of Europe, at least. But is it quite as thorough-going as many assume?

4   Are so-called 'supply-side' economic policies necessarily right-wing?

5   Before the current economic crisis, at least, there was little to suggest that the era of 'tax and spend' in Europe was over: will this all change now or are there reasons to think that it might not?

6   Some see the EU as locking in neoliberalism in Europe. Others see it as an obstacle to free-market, 'Anglo-Saxon' capitalism. Given its performance in the Eurozone crisis, do you think it is really capable of fulfilling either function?

7   Does a move toward the centre-right make electoral sense for Europe's social democratic parties? Even if it does, is it possible that the move is more one of positioning than policies, rhetoric rather than reality?

8   Is where you live likely to make more difference to the kind of welfare the state provides than whether a left- or a right-wing government is in charge?

ONLINE
RESOURCES
AVAILABLE

Visit the companion site at **www.palgrave.com/politics/bale** to access additional learning resources.

Chapter 10

Not wanted but needed – migrants and minorities

We observed in Chapters 2 and 3 how European states were devolving power, sometimes to the extent that traditional distinctions between unitary and federal states seem less and less useful. We also observed that these moves were often, at least in part, a response to claims for autonomy or even independence made by minorities who feel they constitute a nation or even a race apart. But those who feel that they are somehow trapped in the wrong body politic are not the only minorities in Europe. The population of most, if not all, European countries is now made up not just of the descendents of those who lived there centuries ago, but also of those who have arrived much more recently – and, indeed, are still arriving. Whether these minorities are distinctive through **race** or only **ethnicity**, their presence, and the fact that they are being joined by more immigrants every day – at a rate of over two million per year from various sources – is the source of considerable anxiety and friction in many European countries. Migrants and minorities – no matter if they have been here for decades or even centuries – do not always find Europe as welcoming as they might have hoped. Indeed, they routinely encounter misunderstanding, mistrust, and sometimes outright hostility, from the ethnic majorities whose states they share and of which they might even become citizens.

This presents governments of all political stripes in Europe with a dilemma. Their majority populations, it seems clear, are anxious about, not to say hostile towards, any increase in immigration, particularly (though not exclusively) from developing countries and especially when those coming appear to be abusing rights to asylum and family reunification (which actually accounts for around half of all legal migration into Europe). On the other hand, experts are telling politicians that labour and skills-shortages,

Although frequently (and, often, very reasonably) used interchangeably, the terms 'race' and 'ethnicity' do have different origins and connotations. **Race** is essentially about visually obvious physical characteristics that mark out some individuals from others, even if advances in genetics have put paid to the notion – at least at the level of science, if not popular culture – that such differences were somehow immutable and/or more than skin-deep. **Ethnicity** is to do with belonging to a social group that is tied by shared background, culture and language (and perhaps race, as well) and that may see itself (and be seen as) distinctive from the wider society. Inasmuch as it is ever really possible, one can perhaps escape or mask one's ethnicity, should one choose to do so. Persuading others, particularly if they are prejudiced, to ignore one's race might well be more difficult.

combined with the ageing of majority populations whose fertility rates are way below replacement levels (see Chapter 1), make immigration more and more necessary, although few claim it is some kind of magic bullet. Indeed, even if it were, there is no guarantee that the consequent relief of politicians would be shared by their voters or by the media – witness the horrified reaction in some quarters to projections suggesting that (due in part to immigration) the populations of some countries (including the UK's, for instance) might well buck the European trend and actually rise by ten million in the next few decades (see Chapter 1). Some politicians, of course, will choose to side with 'the people' against the experts – one of the essences of populism (see Taggart, 2000). Others argue that democratic leadership sometimes entails leading (or even standing out against) public opinion instead of following and even inflaming it. Most politicians simply try to hold the ring, hoping that, as in times past (see Lucassen, 2006), the incomers currently seen as presenting such a threat will gradually be accepted.

This chapter begins with an account of patterns of migration into Europe, explaining why so many people have chosen, and been able, to make the place their home in the past, and why so many are joining them. It then looks at who Europe's newest arrivals are, what they do and where they live, before going on to examine some of the less than edifying public, political and media responses to their coming, focusing on anxieties about their impact on jobs and welfare, about asylum seekers, about immigration from the new member states of the EU to their richer counterparts in the west, and about Islamist terrorism. Next, the chapter looks at the ways in which European countries have begun, via the EU, to cooperate on immigration. It asks whether this is just one more surrender of sovereignty or yet another way to help preserve it, along with the distinctive immigration regimes that reflect

KEY POINT

Europe is a continent forged by immigration and will continue to be so whether people like it or not: it attracts, and almost certainly needs, people to offset labour shortages and demographic problems.

(but are not wholly determined by) their past choices. The chapter ends by exploring the situation of the Roma minority that has been around in Europe for nearly a thousand years, but is still at the bottom of the heap.

Migration into Europe – then and now

Most of Europe's minorities have always lived there – or, at least, their ancestors have. But Europe is also home to millions of people who came, or whose ancestors came, from other places. Immigration is nothing new in Europe. It has been going on for centuries: the state system whose development we traced in Chapter 1 created national borders, but they were rarely impermeable. European countries might not have encouraged immigration as much as 'settler' societies such as the USA. But they often relaxed their restrictions when the labour market was tight and (perhaps more reluctantly) when claims were made upon them by citizens of their former colonies – Arabs from French North Africa, Afro-Caribbeans and South Asians from the British Commonwealth or Surinamese from the Dutch East Indies (see Box 10.1).

Sometimes the flow of people into Europe has been a gradual, barely contested process, with inter-marriage making a scientific nonsense of the idea of racial purity and bouts of emigration from Europe to the Americas and Australasia balancing out the numbers coming in. At other times, immigration has been more high-profile. Periodically, it has become the kind of influx that – especially when accompanied by media hysteria – causes widespread anxieties about 'overcrowding', about competition for jobs, housing, welfare and sexual partners and about cultural practices (such as forced marriage, honour killing and female circumcision) that many Europeans regard as alien, even barbaric. Migration, like European integration and especially eastern enlargement, has the capacity to both undermine and reinforce people's notions of where they come from, who they are and where they are going (see Spohn and Triandafyllidou, 2002).

For centuries, then, people have moved in and out of Europe without attracting much attention or

BOX 10.1

Out of Africa, but not necessarily everywhere else – European decolonization

France, after almost eight years of fighting, left the Americans to try and sort out Vietnam after 1954. After another eight years of fighting, it left Algeria in 1962, having long disposed of its colonies further south in Africa. It continues, however, to hang on to territorial possessions in the Caribbean, Indian Ocean and in Polynesia – the so called DOM-TOMs. The DOMs (*Départements d'Outre-Mer*) – Guadaloupe, Martinique, French Guyana and Réunion – are fully integrated into France politically. The TOMS (*Territoires d'Outre-Mer*) are still effectively colonies: they are Wallis and Fortuna, French Polynesia (including Tahiti) and the nickel-rich island of New Caledonia, where in recent years an independence movement has forced France into granting it more autonomy.

The UK got out of the Indian subcontinent and Burma (Myanmar) reasonably peacefully, and out of Palestine, as it was then called, rather more violently just after the Second World War. During the 1950s, the British fought limited armed conflicts (but eventually saw the installation of friendly governments) in places such as Malaya, Cyprus, Kenya and southern Arabia. In the 1960s, it not only got out of Africa – rather too hurriedly, some say, given the instability its sudden departures engendered – but also withdrew from a major defence presence in South East Asia. On the other hand, it fought a war to re-take the Falkland Islands that Argentina decided to occupy in 1982. Fifteen years later, in 1997, the UK handed Hong Kong back to China.

The Netherlands withdrew from Dutch East India in 1949, when it became Indonesia. It granted independence to Surinam, next to French Guyana in the northern part of South America, in 1975. **Belgium** was forced out of the Congo in 1960 by nationalist movements, with the chaos surrounding the withdrawal doing much to convince British policy makers that they, too, must accelerate their own withdrawal from Africa.

Portugal pulled out of the African countries of Mozambique and Angola in 1975 when, partly as a result of the strains imposed by trying to hang on to them, there was a peaceful (and eventually democratic) overthrow of the authoritarian regime that had ruled Portugal since the 1930s. It handed over Macau to China in 1999.

Italy and **Germany** both had limited colonial empires, based mainly in Africa, which they were forced to surrender after the Second World War ended in 1945.

Spain lost the last of its South American and Caribbean imperial possessions in the nineteenth century, but continues to hold on to its African outposts of Ceuta and Melilla in what is otherwise Morocco.

doing much to alter, at least visibly, the ethnic balance. But there have also been several waves of immigration, often into particular countries, that have skewed the distribution of the continent's minorities, sometimes temporarily, sometimes permanently. For instance, by the late nineteenth century, Jews had lived in Europe for centuries, although they had often encountered both acute and chronic discrimination. But then the Jewish populations of several countries were swollen by others fleeing 'pogroms' (organized massacres and expulsions that today we might call 'ethnic cleansing' or even genocide) in the Russian empire. East-central Europe and Germany were the obvious places to escape to. Tragically, however, they were also those most afflicted by the Nazi Holocaust of the 1940s (see Chapter 1), once again reducing, in the most terrible way imaginable, the previous expansion.

After the Second World War, waves of immigration were experienced, first, by nations that were vic-

BOX 10.2

Immigration types and terms

Immigration can be *legal* (i.e. people enter countries according to the rules set down by states for accepting them) or *illegal* or *irregular* (i.e. people either enter illicitly without permission or, probably more commonly, enter legally but then overstay). Legal immigration can be split into a number of categories. *Primary immigration* occurs when an individual (perhaps with his or her immediate family) moves to another country, having got its permission to do so, for economic reasons – in other words, to work. *Family reunion* occurs when individuals move to another country (again, with permission) in order to join their relations who are already there, often, but not always, as a result of primary immigration. It is also possible for people to move legally to another country because they have a well-founded fear of persecution (commonly, though not necessarily, by the state) in their own country – this is known as seeking or claiming *asylum*. If the claim is accepted, the claimant will be granted *refugee* status under the 1951 UN convention. It is often the case with such applications, of course, that the person arrives prior to his or her claim being accepted and, in fact, it may turn out to be rejected (possibly because he or she is, in fact, an economic migrant trying to avoid the need for prior permission to enter the labour market). This leaves the individual with the choice of returning home (and he or she may be obliged to do so by the receiving country) or evading the authorities and becoming an *illegal immigrant*. In reality, the application process and any attendant appeal may take time, and the decision of the authorities might be to deny someone refugee status but still allow him or her to stay on other (humanitarian) grounds and/or because deportation would go against *non-refoulement* – a principle of international law which prevents states from returning people to a country where they would be likely to come to harm. In the long term, this might allow the individual concerned to apply for *residency* (the permanent right to remain) or even *citizenship* (the adoption of the receiving country's nationality). This is also a possibility when, as happens in many southern European countries, *amnesties* are granted to illegal immigrants who are offered the chance to 'regularize' their status in return for making themselves known to the authorities and therefore paying tax and insurance contributions – a policy that has proved particularly popular with southern European governments like Spain, Italy, Greece and Portugal but which is heavily criticized by their northern counterparts, who believe it merely encourages illegal migration (see Baldwin-Edwards and Kraler, 2009).

torious and/or possessed colonies in Africa, the Caribbean, and the Indian subcontinent: the 1950s and 1960s saw Afro-Caribbeans and South Asians coming to the UK, and Moroccans, Algerians and Tunisians coming to France. In both countries, they came because labour shortages created demand for (often unskilled) workers at wages that seemed princely compared to what they could earn at home. The same was true, especially from the early 1960s on, in (West) Germany. There, *Gastarbeiter* (guest-workers), often Turkish, poured in to do the relatively low-paid jobs that (in the days of full employment we described in Chapter 1) Germans turned their noses up at but which needed doing if the country's 'economic miracle' was to be sustained. The UK, Germany and France also took in large numbers of Spanish, Portuguese and Italians. They

were either leaving dictatorships (in the case of the first two) or (in the case of all three) the poverty of their native lands. Greeks and Greek Cypriots came for similar reasons, though in smaller numbers. The only countries relatively unaffected by these waves of essentially 'primary' migration (see Box 10.2) were in Scandinavia and the Soviet bloc. In the case of the former, this was because they were too hard to get to and had no historic, colonial links. In the case of the latter, it was because, quite simply, nobody wanted to go there.

Before the end of the Cold War in 1990, then, Europe's immigrants came largely because it made economic sense for those directly concerned. It still does, given the numbers of foreign-born workers in the labour force of most European countries (see Table 10.1). It did not always benefit the underdevel-

Table 10.1 Where they are – foreign population as a percentage of total population

	Foreign-born in population (%)	Foreign-born in labour force (%)
Czech Rep.	6.4	n/a
France	11.6	11.6
Germany	12.9	n/a
Italy	3.9	11.3
Netherlands	11.1	11.6
Poland	2.0	0.3
Spain	14.3	18.5
Sweden	14.4	11.2
UK	11.3	12.9

Note: Most recent data for each country up to 2009.

Source: Data from OECD, *International Migration Outlook* (2011).

oped countries from which they came: after all, they lost skilled, or at least potentially skilled, labour – and they still do, especially in the health sector, for instance. On the other hand, the remittances they sent (and continue to send) back home were useful in economies starved of cash and, in the case of poorer European countries, of the consumer durables that are taken for granted in the richer north.

Since then, however, the situation has become considerably more complicated. A more unsettled geopolitical environment has increased the numbers of people in Africa and the Middle East desperate to flee persecution and civil war, some of whom attempt officially to claim asylum (see Box 10.2). Meanwhile, the economic situation has gone from bad to worse. The insistence on the part of developed countries (often via the multinational agencies that they dominate, such as the IMF and the World Bank) that developing nations pursue what some see as a counterproductive conversion from subsistence to cash economies that will help them to honour overseas loans has made it very difficult for ordinary people. This is particularly the case when, at the same time, critics say, the EU's highly subsidized,

highly protected, agricultural sector is allowed to dump its products in their markets without having to face free and fair competition from their producers (see S. Castles, 2004). Even where people can manage to feed their families, they have little hope that they can attain a standard of living that comes close to what, with the advent of global brand advertising and media, they see being enjoyed – apparently by all – in the prosperous parts of the world. Little wonder, then, say some critics of the developed countries, that more and more people than ever before will do what ever it takes to make a new life for themselves and their families.

All this means that European countries with a history of immigration are finally having to come to terms with the fact that those who have come are unlikely ever to want to go 'home'. It also means that those countries with no history of immigration – often countries, in fact, that supplied immigrants to those that did – are having to adjust to the fact that they, too, are now destinations rather than points of departure. This is most obviously the case in Spain (see Box 10.3). It is also true of Greece, which in 2010 accounted for 90 per cent of all 2010 irregular crossings of the land, sea or air border of the European Union, putting such a huge strain on its system that the European Court of Human Rights requested other member states not to exercise their right to return asylum-seekers to Greece on the grounds that it was where they first entered the EU. Some postcommunist countries now see more people coming into the country than going out, too: this has been the case since the mid 1990s for the Czech Republic, Slovenia, Slovakia and Hungary, although the latter's economic difficulties may see a reversal of the trend; Poland, whose citizens had shown themselves to be particularly mobile after EU accession (see Table 10.2) but whose economy was one of the few to survive the global economic crisis relatively intact, became a net receiver of people in 2010.

Essentially, then, the picture is complicated but the patterns are clear – and neatly summarized in an article by Hooghe *et al.* (2008). The analysis of data covering the quarter of a century between 1980 and 2004 demonstrates that:

migration flows react to economic incentives, mainly with regard to the labor market, but also to

---

BOX 10.3

Spain – from sender to receiver

Spain used to export labour northwards and import tourists southwards. It still does the latter, although more and more of those coming from northern Europe never go home: nearly 400,000 UK citizens (many of them retired; see Casado-Díaz, 2006) now live there, for example – a useful reminder that immigration is offset, at least in part, by citizens who leave to live elsewhere (see Table 10.2). The mass emigration of Spaniards, however, was coming to an end even before their country joined the EU in 1986. Since then, Spain has imported not only tourists from the north, but also labour from the south (see Balch, 2010), notably from Latin America (especially Colombia, Ecuador and Bolivia), many of whom came to work in the construction industry, and from the Maghreb (especially Morocco), many of whom took jobs in 'poly-culture' – the mass cultivation of fruit and salad crops under plastic in southern Spain. Many of the former came in as tourists (often visa-free) and then stayed on illegally. Many of the latter came in illegally in the first place. The favoured route was across the Straits of Gibraltar from northern Morocco, until, that was, Spain spent millions on surveillance equipment for the most vulnerable parts of its southern coast and on reinforcing the huge fences around its African outposts in Ceuta and Melilla. After that, the Canary Islands, just off the Atlantic coast of Africa, have taken over as the main destination for immigrants: getting from there to the Spanish mainland, after all, requires no passport since the islands are fully a part of Spain. In fact, Spain (like Italy) has also tolerated a degree of illegal immigration, which it has regularized through periodic amnesties that have offered hundreds of thousands of people who had managed to evade the authorities to stay permanently. The most recent amnesty, in 2005 which regularized the status of over 600,000 people, infuriated other European governments, especially when they were then asked to help out in the Canary Islands: in their view the boatloads of Africans arriving in 2006 were a natural consequence of the previous year's decision. Spain has also seen an influx from the newest EU member states, and in particular Romania, whose Latinate language made adapting relatively easy. Their arrival has seen the foreign-born population in Spain rise five-fold in just ten years from the turn of the century so that, by the end of the first decade of the millennium, foreigners made up some 14 per cent of the population – up from just two per cent in 2000 (for more detail, see Ros, 2011).

---

cultural and colonial linkages. There is no indication that the importance of the colonial past is declining over time. The response of migration patterns to shortages in the labor market is shown to be highly efficient, while… immigrants are not attracted by high levels of social expenditure.

Europe's immigrants – grim realities and perceptions

Given the role of civil and international conflict in pushing people into migration, we should be forgiven if we often concentrate more on where immigrants come from than who they are. But the latter matters, too. Sociological research suggests that they tend to cluster at either end of the educational spectrum. Some are university graduates filling skills shortages in particular sectors, but Europe also needs unskilled workers willing to do menial jobs, especially in the expanding service and personal (for which read elder) care sector. Research – and common sense – also suggests that immigrants are rarely the poorest of the poor. Most not only come from countries where there is already some economic development, but have had to amass funds to get themselves, legally or otherwise, to Europe in the first place: it can cost tens of thousands of euros to buy illegal entry into Europe, as much as it does to build an average family home in the country of origin. Many media stories about the plight of asylum-seekers ('bogus' or otherwise) feature women and children, either to elicit our sympathy or to provoke our outrage. Far more commonly, in fact, Europe's immigrants are single men in their twenties and thir-

Table 10.2 Where migrants into EU countries come from: the top ten in 2008

EU-citizens		Non-EU citizens	
Romanian	384,000	Moroccan	157,000
Polish	266,000	Chinese	97,000
Bulgarian	91,000	Indian	93,000
German	88,000	Albanian	81,000
Italian	67,000	Ukranian	80,000
French	62,000	Brazilian	62,000
British	61,000	American	61,000
Hungarian	44,000	Turkish	51,000
Dutch	40,000	Russian	50,000
Portugese	38,000	Colombian	49,000

Source: Data from Eurostat (2011: 18)

ties, chosen by the families who help to get that money together because they are seen to have the best chance of making it to, and in, the promised land. If they do, they can then send for family members or at least send back the remittances that a recent study has shown 'significantly reduce the level, depth, and severity of poverty in the developing world' (Adams and Page, 2005: 1645).

Although some use kinship connections and aim for a particular destination, many have only the vaguest idea of where they might end up. Neither do they necessarily want to come forever – indeed, some experts think that stricter immigration regimes actually trap people into not leaving what might otherwise have been a temporary home. Given the restrictive climate, people quite justifiably fear not getting back in again should the planned return home

KEY POINT

Most migrants come to Europe because they are poor, discriminated against or in danger. While the majority contribute positively, they are also over-represented in all sorts of negative statistics. The stereotypes are rarely positive – scrounger, job-stealer, criminal, terrorist – and many people buy into them, just as many people vastly overestimate how many immigrants there are.

not work out. On the other hand, if they do stay, it is often because they find it easy (legally or illegally) to get work. This is one of the reasons why the UK is a relatively popular European destination (and why, by the same token, immigrants there make a positive contribution to GDP and state revenue). Once they do find work, and as long as they regularize their status, many immigrants send for their relations and, in some cases, pick up a spouse from overseas. In Europe, just as in the USA, family reunion is (and this is something worth reminding ourselves of again and again) by far the biggest source of legal migration – and not necessarily one that contributes skilled or even able-bodied immigrants.

Just as they do in the USA, many first-generation immigrants in Europe do badly paid work, often, though not always (see Figure 10.1), because they are less well-educated than the native population – a disadvantage that can persist into the second generation (see Table 10.3). Unlike the USA, however, European countries have high unemployment and more gen-

Figure 10.1 Over here and overqualified: foreign-born and native workers in jobs requiring less education than they possess

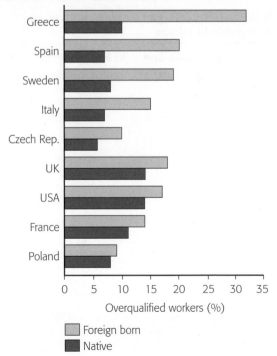

Source: Fundamental Rights Agency (2011a: 41) Note: data not available for Germany or Netherlands.

Table 10.3 People educated only to secondary level or less (as percentage of adult population)

	Native	First generation migrants	Second generation migrants
Germany	8	34	19
France	23	43	26
Netherlands	22	39	29
Sweden	13	29	15
EU-27	24	35	23
Czech Rep.	7	18	29
Italy	42	44	n/a
Spain	43	40	55
UK	25	20	22

Note: Figures are for people aged 25–54; no data for Poland

Source: Data from Eurostat (2011: 132)

Table 10.4 The jobs gap between natives and immigrants in Europe

	(a) Native-born unemployment rate	(b) Foreign-born unemployment rate	Ratio (b : a)
Czech Rep.	7.5	7.4	0.99
UK	7.8	9.1	1.17
Italy	8.1	11.2	1.38
Spain	18.1	29.1	1.61
France	8.6	14.6	1.70
Germany	6.5	11.8	1.82
Netherlands	3.8	8.1	2.13
Sweden	7.1	16.3	2.30

Note: Data is for 2010. No data available for Poland.

Source: OECD, *International Migration Outlook* (2011). Note that these are official statistics: given the fact that immigrants may be more likely to work in the 'black economy', the real gap may be narrower.

erous welfare systems. Because immigrants (at least from some ethnic groups and especially when times are hard) are more likely to be unemployed and therefore on benefits than non-immigrants of working age (see Table 10.4), this feeds into a negative stereotype of the immigrant as a drain on national exchequer – a stereotype that in a number of countries appears to have some truth in it, at least when dependents are taken into account and in the most generous welfare states (see Boeri, 2009). At the same time, and somewhat paradoxically, immigrants are also accused of 'stealing jobs' because in many countries – especially when they were enjoying reasonable employment growth before the financial crisis which hit in 2007/8 – there was a big (and very visible) increase in the number of jobs done by foreign-born workers: according to OECD figures, which compare employment growth for the population as a whole with employment growth among foreign-born workers, the figures for Italy were 14 per cent and 2038 per cent respectively, while for Spain were 58 per cent and 979 per cent, for Sweden 5 and 129 per cent, the Netherlands, 18 and 73 per cent, and the UK, 8 and 52 per cent (OECD, 2007). Moreover, a recent study by the latter's government advisory body on immigration (MAC, 2012: 10) found:

> a tentative negative association between working-age migrants and native employment when the economy is below full capacity…. Between 1995 and 2010, employment of non-British born working age people rose by approximately 2.1 million…. [A]ssociated displacement of British born workers was around 160,000 of the additional 2.1 million jobs held by migrants, or about 1 in 13.

Immigration, then, may well result in an overall rise in GDP, which will result in more jobs for everyone. Equally, however, the idea that some in the native population (typically those with few or no skills and qualifications) might lose out to foreigners is not necessarily a paranoid, right-wing fantasy. On the other hand, it can be argued that a generous and comprehensive welfare state, while it may spawn stories of abuse by those foreigners, may actually serve to compensate and cushion those native-born workers who lose out (at least initially) in a more competitive job market, thereby reducing rather than inflaming anti-immigration sentiment (Crepaz and Damron, 2009).

Figure 10.2 Do immigrants make things better or worse?

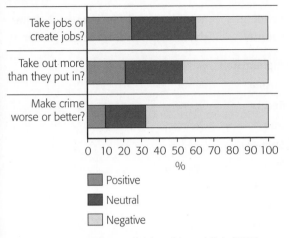

Source: European Social Survey data from Sides and Citrin (2007).

Figure 10.3 Perception is reality? The gap between how many 'foreigners' people think there are and how many there really are

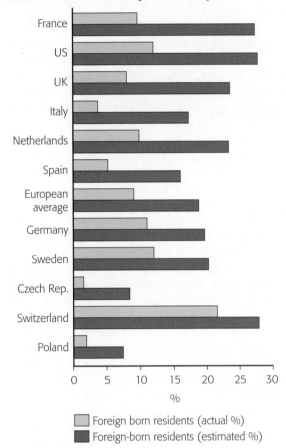

Source: 2002–3 OECD and European Social Survey data from Sides and Citrin (2007).

The perception and the reality also feed into another powerful stereotype – that of immigrants (and those of immigrant origin) as criminals. Given that the children of immigrants often grow up poor and then underperform at school and in the labour market, this can become a vicious circle of deprivation, into which crime – particularly street crime – often enters. For instance, in Rotterdam, in the Netherlands, it has been calculated that nearly eight out of ten who are jailed for such offences are from ethnic minorities. Of course, not everybody in Europe swallows the stereotype whole, but there is enough reality (or perceived reality) in it to mean that plenty of people do buy into it (see Figure 10.2). These perceptions are very difficult to shift, especially because they have some basis in reality, albeit in some countries more than others (see Solivetti, 2012). But the same goes for those that do not. As Figure 10.3 shows, Europeans (like Americans) massively overestimate the numbers of foreign-born people resident in their countries, especially in France and the UK.

Illegal immigration

Although over 1 million people per year still enter the EU legally, the barriers to primary (i.e. economic) immigration were first raised in Europe during the recessions of the 1970s and 1980s. These troubled economic times marked the end of the postwar boom and, partly as a result of the sometimes counterproductive policies pursued to improve matters, saw unemployment return to levels not seen since the 1930s and which would not be seen again until the banking and debt crisis that hit Europe after 2007 (see Chapters 1 and 9). Neither the barriers nor the recessions did much to reduce the push factors for people in developing or conflict-ridden countries: anything was better than where they were, and would-be immigrants were simply driven into increasingly desperate and unlawful measures to get around restrictions. Illegal/irregular immigration into the EU is, in truth, incredibly hard to estimate (see Triandafyllidou, 2010), since it covers those who, whether they slip in unnoticed or initially enter legally and then overstay, effectively disappear, avoiding contact with the authorities, often melting into the communities already established by their (legal) forerunners. A figure commonly quoted in the media, however, is about half a million people per year, with many paying thousands of dollars to 'people-smugglers' or traffickers to help them make it, if not to the European mainland, then to some of its remote islands, often with tragic results.

The routes taken change over time. Indeed illegal migration is commonly compared with the flow of water: if one channel is blocked it will find another. Islands like the Canaries, Malta and Lampedusa in Italy were obvious destinations but the EU and the member states concerned have attempted in recent years (not altogether unsuccessfully) to crack down. By 2012 one of the most popular, at least for those coming from Asia, was the Evros river separating Greece and Turkey, whose waters, journalists from *The Economist* reported, could be crossed in rubber dinghies for around €300 per head. In 2009, local police in Alexandroupolis had registered nearly 9,000 migrants – a figure which ballooned to 47,000 in 2010 and 55,000 in 2011. The biggest single sending country was Pakistan, but there were even migrants trying their luck from the Congo and Algeria in Africa, all of them adding to the estimated half-a-million illegal migrants in Greece. Given the country's economic troubles many of them then attempt to make it further west – either through the Balkans into Hungary and Austria (for €2,800) or straight through from Athens to France in a lorry (for €4,000). Greece and Turkey have long found it difficult to cooperate with each other, which does not make policing the problem any easier – nor does the fact that relations between the EU and Turkey have cooled in recent years (see Chapter 11). But even if security does improve, history teaches us that those who are desperate to get in will find another way – or die trying.

Asylum-seeking

Large numbers of immigrants, however, make it to Europe every year and then claim asylum. Some will

Table 10.5 Favoured destinations of people claiming asylum in EU countries, 2010

Sending country	Most favoured destination	Percentage of claims from sending country
Afghanistan	Germany	29
Russia	Poland	26
Serbia	Germany	38
Iraq	Germany	38
Somalia	Sweden	39
Iran	Germany	29
China	France	35
Pakistan	Greece	30
Nigeria	Italy	21
Syria	Germany	41
Zimbabwe	UK	93

be economic migrants pure and simple, and therefore 'bogus'. Research suggests that the wealth of a country – but, interestingly, not the generosity of its welfare system – does impact on the number of asylum applications it receives (see Neumayer, 2004). But – like Jews from Germany in the 1930s, who also had difficulty persuading authorities in liberal democracies that they were genuinely in need of a place of safety – many will be fleeing for their lives. This is because the number of asylum applications, as well as being related to poverty and discrimination and sheer proximity, is in part a function of civil conflict, state failure and human rights violations (see Neumayer, 2005), although there is often a lagged effect. It therefore comes as no surprise that the top countries of origin for asylum-seekers in EU countries in 2010 were Iraq (10 per cent), Russia and Serbia (7 per cent each), Afghanistan and Turkey (4 per cent each).

On the other hand, their choice of country is rarely random: asylum seekers often make for countries in which there are already communities from their homeland; a common language and colonial connections also count for something (see Table 10.5 and Neumayer, 2004). Sweden, by being particularly welcoming to people from war-torn states like Iraq and Somalia has experienced something of a snowball effect, which explains why a country with a

Table 10.6 Asylum applications and rates of refusal in selected countries

	Total applications p.a.	Percentage of EU total	Percentage of applications rejected
France	56,115	21	80
Sweden	31,225	12	72
Germany	30,400	11	65
UK	23,665	9	70
Italy	20,260	8	54
Netherlands	11,725	4	48
Spain	6,250	2	95
Poland	4,430	2	37
Czech Rep.	1,555	1	77

Source: Data: from Eurostat (2010) The Social Situation in the European Union, p.200.

relatively small population gets so many applications (see Table 10.6). On the other hand (as the same table shows) Sweden is no more generous than most countries, rejecting seven out of ten applications for asylum.

It is also worth pointing out, of course, that European countries' contribution to the problem of displaced persons is nothing like as generous as some claim. Understandably, of course, most Europeans either do not compare their situation with other countries. However, if we do the latter, we can see that certain countries are affected more than others, although the situation varies according to whether the comparison is done on absolute or relative terms (for which see Table 10.7, which provides an indication of the comparative population and financial strains applications represent). In relative terms, or at least in terms of annual applications per head of population, the rankings are very different, with very small countries like Malta and Cyprus, and a relatively small non-member state, Switzerland, appearing to be seriously affected, while the comparative generosity of Sweden becomes even more apparent. On these grounds, the UK, where the press hysteria surrounding asylum seekers has perhaps been greatest, doesn't have that much to

complain about. But it doesn't work like that, largely because it is absolute numbers, their geographical concentration and the peak years that seem to count most – both for ordinary people and (perhaps significantly) for the media they consume. Moreover, as all European states find, it has been one thing to receive an application, another to turn it down and yet another actually to return the person concerned to their country of origin (real or imagined). As politicians and the press never tire of pointing out, many remain regardless of a decision going against them, either because they simply escape the supervision of the authorities or because nowhere else will agree to take them back.

'The numbers game' played in the media involves claim and counterclaims that are very hard to cut-through, not least because there is no one authoritative source of statistics for each country, let alone for Europe as a whole. But it is important, because many Europeans have very little direct contact with migrants and rely for their sense of what is going on (and for many of them what is going wrong) on the

Table 10.7 Countries' capacity to welcome asylum seekers, 2007–11

	Asylum applications per 100 inhabitants	Percentage share (out of 44 advanced democracies)	Applications per $1 of GDP per capita
Malta	20.1	<1	0.3
Sweden	15.6	8	3.9
Cyprus	17.1	1	0.9
Switzerland	9.8	4	1.8
France	3.3	11	6.1
USA	0.9	15	5.9
UK	2.2	7	4.0
Italy	1.8	6	3.6
Netherlands	3.6	3	1.5
Germany	1.9	8	1.4
Poland	1.0	2	1.9
Spain	0.5	1	0.7

Source: Data from UNHCR (2012).

media. Indeed, there is research that suggests that politicians (who may themselves be influenced by newspaper and TV coverage, of course) take account of this: there appears to be a correlation between media coverage and governments taking action to toughen their stances on immigration and integration (see Givens and Luedtke, 2005). Certainly, the media, which made much of the numbers going up, has said relatively little about the fact that from 2002 onwards they appear to have been falling considerably – so much so that they are now only around one-third of their peak in the early 1990s. The UK government achieved a remarkable degree of 'success' in this respect, as well as in reducing the numbers coming in on family grounds, although no-one who relied on the domestic print media for information rather than looking at the statistics across Europe would ever know this. The continental fall may be due to the efforts made by most governments to strengthen their border controls – often, as we shall see, via coordinated action with other receiving states – and to make conditions for asylum seekers (and other immigrants) more onerous. But it is also because civil conflicts in countries close to or in Europe (notably the former Yugoslavia) which help drive asylum applications have reduced in intensity or extent. We should note, of course, that EU member states (which account for eight out of ten claims in Europe) registered 277,400 asylum claims in 2011, which represented a 15 per cent increase on the 240,400 claim registered in 2010 (UNHCR, 2012). On the other hand, it is worth recalling that the 2010 figure represented a drop of 3 per cent on the figure for 2009, which in turn represented a 44 per cent decrease compared to 2008.

Intra-EU migration since enlargement

As asylum appears (rightly or wrongly) to be coming under some kind of control, however, new sources of anxiety have arisen. One of them is the huge increase in legal labour migration prompted by the enlargement of the EU to include much poorer countries from CEE (for background, see Górny and Ruspini, 2004). Once again, some countries are more affected than others. The UK, Ireland and

KEY POINT

Asylum is driven by need, if not always by the imminent threat of persecution that refugee status demands. Some countries seem to get more than their fair share of people seeking that status, although this is disputable if their size is taken into account. Asylum claims have dropped significantly since the peaks seen in the early 1990s and just after the turn of the century.

Sweden decided from the outset that, unlike the rest of the EU-15, they would not introduce restrictions on workers from the postcommunist new member states (the so-called 'A-8'). This meant that anyone from the latter who was not willing to declare themselves self-employed, accept a limited seasonal work permit, or work illegally had only three places they could go if they wanted to earn a western wage. Indeed, given that the power of the trade unions in Sweden seems to have prevented employers from paying immigrants lower wages than their Swedish counterparts, making them less attractive to hire, the choice for many who wished to work in the west effectively came down to the British Isles, although the number of mainly seasonal work permits on offer from Germany still made it a popular destination, as did the ease with which formerly salaried employees could apparently re-define themselves as self-employed. Consequently, the projections made of the numbers who would come to the UK and Ireland were hopelessly inaccurate.

Initial government estimates on how many new EU citizens from CEE would come looking for work in the UK ranged around the 15,000 mark. In the event, over 600,000 from the A-8 registered to work in the UK in the three years following accession, seven out of ten of whom were from Poland. Many of these will, of course, have gone home again, but the numbers of those returning might have been more than made up for by those who do not register

KEY POINT

The distribution of those moving from the postcommunist east to the richer west is also uneven but, interestingly, does not appear to be associated with increased hostility on the part of people in the countries most affected.

Table 10.8 Brits (and others) abroad, 2012

Country of Citizenship	Country of Residence					
	UK	**France**	**Germany**	**Spain**	**Italy**	**Poland**
UK		150,000	104,175	390,880	29,184	764
French	123,000		116,295	122,385	32,956	705
German	297,000	91,000		195,842	42,302	4,446
Spanish	71,000	128,000	111,684		19,094	169
Italian	119,000	174,000	556,145	187,847		672
Polish	550,000	350,000	425,608	85,862	105,608	

Note: Data only includes those officially registered, so numbers are higher in reality.

Source: http://www.guardian.co.uk/news/datablog/2012/jan/26/europe-population-who-lives-where#data

or who declare themselves self-employed. The backlash against this 'flood', especially in right-wing tabloid newspapers which conveniently forget about all those Brits abroad (see Table 10.8) to whom they still like to cater, was predictable and powerful. It led the UK government, notwithstanding a very positive EU report on the economic impact of A-8 migrants (see European Commission, 2006), to join other member states in imposing restrictions on workers from Bulgaria and Romania (the so-called A-2) when those countries joined the EU in 2007. This was just as some member states which had originally imposed restrictions on the A-8 countries in 2004 – Finland, Greece, Italy, the Netherlands, Portugal and Spain – lifted them, while others (Belgium, Denmark, France and Luxembourg) were at least easing them. Only Germany and Austria held out for longer but they created very large seasonal schemes to allow them to employ large numbers of central and eastern Europeans to do the jobs their own workers (notwithstanding continuing high unemployment in Germany) will not do, especially in agriculture. The latter sector, which – especially if involves manual picking – finds it hard to recruit right the way across western Europe, the work being backbreaking and the pay low, is a major source of jobs for migrants, many of whom are unfortunately prone to exploitation by 'gangmasters' who hire them out to growers of flowers, fruit and vegetables with no questions asked.

The new stereotype – migrants and minorities as terrorists

The other contemporary source of anxiety, along with labour migration from 'the new Europe, is Islamist terrorism, especially since the September 11 2001 attacks on New York and Washington were followed by the March 2004 attack in Madrid, the July 2005 bombings in London, the attack on Glasgow airport in June 2007, as well as by numerous plots foiled by police, especially in Germany – the country where the 9-11 attacks were, at least in part, planned. This has contributed to what some analysts refer to as the ongoing 'securitization' of European (and, indeed, global) debates and policy on migration and minorities (see Guild and van Selm, 2005; Huysmans, 2006; Karyotis, 2007), as well as adding yet another to a long list of negative stereotypes with which immigrants have to contend. On the other hand, Islamophobia in Europe has very deep roots, and the spread and visibility of the Islamic population was already the subject of debate in the late 1990s in a number of countries, irrespective of the fact that Muslims – only a small minority of whom approve of, let alone contemplate actually carrying out, radical violence (Leiken, 2012; Pisoiu, 2012) – were not at that stage automatically linked with it (see Box 10.4).

> **BOX 10.4**
>
> ## Islamophobia
>
> It is the extent rather than the existence of European Islamophobia (fear or hatred of Muslims) that is novel. The threat posed by Muslim militancy has long been a familiar tune sung by Europe's populist politicians, particularly in Denmark and Italy. Both countries have a tradition of orchestrated campaigns against the building of mosques – campaigns that have now spread to many European countries (see the special issue on 'Mosque Conflicts in Europe' of the *Journal of Ethnic and Migration Studies*, 31(6) 2005) and resulted in the Swiss voting in a national referendum held in November 2009 to ban the building of minarets. Since 9-11, fears that Europe's Muslims present a clear and present danger have ballooned. Take the Netherlands, where something approaching a moral panic has been going on for a decade. In that year, media reports (backed up by undercover recordings) suggested some of the religious leaders of the country's 800,000 Muslims (who make over 4 per cent of the population) routinely railed against 'the west' and 'western values' such as gender equality and tolerance of homosexuality – attitudes to which remain considerably more conservative among even among the majority of Muslim immigrants who are relatively acculturated to their new European home (see Norris and Inglehart, 2012).
>
> In 2004, people's worst fears were confirmed when outspoken film-maker Theo van Gogh was killed by an Islamist fanatic after his film about the oppression of Muslim women was shown on Dutch TV – a crime which (before she emigrated to the USA) forced one of his collaborators, high-profile MP and apostate, Ayaan Hirsi Ali, into constant police protection (see Buruma, 2007, and Sniderman and Hagendoorn, 2007) – a situation which the charismatic leader of the *Partij voor de Vrijheid*, her former colleague, Geert Wilders, now also finds himself in. On the other hand, Wilders continues to enjoy more liberty than he might have done had a Dutch court not acquitted him on charges of incitement to hatred and discrimination in June 2011 – much to the relief of the Dutch government (for which the PVV was at the time providing vital parliamentary support). Since then there has been talk of banning the wearing of the burqa (which covers the whole body) as a security risk, even though apparently only a few hundred women among the Netherlands' one million Muslims wear it. If this does go ahead it would be following the example of Belgium and France which in 2010 and 2011 passed legislation making it illegal to conceal one's face (and therefore one's identity) in public.

Political responses – populism, priming and 'Catch-22s'

The numbers, concentration and visibility of migrants and minorities in Europe, along with the negative stereotypes (welfare parasite, job-stealer, criminal, terrorist) mean that they are a hot-button political issue in contemporary Europe. Attitudes towards them vary between countries (they seem generally less positive in the EU's new member states) as well as according to sex, education, occupational status and (very significantly) ideological self-placement. These attitudes are not as overwhelmingly hostile as some assume, nor are they necessarily getting worse – especially, interestingly enough, in those countries (the UK, Sweden and Ireland) which have seen big influxes from the new member states in recent years. Nevertheless, there is no doubt that large numbers of Europeans, among elites as well as the so-called masses (see Lahav, 2004: 105–6), are very worried by the situation. These worries, rather than varying much with the numbers of immigrants or levels of unemployment, spring from deeply held preferences for cultural unity and national sovereignty and identity, albeit

KEY POINT

There was Islamophobia in Europe before there was Islamist terrorism, but the latter has almost certainly made things worse.

preferences that are offset by friendships and length of education (see Sides and Citrin, 2007; Hainmueller and Hiscox, 2007). Predictably, Europe's populist politicians have not been slow to pick up on – or even to help drive – these concerns. But the mainstream has had to respond to them, and to some extent has also had a hand in driving them, too.

In the 1990s, parties of the far right, and in particular 'populist radical right parties' (see Mudde, 2007), scored some notable successes, especially in western Europe (see Table 10.9). To many people, these successes are clearly related to xenophobia: in other words, the more hostile to foreigners a country is, the more likely it is to see the far right do well. This is an easy assumption to make – and an understandable one. After all, the one thing such parties have in common is their hostility to immigration (Iversflaten, 2008; see also Almeida, 2010). Moreover,

KEY POINT

In a climate of anxiety, pumped up by the media, populist radical right parties have thrived – but only in some countries, suggesting that it is the skills of the parties concerned, and the reactions of other parties, that matter more than 'objective circumstances'.

that assumption goes well beyond media pundits in Europe: research suggests that the presence of a significant far-right party in a country is enough to discourage would-be asylum seekers from the developing world from trying their luck there, presumably because it suggests they will encounter more hostility there than elsewhere (see Neumayer, 2004). However, back in Europe, perceptions of immigration being a problem or there being too many foreigners in a country – a perception that might or

Table 10.9 'Successful' far-right parties in Europe – electoral performance and parliamentary/government status[a]

Election:	Turn of the century	21st century	Latest	Parliamentary/Government status	
	% (date)	% (date)	% (date)	Previously	Currently
Austria (FPÖ)	26.9 (1999)	10.2 (2002)	17.5 (2008)	Coalition partner	Opposition
(BZÖ)	n/a	n/a	10.7 (2008)	n/a	Opposition
Belgium (VB)	9.9 (1999)	11.6 (2003)	7.7 (2010)	Opposition	Opposition
Bulgaria (Ataka)	n/a	n/a	9.4 (2009)	Opposition	Opposition
Denmark (DF)	12.0 (2001)	13.3 (2005)	12.3 (2011)	Support party	Opposition
France (FN)	14.9 (1997)	11.3 (2002)	13.6 (2012)	No seats	Opposition
Greece (Golden Dawn)	n/a	7.0 (2012)	6.9 (2012)	Opposition	Opposition
Italy (LN)	10.1 (1996)	3.9 (2001)	8.3 (2008)	Coalition partner	Opposition
Netherlands (LPF)[b]	17.0 (2002)	5.7 (2003)	n/a	Coalition partner	No seats
(PVV)	n/a	n/a	10.1 (2012)	Support party	Opposition
Norway (FrP)	15.3 (1997)	14.7 (2001)	22.9 (2009)	Opposition	Opposition
Poland (LPR)	7.9 (2001)	8.0 (2005)	1.3 (2007)	No seats	Finished
Slovakia (SNS)	9.1 (1998)	3.3 (2002)	4.6 (2012)	Opposition	No seats
Sweden (SD)	0.4 (1998)	1.4 (2002)	5.7 (2010)	No seats	Opposition
Switzerland (SVP)	22.5 (1999)	26.6 (2003)	26.6 (2011)	Coalition partner	Coalition partner

Notes: a. Party names are given in full in the List of Abbreviations and Acronyms.
　　b. Not all observers would classify Pim Fortuyn as a right-wing populist, but his party is included.

might not relate to the actual number of foreigners there (see Lahav, 2004: 120) – is, in fact, by no means a guarantee that the far right will do well.

Take Greece: attitudes to immigrants there are among the most hostile in Europe according to most surveys (see Table 10.10). Yet until recently there was little evidence of a far-right breakthrough: the populist Orthodox Rally (LAOS) took only 3.8 per cent of the vote at the 2007 election (though this was up on its score of 2.2 per cent in 2004). This all changed when the extremist Golden Dawn party scored 7 and 6.9 per cent in two elections in 2012. Its performance was widely put down by media commentators to the economic mess the country was in. This is interesting because there is something approaching a consensus among political scientists that – because

support for the far right (and the anti-immigration sentiment it mobilizes on) is more often cultural than it is economic (Lucassen and Lubbers, 2012; McLaren, 2012) – elections where the economy (along with other 'bread and butter' issues favoured by mainstream parties) predominates tend to see the far-right perform relatively poorly (Spies and Franzmann, 2011; see also Bornschier, 2010). In the Greek case, of course, this can perhaps be explained by the fact that the harsh austerity programme which dominated the election was imposed by other countries and international bodies, ensuring that economic and national identity issues were inextricably linked.

Nor are real numbers of foreigners rather than simply exaggerated perceptions or genuine hostility,

Table 10.10 Which countries are least positive towards immigrants and ethnic minorities?

	Percentage **disagreeing** that 'We need immigrants to work in certain sectors of our economy'	Percentage **disagreeing** that 'The arrival of immigrants in Europe can be effective in solving the problem of Europe's ageing population'	Percentage **agreeing** that 'The presence of people from other ethnic groups increases unemployment'	Percentage **disagreeing** that 'Immigrants contribute more in taxes than they benefit from health and welfare services'	Average percentage of immigration- and minority-'negative' responses
Greece	53	67	81	70	68
Czech Rep.	48	51	65	57	55
UK	40	55	59	51	51
Germany	33	52	44	61	48
France	32	47	44	66	47
EU-27 average	37	45	49	51	46
Netherlands	35	45	38	51	42
Italy	32	41	47	48	42
Poland	41	35	48	35	40
Spain	27	23	57	42	37
Sweden	21	29	31	41	31

Notes: Respondents had the option of picking 'it depends' as well 'don't know' and 'agree': this means we have to be more careful than usual to remember not to infer the percentage agreeing from the percentage disagreeing.

Source: *Eurobarometer* 71 (*Future of Europe*), 2010.

a guarantee of far right success. For every Switzerland (see Box 10.5) there are many more countries with high foreign populations (and much more difficult economic and social conditions for that matter) that go for years without the far right making an impact, and although there does in general seem to be a correlation between the foreign born share of the population and the far right's vote share, it is also worth noting that (in keeping with what we have just said about the way the salience of economic concerns can crowd out cultural anxiety) that correlation weakens as the unemployment rate increases (Arzheimer, 2009; Spies and Franzmann, 2011). This suggests that only part of the far right's success can be put down to its nativist (and populist) stance – to its assertion that the nation belongs to those who are born there and is at risk from both outsiders and their ideas, as well as from mainstream politicians and other elites who will sell 'the people' down the river.

Clearly, electoral systems have some impact on success or failure – it is difficult to imagine a pop-

---

BOX 10.5

Too many black sheep? Switzerland's immigration debate

Switzerland is famous for its wealth (some of it stored in the famously secret bank accounts that allegedly still hold wealth looted from European Jews by the Nazis) and for its direct democracy (see Chapter 6). June 2005 also saw a referendum on a challenge to governmental and parliamentary approval of Switzerland joining the Schengen area, meaning that those travelling to and from member countries do not have to show passports, while their governments share information relating to cross-border crime, as well as migration and asylum (see Box 10.9). Turnout among the country's 4.8 million registered voters was 56 per cent and the decision to join was upheld by 55 per cent to 45 per cent. The vote also meant that Switzerland would be allowed automatically to turn back asylum claimants travelling from EU countries. Later on in the year, in September, the Swiss also approved the extension (in 2011) to the ten newest member states of the EU of the right to work freely in Switzerland – a freedom enjoyed by citizens of the pre-accession EU-15 from 2007 onwards.

Notwithstanding its being part of the government, the populist radical right party, the SVP (see Skenderovic, 2007) campaigned for a 'no' vote, building on existing anxieties about immigration in a country that probably gets more than its fair share of asylum seekers (see Table 10.7) and in which non-nationals make up a quarter of its workforce, along with an estimated 100,000 illegals. During the first referendum the SVP joined the 'Association for a Neutral and Independent Switzerland' in a campaign that included the erection of a large-scale Trojan horse in order to reinforce the message that the country would be flooded by foreigners. This was a fairly mild stunt considering how hysterical the debate can get in Switzerland. In December 2002, for instance, Swiss media revealed the plans of one town (Meilen, near Zurich) which had a holding centre for asylum seekers to ban them from places such as schools and sports grounds, to prevent them from congregating in public places, and to forbid them from using the municipal swimming pool unless accompanied by a local resident or local official. According to media reports, this *apartheid*-style regime was based on a map showing no-go areas, indicated on the key by four black men with a line through them.

It should perhaps have come as no surprise, then, when in 2007 the SVP launched an eye-grabbing election poster showing three cartoon white sheep standing on the Swiss flag with one of the sheep raising its rear legs to administer a swift kick to the butt of a fourth, black, sheep effectively shoving it off the map. The SVP increased its vote to almost 29 per cent and remained Switzerland's biggest party when it polled nearly 27 per cent in 2011, after a referendum in late 2010 approved its call for the automatic deportation of any foreigner found to have broken the criminal law.

The Czech Republic (Česko)

Area: 77,300 km² (1.8% of EU-27)

Population: 10.5 million (2% of EU-27)

Religious heritage: Roman Catholic (with Protestant minority)

GDP (2010): €145 billion (1.1% of EU-27)

GDP *per capita* as percentage of EU-27 average: 80

Female representation in parliament and cabinet (end 2011): 22% and 0%

Joined EU: 2004

Top 3 cities: Prague – capital city (1.3 million), Brno (0.4 million), Ostrava (0.3 million).

History: The present-day Czech Republic began life in January 1993, after 75 years as part of a federal state known as Czechoslovakia. The latter was created when the Austro-Hungarian Empire was broken up following the First World War. During the nineteenth century the rise of nationalism in the 'Czech lands' of Bohemia and Moravia made the provinces a thorn in the side of the Germanic Habsburg dynasty. Slovak nationalism also developed in parallel opposition to Hungarian rule in what was eventually to become the Slovak Republic. The exceptions were the German-speaking areas of the Czech lands, later known as the Sudetenland. Claims of discrimination against its inhabitants gave Hitler's Germany an excuse to annex part of what, by the mid-1930s, was one of Europe's most prosperous democracies. When Germany then grabbed the entire country in 1939, Slovakia, already chafing against membership of the rump federal state, declared itself independent. Following Hitler's defeat in 1945, a reunified Czechoslovakia seized

the opportunity to expel 2.5 million ethnic Germans, thousands of whom died on forced marches or in reprisals by Czech paramilitaries. Elections in 1946 brought the Communist Party to power with a degree of mass support unusual in Eastern Europe but, by 1948, it had effectively put an end to democracy. Over the next four decades, the country developed into a repressive regime, punctuated by an attempt at liberalization (known as 'the Prague Spring'), which was crushed by Soviet-led military intervention in August 1968. However, the Soviet-backed regime ultimately found itself unable to resist massive demonstrations (labelled 'people power') which, as elsewhere in Europe, hastened the collapse of the Communist governments in 1989.

After a bloodless handover of power to democratic reformers, dubbed the 'velvet revolution', came the 'velvet divorce' with Slovakia in late 1992. This happened against the wishes of founding president (and former dissident) Václav Havel, whose petition signed by a million Czechoslovak citizens for a referendum was ignored by parliamentary politicians on both sides. Initially the Czech Republic was ruled by coalitions led by the centre-right Civic Democrats (ODS) and then, following corruption scandals in the late 1990s, by the centre-left Social Democrats (ČSSD). The latter, though, have found it hard to find a majority, not least because they cannot work closely with a largely unreformed Communist Party that is still capable of garnering up to a fifth of the vote. In 2010, however, what had been see as one of central and

eastern Europe's most stable party systems was shaken by the entry (at the expense of the Civic Democrats, who lost 15 percentage points compared to 2006, and the Social Democrats, who lost ten) of two new parties – the centre-right TOP 09 and the populist (but not right-wing) VV.

Economy and society: The country's 10 million people have one of the highest standards of living in CEE although clearly still some way below the EU average. This relatively high standing is due not just to tourism but to industry – Czech car-makers and defence, manufacturers have, like banking and property, proved attractive to foreign investors for whom the

WHAT'S IN AN ANTHEM?

Kde domov moj? may well be the only national anthem in the world to have emerged (in the mid-nineteenth century) from a musical comedy, as well as one of the few to end with a question mark. It originally had two verses but the second was replaced by a Slovak verse when the two nations were forced together after the First World War. This was then removed after the 'velvet divorce' of the early 1990s, leaving the anthem with just the one verse, thereby rendering it one of the world's shortest. The lyrics conjure up a rural idyll – waters murmur, pinewoods rustle, spring shines in the orchard and all's well with the world in the beautiful Czech land that the singer calls home.

country's proximity to the huge German market is an obvious plus. A reasonably comprehensive welfare state and fairly moderate economic policies have helped ease the strains of transition on a population that sees itself as largely homogeneous and is generally opposed to sharp growth in social inequalities.

Governance: The Czech Republic is a parliamentary democracy whose government is led by a prime minister appointed, at the suggestion of the speaker of the parliament, by the president. The latter – officially a largely ceremonial head of state – was elected every five years by both chambers of the bicameral parliament, but from 2013 will be directly elected by voters. The more powerful lower house, the Chamber of Deputies, is elected by PR. Members of the upper house, the Senate, however, are elected in single-member constituencies under a two-round majoritarian electoral system. Electoral reform seems to be favoured (in their own interests) by the largest parties but has been successfully resisted by their smaller counterparts.

Foreign policy: The Czechs have devoted themselves to returning to the heart of Europe by achieving membership of NATO, which they joined in 1999, and the EU, of which they became part in May 2004. Other objectives include establishing a reputation for reliability and stability in order to attract foreign investment. Relations with Germany are accorded a high priority in spite of (or perhaps because of) continuing sensitivities on both sides over the expulsion of the Sudeten Germans and the German occupation. Relations with Russia, which in the days of the former Soviet Union kept a tight hold over the Czechs, have, however, come under

KEY CONTEMPORARY CHALLENGE
RIDDING THE COUNTRY OF TRICKY POLITICIANS

The general election saw the arrival in parliament and in government of two relatively new parties which, among other things, promised an end to what many Czechs had come to believe were the endemic dirty tricks and corruption of the conservative and social democratic parties that had run their country – mostly separately but sometimes together – since the Velvet Divorce from Slovakia. Given how thoroughly penetrated both the ODS and the SSD had become by business interests, especially in cities and at the regional level, this was never going to be an easy task. However, few could have guessed quite how quickly hopes would be dashed. The first depressing revelations concerned the smaller of the two new parties, Public Affairs (VV), whose driving force, Vít Bárta, and more specifically his security firm, had, it turned out, been conducting illegal surveillance of politicians from the conservative Civic Democrats, although largely at the behest of their intra-party rivals. Bárta was then accused of planning to use his position in government to enrich his firm and of bribing VV MPs to maintain their loyalty. The ensuing dispute was played out in the media as illicit recordings of calls and meetings between party members were leaked, completely undermining all concerned, not least because some of them made it obvious that the party was bypassing party funding regulations. Bárta, who was eventually sentenced on corruption charges, was forced (along with another colleague) to resign from the government, but a number of VV MPs remained in the coalition by forming a new party – the Liberal Democrats. Meanwhile, the other coalition partners (ODS and TOP 09) experienced problems of their own. Although those problems seemed to have involved financial irregularities on the part of individual ministers rather than the parties as a whole, were not made any easier by the fact that not all of those involved stood down. Whether, in the light of all this, voters were particularly impressed by the government's measures to clean up corruption in the public procurement process and infrastructure projects (including those funded by the EU), seems doubtful at best.

strain as the result of the latter's willingness to host the radar systems for the USA's proposed missile defence system.

Contemporary challenges
- Ridding the country of tricky politicians – some of them from parties pledged to fight corruption (see below)
- Seriously attempting to combat discrimination against Roma minority
- Overcoming the inability of what is still an overly politicized (and, some say, corrupt) public administration to manage and draw down EU funding efficiently
- Tackling a deficit that makes adoption of the euro difficult and a pension system that will struggle as the working population shrinks.

Learning resources. Try Hanley (2006), *The New Right in the New Europe*, which deals with Czech politics since 1989 and Deegan-Krause (2006), *Elected Affinities*, which provides an illuminating comparison with Slovakia. A more general (but still useful) read is Bazant *et al.* (2010), *The Czech Reader*. Keep up to date with the news at www.radio.cz/en/ and http://drseansdiary.wordpress.com/

ulist radical right party making it into the UK parliament, for instance, while proportional representation systems clearly offer more of a chance for such parties to make an initial breakthrough; they might even offer some insurance against a complete wipeout later if things go wrong later on – something that often happens when (as in Austria, for example) the stirring and simplistic promises of opposition can't be delivered in government. Yet give or take some of the differences in electoral thresholds and formulas covered in Chapter 6, the PR systems in use in most countries do not vary sufficiently to explain why some have successful populist radical right parties and some do not (see Carter, 2005).

All of this brings us back to something that might perhaps have been more obvious in the first place had political scientists not been so keen to find more structural explanations that focused, to use the jargon, on the 'demand side' rather than the 'supply side' of politics. Put simply, a good deal of the success or failure of populist radical right parties must be down to how well organized and led they are (see Art, 2011; de Lange and Art, 2011). Obviously, being able to tap into a well of anxiety about immigrants and social breakdown helps. So (especially in the early days) do media outlets which boost the legitimacy and the profile of the far right – perhaps because they believe they have a democratic duty to report on it and the issues it raises, perhaps because they are looking for allies against governments which won't give them what they want commercially, or perhaps simply because they believe anti-immigrant parties provide screaming headlines and good copy (see Art, 2007; Ellinas, 2010; see also Vliegenthart *et al.*, 2012). But ultimately only flexible and competent outfits with savvy leaders can take real advantage of the opportunities with which they are presented (see Mudde, 2007; Norris, 2005; see also Lubbers *et al.*, 2002; van der Brug *et al.*, 2000) – something which emerges even more clearly in detailed studies of far-right parties which fail to break through (see, for example, Goodwin, 2011; Mareš, 2011).

There is another important but often forgotten point to make about those far-right parties that do find success. This is that, in terms of getting into government (if not always in terms of votes), they harm the centre-left more than the centre-right. The latter, although it has traditionally been 'tougher' on

the issue (see Bale, 2008; Gudbrandsen, 2010), obviously has to be careful not to go too far down the anti-immigrant line lest it alienate its business constituency, which is often in favour of anything that fills labour shortages (especially at a knock-down price), and (in the case of Christian democratic parties) a Catholic charity sector known for its good work among newcomers in difficulties. But unlike its counterpart on the left, the mainstream right has fewer dues to pay to progressive values such as liberalism and tolerance. It also has less compunction about getting together in government with more extreme parties on platforms that emphasize the need – and their willingness – to 'do something' about a 'crisis' which they themselves have often done more than a little to talk up in preceding years, thereby helping those more extreme parties to take off in the first place (see Bale, 2003, 2008; Ellinas, 2010; see also Arzheimer and Carter, 2006, and Meguid, 2005). Both mainstream and more populist right-wing politicians, in other words, have, along with the media, helped to 'prime' immigration (and its supposed accomplices – crime, welfare abuse and terrorism) as an issue, helping to boost its salience among voters (see Bohman, 2011; see also Chapter 8). The common wisdom that it is in those countries which maintain what is pejoratively labelled by pundits a 'conspiracy of silence' on the issue that the far right do best is inaccurate: take Scandinavia, where immigration has been talked about quite openly and quite vituperatively for years in Norway and especially Denmark, but not in Sweden (see Box 10.6; see also Odmalm, 2011) where (discounting a flash in the pan in the early 1990s) it took much longer for a populist radical right party to break through.

Interestingly, with the exception of those representing *Ataka* in Bulgaria and the PRM in Romania, not even Europe's populist politicians now justify their hard (some would say hostile) line on immigrants on the explicit grounds of racial difference or superiority. Instead, they talk of 'a clash of cultures', of ways of life that cannot be reconciled when immigrant minorities refuse to 'assimilate' and adopt the dress, customs and ideologies of their host country (see Eatwell, 2000: 411). They also talk about the links between immigration and rising crime and chronic abuse of the welfare state – both issues that the right has traditionally owned. The left is vulner-

Sweden – still immune?

Sweden used to be held up as unusual in that populist radical right parties – with one temporary exception (called New Democracy) in the early 1990s – fared miserably at the polls. This was in spite of the fact that the proportion of the country's population born abroad went from just 4 per cent in 1960 to over 10 per cent by the mid-1990s – thanks not to labour migration (which was strictly limited by the Swedish social democrats and their trade union allies) but to a very generous asylum and family reunification policy. It was also in spite of public concern about immigration (even if it was not traditionally as high as in other European countries) and in spite of a worrying degree of organized racist violence. The poor performance of the far right stood in marked contrast with Sweden's Nordic neighbours, Denmark and Norway, where such parties perform well. At the 2002 election, however, the populist mantle was taken on, a little surprisingly, by the Liberal Party, which focused on welfare dependency among newcomers, arguing that those unable to find work should, after a short period, be repatriated and that those who stayed should be helped to integrate by language and citizenship classes. It seemed to work as an electoral strategy: in a matter of months, the Liberals went from being a party in danger of slipping below Sweden's 4 per cent threshold to 13.4 per cent, trebling its score at the previous election. Some predicted that the genie had escaped from the bottle for a second time: we would, they argued, now see the erosion of the cross-party consensus which seemed to have succeeded – contrary to so much common wisdom elsewhere in Europe concerning the dangers of a 'conspiracy of silence' – in damping down the vote for the far right. They were wrong in one respect: Sweden's mainstream parties continue for the most part not to politicize the issue and (see Green-Pedersen and Odmalm, 2008). However, in 2006 the far-right *Sverigedernokraterna* doubled its vote to just under 3 per cent and in 2010 it made it over the threshold and into parliament, with its 5.7 per cent of the vote garnering it 20 MPs in a parliament of 349.

able on these issues because it is seen as soft, as 'out of touch' with how things really are for ordinary people.

Certainly, many social democrats rightly fear a loss of working-class support to the far right on this issue, notwithstanding the easily forgotten fact that an individual's views on immigration and minorities are in part structured by an individual's left–right orientation (see Lahav, 2004: 127–35). Theoretically, the left faces a 'catch-22'. It faces calls to adopt a more hard-line attitude in order to appear responsive to public anxieties and to prevent the defection to the radical right of some of its 'natural' working-class voters who, perhaps because contemporary social democracy no longer has much to offer them when it comes to redistribution, buy into narratives that blame their current insecurity on crime, fraud, immigration and corrupt and out-of-touch politicians (see Elchardus and Spruyt, 2011; see also Chapter 9). The centre-left in Europe, then, may be just as likely as its centre-right rivals to join rather than beat those who argue for a tougher line on immigration control and integration. Especially in countries where the populist radical right has scored big successes (such as Denmark, Norway, the Netherlands and Austria), social democratic parties have moved to close down the gap by assenting to, or even promoting, a harder line on migration and multiculturalism. But even where the far-right parties have gained less traction, the UK being the most obvious example, social democratic parties (indeed, many mainstream parties) have done the same (see Alonso and Claro de Fonseca, 2012), suggesting perhaps that the move is not simply a reaction to far-right parties but – and some would say this was democracy in action – a response to the very real concerns of the electorate they seek to represent, as well, of course, as an attempt to offset any advantage such concerns may afford their centre-right opponents (see Bale *et al.*, 2010a, 2012).

Ironically, such a response may make things worse in the long run. By toughening its own line on immigration and integration, the centre-left risks rendering legitimate (rather than squeezing out) the very xenophobia its strategy is designed to contain – xenophobia that might then boost support for those parties it is trying to defeat (van Spanje, 2010). This seems to be borne out by recent research conducted in Sweden which uses local politics to generate a sufficient number of cases in which to conduct a rigorous statistical investigation (Dahlström and Sundell, 2012). It finds that

> a tougher stance on immigration on the part of mainstream parties is correlated with more anti-immigrant party support... [M]ainstream parties legitimize anti-immigrant parties by taking a tougher position on immigration. However, the results presented in the paper show that it is not sufficient for one mainstream party to take a tougher position; it is only when the entire political mainstream is tougher on immigration that the anti-immigrant party benefits. What is more, the toughness of the parties on the left seems to be more legitimizing than the toughness of the parties on the right.

One question raised, of course, by the response (and possible contribution) of mainstream parties, left and right, to the success of the far right is how much influence the latter have had on public policy. Certainly, as we note below, there appears to have been a turn away from the official promotion of multiculturalism (although explicit encouragement of the latter was never as great as is sometimes suggested) and more emphasis on integration (if not full assimilation), even if its realization may in fact lie more in the hands of ordinary people than governments (see Box 10.7). And most European countries have made efforts to tighten up their immigration control, even if one can argue that they did this from the early 1970s onwards – before the far right was a political force – and that they are nonetheless still keen (primarily perhaps for economic reasons) to allow 'the right kind of immigrant' in wherever possible. But is this 'restrictive turn' (see Joppke, 2007a) really due to pressure from the radical right inside or outside government (see Howard, 2010; Minkinberg, 2002; Schain, 2006; M.H. Williams, 2006)? Perhaps mainstream parties are responding, in more or less democratic fashion, to real problems (or at least problems that are perceived as real) by the electorate (see Jennings, 2009, and also Bale, 2008)? And they may very well be acting – even on the left – in a manner which is consonant with their ideology and past practice (Hinnfors et al., 2012).

This is a classic conundrum for comparative politics and, indeed, political science as a whole: since an actor was present, how do we judge whether action would have been taken in their absence, and, just because they were present, does that mean that they were responsible? Just because it is a difficult question, however, does not mean it cannot be answered. Indeed, the two most impressive attempts to do so in recent years come to a pretty clear conclusion (Akkerman, 2012; Akkerman and de Lange, 2012). Firstly, although there is considerable between-country and within-country variation, it does seem possible and plausible, at least in those few countries where we have examples, to tie policy changes to the presence of far-right parties that have joined governments (as in Austria, Italy, and the Netherlands) or provided legislative support to them (as in the Netherlands and Denmark). Second, however, not only do right-wing governments pursue more restrictive and assimilationist policies on immigration and integration than left-wing and centrist governments but do so whether or not they contain or are supported by far-right parties. Moreover, even when it comes to those governments which contain or are supported by such parties, the running on policy is as often as not made by the mainstream (centre-) right party or parties rather than their more radical partners.

Less difficult to answer is another, more substantive question related to the issue of populist parties in office; namely, does it do them any good (see Akkerman and de Lange, 2012; Bolleyer et al., 2012)? The answer, at least in the short-term, varies according to which country and party you look at: some win, some lose; generally speaking they do not seem to fare any worse than some other small, radical and often new parties that take the plunge; indeed, they actually fare a little better, all told, than the radical left in this respect. Even if they lose in the short term, however, the inevitable difficulty they experience in converting rash promises into hard choices may not prevent them from staying in the game and maybe even making a comeback at a later date. The fate of the FPÖ in Austria, which was controversially first invited into a coalition in 1999, is a case in point (see Fallend, 2004; Heinisch, 2003; Luther, 2003). The party fell apart and eventually split; however, unlike, say, the LPF in the Netherlands, it lived to fight another day – indeed, if

BOX 10.7

A two-way street: the integration of migrants

The EU's opinion research arm, *Eurobarometer*, is best known for its surveys but it also conducts focus group research. One recent example involved working with both migrants and members of the general public in several states to find out what they thought about integration. There were a few minor differences, but what shines through most from the key findings is how much both sets agreed and a general willingness to admit both a degree of ambivalence about, and a degree of personal (as opposed to governmental) responsibility for, the current situation:

▶ A list of factors that facilitate integration was presented to participants. Among the general public, on average, the top four most important factors that facilitate integration are: 1. Can speak the language; 2. Have a job; 3. Respect local cultures; 4. Enjoy legal status. While among migrants the… factors in order of priority are as follows: 1. Can speak the language; 2. Enjoy legal status; 3. Have a job; 4. Respect local cultures

▶ We asked participants to indicate which of four criteria are most important in deciding who should be eligible to stay in the country. Both the general public and migrants agree that being able to speak or wanting to learn the local language and having a job or job offer are the most important criteria…. Migrants also feel that having family in the country should play a role, whereas the general public are less agreed on this criterion. Several additional criteria were suggested for inclusion by both audiences: notably, a clean criminal record was mentioned by both.

▶ Interestingly, both the general public and migrants feel that citizenship is not necessary for successful integration. Despite the fact that migrants are of the view that having 'legal status' is important in successful integration they did not feel that it was necessary to have citizenship; for most migrants, the benefits gained through citizenship are not outweighed by the costs of relinquishing their own citizenship.

▶ The general public identified many actions that they could do themselves to improve integration within their neighbourhood and their community. Participants from most member states identified the need for a change in the attitude of the general public as the cornerstone to improving integration. In addition there were many relatively small gestures (smiling, saying hello, talking, inviting to everyday activities etc.) that they believed could make migrants feel more welcome and included in society. At work the general public recognized that they could be more sociable and helpful.

▶ We asked migrants how they felt they could improve integration in their neighbourhood and community and they identified changing their own attitude as being something they could do, amongst a variety of other actions. At work, they felt that learning the language better and being more sociable would help to improve integration. However, there was a perception among many migrants that the responsibility for improving integration lies more with the general public than with themselves.

▶ Improving public understanding of the migrant situation is largely believed to be a media issue. Both the general public and migrants feel that negative migrant stereotypes are a result, at least in part, of negative press coverage. Nevertheless, they see the potential to reverse the trend and create a more positive view of migrants and their contribution to society through a more accurate, unbiased and realistic portrayal of migrants.

Source: Qualitative Eurobarometer, *Migrant Integration*, May 2011.

the votes of the two parties that emerged from the split are put together, one can argue that the populist radical right actually gained from its second period in government (see Table 10.9). Reports of the death of the Italian LN have also been exaggerated on a number of occasions, although the crisis provoked by the severe stroke suffered by its leader, the bombastic Umberto Bossi, in 2004 (a calamity from which he eventually recovered), poses another interesting question, can it survive the passing of a dominant, charismatic leader (see Pedahzur and Brichta, 2002)?

This is a dilemma, of course, for populist radical right parties all over Europe but not one that will necessarily lead to failure. In 2006, for example, Carl I. Hagen finally stepped down after 28 years at the helm of the Norwegian Progress Party, one of the best-supported parties of its kind in Europe. His successor, Siv Jensen, managed to lead the party to its best-ever result (22.9 per cent of the vote) in the 2009 general election. And although Progress has since lost some support – possibly because of its association with Anders Behring Breivik, the neo-nazi fanatic behind the shocking murders of 77 people (many of them teenagers) in July 2011, who was formerly a party member – it seems clear that Norway's main conservative party now see it as a potential coalition partner. And if it does get the opportunity to govern, it may well seize it: after all, as a valuable recent study of the Belgian Vlaams Belang reminds us (Pauwels, 2011), being frozen out of power can be just as damaging to radical right parties' support as being invited to share it.

Finally, when thinking about impact, it is worth asking about whether, in or out of office, far-right parties, by their very presence in the system (and especially in parliament), encourage more intolerance towards minorities on the part of the general public. The answer, judging from recent research (Dunn and Singh, 2011), would appear to be a resounding No. Although such parties clearly take advantage of high levels of intolerance in many European countries, their strength is not related to them: how else do we explain, for instance, the lack of success enjoyed by the far-right in the Czech Republic (see Mareš, 2011), which has higher levels of intolerance than many west European countries (although much lower levels than many in eastern and central Europe), while in Denmark, which has one of the lowest levels of intolerance in Europe, the

far-right is a seemingly permanent fixture? Moreover, given how long it has been represented in the Danish parliament, we would by now have been expecting to see an uptick in levels of intolerance, but there has been no such increase. Research looking at these examples as part of a wider cross-national study concludes that the impact of a far-right party in parliament on public tolerance pales into insignificance when set against the fact that most such parties can only operate effectively in party systems and legislatures that contain a diverse range of voices, all of which, by being represented in the media, conditions most people to expect and accept a degree of diversity. In addition, those individuals most likely to be attracted to the far-right's message are already likely to hold attitudes that are already so markedly intolerant that they are unlikely to be rendered much more so by exposure to a far-right party.

Integrating and protecting migrants and minorities

No doubt, if many of today's immigrants did not look so different, were more widely dispersed, and did not insist on their human right to hold onto their religion and culture, things might be easier. European countries might be able to muddle through and let hypocrisy – and, of course, the immigrants themselves and those who live directly alongside them – take the strain. But the problem is, in part, one of visibility, of concentration and of an apparent 'failure' of **integration** or **assimilation** that is subjected to increasing media and political attention. Many of Europe's biggest cities (particularly in western Europe) are now multicultural. They are not, however, always 'melting-pots': different communities live alongside each other but often share little in common. To the middle-class liberal, **multiculturalism** could be a cause for celebration, bringing welcome diversity in the arts, in cuisine and in the economy. Others, whether they live in the cities and resent the changes and the differences or, instead, live outside them and see them as modern-day dens of iniquity, are less welcoming, perhaps distrustful and even downright hostile. Both as a cause and an effect of this negative reaction,

KEY POINT

European governments have begun to place more emphasis on ensuring that immigrants fit into the countries they come to rather than relying on a policy of live and let live. Many have tried to balance this by stepping up anti-discrimination efforts.

Europe's ethnic minorities congregate in particular parts of particular cities. It is also obvious that newly arrived immigrants will set up where they have family and friends, and where there may be jobs. For instance, foreigners constitute around one in ten of the population of the Netherlands, but in Rotterdam the figure is at least one in three.

There is nothing new in this concentration, perhaps. Anyone familiar with the USA will know that certain neighbourhoods in certain cities are often associated with a particular ethnic group. But in the USA, the strong sense of American identity, the stress on English and the drive toward upward mobility, all reinforced by an education system that stresses citizenship and an economic system that makes such mobility possible for so many, tends to work against the establishment of ghettos from which there is no escape. At least, this is the case for people who, whatever their creed, could pass as 'white' (something that has never been true for African-Americans and, at the moment, seems difficult for Latinos and some Asians). In Europe, the state – with the exception of France – is rather more reluctant to force the issue in schools, where minority languages are often protected by law.

Integration is about newcomers fitting peacefully and productively into a host society. **Assimilation** involves minorities and/or migrants adopting the practices, customs, language, manners and even the mores of the host country. **Multiculturalism** implies the preservation and coexistence of separate ethnicities – communities living alongside each other but not necessarily interacting or sharing much in common. Both regimes are ideal types: in reality most European countries – even those supposedly on the two ends of the spectrum like France and the Netherlands (see Bertossi et al., 2012) – have more in common in this respect than the stereotypes suggest.

Welfare can also more easily become a way of life – albeit not a very comfortable one. And many immigrants (and even their children) have little hope of passing as 'white'. Therefore, reassurances that all this is 'just a phase' that has to be gone through every so often are, perhaps understandably, met with rather more scepticism and distrust.

As a response to fears about the threat to security (cultural and physical) posed by the separatism supposedly inherent in multiculturalism, many governments have put an additional premium in recent years on the integration, if not the full-blown assimilation, of minorities. The most obvious way to do this, at least formally, is to grant them citizenship – the only thing, incidentally, that in most countries allows immigrants to vote, at least in national elections (see Box 10.8). It is clear from Table 10.11 that European countries, whether they are located in the tradition of *jus solis* (affording citizenship to all born in the country) or *jus sanguinis* (making it dependent on blood ties), are still creating new citizens, although the rates do vary quite widely: some states are seemingly much keener on getting their foreign-born residents to commit permanently to the country. Each European country allows resident foreigners to gain citizenship in different ways and at different rates, each having its own citizenship requirements based on a sometimes bewildering (and changing) combination of birth and residency requirements (see Bauböck et al., 2006). But in increasing numbers of them these requirements are now moving beyond simply birth and residence to include familiarity with the country and its language being tested before citizenship and even, in some cases, residency is granted (see Wright, 2008) – which could well have the (intended) knock-on effect of making immigration more difficult (see Joppke, 2007b; Joppke et al., 2010; see also Goodman, 2010). From March 2006, all foreigners applying for permanent residency in the Netherlands, for example, have had to pass a test on Dutch language and society – unless, that is, they are citizens of another EU country, Switzerland, the USA, Japan and New Zealand, or if they are a victim of human trafficking. There are similar schemes in other European countries, among them France, Germany and the UK.

Politicians all over Europe, then, have been calling for and putting into place measures that they claim

---

BOX 10.8

Non-nationals and electoral rights in Europe

According to the annual report of the EU's Fundamental Rights Agency published in 2011,

> no Member State gives voting rights to non-national EU citizens in any other elections than municipal and European Parliament elections. Slovenia is the only exception to this as EU citizens from other Member States may vote in elections for the National Council (the second chamber of parliament) where bodies representative of social, economic, professional and local interests are seated. If an EU citizen from another Member State residing in Slovenia belongs to one of these groups he or she will be able to vote and to be elected. In Ireland, United Kingdom (UK) citizens residing in the country may vote in Irish general elections; however, only Irish citizens are entitled to vote in the presidential elections.

Meanwhile, rights for non-EU citizens residing in EU countries vary considerably:

> a great number of EU member states grant, to some extent, third-country nationals the right to political participation at local level – in fact, more than half of the EU member states do so. Belgium, Denmark, Greece, Ireland, the Netherlands and Sweden provide all third-country nationals with the right to vote and the right to stand as a candidate. Luxembourg and Estonia provide third-country nationals with the right to vote but not to stand as a candidate. Some EU member states, such as Finland, Lithuania or Slovakia grant the right to vote and to stand as a candidate to all third-country nationals who have a permanent residence or who hold a long-term residence status. Slovenia and Hungary provide third-country nationals with permanent residence or with long-term residence status with the right to vote but not to stand as a candidate. Finally, several member states provide only citizens of certain third countries with political rights: in Portugal and the UK, certain citizens of certain third countries have the right to vote and to stand as a candidate, while in Spain citizens from certain third countries have the right to vote, but not to stand as a candidate.

---

are designed to improve the integration of immigrants, most notably language and citizenship classes. Again, this is Europeanization, but by learning and following best practice (if that is what it is) rather than driven by the EU. As to the practical results of such measures, beyond providing a measure of reassurance to 'host' populations, it may be too early to tell. Critics on both sides see such attempts as symbolic sops that will make little or no difference. To ardent multiculturalists, they represent an emotive backlash (see Vertovec and Wessendorf, 2009) and a damaging attack on their essentially successful 'live and let live' approach. To those who believe that integration should mean nothing less than complete assimilation into the culture and belief system of the receiving country (assuming for the moment that countries of several million individuals can be said to possess a uniform set of practices and values), the odd citizenship and language class cannot possibly hope to deliver what they want.

But if immigration is to be controlled and immigrants integrated, then native populations presumably have to do their bit, too. Racism leading (at the very least) to discrimination, after all, is by no means a thing of the past in most European countries, even though most EU member states have made considerable progress towards putting systems in place to report on and combat it. A 'framework agreement' was signed in April 2007, following six years of stop–start negotiations, by the justice ministers of the 27 EU states, and commits them to introducing sentences of between one and three years for anyone 'publicly inciting to violence or hatred directed against [persons] defined by reference to race, colour, religion, descent or national or ethnic origin'. The same year also saw the establishment of the EU's Fundamental Rights Agency which uses some of its €20 million annual budget to monitor racism and highlight best practice among member states for tackling it. In a recent

Table 10.11 The granting of citizenship in selected countries, 2009

	Number of Citizenships granted	Citizenships granted per 100 resident foreigners
Sweden	29,500	5.3
Poland	1,800	4.8
UK	203,600	4.8
Netherlands	29,800	4.1
France	135,800	3.6
Switzerland	43,400	2.6
EU-27	776,100	2.4
Italy	59,400	1.5
Spain	79,600	1.4
Germany	96,100	1.3
Czech Rep.	1,100	0.3

Source: Data from UNHCR (2012).

annual report (Fundamental Rights Agency, 2011a), for instance, it noted that:

- discrimination in the area of employment remained prevalent, with cases relating to discrimination in job advertisements, recruitment processes, working conditions and dismissals;
- access to healthcare remained dependent on efforts to overcome language barriers and accommodate cultural diversity. In the case of irregular migrants, access hinged upon whether healthcare personnel were required to report undocumented persons to the authorities;
- although formal legal and administrative barriers to accessing social housing were present in only a few member states, available evidence suggested that minorities continue to live in lower-quality housing resulting from both direct and indirect discrimination;
- segregation in education appeared to remain a problem affecting mainly Roma children in some member states. Barriers to access to education remained for children of undocumented migrants in some member states where school authorities are obliged to collect information

and report on the legal status of students and their parents;

- a number of member states were beginning to move towards the collection of data broken down by race or ethnicity, which is an important development in an effort to record and identify potentially discriminatory practices;
- most member states that collect data on racially motivated crime showed an increase in recorded numbers.

Of course, just because a country has a system and uses it does not mean it has fewer problems with discrimination. Indeed, it might suggest it has more than most: research in France, for instance, suggests that employers routinely ignore or turn down job applications from people with Arab names or addresses in the notorious *banlieues* – the high-rise housing projects on the outskirts of cities and towns. However, lack of progress could well connote a lack of commitment to doing something about problems that do exist.

Policy responses – towards 'Fortress Europe'?

Just as there have been moves between the EU's member states to share (and, to some extent, force the pace on) 'best practice' with regard to discrimination, they have begun to cooperate more closely on immigration – or at least on those aspects of it that they find difficult to manage on their own. They have been spurred on by its salience as a domestic political issue and by the knowledge that, since Europe's internal borders have come down under the *Schengen Agreement* (see Box 10.9), it is much easier for illegal immigrants and asylum seekers to move around the continent and select the country of their choice. Realizing that it would not be enough to nag vulnerable 'gatekeepers' such as Spain and, in particular, Italy (with its 8,000 km coastline) and (lately) Greece to improve security, they began to put in place collective agreements such as the *Dublin Accord* (which insists that asylum seekers must make their claim in the first EU country they arrive in and can be returned there if necessary).

Theoretically, even for non-Schengen states, the national veto on so-called Justice and Home Affairs

---

BOX 10.9

The EU's Schengen Agreement

Although signed in 1985, the provisions of this multilateral agreement designed to promote the free movement of people (primarily as consumers and labourers) first came into force in 1995. By it, EU countries (minus the UK and Ireland), along with Norway, Iceland, Switzerland and tiny Liechtenstein, commit themselves to allowing citizens and those who are legally resident in the 'Schengen' countries to pass between them without needing to show a passport. The *quid pro quo* for this freedom of movement is supposed to be strengthened security at the external borders of the EU. Also important are police cooperation, information-sharing (using the computerized Schengen information system or SIS) and the establishment of a common visa policy. Non-citizens coming into the *Schengen area* as visitors are limited to a three-month stay, will almost certainly need a visa and might need to show means of support. If, for some reason, they are subject to a ban from one Schengen member then that ban applies across the area – which was, why, for instance, Libya's late dictator, Muammar Gaddafi, whose family was banned by Switzerland couldn't make it to Malta in 2010 for what might have been one of his last official visits to Europe. Schengen was incorporated into the Union's *acquis communautaire* (with derogations – get-out clauses – for the UK, Ireland, and also Denmark) by the Amsterdam Treaty in 1997. The entry (with the exception of Cyprus) into Schengen of the countries that joined the EU in 2004 was a major concern, and Romania and Bulgaria (which entered the EU later than their postcommunist counterparts) have had to wait longer in the face of ongoing worries about their ability to police their borders. Ironically, however, the biggest dispute between Schengen countries in recent years arose between two founder members of the EU: in the early summer of 2011, Italy experienced a flood of migrants from Tunisia, which was in the throes of the uprising the media labelled 'The Arab Spring'; when it became clear that no additional help from other member states would be forthcoming, the Italian government issued over 20,000 residence permits that would effectively allow them to travel without travel documents anywhere in the Schengen area; this provoked France to invoke its right to reinstate border controls in an emergency. The spat proved temporary but was seen by some as a sign of things to come.

(JHA) issues has been eroded by bringing as many of them as possible under the first or EC pillar of the EU's three-pillar structure (see Chapter 2). And while the Lisbon Treaty ostensibly gives member states the right to decide on how they handle third-country nationals (TNCs in the jargon) who are seeking work, it also enhanced the involvement of the European Court of Justice in immigration and asylum cases – something which has already seen rulings in cases referred from one country subsequently effect policy in others. Moreover, even states with 'opt-outs' (Denmark) and 'opt-ins' (the UK and Ireland) don't necessarily exercise them in a way which means they stand aside from other member states on such issues (see Adler-Nissen, 2009). On the face of it, then, migration policy is being Europeanized. But, in fact, most informed observers remain convinced that member states have pooled their resources only on those aspects of policy that

they believe will support their main aim, which is to ensure they maintain national control in an area that goes to the heart of sovereignty and which their voters obviously care so much about (see Geddes, 2003; Lahav, 2004).

European states, in other words, are in effect 'contracting out' responsibility for immigration only where it would make little or no sense for them to try to do the job themselves and/or where collective action helps in the construction of a 'first line of defence'. This line began to move outward (via subsidies toward the cost of improved border protection) even before CEE states were formally admitted to the EU in 2004 and 2007. Indeed, it can be argued that the need for secure borders was one of the drivers for enlargement. It then became one of its preconditions, with postcommunist states having to make big changes (and investments) in improved border security and tighter immigration regimes –

DEBATE 10.1

Should immigration be stopped?

YES

- Immigrants disturb the social balance of a nation, bringing with them cultures and religions that are fundamentally incompatible with those of the host population.
- That host population were never given a chance to vote on whether the new arrivals should have come in the first place. Now that they have, and more arrive every day, we are seeing the rise of some very nasty parties. Unless we stop immigration, they will get bigger and bigger.
- Immigrants are more likely to be unemployed, claim welfare benefits and get involved in crime. Even those who are law-abiding and get jobs to support their families place a strain on public services – healthcare and education – and the housing stock. They also hold down the wages of those who are already badly off and discourage government and employers from upskilling their native workforces and introducing technology to improve productivity. Moreover, they are only a short-term answer to an ageing population because they get old, too.
- Immigrants and their descendents represent a security threat.

NO

- It is doubtful whether individual nations and/or states ever possessed timeless and unified cultural identities. The idea that they can continue to do so in a globalized and mediatized world is ridiculous. Indeed, to operate successfully in that world, especially economically, it is essential that a country have as many points of contact with it as possible: multiculturalism is not only inevitable, it is functional.
- It was elected governments that allowed immigration to occur and there are now parties that campaign to stop it: they receive relatively little support and there is no simple correlation between numbers of newcomers and the success of such parties.
- The bulk of immigrants and their descendents get jobs and pay far more in taxes than they ever take out. Besides, without immigrant workers, many of Europe's basic services would collapse – not only garbage collection or street sweeping or transport (or, for that matter, the hospitality industry), but also healthcare. The evidence that they provide a cheap labour force that undercuts native workers and reduces the pressure on the state and on firms to provide training and technology is scanty. And just because they aren't *the* answer to the worker : pensioner ratio, they are a part of the answer,
- It is not immigrants but the violent ideologies that a tiny minority of people will always buy into that pose a terrorist threat.

moves made not just at the behest of the EU acting collectively but also via overlapping bilateral arrangements with the immigration and labour ministries of existing member states (see Guiraudon and Jileva, 2006; Grabbe, 2006: Chapter 7). Whether this has contributed to ensuring that CEE countries still get, for example, only around 10 per cent of the asylum applications of their western counterparts is difficult to say – there are signs that the numbers coming will rise as their economies begin to catch up. The main point is, however, that cooperation on immigration has been far more wholehearted from countries with reasonable (and, in some cases, now realized) prospects of joining the EU than from

those (such as Albania or Morocco) who do not, at least in the short to medium term, have a hope of joining (see Joppke, 2002: 272).

That said, European countries are trying – again, both via the EU and using bilateral agreements – to persuade states which are major sources of (or transit

KEY POINT

European governments have also begun to cooperate on controlling immigration, but only where it suits them (i.e. illegal immigration and asylum). Other aspects of their regimes remain distinctive and firmly under national control.

BOX 10.10

Immigration regimes – still path dependent?

Germany's attitude to immigration and citizenship is rooted in the fact that its main postwar aim was to leave the door open for ethnic Germans who, as a result of the Second World War and the Cold War, were left stranded outside the Federal Republic. This conception of citizenship as being limited to those with blood links rather than being based on birth and residence, also meant, however, that it was very reluctant to offer German nationality (and certainly not joint nationality) to the other immigrants that its powerful economy sucked in as *gastarbeiter* (or guest-workers). As a consequence, there are currently around 7 million 'foreigners' in Germany of whom 1.5 million were born there, many of them as members of a Turkish community numbering nearly 3 million. At the same time, Germany was determined to demonstrate its liberal credentials by running a relatively relaxed asylum regime, which meant, in the early 1990s, that it experienced a huge influx of refugees from the former Yugoslavia. All this left the country with a large number of people who were long-term residents but still foreigners – even if they were born in Germany and were in some ways more 'German' than new arrivals of ethnic Germans from the former Soviet bloc. These anomalies, along with concerns about integration and the recognition that Germany needs immigrants to help tackle long-term population decline (see Chapter 1), meant many politicians, especially on the left, believed the time had come for change. German policy makers, however, operate in a federal and consensual system that gives many 'veto players' a say (see Chapters 3 and 4). This arguably encourages immobilism, making it hard to make changes. Germany has therefore found it difficult to get domestic legislation on matters like citizenship and immigration past voters (whose suspicions were whipped up even by supposedly respectable opposition parties), and past legislators, state parliaments and the Federal Constitutional Court. Difficult, but not impossible: Germany eventually introduced a theoretically more liberal law on citizenship in 2000 and, in 2006, an immigration law that tried to balance the desire to attract more skilled workers from abroad with concerns about encouraging both newcomers and existing minorities to better integrate into German society. Whether this will lead to more people coming to Germany, becoming German, and becoming more German, however, remains to be seen (see Green *et al.,* 2007: Chapter 6; see also Green, 2004). It certainly seems to have done little about public concerns, judging by the millions who bought *Deutschland schafft sich ab* (*Germany Does Itself In*) published by Thilo Sarrazin in August 2010 – a book which argued that the ➡

---

points for) illegal immigrants and asylum seekers to reduce the flow. Ongoing attempts are being made to bring migration issues into the dialogue the EU has with third countries under the Common Foreign and Security Policy (CFSP), as well as into negotiations on development aid, focusing in particular on North Africa and, to a lesser extent, the Middle East (see Chapter 11 and Lavenex and Kunz, 2008). This could mean, to put it bluntly, effectively bribing dictators like Libya's Muammar Gaddafi, to prevent migrants embarking and agreeing to take them back if they were caught – arrangements to which member states turned a blind eye until, that is, the Arab Spring of 2010/2011. There was, however, little support back in 2002 for a UK government suggestion that the EU consider reducing aid to poorer countries who failed

to do enough to stop their citizens emigrating. Neither was support forthcoming when, the following year, the UK (backed again by Spain) suggested that the EU consider Australian-style detention camps outside its borders to which would-be refugees could be deported and then processed. However, a watered-down (and arguably more sensible, as well as more ethical) suggestion – that the EU manage facilities in other parts of the world closer to the flashpoints which produce refugees, and cooperate more with sending and transit countries (Boswell, 2003) – was greeted more sympathetically. European countries are also having some success in getting their immigration officers located at airports and ports in developing countries, either actually checking papers or giving local staff – often airline or

country would be dragged down by its supposedly underachieving but over-breeding Turkish minority and prompted a national controversy during which Chancellor Angela Merkel opined that multiculturalism in Germany had 'failed utterly'.

France, on the other hand, has – since the nineteenth century – had a hang-up about underpopulation, Partly as a consequence of this, and partly as a consequence of its tendency to incorporate its overseas possessions directly into the French state, it has historically made it very easy for immigrants both to come to France in the first place (even if they were *sans papiers*, i.e. illegally) and then for them to bring in family members, as well as for foreigners to gain French citizenship. This, along with the decolonization process in North Africa and the country's relative economic strength in the postwar period, resulted in a large minority population which, even if it feels alienated, has every right to be there, whatever the arguments of the far-right *Front National* (FN). On the other hand, what is (compared to Germany, anyway) a relatively unencumbered state machine has the potential – if not complete freedom (see Hollifield, 1994) – to change direction at the behest of its politicians. Nicolas Sarkozy already had a record of not only tough talk but also tough action on migrants and minorities (see Marthaler, 2008): on his way to winning the presidential election in 2007, he promised to clean up the suburbs dominated by ethnic minorities, tried (controversially) to increase deportations of illegals, and endorsed the suggestion that those who didn't like France were welcome to leave; once in power he created a ministry of Immigration, Integration, National Identity and Co-development, set tougher targets for arrests and deportations, talked of expanding repatriation programmes, making newcomers pass tests on French language and values. On the other hand, Sarkozy talked about the need for more skilled migrants, and made moves towards more explicit recognition of and dialogue with minority groups, and even talked about positive discrimination – things that traditionally were seen as impossible given France's commitment to supposedly 'colour-blind' citizenship. He also raised eyebrows among France's governing elite by appointing as his justice minister Rachida Dati, a judge but, more importantly, a self-made woman of Arab descent who grew up, along with her eleven brothers and sisters, on a tough housing estate in eastern France. She left the Cabinet – though not before shocking people by becoming a single mother and then going back to work just five days after the birth of her daughter – to become an MEP in 2009.

---

shipping company employees – some idea of what to look out for.

In addition, EU member states have taken collective action and built collective institutions to try to crack down on unauthorized immigration. Perhaps the most high-profile of these is *Frontex*, headquartered in Poland, which began its work in 2005 (see Pollack and Slominski, 2009). Originally intended as a training and coordinating body, it has since taken on more operational duties, using both its own aircraft and boats to patrol the Mediterranean routinely in the hope of heading off would-be illegals and asylum seekers heading to Europe from North and West Africa; it has also deployed to try to reduce the number of migrants coming through Turkey to Greece. Cooperation through Frontex has not,

however, prevented rows which occur when migrants get stranded, triggering disputes over who should pick them up, the most infamous of which occurred in June 2007 when nearly 30 Africans had to cling to tuna nets before the Italian navy was eventually prevailed upon to take responsibility. Such cases inevitably bring calls for a system of 'burden-sharing' – mostly ignored – but also for more formal arrangements with poor African countries that would allow more legal recruitment of temporary workers there in exchange for better policing on their part, along with an agreement to take back automatically any of their nationals found to be in Europe illegally.

Just as importantly, European states have also followed each other in 'contracting out' responsibility to private actors, such as airlines and shipping companies, by making them, via so-called 'carrier-sanctions', financially liable for bringing in passengers without appropriate documentation. Many of them have also introduced an expanded 'white list' of those countries from which applications for asylum will be assumed to be unfounded and added countries to their lists of countries from which visas will be required. Many have also made it tougher for asylum seekers to get state benefits and begun to insist on 'integration from abroad' in the sense of requiring, say, foreigners marrying their citizens to take and pass language tests before rather than after arrival. All this is an example of states learning from each other – of Europeanization via best practice, if you like. But this is not full harmonization because learning and cooperation goes only so far and there is no surrender of sovereignty. There may be superficial similarities, but states are unwilling, for instance, to fully harmonize the way they either treat or make decisions on immigrants, citizenship and asylum – indeed, the continuing persistence of wide variations in the rate at which different member states grant refugee status to applicants from the same country (see Neumayer, 2005) is clear proof of their desire and capacity to differ. Each European country, then, continues to operate its own immigration regime with respect to non-EU nationals. These regimes have developed, in a 'path-dependent' manner (see Hansen, 2002), in response to individual states' immigration priorities, history and institutional structure (see Box 10.10).

European states, then, have preserved their competence when it comes to controlling the numbers coming into their countries, just as, for instance, they continue to set their own rules on the employment of non-nationals in their respective public sectors (see Table 10.12). If policy fails to restrict those numbers, it will not be because states have somehow surrendered competence to the EU. Rather, it is because they themselves find it difficult to construct controls that will meet sometimes contradictory objectives simultaneously. First, a regime will have to cope with the sheer unpredictability of migrant flows. Second, states continue to want to run broadly humane asylum, family re-unification and relatively generous welfare arrangements. Third (and related), they want to insulate those arrangements from legal challenge, especially given the ever-increasing role of the courts, national and supranational, in human rights (broadly defined). Fourth, they want enough 'wiggle room' to allow them – either formally, or (especially in southern Europe), informally – to make room for migrants who add to the skills base and/or the flexibility of their domestic labour markets (see Favell and Hansen, 2002; Geddes, 2003). In as much as 'Fortress Europe' (or Fortress Britain, Fortress Germany, Fortress France, etc.), exists, those who man its ramparts are aware that it has to have a drawbridge – not just for humanitarian and legal reasons, but in the knowledge that they can, if needs be, let it down to allow people to trip across. This, for example, was the thinking behind the introduction of the so-called 'Blue Card' – a scheme to encourage settlement of skilled migrants in Europe that would rival the USA's famous 'Green Card'. Typically, however, the European version is hedged with qualifications and 'opt-outs' by the likes of the UK, Ireland and Denmark (Joppke, 2011: 232–33). Indeed, generally speaking (see Cerna, 2009), there are still significant differences between states' HSI (high-skilled immigration) policies – irrespective, incidentally, of which parties are in control

In short, if there is cooperation that appears to involve the compromise of sovereignty, it is essen-

Table 10.12 Public sector regulation regarding restrictions on the employment of non-nationals

Direct application of EU law	Czech Republic
Case-by-case	Germany, UK
Exhaustive/exemplary lists of restricted posts	Sweden, Italy, Netherlands
Not restricted, except for specific posts	Spain, France
Fully restricted	Poland

Source: Fundamental Rights Agency (2011b: 66).

tially self-interested and proceeds only cautiously, extending mainly to asylum and illegal immigration but not necessarily to citizenship (see Vink, 2010) or schemes to attract skilled workers (an area in which states, after all, are in competition). This could of course be what some would regard as a slippery slope toward Europeanization: as one expert points out, states 'first concede authority … in the interest of maximizing control and security' but then find, consistent with the concept of spill-over, that 'as it is sucked into the ambit of supranational actors within the EU, immigration becomes infused with the liberal rights logic of free movement that, in turn, further restricts state authority in this domain, in often unexpected and surprising ways'. One example is the 'upwards-adjustment pressure' generated by a 2007 directive designed to promote labour market mobility, which obliged some countries – notably Germany, Austria, Greece, Italy, Portugal and Spain – to ease their requirements regarding residence for 'third-country nationals', albeit at the same time affording a victory to the growing number of member states (including Germany, Denmark, and the Netherlands) that require those seeking to settle to prove they are willing and able to integrate, often by passing language tests (Joppke, 2011: 225ff; see also Faist and Ette, 2007). Another is the way that the ECJ has effectively undermined Denmark's notoriously strict rules on family reunification by ruling that they contravene EU-wide commitments to free movement of citizens.

As yet, however, what we seem to see is a 'guarded multilateralism' (Messina, 2007: 238) driven by an awareness that public opinion (in some countries anyway) would be suspicious of anything else (see Figure 10. 4) and by the acknowledgement that the national interest is sometimes better promoted, just as it is when it comes to terrorism (see Monar, 2007), by collective rather than independent action. This collective action – whether it be operational (like the Frontex patrols) or more aspirational (like the so-called Hague Programme, which calls for the stepping up of progress towards common policies on asylum, visas and illegal immigration) – might be a response to a problem exacerbated by globalization, namely, the mass movement of people from less to more fortunate parts of the planet. But it does not mean that governments are powerless and inevitably lose their autonomy in the face of global-

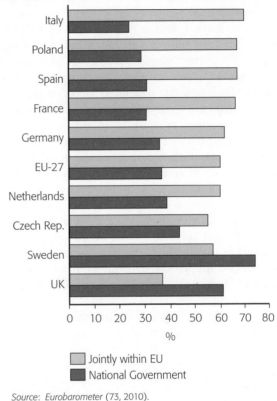

Figure 10.4 Should decisions on immigration be made by national government or jointly within the EU?

Source: *Eurobarometer* (73, 2010).

ization: this assertion is no more valid on migration than it is with regard to welfare (see Chapter 9).

Neither, since we are making the link between the two topics (a link that is often made by populist politicians, screaming media headlines and, indeed, many ordinary Europeans), is it somehow inevitable that hostility to migration and multiculturalism will inevitably undermine support for the welfare state. The question is a serious one (see Banting and Kymlika, 2006) and there is research that seems to show that public support for welfare spending is negatively affected by immigration (Eger, 2010; see also Burgoon *et al.*, 2012). Other research, however is more sceptical, suggesting that that ethnic diversity appears to have a weaker impact on welfare spending in Europe than it does in the USA, mainly because support for it is much greater across all social groups and because social democracy (which doesn't really exist in America) is much more of a force in government (see Mau and Burkhardt, 2009; Taylor-Gooby, 2005). Other research finds that immigration can cut both ways – on the one hand undermining the solidarity associated with support for redistribution, on the other increasing people's sense that their jobs are at risk, thereby boosting support for it (see Finseraas, 2008). Researchers also find that negative attitudes to immigration and support for the welfare state might be correlated, but that (a) there are significant country differences and (b) the perceived presence of immigrants doesn't seem to make much difference (Senik *et al.*, 2009). It is interesting to note, too, that research looking into another piece of common wisdom – namely, that increased ethnic diversity brought about by non-western immigrants will somehow erode social trust – also finds little or no evidence that this is the case (see Lolle and Torpe, 2011; see also Crepaz, 2007). That said, increased migration does seem to decrease support for the welfare state among parties on the right of the political spectrum (Burgoon, 2012) – which, given some voters' tendencies to follow the cue offered by their preferred party, may make a difference to public opinion.

The Roma – Europe's oldest ethnic minority

Unlike other European minorities with claims to nationhood, the claim by some Roma (or Gypsies) that they constitute a nation is based not on territory but on identity. Even then, it is greeted with some scepticism. This is understandable perhaps in view of a widespread tendency among the Roma to see themselves in terms of families or possibly clans rather than a people as a whole. That they do so is not surprising in view of their origins: they came in dribs and drabs. While there is evidence to show that their ancestors had begun arriving in eastern Europe from India in the eleventh century, possibly as mercenaries, there is no recorded mass influx. What we do know is that from very early on (possibly because they were associated with the non-Christian Ottoman empire) they were subject to vicious, often murderous, prejudice. This prejudice, along with restrictions on their liberty (up to and including slavery in Romania until the mid-nineteenth

KEY POINT

One of Europe's oldest minorities, the Roma, are still at the bottom of the heap, living in chronic poverty and subject to prejudice and violence.

century), made it very difficult for them to integrate into the mainstream economy and society. Integration would not have been easy in any case, given their own desire to preserve their language and their physical separation from *gadje* – the non-Roma majority.

This separation continues to a greater or lesser extent in whichever country Europe's 7–9 million Roma find themselves living. As Table 10.13 shows, they are widely but not evenly distributed. Roma are concentrated in southern and (despite Nazi attempts to exterminate them along with the Jews) in central and eastern Europe. Few nowadays are nomadic, but their more settled life has not meant they have caught up in socio-economic or, indeed, political terms with the majorities around them (see Fundamental Rights Agency, 2012). Living, as many do, a ghetto-style existence on the margins of society, and sometimes on the margins of legality, Roma are much more likely than others to suffer poverty (see Figure 10.5), ill-health, to have bigger families and to be uneducated, unemployed, on welfare and in prison. They are also frequently the

Table 10.13 Where most Roma live in Europe

	Estimated Roma population	Roma as proportion of total population (%)
Poland	40,000	0.1
Italy	105,000	0.2
France	350,000	0.6
Spain	725,000	1.6
Greece	200,000	1.8
Czech Rep.	225,000	2.2
Hungary	575,000	5.7
Slovakia	425,000	7.9
Romania	2,100,000	9.7
Bulgaria	750,000	9.8

Source: Liégeois, 2007.

victims not just of discrimination and prejudice (see Box 10.11) but of racially motivated attacks. Their participation in electoral politics is at best minimal. The few political parties that have organized to represent them have found it hard going, not least because they find it difficult to overcome the fragmentation and infighting that some argue characterizes Roma culture more generally.

At a transnational level, however, organization has proved somewhat more successful – and probably needs to given the difficulties of representation in domestic politics (see McGarry, 2010). In the European Parliament, there are a number of MEPs who campaign actively on their behalf, managing to pass a resolution calling for member states and the Commission to prioritize their rights. The International Romani Union (IRU) was given advisory committee status at the UN in 1993 and has now celebrated three decades of work. At its fifth World Congress in Prague in 2000, the IRU demanded the world recognize Roma as a non-territorial nation. It also declared that it would henceforth attempt to organize not just 'embassies' in other countries, but also a parliament or parliaments – something that is perhaps more possible than one might think, given the successful running of such institutions by the *Sami* people (sometimes called Lapplanders) who are spread across four countries in northern Scandinavia and Russia (see Myntti, 2002). It also attempted to progress its claims for compensation for Roma murdered in the *Porajmos* (as they call the Holocaust).

Interestingly, the sponsor of the congress was the Czech government – something which prompted considerable criticism among west European Roma. They single out that country – or at least its population – as being one of the worst offenders against Roma rights (see Box 10.11). Certainly, the Czech Republic seems to have started putting its house in order only as a condition of joining the EU (see Ram, 2003) and after pressure from existing member states complaining that poor treatment in postcommunist countries encouraged asylum-seeking by Roma in the west. That pressure continues to this day, fuelled by moral panics such as the one triggered in Italy after 2007, when so many Roma (mostly from Romania) began arriving that the Italian authorities were forced to construct huge camps in order to contain them, and in France

Figure 10.5 Relatively disadvantaged: Roma at risk of poverty

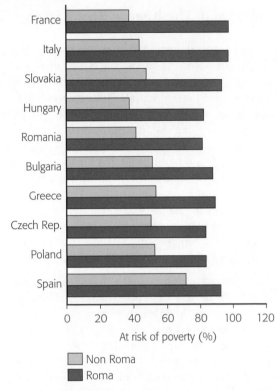

Source: Fundamental Rights Agency (2012).

when, in 2010, the government – to the consternation of the EU – began mass clearing of makeshift camps and deportations back to Romania and Bulgaria. Whether the exhortation to improve things will have much effect given centuries of entrenched disadvantage and discrimination in eastern Europe is a moot point – especially since many suggest that countries joining the EU generally take their foot off the gas on a whole host of issues once they have been granted entry.

While clearly the Roma receive a raw deal in the EU's new member states and current applicants, they have long been subject to serious discrimination in those western countries in which they have a presence, including most obviously Spain and Greece. Certainly, they are rarely accorded any more respect than immigrant minorities, even though they can claim to have been in some European countries longer than many of those who now consider themselves part of the 'native' majority.

BOX 10.11

Bottom of the heap – Roma in the Czech and Slovak Republics

Partly because it seems to contrast so sharply with its reputation (or, at least, the reputation of its liberal former president, the late Václav Havel), the Czech Republic's treatment of its small Roma population has attracted widespread attention in the European media. The new state's beginning was marred by its insistence in 1993 that some 100,000 Roma were, in fact, Slovaks, despite the majority having been horn, apparently, in Czech territory. Fast forward to the present and there are still regular reports of police and officials displaying blatant discrimination towards Roma. Evidence of deliberate and persistent segregation in both education and housing is overwhelming, while the Roma unemployment rate is just under 40 per cent – around four times that for the general population. Hardly surprising then, if many Czech Roma, much to the disquiet of some western Europeans (and their populist newspapers), were keen to leave the country and claim asylum elsewhere on the continent. On the other hand, things were certainly no better for the Roma of Slovakia who, owing to a fertility rate that is more than double that of other Slovaks, are predicted by some demographers to become the majority by the end of the twenty-first century. Both republics made conspicuous efforts to improve in the run-up to EU accession – especially with regard to education, health and even housing.

How effective such measures will be in the long term, let alone the short term, is hard to predict. However earnest the intentions of politicians may be, they cannot turn around centuries of popular prejudice in a few short years. And reports by European monitoring bodies (see Fundamental Rights Agency, 2012) suggest progress is very slow, although they also suggest that the Czech Republic and Slovakia are by no means the only places where discrimination against Roma is rife – and that Roma are not the only ethnic group subject to ancient prejudices. The Global Attitudes Survey conducted by Pew in 2009 found large numbers of respondents admitting to unfavourable attitudes towards Roma in many countries: while they were widespread in the Czech Republic (84 per cent) and Slovakia (78 per cent), they were also common in Hungary (69 per cent), Bulgaria (56 per cent), and Spain (45 per cent) – and shockingly high in Italy (84 per cent). Meanwhile, the numbers holding unfavourable attitudes towards Jews is also depressingly high in some countries, with Lithuania (37 per cent) leading the way, followed by Poland and Hungary (both 29 per cent) and Slovakia (27 per cent).

Interestingly, Roma can claim to be the prototypical postmodern European citizens, scattered throughout a continent and possessing several identities – ethnic, state and European – simultaneously. Yet in other ways, they are more like sub-Saharan Africans – according to the EU's Fundamental Rights Agency (2012) around 40 per cent of Roma live in households where somebody has to go to bed hungry at least once a month and about 45 per cent live in households that lack at least one of the following: an indoor kitchen, indoor toilet, indoor shower or bath and electricity; meanwhile educational attendance and attainment are much poorer than they should be.

Given this, it hardly comes as a surprise to find Roma trying to migrate in order to make a better life elsewhere in Europe. Some just turn up openly looking for work and/or welfare. Other Roma claim asylum but, increasingly, their claims are treated with scepticism. Indeed, it is difficult to see how it can be otherwise: the west European nations they try to get into, after all, can hardly accept that Roma face persecution in the very same countries they have just agreed to admit as functioning liberal democracies to the EU. In some ways, the Roma plight symbolizes the complex difficulties faced by Europe – or, at least, some countries in it – with regard to all minorities. According to many in their native countries, they do not belong there since they exist outside the mainstream majority of 'the nation'. If they manage to make it out to other countries, they suffer and present similar difficulties to other immigrant minorities. Hanging on to their language and their culture, refusing to 'marry out' of it, means they will retain their identity, which is perhaps essential to human happiness. The flipside, however, is their visibility – one of the things that makes it so hard for them to gain acceptance (or at least indifference) rather than hostility.

No use wishing it away

European countries can choose whether they want to be more or less multicultural, at least in the sense of either leaving ethnic minorities to their own devices as long as they obey the law or encouraging them to integrate and even assimilate into the majority population. But they are unlikely to be able to pull up the drawbridge and put a stop to immigration or even achieve their ambition, summed up neatly by former French president, Nicolas Sarkozy, of shifting from the kind of immigration that is suffered to the kind of that is chosen. The reasons are neatly summed up by the OECD's International Migration Outlook (2011: 15):

First, global population will continue to rise, increasing emigration pressures in poorer countries. Environmental deterioration will also encourage emigration from marginal areas. Second, as increased globalization of the economy leads to more globalization of migration, new migration sources and nodes will emerge. In this context, the prevention of massive irregular migration implies the promotion of economic development in origin countries and the strengthening of legal migration channels. Ageing populations … will require some compensatory labour immigration, particularly for labour-intensive personal care occupations. In addition, to maintain economic competitiveness, … countries will continue to compete for migrants with high level skills and qualifications. [C]ountries facing labour shortages will not only have to improve their migration management, but also match international recruitment of workers to labour market needs.

In other words, as with so many other political problems, this is not one that can be solved – only managed, which is one reason why 'European states' immigration policies still hover undecidedly between perfecting the[ir] strategies for keeping out the huddled masses while laying out red carpets for a trickle of highly skilled [workers]' (Joppke, 2012), with the UK (which introduced an Australian-style points-based system in 2008) leading the way when it comes to the latter (Joppke, 2011: 220, 239–40). Those countries which manage the problem best will be more at ease with themselves than those which manage it poorly, and they will almost certainly be better placed to compete and communicate with the rest of the world – something to which we turn in the next and final chapter.

Learning Resources for Chapter 10

Further reading

Anyone interested in immigration in Europe can first set it in global context by reading Castles and Miller (2009), *The Age of* Migration, before turning to Menz (2009), *The Political Economy of Managed Migration* and Boswell and Geddes (2010), *Migration and Mobility in the European Union*. Also very useful are the volumes by Giugni and Passy (2006), *Dialogues on Migration Policy* and the special issue (edited by Boswell, Geddes and Scholten) of the *British Journal of Politics and International Relations*, 13(1), 2011 on 'States, Knowledge and Narratives of Migration.' Messina (2007), *The Logics and Politics of Post-WWII Migration to Western Europe* is also recommended, as are Koopmans and Statham (2009), *Challenging Immigration and Ethnic Relations Politics* and Hampshire (2013), *The Politics of Immigration*. Cohen (2006), *Migration and Its Enemies*, is a stimulating general read and Caldwell (2010), *Reflections on the Revolution in Europe* and Scheffer (2011), *Immigrant Nations* are provocative ones. Howard (2009), *The Politics of Citizenship* and Janoski (2010), *The Ironies of Citizenship* look more specifically how different states have created, changed and maintained different rules on who qualifies for citizenship. Anyone interested in the controversy surrounding Muslim women covering their faces, should read Wallach Scott (2010), *The Politics of the Veil* and Joppke (2009), *Veil: Mirror of Identity*. On patterns of migration, a must-read is the collection edited by Penninx *et al.* (2006), *The Dynamics of International Migration and Settlement in Europe*. On European cooperation on immigration and integration, see the collection edited by Faist and Ette (2007), *The Europeanization of National Policies and Politics of Immigration*, and Geddes (2008), *Immigration and European Integration*. For more on how some mainstream parties have reacted, see the collection edited by Bale (2008), *Immigration and Integration Policy in Europe*. The collection edited by Korkut *et al.* (2013), *The Discourses and Politics of Migration in Europe* is also useful. Several specialist journals cover migration and minority issues: *The Journal of Ethnic and Migration Studies* (JEMS), *Ethnic and Racial Studies*, and *International Migration Review*. The far right receives what is probably disproportionate (but still fascinating) coverage in many political science journals (see Mudde, 2013; Bale, 2012b). As for books, those interested should certainly read Mudde (2007), *Populist Radical Right Parties in Europe*, Norris (2005), *The Rise of the Radical Right*, Carter (2005), *The Extreme Right in Western Europe*, Harrison and Bruter (2011), *Mapping Extreme Right Ideology*, and the recent collection edited by Rydgren (2012), *Class Politics and the Radical Right*. On the continent's Roma population and the challenges it faces, see Liégeois (2007), *Roma in Europe*.

On the web

www.migrationinformation.org – wealth of information on migration

http://eudo-citizenship.eu/databases – everything you ever need to know about how citizenship is regulated, acquired (and lost) in Europe

migration.ucdavis.edu – discussion and news on migration

www.migpolgroup.com – keeps tabs on integration policies in several countries

www.compas.ox.ac.uk – links and working papers on migration

www.migrationwatchuk.org and www.migpolgroup.com – for a sceptical and then a more permissive view

www.unhcr.org and www.ecre.org – refugees and asylum issues

fra.europa.eu – racism and discrimination in Europe

www.som-project.eu/ – research project on the politicization of migration

http://www.extremism-and-democracy.com/ead/ and www.kai-arzheimer.com/extreme-right-western-europe-bibliography.html – academic research on far right and extremist parties

www.errc.org and www.ertf.org – Roma news and issues

Discussion questions

1 Why, historically, have European countries attracted migrants, be they from inside or outside Europe?

2 In recent years, where have migrants to Europe come from, why have they come, and where do they go?

3 Do you think increased immigration in and of itself satisfactorily explains the rise of the far right in Europe?

4 In your opinion, are some European countries right to be more anxious about asylum seekers than others?

5 Europe's population is ageing: can migration help solve the problem?

6 Does the EU undermine or support European countries' attempts to control immigration?

7 How are European countries trying to integrate or assimilate migrants? Is this something you think should be encouraged?

8 Does the historical and present plight of Europe's gypsies – the Roma – give us cause for optimism or pessimism?

ONLINE RESOURCES AVAILABLE

Visit the companion site at **www.palgrave.com/politics/bale** to access additional learning resources.

Chapter 11

Protecting and promoting – Europe's international politics

No exploration of the politics of a continent is complete without an assessment of how the states within it handle – both jointly and severally – their relations with each other and with the rest of the world. Such an assessment is far from easy. Europe contains states of vastly different weights and sizes. Some fought wars against each other, often alongside allies (most obviously the USA) that are now rivals as well as friends. Some have close geographical or colonial relationships with countries that barely even registered on the radar of other states in spite of the fact that they are now part of the same 'ever closer union'. The latter (the EU) is not a permanent member of the UN Security Council. Neither (see Laatikainen and Smith, 2006) does it have much leverage there over the two member states (France and Britain) who are, even though neither can claim the population or the economic power of Germany, which isn't. Not only does each European state have more or less unique ideas (and pretensions) about its interests and its role in the world, it also goes about promoting, playing, and deciding on them in very different ways. Moreover, there are many analysts who would regard it as hopelessly old-fashioned and simplistic to talk about states as if they were unitary and potentially autonomous actors. Lastly, for all the talk of a world that is getting smaller every day, it is still rather a big place: like policy makers, we can only focus on a few aspects of how Europeans operate, and cooperate, within it.

This chapter plunges into these deep, wide and choppy waters – fully aware that they are they are normally home to those specializing in international relations, foreign policy analysis and European integration rather than in comparative politics – by looking at security and defence. It moves on to look at foreign policy – clearly a related area but one in which European states have, on the face of it, been rather more prepared to compromise. Next, it looks at an area in which cooperation is often thought to be even more comprehensive – namely, aid to the developing countries. Finally, after a brief examination of another field apparently characterized by cooperation – the environment – it focuses on one in which European cooperation and compromise is said to have gone furthest; namely, trade. As the chapter moves progressively through the themes, it moves the focus further and further into the world; but it makes no apology for taking as its start- and end-point Europe itself, believing that it is all too easy to forget, particularly when it comes to security, that this is where governments have over the years concentrated most of their efforts and chalked up most of their achievements. The focus at all times is on the interaction between individual state concerns and instruments and the collective action of the EU.

Security and defence – the background

Long before the attacks of 11 September 2001 in New York and Washington, it was fashionable to suggest that the end of the Cold War between 1948 and 1989 (see Chapter 1), far from ushering in a 'new world order' to be overseen by 'the international community', might paradoxically have made the world a more dangerous place (see the yearly *Conflict Barometer* for plentiful evidence of the fact). Threats include 'rogue states' and terrorists, drug- and people-trafficking by organized crime, and civil wars spilling thousands of refugees across vulnerable borders – all of which blur the boundaries between 'external defence' and 'internal security'. Some of these of course are nothing new – as the relatives of hundreds of people who lost their lives as a result of 1970s bombings and shootings in West Germany,

KEY POINT

Europe has a troubled history which still affects the present, notwithstanding the new challenges presented by an ever-wider definition of what constitutes security.

Italy and the UK, or the survivors of the aeroplane hijackings that first became fashionable in that decade, could no doubt attest. Europe has known for a long time that, in a world where extremes of material wealth and spiritual values continue to co-exist, its democracy and its peace and prosperity cannot be taken for granted, but have to be promoted and protected, not least within the continent itself (see Box 11.1).

Security is about perception, about the absence, or at least the minimization, of unacceptable risk not just to life, but to those things that are thought to make it worthwhile or at least easier – freedom and

---

BOX 11.1

Europe's traditional democracy promoters – the CoE and OSCE

The Council of Europe (CoE), founded in 1949, was one of the forerunners of the EU. However, it involved the UK (which did not join the EU until the 1970s) and other countries such as Switzerland and Norway that have never joined the EU. Also, it was always a forum for political, legal and cultural cooperation rather than economic integration. From the early 1990s, its membership swelled to encompass most of postcommunist Europe. It is governed by foreign ministers, but it also has a parliamentary assembly. It was set up to promote parliamentary democracy, human rights and the rule of law, and if possible to set pan-European standards for them. To that end, it has overseen almost 200 binding treaties and conventions, most famously the European Convention for the Protection of Human Rights and Fundamental Freedoms (known as ECHR), which most European countries (including most recently the UK) have incorporated into their domestic law. The convention is overseen by the European Court of Human Rights, a body that is completely distinct from the EU's Court of Justice (ECJ). The ECHR sits in Strasbourg and can be appealed to from member states. The CoE is now tasked, among other things, with assisting postcommunist countries to integrate human rights and the protection of minorities into their reform programmes.

The Organization for Security and Cooperation in Europe (OSCE) was finally established as a permanent body in 1949. With the end of the Cold War, the OSCE was used as a framework in which arms reduction negotiations could take place. Now with a membership of 55 nations that includes Europe, most of the former Soviet Union and the USA and Canada, it has its headquarters in Vienna, but, like the CoE, it is governed by member states' foreign ministers. Its main activities are election monitoring, and the resolution and policing of border disputes in the new democracies of Europe, the Balkans and Eurasia. Given the role played by the EU in some of these regions and activities, some observers worry that the organization is now being sidelined, despite the fact that it potentially has a useful role to play (see van Ham, 2009).

material well-being via access to essentials like food and water and to the raw materials and friendly fellow nations that make trade possible. Providing that security, and providing for the defence of the realm, is one of the most fundamental functions of the state: it has a responsibility to its people and is the guarantor of its own survival. Maintaining armed forces, and holding on to the right to deploy them, is not only one of the symbols of sovereignty, it is also a crucial part of its substance. Hardly surprising, then, that governments do not give up such things lightly, if indeed they are willing to give them up at all (see Hyde-Price, 2007). Most states also know, however, that they are unlikely to be able to protect their people unless they combine their own efforts with those of other states.

They also know that security in the twenty-first century has to be broader than a concern with territorial integrity, and therefore inevitably involves more than the state alone (see Cottey, 2012; Rothschild, 1995). The threat to the latter has receded, though not completely disappeared. Threats to the peaceful and (even in the midst of economic crisis and recession) relatively prosperous way of life led by most Europeans have, on the other hand, multiplied, necessitating a multifaceted, more-than-military response – one that involves Europe projecting not just power but norms, values and institutions. This not only costs money and necessitates interstate and supranational cooperation. It also entails overlapping and contested responsibilities exercised by a mix of actors that are not hierarchically organized and often have different, even contradictory, interests and ways of getting things done. In short, security, like so many other policies (see Chapter 3), might still be guaranteed (if not always effectively) by governments, but it is increasingly delivered via multilevel 'security governance' (see Kirchner and Sperling, 2007).

In Europe, this knowledge is reinforced by often bitter historical experience. But the history of the 150 years prior to 1945 also presented Europe with something of a 'catch-22'. Clearly, maintaining some kind of 'balance of power' between various alliances of states was ultimately insufficient to prevent the outbreak of armed conflict (see Chapter 1). Yet the gap in military potential between France and Germany could not be effectively offset either by Britain (an island) or Russia (which had huge ambi-

tions of its own), meaning that peace and some kind of stability could be achieved only with the help of an extra-European power – the USA – that might one day prove unwilling to assist. The only feasible way out of this *impasse* was to enmesh the continental powers of Germany and France and their smaller allies in an indigenous institution that would effectively ensure their economic interdependence, making them realize that their best interests lay in peaceful cooperation rather than armed conflict. Whatever their criticisms of this institution – now known as the EU – few would deny that it has so far achieved what, beneath both the grand rhetoric and the less edifying wheeling and dealing, was always its primary purpose: to help bring stability and security to a continent that otherwise seemed destined periodically to tear itself apart.

Yet, as critics of the Nobel Peace Prize awarded to the EU in 2012 were quick to point out, the EU and its forerunners were only a necessary rather than a sufficient condition of peace in Europe after 1945. In fact, the absence of war also relied, in depressingly familiar fashion, on a balance of power – this time between the two nuclear-armed superpowers, the Russian-dominated Soviet Union and the USA, with European countries as members either of the Russian-led Warsaw Pact or the US-led NATO (see Chapter 1). To Europe's political and military leaders, concerned about a possible return of US isolationism ushering in either Soviet domination or a return to western European rivalry, NATO had three basic purposes. These were pithily summed up by its first Secretary General: to 'keep the Russians out, the Germans down, and the Americans in' (see Lundestad, 1998a, b). While the definition of European security and the instruments used to strive for it have expanded in recent years, European states have, by and large, not lost sight of those three basics. And for many of the states that have 'rejoined Europe' after first Nazi and then Soviet repression, those basics remain as relevant as they ever were for their western counterparts.

'Old' and 'New' Europe?

The 2003 war in Iraq is often said to have brought into sharp relief two competing visions for European security and defence. For many, these rival

Figure 11.1 How European attitudes to the USA have varied in recent years

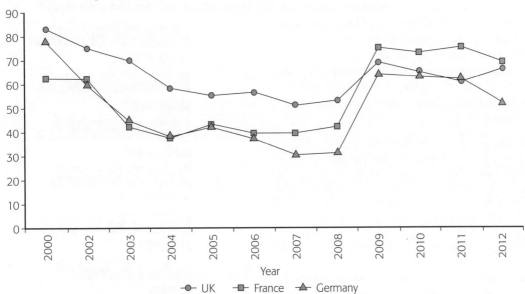

Note: Percentage of respondents saying they had a favourable attitude to the country concerned.

Source: Data from Pew Research Center, *Global Attitudes Survey* (June 2012), http://www.pewglobal.org/files/2012/06/Pew-Global-Attitudes-U.S.-Image-Report-FINAL-June-13-2012.pdf

visions were symbolized in the row over the public letter of support for the USA signed in January 2001 by the prime ministers of Denmark, Hungary, Italy, Poland, Portugal, Spain and the UK, as well as the president of the Czech Republic. This group of countries apparently shared a perspective that during the Cold War was labelled 'Atlanticist'. This perspective holds that European states must implicitly acknowledge their limitations and therefore do nothing which endangers a security relationship with what is now the world's only superpower, the USA. This is then contrasted with the perspective of what American Defense Secretary at the time, Donald Rumsfeld, dismissed as 'old Europe' – espe-

KEY POINT

Distinctions between 'old' and 'new' Europe are not irrelevant but, even though the transatlantic relationship was strained by the Iraq war, they can be overstated. So can the idea that the EU and its member states are preoccupied more with soft than hard power. The European Security Strategy sees a role for both, though military spending is comparatively low.

cially France and Germany. The leadership of the latter came in for particular criticism because it had, claimed Washington, allowed its desire to cosy up to antiwar voters in the general election of 2002 to override its responsibilities to the 'transatlantic alliance' and the US-led 'War on Terror'.

Rumsfeld may have been overstating things, but he may also have had a point. Many postcommunist states did back the Anglo-American position on Iraq for both ideological and material reasons (see Fawn, 2006). And there is an 'old Europe' perspective that holds that the continent should pursue a more independent course, especially in the light of the Iraq conflict and the Bush presidency, both of which (along with stories of the 'extraordinary rendition' of European residents and citizens) appear to have inflicted serious damage on the US's reputation in Europe – damage only repaired by the election of Barack Obama (see Figure 11.1). This alternative perspective is partly driven by objections to a 'unipolar' world dominated by a US 'hyper-power' that some Europeans – albeit (as Figure 11.2 suggests) a minority – hold in cultural contempt (see Markovits, 2005). It might also have something to do with the fact that European countries (which, by the way, did pull together remarkably well when it came to providing aid to rebuild Iraq – see Lewis, 2009) cannot and probably never will project power to the same extent or in the same way as the Americans (see Kagan, 2004). Instead, they place more weight on the value of diplomacy and compromise and on the ideas of **soft power** and **security community**.

> **Soft power** comprises trade and aid, cultural links and institutionalized 'political dialogue' through a web of sometimes overlapping international organizations (such as the OSCE and possibly NATO) that, at least within Europe itself, constitutes what some call a **security community** – an area characterized by such a high level of transactions and communication that conflicts are always resolved peacefully.

But some of these distinctions are too simplistic – and not only on the level of culture. 'Old Europe' is not simply a collection of introverted pacifists and appeasers who habitually shy away from confrontation. In fact, some of those European countries most closely associated with 'old Europe', not least France, argue that both a European security community and European autonomy should be reinforced by a measure of 'hard' (i.e. military) power. And, interestingly, other countries that would escape US criticism, primarily the UK, have some sympathy with this idea. They are, though, more ambivalent about achieving it by bringing security and defence more firmly into the provenance of the EU by, for example, making available sufficient forces and instituting majority voting for the European Security and Defence Policy (ESDP) – renamed Common Security and Defence Policy (CSDP) under the Lisbon Treaty (see Ginsberg and Penska, 2012 and Box 11.2). This is because such a policy could complement American efforts, but it might sometimes diverge from them: theoretically, at least, Europe could decide on some issues not to stand 'shoulder to shoulder' with the USA – something which the UK, keen to maintain its 'special relationship' with the Americans (see Dumbrell, 2006), still tends to do.

On the other hand, just like other Europeans, the British have to at least consider the possibility that the USA might not always be there to keep the peace in Europe – a role which is all too easily underesti-

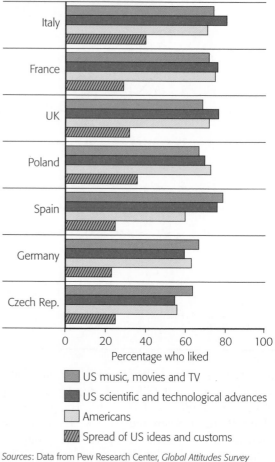

Figure 11.2 Europeans' views on Americans, their culture, science and their ideas

Percentage who liked

- ▓ US music, movies and TV
- ■ US scientific and technological advances
- ▢ Americans
- ▨ Spread of US ideas and customs

Sources: Data from Pew Research Center, *Global Attitudes Survey* (June 2012), http://www.pewglobal.org/files/2012/06/Pew-Global-Attitudes-U.S.-Image-Report-FINAL-June-13-2012.pdf

mated (see Mearscheimer, 2010). This is especially true in the light of America's declared intention, after coming to Europe's aid on several occasions in the 1990s when it proved unable to end civil wars in the former Yugoslavia, to focus less US time, personnel and money on the defence of a continent that many in Washington believe should start looking after itself so that the USA can focus on China's growing power. The question for the UK, and for other European nations, is whether attempts to show that they are more willing than previously to shoulder the burden of their own defence will fuel or forestall US impatience. And could it, in the very long term, even begin to worry the USA that Europe might try to match it militarily, as it is trying to match it politically, economically and diplomatically? Are we seeing the stirrings of a 'European superpower', albeit one not simply based on military might alone (McCormick, 2006; see also Gänzle *et al.*, 2012; Teló, 2006)?

If there is a European challenge to the USA, it will not be military. Most European countries spent the 1990s cashing in on the post-Cold War 'peace dividend' of lower defence spending and are currently reducing their armed forces as a response to the current economic and debt crisis. As a result, they are nowhere near matching or even approaching US defence spending (see Box 11.3). But, just as significant as spending totals, is the way armed forces are organized. The UK and France, because they were global powers and because they continue to want more freedom to respond to crisis situations than might be possible under the CDSP (see Gross, 2011), have more mobile forces that (even after significant cuts in the former's strength) should be able to deploy overseas reasonably rapidly. Most other European states, however, began with rather static, conscript-based forces far less suitable for today's flexible power projection and 'crisis management' scenarios. Defence analysts also argue that research and development (R&D) makes up such a low proportion of spending, and is so fragmented between countries, that European forces risk losing out to technologically superior opposition or remaining forever reliant on American hi-tech equipment that is either expensive to buy or could be denied them should the USA not support their actions.

Still 'the German Question'

But it is not just the USA that is crucial to the calculations of Europe's biggest defence players: France and the UK. The question of Germany is just as important as ever – perhaps even more important than it has been for decades. On the one hand, Germany had to be persuaded (and to persuade its people) that it could and should contribute more and more practically to European defence. On the other, any increased contribution must not allow it to slip the bonds that had seen it safely locked into, rather than dominating, the continent. Germany,

KEY POINT

Few seriously expect Germany to constitute a threat to European peace any longer, but it is seeking to combine its 'civilian power' tradition with a stance more in keeping with its size and weight.

since reunification, has been trying to come to terms with this dilemma itself. Since the 1950s, it had been used to thinking of itself as a 'civilian power' (see Karp, 2009) – a polity that, like Japan and perhaps also the EU, sought multilateral and non-military solutions to international problems – if necessary, through what critics sometimes labelled 'chequebook diplomacy'.

Germany's re-birth as Europe's biggest (and still richest) nation in 1990, however, gave it the confidence to go against its so-called 'coordination reflex' (the tendency not to act without consulting and getting the consent of its EU partners) and recognize Croatia and Slovenia when they declared independence from Yugoslavia. This move was regarded with some concern on the part of other member states, especially France and Britain, who (rightly, it turned out) feared it would ignite a war in the Balkans – one in which none of them wanted to intervene. Ironically, it was this war, and the genocidal atrocities that accompanied it, that (with the help of Federal Constitutional Court rulings in 1994 declaring 'out-of-area' deployment of German armed forces legal) allowed Germany's leaders to persuade enough of its people that it should henceforth play a more active, assertive and military role in world affairs. This new role was symbolized not just by peace-keeping missions in the former Yugoslavia, but also by German participation in NATO bombing raids in Kosovo in 1999 and in the removal of the Taliban regime in Afghanistan that had provided a safe haven for al Quaeda.

Indeed, the negative reaction of the German government to operations in Iraq and Libya (see Box 11.4) has to be seen in the context of the potential of such an unpopular action to undermine its painstaking (and painful) attempt to convince a still sceptical German public that military action abroad is not inherently wrong. Meanwhile, Germany's support for ESDP/CSDP has to be seen in the light

BOX 11.2

European/Common Security and Defence Policy – key dates and events

1992   Maastricht Treaty makes moves towards a common foreign and security policy (CFSP).

1997   EU's Amsterdam Treaty incorporates 'Petersberg Tasks' (humanitarian search and rescue missions, peace keeping, crisis management and 'peace making' by combat forces). The new 'High Representative' appointed to oversee CFSP (ex-head of NATO, Javier Solana) would (in 1999) become the head of the West European Union (WEU), which would, in effect, be incorporated into the EU (basically confirmed by the Nice Treaty of 2000).

1998   France and the UK sign 'St Malo Declaration', outlining the need for more effort on defence by the EU countries (the UK emphasis) and greater autonomy for the EU to carry out missions without NATO (the French emphasis).

1999   EU's Cologne summit notes that 'the Union must have the capacity for autonomous action, backed up by credible military forces, the means to decide to use them, and a readiness to do so, in order to respond to international crises without prejudice to actions by NATO'. Helsinki summit sets 'headline goals' including the creation by December 2003 of an EU 'Rapid Reaction Force' (RRF) for 'Petersberg Task'-style missions. It also sets up military planning/liaison bodies in the Council. Meanwhile Poland, Hungary and the Czech Republic join NATO

2002   Despite ESDP being declared operational, EU peace-keeping force to Former Yugoslav Republic of Macedonia (FYROM) delayed because countries other than France and Belgium insist that ESDP operate on a 'Berlin-plus' basis – i.e. with the ability to call on NATO assets if needed. Delays and disputes also arise because of difficulties raised by NATO (but non-EU) member Turkey, and because of suspicions of smaller EU countries about pretensions to leadership by a *directoire* of France, the UK and Germany, who themselves are in dispute concerning the French desire to stress the autonomy of ESDP from NATO.

2003   France, UK and Germany fall out further over the Iraq war (see Schuster and Maier, 2006). France, Germany, Belgium and Luxembourg hold their own summit meeting on ESDP, hinting at

of that same desire to move towards being a 'normal' country and away from being one that forswears the full range of instruments to protect and promote its considerable economic interests (see Maull, 2006). Europeanizing security and defence policy (see Miskimmon, 2007) offers Germany a way to do this at the same time as reassuring its partners that it will not seek to do anything more than return to normality, hence the country taking a lead role in the EU's contribution to the military operation safeguarding the electoral process in the Democratic Republic of Congo in 2006 and its close cooperation with the UK and France on trying (however unsuccessfully) to talk Iran out of developing a nuclear capability as part of the so-called 'EU-3' (Germany, France and the UK). Such reassurance is aimed not just at western European allies but also at CEE coun-

tries like Poland and the Baltic states which, while grateful to Germany for the role it played in facilitating their accession to the EU, are understandably suspicious of its 'cosying up' to Russia in recent years. At the same time as doing all this, of course, Germany is also having to come to terms with its predominance in the EU itself – something that has become increasingly apparent but all the harder during the Eurozone crisis (see Mayhew *et al.*, 2011). At one and the same time, it is looked to in order to provide a solution and yet resented because (supposedly at least) it is the one country with the power to do so. And within its own borders there are many who are uncomfortable with taking on such a role. No wonder the Federal Republic is Europe's 'reluctant hegemon' (Paterson, 2011; see also Bulmer *et al.*, 2010).

closer integration on defence by core countries and a possible NATO-style 'mutual defence clause' for the EU, obliging them to come to each other's aid militarily if attacked. The USA and the UK are furious, so too are other EU member states. The 'Chocolate makers', as the small group of countries are dismissively labelled, back down and re-stress their commitment to NATO. Henceforth, the 'Berlin-plus' basis (see above; also Reichard, 2006) becomes the consensus. EU 'Operation Concordia', keeping the peace in FYROM, begins in April, with 250 EUFOR troops from 15 member states. June sees the start of 'Operation Artemis', keeping the peace in part of the Congo, involving 1,500 troops (most of them, as with Concordia, French) – the first EU mission outside Europe. At the end of the year, Rome summit agrees to an advanced strategic planning capability for EU, but one that will liaise closely with NATO, which announces the entry in 2004 of the former Soviet states Estonia, Latvia and Lithuania, as well as Slovenia, Slovakia, Bulgaria and Romania. 'European Security Strategy' (Council, 2003) approved.

2004–6 NATO hands responsibility for peace keeping in Bosnia to EU, which launches EUFOR–Althea operation in December 2004. EU cooperates with five ASEAN countries in 2005 to form, in Indonesia, the Aceh Monitoring Mission (AMM) – the first ever ESDP mission in Asia. EUFOR–RDCongo sent in 2006 to support and protect the UN mission overseeing, and civilians participating in, elections in the Democratic Republic of Congo.

2008– EU sends, as EUFOR Tchad/RCA, over 3000 troops to Chad and the Central African Republic to protect refugee camps while a more long-term UN force is readied for deployment. December 2008 sees the launch of Operation Atalanta, the first deployment of a European Naval Force (EUNAVFOR) which, along with a number of other non-EU European countries (including Norway) is tasked with protecting food aid to Somalia and more generally combating piracy off the Horn of Africa – a mission which, in May 2012, saw the first raid (with Somali government permission) on the pirates' land bases. Meanwhile back in Europe, the passing of the Lisbon Treaty, which rechristens the ESDP as the CSDP and incorporates the mutual defence clause of the Treaty of Brussels, leads to the winding up of the WEU in June 2011.

Russia – Eurasia's (ex-?) superpower

Energy supply and security is a vital necessity for the population and the prosperity of Europe (see Egenhofer and Behrens, 2011; Youngs, 2009). But it is increasingly dependent on imports of oil and gas, not only from the Middle East but from central Asia and Eurasia. Because of that, and because of its 143 million consumers, Russia represents a considerable trading opportunity for Europe: even in 2011, according to official Commission figures, the EU accounted for 43 per cent of Russia's imports and took 49 per cent of its exports, while Russia accounted for 12 per cent of the EU's imports and took 7 per cent of its exports. But Russia also repre-

sents a considerable security threat – and, if opinion polls are accurate, continues to be regarded with suspicion by many ordinary Europeans (see Box 11.5). There might be little likelihood (certainly in the short to medium term) of Russia precipitating interstate conflict with European states outside the former Soviet empire, but the Russian Federation contains a number of republics which would like to break away (most notoriously, Chechnya), provoking uncertainty and therefore insecurity. It also borders a number of former Soviet and now 'newly independent states' that, in addition to being geographically close and potentially economically important to the EU, contain very big Russian minorities: examples include Belarus (1 million Russians or 11 per cent of the population), the Ukraine (11 million or 22 per cent) and Kazakhstan

BOX 11.3

Europe's 'meagre' defence spending

The USA has by far the biggest defence budget of any single state on the planet: its spending amounts to around 45 per cent of global defence spending and, if one were to take the top ten spenders, the Americans spend more than the other nine combined. This is not altogether surprising: as a continental power surrounded by vast oceans on either side, the USA necessarily requires a huge navy and air force to defend itself and project its power abroad. Its high spending is also due, in part, to its desire to maintain an edge in technology and, of course, to the upkeep and development of its still-extensive nuclear arsenal. On the other hand, the USA can take advantage of considerable economies of scale, both in terms of its purchasing power and its world-beating and more integrated defence industries – something Europe has decided to try and do something about by creating the European Defence Agency, which reports to the EU's council of (defence) ministers. Although, as Table 11.1 shows, there are considerable variations in the relative and absolute size of each country's armed services, Europe as a whole fields more personnel than the USA. But, as the table also shows, it spends less than half of the US spend, and spending as a proportion of GDP is much lower by comparison: this is true as a whole and of individual countries, although again there are considerable differences in this respect. Looking in more detail reveals that, interestingly, willingness to spend has little to do with the level of threat. Russian military exercises in 2009 revolved around what looked very like the invasion of the three Baltic states, but only one of the three (Estonia) comes close to meeting the 2 per cent target of GDP recommended by NATO.

Table 11.1 EU and US defence spending and military personnel

	Defence spending as percentage of GDP	Defence spending as percentage of of total government spanding	Defence spending *per capita*, € (2005)	Number of military personnel,
USA	4.80	11.20	1,676	1,431,000
UK	2.56	5.03	698	192,000
France	2.01	3.58	605	234,000
Poland	1.81	3.95	167	97,000
EU	1.61	3.20	390	1,620,000
Netherlands	1.43	2.80	510	48,000
Italy	1.40	2.77	358	191,000
Czech Rep.	1.39	3.07	191	23,000
Germany	1.34	2.88	410	246,000
Sweden	1.23	2.32	455	14,000
Spain	1.05	2.33	242	130,000

Note: EU includes all 27 member states apart from Denmark. First three columns relating to it are the EU-average, while the fourth column is the EU total. All figures are for 2010.

Source: Data from European Defence Agency (2012),
http://www.eda.europa.eu/Libraries/Documents/National_Defence_Data_2010_4.sflb.ashx and
http://www.eda.europa.eu/Libraries/Documents/EU-US_Defence_Data_2010.sflb.ashx

(4.5 million or 30 per cent). A number of these states, as well as Russian republics, also harbour their own ethnic conflicts, as well as religious extremists who might respond to global faith-based terrorism. All this creates potential instability not just in Russia itself, but also in Europe's eastern 'near abroad'. It also creates problems further afield. Russia (like the UK and France, we should note) is still one of the world's biggest arms producers and sellers, and has continued to provide several Middle Eastern countries with weapons, and more besides. The nuclear technology which some fear Iran will use to develop WMD was sold to them by a Russia desperate to maintain and increase its trade; meanwhile, the repressive Assad regime in Syria sees Russia – and its state-owned arms companies – as a loyal friend. For its part, Russia, under Vladimir Putin, has become a more nationalistic country and one increasingly keen to recapture at least some of the power and influence that drained away after the end of the Cold War (see Gower and Timmins, 2009).

KEY POINT

A newly assertive Russia and its former empire constitute both an opportunity and something of a threat to Europe. The enlargement of the EU, its energy needs, and the European aspirations of some former Soviet states have complicated relations considerably.

The most obvious way in which Europe deals with this potential instability to its east is the continuation and expansion of NATO – something that should not, incidentally, be taken for granted (see Duke and Haar, 2011) – as well as its extension into a forum for dialogue with Russia in what is called the NATO–Russia Council, established in May 2002. NATO therefore operates both as a workable military alliance and as part of a system of 'multilateral security governance' wherein institutionalized dialogue with potential adversaries can be conducted and their potential risks thereby scaled down (see Smith, 2000). In so doing, it complements European (and US) attempts to involve and enmesh Russia in the institutionalized 'international community' that have cleared the way to its membership of non-security bodies such as the G-8 meetings of the leaders of the world's industrialized

---

BOX 11.4

Europe and Libya

Libya is an important place to many European states: it has large reserves of easily exploitable oil and gas which are located just across the Mediterranean; it is also a major transit country for sub-Saharan African migrants. It was therefore unsurprising that when rebels rose up against its dictator, Europe would take a close interest. While the bulk of military operations against the defeated Gaddafi regime took place under the auspices of NATO, two of the nations that, along with the USA, assumed the biggest burden were European countries, France and the UK. The latter's concerns with regional stability were shared by the former and amplified by France's need to respond to the concerns of French citizens with origins in North Africa. Both were instrumental in pressing the UN Security Council to authorize action, beginning with a resolution calling for a no-fly zone. That resolution was passed without a veto but with five abstentions, including not only Russia and China but also the Federal Republic of Germany. Germany's decision – driven both by domestic public opinion and concerns that action might destabilize rather than stabilize the region – revealed once again how hard it is for the EU to move in lockstep on foreign and defence policy, irrespective of its lofty ambitions, its institutional framework, and its new foreign policy chief, Cathy Ashton. The UK and France were joined by other European NATO allies like Belgium, Bulgaria, Greece, Italy (which came on side only once it realized the game was up for its ally and leading oil-supplier Muammar Gaddafi), the Netherlands, Romania and Spain (all EU member states), as well as by NATO members, Norway and Turkey. Sweden – an EU member state but not part of NATO – also participated in the operation.

---

countries and the World Trade Organization (WTO). On the other hand, Russian dialogue with NATO and its members does not extend to its being granted a say (or even to its being consulted) on military operations that they deem necessary, such as airstrikes in Kosovo in 1999.

The second way Europe deals with the security risk that Russia potentially presents is somewhat old-fashioned, hardly savoury, but, for all that, possibly necessary. It is to allow the Russian Federation what amounts to a 'sphere of influence' over much, though (as the dispute over Ukraine in 2004 and Georgia in 2008 showed) not all, of the territory formerly presided over by the Soviet Union (see Chapter 1). This policy, for example, involves the tacit acceptance (despite formal scoldings) that Russia can do what it likes in the breakaway republic of Chechnya – important to Russia not only in symbolic but also economic terms, since it is the main route for oil from Kazakhstan to Russia's big Black Sea port of Novorossiysk. This tacit acceptance of Moscow's hard-line stance risks offending Islamic extremists; but it also has the considerable advantage – especially in the wake of the massacre of schoolchildren in Beslan in September 2004 – of allowing Europe, the USA and Russia to feel, rightly or wrongly, that they have something in common in the 'War on Terror'.

The third way Europe has attempted to reduce the risk to its security from Russia and the other countries of the former Soviet Union is to provide substantial financial and development assistance, accompanied by political dialogue and promises of improved access to the European single market. EU funding is significant, beginning with the establishment in the early 1990s of the TACIS (Technical Assistance to the CIS) programme. But much of the assistance has been bilateral. German aid to Russia, for instance, is particularly significant – something that might also have something to do with the fact that the country is by far Russia's biggest trading partner. On a political level, the EU and Russia agreed to two summits per year and, at the 2003 St Petersburg summit, it was decided to establish a 'Permanent Partnership Council' (PPC) to promote ministerial contact between member states and Russia. In 2005, the summit came up with so-called 'road-maps' for the closer cooperation. October of the same year saw the first meeting of the EU–Russia Partnership Council on Energy.

But, so far anyway, these frameworks have not done away with genuine clashes of interests and values. Russia, now stronger and much wealthier than it was in the 1990s, is increasingly assertive about defending and promoting its interests, and remains suspicious of anything that smacks of interference in what it regards as its internal affairs or, indeed, those of states it considers as in its own backyard. It was particularly irritated by what it saw as the 'western' meddling that brought about and supported the 'Rose' and 'Orange' revolutions in former Soviet states Georgia and Ukraine in 2003 and 2004 respectively. At the same time, the EU has added members who are determined not to be pushed around by a state they clearly regard as their old enemy and are determined to steer EU policy as far in their direction as possible. Particularly vociferous are the formerly Soviet Baltic states, in which substantial Russian minorities still claim to be discriminated against, and Poland (see Box 11.5). But even one of the newest members, Romania, represents something of a threat to Russian interests by taking an interest in the fate of neighbouring Moldova, where Russia has a military presence. As if this weren't enough, Russia – which declared in 1999 that it was uninterested in ever joining the EU – is concerned (however unlikely it may sound) that the EU will eventually tempt countries that it is recruiting into its own regional organizations, be they economic or military (like the Collective Security Treaty Organization, or CSTO, comprising Russia, Belarus, Kazakhstan, Kyrgyzstan, Tajikistan, Armenia and Uzbekistan). Russia was also clearly outraged by US plans to site infrastructure for its proposed long-range missile defence system not just in the UK but also in the former Soviet bloc states of Poland and the Czech Republic – plans which were abandoned in September 2009, much to the relief of many west European capitals where the whole idea was considered unnecessarily provocative.

On the other hand, argue some observers, Russia is by no means always the victim of bullying. Its military response to Georgia's attempt to reclaim lost territory in South Ossetia by force of arms in August 2008 was, at least privately, seen as understandable by many European countries (on the EU's role, see Whitman and Wolff, 2010b) – one reason perhaps why NATO agreed to restart dialogue with Russia in the NATO-Russia Council a year later in spite of the fact that the former had not fully complied with it armistice obligations. But they had been much less impressed when a couple of years earlier Moscow had decided (literally) to turn off the gas in a price dispute with the Ukraine during the winter of 2005–6.

BOX 11.5

Poland and Russia (and Germany)

Polish–Russian relations have been difficult for quite some time and are reflected – at least in Poland – at the level of public opinion: a Pew Research Center survey in 2009 recorded only 18 per cent of Poles thinking that Russian influence was a good thing while 59 per cent thought it bad; this on-balance negative opinion was shared, though not to quite the same extent in the Czech Republic (24 : 44), Hungary (15 : 42) and Lithuania (22 : 39), but stands in marked contrast to, say, the Ukraine (46 : 25) and Bulgaria (45 : 17). Of course, the Baltic states (particularly Estonia) can also claim to be just as much a victim of what they claim is Russian bullying as Poland. The relationship between Warsaw and Moscow, however, has been under severe strain for some time. It took its first turn for the worse when Poland backed (and persuaded the EU to back) a re-run of the Ukrainian presidential election of 2004 and then supported the eventual winner, leader of the so-called Orange Revolution, Victor Yuschenko, who, six years later, was succeeded anyway by the man who 'beat' him in 2004, the much more Russian-friendly, Viktor Yanukovych.

The relationship deteriorated still further in 2005. In July, Russia made clear its continued support for the Belarussian dictator, Aleksander Lukashenko, whom Poland was accusing of mistreating the hundreds of thousands of ethnic Poles living in his country. In August, diplomats and their families were attacked in both Warsaw and Moscow. In September, Germany and Russia agreed to build a 1,200km (and € 3.5 billion) gas pipeline which, by running partly under the Baltic Sea, would bypass Poland, thereby raising fears that Russia may attempt to deny it access to vital energy supplies. The deal prompted the Polish Foreign Minister into an indirect but ill-judged comparison with the Molotov–Ribbentrop Pact between Nazi Germany and Soviet Russia. This understandably contributed to a worsening of relations between the two EU members, which reached its nadir during difficult negotiations on EU voting reform in 2007: the highly nationalistic government led by the Kaczynski twins had already inflamed things by suggesting that, but for Germany's aggression in the Second World War, Poland would have had a bigger population, thereby fully entitling it to the vote share that others wanted to cut; but things got even worse when the front cover of the Polish weekly *Wprost* (not a government publication, it must be said) proclaimed German Chancellor Angela Merkel the 'Stepmother of Europe' against a photo-shopped image of the twins sucking her bare breasts.

A new post cold war low was reached in 2008 when Poland (notwithstanding the fact that the election held the previous year had seen the ejection of the fiercely nationalistic Law and Justice Party from power) took Georgia's side in its conflict with Russia over South Ossetia. Meanwhile, there was an ongoing war of words between Warsaw and Moscow over the USA's plans to site some of the hardware for its proposed long-range missile defence shield in Poland, with the Russian side making it clear that, if it went ahead (which in the end it did not), Poland (which already seemed to loom ominously large in Russian war-gaming and military exercises) would become a legitimate target. Many feared the worse when, in April 2010, a plane crashed in Russia while carrying the Polish president and many of the country's top military men to a memorial service for the 22,000 Polish officers massacred by the Soviet army in 1940 at Katyn. Fortunately, while a minority of Poles bought into the idea of some sort of malign conspiracy, most saw it as a tragic accident and the sympathetic response of the Russian authorities almost certainly accounted for the striking rise in positive attitudes to Russia among Poles (from 33 in 2009 to 45 per cent in 2010 according to the Pew Center which, by chance, was surveying just as the tragedy occurred). This effectively allowed the Warsaw and Moscow to 'hit the reset button' on their relationship, even if (particularly in the light of a Russian investigation into the accident that many Poles ultimately came to regard as inadequate) the goodwill began to fade after a while. Still, while things are by no means all sweetness and light – one of the first things a visitor passing the presidential palace in Warsaw notices is that it flies not only the Polish and the EU but also the NATO flag – it may be that the two countries can at least learn to co-exist more easily than they have done in recent years.

Russia's action was a sign of its continuing displeasure with the 'orange revolution' regime then in power in Kiev – a regime that later gave way to a more acceptable (in Moscow's eyes anyway) successor. It was also a reminder (and a very tangible one given the drop in gas pressure experienced in western Europe during the dispute) of Europe's heavy reliance on Russian energy. This reliance will only increase as Russian state-sponsored energy giant Gazprom expands into western Europe and into the central Asian republics that European countries once hoped they could deal with in order to bypass Russia. In fact, it would be more accurate to say 'some European countries' because their dependence on gas from the east varies enormously. According to figures compiled by the BBC during the Ukrainian gas dispute in early January 2006, Germany gets around 40 per cent of its gas from Russia and this will increase; the figures for France (around a quarter) and Italy (nearly a third), however, are lower, but those for Austria (75 per cent), Greece and Lithuania (80 per cent), Bulgaria, Slovakia, Lithuania and Finland (90–100 per cent) are much higher. On the other hand Belgium, Ireland, Portugal, Spain, Sweden and the UK import little or no gas from the Russians, while Denmark (like non-EU member Norway) is self-sufficient.

It may be simplistic to suggest that states' relations with Russia are a function of their energy dependence and that variation in the latter will prevent the EU from pursuing a consistent line. True, the German government's decision, taken in the wake of the 2011 Fukushima disaster in Japan, to shut down its remaining nuclear generating capacity (which accounted for over 20 per cent of electricity production) by 2022, might increase the country's dependence on Russia and therefore the potential for disagreements on foreign policy relating towards it with other member states. However, global production of shale and liquefied natural gas (that can be delivered by tanker) may well compensate, making Germany (and other member states) less reliant on Russia. Indeed, this may explain why the EU was able to agree in 2012 on the launching of an antitrust investigation of Russia's state-owned energy giant, Gazprom – much to the Kremlin's chagrin. That said, combined economic and political cooperation between the EU and Russia is proceeding, albeit not as smoothly or as quickly as some

had hoped. It is supposedly being complemented – but also perhaps disrupted – by the announcement at the end of 2003 of the so-called 'European Neighbourhood Policy' (see Whitman and Wolff, 2010a). Reduced to its essentials, the ENP (behind which the EU put € 12 billion in the five years after 2007) sees a number of states bordering the EU offered the prospect not of membership but of 'a stake in the EU's internal market'. Each has an 'Action Plan' detailing the administrative and political reforms (covering things like respect for borders, markets, the rule of law and human and minority rights) that it needs to make in order to qualify for aid from and market access to the EU. Russia is not strictly a part of the policy, having its own 'Strategic Partnership' with the EU, but should share in the economic benefits on offer because it has economic and other relationships with former Soviet states; namely, Moldova, Ukraine, Georgia, Armenia and Azerbaijan. On the other hand, the ENP and the EaP (Eastern Partnership) on offer to countries like Ukraine and Moldova since 2009 (see Bechev, 2011) could prove at one and the same time a source of frustration for the countries concerned, who want more than the EU can give (see Haukkala, 2008), and a source of friction with Russia.

One 'neighbour' that continues to express an interest in joining the EU, notwithstanding its own change of government and the EU's somewhat lukewarm response, is Ukraine, although polls persistently suggest that the plurality of public support in favour is boosted by high support in the west of the country which offsets much more negative feeling in the (pro-Russian) east. Ukraine, at least, has the advantage of being seen by most Europeans, according to opinion polling (see *Special Eurobarometer* 285, 2007), as a neighbour – a feeling that may well have increased in the wake of the highly successful European soccer championships held (jointly with Poland) in the summer of 2012. All the other ENP countries were clearly rejected as such, although it is clear that views vary according to location, with more (though rarely most) people in the Mediterranean member states being prepared to see the North African countries as neighbours and more people in the CEE states doing the same for their easterly 'neighbours'. Across the EU-27, however, a majority of respondents declared 'little or no interest' in what was happening in the ENP countries and did not feel they had values in common with them. Eight out of ten had never heard of the ENP and most believed any help that could be given would end up costing a great deal without many economic benefits accruing to Europe in return. Virtually everyone, however, thought it sensible to pursue good relations with Europe's neighbours, with concerns about organized crime and terrorism and reducing the risk of illegal immigration, war and conflicts in Europe very much to the fore.

On the surface at least, Europeans appear to be sceptical and rational realists. Consistent with the lack of attention paid to foreign countries in their media (see Chapter 7), Europeans don't spend much of their valuable time thinking about them, suspect that dealing with them will involve spending a lot of money that they will never see again, but realize that it may be worth it if it protects them. The latter is very much in keeping with a wider tendency to favour cooperation on issues, such as fighting terrorism, where even the most obtuse of us would have trouble arguing that 'going it alone' makes much sense (see Figure 11.3).

Europe's Mediterranean 'neighbours'

In fact, the idea of a European 'neighbourhood', and the potential economic benefits that might flow from 'neighbourly' behaviour began life as part of Europe's attempt to handle the security risks posed by countries not to its immediate east but to its south, along the Mediterranean (Map 11.1). Those affected include Morocco, Algeria and Tunisia (which historically have been intertwined with France, and to a lesser extent Spain, and which are often collectively referred to as the *Maghreb*), as well as Egypt, Israel, Jordan, Lebanon, Libya, Palestine and sometimes even Syria. Many of them are economically troubled and politically unpredictable, especially in the wake of the Arab Spring of 2011 which saw off a number of dictators who (rather conveniently for the many European countries seemingly content to deal with them) had kept the lid on simmering discontent and anti-Western feeling. They are experiencing a population explosion in spite of the poverty that pervades the

Figure 11.3 Fighting terrorism – Europeans' belief in a collaborative effort

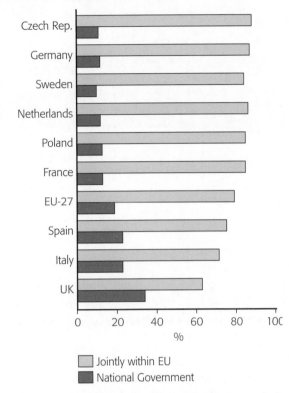

Source: *Eurobarometer*, 73 (2010): 'Decisions on fighting terrorism should be made by the government or jointly within the European Union'.

majority of them, and a number have experienced widespread discontent, if not revolutions, which may give rise to more stable, broadly-based and even democratic regimes but may of course produce regimes whose ideologies are unsympathetic to European values and influence. At the same time, they are a significant source, or at least a conduit, for the energy resources on which Europe relies. Whether they be 'failed' or simply troubled states, they therefore represent a fertile ground for almost everything Europe worries about: maritime pollution, illegal immigration and drug trafficking, and terrorist threats to mainland Europe or, just as seriously, to its energy supply.

Although France maintained postcolonial links with some pretty unsavoury regimes in the region, there was surprisingly little collective thought about the southern Mediterranean until Spain joined the

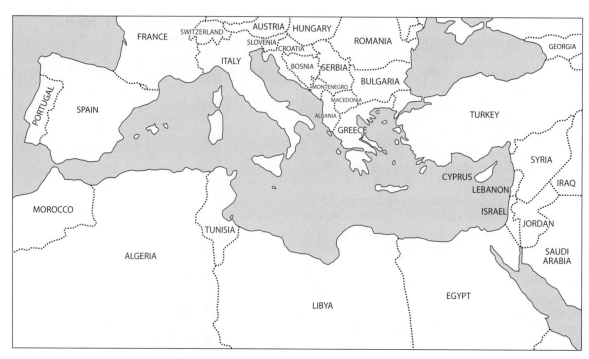

Map 11.1 Europe's Mediterranean neighbourhood

EU in 1986 (see Gillespie, 2000). Spain, like France has a complicated mesh of bilateral security and economic agreements with a number of North African states to its south, and for some time they have played a much bigger role in both its trade and its foreign policy than have states that are often (but often wrongly) assumed to matter more to Spain for cultural reasons, such as those in South America. In the early 1990s, Spain began a concerted attempt (with the French and Italians) to draw the EU's attention to the need to 'do something' for the Mediterranean. Its efforts finally paid off in the so-called 'Barcelona Declaration' of 1995, by and after which the states were offered a much bigger and more comprehensive package of EU assistance – accompanied by political dialogue and promises of

KEY POINT

The ENP that applies to several East European and Eurasian states also applies to the countries of the South Mediterranean: its aim of encouraging political and economic development in order to reduce instability and illegal immigration might be hard to achieve.

'partnership' (see Cardwell, 2011) aimed at securing improvements in human rights and governance.

EU development assistance to the southern Mediterranean runs into the billions. Free trade, too, is supposed to be an important part of the package on offer, although the extent to which the countries in the region actually trade with the EU varies considerably – all the way from Libya and Tunisia (which do 80 per cent of their trade with the EU), through Morocco and Algeria (70 per cent) and Syria (60 per cent) to Israel, the Lebanon and Egypt (25–30 per cent), and finally Jordan (less than 5 per cent). The ENP, then, builds on efforts already in place, but adds political 'conditionality' to the prospect of a bigger economic gain via closer integration with the EU's internal market (see Lavenex and Schimmelfennig, 2011). However, if one regards poverty as the main source of instability, then simply encouraging trade and providing development assistance (and attaching strings to both) is unlikely to prove a quick fix to the security risks posed by the southern Mediterranean. Israel's GDP *per capita* may, according to IMF figures for 2011, reach well over 90 per cent of the EU average but, with the exception of Lebanon (see Ruffa, 2011), where it is now 50 per cent, not one of the Southern Mediterranean countries can claim to reach even 30 per cent.

These differences – plus bilateral relationships – already mean that each country is treated rather differently, rendering the ENP more of 'a policy for neighbours rather than a neighbourhood policy' (Smith, 2005a: 771). On the other hand, the ENP, by providing off-the-shelf regulatory regimes, promoting good policy and opening up markets can potentially help each neighbour progress economically as well as politically (see Dodini and Fantini, 2006). But this will take time. Right now, the fear is that the extreme poverty of many of the countries involved will lead to ever-greater migratory pressure. This, combined with heightened concerns about Islamist terrorism, could mean that ENP ends up reinforcing the impression that, whatever the rhetoric, the EU will end up as a 'gated community' – prepared to pay to keep 'undesirables' at a safe and well-policed distance but never to welcome them inside, other than as temporary (and even then not particularly trusted) servants (see Zaiotti, 2007).

These risks are why many would argue that 'soft power' instruments such as trade and aid have, in the end, to be backed up by 'hard power' – military threats or even actual force. In fact, when it comes to the Middle East, Europeans probably need to be as much, if not more, interested in that region's oil than the nation many of them like to think of as the 'bad guy', the USA. In fact, Europe consumes over three times the amount of oil it produces and is more reliant on Arab energy suppliers than the Americans. Along with the need to keep onside what in some countries is a sizable Muslim population (see Chapter 1), this may well be why European countries have been so keen to try to counterbalance US backing of Israel in the drawn-out Palestinian peace process (see Musu, 2010) – a stance that helped Cathy Ashton, the EU's High Representative (its foreign policy chief) attain considerably more in the way of trust from her Arab interlocutors than they afforded to former British prime minister, Tony Blair, the envoy of 'the Quartet (the USA, Russia, the UN and the EU). This is also why even those governments critical of America's policy in the Middle East have to help clear up the mess they believe it has created in places such as Iraq. In any case, their

doing so, some wryly observe, fits nicely into the pattern created after the US interventions in the former Yugoslavia whereby 'America fights and Europe does the dishes' by providing the bulk of men and money for peacekeeping. Rather less pejoratively (though employing rather more jargon), we might talk of complementarity, with Europe bringing increasingly sophisticated, integrated civilian–military preventative and postconflict capacity to the party (see Whitman and Wolff, 2012).

Towards a European army?

Actually, one can question how hard and fast and set in stone this putative division of labour between Europe and the USA really is (see Flockhart, 2011). True, European countries did indeed provide most of the 'stabilization force' that initially came in once the Americans had toppled the Taliban regime in Afghanistan, while the EU and its member states have provided around a third of the total international aid to the country. But, although their commitment has clearly waned since (see Duke and Haar, 2011: 408–412), Europeans (especially the British) did suffer military losses in Afghanistan – one of the reasons that the debate about involvement in the Netherlands became so heated that it helped lead to the collapse of that country's ruling coalition in February 2010. Conversely, the USA remains heavily involved, on the ground as well as at the diplomatic level (see US Mission to Pristina, 2007), in trying to achieve lasting peace in Kosovo, much to the chagrin of Russia and China that which fear the granting of independence (supervised by the EU and the UN) will set a worrying precedent. Moreover, even assuming the clichéd EU–USA division of labour – between a USA specializing in 'hard power' and a Europe that is better at 'soft power' – exists, can it go on for ever? The question raises once again the extent to which Europe is willing to both share the burden with the USA (the UK emphasis) and/or assume some degree of autonomy from it (the French emphasis, although not one that prevented the two republics cooperating on Libya).

This, as we have seen, is what ESDP/CSDP, if only in part (see Selden, 2010), is about. Whether Europe actually needs or finds it convenient to use it in an operational as well as a symbolic sense, however, remains to be seen. For one thing, however much commentators talk about Sweden, Finland, Austria and Ireland supposedly moving toward 'postneutrality' in what seems to be a more dangerous world, there seems little prospect of them surrendering their neutrality soon. This means that they may pick and choose missions, preferring perhaps to contribute to the non-military side of putative European operations. For another, experience also suggests that the key to things working is as much political as institutional. Unless big players, big contributors and big strategic thinkers such as France, Germany and Britain form some kind of informal trilateral *directoire* (and are allowed to do so by the other member states), ESDP/CSDP will not develop any grand coherence even though particular missions (see Box 11.2 and Merlingen and Ostrauskaite, 2010) will continue (see Menon, 2004).

KEY POINT

Despite developments and missions carried out under auspices of the European/Common Security and Defence Policy (ESDP/CSDP), a European army, though not as much of a pipe-dream as some suggest, is still a long way off.

Experience also suggests that – especially in times of crisis – institutions, or indeed the lack of them, will not stop the formation of ad hoc 'coalitions-of-the-willing' making use of national rather than multinational military assets (see Duke, 2000: 29). This is true whether they involve countries outside Europe, as in Iraq or Libya, or inside, as in the little remembered Italian-led intervention in Albania in 1997, undertaken in order to prevent a breakdown in state control turning into complete anarchy. Neither will institutional membership prevent those states in Europe with global pasts and therefore global pretensions projecting their power (albeit in ways that they think are for the best) in smaller conflicts well away from Europe. The sending of British troops to Sierra Leone to shore up a UN force in trouble is one example. France's on–off intervention in its former colony, Côte d'Ivoire, which saw military intervention (along with the UN) in 2010 in order to force the country's president to make way for his successor, is another.

What ESDP/CSDP is certainly *not* about – at least in the foreseeable future – is establishing EU control over the defence capability of its member states, forcing them to say 'yes' to what other states want them to do or preventing them from saying 'no'. Neither, for the moment, is it trying to balance rather than simply complement NATO or to swap the intergovernmental logic of the latter with the supranational logic that some see as inherent in the EU (see Duke and Haar, 2011). True, there now exists a *Eurocorps,* based on soldiers from France, Germany, Spain, Belgium and Luxembourg. Although this was set up separately from ESDP/CSDP since the coming to force of the Treaty of Strasbourg in 2009 and various motions by the European Parliament inviting other member states to contribute, it has arguably made a further step forward towards becoming (albeit in miniature or in embryo) a European army. There are also, since 2007, 'EU battlegroups' – rapid reaction forces made up from several member states which are assigned for exclusive EU use on a six-monthly rotation basis. There is also a civil-military planning cell, run by the (currently British-commanded) EU Military Staff (EUMS), which aims to improve the EU's ability to deploy such collective resources quickly. There have been complaints, too, (for example, from NATO's Secretary General in a speech in late January 2007) that cooperation between his organization and the EU remained very narrow. However, the decision-making basis for ESDP/CSDP remains intergovernmental (see Chapter 2). It may now be possible for some states to go ahead with a mission should others who do not support it choose to let them to get on with it; but if they want to, they can still veto any operation. Neither, we should note, does the supranational Commission, which is at least consulted on and can make suggestions in EU foreign policy, have any formal role in CSDP.

In any case, a report on ESDP approved by all heads of state and government at the EU's Nice summit in 2000 (see UK House of Lords, 17 January 2002, *Hansard,* Column 1210) made three things crystal clear. First, that 'NATO remains the basis of the collective defence of its members. Second, that [t]he development of the ESDP will contribute to the vitality of a renewed transatlantic link'. And, third, that it 'does not involve the establishment of a European army. The commitment of national

Figure 11.4 'Should decisions on defence and foreign affairs be made by national government or jointly within the EU?'

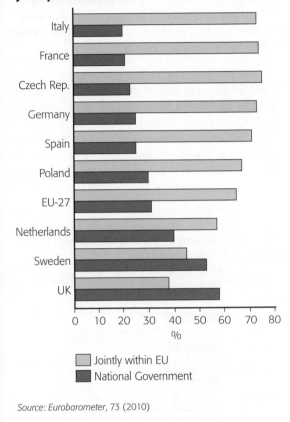

Source: *Eurobarometer*, 73 (2010)

within a European command, no amount of planning for a European security identity will field a single battalion.

This, of course, is the ultimate test. And, strangely enough, there are signs that, even if Europeans don't appear to want it, many of them regard some kind of European army as something that will eventually come about (see Figure 11.5). This is not perhaps entirely unreasonable if one considers how European integration has proceeded since the late 1950s via a series of treaties which, almost with each new document, set out new goals and, in keeping with those goals, inexorably expand the range of activities which are carried out in common – one of the reasons that so many Eurosceptics fret about

Figure 11.5 'Do you think that, fifty years from now, the EU will have its own army?'

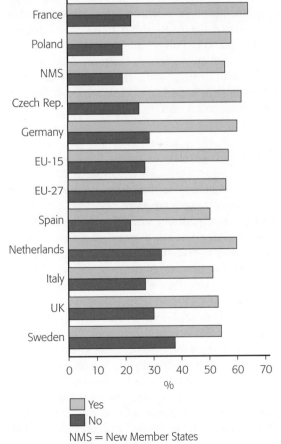

NMS = New Member States

Source: *Eurobarometer*, 67 (2007)

resources by Member States to [its] operations will be based on their sovereign decisions.' It is difficult to see how in the short to medium term this can be got around, although it is of course possible (as, arguably, they have done with Eurocorps) for the states concerned to effectively pool their sovereignty. Moreover, significant numbers of European people do not want it to be got around, especially in western European countries and particularly in Scandinavia and the UK (see Figure 11.4). Nor, one suspects, do their leaders, civil and military. As one US ambassador to the EU put it in the early 1990s (see Duke, 2000: 188):

Until the major European nations, including Germany, are prepared to send their young men abroad to fight, and to die if necessary, in a European cause, under a European flag, and

article 42 of the Lisbon Treaty. This states that 'The common security and defence policy shall include the progressive framing of a common defence policy. This will lead to a common defence, when the European Council, acting unanimously, so decides.' And it goes on to note 'If a Member State is the victim of armed aggression on its territory, the other Member States shall have towards it an obligation of aid and assistance by all the means in their power.' On the other hand, the same article – as well as making the need for unanimity clear – is careful to note that 'Commitments and cooperation in this area shall be consistent with commitments under the North Atlantic Treaty Organisation, which, for those States which are members of it, remains the foundation of their collective defence and the forum for its implementation.' Moreover, with the frankly tiny exception of the *Eurocorps*, there is as yet little sign of movement towards anything like a collectivization of Europe's military 'strength'. Indeed, the most tangible cooperation on the continent is bilateral, namely the relationship between its biggest defence players, France and the UK, which in November 2010 signed a Defence and Security Cooperation Treaty, paving the way for joint work and training in areas like nuclear weapons, carriers and rapid reaction operations.

Foreign policy

The right to determine their own defence policies is clearly something European states are keen to protect. When it comes to foreign policy – often a rather less highly charged area – there is a similar concern to preserve their sovereignty. But there is also, too, more of a recognition – at a mass as well as an elite level (see Figure 11.6) – that cooperation with other states, particularly if they are also in the EU, can be beneficial. Even before the formal declaration in the Maastricht Treaty signed in 1992 that the EU would establish (albeit intergovernmentally rather than supranationally) a 'Common Foreign and Security Policy' (widely known as CFSP), member states were engaging in what had become known as 'European Political Cooperation' or EPC.

Yet much of the potential afforded by the CFSP for common action – and for the EU to assert its 'presence' and its 'actorness' (see Allen and Smith,

1998; Bretherton and Vogler, 2005; Hill, 1993) – remains unrealized, as various audits undertaken by academic observers, more or less ruefully note. There are many reasons for this. At the level of process, the insistence by EU member states on a clear distinction between the EU's foreign policy, on the one hand, and its trade and aid policies, on the

Figure 11.6 'Are you for or against a common foreign policy among the Member States of the EU towards other countries?'

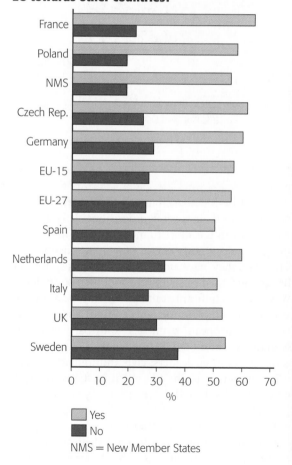

Source: Eurobarometer, 67 (2007)

other, means that many of the instruments that they themselves routinely use to support their bilateral aims cannot be brought to bear by the EU. This, plus the fact that, until the coming into force of the Lisbon Treaty, the EU lacked a constitutionally and internationally recognized 'legal personality' that would allow it to act more cohesively in global forums, also often means that it has to be content with 'declaratory diplomacy'. Yet even when it manages to go further, and (say) impose sanctions on a foreign regime abusing human rights – a weapon for which the EU reaches a little too frequently for some critics – the hard-won consensus for that action often frays under pressure from contradictory national interests (see Brummer, 2009). As long as state interests remain so diverse and potentially contradictory, then no amount of institutional tinkering can compensate for the lack of political will that, ultimately, lies behind what some see as the failure of the CFSP.

That said, we should think twice before portraying the national interest vs CFSP as some sort of simple zero-sum game. Indeed, it is clear that European cooperation offers individual states or groups of states opportunities to better pursue their national interests, at least where they are perceived to coincide with those of the rest. For instance, states such as France, the UK, Portugal and Belgium can use the CFSP to speak and act on African questions without necessarily drawing attention to (and fire for) supposedly 'neocolonial' attitudes. Meanwhile, states such as Ireland, Austria, Finland and Sweden can use participation in the CFSP at least to finesse, if not necessarily to transcend, their non-aligned or neutral stances (see Manners and Whitman, 2000). The release in the summer of 2007 of six Bulgarian healthcare workers Libya had held for seven years was almost certainly accelerated by Bulgaria joining the EU at the start of that year, and perhaps by the (then) French 'first lady' Cecilia Sarkozy, who went to Libya 'as a woman, as a mother' to secure their release. Likewise, the EU's collective condemnation of attacks on Danish embassies in the wake of the crisis caused by Danish newspapers and magazines publishing cartoons of the Prophet Mohammed almost certainly prevented the row turning into a bigger trade boycott against a small member state. Similarly, the immediate EU backing of the UK's demand that Iran release a handful of captured British sailors in the spring of 2007 was probably also useful – although the absence of any concomitant threat of sanctions unfortunately spoke volumes about the unwillingness of certain member states to sacrifice their commercial relationships with Tehran.

Neither should we think of European countries' foreign policy elites as somehow insulated from each other. Far from it: observers draw attention to the effect of Europeanization on the tendency of states in Europe to consult each other almost as a reflex and often before their traditional allies. For example, Scandinavian policy makers will tend to think 'European' rather than simply 'Nordic', while those in the UK might now think of consulting their partners across the Channel rather than going across the Atlantic first (see Manners and Whitman, 2000: 249). On the other hand, the extent to which socialization into collective habits, norms and identities has taken place is easily overdone, especially with regard to policy makers from larger member states such as France, Germany and the UK. This is irrespective of the fact that they have been in the community as long (or in some cases longer) than some of the member states in which that socialization is more noticeable (Manners and Whitman, 2000: 251–2).

This points to a more general pattern among EU member states. States with more global interests, such as France and Britain, tend to be rather more reticent about foreign policy convergence than often (but not always) smaller states with a more exclusive European focus, such as (prototypically) Belgium or Italy. The latter realize that Europe could – theoretically at least (see Steinmetz and Wivel, 2010) – afford them far more say in world affairs than they could ever hope to get acting alone; the former that the less intergovernmental the process, the less likely a putative European policy is to reflect the interests of the larger member states. Located between these two extremes are three groups. First, there are the states with a more 'Atlanticist' focus but that also like to think of themselves as good Europeans (Denmark, the Netherlands, Portugal, and Spain). Second, there are states with a particular regional focus and/or a tradition of neutralism (Austria, Finland, Ireland and Sweden) or at least multilateralism (Germany). Third, there are the postcommunist states: they are concerned to be good Europeans

Sweden (Sverige)

Area: 410,900 km² (9.8% of EU-27)
Population: 9.5 million (1.9% of EU-27)
Religious heritage: Protestant
GDP (2010): €347 billion (2.8% of EU-27)
GDP *per capita* as percentage of EU-27 average: 126
Female representation in parliament and cabinet (end 2011): 45% and 50%
Joined EU: 1995
Top 3 cities: Stockholm – capital city (0.9 million), Gothenburg (0.5 million); Malmö (0.3 million).

History: Sweden's early history was bound up with that of the other Nordic countries. It conquered Finland in the thirteenth century, but was then subsumed into the kingdom of Denmark. It regained its independence in the early sixteenth century under a king elected by its parliament, the *Riksdag*. For the next one hundred and fifty years, it went from strength to strength, conquering territory in modern-day Estonia, Latvia, Russia, Germany and Poland, and even pushing into what is now the Czech Republic during the high point of its power, the Thirty Years' War (1618–48). After this, it began to lose out to other powers, most notably Russia, to which it was forced to cede Finland in 1809. Things looked up soon after when the *Riksdag* elected a high-ranking French soldier as regent and then king, creating the line of Bernadotte, which still reigns in Sweden today. As a reward for siding with Britain and Prussia (now part of Germany) against the French dictator, Napoleon Bonaparte, Sweden was granted effective control over the kingdom of Norway

– a situation that lasted until 1905 when the Norwegians peacefully regained their independence. The nineteenth century saw Sweden adopt, first, a liberal constitution, then (in the 1860s) parliamentary government and, finally, a fully fledged democracy after the First World War (1914–18).

Sweden did not take part in that conflict and likewise remained neutral in the Second World War (1939–45), managing to escape the occupation endured by its Nordic neighbours and to develop its economy by trading with the combatants. If neutrality was the first defining feature of the twentieth century for Sweden, the second was the unparalleled political hegemony of its social democratic party, SAP. The SAP effectively ran Sweden from 1932 to 1976. During this period it pioneered anti-recessionary public spending and then went on to construct the third defining feature of Sweden in the twentieth century, its highly comprehensive welfare state. Even since wresting power from the SAP in the mid-1970s, the so-called 'bourgeois' parties of the centre-right, led by the conservative Moderates, have only managed to govern Sweden three times – once between 1976 and 1982, then between 1991 and 1994, and finally, after over a decade of the social democrats being kept in office by the smaller, more radical Left Party and the Greens, since 2006.

Economy and society: Sweden's citizens are some of the richest in Europe, with a *per capita GDP* a quarter above the EU average. Much of their income,

however, is swallowed up by taxes to pay for the welfare state, although the universal nature of many of the benefits it offers (in both cash and in kind) means that support for it remains high, even amongst those who pay most. Historically, Sweden has been able to afford its wrap-around welfare provision because it has a very competitive international trading sector which, although privately owned, seems to benefit from the stable economic environment; industrial harmony and active labour market policies facilitated by the state. Things are not perfect, of course: there is unemployment, much of it disproportionately affecting Sweden's half a million or so immigrant population, many of whom arrived only after the 1980s from places such as the former

WHAT'S IN AN ANTHEM?

The vaguely Tolkeinesque *Du gamla, Du fria* dates back to the nineteenth century, which is partly why neither of the two official verses mentions Sweden by name but instead refers to the 'ancient ... free ... [and] mountainous north'. The first verse goes on to talk of the 'green meadows' of 'the most beautiful land on earth', before recalling, in the second, the great days of yore when the place was honoured throughout the world. It reinforces the stereotype of a nation no longer interested in conquest and more concerned with keeping itself clean and green.

Yugoslavia, the Middle East and Somalia. Until their arrival, Sweden was unusually ethnically homogeneous – a homogeneity that also applied to religion: over nine out of ten Swedes still identify, even if only minimally, with the state Lutheran (Protestant) church which is financed through the tax system.

Governance: Sweden is a parliamentary democracy and a constitutional monarchy. Its unicameral legislature reflects the relatively consensual nature of Swedish political life. Its procedures, like policy making more generally, encourage consultation with outside interests, especially the powerful unions (to which most people belong) and employers' organizations, although the latter have cooled somewhat toward government-facilitated economic planning in recent years. Responsibility for many state functions is exercised by agencies, often at the regional or county level. Strong respect for due process has not precluded adaptation and innovation: Sweden undertook a major overhaul of its constitution as recently as the mid-1970s, and was the pioneer of the *ombudsman* system designed to help citizens redress grievances against public bodies without expensive recourse to the law – a system that has since spread to other countries.

Foreign policy: Sweden put off joining the EU until 1995. By then, the end of the Cold War had calmed concerns about membership undermining its neutral, non-aligned stance. Nevertheless, the country rejected adopting the euro in a referendum in 2003. Sweden still declines to join NATO, but is active in a non-combat role in humanitarian interventions all over the world.

A KEY CONTEMPORARY CHALLENGE
REFORMING BUT STILL PRESERVING THE WELFARE STATE

Sweden is famous the world over for its supposedly 'cradle-to-grave' welfare state but understandably has concerns lest it hinder the country's ability to compete in an open economy, in part by crippling business with high taxes, in part by discouraging its inhabitants from working – or working as hard as they otherwise might do. It was these concerns that helped bring a centre-right coalition to power in 2006. That coalition, re-elected in 2010, enjoyed considerable success in boosting employment and growth, in spite of the difficult economic climate that the world has experienced since 2008. It has also shrunk the proportion of national income swallowed by the state and has overseen the country's rise in league tables of economic competitiveness. It achieved all this in part by 'making work pay' by reducing taxes on earned income for both low- and high-earners and introducing tax-deductibility on domestic services like cleaning and renovation. Benefits have been reduced, while the retirement age has been raised to 67. In health care, more publicly-funded services are now privately delivered. Concerned parents and canny, profit-seeking entrepreneurs were also encouraged to found so-called free schools, again funded by the tax-payer but liberated from government control.

Clearly, not everything has worked perfectly and certainly not as perfectly as some of the glowing press commentary from conservative pundits (especially in the UK) suggests – indeed some argue that public services have deteriorated rather than improved as a result of introducing competition. Nevertheless, it is clear, not least from the difficulties experienced by the Social Democrats in coming up with a credible response to the government's programme, that the Swedish Prime Minister, Fredrik Reinfeld and his (famously pony-tailed and ear-ring sporting) Finance Minister, Anders Borg, have managed to convince enough Swedes – for the moment anyway – that they have retained the best of both worlds: a dynamic economy and a safety net which is not just secure but still pretty comfortable.

Contemporary challenges
- Reforming but still preserving the welfare state (see box above).
- Integrating ethnic minorities, particularly when it comes to the labour market.
- Reconciling continued state support for family reunification for refugees with constraints on local communities' resources and capacity.
- Ensuring the survival of (and service-delivery to) communities in sparsely populated areas, especially when their plight is of little interest to the urban majority.

Learning resources: Start with Larsson and Bäck (2008), *Governing and Governance in Sweden*. After that, try Arter (2006), *Democracy in Scandinavia*, Ingebritsen (2006), *Scandinavia in World Politics* and Hilson (2008), *The Nordic Model*. You can keep up with the news at http://sverigesradio.se/sida/default.aspx?programid=2054.

and, to some extent, share the anxieties of other smaller states that a purely intergovernmental 'European foreign policy' will be dominated by larger states; but they are also determined to preserve the sovereignty that they have only just won back after years of Soviet domination.

It is also important to remember that Europeanization, and the variation in the extent to which it seems to have affected the foreign policy making of EU member states (see Wong and Hill, 2011), is by no means the only factor impacting on such policy making. Any list would have to include the following questions (see Manners and Whitman, 2000: 252–61): How important is parliamentary oversight on foreign policy: practically unimportant as in France and the UK, or a potential constraint, as in the Nordic countries? To what extent do subnational governments get involved: not at all, as in most states, or increasingly often as in the federal states such as Belgium or Germany? Do parties make a difference: who would argue with the assertion that the election of a Socialist government in Spain in 2004 very swiftly reoriented Spain back to a more 'European' as opposed to 'Atlanticist' foreign policy orientation? Does this indicate that foreign policy – traditionally rather an elitist forum (a policy community rather than an issue network, to use the language of Chapter 8) – is becoming more generally politicized and even rising in salience among voters? Does this explain how and why German governments, of whatever stripe, continue to be constrained by public opinion from taking even multilateral military action, with Libya being only the most recent example and Afghanistan an exception that proves the rule? How influential are pressure groups: do defence industry lobbies push some countries (France and Britain) in one direction, while internationalist trade unions try to push other governments (Sweden, Germany) in another? How extensive is prime ministerial (or, in the case of France, presidential) intervention in foreign policy: is the foreign minister and his department very much in charge (as in, say, the Netherlands) or do they have to work hand in hand with the head of government (as in the UK, France, Germany and, increasingly, Italy)? And what about the bureaucratic politics and foreign ministries (see Hocking and Spence, 2002): to what extent are they under pressure financially and losing exclusive competence over foreign (and especially European affairs) to a whole range of departments who find themselves consulting with their opposite numbers in other member states?

Most of these issues, of course, pertain to foreign policy makers 'at home' in Europe. There is less research on the Europeanization of those who carry out those policies 'in country' outside Europe. What work there is (see Bale, 2000, 2004) suggests a familiar pattern. By and large, diplomats from smaller states are keener on cooperation with their fellow ambassadors than those from larger states; meanwhile, all states see the multilateral approach as a more or less useful addition to, rather than as a substitute for, their primarily bilateral approaches. Material, and not merely symbolic, obstacles remain in the way of any moves toward the truly integrated, 'European' diplomacy envisaged by the establishment under the Lisbon Treaty of the EU's External Action Service (see Blockmans and Laatsit, 2012; Spence, 2012). The EEAS, despite working direct to the EU's Foreign Policy chief (formally the High Representative of the Union for Foreign Affairs and Security Policy), is in its infancy, and many of its staff will continue to be on secondment from member states. On the other hand, it was given something of a head-start by assuming control of the European Commission delegations already operating in over 120 countries, most of which will now become EU embassies. Whether these will eventually subsume national diplomatic delegations, however, is a moot point. Such a move might make sense in terms of upfront cost savings, but individual European countries would lose the considerable commercial benefit of their own flag-waving public diplomacy. It would also demand changes from a group of relatively insulated and privileged civil servants.

None of this makes it any easier for Europe to 'speak with one voice' in or to the rest of the world, notwithstanding the appointment. None of it means, however, that European foreign policy is necessarily a mess. But it is necessarily messy. All-in-all, the words of perhaps the preeminent analyst of European foreign policy (Hill, 1998: 48–9) stil hold good today, namely that

We cannot know where the European foreign policy system is heading ... What is clear, however, is the interplay taking place between the national and the collective ... This has produced a pattern of multilevel diplomacy in which the various elements sometimes, compete, sometimes reinforce each other, and sometimes merely coexist.

Europe in the developing countries

Europe may spend less than two thirds of what the USA spends on the military, but it prides itself on spending at least twice as much on development assistance. Indeed, European countries provide over half of what governments around the world give in aid to developing countries. The UN target is that donor countries should be giving 0.7 per cent of their gross national income (GNI), although only a handful of countries (all of them in northern Europe) actually meet that target. In September 2005, the EU adopted its own target for member states of 0.51 per cent by 2010, although,

as Table 11.2 shows, that has clearly not been reached even by some relatively large and rich countries, let alone by newer member states (for which, see Horký and Lightfoot, 2012). Depending on the country concerned, a significant (though generally falling) proportion of this overseas development assistance (ODA) is still provided on a bilateral basis to particular countries – often those with colonial links – although, on the upside, less and less of it is now tied to the recipient doing some sort of business with the donor. An increasing proportion of Europe's development assistance, most of it going to sub-Saharan Africa and the so-called LDCs or least developed countries (see Figure 11.7), now comes through the EU. It is managed on member state's behalf by the Commission as the 'European Development Fund' (EDF) and goes to some 650 million people living in seventy-seven African, Caribbean and Pacific nations – the so-called 'ACP countries' – under an agreement signed at Cotonou in June 2000 that came into force in April 2003 for a twenty-year period, subject to five-yearly reviews.

Table 11.2 Who spends how much on aid, and where and how they spend it

	ODA (%GNI) 2010	ODA (US$ billion) 2010	ODA spent bilaterally (2010) (%)	Tied aid as % of ODA (2009) (%)	Top three recipients	ODA per capita (US$) 2010
Sweden	0.97	4.527	64	0	Tanzania, Mozambique, Afghanistan	485
Netherlands	0.81	6.531	75	14	Indonesia, Afghanistan, Sudan	394
UK	0.56	13.763	64	0	India, Iraq, Afghanistan	222
France	0.50	12.916	60	14	Ivory Coast, French Polynesia, China	200
Germany	0.38	12.723	63	2	Iraq, China, India	156
Spain	0.43	5.197	68	27	Guatemala, Morocco, Nicaragua	113
Italy	0.15	3.111	30	28	Iraq, Afghanistan Ethiopia	52
Czech Rep.	0.12	0.224	47	n/a	Afghanistan, Mongolia, Serbia	21
Poland	0.08	0.378	25	n/a	n/a	10
EU	n/a	12.986	n/a	n/a	Turkey, Palestine, Afghanistan	26
USA	0.21	30.154	87	28	Afghanistan, Iraq, Sudan	98

Notes: n/a = Not available.

Source: Data from OECD, *Development Cooperation Report*, 2011.

Figure 11.7 Where ODA channelled through the EU goes

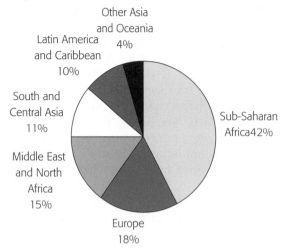

Other Asia and Oceania 4%

Latin America and Caribbean 10%

South and Central Asia 11%

Middle East and North Africa 15%

Europe 18%

Sub-Saharan Africa 42%

Note: Figures exclude unspecified destinations and unallocated income.

Source: OECD, OECD, *Development Cooperation Report*, 2011.

KEY POINT

European states, both bilaterally and through the EU, provide a massive amount of aid to the developing world, although the good they do has to be offset against their continued protectionism.

The Cotonou Agreement is the latest in a long line of agreements under which the EU and its forerunners have provided ODA and preferential access to European markets to countries which, more often than not, are former colonies of member states. Unfortunately, while the assistance provided to the ACP should not be sniffed at, the Commission itself noted prior to Cotonou that the results were pretty meagre in terms of the overall EU development goals (namely, to reduce poverty and produce sustainable socio-economic development in the countries helped, to facilitate their integration into the world economy and to support democracy and human rights). Moreover, under 10 per cent of African trade is intra-African: most African nations (indeed, most ACP nations) are still exporting to and importing from Europe instead of, as it were, building indigenous (and possibly economically more rational) trade networks. ACP countries' share of the EU market continues to be over-concentrated in a few commodities and dropped significantly from the 1970s right through to the late 1990s. Since then another actor – China – has appeared on the scene and shown itself very keen (without worrying too much about the kind of regimes it deals with) to trade with and provide aid to African countries in

order, among other things, to gain access to valuable raw materials as well as new markets (see Brautigam, 2009; Men and Barton, 2011).

Irrespective of outcomes, there has been considerable criticism of the way in which, over the years, Europe's development assistance has been managed. First, there is the overlap and duplication between EU programmes, the bilateral efforts of member states and the work of non-European governments, other international organizations and non-governmental organizations (NGOs). Second, there is the corruption and misspending in the developing countries themselves. These criticisms led to the establishment of EuropeAid, an EU agency tasked with coordinating and implementing the EU effort – an arrangement that appears to be improving matters considerably. Coordination will always be an issue, of course, but most analysts believe that a 'mixed economy' of donors is healthy, even if there is some risk of overlap. They also point to the fact that the EU has considerable advantages over bilateral providers. For instance (although this could change with an increased security and foreign policy presence), it is seen by most receiving countries as 'neutral' rather than 'neocolonial'. In addition, the fact that the EU, via the Commission, is responsible for negotiating multilateral trade agreements (see below) means it is in a better position than single countries to ensure coherence between these agreements and aid packages. Another advantage of EU action in this area is that 'tied aid' is even further reduced, even if it is not yet completely eliminated.

The other big change that has come about in recent years is the increasing 'conditionality' attached to development assistance coming from European countries and the EU (see Holland and Doidge, 2012). While some of the conditions have to do with promoting economic reform, most of them are to do with good governance (transparency and accountability) and, increasingly, human rights and gender equality. This is part of an overall trend towards including a political dimension in the aid relationship. Also important, but rather less trumpeted, is the encouragement of trade liberalization. This has to happen so that most, if not all, ACP countries, and their trade relationships with European countries that are still inclined to grant them non-reciprocal, special treatment, can meet ever-stricter WTO rules. The downside of this will be that their markets will be open to the advanced industrialized countries. The upside of this is the granting to the least-developed countries (or LDCs) practically free access to European markets. The fact that free access will apply only to the poorest of the poor raises the critical question of coherence. Put bluntly, European countries give with one hand but take away with the other by continuing to protect markets – particularly agricultural markets – in which developing countries could well enjoy a comparative advantage if they were granted full and unfettered access.

Another, recent criticism is that Europe is increasingly using aid as a tool of foreign and security policy, meaning that its 'near abroad' will get an unfair share compared with those far-away countries which need it more. Those concerned with security are, of course, right to point to the fact that, as the European Security Strategy of 2003 (see Box 11.2) put it, 'security is a precondition of development'. But many in the development community suspect that the security to be protected is less that of the developing countries than that of Europe itself. Only the naive would expect or demand no linkage between development assistance and foreign and security policy, but many would argue it would be misguided if long-term goals such as poverty reduction (which might eventually contribute to a more secure world) were made subordinate to immediate security priorities. In any case, controlling and/or reducing the flow of migrants into Europe (see Chapter 10) can also be seen as a security priority, which aid to the sending countries (especially if made conditional) might address (Boswell, 2003).

Critical voices in the development community also argue that the newer member states (whose commitment to and capacity for helping the poorest countries is probably lower than that of their richer counterparts in western Europe) should not deflect EU efforts even further away from the far-away poor to the non-EU countries of eastern Europe. This would be understandable – they have closer trading relationships and obvious security concerns – but

would be a very negative consequence of enlargement. Those concerned with the far-away poor are probably also right to worry that the security focus of the EU as a whole on Islamic North Africa and the Middle East also risks diverting its attention from the ACP. On the other hand, it has long been a criticism of EU assistance policy that (at least as far as EDF financing goes, and owing in no small part to the initial influence of the French) it has been over-concentrated on the ACP, leaving out massive areas of poverty in Asia and, to a lesser extent, in Latin America. Meanwhile, overlaying these distributional disputes are concerns that still relatively well-off European countries are making cuts in overseas aid as part of their efforts to reduce their budget deficits or, just as bad, using their current difficulties as an excuse for their failure to up their contributions even during the years of plenty; they are also (in addition to diverting spending to those countries seen to present a security threat) spending more of it at home via assistance to refugees – an activity which technically counts as ODA but which some would argue scarcely deserves the name (see AidWatch, 2012).

These criticisms notwithstanding, few would begrudge the EU making the most of its aid role, even if it can sometimes seem part of its wider ambitions as a global player (see Gänzle, et al., 2012). Admittedly, its efforts are far from perfect and it has a nasty habit, first, of forgetting that much of 'its' spending is actually done by individual member states and, second, of making comparisons with the USA only on publicly-provided aid (see Table 11.2) when the Americans spend almost four times as much on privately provided aid as the Europeans. Nevertheless, the EU is clearly a major player in the developing world, and it does seem to be the case that Europe's aid and development policies have been subject over the years to Europeanization. Many countries – including some of the most generous – still handle most of their ODA bilaterally (see Table 11.2). Yet increasingly, all of them try to help LDCs in a way that attempts not to cross-cut or duplicate EU efforts. This would seem not only to make sense, but also to be in keeping with the wishes of most of their citizens. A special Eurobarometer survey (no.343) conducted in 2010 found that on average only a quarter of respondents on average thought that humanitarian (note, not development) aid would be more efficiently provided separately by member state governments than by the EU with well over half preferring the latter option. This does not mean, however, that individual European countries will eventually subsume their own efforts into a collective EU operation: as with diplomacy, there are both symbolic and bottom-line reasons for continuing to maintain a national presence in the world.

Europe and the global environment

Europe, as we noted in Chapter 1, leaves a big environmental footprint on the world. Its citizens, its industries (and its highly subsidized farm animals!) are responsible for billions of tons of sometimes toxic waste, for depleting fish stocks, eroding soil and for around 15 per cent of world emissions of greenhouse gases. With the growing realization that the latter, in particular, are contributing to global warming, European countries have, in recent years, come to realize that environmental policy cannot be pursued simply at a national, nor even just a regional, EU-wide level. Of course, they still have a lot to learn and a lot to do at those levels (see Jordan *et al.*, 2010; Knill and Liefferink, 2007), even though they have taken the opportunity offered by EU enlargement to force the relatively high standards of the northern part of the continent onto the southern and eastern parts. But the EU has also turned its attention further afield: it puts pressure on those countries who wish to join it (or at least establish a close relationship with it) to become 'greener' (Knill and Tosun, 2009) and sees itself as a world leader and global agenda-setter on the environment and climate change

The EU and its member states have pursued this role in spite of manifold and manifest difficulties caused by the 'mixed competence' (between the EU and national governments) that characterizes policy and the capacity to make international agreements in this area, as well as the big inconsistencies in

KEY POINT

Environmental policy is another area where Europe takes the lead, although it is by no means perfect and continues to have trouble persuading its allies to follow that lead.

European countries' taxation and energy regimes (see Bretherton and Vogler, 2005). This is partly due to the seriousness of the situation, and partly due to the fact that European unity is seen as the only way of (a) governments persuading their own populations and business sectors to make sacrifices; and (b) getting foreign powers (not least the USA and Japan) to agree to do so. But whatever its causes, this unity was crucial in getting the agreement to cut greenhouse gas emissions that was affirmed in the UN-based Kyoto Treaty which was negotiated in 1997 and eventually (with the assistance of Russia but not the USA) came into force in 2005. Along with what was widely perceived as the intransigence of the USA during the negotiations, this could well have contributed at least a little to the 'presence' – or, at least, the recognition – of the EU in the world, and perhaps even the generally favourable attitudes other countries' populations (including, incidentally, those living in Russia) seem to have of it (see Figure 11.8).

Figure 11.8 Other countries' views of the EU

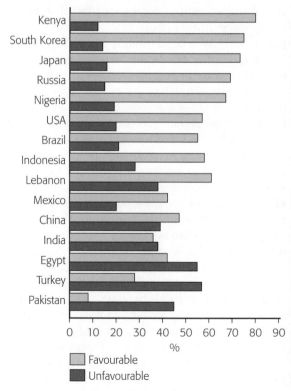

Source: PewResearchCenter, *Global Attitudes Survey* (June 2010) http://www.pewglobal.org/2010/06/17/chapter-6-opinions-about-european-leaders-and-nations/

How much this impression is based on knowledge, however, is a moot point: a more detailed opinion survey carried out by Gallup in the USA in May 2004 might have made depressing reading for the EU: 77 per cent of Americans admitted to knowing very little or nothing about it (for instance, that its population is larger than that of the USA). On the other hand, although the USA was rated more positively than the EU on promoting peace and economic growth, and fighting poverty and terrorism, the EU was rated by Americans as better on 'protection of the environment'.

The EU, in the knowledge that most of its citizens realize it has a role alongside their national governments on what is the ultimate cross-border issue (see Figure 11.9), has continued to commit itself to cut CO_2 emissions faster than other countries and regions in the hope that it can persuade them to follow suit. Whether this will work still remains to be seen. USA intransigence on global warming is beginning to crumble only very slowly in the face of overwhelming scientific evidence that climate change is 'man-made', and the developing nations, China and India especially, remain huge obstacles to progress. Indeed, Europe's lack of influence over them was once again revealed at the so-called COP-15 summit in Copenhagen in 2009. Despite the best efforts of European negotiators, all that could be achieved was a non-binding accord on reducing emissions and providing help to developing countries, characterized by vague targets and even vaguer promises about how they might be achieved – all of them hammered out in a backroom deal between the USA, China, India, Brazil and South Africa which was then presented as a fait-accompli to European governments who in the end decided that any deal was better than none. That said, those countries – or more precisely their airlines – have not been able to avoid being billed by the EU for the notional price of the carbon used when they fly in and out of Europe. Where Europe has leverage, it is apparently prepared to use it.

Europe as a global trader

Europe expects to have some clout because it is one of the wealthiest places on the planet – one of the reasons, incidentally, that it can afford to spend so

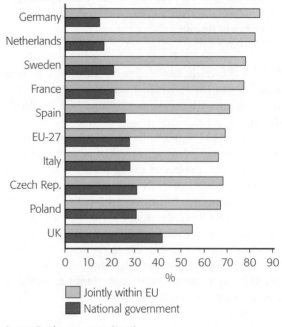

Figure 11.9 'Should decisions on protecting the environment be made by national government or jointly within the EU?'

Source: Eurobarometer, 73 (2010)

much on overseas aid. The continent might only contain 5 per cent of the world's population, but it produces nearly one-third of the world's economic output, accounts for about one-fifth of all trade flows (indeed, nearer a half if one includes intra-EU trade), and at least one-third of the world's foreign direct investment (FDI), including between half and three-quarters of that flowing into the USA. Not only this, but trade is the one area in which the EU has really got its act together. Member states – although they often remain in the room looking over its shoulder – allow the European Commission to act as their single negotiator in world trade forums such as the WTO and in the bilateral negotiations which, after the failure of the Doha round to achieve a multilateral deal (see Poletti, 2012), have become more common. Consequently, its voice has to be listened to, even by a country such as the USA, which in other areas can do almost as it likes. And this is likely to remain as much the case after the Lisbon Treaty as before it since, apart from increasing the involvement of the European Parliament and possibly the new High Representative and the External Action

Europe is the biggest trade bloc in the world and increasingly acts accordingly, sometimes putting commercial interests above the foreign policy wishes of its allies.

Service (EEAS) in trade matters, it makes very little difference to Europe's evident determination to carry on speaking with one voice on trade (see Woolcock, 2010).

If even the USA has to listen, so, too, do less powerful countries. Many of these like to present themselves to their publics as doing battle with 'Fortress Europe'. This apparently protectionist behemoth seems to them determined to protect the interests of its producers (particularly, via the hated CAP, its agricultural producers), even if it means denying its consumers access to the cheap imports that third countries are dying to provide. This could be a misleading impression: even though things continue to move slowly on agriculture, the EU is (relatively speaking) no longer so bent on protection (see Woolcock, 2009). But it is a persistent impression, albeit one that competes with other images conjured up by the EU (some more positive, some less so) in other parts of the world (see Lucarelli and Fioramonti, 2011) including places where it would hope to generate more awareness than it currently does (see Chaban and Holland, 2008).

This notwithstanding, the trade and investment links between the EU and other advanced industrial and rapidly industrializing countries are highly significant. For instance, China and Europe might have public slanging matches over allegedly unequal access to their respective domestic markets (peaking in the so-called 'Bra wars' of 2005), but that is partly because they are each other's second biggest trading partners. Whereas two decades ago trade between the two was minimal, official figures from 2011 show exports of goods and services from EU member states to China running at €160 billion per annum (around 9 per cent of the EU-27's total exports), with imports at €210 billion (around 17 per cent of the EU's total imports) – a deficit accounted for largely by the fact that Europe imports far more manufactured goods from China than China imports services from Europe. Some 11 per cent of Japan's imports in 2010 came from EU countries, to which it sent 13 per

cent of its total exports. For India in 2011 the figures were 12 and 19 per cent, and for Brazil 22 per cent and 21 per cent respectively – and trade with the latter should become all the more valuable if the mooted Association agreement between the EU and Latin America's free trade area, Mercosur, comes to fruition. In Australia, EU countries account for 19 per cent of the country's imports and 8 per cent of exports, in New Zealand 15 and 11 per cent, and in Canada 12 and 9 per cent respectively. It is these kinds of volumes that guarantee Europe – or, at least, European countries – a significant 'presence'. So does the fact that many overseas financial institutions now hold currency reserves in euros, notwithstanding the eurozone's recent troubles. Indeed, it could well be the case that the € sign is as familiar to non-Europeans as the blue flag with twelve gold stars.

Trade between the country whose currency is presently the world leader, the USA, and countries belonging to the European Union is highly significant and currently runs in favour of the EU-27. Exports from those countries to the USA in 2011 were worth €261 billion (goods) and €127 billion (services) and, in turn, they imported €184 billion (goods) and €131 billion (services) from the USA. Put another way, the USA accounted for some 11 per cent of the EU's imports and 17 per cent of its exports, while the EU accounted for 17 per cent of US imports and 19 per cent of US exports. Moreover, according to the Commission's Trade Directorate General,

Total US investment in the EU is three times higher than in all of Asia and EU investment in the US is around eight times the amount of EU investment in India and China together. Investments are thus the real driver of the transatlantic relationship, contributing to growth and jobs on both sides of the Atlantic. This can also be illustrated with approximately 15 million jobs linked to the transatlantic economy. It is estimated that a third of the trade across the Atlantic actually consists of intra-company transfers.

Nor is this just a relationship *à deux,* either. Between them, the EU and the USA are easily the world's most successful capitalist economies. As such, they go some way to determining the trading and financial framework for the rest of the world.

None of this, of course, prevents Europe and the USA falling out over trade. There have been big bilateral rows between the USA and Europe over steel tariffs (in 2002), GM crops and animal growth hormones (ongoing), Cuba (also ongoing), jumbo jets and audiovisual services (likewise) and (strange, but true) bananas. Things are not helped either by accusations by American commentators and policy makers that Europeans are rather keener than they should be to see 'the flag following trade' rather than using economic clout to achieve foreign policy objectives or to reward good behaviour on the part of foreign regimes. Although these accusations might to some extent be motivated by the fact that the EU is now no pushover in international trade negotiations (see Meunier, 2007), American critics have a point. What they see as Europe's intransigence goes right back to the reluctance among European states to support Israel in the 1973 war with Arab countries, partly (though not purely) because they feared a backlash by oil-producing states. Americans were also enraged by European states' refusal to stop importing gas from the Soviet Union following its role in suppressing the 1981 liberalization of the then communist regime in Poland. Europe's determination to ignore the US boycott of Cuba, with which it has trade, tourism and (Spanish) cultural links, has also been a problem. And, much to the irritation of some in the USA, European states, both collectively and individually, continue to attempt a constructive dialogue with the Islamic regime in (oil- and gas-rich) Iran and not to allow 'local difficulties' in Tibet and Taiwan to interfere in relations with the economic powerhouse that is China. Indeed, one of the lowest points in transatlantic relations in recent years came about when, in 2005, European countries, especially those with big and increasingly pan-European defence industries (see Epstein and Gheciu, 2006: 323–8), looked as if they might lift the US-led arms embargo on China – a possibility that was only averted when the American administration (after its so-called European 'charm offensive' in early 2005 appeared to alter little more than the mood music) made it clear in no uncertain terms that it would have huge negative repercussions.

But things are changing. It would be naive to think that centuries-old European pragmatism is ever likely to give way to wide-eyed idealism. But European governments, particularly acting together as the EU, are beginning to realize that their collective interests (in the trade as well as the security field) could well lie in investing more political content in what previously have been very much economic relationships, perhaps via bilateral forums or perhaps via contacts with Asian regional cooperation organizations like ASEAN and ASEM in East and South East Asia (see Wiessala, 2006). If anything, given heightened fears over migration, and over WMD in North Korea, collective diplomacy in those regions will probably increase, as will the tendency to insist that any agreements entered into by the EU with other countries include conditions on progress toward human rights and democracy – something the EU already tries to promote around the world through initiatives like the European Instrument for Democracy and Human Rights (EIDHR), which had a budget of €1.104 million for 2007–2013 and covered over 100 countries.

But we should be careful. For one thing, there is evidence that the European states' commitment to conditionality is more rhetorical than real where it clashes with their economic or strategic interests (Smith, 2005b). For another, EU specialists are bound to stress the role of collective, as opposed to bilateral, diplomacy between individual member states and the countries concerned. Similarly, it is all very well for the EU to claim that it accounts for a large chunk of world trade and therefore enjoys massive presence; but it is a little misleading. Obviously, the EU helps provide the framework for those trade flows; but we must not forget that it is individual member states and the companies within them that actually do the business. It is rather like UEFA (the body which regulates soccer in Europe) claiming credit for all the goals scored and wins notched up by European countries in the World Cup finals which, via its association with FIFA (the world governing body), it goes some way to helping stage every four years. Clearly, at least some of the audience will recognize the collective brand, but many more of them will be aware of the nations of which it is composed. This could change, however, as the EU, frustrated at lack of progress in the WTO, begins to look toward doing bilateral deals with single countries, including India (Woolcock, 2009, 2010).

Lest we forget – the enlargement and domestication of international politics

'Europe' in the world, then, is a complex mix of individual states and the European Union of which the majority are a part. And it is about the interaction between national foreign policies, CFSP (and ESDP), and the 'external relations' of the EU when it operates in the trade (and increasingly perhaps) the aid and the environmental field. There is no reason to think this will change any time soon. Certainly, we should be careful not to presume that foreign policy in Europe is somehow on an inevitable evolutionary progress towards eventual integration. Doing so will only disappoint, since the gap between expectations and capability is unlikely to disappear (see Hill, 1993). As Smith (2004) argues (see also Hill, 1998), it could be that the 'part-formed foreign policy' of the EU will always be expressed as much by supposedly non-foreign-policy instruments such as trade and aid, and that it is pointless, in the absence of a collective 'European interest' to expect it to take on the forms we traditionally associate with states – states that, in any case, wish to cling on to those forms even in the 'postmodern' or 'postsovereign' age.

KEY POINT

Enlargement of the EU is probably the biggest foreign policy success of the last half-century, rendering Europe more secure than it has ever been. Whether enlargement, and Europe's relative standing in the world, can continue forever is another matter.

But whatever 'Europe's' place in the wider world, the biggest success story with regard to defence, foreign policy and even development aid, has been Europe itself. Prior to the founding and development of what is now the EU, most European countries regarded their immediate neighbours as part of the rest of the world. That is no longer the case: within Europe, international politics have been substantially 'domesticated'. It is not just that European states – even those states that retain global interests and/or wish to maintain a close relationship with

Figure 11.10 It all depends which country: EU residents' attitudes to future EU enlargement

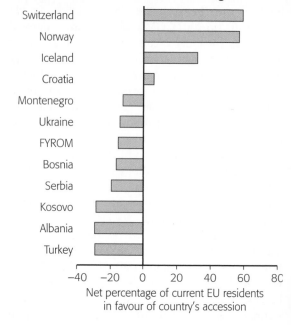

Net percentage of current EU residents in favour of country's accession

Source: Eurobarometer, 74 (2010).

the USA – no longer consider armed conflict between themselves as even an outside possibility. It is also that, at the very least, they reflexively think about the mutual consequences of their following their own interests and, in some, cases hesitate even to define those interests without or before consultation (Aggestam, 2000: 71). And even where those interests would appear to differ, they will often lay them aside for what they consider as more important in the long term; namely, a security and a prosperity that they recognize is best guaranteed collectively. The EU, probably more even than organizations such as the OSCE, contributes to a European security community.

The most obvious recent example of this, of course, is EU enlargement. This was achieved not just because of the long-term economic potential of expanding the single market. It also fitted with the even longer-term foreign policy goal – albeit not one always very consciously or consistently pursued – of 'securing' the 'near abroad' by 'locking-in' democracy, just as it was locked-in in Spain, Portugal and Greece in the 1980s and in the previously non-democratic states of western Europe after the

DEBATE 11.1
Should Turkey join the EU?

YES

- Turkey has played an integral part in European history and has grown closer to Europe in recent times. It is an officially secular state and an increasingly stable democracy. By denying Turkey entry, the EU would send a signal to the Islamic world that ultimately its religion is a sticking point.
- Turkey, a long-term and loyal member of NATO for half a century, would provide a buffer zone against, and a bridgehead into, potentially unstable (but also potentially lucrative) parts of the world. Turkish entry would be looked on favourably by the USA.
- Incorporating Turkey into the EU would help consolidate democracy there and improve its economy, thereby reducing any potential risk to its European neighbours
- Turkey's population is much younger than that of the current EU member states and would help with the demographic crunch that is fast approaching.
- Turkey will have to meet EU criteria before it can join. If and when it does join, institutional fixes and transition periods can, if necessary, be put in place.

NO

- The first obstacle is Turkey's sheer size: in under a decade its population will match Germany's, and is already bigger than the combined population of the ten states that joined the EU in 2004. This would give Turkey a big say in EU institutions.
- Turkey's poverty (its unevenly distributed *per capita* income is only around a quarter of the EU average) would see it swallow up large amounts of EU regional funding.
- Imagine Europeans' anxiety if Turks, of whom there are already millions in Germany and elsewhere, are granted free movement and the right to work in Europe. The EU's absorption capacity is not infinite; better a deal that stops short of full membership.
- Turkey's Islamic culture – given a boost by religiously oriented governments in recent years – means that it simply does not belong in Europe, which has its roots in Christianity and a more secular enlightenment tradition of respecting the rights of the individual. And what about the danger of importing Islamic terrorism?

Second World War. Even the prospect of membership, it seems, is enough to persuade potentially troublesome states, especially in the Balkans, to 'behave themselves' – witness the progress of Croatia, which was offered membership in the EU after less than a decade of being declared a candidate country, and more recently Serbia, which once membership became a realistic prospect finally began to take the search for those wanted for war crimes in Bosnia seriously.

The enlargement that took place in 2004, we should also note, was achieved – particularly as accession became a reality – without the support of the majority in some of the biggest countries of what was then the EU-15 (see *Eurobarometer 61*). Hopefully, experience will show that their leaders really did 'know best'. However, they may be less able to insulate themselves against public opinion – and, indeed, their own prejudices – when it comes to enlarging the EU to include a country like Turkey,

whose claim to be part of 'us' rather than 'them' (see Neumann, 1998) is, for many, less persuasive (see Debate 11.1 and Scherpereel, 2010b). Turkey has been formally associated with the EU since 1963 and first applied to join in 1987 (see Müftüler-Bac, 1997). After a customs union took effect in 1996, Turkey was finally accepted as a candidate country in 1999, since when it has accelerated economic and political reforms (see Hughes, 2004). Negotiations began in earnest in 2005, although in 2006 they ran into difficulty over Cyprus (see Chapter 2). The previous year, the prospect of Turkish accession appeared to have contributed to the negative result of the Dutch and especially the French referendums on the EU's Constitutional Treaty in 2005. Meanwhile, the negative rhetoric coming from some European countries, plus the realization that compromises to its sovereignty and way of life will have to be made before it can join, are beginning to dampen EU-enthusiasm among the Turkish population. Commenting on its Global Attitudes Survey in 2010, the respected Pew Research Center, based in the USA, noted that

> Turkey has long hoped to join the EU, but Turkish public sentiment… remains decidedly unenthusiastic. Currently, only 28% of Turks hold a positive view of the EU,… down substantially from 2004 (58% favorable). Moreover, while a majority (54%) of Turks are still in favor of Turkey becoming an EU member, this is substantially fewer than in 2005 (68%). The intensity of Turkish interest in joining the EU has also dropped substantially. Far fewer Turks now strongly favor (16%) their country's accession to the EU than in 2005 (31% strongly favor).

If Turkish enthusiasm continues to wane and Turkish cynicism continues to rise – and it is hard not to share the feeling that all the cementing of democracy has done is to remove Europe's last big excuse for delay rather than actually opening the door – the opportunities created by that country's accession, both for Turkey and other European countries, will never be fully realized. Doubtless, some Europeans will regard that as a lucky escape. Others will see it as an historic chance stupidly missed.

Support for further enlargement among the EU's population is questionable, especially in the larger, older member states whose politicians are insisting that the EU have regard to its so-called 'absorption capacity' – an insistence that has hardened in the wake of a widespread feeling that Romania and Bulgaria were allowed in without doing enough to end their chronic corruption problems, while Cyprus should have been obliged to find a workable solution to its arguments with Turkey before rather than after joining. Judging by the widespread apathy that greeted the accessions of 2004 and 2007, as well as the lack of enthusiasm in some key member states for more – depending, of course, which country we are talking about (see Figure 11.10) – a degree of 'enlargement fatigue' is now affecting European publics. The problem with responding to this by declaring an end to new accessions is that, by effec-

tively fixing what become finite borders, the EU will lose some, though not all (see Epstein and Sedelmeier, 2008), of its capacity to exert leverage over the behaviour of aspirant states. Losing that capacity will do nothing to enhance European security, whether one defines it narrowly as territorial defence or more broadly as providing a environment in which nearly half a billion sometimes very different people can continue to pursue their personal and political aspirations in comparative safety and comfort.

Which brings us neatly to our final point. Europeans – especially those in the west – have grown accustomed to their relative wealth and the position in the world that comes with it. Many of them assume that the latter will be maintained diplomatically over the next century, whether it be by their own country or by the EU collectively. But are they right? Or are they complacent? By the end of the century, less than one in twenty of the world's population will be European. And European countries' wealth might not look quite so impressive in comparison to that of rising powers like China, India and Brazil, let alone the existing superpower, the USA. Consequently, the ability of Europeans to help set the global agenda and secure and promote their values and interests could diminish, at least in relative terms. One early demonstration of this was the failure in early 2006 of either India or the USA to forewarn most European governments of a nuclear technology deal between them that seemed to ignore the fact that India is not a signatory to the non-proliferation treaty and therefore may legitimately exploit such cooperation for military purposes. Another, is the deal on global emissions, which, as we have already mentioned, was struck at Copenhagen in 2009 by those two countries, along with China, South Africa and Brazil, without consulting European 'allies'. It is not immediately obvious that acting in even greater consort through the EU rather than maintaining the current combination of bilateral and multilateral action will have much more impact on these profound global shifts in influence. Politics matters in many ways (see Chapter 9), but it cannot achieve miracles.

Learning Resources for Chapter 11

Further reading

The literature on EU and European foreign policy is massive: two excellent places to start, however, are provided by Cameron (2012), *An Introduction to European Foreign Policy* and the volume edited by Hill and Smith (2011), *International Relations and the European Union*. The collections edited by Tiersky and van Oudenaren (2010), *European Foreign Policies*, and by Wong and Hill (2011), *National and European Foreign Policies: Towards Europeanization* represent good next ports of call, the latter especially because it mixes country case studies and wider, collective considerations. Highly recommended, too, are an article on the EU's 'liberal grand strategy' by Michael E. Smith (2011) and Youngs (2010), *The EU's Role in World Politics*. A useful overview is provided by the chapter by Whitman and Steward in Jones *et al.* (2011) *Developments in European Politics Two*. The regular chapters on the EU's relationship with 'the wider Europe' and the rest of the world in the *JCMS Annual Review of the European Union* are a great way of keeping up to speed with current and recent events. For more on the international politics of Central and Eastern Europe, see Fawn, 2013.

On defence and security, see Ginsberg and Penska (2012), *The European Union in Global Security* and Kirchner and Sperling (2007), *EU Security Governance*, as well as the collection edited by Kurowska and Breuer (2011), *Explaining the EU's Common Security and Defence Policy* and a special issue of the *Journal of European Public Policy* on CFSP, edited by Sjursen (2011). Also recommended is the collection edited by Whitman (2011), *Normative Power Europe* and the chapter on counter-terrorism by Spencer in Jones *et al.* (2011), *Developments in European Politics Two*. On development and aid, see the special issue on 'The New Season of EU Development Policy' edited by Carbone (2008) in the journal *Perspectives on European Politics and Society*, as well as Holland and Doidge (2012), *Development Policy of the European Union*. On trade, but also wider issues of 'economic diplomacy', try Woolcock (2012), *European Union Economic Diplomacy*.

Those interested in Europe in particular parts of the world should consult the following: on the transatlantic relationship, see Lagadec (2012), *Transatlantic Relations in the 21st Century* and Hamilton and Burwell (2009), *Shoulder to Shoulder*. On Asia in general, see Gaens *et al.* (2009), *The Role of the European Union in Asia* and on Japan in particular Ueta and Remacle (2008), *Tokyo–Brussels Partnership*; on the Middle East, Müller (2012), *EU Foreign Policymaking and the Middle East Conflict*; on the Mediterranean, see the special issue of the journal *Democratization* on 'The European Union's Democratization Agenda in the Mediterranean: a Critical Inside-Out Approach' edited by Pace and Seeberg (2009), although bear in mind things have changed (and, indeed, will have to change) in the wake of the 'Arab Spring' (see Bauer, 2011); on China, see the collection edited by Pan (2012), *Conceptual Gaps in China-EU Relations*; on Russia, see the collections edited by Kanet (2010), *Russian Foreign Policy in the 21st Century*, by Gower and Timmins (2009), *Russia and Europe in the Twenty-First Century: An Uneasy Partnership*, and by David *et al.* (2013) *National Perspectives on Russia*; on Africa, see Sicurelli (2010), *The European Union's Africa Policies*; and on Latin America, see the collection edited by Ruano (2012), *The Europeanization of National Foreign Policies towards Latin America*. For more on the Turkish question, see the two consecutive special issues of the journal *South European Society and Politics* edited in 2011 by Avcı and Çarkoğlu.

On the web

www.oecd.org/dac/ and **http://ec.europa.eu/europeaid/index_en.htm** – development issues and statistics

ecfr.eu – pan-European think-tank on foreign and international affairs

europeangeostrategy.ideasoneurope.eu/ – short but interesting blogs and interviews (and more links) on European foreign, security and military policy

www.iss.europa.eu/home/ – EU sponsored think tank on security issues
http://www.ceps.be/ – Centre for European Policy Studies, a think tank which includes specialists on Energy, Foreign and Defence Policy, the European Neigbourhood Programme and Trade.
http://eeas.europa.eu/index_en.htm – EU foreign policy via the European External Action Service
www.eurocorps.org – EU's military force
ec.europa.eu/trade – European trade statistics and analysis
www.iea.org/ – all things energy
www.consilium.europa.eu/eeas/security-defence?lang=en – info. on CSDP and ESDP missions
www.hiik.de/en/konfliktbarometer/index.html – monitors conflicts worldwide
http://www.eidhr.eu/home – The EU's democracy and human rights promotion
aidwatch.concordeurope.org – monitors and lobbies governments and the EU on aid issues

Discussion questions

1   Do you think that Europe is a safer place to live in now compared with at the height of the Cold War?

2   In the build up to the war in Iraq, some US politicians claimed there was a difference between 'Old' and 'New' Europe. What did they mean and were they right?

3   Can and should European countries act together to integrate and build up a European security and defence capability?

4   What is Europe's policy on relations with Russia? Do you think it has been successful?

5   How and why is Europe becoming more serious about its relations with the countries of the southern Mediterranean?

6   What are the arguments – and what is the evidence – for and against a Europeanization of foreign policy?

7   The EU makes a good deal of its role both in helping developing countries and on environmental issues. In your view, is it right to do so?

8   Is Europe's foreign policy really driven by its trading and energy interests? If so, is that so very wrong?

9   Conflicts between the continent's countries are no longer military but simply domestic disputes: will it always be like that from now on?

ONLINE RESOURCES AVAILABLE

Visit the companion site at www.palgrave.com/politics/bale to access additional learning resources.

References

A

Aars, Jacob and Strømsnes, Kristin (2007) 'Contacting as a Channel of Political Involvement: Collectively Motivated, Individually Enacted', *West European Politics*, 30(1), pp. 93–120.

Aarts, Kees and Semetko, Holli A. (2003) 'The Divided Electorate: Media Use and Political Involvement', *Journal of Politics*, 65(3), pp. 759–84.

Aarts, Kees, Blais, André and Schmitt, Hermann (eds.) (2011) *Political Leaders and Democratic Elections* (Oxford: Oxford University Press).

Abdedi, Amir (2009) *Anti-Political Establishment Parties: a Comparative Analysis* (Abingdon: Routledge).

Achterberg, Peter (2006) 'Class Voting in the New Political Culture: Economic, Cultural and Environmental Voting in 20 Countries', *International Sociology*, 21(2), pp. 237–61.

Adam, Silke and Maier, Michaela (2010) 'Personalization of Politics: A Critical Review and Agenda for Research', in Charles Salmon (ed) *Communication Yearbook 34* (Abingdon: Routledge).

Adams, R.H. and Page, J. (2005) 'Do International Migration and Remittances Reduce Poverty in Developing Countries?', *World Development*, 33(10), pp. 1645–69.

Adler-Nissen, R. (2009) 'Behind the Scenes of Differentiated Integration:Circumventing National Opt-Outs in Justice and Home Affairs', *Journal of European Public Policy*, 16(1), pp. 62–80.

Aggestam, Lisbeth (2000) 'Germany', in Ian Manners and Richard G. Whitman (eds), *The Foreign Policies of European Union Member States* (Manchester: Manchester University Press).

Agranoff, Robert (1996) 'Federal Evolution in Spain', *International Political Science Review*, 17(4), pp. 385–401.

Aidukaite, Jolante (2011) 'Welfare reforms and socio-economic trends in the 10 new EU member states of Central and Eastern Europe', *Communist and Post-Communist Studies*, 44 (3) pp. 211–219.

AidWatch (2012) *Aid We Can: Annual Report 2012* (Brussels: Concord), available online at http://aidwatch.concordeurope.org/static/files/assets/3f200cc4/report.pdf.

Akkerman, Tjitske (2012) 'Comparing Radical Right Parties in Government: Immigration and Integration Policies in Nine Countries (1996–2010)', *West European Politics*, 35(3), pp. 511–529.

Akkerman, Tjitske and de Lange, Sarah L. (2012) 'Radical Right Parties in Office: Incumbency Records and the Electoral Cost of Governing', *Government and Opposition*, 47(4), pp. 574–596.

al-Azmeh, Aziz and Fokas, Effie (2007) *Islam in Europe: Diversity, Identity and Influence* (Cambridge: Cambridge University Press).

Albertazzi, Daniele and McDonnell, Duncan (eds) (2007) *Twenty-First Century Populism: The Spectre of Western European Democracy* (Basingstoke: Palgrave Macmillan).

Allan, James P. and Scruggs, Lyle (2004) 'Political Partisanship and Welfare State Reform in Advanced Industrial Societies', *American Journal of Political Science*, 48(3), pp. 496–512.

Allen, David and Smith, Michael (1998) 'The EU's Security Presence: Barrier, Facilitator, or Manager?', in Carolyn Rhodes (ed) *The European Union in the World Community* (Boulder, CO: Lynne Rienner).

Allern, Elin Haugsgjerd and Pedersen, Karina (2007) 'The Impact of Party Organizational Changes on Democracy', *West European Politics*, 30(1), pp. 69–92.

Allern, Elin Haugsgjerd, Aylott, Nicholas and Christiansen, Flemming Juul (2007) 'Social Democrats and Trade Unions in Scandinavia: the Decline and Persistence of Institutional Relationships', *European Journal of Political Research*, 46(5), pp. 607–635.

Allern, Elin Haugsgjerd and Aylott, Nicholas (2009) 'Overcoming the Fear of Commitment: Pre-electoral Coalitions in Norway and Sweden', *Acta Politica*, 44(3), pp. 259–285.

Allern, Elin Haugsgjerd and Bale, Tim (eds.) (2012) 'Political Parties and Interest Groups: Qualifying the Common Wisdom', special issue of *Party Politics*, 18(1).

Almeida, Dimitri (2010) 'Europeanized Eurosceptics? Radical Right Parties and European Integration', *Perspectives on European Politics and Society*, 11(3), pp. 237–253.

Almond, Gabriel and Verba, Sidney (1963) *The Civic Culture: Political Attitudes and Democracy in Five Nations* (Princeton, NJ: Princeton University Press).

Alonso, Sonia (2012) *Challenging the State: Devolution and the Battle for Partisan Credibility: A Comparison of Belgium, Italy, Spain, and the United Kingdom* (Oxford: Oxford University Press).

Alonso, Sonia and Claro de Fonseca, Saro (2012), 'Immigration, Left and Right', *Party Politics*, 18(6), pp. 865–884.

Alter, Karen J. (2003) *Establishing the Supremacy of European Law: The Making of an International Rule of Law in Europe* (Oxford: Oxford University Press).

Alvarez, Michael R., Garrett, Geoffrey and Lange, Peter (1991) 'Government Partisanship, Labor Organization and Macroeconomic Performance', *American Political Science Review*, 85(2), pp. 539–56.

Amable, Bruno, Gatti, Donatella and Schumacher, Jan (2006) 'Welfare-State Retrenchment: The Partisan Effect Revisited', *Oxford Review of Economic Policy*, 22(3), pp. 426–44.

Anckar, Carsten (1997) 'Determinants of Disproportionality and Wasted Votes', *Electoral Studies*, 16(4), pp. 501–15.

Anderson, Benedict (1991) *Imagined Communities: Reflections on the Origin and Spread of Nationalism* (London: Verso).

Anderson, Christopher J. and Beramendi, P. (2012) 'Left Parties, Poor Voters, and Electoral Participation in Advanced Industrial Societies', *Comparative Political Studies*, 45(6), pp. 714–746.

Anderson, Jeffrey J. and Langenbacher, Eric (eds) (2010) *From the Bonn to the Berlin Republic: Germany at the Twentieth Anniversary of Unification* (New York: Berghahn Books).

Anderson, K.M. (2001) 'The Politics of Retrenchment in a Social Democratic Welfare State: Reform of Swedish Pensions and Unemployment Insurance', *Comparative Political Studies*, 34(9), pp. 1063–91.

Andeweg, Rudy B. (2000) 'Ministers as Double Agents? The Delegation Process Between Cabinet and Ministers', *European Journal of Political Research*, 37(3), pp. 377–95.

Andeweg, Rudy B. and Irwin, Galen A. (2009) *Governance and Politics of the Netherlands,* 3rd edn (Basingstoke and New York: Palgrave Macmillan).

Andeweg, Rudy B., De Winter Lieven, and Dumont, Patrick (eds.) (2011) *Puzzles of Government Formation: Coalition Theory and Deviant Cases* (Abingdon: Routledge).

Andrews, Josephine T. and Jackman, Robert W. (2005) 'Strategic Fools: Electoral Rule Choice under Extreme Uncertainty', *Electoral Studies*, 24, pp. 65–84.

Ansell, Ben W. (2010) *From the Ballot to the Blackboard: The Redistributive Political Economy of Education* (Cambridge: Cambridge University Press).

Armingeon, Klaus (2007) 'Political Participation and Associational Involvement', in Jan van Deth, José Ramón Montero and Anders Westholm (eds), *Citizenship and Involvement in European Democracies* (London: Routledge).

Art, David (2007) 'Reacting to the Radical Right: Lessons from Germany and Austria', *Party Politics,* 13(3), pp. 331–49.

Art, David (2011) *Inside the Radical Right: The Development of Anti-Immigrant Parties in Western Europe* (Cambridge: Cambridge University Press).

Arter, David (ed.) (2001) *From Farmyard to City Square: The Electoral Adaptation of the Nordic Agrarian Parties* (Aldershot: Ashgate).

Arter, David (2006) *Democracy in Scandinavia: Consensual, Majoritarian or Mixed?* (Manchester: Manchester University Press).

Arts, Will, Hagneaars, Jacques and Halman, Loek (2004) *The Cultural Diversity of European Unity: Findings, Explanations and Reflections from the European Values Survey* (Leiden: Brill).

Arzheimer, Kai (2006) 'Dead Men Walking? Party Identification in Germany, 1977–2002', *Electoral Studies*, 25(4), pp. 791–807.

Arzheimer, Kai (2009) 'Contextual Factors and the Extreme Right Vote in Western Europe, 1980–2002', *American Journal of Political Science*, 53(2), pp. 259–75.

Arzheimer, Kai and Carter, Elisabeth (2006) 'Political Opportunity Structures and Right-Wing Extremist Party Success', *European Journal of Political Research*, 45(3), pp. 419–43.

Asp, Kent (1983) 'The Struggle for the Agenda: Party Agenda, Media Agenda, and Voter Agenda in the 1979 Swedish Election Campaign', *Communication Research*, 10(3), pp. 333–55.

Astudillo Ruiz, Javier (2002) 'The Spanish Experiment: A Social Democratic Party–Union Relationship in a Competitive Union Context', Harvard Centre for European Studies, Working Paper 83.

Atchison, Amy and Down, Ian (2009) 'Women Cabinet Ministers and Female-Friendly Social Policy', *Poverty & Public Policy*, 1(2).

Avcı, Gamze and Çarko lu, Ali (eds.) (2011) 'Turkey and the European Union: Accession and Reform', special issue of *South European Politics*, 16(2 and 3), pp. 209–364 and 365–512.

Avdagic, Sabina, Rhodes, Martin and Visser, Jelle (2011) *Social Pacts in Europe: Emergence, Evolution, and Institutionalization* (Oxford: Oxford University Press).

Avdagic, Sabina (2013) 'Partisanship, Political Constraints, and Employment Protection Reforms in an Era of Austerity', *European Political Science Review*.

Avdagic, Sabina and Crouch, Colin (2006) 'Organized Economic Interests: Diversity and Change in an Enlarged Europe', in Paul Heywood, Erik Jones, Martin Rhodes and Ulrich Sedelmeier (eds), *Developments in European Politics* (Basingstoke: Palgrave Macmillan).

B

Baccaro, L. (2002) 'Negotiating the Italian Pension Reform with the Unions: Lessons for Corporatist Theory', *Industrial and Labour Relations Review,* 55(3), pp. 413–31.

Bache, Ian (2007) *Europeanization and Multilevel Governance Cohesion Policy in the European Union and Britain* (Lanham: Rowman and Littlefield).

Bache, Ian George, Stephen and Bulmer, Simon. (2011) *Politics in the European Union*, 3rd edn (Oxford: Oxford University Press).

Bäck, Hanna, Debus, Marc and Dumont, Patrick (2011) 'Who Gets What in Coalition Governments? Predictors of Portfolio Allocation in Parliamentary Democracies', *European Journal of Political Research* 50(4), pp. 441–478.

Badescu, Gabriel and Neller, Katja (2007) 'Explaining Associational Involvement', in Jan van Deth, José Ramón Montero and Anders Westholm (eds) *Citizenship and Involvement in European Democracies* (London: Routledge).

Badinger, Harald and Breuss, Fritz (2003) 'What has Determined the Rapid Post-war Growth of intra-EU Trade?', IEF Working Paper 48, Wirtschaftsuniversität Wien.

Bailey, David J. (2009) *The Political Economy of European Social Democracy* (Abingdon: Routledge).

Bailey, Ric (2012) *Squeezing out the Oxygen – or Reviving Democracy? The History and Future of TV Election Debates in the UK* (Oxford: Reuters Institute), available online at http://reutersinstitute.politics.ox.ac.uk/fileadmin/documents/Publications/Working_Papers/History_and_Future_of_TV_Election_Debates.pdf.

Bajomi-Lázár, Péter (2008) 'The Consolidation of Media freedom in Post-communist Countries', in Karol Jakubowicz, Miklos Sükösd (eds.) *Finding the Right Place on the Map. Central and Eastern European Media Change in a Global Perspective* (Chicago: University of Chicago Press, 2008).

Baker, C. Edwin (2007) *Media Concentration and Democracy: Why Ownership Matters* (Cambridge: Cambridge University Press).

Bakke, Elisabeth and Peters, Ingo (eds.) (2011) *20 Years since the Fall of the Berlin Wall: Transitions, State Break-Up and Democratic Politics in Central Europe and Germany* (Berlin: BWV).

Balch, Alex (2010) *Managing Labour Migration in Europe: Ideas, Knowledge and Policy Change* (Manchester: Manchester University Press).

Baldassarri, Delia and Schadee, Hans (2006) 'Voter Heuristics and Political Cognition in Italy: An Empirical Typology', *Electoral Studies*, 25(3), pp. 448–66.

Baldini, Gianfranco (2011) 'The Different Trajectories of Italian Electoral Reforms', *West European Politics*, 34(3), pp. 644–66.

Baldini, Gianfranco and Pappalardo (2008) *Elections, Electoral Systems and Volatile Voters* (Basingstoke: Palgrave Macmillan).

Baldwin, Peter (2009) *The Narcissism of Minor Differences: How America and Europe are Alike* (New York: Oxford University Press).

Baldwin-Edwards, Martin and Kraler, Albert (2009) *REGINE – Regularisations in Europe* (Amsterdam: University of Amsterdam Press).

Bale, Tim (2000) 'Field-level CFSP: EU Diplomatic Cooperation in Third Countries', *Current Politics and Economics of Europe*, 10(2), pp. 187–212; also available at http://www.lse.ac.uk/Depts/intrel/pdfs/EFPU%20Working%20Paper%204.pdf.

Bale, Tim (2003) 'Cinderella and her Ugly Sisters: The Mainstream and Extreme Right in Europe's Bipolarising Party Systems', *West European Politics*, 26(3), pp. 67–90.

Bale, Tim (2004) 'Business as Usual? Europe's Overseas Diplomacy in the Age of CFSP', in Martin Holland (ed.), *Common Foreign and Security Policy: The First Ten Years* (London: Continuum).

Bale, Tim (2006) 'Between a Soft and a Hard Place? The Conservative Party, Valence Politics, and the Need for a New "Eurorealism"', *Parliamentary Affairs*, 59(3), pp. 385–400.

Bale, Tim (2007) 'Are Bans on Political Parties Bound to Turn Out Badly? A Comparative Investigation of Three "Intolerant" Democracies: Turkey, Spain and Belgium', *Comparative European Politics*, 5(2), pp. 141–57.

Bale, Tim (ed.) (2008) *Immigration and Integration Policy in Europe: Why Politics – and the Centre-Right – Matter*, (London: Routledge).

Bale, Tim (2011) *The Conservative Party from Thatcher to Cameron* (Cambridge: Polity).

Bale, Tim (2012a) *The Conservatives since 1945: the Drivers of Party Change* (Oxford: Oxford University Press).

Bale, Tim (2012b) 'Supplying the Insatiable Demand: Europe's Populist Radical Right', *Government and Opposition*, 47(2), pp. 256–274.

Bale, Tim and Bergman, Torbjörn (2006) 'Captives no Longer, but Servants Still? Contract Parliamentarism and the New Minority Governance in Sweden and New Zealand', *Government and Opposition*, 41(3), pp. 422–49.

Bale, Tim and Dunphy, Richard (2011) 'In From the Cold? Left Parties and Government Involvement since 1989', *Comparative European Politics*, 9(3), pp. 269–291.

Bale, Tim, Green-Pedersen, Christoffer, Krouwel, André, Luther, K. Richard and Sitter, Nick (2010a) 'If you Can't Beat Them, Join Them? Explaining Social Democrats' Responses to the Challenge from the Populist Radical Right in Western Europe', *Political Studies*, 58(3), pp. 410–26.

Bale, Tim, Hanley, Sean, and Szczerbiak, Aleks (2010b) '"May Contain Nuts"? The Reality behind the Rhetoric Surrounding the British Conservatives', *Political Quarterly*, 81(1) pp. 85–98.

Bale, Tim, Hough, Dan and van Kessel (2012) 'In or Out of Proportion? Labour and Social Democratic Parties' Responses to the Radical Right', in Jens Rydgren (ed.) *Class Politics and the Radical Right* (Abingdon: Routledge).

Bale, Tim and Kopecký, Petr (1998) 'Can Young Pups Teach an Old Dog New Tricks? Legislative Lessons for Britain from Eastern Europe's New Constitutional Democracies', *Journal of Legislative Studies*, 4(2), pp. 159–78.

Bale, Tim and Krouwel, Andre (2013) 'Down but Not Out: A Comparison of Germany's CDU/CSU with Christian Democratic Parties in Austria, Belgium, Italy and the Netherlands', *German Politics*.

Bale, Tim and Szczerbiak, Aleks (2008) 'Why Is There No Christian Democracy In Poland – And Why Should We Care?', *Party Politics*, 14(4), pp. 479–500.

Bale, Tim and van Biezen, Ingrid (2007) 'Political Data in 2006', *European Journal of Political Research*, 46(7–8).

Bale, Tim, Webb, Paul and Taggart, Paul (2006) 'You Can't Always Get What You Want: Populism and the Power Report', *Political Quarterly*, 77(2), pp. 195–203.

Balme, Richard and Chabent, Didier (2008) *European Governance and Democracy: Power and Protest in the EU* (Lanham: Rowman and Littlefield).

Banting, Keith and Kymlika, Will (eds) (2006) *Multiculturalism and the Welfare State: Recognition and Redistribution in Contemporary Democracies* (Oxford: Oxford University Press).

Bara, Judith (2005) 'A Question of Trust: Implementing Party Manifestos', *Parliamentary Affairs*, 58(3), pp. 585–599.

Barany, Zoltan (2002) *The East European Gypsies: Regime Change, Marginality, and Ethnopolitics* (Cambridge: Cambridge University Press).

Barisione, Mauro (2009) 'So, What Difference Do Leaders Make? Candidate's Images and the "Conditionality" of Leader Effects on Voting', *Journal of Elections, Public Opinion and Parties*, 19(4), pp. 473–500.

Barnett, Steven (2002) 'Will a Crisis in Journalism Provoke a Crisis in Democracy?', *Political Quarterly*, 2(4), pp. 400–8.

Barrett, David B., Kurian, George T. and Johnson, Todd M. (2001) *World Christian Encyclopedia: A Comparative Survey of Churches and Religion in the Modern World*, 2nd edn (New York: Oxford University Press).

Bartlett, Jamie, Birdwell, Jonathan and Littler, Mark (2011) The New Face of Digital Populism (London: Demos), available online at http://www.demos.co.uk/publications/thenewfaceofdigitalpopulism.

Bartolini, Stefano (2007) *Restructuring Europe: Centre Formation, System Building, and Political Structuring Between the Nation State and the European Union* (Oxford: Oxford University Press).

Batory, Agnes and Sitter, Nick (2004) 'Cleavages, Competition and Coalition-building: Agrarian Parties and the European Question in Western and East Central Europe', *European Journal of Political Research*, 43(4), pp. 523–46.

Bauböck, Rainer, Ersboll, Eva, Groenendijk, Kees and Waldrauch, Harald (2006) *Acquisition and Loss of Nationality: Policies and Trends in 15 European Countries: Comparative Analyses* (Amsterdam: Amsterdam University Press).

Bauer, Patricia (2011) 'The Transition of Egypt in 2011: A New Springtime for the European Neighbourhood Policy?',

Perspectives on European Politics and Society, 12(4), pp. 420–439.

Baun, Michael and Marek, Dan (2006) 'Regional Policy and Decentralization in the Czech Republic', *Regional and Federal Studies*, 16(4), pp. 409–28.

Bazant, Jan, Bazantová, Nina and Starn, Frances (eds) (2010) *The Czech Reader: History, Culture, Politics* (Durham, NC: Duke University Press).

BBC (2006) 'Excerpts: Hungarian "Lies" Speech', available at http://news.bbc.co.uk/1 /hi/world/europe/5359546.stm.

BBC (2007) 'Migrant Workers: What We Know', available at, http://news.bbc.co.uk/1 /hi/uk/6957171.stm.

Bechev, Dimitar (2011) 'Of power and Powerlessness: The EU and its Neighbours', *Comparative European Politics*, 9 (4), pp. 414–431.

Becker, Rolf and Saalfeld, Thomas (2004) 'The Life and Times of Bills', in Herbert Döring and Mark Hallerberg (eds) *Patterns of Parliamentary Behaviour* (Aldershot: Ashgate).

Behmer, Markus (2009) 'Measuring Media Freedom: Approaches of International Comparison', in Andrea Czepek, Melanie Hellwig and Eva Nowak (eds.) *Press Freedom and Pluralism in Europe: Concepts and Conditions* (Bristol: Intellect).

Bekke, Hans A.G.M. and van der Meer, Frits M. (eds) (2000) *Civil Service Systems in Western Europe* (Aldershot: Edward Elgar).

Bekkers, Rene (2005) 'Participation in Voluntary Associations: Relations with Resources, Personality, and Political Values', *Political Psychology*, 26(3), pp. 439–54.

Bell, David S. (2002) *French Politics Today* (Manchester: Manchester University Press).

Bell, John (2010) *Judiciaries within Europe: a Comparative Review* (Cambridge: Cambridge University Press).

Bennie, Lynne G. (1998) 'Brent Spar, Atlantic Oil and Greenpeace', *Parliamentary Affairs*, 51(3), pp. 397–410.

Bergh, Johannes and Bjørklund, Tor (2011) 'The Revival of Group Voting: Explaining the Voting Preferences of Immigrants in Norway', *Political Studies*, 59, pp. 308–27.

Bergqvist, Christina (2011) 'The Nordic Countries', in Gretchen Bauer and Manon Tremblay (eds) *Women in Executive Power: a Global Overview* (Abingdon: Routledge).

Bernhagen, Patrick (2007) *The Political Power of Business: Structure and Information in Public Policymaking* (London: Routledge).

Bernhagen, Patrick and Marsh, Michael (2007) 'Voting and Protesting: Explaining Citizen Participation in Old and New European Democracies', *Democratization*, 14(1), pp. 44–72.

Bernhard, William and Leblang, David (2006) *Democratic Processes and Financial Markets: Pricing Politics* (Cambridge: Cambridge University Press).

Bertossi, Christophe, Duyvendak, Jan Willem and Schain, Martin (eds) (2012), 'The Problems with National Models of Integration: A Franco–Dutch Comparison', special issue of *Comparative European Politics*, 10(3), pp. 237–376.

Best, Heinrich and Higley, John (2010) 'Democratic Elitism Reappraised', in Heinrich Best and John Higley (eds.) *Democratic Elitism: New Theoretical and Comparative Perspectives* (Leiden: Brill).

Best, Robin E. (2011) 'The Declining Electoral Relevance of Traditional Social Groups', *European Political Science Review*, 3(2), pp. 279–300.

Best, Robin E. (2012) 'The Long and the Short of It: Electoral Institutions and the Dynamics of Party System Size, 1950–2005', *European Journal of Political Research*, 51(2), pp. 141–165.

Bevan, Shaun, John, Peter and Jennings, Will (2011) 'Keeping Party Programmes on Track the Transmission of the Policy Agendas of Executive Speeches to Legislative Outputs in the United Kingdom', *European Political Science Review*, 3(3), pp. 395–417..

Bevir, Mark, Rhodes, R.A.W. and Weller, Patrick (2003) 'Comparative Governance: Prospects and Lessons', *Public Administration*, 81(1), pp. 191–210.

Beyers, Jan (2002) 'Gaining and Seeking Access: The European Adaptation of Domestic Interest Associations', *European Journal of Political Research*, 41 (5), pp. 585–612.

Beyers, Jan (2004) 'Voice and Access: Political Practices of European Interest Associations', *European Union Politics*, 5(2), pp. 211–40.

Beyers, Jan and Kerremans, Bart (2004) 'Bureaucrats, Politicians, and Societal Interests: How is European Policy Making Politicized?', *Comparative Political Studies*, 37(10), pp. 1119–50.

Beyers, Jan, Eising, Rainer and Maloney, William (2008) 'The Politics of Organised Interests in Europe: Lessons from EU Studies and Comparative Politics', special issue of *West European Politics*, 31(6), pp. 1103–1302.

Billig, Michael (1995) *Banal Nationalism* (London: Sage).

Biltereyst, Daniel and Desmet, Lieve (2010) 'Reconsidering the Paradox of Parochialism and the Shrinking News Agenda', in Gripsund, Jostein and Weibull, Lennart (eds.) *Media, Markets and Public Spheres* (Bristol: Intellect).

Binderkrantz, Anne Skorkjær (2005) 'Interest Group Strategies: Navigating Between Privileged Access and Strategies of Pressure', *Political Studies*, 53, pp. 694–715.

Binderkrantz, Anne Skorkjær (2009) 'Membership Recruitment and Internal Democracy in Interest Groups: Do Group-Membership Relations Vary Between Group Types?', *West European Politics*, 32(3), pp. 657–678.

Binderkrantz, Anne Skorkjær (2012) 'Interest Groups in the Media: Bias and Diversity over Time', *European Journal of Political Research*, 51(1), pp. 117–139.

Birch, Sarah, Millard, Frances, Popescu, Marina and Williams, Kieran (2002) *Embodying Democracy: Electoral System Design in Post-Communist Europe* (Basingstoke: Palgrave Macmillan).

Birdlife International (2007) available at http://www.birdlife.org.

Blair, Tony and Schröder, Gerhard (1999) *Europe: The Third Way/Die Neue Mitte*, available on numerous websites, e.g. http://www.iedm.org/library/blair_en.html.

Blais, André and Loewen, Peter John (2009) 'The French Electoral System and its Effects', *West European Politics*, 32(2), pp. 345–359.

Blais, André, Blake, Donald and Dion, Stéphane (1996) 'Do Parties Make a Difference? A Reappraisal', *American Journal of Political Science*, 40(2), pp. 514–20.

Blais, André, Kim, Jiyoon and Foucault, Martial (2010) 'Public Spending, Public Deficits and Government Coalitions', *Political Studies*, 58, pp. 829–846.

Blanden, Jo, Gregg, Paul and Machin, Stephen (2005) *International Mobility in Europe and North America* (London: LSE Centre for Economic Performance).

Blockmans, Steven and Laatsit, Marja-Liisa (2012) 'The European External Action Service: Enhancing Coherence in EU External Action?', in Cardwell, Paul James (ed.) *EU External Relations Law and Policy in the Post-Lisbon Era* (The Hague: TMC Asser Press).

Blondel, Jean and Müller-Rommel, Ferdinand (eds) (1997) *Cabinets in Western Europe* (Basingstoke: Palgrave Macmillan).

Blondel, Jean and Müller-Rommel, Ferdinand (2001) *Cabinets in Eastern Europe* (Basingstoke: Palgrave Macmillan).

Blondel, Jean, Müller-Rommel, Ferdinand and Malová, Darina (2007) *Governing New European Democracies* (Basingstoke: Palgrave Macmillan).

Blondel, Jean, Sinnott, Richard and Svensson, Palle (1998) *People and Parliament in the European Union: Participation, Democracy and Legitimacy* (Oxford: Clarendon Press).

Blondel, Jean and Thiébault, Jean-Louis with Czernicka, Katarzyna, Inoguchi, Takashi Ukrist, Pathmanand, and Venturino, Fulvio, (2009) *Political Leadership, Parties and Citizens: The Personalisation of Leadership* (Abingdon: Routledge).

Blühdorn, Ingolfur (2009) 'Reinventing Green Politics: On the Strategic Repositioning of the German Green Party', *German Politics*, 18(1), pp. 36–54.

Boeri, Tito. (2009) Immigration to the Land of Redistribution. IZA Discussion Paper No. 4273, available online at http://ssrn.com/abstract=1434607.

Bohle, Dorothee and Greskovits, Béla (2007) 'Neoliberalism, Embedded Neoliberalism and Neocorporatism: Towards Transnational Capitalism in Central-Eastern Europe', *West European Politics*, 30(3), pp. 443–466.

Bohle, Dorothee and Greskovits, Béla (2012) *Capitalist Diversity on Europe's Periphery* (Ithaca, NY: Cornell University Press).

Bohman, Andrea (2011) 'Articulated Antipathies: Political Influence on Anti-immigrant Attitudes', *International Journal of Comparative Sociology*, 52(6): 457–477.

Boix, Carles (1998) *Political Parties, Growth and Equality: Conservative and Social Democratic Economic Strategies in the World Economy* (Cambridge: Cambridge University Press).

Boix, Carles (1999) 'Setting the Rules of the Game: The Choice of Electoral Systems in Advanced Democracies', *American Political Science Review*, 93(3), pp. 609–24.

Bolleyer, Nicole (2012) 'The Partisan Usage of Parliamentary Salaries: Informal Party Practices Compared', *West European Politics*, 35(2), pp. 209–237.

Bolleyer, Nicole, van Spanje, Joost and Wilson, Alex (2012) 'New Parties in Government: Party Organisation and the Costs of Public Office', *West European Politics*, 35(5), pp. 971–998.

Bolzendahl, Catherine (2009) 'Making the Implicit Explicit: Gender Influences on Social Spending in Twelve Industrialized Democracies, 1980–99', *Social Politics*, 16(1), pp. 40–81.

Bomberg, Elizabeth (2002) 'The Europeanisation of Green Parties: Exploring the EU's Impact', *West European Politics*, 25(3), pp. 29–50.

Bomberg, Elizabeth and Carter, Neil (2006) 'The Greens in Brussels: Shaping or shaped?', *European Journal of Political Research*, 45(s1), pp. 99–125.

Bongiovanni, Francesco M. (2012) *The Decline and Fall of Europe* (Basingstoke: Palgrave Macmillan).

Bonoli, Giuliano (2004) 'Social Democratic Party Policies in Europe: Towards a Third Way?', in Giuliano Bonoli and Martin Powell (eds), *Social Democratic Party Policies in Contemporary Europe* (London: Routledge/ECPR).

Bonoli, Giuliano (2007) 'Time Matters: Postindustrialization, New Social Risks, and Welfare State Adaptation in Advanced Industrial Democracies', *Comparative Political Studies*, 40(5), pp. 495–520.

Bonoli, Giuliano and Powell, Martin (eds) (2004) *Social Democratic Party Politics in Contemporary Europe* (London: Routledge).

Bornschier, Simon (2010) *Cleavage Politics and the Populist Right: The New Cultural Conflict in Western Europe* (Baltimore: Temple).

Borraz, O. and John, P. (2004) 'The Transformation of Urban Political Leadership in Western Europe', *International Journal of Urban and Regional Research*, 28(1), pp. 107–20.

Bortolotti, Bernard and Siniscalco, Dominico (2004) *The Challenges of Privatization: An Internal Analysis* (Oxford: Oxford University Press).

Börzel, Tanja A. (2010) 'Civil Society on the rise? EU Enlargement and Societal Mobilization in Central and Eastern Europe', special issue of *Acta Politica*, 45(1–2), pp. 1–267.

Börzel, Tanja A., Hofmann, Tobias and Panke, Diana (2012) 'Caving In or Sitting It Out? Longitudinal Patterns of Non-Compliance in the European Union', *Journal of European Public Policy*, 19(4), pp. 454–471.

Börzel, Tanja and Sedelmeier, U. (2006) 'The EU Dimension in European Politics', in Paul Heywood, Erik Jones, Martin Rhodes and Ulrich Sedelmeier (eds), *Developments in European Politics* (Basingstoke: Palgrave Macmillan).

Boswell, Christina (2003) 'The "External Dimension" of EU Immigration and Asylum Policy', *International Affairs*, 79(3), pp. 619–38.

Boswell, Christina and Geddes, Andrew (2010) *Migration and Mobility in the European Union* (Basingstoke: Palgrave Macmillan).

Boswell, Christina, Geddes, Andrew and Scholten, Peter (2011) 'States, Knowledge and Narratives of Migration: the Construction of Migration in European Policy making', special issue of *British Journal of Politics and International Relations*, 13(1), pp. 1–126.

Boucek, Françoise (2012) *Factional Politics: How Dominant Parties Implode or Stabilize* (Basingstoke: Palgrave Macmillan).

Bouwen, Pieter (2002) 'Corporate Lobbying in the European Union: The Logic of Access', *Journal of European Public Policy*, 9(3), pp. 365–90.

Bouwen, Pieter and McCown, Margaret (2007) 'Lobbying versus Litigation: Political and Legal Strategies of Interest Representation in the European Union', *Journal of European Public Policy*, 14(3), pp. 422–43.

Bowler, Shaun, Donovan, Todd and Hanneman, Robert (2003) 'Art for Democracy's Sake? Group Membership and Political Engagement in Europe', *Journal of Politics*, 65(4), pp. 1111–29.

Bradley, David, Huber, Evelyne, Moller, Stephanie, Nielsen Francois and Stephens, John D. (2003) 'Distribution and Redistribution in Postindustrial Democracies', *World Politics*, 55(2), pp. 193–228.

Brady, David (2003) 'The Politics of Poverty: Left Political Institutions, the Welfare State, and Poverty', *Social Forces*, 82(2), pp. 557–88.

Brandenburg, Heinz (2002) 'Who Follows Whom? The Impact of Parties on Media Agenda Formation in the 1997 British General Election Campaign', *Harvard International Journal of Press/Politics*, 7(3), pp. 34–54.

Brants, Kees and Siune, Karen (1998) 'Politicization in Decline', in Denis McQuail and Karen Siune (eds), *Media Policy: Convergence, Concentration and Commerce* (London: Sage).

Brants, Kees, de Vreese, Claes, Möller, Judith, and van Praag, Philip (2010) 'The Real Spiral of Cynicism? Symbiosis and Mistrust between Politicians and Journalists', *International Journal of Press/Politics*, 15(1), pp. 25–40.

Brants, Kees and Voltmer, Katrin (2011), *Political Communication in Postmodern Democracy: Challenging the Primacy of Politics* (Basingstoke: Palgrave Macmillan).

Bräuninger, Thomas and Debus, Marc (2009) 'Legislative Agenda-setting in Parliamentary Democracies', *European Journal of Political Research*, 48(6), pp. 804–839.

Brautigam, Deborah (2009) *The Dragon's Gift: The Real Story of China in Africa* (Oxford: Oxford University Press).

Breen, Richard (ed.) (2004) *Social Mobility in Europe* (Oxford: Oxford University Press).

Bretherton, Charlotte and Vogler, John (2005) *The European Union as a Global Actor*, 2nd Edition (London: Routledge).

Brettschneider, Frank (1997) 'The Press and the Polls in Germany, 1980–1994: Poll Coverage as an Essential Part of Election Campaign Reporting', *International Journal of Public Opinion Research*, 9(3), pp. 248–65.

Brettschneider, Frank, Neller, Katya and Anderson, Christopher J. (2006) 'Candidate Images in the 2005 German National Election', *German Politics*, 15(4), pp. 481–99.

Bridgen, Paul and Meyer, Traute (2009) 'The Politics of Occupational Pension Reform in Britain and the Netherlands: The Power of Market Discipline in Liberal and Corporatist Regimes', *West European Politics*, 32(3), pp. 586–610.

Brighton, Paul and Foy, Dennis (2007) *News Values* (London: Sage).

Brookes, Rod, Lewis, Justin and Wahl-Jorgensen, Karin (2004) 'The Media Representation of Public Opinion: British Television News Coverage of the 2001 General Election', *Media, Culture & Society*, 26(1), pp. 63–80.

Brooks, Clem and Manza, Jeff (2007) *Why Welfare States Persist: The Importance of Public Opinion in Democracies* (Chicago: University of Chicago Press).

Brooks, Clem, Nieuwbeerta, Paul and Manza, Jeff (2006) 'Cleavage-Based Voting Behavior in Cross-National Perspective: Evidence from Six Postwar Democracies', *Social Science Research*, 35(1), pp. 88–128.

Brouard, Sylvain (2009) The Politics of Constitutional Veto in France: Constitutional Council, Legislative Majority and Electoral Competition, *West European Politics*, 32(2), pp. 384–403.

Brouard, Sylvain, Appleton, Andrew M. and Mazur, Amy G. (eds.) (2008), *The French Fifth Republic at Fifty: Beyond Stereotypes* (Basingstoke: Palgrave Macmillan).

Broughton, David and Ten Napel, Hans-Martien (2000) *Religion and Mass Electoral Behaviour in Europe* (London: Routledge).

Brummer, Klaus (2009) 'Imposing Sanctions: The Not So "Normative Power Europe"', *European Foreign Affairs Review*, 14, pp. 191–207.

Bruszt, László (2002) 'Making Markets and Eastern Enlargement: Diverging Convergence', *West European Politics*, 25(2), pp. 121–40.

Bruszt, László (2008) 'Multi-level Governance—the Eastern Versions: Emerging Patterns of Regional Developmental Governance in the New Member States, *Regional & Federal Studies*, 18(5), pp. 607–627.

Bruter, Michael (2005) *Citizens of Europe? The Emergence of a Mass European Identity* (Basingstoke: Palgrave Macmillan).

Bruter, Michael and Harrison, Sarah (2009) *The Future of our Democracies: Young Party Members in Europe* (Basingstoke: Palgrave).

Buckley, Fiona and Galligan, Yvonne (2011) 'Western Europe', in Gretchen Bauer and Manon Tremblay (eds) *Women in Executive Power: a Global Overview* (Abingdon: Routledge).

Budge, Ian and Keman, Hans, (1990) 'New Concerns for Coalition Theory: Allocation of Ministries and Segmental Policy making; A Comparative Analysis', *Acta Politica*, 90(2), pp. 151–85.

Budge, Ian and McDonald, Michael D. (2006) 'Choices Parties Define: Policy Alternatives in Representative Elections, 17 Countries 1945–1998', *Party Politics*, 12(4), pp. 451–66.

Budge, Ian, McDonald, Michael D., Pennings, Paul and Keman, Hans (2012) *Organizing Democratic Choice: Party Representation Over Time* (Oxford: Oxford University Press).

Bull, Martin and Pasquino, Gianfranco (2007) 'A Long Quest in Vain: Institutional Reforms in Italy', *West European Politics*, 30(4), pp. 670–691.

Burgoon, Brian (2012) 'Partisan Embedding of Liberalism: How Trade, Investment and Immigration Affect Party Support for the Welfare State', *Comparative Political Studies*, 45(5), pp. 606–635.

Burgoon, Brian, Koster, Ferry and van Egmond, Marcel (2012) 'Support for Redistribution and the Paradox of Immigration', *Journal of European Social Policy*. 22(3), pp. 288–304.

Buruma, Ian (2007) *Murder in Amsterdam: The Death of Theo van Gogh and the Limits of Tolerance* (London: Atlantic Books).

Busemeyer, Marius R. (2009a) 'Social Democrats and the New Partisan Politics of Public Investment in Education', *Journal of European Public Policy*, 16(1), pp. 107–126.

Busemeyer, Marius R. (2009b) From Myth to Reality: Globalisation and Public Spending in OECD Countries Revisited', *European Journal of Political Research*, 48(4), pp. 455–482.

Bühlmann, Marc and Lisa Schädel (2012) Representation Matters: the impact of descriptive women's representation on the political involvement of women, *Representation*, 48(1), pp. 101–114.

Bulmer, Simon, Jeffery, Charlie and Padgett, Stephen (eds.) (2010) *Rethinking Germany and Europe: Democracy and Diplomacy in a Semi-Sovereign State* (Basingstoke: Palgrave Macmilan).

C

Caiani, Manuela and Parenti, Linda (2009) 'The Dark Side of the Web: Italian Right-Wing Extremist Groups and the Internet', *South European Society and Politics*, 14(3), pp. 273–294.

Caldwell, Christopher (2010) *Reflections on the Revolution in Europe: Immigration, Islam and the West* (Harmondsworth, Penguin).

Callaghan, John (2000) *The Retreat of Social Democracy* (Manchester: Manchester University Press).

Callinicos, Alex (2001) *Against the Third Way* (Cambridge: Polity Press).

Cameron, Fraser (2012) *An Introduction to European Foreign Policy, 2nd Edition* (Abingdon: Routledge).

Campbell, John L. and Pedersen, Ove K. (2007) 'The Varieties of Capitalism and Hybrid Success: Denmark in the Global Economy', *Comparative Political Studies*, 40(3), pp. 307–332.

Campbell, Rosie (2004) 'Gender, Ideology and Issue Preference: Is There Such a Thing as a Political Women's Interest in Britain?', *British Journal of Politics and International Relations*, 6, pp. 20–46.

Camyar, Isa (2010) 'Europeanization, Domestic Legacies and Administrative Reforms in Central and Eastern Europe: a Comparative Analysis of Hungary and the Czech Republic', *Journal of European Integration*, 32(2), pp. 137–155.

Caramani, Daniele, Deegan-Krause, Kevin and Murray, Rainbow (2012), 'Political Data in 2011', *European Journal of Political Research*, 51(7–8), pp. 3–23.

Carbone, Maurizio (ed) (2008) 'The New Season of EU Development Policy', special issue of *Perspectives on European Politics and Society*, 9(2), pp. 111–255.

Cardwell, Paul James (2011) 'EuroMed, European Neighbourhood Policy and the Union for the Mediterranean: Overlapping Policy Frames in the EU's Governance of the Mediterranean', *JCMS: Journal of Common Market Studies*, 49(2), pp. 219–241.

Careja, Romana and Patrick Emmenegger (2009) 'The Politics of Public Spending in Post-Communist Countries', *East European Politics & Societies*, 23(2) 165–184.

Carey, John M. and Hix, Simon (2011) 'The Electoral Sweet Spot: Low-Magnitude Proportional Electoral Systems', *American Journal of Political Science*, 55(2), pp. 383–397.

Carter, Elisabeth (2005) *The Extreme Right in Western Europe* (Manchester: Manchester University Press).

Carter, Elisabeth and Farrell, David M. (2010) 'Electoral Systems and Election Management', in Lawrence LeDuc, Righard G. Niemi and Pippa Norris (eds), *Comparing Democracies, 3: Elections and Voting in the 21st Century* (Thousand Oaks, CA: Sage Publications).

Carty, R. Kenneth (2004) 'Parties as Franchise Systems: The Stratarchical Organizational Imperative', *Party Politics*, 10(1), pp. 5–24.

Casado-Díaz, M.A. (2006) 'Retiring to Spain: an Analysis of Differences among North European Nationals', *Journal of Ethnic and Migration Studies*, 32(8), pp. 1321–39.

Casal Bértoa, Fernando (2013) 'Party Systems and Cleavage Structures Revisited: a Sociological Explanation of Party System Institutionalization in East Central Europe', *Party Politics*.

Cassese, Sabino (1999) 'Italy's Senior Civil Service: An Ossified World', in Edward C. Page and Vincent Wright (eds), *Bureaucratic Elites in Western European States* (Oxford: Oxford University Press).

Castells, Manuel (2009) *Communication Power* (Oxford: Oxford University Press).

Castiglione, Dario, van Deth, Jan W. and Wolleb, Guglielmo (2008) *The Handbook of Social Capital* (Oxford: Oxford University Press).

Castles, Francis (2004) *The Future of the Welfare State: Crisis Myths and Crisis Realities* (Oxford: Oxford University Press).

Castles, Stephen (2004) 'Why Migration Policies Fail', *Ethnic and Racial Studies*, 27(2), pp. 205–27.

Castles, Stephen and Miller, Mark J. (2009) *The Age of Migration, 4th Edition* (Basingstoke: Palgrave Macmillan).

Caul, Miki L. and Gray, Mark M. (2000) 'From Platform Declarations to Policy Outcomes: Changing Party Profiles and Partisan Influence over Policy', in Russell J. Dalton and Martin P. Wattenberg (eds), *Parties without Partisans: Political Change in Advanced Industrial Democracies* (Oxford: Oxford University Press), pp. 208–37.

CCS (2004) http://www.lse.ac.uk/collections/CCS/introduction.htm#generated-subheading2

Cerami, Alfio (2010) 'The Politics of Social Security Reforms in the Czech Republic, Hungary, Poland and Slovakia', in Bruno Palier (ed) *A Long Goodbye to Bismark? The Politics of Welfare Reform in Continental Europe* (Amsterdam: Amsterdam University Press), available online at http://dare.uva.nl/document/183117

Cerna, Lucie (2009) 'The Varieties of High-skilled Immigration policies: Coalitions and Policy Outputs in Advanced Industrial Countries', *Journal of European Public Policy*, 16(1), pp. 144–161.

Chaban, Natalia and Holland, Martin (eds) (2003) *The European Union and the Asia-Pacific: Media, Public and Elite Perceptions of the EU* (Abingdon: Routledge).

Chadwick, Andrew and Howard, Philip N. (eds.) (2009) *The Routledge Handbook of Internet Politics* (Abingdon: Routledge).

Chalaby, Jean K. (2002) 'Transnational Television in Europe: The Role of Pan-European Channels', *European Journal of Communication,* 17(2), pp. 183–203.

Chalaby, Jean K. (2009) *Transnational Television in Europe: Reconfiguring Global Communications Networks* (London: IB Tauris).

Charalambous, Giorgos (2011) 'Realignment and Entrenchment: the Europeanisation of Rifondazione Comunista', *Perspectives on European Politics and Society*, 12(1), pp. 29–51.

Chawla, Mukesh, Bechterman, Gordon and Banerji, Arup (2007) *From Red to Grey: The 'Third Transition' of Ageing Populations in Eastern Europe and the Former Soviet Union* (Washington, DC: World Bank).

Checkel, Jeffrey and Katzenstein, Peter J. (eds.) (2009) *European Identity* (Cambridge: Cambridge University Press).

Childs, Sarah and Webb, Paul (2011) *Sex, Gender and the Conservative Party: From Iron Lady to Kitten Heels* (Basingstoke: Palgrave).

Christensen, Tom and Lægreid, Per (eds.) (2011) *The Ashgate Research Companion to New Public Management* (Aldershot: Ashgate).

Christmas-Best, Verona and Kjær, Ulrik (2007) 'Why So Few and Why So Slow? Women as Parliamentary Representatives in Europe from a Longitudinal Perspective', in Maurizio Cotta and Heinrich Best (eds) *Democratic Representation in Europe: Diversity, Change, and Convergence* (Oxford: Oxford University Press).

Church, Clive H. (2004) *The Politics and Government of Switzerland* (Basingstoke: Palgrave Macmillan).

Cichowski, Rachel A. (2007) *The European Court and Civil Society: Litigation, Mobilization and Governance* (Cambridge: Cambridge University Press).

Cini, Michelle and Perez-Solorzano Borragan, Nieves (eds) (2009) *European Union Politics* (Oxford: OUP).

Clark, David (1998) 'The Modernization of the French Civil Service: Crisis, Change and Continuity', *Public Administration*, 76(1), pp. 97–116.

Clark, Michael (2009) 'Valence and Electoral Outcomes in Western Europe, 1976–1998', *Electoral Studies*, 28(1), pp. 111–122.

Clift, Ben (2001) 'The Jospin Way', *Political Quarterly*, 72(2), pp. 170–9.

Clift, Ben (2002) 'Social Democracy and Globalisation: The Case of France and the UK', *Government and Opposition*, 37(4), pp. 466–500.

Clifton, Judith, Comín, Francisco and Díaz Fuentes, Daniel (2006) 'Privatizing Public Enterprises in the European Union 1960–2002: Ideological, Pragmatic, Inevitable?', *Journal of European Public Policy*, 13(5), pp. 736–56.

Coen, David and Richardson, Jeremy (eds.) (2009) *Lobbying the European Union: Institutions, Actors, and Issues* (Oxford: Oxford University Press).

Coffé, Hilde and Need, Ariana (2010) 'Similarity in Husbands' and Wives' Party Family Preference in the Netherlands', *Electoral Studies*, 29 (2), pp. 259–268.

Cohen, Robin (2006) *Migration and Its Enemies: Global Capital, Migrant Labour and the Nation-state* (Aldershot: Ashgate).

Cole, Alistair (1999) 'The *service publique* under Stress', *West European Politics*, 22(4), pp. 166–84.

Cole, Alistair and Drake, Helen (2000) 'The Europeanization of the French Polity: Continuity, Change and Adaptation', *Journal of European Public Policy*, 7(1), pp. 26–43.

Cole, Alistair, Le Gales, Patrick and Levy, Jonah (2008) *Developments in French Politics 4* (Basingstoke: Palgrave Macmillan).

Coleman, Stephen (2003) *A Tale of Two Houses – The House of Commons, the Big Brother House and the People at Home* (London: Hansard Society).

Coleman, Stephen (2005) 'Blogs and the New Politics of Listening', *Political Quarterly*, 76(2), pp. 272–80.

Coleman, Stephen and Blumler, Jay G. (2009) *The Internet and Democratic Citizenship: Theory, Practice and Policy* (Cambridge: Cambridge University Press).

Coleman, Stephen, Anthony, Scott and Morrison, David E. (2009) *Public Trust in the News: a Constructivist Study of the Social Life of the News* (Oxford: Reuters Institute), available online at http://reutersinstitute.politics.ox.ac.uk/fileadmin/documents/Publications/Public_Trust_in_the_News.pdf.

Coleman, Stephen, Kuik, Anke, and van Zoonen, Liesbet (2009) 'Laughter and Liability: The Politics of British and Dutch Television Satire', *British Journal of Politics & International Relations*, 11(4), pp. 652–665.

Collins, Neil and Butler, Patrick (2004) 'Political Mediation in Ireland: Campaigning between Traditional and Tabloid Markets', *Parliamentary Affairs*, 57(1), pp. 93–107.

Colomer, Josep M. (2011) 'The More Parties, the Greater Policy Stability', *European Political Science*, 11(2), pp. 229–243.

Compston, Hugh (2006) *King Trends and the Future of Public Policy* (Basingstoke: Palgrave Macmillan).

Conant, Lisa J. (2002) *Justice Contained: Law and Politics in the European Union* (Ithaca, NY: Cornell University Press).

Conceição, Pedro, Ferreira, Pedro and Galbraith, James K. (2001) 'Inequality and Unemployment in Europe: The American Cure', in James K. Galbraith and Maureen Berner (eds), *Inequality and Industrial Change: A Global View* (Cambridge: Cambridge University Press).

Conti, Nicoló and Memoli, Vincenzo (2012) 'The Multi-faceted Nature of Party-based Euroscepticism', *Acta Politica*, 47(2), pp. 91–112.

Cook, Linda J. (2007) *Postcommunist Welfare States: Reform Politics in Russia and Eastern Europe* (Ithaca, NY: Cornell University Press).

Cook, Linda J. (2010) 'Eastern Europe and Russia', in Francis G. Castles, Stephan Leibfried, Jane Lewis, Herbert Obinger, and Christopher Pierson (eds) *The Oxford Handbook of the Welfare State* (Oxford: Oxford University Press).

Cooper, Ian (2012) 'A "Virtual Third Chamber" for the European Union? National Parliaments after the Treaty of Lisbon'. *West European Politics*, 35(3), 441–465.

Copeland, Paul (2012) 'EU Enlargement, the clash of capitalisms and the European social model', *Comparative European Politics*, 10(4), pp. 476–504.

Corbett, Richard, Jacobs, Francis and Shackleton, Michael (2011) *The European Parliament* (London: John Harper).

Cordell, Karl and Wolff, Stefan (eds) (2004) *The Ethnopolitical Encyclopaedia of Europe* (Basingstoke: Palgrave Macmillan).

Corry, Dan, Valero, Anna, van Reenan, John (2012) 'The UK's Economic Performance under Labour', *Renewal*, 20(1), pp. 56–69.

Costa, Olivier and Kerrouche, Eric (2009) 'Representative Roles in the French National Assembly: the Case for a Dual Typology?', *French Politics* 9(3–4), pp. 219–242.

Costa Lobo, Marina (2006) 'Short-Term Voting Determinants in a Young Democracy: Leader Effects in Portugal in the 2002 Legislative Elections', *Electoral Studies*, 25(2), pp. 270–86.

Cotta, Maurizio and Best, Heinrich (eds) (2007) *Democratic Representation in Europe: Diversity, Change, and Convergence* (Oxford: Oxford University Press).

Cottey, Andrew (2012) *Security in 21st Century Europe* (Basingstoke: Palgrave Macmillan).

Couldry, Nick, Livingstone, Sonia and Markham, Tim (2010) *Media Consumption and Public Engagement: Beyond the Presumption of Attention* (Basingstoke: Palgrave Macmillan).

Council of the European Union (2003) *European Security Strategy*, available at http://www.consilium.europa.eu/uedocs/cmsUpload/78367.pdf.

Cowles, Maria Green, Caporaso, James and Risse, Thomas (eds) (2001) *Transforming Europe: Europeanization and Domestic Change* (Ithaca, NY: Cornell University Press).

Cramme, Olaf and Diamond, Patrick (2012) *After the Third Way: The Future of Social Democracy in Europe* (London: IB Tauris).

Crepaz, Markus M.L. (2007) *Trust Beyond Borders: Immigration, the Welfare State, and Identity in Modern Societies* (Ann Arbor: University of Michigan Press).

Crepaz, Markus M.L. and Damron, Regan (2009) Constructing Tolerance: How the Welfare State Shapes Attitudes About Immigrants, *Comparative Political Studies*, 42(3), pp. 437–463.

Cronin, James, Ross George, Shoch, James (eds) (2011) *What's Left of the Left: Democrats and Social Democrats in Challenging Times* (London: Duke University Press).

Crouch, Colin (1999) *Social Change in Western Europe* (Oxford: Oxford University Press).

Crouch, Colin (2004) *Post-Democracy* (Cambridge: Polity).

Crouch, Colin (2011) *The Strange Non-Death of Neo-Liberalism* (Cambridge: Polity).

Crowley, Stephen and Stanojevi, Miroslav (2011) *Varieties of Capitalism, Power Resources, and Historical Legacies: Explaining the Slovenian Exception*, Politics and Society, 39(2), pp. 268–295.

Csergo, Zsuzsa and Goldgeier, James M. (2004) 'Nationalist Strategies and European Integration', *Perspectives on Politics*, 2(1), pp. 21–37.

Culpepper, Pepper D. (2011) *Quiet Politics and Business Power: Corporate Control in Europe and Japan* (Cambridge: Cambridge University Press).

Curran, James (2002) *Media and Power* (London: Routledge).

Curran, James, Iyengar, Shanto, Lund, Anker Brink and Salovaara-Moring, Inka (2009) 'Media System, Public Knowledge and Democracy: A Comparative Study', *European Journal of Communication*, 24(1), pp. 5–26.

Curtice, John and Shiveley, W. Phillips (2009) 'Who Represents Us Best? One Member or Many?', in Hans-Dieter Klingemann (ed.) *The Comparative Study of Electoral Systems* (Oxford: Oxford University Press).

Curzon Price, Victoria (2004) 'Industrial Policy', in Ali M. El-Agraa, (ed.), *The European Union: Economics and Policy*, 7th edn (London: Prentice-Hall/FT).

Cusack, Thomas R. and Beramendi, Pablo (2006) 'Taxing Work', *European Journal of Political Research*, 45(1), pp. 43–73.

Czepek, Andrea, Hellwig, Melanie and Nowak, Eva (eds.) (2009) *Press Freedom and Pluralism in Europe: Concepts and Conditions* (Bristol: Intellect).

D

d'Haenens, Leen, Sousa, and Hultén, Olof (2011) 'From Public Service Broadcasting to Public Service Media', in Trappel, Josef, Meier, Werner A., D'Haenens, Leen, Steemers, Jeanette, Thomass, Barbara (eds.) *Media in Europe Today* (Bristol: Intellect).

Dahlgren, Peter (2009) *Media and Political Engagement: Citizens, Communication and Democracy* (Cambridge: Cambridge University Press).

Dahlström, Carl (2011) 'Who Takes the Hit? Ministerial Advisers and the Distribution of Welfare State Cuts', *Journal of European Public Policy*, 18(2), pp. 294–310.

Dahlström, Carl and Sundell, Anders (2012) 'A Losing Gamble. How Mainstream Parties Facilitate Anti-Immigrant Party Success', *Electoral Studies*, 31(2), pp. 353–363.

Dalton, Russell J. (2000) 'The Decline of Party Identification', in Russell J. Dalton and Martin P. Wattenberg (eds), *Parties without Partisans: Political Change in Advanced Industrial Democracies* (Oxford: Oxford University Press).

Dalton, Russell J. (2002) 'Political Cleavages, Issues and Electoral Change', in Lawrence LeDuc, Righard Niemi and Pippa Norris (eds), *Comparing Democracies*, 2nd edn (Thousand Oaks, CA: Sage Publications).

Dalton, Russell J. (2009) 'Economics, Environmentalism and Party Alignments: a Note on Partisan Change in Advanced Industrial Democracies', *European Journal of Political Research*, 48(2), pp. 161–175.

Dalton, Russell J. (2010) 'Ideology, Partisanship, and Democratic Development', in Lawrence LeDuc, Righard G. Niemi and Pippa Norris (eds), *Comparing Democracies, 3: Elections and Voting in the 21st Century* (Thousand Oaks, CA: Sage Publications).

Dalton, Russell J., Farrell, David and McAllister, Ian (2011) *Political Parties and Democratic Linkage. How Parties Organize Democracy* (Oxford: Oxford University Press).

Dalton, Russell J., McAllister, Ian and Wattenberg, Martin P. (2000) 'The Consequences of Partisan Dealignment', in Russell J. Dalton and Martin P. Wattenberg (eds), *Parties without Partisans: Political Change in Advanced Industrial Democracies* (Oxford: Oxford University Press).

Dalton, Russell J., McAllister, Ian and Wattenberg, Martin P. (2002) 'The Consequences of Partisan Dealignment', in Russell J. Dalton and Martin P. Wattenberg (eds), *Parties without Partisans: Political Change in Advanced Industrial Democracies* (Oxford: Oxford University Press).

Dalton, Russell J. and Wattenberg, Martin P. (eds) (2002) *Parties without Partisans: Political Change in Advanced Industrial Democracies* (Oxford: Oxford University Press).

Dalton, Russell J. and Weldon, Steven (2005) 'Public Images of Political Parties: A Necessary Evil?', *West European Politics*, 28(5), pp. 931–51.

Damgaard, Erik and Jensen, Henrik (2005) 'Europeanisation of Executive–Legislative Relations: Nordic Perspectives', *Journal of Legislative Studies*, 11(3–4), pp. 394–411.

Damgaard, Erik and Mattson, Ingvar (2004) 'Conflict and Consensus in Committees', in Herbert Döring and Mark Hallerberg (eds), *Patterns of Parliamentary Behaviour* (Aldershot: Ashgate).

Dancygier, Rafaela and Saunders, Elizabeth M. (2006) 'A New Electorate? Comparing Preferences and Partisanship between Immigrants and Natives', *American Journal of Political Science*, 50(4), pp. 962–81.

Dardanelli, Paolo (2012) 'Europeanization and the Unravelling of Belgium: A Comparative Analysis of Party Strategies', *Acta Politica*, 47(2), pp. 181–209.

David, Maxine, Gower, Jackie and Haukkala, Hiski (eds) (2013) *National Perspectives on Russia: European Foreign Policy in the Making* (Abingdon: Routledge).

Davies, Nick (2008) *Flat Earth News* (London: Chatto and Windus).

Davies, Norman (2007) *Europe East and West* (London: Pimlico).

Davis, Aeron (2010) *Political Communication and Social Theory* (Abingdon: Routledge).

Dawisha, Karen and Deets, Stephen (2006) 'Political Learning in Post-Communist. Elections', *East European Politics and Society*, 20(4), pp. 691–728.

De Bens, Els (2007) 'Developments and Opportunities of the European Press Industry', in Werner A. Meier and Josef Trappel (eds.) *Power, Performance and Politics* (Baden Baden: Nomos).

De Bens, Els and Østbye, Helge (1998) 'The European Newspaper Market', in Denis McQuail and Karen Siune (eds), *Media Policy: Convergence, Concentration and Commerce* (London: Sage).

de Lange, Sarah L. (2007) 'A New Winning Formula? The Programmatic Appeal of the Radical Right', *Party Politics*, 13(4), pp. 411–35.

de Lange, Sarah L. and Art, David (2011) 'Fortuyn versus Wilders: An Agency-Based Approach to Radical Right Party Building', *West European Politics*, 34(6), pp. 1229–49.

de Rooij, Eline A. (2012) 'Patterns of Immigrant Political Participation: Explaining Differences in Types of Political Participation between Immigrants and the Majority Population in Western Europe', *European Sociological Review*, 28(4), pp. 455–481.

de Vreese, Claes H. (2001) 'Election Coverage: New Directions for Public Broadcasting', *European Journal of Communication*, 16(2), pp. 155–80.

de Vreese, Claes H. (2005) 'The Spiral of Cynicism Reconsidered: The Mobilizing Function of News', *European Journal of Communication*, 20(3), pp. 283–301.

de Vreese, Claes H. (2007) 'A Spiral of Euroscepticism: the Media's Fault?', *Acta Politica*, 42(2–3), pp. 271–86.

de Vreese, Claes H., Banducci, S., Semetko, H.A. and Boomgaarden, Hajo G. (2006) 'The News Coverage of the 2004 European Parliamentary Election Campaign in 25 Countries', *European Union Politics*, 7(4), pp. 477–504.

de Vreese, Claes H. and Boomgaarden, Hajo, G. (2006a) 'Media Message Flows and Interpersonal Communication: The Conditional Nature of Effects on Public Opinion', *Communication Research*, 33(1), pp. 19–37.

de Vreese, Claes H. and Boomgaarden, Hajo, G. (2006b) 'Media Effects on Public Opinion about the Enlargement of the European Union', *Journal of Common Market Studies*, 44(2), pp. 419–36.

de Vreese, Claes H. and Boomgaarden, Hajo G., eds, (2009) 'Symposium – Religion and the European Union', *West European Politics*, 32 (6), pp. 1181–1283.

de Vries, Catherine E. (2010) 'EU Issue Voting: Asset or Liability? How European Integration Affects Parties' Electoral Fortunes', *European Union Politics*, 11(1), pp. 89–117.

De Vries, Catherine E. and Hobolt, Sara B. (2012) 'Do Voters Blame Governments for Social Spending Cuts? Evidence from a Natural Experiment', Paper presented to the Annual Conference of the Political Studies Association specialist group on Elections, Public Opinion and Parties, Oxford, 7–9 September.

de Winter, Lieven, Gómez-Reino, M. and Lynch, P. (eds) (2006) *Autonomist Parties in Europe: Identity Politics and the Revival of the Territorial Cleavage* (Barcelona: Institut de Ciències Polítiques i Socials).

De Winter, Lieven (2004) 'Government Declarations and Law Production', in Herbert Döring and Mark Hallerberg (eds) *Patterns of Parliamentary Behavior: Passage of Legislation Across Western Europe* (Aldershot: Ashgate).

de Wilde, Pieter (2011) No Effect, Weapon of the Weak or Reinforcing Executive Dominance? How Media Coverage Affects National Parliaments' Involvement in EU Policy-Formulation', *Comparative European Politics*, 9(2), pp. 123–144.

Deacon, Bob (2000) 'Social Policy in Eastern Europe: The Impact of Political Globalisation', *Journal of European Social Policy*, 10(2), pp. 146–61.

Deacon, Bob (2005) 'From "Safety Nets" back to "Universal Social Provision": Is the Global Tide Turning?', *Global Social Policy*, 5(1), pp. 19–28.

Debus, Marc (2009) Pre–electoral Commitments and Government Formation, *Public Choice*, 138(1–2), pp. 45–64.

Deegan-Krause, Kevin (2006) *Elected Affinities: Democracy and Party Competition in Slovakia and the Czech Republic* (Stanford University Press).

Deegan-Krause, Kevin and Enyedi, Zsolt (2010): Agency and the Structure of Party Competition: Alignment, Stability and the Role of Political Elites, *West European Politics*, 33(3), pp. 686–710.

Dekker, Paul and van den Broek, Andries (2005) 'Involvement in Voluntary Associations in North America and Western Europe: Trends and Correlates, 1981–2000', *Journal of Civil Society*, 1(1), pp. 45–59.

della Porta, Donatella and Caiani, Manuela (2007) 'Europeanization from Below? Social Movements and Europe', *Mobilization*, 12(1), pp. 1–20.

della Porta, Donatella and Diani, Mario (2005) *Social Movements: An Introduction* (Oxford: Blackwell).

della Porta, Donatella and Tarrow, Sidney (2005) *Transnational Protest and Global Activism* (Lanham: Rowman & Littlefield).

Delli Carpini, Michael X. and Williams, Bruce (1994) 'Fictional and Non-Fictional Television Celebrates Earth Day', *Cultural Studies*, 8, pp. 74–98.

Demmke, Christoph and Moilanen, Timo (2010) *Civil Services in the EU of 27: Reform Outcomes and the Future of the Civil Service* (Oxford: Peter Lang).

Denemark, David (2002) 'Television Effects and Voter Decision Making in Australia: A Reexamination of the Converse Model', *British Journal of Political Science*, 32(4), pp. 663–90.

Depauw, Sam and Martin, Shane (2009) 'Legislative Party Discipline and Cohesion in Comparative Perspective', in Giannetti, Daniella and Benoit, Kenneth (eds.) *Intra-Party Politics and Coalition Governments* (Routledge: London).

Derlien, Hans-Ulrich (2008) 'The German Public Service: Between Tradition and Transformation', in Derlien and B. Guy Peters (eds.) *The State at Work Volume 1: Public Sector Employment in Ten Western Countries* (Cheltenham: Edward Elgar).

Deschouwer, Kris (2006) 'Political Parties as Multi-level Organizations', in Richard Katz and William Crotty (eds) *Handbook of Political Parties* (London: Sage).

Detterbeck, Klaus (2005) 'Cartel Parties in Western Europe?', *Party Politics*, 11(2), pp. 173–91.

Dewan, Torun and Dowding, Keith (2005) 'The Corrective Effect of Ministerial Resignations on Government Popularity', *American Journal of Political Science*, 49(1), pp. 46–56.

Diani, Mario and McAdam, Doug (eds) (2003) *Social Movements and Networks: Relational Approaches to Collective Action* (Oxford: Oxford University Press).

Diedrichs, Udo, Reiners Wulf and Wessels, Wolfgang (2011) 'New Modes of Governance: Policy Developments and the Hidden Steps of European Integration', in Adrienne Héritier and Martin Rhodes (eds) *New Modes of Governance in Europe: Governing in the Shadow of Hierarchy* (Basingstoke: Palgrave Macmillan).

Díez Medrano, Juan and Gutierrez, Paula (2001) 'Nested Identities: National and European Identity in Spain', *Ethnic and Racial Studies*, 24(5), pp. 753–78.

Dimitrakopoulos, Dyonissis, G. (2001) 'Incrementalism and Path Dependence: European Integration and Institutional Change in National Parliaments', *Journal of Common Market Studies*, 39(3), pp. 405–22.

Dimitrakopoulos, Dionyssis G. (ed.) (2010) *Social Democracy and European Integration: the Politics of Preference Formation* (Abingdon: Routledge).

Dobre, Ana Maria (2009) 'The Dynamics of Europeanisation and Regionalisation: Regional Reform in Romania', *Perspectives on European Politics and Society*, 10(2), pp. 181–194.

Dodini, Michaela and Fantini, Marco (2006) 'The EU Neighbourhood Policy: Implications for Economic Growth and Stability', *Journal of Common Market Studies*, 44(3), pp. 507–32.

Dogan, Mattei (2001) 'Class, Religion, Party: Triple Decline of Electoral Cleavages in Western Europe', in Lauri Karvonen and Stein Kuhnle (eds), *Party Systems and Voter Alignments Revisited* (London: Routledge).

Dolezal, Martin (2010): Exploring the Stabilization of a Political Force: The Social and Attitudinal Basis of Green Parties in the Age of Globalization, *West European Politics*, 33(3), pp. 534–552.

Dollery, Brian E. and Robotti, Lorenzo (eds.) (2008) *The Theory and Practice of Local Government Reform* (Cheltenham: Edward Elgar).

Donders, Karen (2011) *Public Service Media and Policy in Europe* (Basingstoke: Palgrave Macmillan).

Donovan, Todd and Karp, Jeffrey (2006) 'Popular Support for Direct Democracy', *Party Politics*, 12(5), pp. 671–88.

Donsbach, Wolfgang (1995) 'Lapdogs, Watchdogs and Junkyard Dogs', *Media Studies Journal*, 9(4), pp. 17–30.

Donsbach, Wolfgang and Patterson, Thomas, E. (2004) 'Political News Journalists: Partisanship, Professionalism, and Political Roles in Five Countries', in Frank Esser and Barbara Pfetsch (eds) *Comparing Political Communication: Theories, Cases, and Challenges* (Cambridge: Cambridge University Press).

Doorenspleet, Renske (2005) 'Electoral Systems and Democratic Quality: Do Mixed Systems Combine the Best or the Worst of Both Worlds? An Explorative Quantitative Cross-national Study', *Acta Politica*, 40(1), pp. 28–49.

Döring, Herbert (ed.) (1995) *Parliaments and Majority Rule in Western Europe* (New York: St Martin's Press).

Döring, Herbert and Hallerberg, Mark (eds) (2004) *Patterns of Parliamentary Behaviour* (Aldershot: Ashgate).

Dover, Caroline and Barnett, Stephen (2004) *The World on the Box* (London: 3WE).

Dow, Jay K. (2011) 'Party-System Extremism in Majoritarian and Proportional Electoral Systems', *British Journal of Political Science*, 41(2), pp. 341–61.

Dowding, Keith (2005) 'Why do People Vote? Five Types of Answer and a Suggestion', *British Journal of Politics and International Relations*, 7(3), pp. 442–59.

Dowding, Keith and Dumont, Patrick (eds.) (2008) *The Selection of Ministers in Europe: Hiring and Firing* (Abingdon: Routledge).

Down, Ian and Wilson, Carole J. (2010) 'Opinion Polarization and Inter-Party Competition on Europe', *European Union Politics*, 11(1), pp. 61–87.

Downey, John (2012) 'Transnational Capital, Media Differentiation, and Institutional Isomorphism in Central and Eastern European Media Systems', in Downey, John and Mihelj, Sabina (eds) *Central and Eastern European Media in Comparative Perspective* (Aldershot: Ashgate).

Downs, Anthony (1972) 'Up and Down with Ecology: "The Issue Attention Cycle"', *The Public Interest*, 28, pp. 38–50, available at http://www.anthonydowns.com/ upanddown.htm.

Drake, Helen (2011) *Contemporary France* (Basingstoke: Palgrave Macmillan).

Druckman, James N. and Roberts, Andrew (2007) 'Communist Successor Parties and Coalition Formation in Eastern Europe', *Legislative Studies Quarterly*, 32(1), pp. 5–31.

Drummond, Andrew (2006) 'Electoral Volatility and Party Decline in Western Democracies: 1970–1995', *Political Studies*, 54(3), pp. 628–47.

Duch, Raymond M. and Stevenson, Randy (2006) 'Assessing the Magnitude of the Economic Vote over Time and Across Nations', *Electoral Studies*, 25(3), pp. 528–47.

Duch, Raymond M., May, Jeff and Armstrong, David A. (2010) 'Coalition-directed Voting in Multiparty Democracies', *American Political Science Review*, 104(4), pp. 698–719.

Duke, Simon (2000) *The Elusive Quest for European Security: From EDC to CFSP* (Basingstoke: Palgrave Macmillan).

Duke, Simon and Haar, Roberta (2011) 'Still at the Crossroads: Europe, the United States, and NATO', in Tiersky, Ronald and Jones, Erik (eds) *Europe Today: a Twenty-First Century Introduction* (Lanham, MA: Rowman and Littlefield).

Dumbrell, John (2006) *A Special Relationship: Anglo-American Relations from the Cold War to Iraq* (Basingstoke: Palgrave Macmillan).

Duncan, Fraser (2006) 'A Decade of Christian Democratic Decline: The Dilemmas of the CDU, ÖVP and CDA in the 1990s', *Government and Opposition*, 41(4), pp. 469–90.

Duncan, Fraser (2007) '"Lately, Things Just Don't Seem the Same". External Shocks, Party Change and the Adaptation of the Dutch Christian Democrats during "Purple Hague" 1994–8', *Party Politics*, 13(1), pp. 69–87.

Dunleavy, Patrick (1991) *Democracy, Bureaucracy and Public Choice: Economic Explanations in Political Science* (Hemel Hempstead: Harvester Wheatsheaf).

Dunn, Kris and Singh, Shane. (2011) 'The surprising non-impact of radical right-wing populist party representation on public tolerance of minorities'. *Journal of Elections, Public Opinion and Parties*, 21(3), pp. 313–331.

Dunphy, Richard (2004) *Contesting Capitalism? Left Parties and European Integration* (Manchester: Manchester University Press).

Dunphy, Richard and Bale, Tim (2007) 'Red Flag Still Flying? Explaining AKEL – Cyprus's Communist Anomaly', *Party Politics*, 13(3), pp. 287–304.

Dunphy, Richard and Bale, Tim (2011) 'The Radical Left In Coalition Government: Towards A Comparative Measurement Of Success And Failure', *Party Politics*, 17(4), pp. 488–504.

Dutton, William H. (ed) (2013) *Politics and the Internet* (Abingdon: Routledge).

Duvanova, Dinissa S. (2009) 'Business Representation in Eastern Europe: the Failure of Corporatism?', in Conor McGrath (ed) *Interest Groups and Lobbying in Europe* (Lampeter: Edwin Mellen Press).

Duverger, Maurice (1954) *Political Parties: Their Organization and Activity in the Modern State* (London: Methuen).

E

Earnshaw, David and Judge, David (2002) 'No Simple Dichotomies: Lobbyists and the European Parliament', *Journal of Legislative Studies*, 8(4), pp. 61–79.

Eatwell, Roger (2000) 'The Rebirth of the Extreme Right in Western Europe', *Parliamentary Affairs*, 53(3), pp. 407–25.

Ecker-Ehrhardt, Matthias (2010) 'Aid Organizations, Governments and the Media: the Critical Role of Journalists in Signalling Authority Recognition', in Koch-Baumgarten, Sigrid and Voltmer, Katrin (eds.) (2010) *Public Policy and Mass Media: The Interplay of Mass Communication and Political Decision Making* (Abingdon: Routledge).

Egeberg, Morten (2008) 'European Government(s): Executive Politics in Transition?', *West European Politics*, 31(1–2), pp. 235–257.

Egenhofer, Christian and Behrens, Arlo (2011) 'Resource Politics: the Rapidly Shifting European Engergy Policy Agenda', in Erik Jones, Paul M. Heywood, Martin Rhodes, and Ulrich Sedelmeier (eds) *Developments in European Politics Two* (Basingstoke: Palgrave Macmillan).

Eger, Maureen A. (2010) 'Even in Sweden: the Effect of Immigration on Support for Welfare State Funding', *European Sociological Review*, 26(2), pp. 203–217.

Eide, Elisabeth, Kunelius, Risto and Phillips, Angela (eds.) (2008) *Transnational Media Events: the Mohammed Cartoons and the Imagined Clash of Civilizations* (Gothenburg: Nordicom).

Eising, Rainer and Kohler-Koch, Beate (1999) 'Introduction: Network Governance in the European Union', in Beate Kohler-Koch and Rainer Eising (eds), *The Transformation of Governance in the European Union* (London: Routledge/ECPR).

Elazar, D.J. (1997) 'Contrasting Unitary and Federal Systems', *International Political Science Review*, 18(3), pp. 237–51.

Elchardus, Mark and Spruyt, Bram (2012) 'The Contemporary Contradictions of Egalitarianism: an Empirical Analysis of the Relationship between the Old and New Left/Right Alignments', *European Political Science Review*, 4(2), pp. 217–239.

Elff, Martin (2007) 'Social Structure and Electoral Behavior in Comparative Perspective: The Decline of Social Cleavages in Western Europe Revisited', *Perspectives on Politics*, 5(2), pp 277–294.

Elgie, Robert (2011) *Semi-Presidentialism: Sub-Types And Democratic Performance* (Oxford: Oxford University Press).

Elgie, Robert, and Moestrup, Sophia (eds.) (2008) *Semi-Presidentialism in Central and Eastern Europe* (Manchester: Manchester University Press).

Elias, Anwen (2009) *Minority Nationalist Parties and European Integration* (Abingdon: Routledge).

Elias, Anwen and Tronconi, Filippo (2011) 'From Protest to Power: Autonomist Parties in Government', *Party Politics*, 17(4), pp. 505–524.

Elkins, Zachary, Ginsburg, Tom and Melton, James (2009) *The Endurance of National Constitutions* (Cambridge: Cambridge University Press).

Ellinas, Antonis (2010) *The Media and the Far Right in Western Europe: Playing the Nationalist Card* (Cambridge: Cambridge University Press).

Elster, Jon (1986) 'Introduction', in Jon Elster (ed.), *Rational Choice* (Oxford: Blackwell).

Elvestad, Eiri and Blekesaune, Arild (2008) 'Newspaper Readers in Europe: A Multilevel Study of Individual and National Differences', *European Journal of Communication*, 23(4), pp. 425–447.

Emmott, Bill (2012) *Good Italy, Bad Italy: Why Italy Must Conquer its Demons to Face the Future* (New Haven, CT: Yale University Press).

Ennser, Laurenz (2012) 'The Homogeneity of West European Party Families. The Radical Right in Comparative Perspective', *Party Politics*, 18(2), pp. 151–171.

Epperly, Brad (2011), 'Institutions and Legacies: Electoral Volatility in the Postcommunist World', *Comparative Political Studies*, 44(7), pp. 829–853.

Epstein, Rachel and Gheciu, Alexandra (2006) 'Beyond Territoriality: European Security after the Cold War', in Paul Heywood, Erik Jones, Martin Rhodes and Ulrich Sedelmeier (eds), *Developments in European Politics* (Basingstoke: Palgrave Macmillan).

Epstein, Rachel A. and Sedelmeier, Ulrich (eds) (2008) 'Beyond Conditionality: International Institutions in Postcommunist Europe after Enlargement', special issue of the *Journal of European Public Policy*, 15(2), pp. 795–955.

Ericson, Richard, Baranek, Patricia and Chan, Janet B.L. (1989) *Negotiating Control: A Study of News Sources* (Toronto: University of Toronto Press).

Erne, Roland (2008) *European Unions: Labor's Quest for a Transnational Democracy* (Ithaca, NY: Cornell University Press).

Ertman, Thomas (2009) 'Western European Party Systems and the Religious Cleavage', in Kees van Kersbergen and Philip Manow (eds.) (2009) *Religion, Class Coalitions, and Welfare States* (Cambridge: Cambridge University Press).

Esmer, Yilmaz and Pettersson, Thorleif (2007) 'The Effects of Religion and Religiosity on Voting Behaviour', in Dalton, Russell and Klingemann, Hans-Dieter (eds.) *The Oxford Handbook of Political Behaviour* (Oxford: Oxford University Press).

Esping-Andersen, Gøsta (1990) *The Three Worlds of Welfare Capitalism* (Cambridge: Polity Press).

Esping-Andersen, Gøsta (2009) *Incomplete Revolution: Adapting Welfare States to Women's New Roles* (Cambridge: Polity Press).

Esser, Frank (2008) 'Dimensions of Political News Cultures: Sound Bite and Image Bite News in France, Germany, Great Britain, and the United States', *International Journal of Press/Politics*, 13(4), pp. 401–428.

Esser, Frank, Reinemann, Carsten and Fan, David (2000) 'Spin Doctoring in British and German Election Campaigns: How the Press is being Confronted with a New Quality of Political PR', *European Journal of Communication*, 15(2), pp. 209–39.

Esser, Frank, Reinemann, Carsten and Fan, David (2001) 'Spin Doctors in the United States, Great Britain, and Germany: Metacommunication about Media Manipulation', *Harvard International Journal of Press/Politics*, 6(1), pp. 16–45.

Esser, Frank and Pfetsch, Barbara (eds) (2004) *Comparing Political Communication: Theories, Cases, and Challenges* (Cambridge: Cambridge University Press).

EUMAP (2009) *Television Across Europe: More Channels, Less Independence Follow-Up Reports* 2008, available at http://www.soros.org/initiatives/media/articles_publications/publications/television_20090313.

European Commission (2006) http://ec.europa.eu/employment_social/news/2006/feb/ report_en.pdf.

European Commission (2007) *Towards Common Principles of Flexicurity,* available at http://ec.europa.eu/employment_social/employment_strategy/flexicurity%20media/flexicurity-publication_2007_en.pdf.

Eurostat (2011) *Migrants in Europe: a statistical portrait of the first and second generation* (Luxembourg: European Union), available at http://epp.eurostat.ec.europa.eu/cache/ITY_OFFPUB/KS-31-10-539/EN/KS-31–10–539–EN.PDF.

Evans, Geoffrey (1999) *The End of Class Politics?: Class Voting in Comparative Context* (Oxford: Oxford University Press).

Evans, Geoffrey (2006) 'The Social Bases of Political Divisions in Post-Communist Eastern Europe, *Annual Review of Sociology,* 32, pp. 245–70.

Evans, Jocelyn A.J. (ed.) (2002) *The French Party System* (Manchester: Manchester University Press).

Evans, Jocelyn, A.J. (2003) *Voters and Voting: An Introduction* (London: Sage).

Evans, Jocelyn A.J. (2004) 'Ideology and Party Identification: A Normalisation of French Voting Anchors?', in Michael Lewis-Beck (ed.), *The French Voter* (Basingstoke: Palgrave Macmillan).

F

Faas, T. and Maier, J. (2004) 'Chancellor-candidates in the 2002 Televised Debates', *German Politics,* 13(2), pp. 300–16.

Fabbrini, Sergio (2011) 'When Media and Politics Overlap: Inferences from the Italian Case', *Government and Opposition,* 46(3), pp. 345–364.

Fairbrass, J. and Jordan, A. (2001) 'Protecting Biodiversity in the European Union: National Barriers and European Opportunities', *Journal of European Public Policy,* 8(4), pp. 499–518.

Faist, Thomas and Ette, Andrew (2007) *The Europeanization of National Policies and Politics of Immigration* (Basingstoke: Palgrave Macmillan).

Falkner, Gerda (2000a) 'How Pervasive are Euro-politics? Effects of EU Membership on a New Member State', *Journal of Common Market Studies,* 38(2), pp. 223–50.

Falkner, Gerda (2000b) 'The Council or the Social Partners? EC Social Policy between Diplomacy and Collective Bargaining', *Journal of European Public Policy,* 7(5), pp. 705–24.

Falkner, Gerda (2009) 'The European Union's Social Dimension', in Michelle Cini and Nieves Perez-Solorzano Borragan (eds.) (2009) *European Union Politics* (Oxford: OUP).

Falkner, Gerda (2010) 'Institutional Performance and Compliance with EU Law: Czech Republic, Hungary, Slovakia and Slovenia', *Journal of Public Policy,* 30(1), pp. 101–116.

Falkner, Gerda, Treib, Oliver, Hartlapp, Miriam and Leiber, Simone (2004) 'Non-Compliance with EU Directives in the Member States: Opposition through the Backdoor?', *West European Politics,* 27(3), pp. 452–73.

Fallend, Franz (2004) 'Are Right-Wing Populism and Government Participation Incompatible? The Case of the Freedom Party of Austria', *Representation,* 40(2), pp. 1156–30.

Farrell, David M. (2011) *Electoral Systems: A Comparative Introduction* (Basingstoke: Palgrave Macmillan).

Farrell, David M. and Schmitt-Beck, Rüdiger (2002) *Do Political Campaigns Matter? Campaign Effects in Elections and Referendums* (London: Routledge).

Favell A. and Hansen R. (2002) 'Markets against Politics: Migration, EU Enlargement and the Idea of Europe', *Journal of Ethnic and Migration Studies,* 28(4), pp. 581–601.

Fawn, Rick (2006) 'Alliance Behaviour, the Absentee Liberator and the Influence of Soft Power: Post-communist State Positions over the Iraq War in 2003', *Cambridge Review of International Affairs,* 19(3), pp. 465–80.

Fawn, Rick (2013) 'The International Politics of Central and Eastern Europe', in Paul G. Lewis and Judy Batt (eds) *Developments in Central and East European Politics 5* (Basingstoke: Palgrave Macmillan).

Feigenbaum, Harvey, Henig, Jeffrey and Hamnett, Chris (1998) *Shrinking the State: The Political Underpinnings of Privatization* (Cambridge: Cambridge University Press).

Fella, Stefano and Ruzza, Carlo (2011) *Re-Inventing the Italian Right: Territorial Politics, Populism and 'Post-Fascism'* (Abingdon: Routledge).

Fenger, HJM (2007) 'Welfare regimes in Central and Eastern Europe: Incorporating post-communist countries in a welfare regime typology', Contemporary Issues and Ideas in Social Sciences, 3(2), available online at http://journal.ciiss.net/index.php/ciiss/article/view/45/37

Ferge, Zsuzsa (2001) 'Welfare and "Ill-fare" Systems in Central and Eastern Europe', in Robert Sykes, Bruno Palier and Pauline M. Prior (eds), *Globalization and European Welfare States: Challenges and Change* (Basingstoke: Palgrave Macmillan).

Ferguson, Ross and Howell, Milica (2004) *Political Blogs – Craze or Convention?* (London: Hansard Society), available at http://www.hansardsociety.org.uk/assets/Final_Blog_Report_pdf.

Fielden, Lara (2012) Regulating the Press. A Comparative Study of International Press Councils (Oxford: Reuters Institute), available online at http://reutersinstitute.politics.ox.ac.uk/file admin/documents/Publications/Working_Papers/Regulating_the_Press.pdf.

Fink, Simon (2009) 'Churches as Societal Veto Players: Religious Influence in Actor-Centred Theories of Policy making', *West European Politics,* 32(1), pp. 77–96.

Finseraas, Henning (2008) 'Immigration and Preferences for Redistribution: An Empirical Analysis of European Survey Data', *Comparative European Politics,* 6(4), pp. 407–431.

Firmstone, Julie (2009) 'Influences on the Editorial Opinions of the British Press towards the European Union', in Charles, Alec (ed.) Media in the Enlarged Europe: Politics, Policy and Industry (Bristol: Intellect).

Fish, M. Steven and Kroenig, Matthew (2011) *The Handbook of National Legislatures: A Global Survey* (Cambridge: Cambridge University Press).

Fitjar, Ruhne Dahl (2010) 'Explaining variation in sub-state regional identities in Western Europe', *European Journal of Political Research*, 49, pp. 522–544.

Flavin, Patrick and Radcliff, Benjamin (2011) 'Labor Union Membership and Voting Across Nations', *Electoral Studies*, 30, pp. 633–641.

Flockhart, Trine (2011) '"Me Tarzan – You Jane": The EU and NATO and the Reversal of Roles', *Perspectives on European Politics and Society*, 12(3), pp. 263–282.

Forest, Maxime (2011) 'Central and Eastern Europe', in Gretchen Bauer and Manon Tremblay (eds) *Women in Executive Power: a Global Overview* (Abingdon: Routledge).

Foret, François and Itçaina, Xabier (2011) *Politics of Religion in Western Europe. Modernities in Conflict?* (Abingdon: Routledge).

Franceschet, Susan, Krook, Mona Lena and Piscopo, Jennifer M (eds) (2012) *The Impact of Gender Quotas* (Oxford: Oxford University Press).

Franklin, Mark N. (2001a) 'How Structural Factors Cause Turnout Variations at European Parliament Elections', *European Union Politics*, 3(2), pp. 309–28.

Franklin, Mark N. (2001b) 'European Elections and the European Voter', in Jeremy Richardson (ed.), *European Union: Power and Policy making*, 2nd edn (London: Longman).

Franklin, Mark N. (2002) 'The Dynamics of Electoral Participation', in Lawrence LeDuc, Richard Niemi and Pippa Norris (eds), *Elections and Voting in Global Perspective 2* (Thousand Oaks, CA: Sage).

Franklin, Mark N. (2004) *Voter Turnout and the Dynamics of Electoral Competition in Established Democracies since 1945* (New York: Cambridge University Press).

Franklin, Mark N., MacNie, Thomas and Valen, Henry (eds) (1992) *Electoral Change: Responses to Evolving Social and Attitudinal Structures in Western Countries* (Cambridge: Cambridge University Press).

Frankland, E. Gene Frankland, Lucardie Paul, Rihoux, Benoît (eds.) (2008) *Green Parties in Transition: The End of Grass-roots Democracy?* (Aldershot: Ashgate).

Franks, Suzanne (2006) 'Lacking a Clear Narrative: Foreign Reporting after the Cold War', in John Lloyd and Jean Seaton (eds), *What Can be Done? Making the Media and Politics Better* (Oxford: Blackwell).

Friedman, Jeffrey (ed.) (1996) *The Rational Choice Controversy: Economic Models of Politics Reconsidered* (New Haven, CT: Yale University Press).

Fuchs, Christian (2009) 'The Role of Income Inequality in a Multivariate Cross-National Analysis of the Digital Divide', *Social Science Computer Review*, 27(1), pp. 41–58.

Fuchs, Dieter and Klingemann, Hans-Dieter (2002) 'Eastward Enlargement of the European Union and the Identity of Europe', *West European Politics*, 25(2), pp. 19–54.

Fuchs, Susanne and Offe, Claus (2008) *Welfare State Formation in the Enlarged European Union: Patterns of Reform in the Post-Communist New Member States*, Hertie School of Governance Working Paper No. 14.

Fundamental Rights Agency (2011a) *Migrants, minorities and employment Exclusion and discrimination in the 27 Member States of the European Union* (Luxembourg: European Union), also available at http://fra.europa.eu/fraWebsite/attachments/pub-migrants-minorities-employment_EN.pdf.

Fundamental Rights Agency (2011b) Migrants, minorities and employment Exclusion and discrimination in the 27 Member States of the European Union (Luxembourg: European Union), http://fra.europa.eu/fraWebsite/attachments/pub-migrants-minorities-employment_EN.pdf.

Fundamental Rights Agency (2012) *The Situation of Roma in 11 EU Member States* (Luxembourg: European Union), also available at http://fra.europa.eu/fraWebsite/attachments/FRA-2012-Roma-at-a-glance_EN.pdf.

G

Gabel, Matthew J. and Anderson, Christopher J. (2002) 'The Structure of Citizen Attitudes and the European Political Space', *Comparative Political Studies*, 35(8), pp. 893–913.

Gaddis, John Lewis (2007) *The Cold War* (London: Penguin).

Gaens, Bart, Jokela, Juha and Limnel, Eija (eds) (2009) *The Role of the European Union in Asia* (Farnham: Ashgate).

Gains, Francesca (2003) 'Executive Agencies in Government: The Impact of Bureaucratic Networks on Policy Outcomes', *Journal of Public Policy*, 23(1), pp. 55–79.

Gallagher, Michael (2008) Electoral systems website, http://www.tcd.ie/Political_Science/staff/michael_gallagher/El Systems/index.php.

Gallagher, Michael, Laver, Michael and Mair, Peter (2011) *Representative Government in Modern Europe* (New York: McGraw-Hill).

Gallagher, Michael and Marsh, Michael (eds.) (2011) *How Ireland Voted 2011: The Full Story of Ireland's Earthquake Election* (Basingstoke: Palgrave Macmillan).

Gallagher, Michael and Mitchell, Paul (eds) (2005) *The Politics of Electoral Systems* (Oxford: Oxford University Press).

Gamson, William A. (2004) 'Bystanders, Public Opinion, and the Media', in David A. Snow, Sarah Soule and Hanspeter Kriesi (eds) (2004), *The Blackwell Companion to Social Movements* (Oxford: Blackwell).

Ganghof, Steffen (2006) *The Politics of Income Taxation: A Comparative Analysis of Advanced Industrial Countries* (Colchester: ECPR Press).

Gänzle, Stefan Grimm, Sven, Makhan, Davina (eds) (2012) *The European Union and Global Development: An 'Enlightened Superpower' in the Making?* (Basingstoke: Palgrave Macmillan).

Garbaye, Romain (2005) *Getting Into Local Power: The Politics of Ethnic Minorities in British and French Cities* (Oxford: Blackwell).

Garnett, Mark and Lynch, Philip (2012) *Exploring British Politics* (London: Pearson Longman).

Garrett, Geoffrey (1998) 'Global Markets and National Politics: Collision Course or Virtuous Circle', *International Organization*, 52(4), pp. 787–824.

Garzia, Diego (2012) 'Party and Leader Effects in Parliamentary Elections', *Politics*, 32(2), pp. 175–185.

Gaskins, Benjamin and Jerit, Jennifer (2012) 'Internet News: Is It a Replacement for Traditional Media Outlets?', *International Journal of Press/Politics*, 17(2), pp. 190–213.

Gavin, Neil (2010a) 'Closing the Circle. A Case Study in the Role of Spin in the Policy Cycle', in Koch-Baumgarten, Sigrid and Voltmer, Katrin (eds.) *Public Policy and Mass Media: The*

Interplay of Mass Communication and Political Decision Making (Abingdon: Routledge).

Gavin, Neil (2010b) 'Pressure Group Direct Action on Climate Change: the Role of the Media and the Web in Britain – a case study', *British Journal of Politics and International Relations*, 12, pp. 459–475.

Gavin, Neil and Sanders, David (2003) 'The Press and its Influence on British Political Attitudes under New Labour', *Political Studies*, 51(3), pp. 573–91.

Gaxie, Daniel, Hubé, Nicolas, and Rowell, Jay (2011) *Perceptions of Europe: A Comparative Study of European Attitudes* (Colchester: ECPR Press).

Geddes, Andrew (2003) *The Politics of Migration and Immigration in Europe* (London: Sage).

Geddes, Andrew (2008) *Immigration and European Integration: Beyond Fortress Europe?* (Manchester: Manchester University Press).

Genschel, Philipp (2004) 'Globalization and the Welfare State: a Retrospective', *Journal of European Public Policy*, 11(4), pp. 613–36.

Genschel, Philipp and Jachtenfuchs, Markus (2011) 'How the European Union Constrains the State: Multilevel Governance of Taxation', *European Journal of Political Research*, 50, pp. 293–314.

Gertner, Jon (2004) 'The Very, Very Personal is the Political', *New York Times Magazine*, 15 February.

Geys, Benny (2006) 'Explaining Voter Turnout: a Review of Aggregate-Level Research', *Electoral Studies*, 25(4), pp. 637–63.

Ghemawat, Pankaj (2011) World 3.0: Global Prosperity and How to Achieve It (Cambridge, MA: Harvard Business School Press).

Gibson, Rachel and Harmel, Robert (1998) 'Party Families and Democratic Performance: Extraparliamentary vs Parliamentary Group Power', *Political Studies*, 46(3), pp. 633–50.

Gibson, Rachel, Nixon, Paul and Ward, Stephen (eds) (2003) *Political Parties and the Internet: Net Gain?* (London: Routledge).

Gibson, Rachel, Römmele, Andrea and Ward, Stephen (2003) 'German Parties and Internet Campaigning in the 2002 Federal Election', *German Politics*, 12(1), pp. 79–108.

Giddens, Anthony (1990) *The Consequences of Modernity* (Stanford: Stanford University Press).

Giger, Nathalie and Nelson, Moira (2010), 'The Electoral Consequences of Welfare State Retrenchment: Blame Avoidance or Credit Claiming in the Era of Permanent Austerity?', *European Journal of Political Research*, 50, pp. 1–23.

Giger, Nathalie Rosset, Jan and Bernauer, Julian (2012) 'The Poor Political Representation of the Poor in a Comparative Perspective', *Representation*, 48 (1), pp. 47–61.

Gijsberts, Mérova and Nieuwbeerta, Paul (2000) 'Class Cleavages in Party Preferences in the New Democracies in Eastern Europe: A Comparison with Western Democracies', *European Societies*, 2(4), pp. 397–430.

Gillespie, Richard (2000) *Spain and the Mediterranean: Developing a European Policy towards the South* (Basingstoke: Palgrave Macmillan).

Gimenez-Nadal, Jose Ignacio and Sevilla, Almudena (2012) 'Trends in time allocation: A cross-country analysis', *European Economic Review*, 56(6), pp. 1338–1359.

Ginsberg, Roy H. and Penska, Susan E (2012) *The European Union in Global Security: the Politics of Impact* (Basingstoke: Palgrave Macmillan).

Ginsborg, Paul (2004) *Silvio Berlusconi: Television, Power and Patrimony* (London: Verso).

Giugni, Marco and Passy, Florence (eds) (2006) *Dialogues on Migration Policy* (Lanham: Lexington Books).

Givens, Terri and Luedtke, Adam (2005) 'European Immigration Policies in Comparative Perspective: Issue Salience, Partisanship and Immigrant Rights', *Comparative European Politics*, 3, pp. 1–22.

Glasgow, Garrett, Golder, Matt and Golder, Sona N. (2011) 'Who "Wins"? Determining the Party of the Prime Minister', *American Journal of Political Science*, 55(4), pp. 936–953.

Global Media Monitoring Project (2010) *Who Makes the News?*, available at http://www.whomakesthenews.org.

Goerres, Achim (2007) 'Why are Older People More Likely to Vote? The Impact of Ageing on Electoral Turnout in Europe', *British Journal of Politics and International Relations*, 9(1), pp. 90–1.

Goetz, Klaus H. (2001) 'Making Sense of Post-Communist Central Administration: Modernization, Europeanization or Latinization', *Journal of European Public Policy*, 8(6), pp. 1032–51.

Goetz, Klaus H. (2006) 'Power at the Centre: the Organization of Democratic Systems', in Paul Heywood, Erik Jones, Martin Rhodes and Ulrich Sedelmeier (eds) (2006) *Developments in European Politics* (Basingstoke: Palgrave Macmillan).

Goetz, Klaus H. and Zubek, Radoslav (2007) 'Government, Parliament and Lawmaking in Poland 1997–2001', *Journal of Legislative Studies*, 13(4), pp. 517–38.

Golder, Matt and Stramski, Jacek (2010) 'Ideological Congruence and Electoral Institutions', *American Journal of Political Science*, 54(1), pp. 90–106.

Golder, Sona N. (2010) 'Bargaining Delays in the Government Formation Process', *Comparative Political Studies*, 43(1), pp. 3–32.

Goodin, Robert, Headey, Bruce, Muffels, Ruud and Dirven, Henk-Jan (1999) *The Real Worlds of Welfare Capitalism* (Cambridge: Cambridge University Press).

Goodman, Sara W. (2010) 'Integration Requirements for Integration's Sake? Identifying, Categorising and Comparing Civic Integration Policies', *Journal of Ethnic and Migratio Studies*, 36(5), pp. 753–72.

Goodwin, Jeff, Jasper, James M. and Polleta, Francesca (eds) (2001) *Passionate Politics: Emotions and Social Movements* (Chicago: University of Chicago Press).

Goodwin, Matthew (2011) *New British Fascism: Rise of the British National Party:* (Abingdon: Routledge).

Górny, Agata and Ruspini, Paolo (eds) (2004) *Migration in the New Europe: East–West Revisited* (Basingstoke: Palgrave Macmillan).

Gould, John A. (2011) *The Politics of Privatization: Wealth and Power in Postcommunist Europe* (Boulder: Lynne Rienner, 2011).

Gower, Jackie and Timmins, Graham (eds) (2009) *Russia and Europe in the Twenty-First Century: An Uneasy Partnership* (London: Anthem Press).

Grabbe, Heather (2006) *The EU's Transformative Power: Europeanization through Conditionality in Central and Eastern Europe* (Basingstoke: Palgrave Macmillan).

Grant, Wyn and Stocker, Tim (2009) 'Politics of Food: Agro-Industry Lobbying in Brussels', in David Coen and Jeremy Richardson (eds.) *Lobbying the European Union: Institutions, Actors, and Issues* (Oxford: Oxford University Press).

Gray, Pat and t'Hart, Paul (eds) (1998) *Public Policy Disasters in Western Europe* (London: Routledge).

Graziano, Paolo and Vink, Maarten (eds) (2006) *Europeanization: New Research Agendas* (Basingstoke: Palgrave Macmillan).

Green, Donald P. and Shapiro, Ian (1994) *Pathologies of Rational Choice Theory: A Critique of Applications in Political Science* (New Haven: Yale University Press).

Green, Jane (2007) 'When Voters and Parties Agree: Valence Issues and Party Competition', *Political Studies*, 55(3), pp. 629–55.

Green, Simon (2004) *The Politics of Exclusion: Institutions and Immigration Policy in Contemporary Germany* (Manchester: Manchester University Press).

Green, Simon and Turner, Ed, (eds.) (2013) 'The CDU/CSU', special issue of *German Politics*.

Green, Simon, Hough, Dan, Miskimmon, Mister, Timmins, Graham (2007) *The Politics of the New Germany* (London: Routledge).

Green-Pedersen, Christoffer (1999) 'The Danish Welfare State under Bourgeois Reign', *Scandinavian Political Studies*, 22(3), pp. 243–60.

Green-Pedersen, Christoffer (2001) 'Welfare-state Retrenchment in Denmark and the Netherlands, 1982–1998: The Role of Party Competition and Party Consensus', *Comparative Political Studies*, 34(9), pp. 963–85.

Green-Pedersen, Christoffer (2010) 'Bringing Parties Into Parliament: the Development of Parliamentary Activities in Western Europe', *Party Politics*, 16(3), pp. 347–369.

Green-Pedersen, Christoffer and Stubage, Rene (2010) 'The Political Conditionality of Mass Media Influence: When Do Parties Follow Mass Media Attention?', *British Journal of Political Science*, 40(3), pp. 663–677.

Green-Pedersen, Christoffer and Odmalm, Pontus (2008) 'Going Different Ways? Right-wing Parties and the Immigrant Issue in Denmark and Sweden', *Journal of European Public Policy*, 15(3).

Green-Pedersen, Christoffer, van Kersbergen Kees and Hemerijck, Anton (2001) 'Neo-liberalism, the "Third Way" or What? Recent Social Democratic Welfare Policies in Denmark and the Netherlands', *Journal of European Public Policy*, 8(2), pp. 307–25.

Greenwood, Justin (2011) *Interest Representation in the European Union, 3rd edition* (Basingstoke: Palgrave Macmillan).

Greer, Scott L. (2007) *Nationalism and Self-government* (Albany: SUNY Press).

Gross, Eva (2011), *The Europeanization of National Foreign Policy: Continuity and Change in European Crisis Management* (Basingstoke: Palgrave Macmillan).

Gross, Peter (2004) 'Between Reality and Dream: Eastern European Media Transition, Transformation, Consolidation, and Integration', *East European Politics and Societies*, 18(1), pp. 110–31.

Grzymala-Busse, Anna (2013) 'Why there is (almost) no Christian Democracy in post-communist Europe', *Party Politics*, 19(2).

Gualmini, Elisabetta and Rhodes, Martin (2011) 'Welfare States in Trouble: Policy Reform in a Period of Crisis', in Erik Jones, Paul Heywood, Martin Rhodes and Ulrich Sedelmeier (eds), *Developments in European Politics Two* (Basingstoke: Palgrave Macmillan).

Guarnieri, Carlo and Pederzoli, Patrizia (2002) *The Power of Judges: A Comparative Study of Courts and Democracy* (Oxford: Oxford University Press).

Gudbrandsen, Frøy (2010) 'Partisan Influence on Immigration: The Case of Norway', *Scandinavian Political Studies*, 33(3), pp. 248–270.

Gugiu, Mihaiela Ristei (2012) 'EU Enlargement and Anticorruption: Lessons Learned from Romania', *Journal of European Integration*, 34(5), pp. 429–446.

Guibernau, Montserrat (2007) *The Identity of Nations* (Cambridge: Polity).

Guild, Elspeth and van Selm, Joanne (eds) (2005) *International Migration and Security: Opportunities and Challenges* (London: Routledge).

Guiliani, Marco and Jones, Erik (eds) (2010) *Italian Politics 2010: Managing Uncertainty* (New York: Berghahn Books).

Guillén, Mauro F and Suarez, Sandra L. (2005) 'Explaining the Global Digital Divide: Economic, Political and Sociological Drivers of Cross-National Internet Use', *Social Forces*, 84(2), pp. 681–708.

Guiraudon, Virginie and Jileva, Elena (2006) 'Immigration and Asylum', in Paul Heywood *et al.* (eds) (2006) *Developments in European Politics* (Basingstoke: Palgrave Macmillan).

Gulbrandsen, Trygve (2010) 'Political Versus Media Elites in Norway', in Heinrich Best and John Higley (eds.) *Democratic Elitism: New Theoretical and Comparative Perspectives* (Leiden: Brill).

Gunther, Richard, Montero, José Ramón, and Wert, José Ignacio (2000) 'The Media and Politics in Spain: from Dictatorship to Democracy', in Richard Gunther and Anthony Mughan (eds) *Democracy and the Media: A Comparative Perspective* (Cambridge: Cambridge University Press).

Gunther, Richard, Montero, José Ramón and Linz, Juan J. (2002) *Political Parties: Old Concepts and New Challenges* (Oxford: Oxford University Press).

Gunther, Richard and Montero, José Ramón (2009) *The Politics of Spain.* (Cambridge: Cambridge University Press).

Gunther, Richard and Mughan, Anthony (eds) (2000) *Democracy and the Media: A Comparative Perspective* (Cambridge: Cambridge University Press).

Gustavsson, Sverker and Lewin, Lerf (1996) *The Future of the Nation State* (London: Routledge).

Gwiazda, Anna (2009) 'Poland's Quasi-Institutionalized Party System: The Importance of Elites and Institutions', *Perspectives on European Politics and Society*, 10(3), pp. 350–376.

H

Habermas, Jürgen (1989) *The Structural Transformation of the Public Sphere* (Cambridge: Polity).

Hagemann, Sara and Hoyland, Bjorn (2008) 'Parties in the Council?', *Journal of European Public Policy*, 15(8), pp. 1205–1221.

Hainmueller, J., and Hiscox, M.J. (2007) Educated Preferences: Explaining Attitudes toward Immigration in Europe, *International Organization*, 61 (2), pp. 399–442.

Hall, Peter A. and Soskice, David (2001) 'An Introduction to Varieties of Capitalism', in Peter A. Hall and David Soskice (eds), *Varieties of Capitalism: The Institutional Foundation of Comparative Economic Advantage* (Oxford: Oxford University Press).

Hallin, Daniel C. and Mancini, Paolo (2004) *Comparing Media Systems: Three Models of Media and Politics* (Cambridge: Cambridge University Press).

Halman, Loek and Riis, Ole (2002) *Religion in a Secularizing Society: The Europeans' Religion at the end of the 20th Century* (Leiden and Boston: Brill).

Hamman, Kerstin and Kelly, John (2007) 'Party Politics and the Reemergence of Social Pacts in Western Europe', *Comparative Political Studies*, 40(8), pp. 971–994.

Hamman, Kerstin and Kelly, John (2010) *Parties, Elections, and Policy Reforms in Western Europe. Voting for Social Pacts* (Abingdon: Routledge).

Hamilton, Daniel S. and Burwell, Frances (2010) Shoulder to Shoulder: Forging a U.S.–EU Strategic Partnership. (Washington, DC: Brookings Institute).

Hampshire, James (2013) *The Politics of Immigration: Contradictions of the Liberal State* (Cambridge: Polity Press).

Hanitzsch, Thomas, Hanusch, Folker, Mellado, Claudia, Anikina, Maria, Berganza, Rosa, Cangoz, Incilay, Coman, Mihai, Hamada, Basyouni, Elena Hernández, María, Karadjov, Christopher D., Virginia Moreira, Sonia, Mwesige, Peter G., Plaisance, Patrick Lee, Reich, Zvi, Seethaler, Josef, Skewes, Elizabeth A., Vardiansyah Noor, Dani and Kee Wang Yuen, Edgar (2011) 'Mapping Journalism Cultures across Nations', *Journalism Studies*, 12(3), pp. 273–293.

Hanké, Bob (2011) 'Varieties of European Capitalism and their Transformation', in Erik Jones, Paul Heywood, Martin Rhodes and Ulrich Sedelmeier (eds), *Developments in European Politics Two* (Basingstoke: Palgrave Macmillan).

Hanley, David (ed.) (1994) *Christian Democracy in Europe: A Comparative Perspective* (London: Pinter).

Hanley, David (2007) *Beyond the Nation State: Parties in the Era of European Integration* (Basingstoke: Palgrave Macmillan).

Hanley, Sean (2006) *The New Right in the New Europe* (London: Routledge).

Hanretty, Chris (2011) *Public Broadcasting and Political Interference* (Abingdon: Routledge).

Hansen, R. (2002) 'Globalization, Embedded Realism and Path Dependence: The Other Immigrants to Europe', *Comparative Political Studies*, 35(3), pp. 259–83.

Hantrais, Linda (2007) 'Welfare Policies', in Colin Hay and Anand Menon, *European Politics* (Oxford: Oxford University Press).

Harcourt, Alison J. (2003) 'Europeanization as Convergence: The Regulation of Media Markets in the European Union', in Kevin Featherstone and Claudio Radaelli (eds), *The Politics of Europeanization* (Oxford: Oxford University Press).

Harcourt, Alison J. (2005) *The European Union and the Regulation of Media Markets* (Manchester: Manchester University Press).

Harcourt, Alison J. (2012) 'Transnational Media Regulation in Central and Eastern Europe', in Sabina Mihelj and John Downey (eds.) *Central and Eastern European Media in Comparative Perspective* (Farnham: Ashgate).

Hardy, Jonathan (2008) *Western Media Systems* (Abingdon: Routledge).

Hargreaves Heap, Shaun, Hollis, Martin, Lyons, Bruce, Sugden, Robert and Weale, Albert (1992) *The Theory of Choice: A Critical Guide* (Oxford: Blackwell, 1992).

Harguindéguy, Jean-Baptiste (2007) 'Cross-border Policy in Europe: Implementing INTERREG III-A, FrancSpain', *Regional and Federal Studies*, 17(3), pp. 3 17–334.

Harrison, Jackie (2012) 'The sacking of anti-austerity journalists is part of a worrying trend for press freedom in Spain', http://blogs.lse.ac.uk/europpblog/2012/09/05/spain-press-freedom/

Harrison, Sarah and Bruter, Michael (2011) *Mapping Extreme Right Ideology: An Empirical Geography of the European Extreme Right* (Basingstoke: Palgrave Macmillan).

Hassel, Anke (2009) 'Policies and Politics in Social Pacts in Europe', *European Journal of Industrial Relations*, 15(1), pp. 7–26.

Haukkala, Hiski (2008) 'The European Union as a Regional Normative Hegemon: The Case of European Neighbourhood Policy', *Europe–Asia Studies*, 60(9), pp. 1601–1622.

Haupt, Andrea B. (2007) 'What is Right for the Right? Austrian and German Catch-All Parties' Responses to Globalization, Unpublished MS, available at http://psweb.sbs.ohio-state.edu/faculty/haupt/right.pdf.

Haynes, Jeffrey (ed.) (2009) *The Routledge Handbook of Religion and Politics* (Abingdon: Routledge).

Hays, Jude (2009) *Globalization and the New Politics of Embedded Liberalism* (Oxford: Oxford University Press).

Hayward, Jack (1982) 'Mobilising Private Interests in the Service of Public Ambitions: The Salient Element in the Dual French Policy Style', in Jeremy J. Richardson (ed.), *Policy Styles in Western Europe* (London: George Allen & Unwin).

Hazan, Reuven and Rahat, Gideon (2010) *Democracy within Parties: Candidate Selection Methods and their Political Consequences* (Oxford: Oxford University Press).

Hazell, Robert and Yong, Ben (2012) *The Politics of Coalition: How the Conservative–Lib Dem Government Works* (London: Hart Publishing).

Heidar, Knut and Koole, Ruud (2000) *Parliamentary Party Groups in European Democracies: Political Parties Behind Closed Doors* (London: Routledge).

Heinderyckx, F. (1993) 'TV News Programmes in Western Europe', *European Journal of Communication*, 8(4), pp. 425–50.

Heine, Sophie (2010) 'Left versus Europe? The Ideologies Underlying the Left's 'No' to the Constitutional Treaty in France and Germany', *Perspectives on European Politics and Society*, 11(3), pp. 313–332.

Heinelt, Hubert and Bertrana, Xavier (eds.) (2011) *The Second Tier of Local Government in Europe: Provinces, Counties, Départements and Landkreise in Comparison* (Abingdon: Routledge).

Heinisch, Richard (2003) 'Success in Opposition – Failure in Government: Exploring the Performance of the Austrian Freedom Party and other European Right-wing Populist Parties in Public Office', *West European Politics*, 26(3), pp. 91–130.

Heipertz, Martin and Verdun, Amy (2003) *Ruling Europe: Theory and Politics of the Stability and Growth Pact, Draft Report* (Cologne: Max Planck Institute), available at http://www.mpifg-koeln.mpg.de/people/hz/Dokumente/hz-av_gesamt.pdf.

Held, David (1987) *Models of Democracy* (Stanford: Stanford University Press).

Held, David, McGrew, Anthony, Goldblatt, David and Perraton, Jonathan (1999) *Global Transformations: Politics, Economics and Culture* (Cambridge: Polity Press).

Hellwig, Timothy (2010) 'Elections and the Economy', in Lawrence LeDuc, Righard G. Niemi and Pippa Norris (eds), *Comparing Democracies, 3: Elections and Voting in the 21st Century* (Thousand Oaks, CA: Sage Publications).

Helms, Ludger (2005) *Presidents, Prime Ministers and Chancellors: Executive Leadership in Western Democracies* (Basingstoke: Palgrave Macmillan).

Helms, Ludger (2006) 'The Changing Parameters of Political Control in Western Europe', *Parliamentary Affairs*, 59(1), pp. 78–97.

Helms, Ludger (2012) 'Democratic Political Leadership in the New Media Age: A Farewell to Excellence?', *British Journal of Politics and International Relations*, 14(4), pp. 651–670.

Hemerijck, Anton, Keune, Maarten and Rhodes, Martin (2006) 'European Welfare States: Diversity, Challenges and Reforms', in Paul Heywood, Erik Jones, Martin Rhodes and Ulrich Sedelmeier (eds), *Developments in European Politics* (Basingstoke: Palgrave Macmillan).

Hemerijck, Anton and Visser, Jelle (2001) 'Dutch Lessons in Social Pragmatism', in Stuart White (ed.), *New Labour: The Progressive Future?* (Basingstoke: Palgrave Macmillan).

Henderson, Ailsa and White, Linda A. (2004) 'Shrinking Welfare States? Comparing Maternity Leave Benefits and Child Care Programs in European Union and North American Welfare States, 1985–2000', *Journal of European Public Policy*, 11(3), pp. 497–519.

Hendricks, John Allen (ed.) (2012) *The Palgrave Handbook of Global Radio* (Basingstoke: Palgrave Macmillan).

Henjak, Andrija (2010) 'Political Cleavages and Socio-economic Context: How Welfare Regimes and Historical Divisions Shape Political Cleavages', *West European Politics*, 33(3), pp. 474–504.

Hepburn, Eve (2010) *Using Europe: Territorial Party Strategies in a Multi-level System* (Manchester: Manchester University Press).

Héritier, Adrienne, Kerwer, Dieter, Knill, Christopher, Lehmkuhl, Dirk, Teutsch, Michael and Douillet, Anne-Cécile (2001) *Differential Europe: The European Union Impact on National Policy Making* (Lanham: Rowman & Littlefield).

Hertner, Isabelle (2011) 'Are European Election Campaigns Europeanized? The Case of the Party of European Socialists in 2009', *Government and Opposition*, 46(3), pp. 321–344.

Heyns, Barbara (2005) 'Emerging Inequalities in Central and Eastern Europe', *Annual Review of Sociology*, 31: 163–97.

Heywood, Paul, Erik Jones, Martin Rhodes and Ulrich Sedelmeier (eds), (2006) *Developments in European Politics* (Basingstoke: Palgrave Macmillan).

Hicks, Alexander (1999) *Social Democracy and Welfare Capitalism: A Century of Income Security Politics* (Ithaca, NY: Cornell University Press).

Hill, Christopher (1993) 'The Capability–Expectations Gap, or Conceptualising Europe's Global Role', *Journal of Common Market Studies*, 31(3), pp. 305–28.

Hill, Christopher (1998) 'Convergence, Divergence and Dialectics: National Foreign Policies and the CFSP', in Jan Zielonka (ed.), *Paradoxes of European Foreign Polity* (London: Kluwer).

Hill, Christopher and Smith, Michael (eds) (2011) *International Relations and the European Union* (Oxford: Oxford University Press).

Hilson, C. (2002) 'New Social Movements: The Role of Legal Opportunity', *Journal of European Public Policy*, 9(2), pp. 238–55.

Hilson, Mary (2008) *The Nordic Model: Scandinavia since 1945* (London: Reaktion Books).

Hindman, Matthew (2008) *The Myth of Digital Democracy* (Princeton, NJ: Princeton University Press).

Hinnfors, J. Spehar, A. and Bucken-Knapp, G. (2012) The missing factor: why social democracy can lead to restrictive immigration policy', *Journal of European Public Policy*, 19(4), pp. 583–603.

Hino, Airo (2012) *New Challenger Parties in Western Europe. A Comparative Analysis* (Abingdon: Routledge).

Hirschl, Ran (2004) *Toward Juristocracy: The Origins and Consequences of the New Constitutionalism* (Cambridge: Harvard University Press).

Hirschl, Ran (2008) 'The Judicialization of Mega-Politics and the Rise of Political Courts', *Annual Review of Political Science*, 11: 93–118.

Hix, Simon (2002) 'Parliamentary Behavior with Two Principals: Preferences, Parties, and Voting in the European Parliament', *American Journal of Political Science*, 46(3), pp. 688–98.

Hix, Simon (2008) 'Towards a Partisan Theory of EU politics', *Journal of European Public Policy*, 15(8), pp. 1254–1265.

Hix, Simon and Goetz, Klaus (2000) *Europeanized Politics? European Integration and National Political Systems* (London: Frank Cass).

Hix, Simon and Høyland, Bjørn (2011) *The Political System of the European Union*, 3rd edn (Basingstoke: Palgrave Macmillan).

Hix, Simon, Kreppel, Amy and Noury, Abdul (2003) 'The Party System in the European Parliament: Collusive or Competitive?', *Journal of Common Market Studies*, 41(2), pp. 309–31.

Hix, Simon, Noury, Abdul G., and Roland, Gerard (2007) *Democratic Politics in the European Parliament* (Cambridge: Cambridge University Press).

Hloušek, Vít and Kopeček, Lubomír (2010) *Origin, Ideology and Transformation of Political Parties. East-Central and Western Europe Compared* (Aldershot: Ashgate).

Hobolt, Sara Binzer (2009) *Europe in Question: Referendums on European Integration* (Oxford: Oxford University Press).

Hocking, Brian and Spence, David (2002) *Foreign Ministries in the European Union* (Basingstoke: Palgrave Macmillan).

Holbrook, Andrew and Hill, Timothy G. (2005) 'Agenda-Setting and Priming in Prime Time Television: Crime Dramas as Political Cues', *Political Communication*, 22(3), pp. 277–95.

Holland, Martin and Doidge, Matthew (2012) *Development Policy of the European Union* (Basingstoke: Palgrave Macmillan).

Hollifield, James F. (1994) 'Immigration and Republicanism in France: The Hidden Consensus', in Wayne A. Cornelius, Philip L. Martin and James F. Hollifield (eds), *Controlling Immigration: A Global Perspective* (Stanford: Stanford University Press).

Holmes, Michael and Lightfoot, Simon (2007) 'The Europeanisation of Left Political Parties: Limits to Adaptation and Consensus', Capital and Class, 31(3), pp. 141–158.

Holmes, Michael and Lightfoot, Simon (2011) 'Limited Influence? The Role of the Party of European Socialists in Shaping Social Democracy in Central and Eastern Europe', *Government and Opposition*, 46(1), pp. 32–55.

Holtz-Bacha, Christina (2004) 'Germany: How the Private Life of Politicians got into the Media', *Parliamentary Affairs*, 57(1), pp. 41–52.

Hönnige, Christoph (2009) 'The Electoral Connection: How the Pivotal Judge Affects Oppositional Success at European Constitutional Courts', *West European Politics*, 32(5), pp. 963–984.

Hooghe, Liesbet (2007) 'What Drives Euroskepticism? Party–Public Cueing, Ideology and Strategic Opportunity', *European Union Politics,* 8, pp. 5–12.

Hooghe, Liesbet and Marks, Gary (2001) *Multi-level Governance and European Integration* (Lanham: Rowman & Littlefield).

Hooghe, Liesbet and Marks, Gary (eds) (2007) 'Understanding Euroscepticism', *Acta Politica,* Special issue, 42(2–3).

Hooghe, Liesbet and Marks, Gary (2009) 'A Postfunctionalist Theory of European Integration: From Permissive Consensus to Constraining Dissensus', *British Journal of Political Science*, 39(1), pp. 1–23.

Hooghe, Liesbet, Marks, Gary and Wilson, Carole J. (2002) 'Does Left/Right Structure Party Positions in European Integration?', *Comparative Political Studies,* 35(8), pp. 965–89.

Hooghe, Marc (2002) 'Watching Television and Civic Engagements: Disentangling the Effects of Time, Programs, and Stations', *Harvard International Journal of Press/Politics*, 7(2), pp. 84–104.

Hooghe, Marc, Maddens, B. and Noppe, J. (2006) 'Why Parties Adapt: Electoral Reform, Party Finance and Party Strategy in Belgium', *Electoral Studies,* 25(2), pp. 351–68.

Hooghe, Marc and Stolle, Dietland (2003) *Generating Social Capital: Civil Society and Institutions in Comparative Perspective* (Basingstoke: Palgrave Macmillan).

Hooghe, Marc, Trappers, Ann, Meuleman, Bart, Reeskens, Tim (2008) 'Migration to European Countries: a Structural Explanation of Patterns, 1980–2004', *International Migration Review,* 42(2), pp. 476–504.

Hopkin, Jonathan (1999) *Party Formation and Democratic Transition in Spain: The Creation and Collapse of the Union of Democratic Centre* (Basingstoke: Palgrave Macmillan).

Hopkin, Jonathan (2011) 'Elections and Electoral Systems', in Erik Jones, Paul Heywood, Martin Rhodes and Ulrich Sedelmeier (eds), *Developments in European Politics Two* (Basingstoke: Palgrave Macmillan).

Hopkin, Jonathan and Paolucci, Caterina (1999) 'The Business Firm Model of Party Organisation: Cases from Spain and Italy', *European Journal of Political Research,* 35(3), pp. 307–38.

Hopkin, Jonathan and van Houten, Pieter (eds) (2009) 'Decentralization and State-wide Parties', special issue of *Party Politics,* 15 (2).

Hopkins, Thomas D. (1998) 'The Czech Republic's Privatization Experience', in Demetrius S. Iatridis and June Gary Hopps (eds), *Privatization in Central and Eastern Europe: Perspectives and Approaches* (London: Praeger).

Hopmann, David N., Elmelund-Præstekær, Christian, Albæk, Erik, Vliegenthart, Rens and de Vreese, Claes H. (2012) 'Party Media Agenda-setting. How Parties Influence Election News Coverage', *Party Politics*, 18(2), pp. 173–191.

Horký, Ondřej and Lightfoot, Simon 'From Aid Recipients to Aid Donors?: Development Policies of Central and Eastern European States', special issue of *Perspectives on European Politics and Society*, 13(1), pp.1–130.

Horne, Cynthia M. (2012) 'Assessing the Impact of Lustration on Trust in Public Institutions and National Government in Central and Eastern Europe', *Comparative Political Studies*, 45(4), pp. 412–446.

Horvat, Pia and Evans, Geoffrey (2011) 'Age, Inequality, and Reactions to Marketization in Post-Communist Central and Eastern Europe', *European Sociological Review*, 27(6), pp. 708–727.

Hough, Dan (2005) 'Third Ways or New Ways? The Social Democratic Left in East Central Europe', *Political Quarterly*, 76(2), pp. 253–63.

Hough, Dan, Koß, M. and Olsen, J. (2007) *The Left Party in Contemporary German Politics* (Basingstoke: Palgrave Macmillan).

Hough, Dan (2013) *Corruption, Anti-Corruption and Governance* (Basingstoke: Palgrave).

Howard, Marc Morjé (2003) *The Weakness of Civil Society in Post-Communist Europe* (Cambridge: Cambridge University Press).

Howard, Marc Morjé (2009) *The Politics of Citizenship in Europe* (Cambridge: Cambridge University Press).

Howard, Marc Morjé (2010) 'The Impact of the Far Right on Citizenship Policy in Europe: Explaining Continuity and Change', *Journal of Ethnic and Migration Studies*, 36(5), pp. 735–51.

Howard, Marc Morjé and Gilbert, Leah (2008) 'A Cross-National Comparison of the Internal Effects of Participation in Voluntary Organizations', *Political Studies*, 56(1), pp.12–32.

Howarth, David (ed.) (2004) 'The Stability and Growth Pact', *Journal of European Public Policy,* Special issue, 11(5).

Hsu, Ronald (ed) (2010) *Ethnic Europe: Mobility, Identity, and Conflict in a Globalized World* (Stanford: Stanford University Press).

Huber, Evelyne and Stephens, John D. (2001) *Development and Crisis of the Welfare State: Parties and Policies in Global Markets* (Chicago: University of Chicago Press).

Hug, Simon (2002) *Voices of Europe: Citizens, Referendums, and European Integration* (Lanham: Rowman & Littlefield).

Hughes, James, Sasse, Gwendolyn and Gordon, Claire (2004) *Europeanization and Regionalization in the EU's Enlargement to Central and Eastern Europe: The Myth of Conditionality* (Basingstoke: Palgrave Macmillan).

Hughes, Kirsty (2004) *Turkey and the European Union: Just Another Enlargement? Exploring the Implications of Turkish Accession* (Brussels: Friends of Europe Working Papers), June, available at http://www.friendsofeurope.org.

Humphreys, Peter (2009) 'EU Audio-visual Policy, Cultural Diversity and the Future of Public Service Broadcasting', in Jackie Harrison and Bridgette Wessels (eds.) *Mediating Europe:*

New Media, Mass Communications and the European Public Sphere (Oxford: Berghahn Books).

Huysmans, Jef (2006) *The Politics of Insecurity: Fear, Migration and Asylum in the EU* (London: Routledge).

Hyde-Price, Adrian (2007) *European Security in the Twenty-First Century: The Challenge of Multipolarity* (London: Routledge).

I

Iankova, Elena A. (2002) *Eastern European Capitalism in the Making* (Cambridge: Cambridge University Press).

Iatridis, Demetrius S. and Hopps, June Gary (eds) (1998) *Privatization in Central and Eastern Europe: Perspectives and Approaches* (London: Praeger).

Ibrahim, Yasmin (2009) 'The Mediated "Ummah" in Europe: The Islamic Audience in the Digital Age', in Charles, Alec (ed.) *Media in the Enlarged Europe: Politics, Policy and Industry* (Bristol: Intellect).

IDEA (2007) Voter Turnout Website, http://www.idea.int/vt/index.cfm.

Ignazi, Piero (2003) *Extreme Right Parties in Western Europe* (Oxford: Oxford University Press).

Ilie, Cornelia (ed.) (2010) *European Parliaments under Scrutiny: Discourse Strategies and Interaction Practices* (Amsterdam: John Benjamin's).

Imbeau, L. M., Pétry, F. and Lamari, M. (2001) 'Lefright Party Ideology and Government Policies: A Meta Analysis', *European Journal of Political Research*, 40(1), pp. 1–29.

Imig, Doug (2002) 'Contestation in the Streets: European Protests and the Emerging Euro-polity', *Comparative Political Studies,* 35(8), pp. 914–33.

Indridason, Indridi (2008) 'Does Terrorism Influence Domestic Politics? Coalition Formation and Terrorist Incidents', *Journal of Peace Research*, 45(2), pp. 241–260.

Ingebritsen, Christine (2006) *Scandinavia in World Politics* (Lanham: Rowman & Littlefield).

Inglehart, Ronald and Catterberg, Gabriela (2002) 'Trends in Political Action: the Developmental Trend and the Post-Honeymoon Decline', *International Journal of Comparative Sociology,* 43(3–5), pp. 300–16.

Inglehart, Ronald and Norris, Pippa (2000) 'The Development Theory of the Gender Gap: Women's and Men's Voting in Global Perspective', *International Political Science Review,* 21(4), pp. 441–63.

Inglehart, Ronald and Rabier, Jacques-Rene (1986) 'Political Realignment in Advanced Industrial Society: From Class-based Politics to Quality of Life Politics', *Government and Opposition,* 21, pp. 456–79.

Inglehart, Ronald and Welzel, Christian (2005) *Modernization, Cultural Change, and Democracy. The Human Development Sequence* (Cambridge: Cambridge University Press).

IPG (2010) *The Future of Social Democracy* (Berlin: IPG), available online at http://www.fes.de/ipg/sets_e/arc_e.htm.

Irwin, Galen A. and van Holsteyn, Joop J.M. (2012) 'Strategic Electoral Considerations under Proportional Representation', *Electoral Studies*, 31(1), pp. 184–191.

Iversen, Torben and Soskice, David (2006) 'Electoral Institutions and the Politics of Coalitions: Why Some Democracies Redistribute More Than Others', *American Political Science Review,* 100 (2), pp. 165–81.

Iversflaten, Elisabeth (2008) 'What Unites Right-Wing Populists in Western Europe? Re-Examining Grievance Mobilization Models in Seven Successful Cases', *Comparative Political Studies*, 41(1), pp. 3–23.

J

Jacoby, Wade (2010) 'Managing globalization by managing Central and Eastern Europe: the EU's backyard as threat and opportunity', *Journal of European Public Policy*, 17(3), pp.416–432.

Jagers, Jan and Walgrave, Stefaan (2007) 'Populism as Political Communication Style: An Empirical Study of Political Parties' Discourse in Belgium', *European Journal of Political Research,* 46(3), pp. 319–45.

Jahn, Detlef and Müller-Rommel, Ferdinand (2010) 'Political Institutions and Policy Performance: a Comparative Analysis of Central and Eastern Europe', *Journal of Public Policy*, 30(1), pp. 23–44.

Jakubowicz, Karol (2004) 'Ideas in Our Heads. Introduction of PSB as Part of Media System Change in Central and Eastern Europe', *European Journal of Communication*, 19(1), pp. 53–74.

Janoski, Thomas (2010) *The Ironies of Citizenship: Naturalization and Integration in Industrialized Countries* (Cambridge: Cambridge University Press).

Jasiewicz, Krysztof (2009) 'The Past is Never Dead: Identity, Class and Voting Behaviour in Contemporary Poland', *East European Politics and Societies*, 23(4) pp. 491–508.

Jenkins, Philip (2007) *God's Continent: Christianity, Islam, and Europe's Religious Crisis* (Oxford: Oxford University Press).

Jennings, Will (2009) 'The Public Thermostat, Political Responsiveness and Error-Correction: Border Control and Asylum in Britain, 1994–2007', *British Journal of Political Science*, 39(4), pp. 847–870.

Jensen, Carsten (2010) 'Issue Compensation and Right-Wing Government Social Spending', *European Journal of Political Research*, 49, pp. 282–299.

Jensen, Carsten (2011a) 'Negotiated Expansion: Left-Wing Governments, Corporatism and Social Expenditure in Mature Welfare States', *Comparative European Politics*, 9, pp. 168–190.

Jensen, Carsten (2011b) "Catching up by transition: globalization as a generator of convergence in social spending', *Journal of European Public Policy*, 18(1), pp. 106–21.

Johansson, Karl Magnus (2008) External Legitimization and Standardization of National Political Parties: the Case of Estonian Social Democracy, *Journal of Baltic Studies*, 39(2), pp. 157–183.

Johansson, Karl Magnus and Tallberg, Jonas (2010) 'Explaining Chief Executive Empowerment: EU Summitry and Domestic Institutional Change', *West European Politics*, 33(2), pp. 208–236.

Johansson, Karl Magnus and Zervakis A. Peter (eds) (2002) *European Political Parties between Cooperation and Integration 2002* (Baden-Baden: Nomos Verlag).

Johns, Robert and Shephard, Mark (2007) 'Gender, Candidate Image and Electoral Preference', *British Journal of Politics and International Relations*, 9(3), pp. 434–60.

Jones, Erik (2002) *The Politics of Economic and Monetary Union: Integration and Idiosyncrasy* (Lanham: Rowman & Littlefield).

Jones, Erik (2011) 'Europe and the Global Economic Crisis', in Tiersky, Ronald and Jones, Erik (eds) *Europe Today: a Twenty-First Century Introduction* (Lanham, MA: Rowman and Littlefield).

Jones, Erik, Heywood, Paul Rhodes, Martin and Sedelmeier, Ulrich (eds) (2011) *Developments in European Politics Two* (Basingstoke: Palgrave Macmillan).

Joppke, Christian (2002) 'European Immigration Policies at the Crossroads', in Paul Heywood, Erik Jones and Martin Rhodes (eds), *Developments in West European Politics* (Basingstoke: Palgrave Macmillan).

Joppke, Christian (2007a) 'Beyond National Models: Civic Integration Policies for Immigrants in Western Europe', *West European Politics*, 30 (1): 1–22.

Joppke, Christian (2007b) 'Transformation of Immigrant Integration: Civic Integration and Antidiscrimination in the Netherlands, France and Germany', *World Politics*, 59, pp. 243–73.

Joppke, Christian (2009) *Veil: Mirror of Identity* (Cambridge: Polity Press).

Joppke, Christian (2011) 'European Immigration Policies: Between Stemming and Soliciting Still', in Erik Jones, Paul M. Heywood, Martin Rhodes, and Ulrich Sedelmeier (eds.) *Developments in European Politics Two* (Basingstoke: Palgrave Macmillan).

Joppke, Christian *et al.* (2010) 'How Liberal are Citizenship Tests – EUDO Citizenship Forum', http://eudo-citizenship.eu/citizenship-forum/255-how-liberal-are-citizenship-tests.

Jordan, Andrew and Adelle, Camilla (2012) *Environmental Policy in the EU: Actors, Institutions and Processes* (Abingdon: Routledge).

Jordan, Andrew, Huitema, Dave, van Asselt, Harro, Rayner, Tim and Berkhout, Frans (eds) (2010) *Climate Change Policy in the European Union: Confronting the Dilemmas of Mitigation and Adaptation?* (Cambridge: Cambridge University Press).

Jordan, Grant and Maloney, William (1997) *Protest Businesses? Mobilising Campaigning Groups* (Manchester: Manchester University Press).

Jordan, Grant and Maloney, William (2006) '"Letting George Do It": Does Olson Explain Low Levels of Participation?', *Journal of Elections, Public Opinion and Parties*, 16(2), pp. 115–39.

Jouët, Josiane (2010) 'French Media: Policy Regulation and the Public Sphere', in Gripsund, Jostein and Weibull, Lennart (eds.) *Media, Markets and Public Spheres* (Bristol: Intellect).

Judt, Tony (2007) *Postwar: A History of Europe Since 1945* (London: Pimlico).

K

Kagan, Robert (2004) *Paradise and Power: America and Europe in the New World Order* (New York: Atlantic Books).

Kaid, Lynda and Holz-Bacha, Christina (2006) *The Sage Handbook of Political Advertising* (London: Sage).

Kalogeropoulou, Efthalia (1989) 'Election Promises and Government Performance in Greece: PASOK's Fulfilment of its 1981 Election Pledges', *European Journal of Political Research*, 17(3), pp. 289–311.

Kam, Christopher J. (2009) *Party Discipline and Parliamentary Politics* (Cambridge, Cambridge University Press).

Kam, Christopher J., Bianco, William T., Sened, Itai and Smyth, Regina (2010) 'Ministerial Selection and Intraparty Organization in the Contemporary British Parliament', *American Political Science Review*, 104(2), pp. 289–306.

Kanet, Roger E. (2010) *Russian Foreign Policy in the 21st Century* (Basingstoke: Palgrave Macmillan).

Kantola, A. (2006) 'On the Dark Side of Democracy: the Global Imaginary of Financial Journalism', in B. Cammmaerts and N. Carpentier (eds.) *Reclaiming the Media: Communication, Rights and Democratic Media Roles* (Bristol: Intellect).

Karp, Jeffrey A. and Hobolt, Sara B. (eds.) (2010) 'Special Symposium: Voters and Coalition Governments', *Electoral Studies*, 29(3), pp. 299–391.

Karp, Regina (2009) 'Germany: A "Normal" Global Actor?', *German Politics*, 18(1), pp. 12–35.

Karvonen, Erkki (2009) 'Entertainmentization of the European Public Sphere and Politics', in Jackie Harrison and Bridgette Wessels (eds.) *Mediating Europe: New Media, Mass Communications and the European Public Sphere* (Oxford: Berghahn Books).

Karvonen, Lauri (2004) 'Preferential Voting: Incidence and Effects', *International Political Science Review*, 25(2), pp. 203–26.

Karvonen, Lauri (2010) *The Personalisation of Politics* (Colchester: ECPR Press).

Karyotis, Georgios (2007) 'European Migration Policy in the Aftermath of September 11: The Security–Migration Nexus', *Innovation*, 20(1), pp. 1–17.

Katz, Richard and Crotty, William (eds) (2006) *Handbook of Party Politics* (London: Sage).

Katz, Richard and Mair, Peter (1995) 'Changing Models of Party Organization and Party Democracy: The Emergence of the Cartel Party', *Party Politics*, 1(1), pp. 8–28.

Kaufman, Bruno and Waters, M. Dane (2004) *Direct Democracy in Europe: A Comprehensive Reference Guide to the Initiative and Referendum Process in Europe* (Durham, NC: Carolina Academic Press).

Kavada, Anastasia (2005) 'Civil Society Organizations and the Internet: the Case Studies of Oxfam, Amnesty International and the World Development Movement', in W. de Jong, M. Shaw and N. Stammers (eds.) *Global Activism, Global Media* (London: Pluto Press).

Kayser, Mark Andreas and Wlezien, Christopher (2011) 'Performance Pressure: Patterns of Partisanship and the Economic Vote', *European Journal of Political Research*, 50, pp. 365–394.

Keane, John (2009) *The Life and Death of Democracy* (New York: Norton).

Keating, Michael (2000) *The New Regionalism in Western Europe: Territorial Restructuring and Political Change* (Aldershot: Edward Elgar).

Keating, Michael (2001) *Nations Against the State: The New Politics of Nationalism in Quebec, Catalonia and Scotland* (Basingstoke: Palgrave Macmillan).

Keating, Michael (2006) 'Territorial Politics in Europe', in Paul Heywood, Erik Jones, Martin Rhodes and Ulrich Sedelmeier (eds), *Developments in European Politics* (Basingstoke: Palgrave Macmillan).

Keating, Michael and Hooghe, Liesbet (1996) 'By-passing the Nation State? Regions and the EU Policy Process', in Jeremy Richardson (ed.), *European Union: Power and Policy Making* (London: Routledge), pp. 216–29.

Keating, Michael, Loughlin, John and Deschouwer, Kris (2005) *Culture, Institutions and Economic Development* (Aldershot: Edward Elgar).

Keating, Michael and Wilson, Alex (2009) 'Renegotiating the State of Autonomies: Statute Reform and Multi-level Politics in Spain', *West European Politics*, 32(3), pp. 536–558.

Kelemen (2011) *Eurolegalism: The Transformation of Law and Regulation in the European Union* (Cambridge, MA: Harvard University Press).

Kelemen, R. Daniel and Schmidt, Suzanne (eds.) (2012) *Perpetual Momentum? Reconsidering the Power of the European Court of Justice*, special issue of the *Journal of European Public Policy*, 19 (1).

Kelley, Judith (2004) 'International Actors on the Domestic Scene: Membership Conditionality and Socialization by International Institutions', *International Organization, 58*, pp. 425–57.

Keman, Hans (2002a) 'The Low Countries: Confrontation and Coalition in Segmented Societies', in Josep M. Colomer (ed.), *Political Institutions in Europe* (London: Routledge).

Keman, Hans (2002b) *Comparative Democratic Politics* (Oxford: Oxford University Press).

Keman, Hans (2003) 'Explaining Miracles: Third Ways and Work and Welfare', *West European Politics*, 26(2), pp. 115–35.

Keman, Hans (2010) 'Fading Away of State Support to the Economy? A Comparative Analysis of the OECD World (1980–2002)', *Comparative European Politics*, 8, pp. 281–303.

Keman, Hans (2011) 'Third Ways and Social Democracy: The Right Way to Go?', *British Journal of Political Science*, 41(3), pp. 671–680.

Kemmerling, Achim (2010) 'Does Europeanization Lead to Policy Convergence? The Role of the Single Market in Shaping National Tax Policies', *Journal of European Public Policy*, 17(7), pp. 1058–1073.

Kenig, Ofer (2009) Democratization of Party Leadership Selection: Do Wider Selectorates Produce More Competitive Contests?', *Electoral Studies*, 28(2), pp. 240–247.

Kenworthy, Lane (2004) *Egalitarian Capitalism: Jobs, Incomes and Growth in Affluent Countries* (New York: Russell Sage Foundation).

Kenworthy, Lane and Pontusson, Jonas (2005) 'Rising Inequality and the Politics of Redistribution in Affluent Countries', *Perspectives on Politics*, 3(3), pp. 449–71.

Kepplinger, Hans Mathias (2007) 'Reciprocal Effects: Towards a Theory of Mass Media Effects on Decision Makers', *Harvard Journal of Press/Politics*, 12(2), pp. 3–23.

Ker-Lindsay, James (2006) 'Presidential Power and Authority in the Republic of Cyprus', *Mediterranean Politics*, 11(1), pp. 21–37.

Ker-Lindsay, James (2011) *Kosovo: The Path to Contested Statehood in the Balkans* (London: IB Tauris).

Kersting, Norbert, Caulfield, Janice, Nickson, R. Andrew, Olowu), Dele, and Wollmann, Hellmut (2009) *Local Governance Reform in Global Perspective* (Wiesbaden: VS Verlag Für Sozialwisseenchaften).

Keune, Maarten (2006) 'The European Social Model and Enlargement', in M. Jepsen and A. Serrano (eds), *Unwrapping the European Social Model* (Bristol: Policy Press).

Kim, HeeMin, Powell, G. Bingham, Fording, Richard C. (2010) 'Electoral Systems, Party Systems, and Ideological Representation: An Analysis of Distortion in Western Democracies', *Comparative Politics*, 42(2), pp. 167–185.

King, Anthony (1975) 'Overload: Problems of Governing in the 1970s', *Political Studies*, 23(2–3), pp. 284–96.

King, Anthony (1976) 'Modes of Executive–Legislative Relations: Great Britain, France and West Germany', *Legislative Studies Quarterly*, 1(1), pp. 11–36.

King, Anthony (1994) '"Chief Executives" in Western Europe', in Ian Budge and David McKay (eds), *Developing Democracy: Comparative Research in Honour of J.F.P. Blondel* (London: Sage).

King, Anthony (ed.) (2002) *Leaders' Personalities and the Outcomes of Democratic Elections* (Oxford: Oxford University Press).

King, Anthony (2009) *The British Constitution* (Oxford: Oxford University Press).

Kirchheimer, Otto (1966) 'The Transformation of the Western European Party System', in Joseph La Palombara and Myrah Weiner (eds), *Political Parties and Political Development* (Princeton, NJ: Princeton University Press).

Kirchner, Emil J. and Sperling, James (2007) *EU Security Governance* (Manchester: Manchester University Press).

Kitschelt, Herbert (1994) *The Transformation of European Social Democracy* (Cambridge: Cambridge University Press).

Kitschelt, Herbert (2000) 'Citizens, Politicians, and Party Cartellization: Political Representation and State Failure in Post Industrial Democracies', *European Journal of Political Research*, 37, pp. 149–79.

Kittel, Bernhard and Obinger, Herbert (2003) 'Political Parties, Institutions, and the Dynamics of Social Expenditure in Times of Austerity', *Journal of European Public Policy*, 10(1), pp. 20–45.

Kittilson, Miki Caul (2006) *Challenging Parties, Changing Parliaments: Women and Elected Office in Contemporary Western Europe* (Columbus: Ohio State University Press).

Kittilson, Miki Caul (2011) 'Women, Parties and Platforms in Post-industrial Democracies, *Party Politics*, 17(1), pp. 66–92.

Klausen, Jytte (2005) *The Islamic Challenge: Politics and Religion in Western Europe* (Oxford: Oxford University Press).

Kleinnijenhuis, Jan, Maurer, Marcus, Kepplinger, Hans Mathias and Oegema, Dirk (2001) 'Issues and Personalities in German and Dutch Television News: Patterns and Effects', *European Journal of Communication*, 16(3), pp. 337–59.

Kleis Nielsen, Rasmus with Linnebank, Geert (2011) *Public Support for the Media: A Six-Country Overview of Direct and Indirect Subsidies* (Oxford: Reuters Institute), available online at http://reutersinstitute.politics.ox.ac.uk/fileadmin/documents/Publications/Working_Papers/Public_support_for_Media.pdf.

Klich, Jacek (1998) 'The Concept of Mass Privatization in Poland: Theoretical and Practical Considerations', in Demetrius S. Iatridis and June Gary Hopps (eds), *Privatization in Central and Eastern Europe: Perspectives and Approaches* (London: Praeger).

Klimlkiewicz, Beata (2009) 'Is the Clash of Realities Leading Nowhere? Media Pluralism in European Regulatory Policies', in Andrea Czepek, Melanie Hellwig and Eva Nowak (eds.) *Press Freedom and Pluralism in Europe: Concepts and Conditions* (Bristol: Intellect).

Klingemann, Hans-Dieter (ed.) (2009) *The Comparative Study of Electoral Systems* (Oxford: Oxford University Press).

Klitgaard, Michael B. (2007) 'Why are They Doing It? Social Democracy and Market-Oriented Welfare State Reforms', *West European Politics*, 30(1), pp. 172–94.

Klüver, Heike (2011) 'The Contextual Nature of Lobbying: Explaining Lobbying Success in the European Union', *European Union Politics*, 12(4), pp. 483–506.

Knill, Christoph and Liefferink, Duncan (2007) *Environmental Politics in the European Union: Policy making, Implementation and Patterns of Multi-level Governance* (Manchester: Manchester University Press).

Knill, Christoph and Tosun, Jale (2009) 'Hierarchy, Networks, or Markets: How Does the EU Shape Environmental Policy Adoptions Within and Beyond Its Borders?', *Journal of European Public Policy*, 16(6), pp. 873–894.

Knill, Christoph, Debus, Marc and Heichel, Stephan (2010) Do Parties Matter in Internationalised Policy Areas? The Impact of Political Parties on Environmental Policy Outputs in 18 OECD Countries, 1970–2000', *European Journal of Political Research*, 49, pp. 301–336.

Knutelská, Viera (2011) 'Working Practices Winning Out over Formal Rules: Parliamentary Scrutiny of EU Matters in the Czech Republic, Poland and Slovakia', *Perspectives on European Politics and Society*, 13(3), 320–339.

Knutsen, Oddbjørn (2004) 'Religious Denomination and Party Choice in Western Europe: A Comparative Longitudinal Study from Eight Countries, 1970–97', *International Political Science Review*, 25(1), pp. 97–128.

Knutsen, Oddbjørn (2005) 'The Impact of Sector Employment on Party Choice: A Comparative Study of Eight West European Countries', *European Journal of Political Research*, 44(4), pp. 593–621.

Knutsen, Oddbjørn (2006) *Class Voting in Western Europe: A Comparative Longitudinal Study* (Lanham: Lexington Books).

Knutsen, Oddbjørn (2010) 'The Regional Cleavage in Western Europe: Can Social Composition, Value Orientations and Territorial Identities Explain the Impact of Region on Party Choice?', *West European Politics*, 33(3), pp. 553–585.

Knutsen, Oddbjørn and Scarbrough, Elinor (1995), 'Cleavage Politics', in Jan W. van Deth and Elinor Scarbrough (eds), *The Impact of Values* (Oxford: Oxford University Press).

Koole, Karin and Vis, Barbara (2012) 'Working Mothers and the State: Under Which Conditions do Governments Spend Much on Maternal Employment Supporting Policies?', COMPASSS WP Series 2012–71, available online at http://www.compasss.org/wpseries/KooleVis2012.pdf).

Koopmans, Ruud (2004) 'Integrated Report: Cross-National, Cross-Issue, Cross-Time', Project report for the EU-funded project *The Transformation of Political Mobilisation and Communication in European Public Spheres*, available at http://europub.wz-berlin.de/project%20reports.en.htm.

Koopmans, Ruud and Erbe, Jessica (2004) 'Towards a European Public Sphere', *Innovation: The European Journal of Social Sciences*, 17(2), pp. 97–118.

Koopmans, Ruud and Statham, Paul (eds) (2009) *Challenging Immigration and Ethnic Relations Politics: Comparative European Perspectives* (Oxford: Oxford University Press).

Kopecký, Petr (2007) 'Structures of Representation', in Stephen White, Paul G. Lewis and Judy Batt (eds) *Developments in Central and East European Politics* (Basingstoke: Palgrave Macmillan).

Kopecký, Petr and Mudde, Cas (2002) *Uncivil Society: Contentious Politics in Post-communist Europe* (London: Routledge).

Kopecký, Petr, Mair, Peter and Spirova, Maria (2012) *Party Patronage and Party Government in European Democracies* (Oxford: Oxford University Press).

Korkut, Ulmut, Bucken-Knapp, Gregg, Hinnfors, Jonas, McGarry, Aidan and Drake, Helen (eds) (2013) *The Discourses and Politics of Migration in Europe* (New York: Palgrave/NYU).

Korpi, Walter and Palme, Joakim (2003) 'New Politics and Class Politics in the Context of Austerity and Globalization: Welfare State Regress in 18 Countries, 1975–95', *American Political Science Review*, 97(3), pp. 425–46.

Koß, Michael (2010) *The Politics of Party Funding: State Funding to Political Parties and Party Competition in Western Europe* (Oxford: Oxford University Press).

Kostadinova, Tatiana (2003) 'Voter Turnout Dynamics in Post-communist Europe', *European Journal of Political Research*, 42(6), pp. 741–60.

Krašovec, Alenka and Haughton, Tim (2011) 'Money, Organization and the State: the Partial Cartelization of Party Politics in Slovenia', *Communist and Post-Communist Studies, Communist and Post-Communist Studies*, 44(3), pp. 199–209.

Kreuzer, Marcus (2010) 'Historical Knowledge and Quantitative Analysis: The Case of the Origins of Proportional Representation', *American Political Science Review*, 104(2), pp. 369–392.

Kriesi, Hanspeter (1998) 'The Transformation of Cleavage Politics', *European Journal of Political Research*, 33, pp. 165–85.

Kriesi, Hanspeter (2007) 'The Role of European Integration in National Election Campaigns', *European Union Politics*, 8(1), pp. 83–108.

Kriesi, Hanspeter (2012) Personalization of National Election Campaigns, *Party Politics*, 18(6), pp. 825–844.

Kriesi, Hanspeter, Armingeon, Klaus, Siegrist, Hannes and Wimmer, Andreas (eds) (2003) *Nation and National Identity: The European Experience in Perspective* (West Lafayette: Purdue University Press).

Kriesi, Hanspeter, Grande, Edgar, Lachat, Romain, Dolezal, Martin, Bornschier, Simon and Frey, Timotheos (2008) *West European Politics in the Age of Globalization* (Cambridge: Cambridge University Press).

Kriesi, Hanspeter, Koopmans, Ruud, Duyvendak, Jan Willem and Giugni, Marco G. (1995) *New Social Movements in Western Europe: A Comparative Analysis* (London: UCL Press).

Kriesi, Hanspeter and Trechsel, Alexander H. (2008) *The Politics of Switzerland: Continuity and Change in a Consensus Democracy* (Cambridge: Cambridge University Press).

Kriesi, Hanspeter, Tresch, Anke, and Jochum, Margit (2007) 'Going Public in the European Union: Action Repertoires of Western European Collective Political Actors', *Comparative Political Studies*, 40(1), pp. 48–73.

Krönig, Jürgen (2006) 'Hotting it up', in John Lloyd and Jean Seaton (eds), *What Can be Done? Making the Media and Politics Better* (Oxford: Oxford Blackwell).

Krook, Mona Lena (2009) *Quotas for Women and Politics. Gender and Candidate Selection Reform Worldwide* (New York: Oxford University Press).

Krook, Mona Lena and Mackay, Fiona (eds) (2010) *Gender, Politics and Institutions: Towards a Feminist Institutionalism* (Basingstoke: Palgrave Macmillan).

Krook, Mona Lena and O'Brien, Diana Z. (2012) 'All the President's Men? The Appointment of Female Cabinet Ministers Worldwide', *Journal of Politics*, 74(3), pp. 840–855.

Krouwel, André (2006) 'Party Models', in Richard Katz and William Crotty (eds) (2006) *Handbook of Party Politics* (London: Sage).

Krouwel, André (2012) *Party Transformations in European Democracies* (Albany: SUNY Press).

Kselman, Thomas and Buttigieg, Joseph A. (eds) (2003) *European Christian Democracy: Historical Legacies and Comparative Perspectives* (Notre Dame: University of Notre Dame Press).

Kuhlmann, S. (2009) 'Reforming Local Government in Germany: Institutional Changes and Performance Impacts', *German Politics*, 18(2), 226–245.

Kuhn, Raymond (2004a) '"Les médias, c'est moi." President Sarkozy and News Media Management', *French Politics*, 8, pp. 355–376.

Kuhn, Raymond (2004b) '"Vive la difference"? The Mediation of Politicians' Public Images and Private Lives in France', *Parliamentary Affairs*, 57(1), pp. 24–40.

Külachi, Erol (2012) *Europeanisation and Party Politics: How the EU Affects Domestic Actors, Patterns and Systems* (Colchester: ECPR Press).

Kurowska, Xymena and Breuer, Fabian (2011) *Explaining the EU's Common Security and Defence Policy: Theory in Action* (Basingstoke: Palgrave Macmillan).

Kurzer, Paulette (2001) *Markets and Moral Regulation: Cultural Change in the European Union* (Cambridge: Cambridge University Press).

Kvist, Jon and Greve, Bent (2011) 'Has the Nordic Welfare Model Been Transformed?', *Social Policy and Administration*, 45(2), pp. 146–160.

L

Laatikainen, Katie and Smith, Karen E. (2006) *The European Union at the United Nations* (Basingstoke; Palgrave Macmillan).

Ladrech, Robert (2002) 'Europeanization and Political Parties: Towards a Framework for Analysis', *Party Politics*, 8(4), pp. 389–403.

Ladrech, Robert (2010) *Europeanization and National Politics* (Basingstoke: Palgrave Macmillan).

Lagadec, Erwan (2012), *Transatlantic Relations in the 21st Century: Europe, America and the Rise of the Rest* (Abingdon: Routledge).

Lahav, Gallya (2004) *Immigration and Politics in the New Europe: Reinventing Borders* (Cambridge: Cambridge University Press).

Lahusen, Christian (2004) 'Joining the Cocktail Circuit: Social Movement Organizations at the European Union', *Mobilization*, 9(1), pp. 55–71.

Laitin, David D. (2002) 'Culture and National Identity: "The East" and European Integration', *West European Politics*, 25(2), pp. 55–80.

Landtsheera, Christ'l De, De Vries, Philippe and Vertessen, Dieter (2008) 'Political Impression Management: How Metaphors, Sound Bites, Appearance Effectiveness, and Personality Traits Can Win Elections', *Journal of Political Marketing*, 7(3–4), pp. 217–238.

Langer, Ana Ines (2012) *The Personalisation of Politics in the UK: Mediated Leadership from Attlee to Cameron* (Manchester: Manchester University Press).

Lanzieri, Giampolo (2011) *The Greying of the Baby Boomers: a Century Long Review of Ageing in European Populations* (Eurostat: Statistics in Focus 23/2011).

Laqueur, Walter (2012) *After the Fall* (Thomas Dunne).

Larsson, Torbjörn and Bäck, Henry (2008) *Governing and Governance in Sweden* (Lund: Studentlitteratur).

Lavenex, Sandra and Kunz, Rahel (2008): 'The Migratio-Development Nexus in EU External Relations', *Journal of European Integration*, 30(3), pp.439–457.

Lavenex, Sandra and Schimmelfennig, Frank (eds) (2011) 'EU Democracy Promotion in the Neighbourhood: From Leverage to Governance?', special issue of *Democratization*, 18(4), pp. 885–1054.

Lawson, Kay (ed.) (2010) *Political Parties and Democracy Volume Two: Europe* (New York: Praeger).

Lawson, Kay and Merkl, Peter (2007) *When Political Parties Prosper: The Uses of Electoral Success* (Boulder: Lynne Rienner).

Leconte, Cécile (2010) *Understanding Euroscepticism* (Basingstoke: Palgrave Macmillan).

LeDuc, Lawrence (2003) *The Politics of Direct Democracy: Referendums in Global Perspective* (Toronto: Broadview Press).

Lees-Marshment, Jennifer, Rudd, Chris and Strömbäck, Jesper (2011) *Global Political Marketing* (Abingdon: Routledge).

Leiken, Robert S. (2012) *Europe's Angry Muslims* (New York: Oxford University Press).

Lelieveldt, Herman and Caiani, Manuela (2007) 'The Political Role of Associations', in William A. Maloney and Sigrid Roßteutscher (eds), *Social Capital and Associations in European Democracies: A Comparative Analysis* (London: Routledge).

Levy, Mark R. (1981) 'Disdaining the News', *Journal of Communication*, 31(3), pp. 24–31.

Lewanski, Rudolf (1999) 'Italian Administration in Transition', *South European Society and Politics*, 4(1), pp. 97–131.

Lewanski, Rudolf (2000) 'The Development and Current Features of the Italian Civil Service System', in Hans A.G.M. Bekke and Frits M. van der Meer (eds), *Civil Service Systems in Western Europe* (Aldershot: Edward Elgar).

Lewis, Jeffrey (2009) 'EU Policy on Iraq: The Collapse and Reconstruction of Consensus-Based Foreign Policy', *International Politics*, 46, pp. 432–450.

Lewis, Paul G. and Mansfeldova, Zdenka (eds) (2007) *The European Union and Party Politics in Central and Eastern Europe* (Basingstoke: Palgrave Macmillan).

Lewis, Paul G. and Batt, Judy (eds) (2013) *Developments in Central and East European Politics 5* (Basingstoke: Palgrave Macmillan).

Leyenaar, Monique and Hazan, Reuven Y. (eds) (2011) 'Understanding Electoral Reform', special issue of *West European Politics*, 34(3), pp. 437–663.

Liégeois, Jean-Pierre (2007) *Roma in Europe* (Strasbourg: Council of Europe), also available at http://book.coe.int/sysmodules/RBS_fichier/admin/download.php?fileid=3017

Lightfoot, Simon (2005) *Europeanizing Social Democracy? The Rise of the Party of European Socialists* (London: Routledge).

Lijphart, Arend (1999) *Patterns of Democracy: Government Forms and Performance in Thirty-six Countries* (New Haven, CT: Yale University Press).

Lindberg, Björn, Rasmussen, Anne and Wantjen, Andreas (eds) (2008) 'The Role of Political Parties in the European Union', special issue of the *Journal of European Public Policy*, 15(8), 2008, pp. 1107–1265.

Lindblom, Charles (1977) *Politics and Markets* (New York: Basic Books).

Lindbom, Anders (2008) 'The Swedish Conservative Party and the Welfare State: Institutional Change and Adapting Preferences', *Government and Opposition*, 43(4), pp. 539–560.

Linder, Wolf (2010) *Swiss Democracy: Possible Solutions to Conflict in Multicultural Societies* (Basingstoke: Palgrave Macmillan).

Lipset, Seymour Martin and Rokkan, Stein (1967) 'Cleavage Structures, Party Systems and Voter Alignments: An Introduction', in Seymour Martin Lipset and Stein Rokkan (eds), *Party Systems and Voter Alignments: Cross-National Perspectives* (New York: Free Press).

Lipsmeyer, Christine S. and Pierce, Heather Nicole (2011) 'The Eyes that Bind: Junior Ministers as Oversight Mechanisms in Coalition Governments', *Journal of Politics*, 73(4), pp. 1152–1164.

Lloyd, John (2004) *What the Media are Doing to Our Politics* (London: Constable).

Lloyd, John (2005) 'The Epiphany of Joe Trippi', *Political Quarterly*, 76, pp. 33–45.

Lolle, Henrik and Torpe, Lars (2011), 'Growing ethnic diversity and social trust in European societies', *Comparative European Politics*, 9, pp. 191–216.

Lord, Christopher (2004) *A Democratic Audit of the European Union* (Basingstoke: Palgrave Macmillan).

Loughlin, John, Hendriks, Frank, and Lidström, Anders (eds.) (2011) *The Oxford Handbook of Local and Regional Democracy in Europe* (Oxford: Oxford University Press).

Louw, Eric (2005) *The Media and Political Process* (London: Sage).

Lubbers, Marcel, Gijsberts, Merove and Scheepers, Peer (2002) 'Extreme Right-wing Voting in Europe', *European Journal of Political Research*, 41(3), pp. 345–78.

Lucarelli, Sonia and Fioramonti, Lorenzo (eds) (2011) *External Perceptions of the European Union as a Global Actor* (Abingdon: Routledge).

Lucassen Geertje and Lubbers, Marcel (2012) 'Who Fears What? Explaining Far-Right-Wing Preference in Europe by Distinguishing Perceived Cultural and Economic Ethnic Threats', *Comparative Political Studies*, 45(5), 547–574.

Lucassen, L. (2006) *The Immigrant Threat: the Integration of Old and New Migrants in Western Europe since 1850* (Chicago: University of Illinois Press).

Lukowski, Jerzy and Zawadzki, Hubert (2006) *A Concise History of Poland* (Cambridge: Cambridge University Press).

Lundell, Krister (2004) 'Determinants of Candidate Selection: The Degree of Centralization in Comparative Perspective', *Party Politics*, 10(1), pp. 25–47.

Lundestad, Geir (1998a) *Empire by Integration: The United States and European Integration, 1945–1997* (Oxford: Oxford University Press).

Lundestad, Geir (1998b) *No End to Alliance. The United States and Western Europe: Past, Present and Future* (Basingstoke: Palgrave Macmillan).

Luther, Kurt Richard (2003) 'The Self-Destruction of a Right-Wing Populist Party? The Austrian Parliamentary Election of 2002', *West European Politics*, 26(3), pp. 91–130.

Luther, Kurt Richard and Müller-Rommel, Ferdinand (eds) (2002) *Political Parties in the New Europe: Political and Analytical Challenges* (Oxford: Oxford University Press).

M

MAC (2012) Analysis of the Impacts of Migration (London: UKBA), available online at http://www.ukba.homeoffice.gov.uk/aboutus/workingwithus/indbodies/mac/reports-publications/

Machill, Marcel, Beiler, Markus and Fischer, Corinna (2006) 'Europe-Topics in Europe's Media. The Debate about the European Public Sphere: A Meta-Analysis of Media Content Analyses', *European Journal of Communication*, 21(1), pp. 57–88.

MacInnes, John (2006) 'Work–Life Balance in Europe: A Response to the Baby Bust or Reward for the Baby Boomers?', *European Societies*, 8(2), pp. 223–49.

Madeley, John T.S. (2011) 'Religion Related Issues in European Politics and Law', in Erik Jones, Heywood, Paul M, Martin Rhodes and Ulrich Sedelmeier (eds), *Developments in European Politics Two* (Basingstoke: Palgrave Macmillan).

Magone, José M. (2008) *Contemporary Spanish Politics* (London: Routledge).

Mahler, Vincent A. (2004) 'Economic Globalization, Domestic Politics, and Income Inequality in the Developed Countries: A Cross-National Study', *Comparative Politics*, 37(9), pp. 1025–53.

Mainwaring, Scott and Zoco, Edurne (2007) 'Political Sequences and the Stabilization of Interparty Competition Electoral Volatility in Old and New Democracies', *Party Politics*, 13(2), pp. 155–78.

Mair, Peter (1996) 'Party Systems and Structures of Competition', in Lawrence le Dine, Richard G. Niemi and Pippa Norris (eds), *Comparing Democracies: Elections and Voting in Comparative Perspective* (London: Sage).

Mair, Peter (2000) 'The Limited Impact of Europe on National Party Systems', *West European Politics*, 23 (4), pp. 27–51.

Mair, Peter (2001) 'The Green Challenge and Political Competition: How Typical is the German Experience?', *German Politics*, 10(2), pp. 99–116.

Mair, Peter (2006a) 'Political Parties and Party Systems', in Paolo Graziano and Maarten Vink, (eds), *Europeanization: New Research Agendas* (Basingstoke: Palgrave Macmillan).

Mair, Peter (2006b) 'Ruling the Void: The Hollowing of Western Democracy', *New Left Review*, 42, pp. 25–52.

Mair, Peter and Mudde, Cas (1998) 'The Party Family and its Study', *Annual Review of Political Science*, 1, pp. 211–29.

Mair, Peter, Müller, Wolfgang and Plasser, Fritz (eds) (2004) *Political Parties and Electoral Change* (London: Sage).

Majone, Giandomenico (1996) *Regulating Europe* (London: Routledge).

Malgin, Artem (2002) 'The Commonwealth of Independent States: Summary of a Decade', *Russian Politics and Law*, 40(5), pp. 43–54.

Maloney, William A. and Roßteutscher, Sigrid (eds) (2007a) *Social Capital and Associations in European Democracies: A Comparative Analysis* (London: Routledge).

Maloney, William A. and Roßteutscher, Sigrid (2007b) 'Associations, Participation and Democracy', in William A. Maloney and Sigrid Roßteutscher (eds), *Social Capital and Associations in European Democracies: A Comparative Analysis* (London: Routledge).

Mancini, Paolo (2011) *Between Commodification and Lifestyle Politics: Does Silvio Berlusconi provide a New Model of Politics for the Twenty-First Century?* (Oxford: Reuters Institute).

Manners, Ian and Whitman, Richard G. (eds) (2000) *The Foreign Policies of European Union Member States* (Manchester: Manchester University Press).

Mansergh, Lucy and Thomson, Robert (2007) 'Election Pledges, Party Competition and Policymaking', *Comparative Politics* 39(3), pp. 311–30.

Mansfeldová, Zdenka (2011) 'Central European Parliaments over Two Decades – Diminishing Stability? Parliaments in Czech Republic, Hungary, Poland, and Slovenia', *Journal of Legislative Studies*, 17(2), 128–146.

March, Luke (2011) *Radical Left Parties in Europe* (Abingdon: Routledge).

Mareš, Miroslav (2011) 'Czech Extreme Right Parties: An Unsuccessful Story', *Communist and Post-Communist Studies*, 44(4), pp. 283–298.

Marien, Sofie, Hooghe, Marc, and Quintelier, Ellen. (2010) 'Inequalities in Non institutionalised Forms of Political Participation: A Multi level Analysis of 25 countries', *Political Studies*, 58(1), pp. 187–213.

Markovits, Andrei (2005) *European Anti-Americanism and Anti-Semitism in a Changing Transatlantic Relationship* (Princeton, NJ: Princeton University Press).

Marks, Gary and Steenbergen, Marco R. (eds) (2004) *European Integration and Political Conflict* (Cambridge: Cambridge University Press).

Marquand, David (2011) *The End of the West. The Once and Future Europe* (Princeton, NJ: Princeton University Press).

Marsh, Michael (2007) 'Candidates or Parties? Objects of Electoral Choice in Ireland', *Party Politics*, 13(4), pp. 500–27.

Martell, Luke (2001) 'Capitalism, Globalization and Democracy: Does Social Democracy have a Role?', in Luke Martell (ed.), *Social Democracy: Global and National Perspectives* (Basingstoke: Palgrave Macmillan).

Martell, Luke (2010) *The Sociology of Globalization* (Cambridge: Polity Press).

Martens, Maria (2008) 'Runaway Bureaucracy? Exploring the Role of Nordic Regulatory Agencies in the European Union', *Scandinavian Political Studies*, 31(1), pp. 27–43.

Marthaler, Sally (2008) 'Nicolas Sarkozy and the Politics of French Immigration Policy', *Journal of European Public Policy*, 15(3).

Martin, Lanny W. and Stevenson, Randolph T. (2010) 'The Conditional Impact of Incumbency on Government Formation', *American Political Science Review*, 104(3), pp. 503–18.

Martin, Lanny W. and Vanberg Georg (2011) *Parliaments and Coalitions: the Role of Legislative Institutions in Multiparty Governance* (Oxford: Oxford University Press).

Martin, Shane (2008) 'Two Houses: Legislative Studies and the Atlantic Divide', *PS: Political Science & Politics*, 41(3), pp 557–565.

Martin, Shane (ed.) (2011) *Parliamentary Questions*, special issue of the *Journal of Legislative Studies*, 17(3).

Martinez-Herrera, Enric and Miley, Thomas Jeffrey (2010) 'The Constitution and the Politics of National Identity in Spain', *Nations and Nationalism*, 16(1), pp. 6–30.

Martinsen, Dorte Sindbjerg (2011) 'Judicial policy-making and Europeanization: The Proportionality of National Control and Administrative Discretion', *Journal of European Public Policy*, 18(7), pp. 944–961.

Marx, Paul and Schumacher, Gijs (2013) 'Will to Power? Intra-Party Conflict in Social Democratic Parties and the Choice for Neoliberal Policies in Germany, the Netherlands and Spain', *European Political Science Review*,

Marziali, Valeria (2009) 'Lobbying in the EU: Between Strengthening Legitimacy and Increasing Transparency', in Conor McGrath (ed) *Interest Groups and Lobbying in Europe* (Lampeter: Edwin Mellen Press).

Massetti, Emanuele (2006) 'Electoral Reform in Italy: From PR to Mixed System and (Almost) Back Again', *Representation*, 42(3), pp. 261–9.

Mateju, P. and Vlachová, K. (1998) 'Values and Electoral Decisions in the Czech Republic', *Communist and Post-Communist Studies*, 31(3), pp. 249–69.

Mateo-Diaz, Mercedes (2005) *Representing Women? Female Legislators in West European Parliaments* (Colchester: ECPR Press).

Matland, Richard E. and Studlar, Donley T. (2004) 'Determinants of Legislative Turnover: A Cross-National Analysis', *British Journal of Political Science*, 34, pp. 87–108.

Mattson, Ingvar and Strøm, Kaare (2004) 'Committee Effects on Legislation', in Herbert Döring and Mark Hallerberg (eds), *Patterns of Parliamentary Behaviour* (Aldershot: Ashgate).

Mau, Steffen and Burkhardt, Christoph (2009) 'Migration and Welfare State Solidarity in Western Europe', *Journal of European Social Policy*, 19(3), pp. 213–229.

Mau, Steffen and Verwiebe, Roland (2010) *European Societies: Mapping Structure and Change* (Bristol: Policy Press).

Maull, Hanns, W. (ed.) (2006) *Germany's Uncertain Power: Foreign Policy of the Berlin Republic* (Basingstoke: Palgrave Macmillan).

Maurer, Andreas, Mittag, Jürgen and Wessels, Wolfgang (2003) 'National Systems' Adaptation to the EU System: Trends, Offers, and Constraints', in Beate Kohler-Koch (ed.), *Linking EU and National Governance* (Oxford: Oxford University Press).

Mayhew, Alan, Oppermann, Kai and Hough, Dan (2011) *German foreign policy and leadership of the EU – 'You can't always get what you want ... but you sometimes get what you need*', Sussex European Institute Working Paper, 119.

Mazower, Mark (2008) *Dark Continent: Europe's Twentieth Century* (Harmondsworth: Penguin).

Mazzoleni, Gianpietro (1987) 'Media Logic and Parry Logic in Campaign Coverage: The Italian General Election of 1983', *European Journal of Communication*, 2(1), pp. 81–103.

Mazzoleni, Gianpietro, Stewart, Julianne and Horsfield, Bruce (eds) (2003) *The Media and Neo Populism: A Contemporary Comparative Analysis* (London: Praeger).

McAdam, Doug, McCarthy, John D. and Zald, Mayer N. (eds) (1996) *Comparative Perspectives on Social Movements: Political Opportunities, Mobilizing Structures, and Cultural Framings* (New York: Cambridge University Press).

McAllister, Ian and White, Stephen (2007) 'Political Parties and Democratic Consolidation in Post-Communist Societies', *Party Politics*, 13(2), pp. 197–216.

McCarthy, John D. and Zald, Mayer N. (1977) 'Resource Mobilization and Social Movements: A Partial Theory', *American Journal of Sociology*, 8(6), pp. 1212–41.

McCormick, John (2006) *The European Superpower* (Basingstoke: Palgrave Macmillan).

McCormick, John (2007) *Contemporary Britain*, 2nd edn (Basingstoke: Palgrave Macmillan).

McCormick, John (2011) *Understanding the European Union*, 5th edn (Basingstoke: Palgrave Macmillan).

McDonald, Michael D., Budge, Ian and Best, Robin E. (2012) 'Electoral Majorities, Political Parties, and Collective Representation', *Comparative Political Studies*, 45 (9), pp. 1104–113

McGarry, Aidan (2010) *Who Speaks for Roma? Political Representation of a Transnational Minority Community* (New York: Continuum).

McGarry, John and Keating, Michael (eds) (2006) *European Integration and the Nationalities Question* (London: Routledge).

McGowan, Francis (2001) 'Social Democracy and the European Union: Who's Changing Whom?', in Luke Martell (ed.), *Social Democracy: Global and Local Perspectives* (Basingstoke: Palgrave Macmillan).

McLaren, Lauren (2012) 'Public Opinion on Immigration in Europe', in Gary P. Freeman, Randall Hansen and David L. Leal (eds) *Immigration and Public Opinion in Liberal Democracies* (Abingdon: Routledge).

McMenamin, Iain (2002) 'Polish Business Associations: Flattened Civil Society or Super Lobbies?', *Business and Politics*, 4, pp. 299–315.

McMenamin, Iain (2011) Liberal Market Economies, Business, and Political Finance: Britain under New Labour, *West European Politics*, 34(5), pp. 1021–1043.

McNair, Brian, Hibberd, Matthew and Schlesinger, Philip (2002) 'Public Access Broadcasting and Democratic Participation in the Age of Mediated Politics', *Journalism Review*, 3(3), pp. 407–22.

Mearscheimer, John J. (2010) 'Why is Europe Peaceful Today?', *European Political Science*, 9, pp. 387–97.

Meehan, Elizabeth (1993) 'Citizenship and the European Community', *Political Quarterly*, 64(2), pp. 172–86.

Meguid, Bonnie (2005) 'Competition between Unequals: The Role of Mainstream Party Strategy in Niche Party Success', *American Political Science Review*, 99(3), pp. 347–59.

Meier, Werner A. (2007) 'National and Transnational Media Ownership Concentration in Europe: a Burden for Democracy?', in Werner A. Meier and Josef Trappel (eds.) *Power, Performance and Politics* (Baden Baden: Nomos).

Meier, Werner A. (2011) 'From Media Regulation to Democratic Media Governance', in Trappel, Josef, Meier, Werner A., D'Haenens, Leen, Steemers, Jeanette, Thomass, Barbara (eds.) *Media in Europe Today* (Bristol: Intellect).

Men, Jing and Barton, Benjamin (eds) (2010) *China and the European Union in Africa* (Farnham: Ashgate).

Menon, Anand (2004) 'From Crisis to Catharsis: ESDP after Iraq', *International Affairs*, 80(4), pp. 631–49.

Menz, Georg (2009) *The Political Economy of Managed Migration: Nonstate Actors, Europeanization, and the Politics of Designing Migration Policies* (Oxford: Oxford University Press).

Menz, Georg (2011): Revisiting the Configurational Theory of Policy Concertation: Analysing the Renaissance of Concertation in Western Europe, *Perspectives on European Politics and Society*, 12(2), pp. 180–196.

Merkel, Wolfgang (1992) 'After the Golden Age', in Christian Lemke and Gary Marks (eds) *The Crisis of Socialism in Europe* (Durham, NC: Duke University Press).

Merkel, Wolfgang, Petring, Alexander, Henkes, Christian, and Engle, Christoph (2008) *Social Democracy in Power: The Capacity to Reform* (Abingdon: Routledge).

Merlingen, Michael and Ostrauskaite, Rasa (eds) (2010) *European Security and Defence Policy: An Implementation Perspective* (Abingdon: Routledge).

Messina, Anthony M. (2007) *The Logics and Politics of Post-WWII Migration to Western Europe* (Cambridge: Cambridge University Press).

Messmer, William B. (2003) 'Taming Labour's MEPs', *Party Politics*, 9(2), pp. 201–18.

Meunier, Sophie (2007) *Trading Voices: The European Union in International Commercial Negotiations* (Princeton, NJ: Princeton University Press).

Meunier, Sophie and McNamara, Kathleen R. (eds) (2007) *Making History: European Integration and Institutional Change at Fifty* (Oxford: Oxford University Press).

Meyer-Sahling, Jan-Hinrik (2011) 'The Durability of EU Civil Service Policy in Central and Eastern Europe after Accession', *Governance*, 24(2), pp. 231–260.

Michels, Robert (1962) *Political Parties: A Sociological Study of the Oligarchical Tendencies of Modern Democracy* (New York: Free Press), also available at http://religionanddemocracy.lib.virginia.edu/library/tocs/MichPoli.html.

Miley, Thomas Jeffrey (2007) 'Against the Thesis of the "Civic Nation": The Case of Catalonia in Contemporary Spain', *Nationalism and Ethnic Politics*, 13(1), pp. 1–37.

Millard, Frances (2004) *Elections, Parties and Representation in Post-Communist Europe* (Basingstoke: Palgrave Macmillan).

Milner, Henry (2002) *Civic Literacy: How Informed Citizens Make Democracy Work* (London: Tufts University Press).

Minkinberg, Michael (2002) 'The New Radical Right in the Political Process: Interaction Effects in France and Germany', in M. Schain, A. Zolberg and P. Hossay (eds), *Shadows Over Europe: The Development and Impact of the Extreme Right Wing in Western Europe* (Basingstoke: Palgrave Macmillan).

Minkenberg, Michael (2010) Party Politics, Religion and Elections in Western Democracies, *Comparative European Politics*, 8(4), pp. 385–414.

Minkenberg, Michael (2011) 'Church–State Regimes and Democracy in the West: Convergence vs. Divergence', paper delivered to the ECPR conference in Reykjavik, Iceland, Aug. 25–27, 2011, available online at http://www.ecprnet.eu/MyECPR/proposals/reykjavik/uploads/papers/872.pdf.

Miskimmon, Alister (2007) *Germany and the Common Foreign and Security Policy of the European Union: Between Europeanization and National Adaptation* (Basingstoke: Palgrave Macmillan).

Mitchell, Paul (2005) 'United Kingdom: Plurality Rule under Siege', in Michael Gallagher and Paul Mitchell (eds), *The Politics of Electoral Systems* (Oxford: Oxford University Press).

Molina, Oscar and Rhodes, Martin (2007) 'Industrial Relations and the Welfare State in Italy: Assessing the Potential of Negotiated Change', *West European Politics*, 30(4), pp. 803–829.

Monar, Jörg (2007) 'Common Threat and Common Response? The European Union's Counter-Terrorism Strategy and its Problems', *Government and Opposition*, 42(3), pp. 292–313.

Moore, Carolyn (2008a) 'A Europe of the Regions vs. the Regions in Europe: Reflections on Regional Engagement in Brussels', *Regional and Federal Studies*, 18(5), pp. 517–535.

Moore, Carolyn (2008b) 'Beyond Conditionality? Regions from the New EU Member States and their Activities in Brussels', *Comparative European Politics*, 6, pp. 212–234.

Morales, Laura and Geurts, Peter (2007) 'Associational Involvement', in Jan van Deth, José Ramón Montero and Anders Westholm (eds), *Citizenship and Involvement in European Democracies: A Comparative Analysis* (Abingdon: Routledge).

Morales, Laua and Giugni, Marco (eds) (2010) *Social Capital, Political Participation and Migration in Europe: Making Multicultural Democracy Work?* (Basingstoke: Palgrave Macmillan).

Moran, Michael (2005) *Politics and Governance in the UK* (Basingstoke: Palgrave Macmillan).

Moran, Michael, Rein, Martin and Goodin, Robert E. (2008) *The Oxford Handbook of Public Policy* (Oxford: Oxford University Press).

Motzkin, Gabriel and Fischer, Yochi (eds.) (2008) *Religion and Democracy in Contemporary Europe* (London: Alliance Publishing Trust).

Mrozowicki, Adam and van Hootegem, Geert (2008) 'Unionism and Workers' Strategies in Capitalist Transformation: the Polish Case Reconsidered', *European Journal of Industrial Relations*, 14(2), pp. 197–216.

Mudde, Cas (2004) 'The Populist Zeitgeist', *Government and Opposition*, 39(4), pp. 542–563.

Mudde, Cas (2007) *Populist Radical Right Parties in Europe* (Cambridge: Cambridge University Press).

Mudde, Cas (2013) 'Three Decades of Populist Radical Right Parties in Western Europe: So What?', *European Journal of Political Research*, 52(1), pp. 1–19.

Mudde, Cas and Rovira Kaltwasser, Cristóbal (2012) *Populism in Europe and the Americas: Threat or Corrective for Democracy?* (Cambridge: Cambridge University Press).

Mughan, Anthony (2000) *Media and the Presidentialization of Parliamentary Elections* (Basingstoke: Palgrave Macmillan).

Mughan, Anthony (2009) 'Partisan Dealignment, Party Attachments and Leader Effects', *Journal of Elections, Public Opinion and Parties*, 19(4), pp. 413–431.

Mullard, Maurice and Swaray, Raymond (2010) 'New Labour Legacy: Comparing the Labour Governments of Blair and Brown to Labour Governments since 1945', *Political Quarterly*, 81(4), pp. 511–521.

Murray, Rainbow (2007) 'How Parties Evaluate Compulsory Quotas: A Study of the Implementation of the "Parity" Law in France', *Parliamentary Affairs*, 60(4), pp. 568–84.

Murray, Rainbow (2010) *Parties, Gender Quotas and Candidate Selection in France* (Basingstoke: Palgrave).

Musu, Costanza (2010) *European Union Policy Towards The Arab–Israeli Peace Process: The Quicksands of Politics* (Basingstoke: Palgrave Macmillan).

Müftüler-Bac, Meltem (1997) *Turkey's Relations with a Changing Europe* (Manchester: Manchester University Press).

Müller, Patrick (2012) *EU Foreign Policymaking and the Middle East Conflict: the Europeanization of National Foreign Policy* (Abingdon: Routledge).

Müller, Wolfgang C. and Saalfield, Thomas (eds) (1997) *Members of Parliament in Western Europe: Roles and Behaviour* (London: Frank Cass).

Müller, Wolfgang C. and Strøm, K. (eds) (2000) *Coalition Governments in Western Europe* (Oxford: Oxford University Press).

Myntti, Kristian (2002) 'The Sami Cultural Autonomies in the Nordic Countries', in Kinga Gál (ed.), *Minority Governance in Europe* (Budapest: Local Government and Public Service Reform Initiative/Open Society Institute).

N

Nassmacher, Karl-Heinz (2009) *The Funding of Party Competition: Political Finance in 25 Democracies* (Baden-Baden: Nomos).

Naurin, Elin (2011) *Election Promises, Party Behaviour and Voter Perceptions* (Basingstoke: Palgrave Macmillan).

NEC Estonia (2012) http://www.vvk.ee/voting-methods-in-estonia/engindex/

Negrine, Ralph (1998) *Parliament and the Media: A Study of Britain, Germany and France* (London: Pinter).

Negrine, Ralph, Mancini, Paolo, Holtz-Bacha, Christina and Papathanassopoulos, Stylianos (eds.) (2007) *The Professionalisation of Political Communication* (Bristol: Intellect).

Neuhold, Christine and de Ruiter, Rik (2010) 'Out of REACH? Parliamentary Control of EU Affairs in the Netherlands and the UK', *Journal of Legislative Studies*, 16(1), pp. 57–7.

Neumann, Iver B. (1998) *Uses of the Other: 'The East' in European Identity Formation* (Minneapolis: University of Minnesota Press).

Neumayer, Eric (2004) 'Asylum Destination Choice. What Makes Some West European Countries More Attractive than Others?', *European Union Politics*, 5(2), pp. 155–80.

Neumayer, Eric (2005) 'Asylum Recognition Rates in Western Europe: Their Determinants, Variation, and Lack of Convergence', *Journal of Conflict Resolution*, 49(1), pp. 43–66.

Neunreither, Karlheinz (2005) 'The European Parliament and National Parliaments: Conflict or Cooperation?', *Journal of Legislative Studies*, 11(3–4), pp. 466–489.

Newell, James (2000) *Parties and Democracy in Italy* (Aldershot: Dartmouth).

Newell, James (2010) *The Politics of Italy: Governance in a Normal Country* (Cambridge: Cambridge University Press).

Newton, Kenneth (2006) 'May the Weak Force Be With You: The Power of the Mass Media in Modern Politics', *European Journal of Political Research*, 45, pp. 209–34.

Newton, Kenneth and Artingstall, Nigel (1994) 'Government and Private Censorship in Nine Western Democracies', in Ian Budge and David McKay (eds), *Developing Democracy: Comparative Research in Honour of J.F.P. Blondel* (London: Sage).

Newton, Kenneth and Brynin, Malcolm (2001) 'The National Press and Party Voting in the UK', *Political Studies*, 49(2), pp. 265–85.

Neyer, Jürgen and Wolf, Dieter (2003) 'Horizontal Enforcement in the EU: The BSE Crisis and the Case of State Aid Control', in Beate Kohler-Koch (ed.), *Linking EU and National Governance* (Oxford: Oxford University Press).

Nieuwbeerta, Paul and De Graaf, Nan Dirk (1999) 'Traditional Class Voting in 20 Postwar Societies', in Geoffrey Evans, *The End of Class Politics?: Class Voting in Comparative Context* (Oxford: Oxford University Press).

Nikolenyi, Csaba (2011) 'When Electoral Reform Fails: The Stability of Proportional Representation in Post-Communist Democracies', *West European Politics*, 34(3), pp. 607–625.

Nord, Lars (2006) 'Still the Middle Way: A Study of Political Communication Practices in Swedish Election Campaigns', *Harvard International Journal of Press/Politics*, 11(1), pp. 64–76.

Norris, Pippa (2000) *A Virtuous Circle: Political Communication in Postindustrial Societies* (Cambridge: Cambridge University Press).

Norris, Pippa (2001) *Digital Divide: Civic Engagement, Information Poverty and the Internet Worldwide* (Cambridge: Cambridge University Press).

Norris, Pippa (2002) *Democratic Phoenix: Reinventing Political Activism* (Cambridge: Cambridge University Press).

Norris, Pippa (2004a) 'Global Political Communication: Good Governance, Human Development, and Mass Communication', in Frank Esser and Barbara Pfetsch (eds), *Comparing Political Communication: Theories, Cases, and Challenges* (Cambridge University Press).

Norris, Pippa (2004b) *Electoral Engineering: Voting Rules and Political Behaviour* (Cambridge: Cambridge University Press.

Norris, Pippa (2005) *The Rise of the Radical Right* (Cambridge: Cambridge University Press).

Norris, Pippa (2006) 'Recruitment', in Richard Katz and William Crotty (eds) *Handbook of Party Politics* (London: Sage).

Norris, Pippa (2011a) *Democratic Deficit: Critical Citizens Revisited* (Cambridge: Cambridge University Press).

Norris, Pippa (2011b) 'Political Activism', in Erik Jones, Heywood, Paul M, Martin Rhodes and Ulrich Sedelmeier (eds), *Developments in European Politics Two* (Basingstoke: Palgrave Macmillan).

Norris, Pippa and Inglehart, Ronald (2011) *Sacred and Secular: Religion and Politics Worldwide, 2nd Edition* (Cambridge: Cambridge University Press).

Norris, Pippa and Inglehart, Ronald (2012) Muslim Integration into Western Cultures: Between Origins and Destinations', *Political Studies*, 60(2), pp. 228–251.

Norton, Philip (ed.) (1999) *Parliaments and Governments in Western Europe* (London: Frank Cass).

Núñez, Xosé-Manoel (2001) 'What is Spanish Nationalism Today? From Legitimacy Crisis to Unfulfilled Renovation (1975–2000)', *Ethnic and Racial Studies*, 24(5), pp. 719–52.

Nygård, Mikael (2006) 'Welfare-Ideological Change in Scandinavia: A Comparative Analysis of Partisan Welfare State Positions in Four Nordic Countries, 1970–2003', *Scandinavian Political Studies*, 29(4), pp. 356–85.

O

O'Brennan, John and Raunio, Tapio (eds) (2009) *National Parliaments within the Enlarged European Union: From 'Victims' of Integration to Competitive Actors?* (Abingdon: Routledge).

O'Donnell, R. (2001) 'Towards Post-corporatist Concertation in Europe', in Helen Wallace (ed.), *Interlocking Dimensions of European Integration* (London: Pinter).

O'Dwyer, Conor (2006) *Runaway State-Building: Patronage Politics and Democratic Development* (Baltimore: Johns Hopkins University Press).

O'Dwyer, Conor and Koval ik, Branislav (2007) 'And the Last Shall be First: Party System Institutionalization and Second Generation Economic Reform in Postcommunist Europe', *Studies in Comparative International Development*, 41(3), pp. 3–26.

O'Malley, Eoin (2010), 'Punch Bags for Heavyweights? Minor Parties in Irish Government', *Irish Political Studies*, 25(4), pp. 539–561.

Odmalm, Pontus (2011) 'Political Parties and "the Immigration Issue": Issue Ownership in Swedish Parliamentary Elections 1991–2010', *West European Politics*, 34(5), pp. 1070–91.

OECD (2007) DAC Peer Review of the European Community, 2007, available at http://www.oecd.orgiclataoecd/57/6/3896 5119.pdf.

OECD (2011) Communications Outlook, 2011, available at http://www.keepeek.com/Digital-Asset-Management/oecd/science-and-technology/oecd-communica-tions-outlook-2011-comms-outlook-2011-en.

OECD Better Life Index (2012) http://www.oecdbetterlifeindex. org.

Ofcom (2007) The Communications Market, http://www.ofcom.org.uk/research/cm/cmr07/

Ohmae, Kenichi (1996) *The End of the Nation State: The Rise of Regional Economies* (London: HarperCollins).

Olcott, Martha Brill, Åslund, Anders and Garnett, Sherman W. (2000) *Getting It Wrong: Regional Cooperation and the Commonwealth of Independent States* (Washington, DC: Carnegie Endowment for International Peace).

Olsen, Jonathan, Koß, Michael, Hough, Dan (2010) *Left Parties in National Governments* (Basingstoke: Palgrave).

Olson, David and Ilonszki, Gabriella (eds) (2011) 'Post-Communist Parliaments: Change and Stability in the Second Decade', special issue of the *Journal of Legislative Studies*, 17(2).

Olson, Mancur (1982) *The Rise and Decline of Nations: Economic Growth, Stagflation, and Social Rigidities* (New Haven, CT: Yale University Press).

Ongaro, Edoardo (2009) *Public Management Reform and Modernization: Trajectories of Administrative Change in Italy, France, Greece, Portugal and Spain* (Cheltenham: Edward Elgar).

Ongaro, Edoardo (2011) 'The Role of Politics and Institutions in the Italian Administrative Reform Trajectory', *Public Administration*, 89(3), pp. 738–755.

Ost, David (2009) 'The Consequences of Postcommunism: Trade Unions in Eastern Europe's Future', *East European Politics and Societies*, 23(1), pp. 13–33.

Ots, Mart (2009) 'Efficient Servants of Pluralism or Marginalized Media Policy Tools? The Case of Swedish Press Subsidies', *Journal of Communication Inquiry*, 33(4), pp. 376–392.

Outhwaite, William (2008) *European Society* (Cambridge: Polity).

P
_____

Pace, Michelle and Seeberg, Peter (ed). (2009) 'The European Union's Democratization Agenda in the Mediterranean: a Critical Inside-Out Approach', special issue of *Democratization*, 16(1).

Pacek, Alexander C., Grigore Pop-Eleches and Joshua A. Tucker (2007) 'Disenchanted or Discerning: Voter Turnout in Post-Communist Countries', Unpublished MS, available at http://homepages.nyu.edu/~jat7/Turnout_PPT_2006.pdf.

Padgett, Stephen (2000) *Organizing Democracy in Eastern Germany: Interest Groups in Post-Communist Society* (Cambridge: Cambridge University Press).

Pagden, Anthony (ed.) (2002) *The Idea of Europe: From Antiquity to the European Union* (Cambridge: Cambridge University Press).

Page, Edward C. and Wouters, Linda (1995) 'The Europeanisation of the National Bureaucracies', in Jon Pierre (ed.), *Bureaucracy in the Modern State: An Introduction to Comparative Public Administration* (Aldershot: Edward Elgar).

Page, Edward C. and Wright, Vincent (1999) *Bureaucratic Elites in Western European States: A Comparative Analysis of Top Officials* (Oxford: Oxford University Press).

Page, Edward and Wright, Vincent (eds) (2006) *From the Active to the Enabling State: The Changing Role of Top Officials in European Nations* (Basingstoke: Palgrave Macmillan).

Painter, Martin and Peters, B. Guy (eds.) (2010) *Tradition and Public Administration* (Basingstoke: Palgrave Macmillan).

Palier, Bruno (ed) (2010) *A Long Goodbye to Bismarck? The Politics of Welfare Reform in Continental Europe* (Amsterdam: Amsterdam University Press) available online at http://dare.uva.nl/document/183117.

Palmer, Jerry (2002) 'News Production: News Values', in Adam Briggs and Paul Cobley (eds), *The Media: An Introduction* (London: Longman).

Pan, Zhongqi (ed) (2012) *Conceptual Gaps in China–EU Relations: Global Governance, Human Rights and Strategic Partnerships* (Basingstoke: Palgrave Macmillan).

Panara, Carlo and De Becker, Alexander (eds.) (2010) *The Role of the Regions in EU Governance* (London: Springer).

Panayi, Panikos (1999) *An Ethnic History of Europe since 1945: Nations, States and Minorities* (London: Longman Pearson).

Panebianco, Angelo (1988) *Political Parties: Organisation and Power* (Cambridge: Cambridge University Press).

Pankowski, Rafal (2011) *The Populist Radical Right in Poland. The Patriots* (Abingdon: Routledge).

Papadopoulos, Yannis (2001) 'How Does Direct Democracy Matter? The Impact of Referendum Votes upon Politics and Policy making', *West European Politics*, 24(2), pp. 35–58.

Pardos-Prado, Sergi (2012) 'Valence Beyond Consensus: Party Competence and Policy Dispersion from a Comparative Perspective', *Electoral Studies*, 31 (2), pp. 342–352.

Parker, David (ed.) (1998) *Privatisation in the European Union: Theory and Policy Perspectives* (London: Routledge).

Parsons, Nick (2012) 'Legitimizing Illegal Protest: The Permissive Ideational Environment and 'Bossnappings' in France', *British Journal of Industrial Relations*, DOI: 10.1111/j.1467-8543.2012.00899.x.

Passarelli, Gianluca (2010) 'The Government in Two Semi-Presidential Systems: France and Portugal in a Comparative Perspective', *French Politics*, 8, pp.402–428.

Paterson, William E. (2011) 'The Reluctant Hegemon? Germany Moves Centre Stage in the European Union', *JCMS: Journal of Common Market Studies*, 49(s1), pp. 57–75.

Pattie, Charles and Johnston, Ron (2011) 'A Tale of Sound and Fury, Signifying Something? The Impact of the Leaders' Debates in the 2010 UK General Election', *Journal of Elections, Public Opinion and Parties*, 21(2), pp, 147–177.

Paul, T.V., Ikenberry, John and Hall, John (2003) *The Nation State in Question* (Princeton, NJ: Princeton University Press).

Pauwels, Teun (2011) 'Explaining the Strange Decline of the Populist Radical Right Vlaams Belang in Belgium: The Impact of Permanent Opposition', *Acta Politica*, 46, pp. 60–82.

Pedahzur, Ami and Brichta, Avraham (2002) 'The Institutionalization of Extreme Right-Wing Charismatic Parties: A Paradox?', *Party Politics*, 8(1), pp. 31–49.

Pedersen, Helene Helboe (2010a) 'Differences and Changes in Danish Party Organisations: Central Party Organisation versus Parliamentary Party Group Power', *Journal of Legislative Studies*, 16(2), pp. 233–250.

Pedersen, Helene Helboe (2010b) 'How Intra-Party Power Relations Affect the Coalition Behaviour of Political Parties', *Party Politics*, 16(6), pp. 737–754.

Pedersen, Karina and Saglie, Jo (2005) 'Technology in Ageing Parties: Internet Use in Danish and Norwegian Parties', *Party Politics*, 11(3) 3, 359–77.

Pelizzo, Riccardo and Stapenhurst, Frederick (2011) *Parliamentary Oversight Tools: a Comparative Analysis* (Abingdon: Routledge).

Pellikaan, Huib (2010) 'The Impact of Religion on the Space of Competition: The Dutch Case', *Politics and Religion*, 3, pp. 469–494.

Penninx, R., Berger, M. and Kraal, K. (eds) (2006) *The Dynamics of International Migration and Settlement in Europe* (Amsterdam: Amsterdam University Press).

Pérez-Solórzano Borragán, Nieves (2006) 'Post-Communist Interest Politics: A Research Agenda', *Perspectives on European Politics and Society*, 7(2), pp. 134–54.

Péteri, György (2000) 'Between Empire and Nation-state: Comments on the Pathology of State Formation during the "Short Twentieth Century"', *Contemporary European History*, 9(3), pp. 367–84.

Peters, B. Guy (2001) *The Politics of Bureaucracy* (London: Routledge).

Peters, B. Guy (2007) 'Executives', in Colin Hay and Anand Menon (eds) *European Politics* (Oxford: Oxford University Press).

Peters, B. Guy and Pierre, Jon (eds) (2000) *Governance, Politics and the State* (Basingstoke: Palgrave Macmillan).

Peters, B. Guy and Pierre, Jon (eds) (2004) *The Politicization of the Civil Service in Comparative Perspective: A Quest for Control* (London: Routledge).

Peters, B. Guy and Wright, Vincent (2000) *Administering the Summit: Administration of the Core Executive in Developed Countries* (Basingstoke: Palgrave Macmillan).

Petersson, Olof, Djerf-Pierre, Monika, Holmberg, Sören, Strømbäck, Jesper and Weibull, Lennart (2006) 'Media and Elections in Sweden' (SNS Förlag), available at www.sns.se/document/dr_2006_english_web.pdf.

Pétry, François and Collette, Benoît (2009) 'Measuring How Political Parties Keep Their Promises: A Positive Perspective from Political Science', *Studies in Public Choice*, 15(2), pp. 65–80.

PewResearchCenter, available at http://pewglobal.org/reports/pdf/256.pdf.

Pfetsch, B. (1996) 'Convergence through Privatization? Changing Media Environments and Televised Politics in Germany', *European Journal of Communication*, 11(4), pp. 427–51.

Phelan, Craig (ed) (2007) *Trade Union Revitalisation: Trends and Prospects in 34 Countries* (Bern: Peter Lang).

Pickerill, Jenny (2010) *Cyberprotest: Environmental Activism Online* (Manchester: Manchester University Press).

Pierre, Jon (ed.) (1995) *Bureaucracy in the Modern State: An Introduction to Comparative Public Administration* (Aldershot: Edward Elgar).

Pierson, Christopher (2001) *Hard Choices: Social Democracy in the Twenty-First Century* (Cambridge: Polity Press).

Pierson, Paul (1996) 'The New Politics of the Welfare State', *World Politics*, 48 (2), pp. 143–79.

Pilet, Jean-Benoit and Bol, Damien (2011) 'Party Preferences and Electoral Reform: How Time in Government Affects the Likelihood of Supporting Electoral Change', *West European Politics*, 34(3), pp. 568–586.

Pisoiu, Daniela (2012) *Islamist Radicalisation in Europe: An Occupational Change Process* (Abingdon: Routledge).

Pissarides, Christopher, Garibaldi, Pietro, Olivetti, Claudia, Petrongolo, Barbara and Wasmer, Etienne (2004) 'Women in the Labour Force: How Well is Europe Doing?', in Tito Boeri, Daniela Del Boca and Christopher Pissarides (eds), *Women at Work: An Economic Perspective. A Report for the Fondazione Rodolfo Debenedetti* (Oxford: Oxford University Press).

Pitschel, Diana and Bauer, Michael Bauer (2009) 'Subnational Governance Approaches on the Rise—Reviewing a Decade of Eastern European Regionalization Research', *Regional and Federal Studies*, 19(3), pp. 327–347.

Plasser, Fritz and Plasser, Gunda (2002) *Global Political Campaigning: A Worldwide Analysis of Campaign Professionals and their Practices* (Westport: Greenwood/Praeger).

Poguntke, Thomas, Aylott, Nicholas, Carter, Elisabeth, Ladrech, Robert and Luther, Kurt Richard (eds) (2006) *The Europeanization of National Political Parties: Power and Organizational Adaptation* (London: Routledge).

Poguntke, Thomas and Webb, Paul (eds) (2004) *The Presidentialization of Politics: A Comparative Study of Modern Democracies* (Oxford: Oxford University Press).

Poitras, Guy E. (2003) 'Resisting Globalization: The Politics of Protest in the Global Political Economy', *International Politics*, 40(3), pp. 409–24.

Poletti, Arlo (2012) *The European Union and Multilateral Trade Governance: The Politics of the Doha Round* (Abingdon: Routledge).

Pollack, Johannes and Slominski, Peter (2009) 'Experimentalist but not Accountable Governance? The Role of Frontex in Managing the EU's External Borders', *West European Politics*, 32(5), pp. 904–924.

Pollitt, Christopher and Bouckaert, Geert (2011) *Public Management Reform: A Comparative Analysis – New Public Management, Governance, and the Neo-Weberian State* (Oxford: Oxford University Press).

Pollitt, Christopher, Talbot, Colin, Caulfield, Janice and Smullen, Amanda (2007a) *Agencies: How Governments Do Things Through Semi-Autonomous Organizations* (Basingstoke: Palgrave Macmillan).

Pollitt, Christopher, van Thiel, Sandra and V.M.F. Homburg (eds) (2007b) *The New Public Management in Europe: Adaptation and Alternatives* (Basingstoke: Palgrave Macmillan).

Poloni-Staudinger, Lori (2009) 'We All Need Friends': Elite Alliances and the Activity Choices of Environmental Groups in the United Kingdom, France and Germany', in Conor McGrath (ed) *Interest Groups and Lobbying in Europe* (Lampeter: Edwin Mellen Press).

Ponce, Aldo F. and Scarrow, Susan E. (2011): Who Gives? Partisan Donations in Europe, *West European Politics*, 34(5), pp. 997–102.

Pontusson, Jonas (2005) *Inequality and Prosperity: Social Europe vs. Liberal America* (Ithaca, NY: Cornell University Press).

Pontusson, Jonas and Rueda, David (2010) 'The Politics of Inequality: Voter Mobilization and Left Parties in Advanced Industrial States', *Comparative Political Studies*, 43(6), pp. 675–705.

Pop-Eleches, Grigoire (2010) 'Throwing out the Bums: Protest Voting and Unorthodox Parties after Communism', *World Politics*, 62(2), pp. 221–260.

Poppe, Christian and Kjærnes, Unni (2003) *Trust in Food in Europe: A Comparative Analysis* (Oslo: National Institute for Consumer Research).

Praud, Jocelyne (ed) (2012) Symposium on Gender Parity and Quotas in European Politics, *West European Politics*, 35(2).

Preston, Paul (2013) *The Spanish Holocaust: Inquisition and Extermination in Twentieth Century Spain* (London: Harper Press).

Procházka, Radoslav (2002) *Mission Accomplished: On Founding Constitutional Adjudication in Central Europe* (Budapest: Central European University Press).

Przeworski, Adam and Wallerstein, Michael (1988) 'Structural Dependence of the State on Capital', *American Political Science Review*, 82: 11–29.

Psychogiopoulou, Evangelia (2012) *Understanding Media Policies: a European Perspective* (Basingstoke: Palgrave Macmillan).

Putnam, Robert D. (1988) 'Diplomacy and Domestic Politics: The Logic of Two Level Games', *International Organization*, 42(3), pp. 427–60.

Putnam, Robert D. (2000) *Bowling Alone: The Collapse and Revival of American Community* (New York: Simon & Schuster).

Putnam, Robert, D., Leonardi, Robert and Nanetti, Raffaella, Y. (2000) *Making Democracy Work: Civic Traditions in Modern Italy* (Princeton, NJ: Princeton University Press).

Q

QAA (2000) *Politics and International Relations Subject Benchmark Statement* (Gloucester: Quality Assurance Agency for Higher Education), available at http://www.qaa.ac.uk/crnt-work/benchmark/politics.pdf.

Quittkat, Christine (2009) 'The Europeanization of Professional Interest Intermediation: National Trade Associations in a French–German Comparison', in Conor McGrath (ed) *Interest Groups and Lobbying in Europe* (Lampeter: Edwin Mellen Press).

Qvortrup, Mads (2002, 2005) *A Comparative Study of Referendums: Government by the People* (Manchester: Manchester University Press).

Qvortrup, Mads (2007) *The Politics of Participation* (Manchester: Manchester University Press).

R

Raadschelders, Jos C.N., Toonen, Theo A.J. and van der Meer, Frits M. (eds.) (2007) *The Civil Service in the 21st Century: Comparative Perspectives* (Basingstoke: Palgrave Macmillan).

Rai, Shirin M. (ed.) (2010) *Ceremony and Ritual in Parliament*, special issue of the *Journal of Legislative Studies*, 16(3).

Rallings, Colin (1987) 'The Influence of Election Programmes: Britain and Canada, 1945–79', in Ian Budge, David Robertson and Derek Hearl (eds), *Ideology, Strategy and Party Changes: Spatial Analysis of Post-War Election Programmes in 19 Democracies* (Cambridge: Cambridge University Press).

Ram, M. (2003) 'Democratization through European Integration: The Case of Minority Rights in the Czech Republic and Romania', *Studies in Comparative International Development*, 38(2), pp. 28–56.

Ramet, Sabrina P. (ed.) (2010), *Central and Southeast European Politics since 1989* (Cambridge: Cambridge University Press).

Rauh, Christian, Kirchner, Antje and Kappe, Roland (2011) 'Political Parties and Higher Education Spending: Who Favours Redistribution?', *West European Politics*, 34(6), pp. 1185–1206.

Raunio, Tapio (2011) 'The Gatekeepers of European Integration? The Functions of National Parliaments in the EU Political System', *Journal of European Integration*, 33(3), pp. 303–321.

Rawcliffe, Peter (1998) *Environmental Pressure Groups in Transition* (Manchester: Manchester University Press).

Reeves, Minou (2003) *Muhammad in Europe: A Thousand Years of Western Myth-Making* (New York University Press).

Reichard, Michael (2006) *The EU–NATO Relationship: A Legal and Political Perspective* (Aldershot: Ashgate).

Renwick, Alan (2011) Electoral Reform in Europe since 1945, *West European Politics*, 34(3), pp. 456–477.

Rhodes, R.A.W. (1997) *Understanding Governance: Policy Networks, Governance, Reflexivity and Accountability* (Buckingham: Open University Press).

Rhodes, R.A.W. (2002) 'Globalization, EMU and Welfare State Futures', in Erik Jones, Paul Hayward and Martin Rhodes (eds), *Developments in West European Politics* (Basingstoke: Palgrave Macmillan).

Rhodes, R.A.W. and Weller, P. (eds) (2001) *The Changing World of Top Officials: Mandarins or Valets?* (Buckingham: Open University Press).

Richardson, Jeremy (2001) 'Policy making in the EU: Familiar Ambitions in Unfamiliar Settings', in Anand Menon and Vincent Wright (eds), *From the Nation State to Europe?* (Oxford: Oxford University Press).

Richardson, Jeremy, Gustafsson, Gunnel and Jordan, Grant (1982) 'The Concept of Policy Style', in Jeremy Richardson (ed.), *Policy Styles in Western Europe* (London: George Allen & Unwin).

Riddell, Peter (2006) 'The Rise of the Ranters: Saving Political Journalism', in John Lloyd and Jean Seaton (eds), *What Can Be Done? Making the Media and Politics Better* (Oxford: Blackwell).

Rihoux, B. and Rüdig, Wolfgang (eds) (2006) 'The Greens in Power', *European Journal of Political Research*, Special issue, 45.

Risse, Thomas (2010) *A Community of Europeans? Transnational Identities and Public Spheres* (Ithaca, NY: Cornell University Press).

Roberts, Andrew (2008) 'Hyperaccountability: Economic Voting in Central and Eastern Europe', *Electoral Studies*, 27(3), pp. 533–546.

Roberts, Andrew (2009) *The Quality of Democracy in Eastern Europe* (Cambridge: Cambridge University Press).

Rodgers, Jayne (2003) *Spatializing International Politics: Analysing Activism on the Internet* (London: Routledge).

Rohrschneider, Robert and Whitefield, Stephen (2009) 'Understanding Cleavages in Party Systems: Issue Position and Issue Salience in 13 Post-Communist Democracies', *Comparative Political Studies*, 42(2), pp. 280–313.

Roller, Elisa (2004) 'Conflict and Cooperation in EU Policy making: The Case of Catalonia', *Perspectives on European Politics and Society*, 5(1), pp. 81–102.

Roncarolo, Franca (2004) 'Mediation of Italian Politics and the Marketing of Leaders' Private Lives', *Parliamentary Affairs*, 57(1), pp. 108–17.

Rootes, Christopher (2004) 'Is There a European Environmental Movement?', in Brian Baxter, John Barry and Richard Dunphy (eds), *Europe, Globalisation and Sustainable Development* (London: Routledge).

Ros, Virginia (2011) 'Demographics of Immigration: Spain', SOM Working Papers, 2011–08, available at https://sites.google.com/site/somprojecteu/working-papers/2011

Ross, George (2011) *The European Union and its Crises: Through the Eyes of the Brussels Elite* (Basingstoke: Palgrave Macmillan).

Ross, George, Hoffman, Stanley and Malzacher, Sonja (1987) *The Mitterrand Experiment* (Cambridge: Polity Press).

Ross, Karen (2004) 'Political Talk Radio and Democratic Participation: Caller Perspectives on Election Call', *Media Culture and Society*, 26(6), pp. 785–801.

Rössler, Patrick (2004) 'Political Communication Messages: Pictures of Our World on International Television News', in Frank Esser and Barbara Pfetsch (eds) *Comparing Political Communication: Theories, Cases, and Challenges* (Cambridge: Cambridge University Press).

Rössler, Patrick (2006) 'Political Communication Messages: Pictures of our World on International Television News', in Frank Esser and Barbara Pfetsch (eds), *Comparing. Political Communication: Theories, Cases and Challenges* (Cambridge: Cambridge University Press).

Rothschild, Emma (1995) 'What Is Security?', *Daedalus,* 124(3), pp. 53–98.

Rouban, Luc (1995) 'Public Administration at the Crossroads: The End of French Exceptionalism', in Jon Pierre (ed.), *Bureaucracy in the Modern State: An Introduction to Comparative Public Administration* (Adershot: Edward Elgar).

Rovny, Jan, and Edwards, Erica E. (2012) 'Struggle Over Dimensionality: Political Competition in Western and Eastern Europe', *East European Politics and Societies,* 26(1), pp. 56–74.

Ruano, Lorena (ed.) (2012) *The Europeanization of National Foreign Policies towards Latin America* (Abingdon: Routledge).

Rucht, Dieter (2003) 'The Changing Role of Political Protest Movements', *West European Politics,* 26(4), pp. 153–78.

Rueda, David (2007) *Social Democracy Inside Out: Partisanship and Labor Market Policy in Industrialized Democracies* (Oxford: Oxford University Press).

Rueschemeyer, Marylin and Wolchik, Sharon L. (eds) (2009) *Women in Power in Post-Communist Parliaments* (Bloomington: Indiana University Press).

Ruffa, Chiara (2011) 'Realist–normative power Europe? Explaining EU policies toward Lebanon from an IR perspective', *Comparative European Politics,* 9(3), pp. 562–580.

Ruzza, Carlo (2004) *Europe and Civil Society: Movement Coalitions and European Governance* (Manchester: Manchester University Press).

Ryan, Johnny (2007) *Countering Militant Islamist Radicalization on the Internet* (Dublin: Institute of European Affairs).

Ryan, Rosalind (2008) 'How the Muhammad Cartoon Row Escalated', *Guardian,* 12 February 2008.

Rydgren, Jens (ed.) (2012) *Class Politics and the Radical Right* (Abingdon: Routledge).

Ryfe, David M. and Blach-Ørsten, Mark (eds.) (2011) 'Special Issue: Journalism as an Institution', *Journalism Studies,* 12(1), pp. 1–118.

S

Saalfeld, Thomas (2006) 'Conflict and Consensus in Germany's Bicameral System: A Case Study of the Passage of the 'Agenda 2010'', *Debatte,* 14(3), pp. 247–69.

Saalfeld, Thomas (2010) 'Veto Players, Agenda Control and Cabinet Stability in 17 European Parliaments, 1945–1999', in Thomas König, George Tsebelis and Marc Debus (eds), *Reform Processes and Policy Change: Veto Players and Decision-Making in Modern Democracies* (Springer).

Sadurski, Wojciech (2009) *Twenty Years After the Transition: Constitutional Review in Central and Eastern Europe* (Sydney University Legal Studies Research Paper No. 09/69), available at http://ssrn.com/abstract=1437843

Saggar, Shamit (2000) *Race and Electoral Politics in Britain* (London: UCL Press).

Salmond, Rob (2006) 'Proportional Representation and Female Parliamentarians', *Legislative Studies Quarterly,* 31(2), pp. 175–204.

Sambrook, Richard (2010) *Are Foreign Correspondents Redundant? The Changing Face of International News* (Oxford: Reuters Institute), available online at http://reutersinstitute.politics.ox.ac.uk/fileadmin/documents/Publications/Challenges/Are_Foreign_Correspondents_Redundant.pdf.

Sanders, Karen (2009) *Communicating Politics in the Twenty First Century* (Basingstoke: Palgrave Macmillan).

Sanders, Karen with Canel, Maria José (2004) 'Spanish Politicians and the Media: Controlled Visibility and Soap Opera Politics', *Parliamentary Affairs,* 57(1), pp. 196–208.

Sandvoss, Cornel, Harrington, C. Lee and Gray, Jonathan (2012) 'Not Necessarily the News? Global Approaches to News Parody and Political Satire', special issue of *Popular Communication,* 10(1–2), pp. 1–182.

Sanford, George (2002) *Democratic Government in Poland: Constitutional Politics Since 1989* (Basingstoke: Palgrave Macmillan).

Sano, Joelle and Williamson, John (2008) 'Factors Affecting Union Decline in 18 OECD Countries and their Implications for Labor Movement Reform', *International Journal Of Comparative Sociology,* 49(6), pp. 479–500.

Sapir, André (1996) 'Globalization and the Reform of European Social Models', *Journal of Common Market Studies,* 44(2), pp. 369–90.

Sartori, Giovanni (1997) *Comparative Constitutional Engineering: An Inquiry into Structures, Incentives and Outcomes* (Basingstoke: Palgrave Macmillan).

Sassoon, Donald (1997) *One Hundred Years of Socialism: The West European Left in the Twentieth Century* (London: Fontana).

Savigny, Heather (2008) *The Problem of Political Marketing* (New York: Continuum).

Scarrow, Susan E. (1994) 'The "Paradox of Enrolment": Assessing the Costs and Benefits of Party Membership', *European Journal of Political Research,* 25(1), pp. 41–60.

Scarrow, Susan E. (2007) 'Political Finance in Comparative Perspective', *Annual Review of Political Science,* 10, pp. 193–210.

Scarrow, Susan E. (2010) 'Political Parties and Party Systems', in Lawrence LeDuc, Righard G. Niemi and Pippa Norris (eds), *Comparing Democracies, 3: Elections and Voting in the 21st Century* (Thousand Oaks, CA: Sage Publications).

Scarrow, Susan E. and Gezgor, Burcu (2010) 'Declining memberships, changing members? European political party members in a new era', *Party Politics,* 16(6), pp. 823–843.

Scarrow, Susan E. and Kittilson, Miki Caul (2003) 'Political Parties and the Rhetoric and Realities of Democratization', in Russell Dalton, Bruce Cain and Susan Scarrow (eds), *Democracy Transformed? Expanding Citizen Access in Advanced Industrial Democracies* (Oxford: Oxford University Press).

Schain, Martin (2006) 'The Extreme-right and Immigration Policy making: Measuring Direct and Indirect Effects', *West European Politics,* 29(2), pp. 270–89.

Scheffer, Paul (2011) *Immigrant Nations* (Cambridge: Polity).

Scherpereel, John A. (2008) *Governing the Czech Republic and Slovakia: Between State Socialism and the European Union* (Boulder: FirstForum Press).

Scherpereel, John A. (2010a) EU Cohesion Policy and the Europeanization of Central and East European Regions, *Regional and Federal Studies,* 20(1), pp. 45–62.

Scherpereel, John A. (2010b) 'European Culture and the European Union's 'Turkey Question', *West European Politics*, 33(4), pp. 810–829.

Scheuer, Steen (2011) Union Membership Variation in Europe: A Ten-country Comparative Analysis', *European Journal of Industrial Relations*, 17(1), pp. 57–73.

Scheve, Kenneth and Stasavage, David (2009) 'Institutions, Partisanship, and Inequality in the Long Run', *World Politics*, 61(2), pp. 215–253.

Schlesinger, Philip and Kevin, Deirdre (2000) 'Can the European Union become a Sphere of Publics?', in Erik Oddvar Eriksen and John Erik Fossum (eds), *Democracy in the European Union: Integration through Deliberation?* (London: Routledge).

Schludi, Martin (2005) *The Reform of Bismarkian Pension Systems: A Comparison of Pension Politics in Austria, France, Italy, and Sweden* (Amsterdam: Amsterdam University Press).

Schmidt, Manfred G. (1996) 'When Parties Matter: A Review of the Possibilities and Limits of Partisan Influence on Public Policy', *European Journal of Political Research*, 30(2), pp. 155–83.

Schmidt, Manfred G. (2002) 'The Impact of Political Parties, Constitutional Structures and Veto Players in Public Policy', in Hans Keman (ed.), *Comparative Democratic Politics* (London: Sage).

Schmidt, Vivien A. (1999) 'National Patterns of Governance under Siege: The Impact of European Integration', in Beate Kohler Koch and Rainer Eising (eds), *The Transformation of Governance in the European Union* (London: Routledge/ECPR).

Schmidt, Vivien A. (2001) 'The Politics of Adjustment in France and Britain: When Does Discourse Matter?', *Journal of European Public Policy*, 8(2), pp. 247–64.

Schmidt, Vivien A. (2006) *Democracy in Europe: The EU and National Politics* (Oxford: Oxford University Press).

Schmidtke, Oliver (2002) *The Third Way Transformation of Social Democracy* (London Ashgate).

Schmitt, Hermann and Holmberg, Sören (1995) 'Political Parties in Decline?', in Hans-Dieter Klingemann and Dieter Fuchs (eds), *Citizens and the State* (Oxford: Oxford University Press).

Schmitt-Beck, Rüdiger (2004) 'Personal Communication Effects: the Impact of Mass Media and Personal Conversations on Voting', in Frank Esser and Barbara Pfetsch (eds), *Comparing Political Communication: Theories, Cases, and Challenges* (Cambridge: Cambridge University Press).

Schoen, Harald (2007) 'Campaigns, Candidate Evaluations, and Vote Choice: Evidence from German Federal Election Campaigns, 1980–2002', *Electoral Studies*, 26(2), pp. 324–37.

Schöpflin, George (1995) 'Nationalism and Ethnicity in Europe, East and West', in Charles A. Kupchan (ed.), *Nationalism and Nationalities in the New Europe* (Ithaca, NY: Cornell University Press).

Schudson, Michael (2003) *The Sociology of News* (New York: W. W. Norton).

Schudson, Michael (2008) *Why Democracies Need an Unlovable Press* (Cambridge: Polity Press).

Schulz, Winfried (2004) 'Reconstructing Mediatization as an Analytical Concept', *European Journal of Communication*, 19(1), pp. 87–101.

Schulz, Winfried, Zeh, Reimar and Quiring, Oliver (2005) 'Voters in a Changing Media Environment: A Data-Based Retrospective on Consequences of Media Change in Germany', *European Journal of Communication*, 20(1), pp. 55–88.

Schulz-Forberg, Hagen and Stråth, Bo (2012) *The Political History of European Integration: the Hypocrisy of Democracy-Through-Market* (Abingdon: Routledge).

Schumacher, Gijs (2011) 'Signalling a Change of Heart? How Parties' Short-Term Ideological Shifts Explain Welfare State Reform', *Acta Politica*, 46(4), pp. 331–352.

Schumacher, Gijs, Vis, Barbara, van Kersbergen, Kees (2013), 'Political Parties' Welfare Image, Electoral Punishment and Welfare State Retrenchment', *Comparative European Politics*, 11(1), pp. 1–21.

Schuster, Jürgen and Maier, Herbert (2006) 'The Rift: Explaining Europe's Divergent Iraq Policies in the Run-Up to the American-Led War on Iraq', *Foreign Policy Analysis*, 2(3), pp. 223–44.

Schweitzer, Eva Johanna (2012) 'The Mediatization of E-Campaigning: Evidence From German Party Websites in State, National, and European Parliamentary Elections 2002–2009', *Journal of Computer-Mediated Communication*, 17(3), pp. 283–302.

Schwindt-Bayer, Leslie A. (2005) 'The Incumbency Disadvantage and Women's Election to Legislative Office', *Electoral Studies*, 24, pp. 227–44.

Sciarini, Pascal, Fischer, Alex and Nicolet, Sarah (2004) 'How Europe Hits Home: Evidence from the Swiss Case', *Journal of European Public Policy*, 11(3), pp. 353–78.

Scott, James Wesley (2006) *EU Enlargement, Region Building and Shifting Borders of Inclusion and Exclusion* (Aldershot: Ashgate).

Scott, Joan Wallach (2010) *The Politics of the Veil* (Princeton, NJ: Princeton University Press).

SCP (2004) *Public Sector Performance. An International Comparison of Education, Health Care, Law and Order and Public Administration* (The Hague: Social and Cultural Planning Office of the Netherlands), available online at www.scp.nl/english/dsresource?objectid=22049&type=pdf.

Scruggs, Lyle and Allan, James P. (2006a) 'Welfare-state Decommodification in 18 OECD Countries: A Replication and Revision', *Journal of European Social Policy*, 16(1), pp. 55–72.

Scruggs, Lyle and Allan, James P. (2006b) 'The Material Consequences of Welfare States: Benefit Generosity and Absolute Poverty in 16 OECD Countries', *Comparative Political Studies*, 39(7), pp. 880–904.

Sedelius, Thomas and Ekman, Joakim (2010) 'Intra-executive Conflict and Cabinet Instability: Effects of Semi-Presidentialism in Central and Eastern Europe', *Government and Opposition*, 45(4), pp. 505–530.

Selb, Peter (2009) 'A Deeper Look at the Proportionality – Turnout Nexus', *Comparative Political Studies*, 42(4), pp. 527–548.

Selden, Zachary (2010) 'Power is Always in Fashion: State-Centric Realism and the European Security and Defence Policy', *JCMS: Journal of Common Market Studies*, 48(2), pp. 397–416.

Semetko, Holli A. (2000) 'Great Britain: The End of News at Ten and the Changing News Environment', in Richard Gunther and Anthony Mughan (eds), *Democracy and the Media: A Comparative Perspective* (Cambridge: Cambridge University Press).

Semetko, Holli A., Vreese, Claes H. de and Peter, Jochen (2000) 'Europeanised Politics – Europeanised Media? European

Integration and Political Communication', *West European Politics*, 23(4), pp. 121–41.

Semetko, Holli and Scammell, Margaret (eds.) (2012) *The SAGE Handbook of Political Communication* (London: Sage).

Senik, Claudia, Stichnoth, Holger and van der Straeten, Karine (2009) 'Immigration and Natives' Attitudes towards the Welfare State: Evidence from the European Social Survey', *Social Indicators Research*, 91(3), pp. 345–370.

Setälä, Maija (1999) *Referendums and Democratic Government: Normative Theory and the Analysis of Institutions* (Basingstoke: Palgrave Macmillan).

Setälä, Maija and Schiller, Theo (eds) (2009) *Referendums and Representative Democracy: Responsiveness, Accountability and Deliberation* (Abingdon: Routledge).

Shehata, Adam (2010) 'Pathways to Politics: How Media System Characteristics Can Influence Socioeconomic Gaps in Political Participation', *International Journal of Press/Politics*, 15(3), pp. 295–318.

Sicurelli, Daniela (2010) *The European Union's Africa Policies* (Farnham: Ashgate).

Sides, John and Citrin, Jack (2007) 'European Opinion about Immigration: The Role of Identities, Interests and Information', *British Journal of Political Science*, 37, pp. 477–504.

Sieberer, Ulrich (2011) 'The Institutional Power of Western European Parliaments: a Multidimensional Analysis', *West European Politics*, 34(4), pp. 731–754.

Sissenich, Beate (2010) 'Weak States, Weak Societies: Europe's East–West gap', *Acta Politica*, 45(1–2), pp. 11–40.

Sitter, Nick (2003) 'Cleavages, Party Strategy and Party System Change in Europe, East and West', in Paul Lewis and Paul Webb (eds), *Pan European Perspectives on Party Politics* (Leiden: Brill).

Siune, Karen, Svensson, Palle and Tongsgaard, Ole (1994) 'The European Union: The Danes Said "No" in 1992 but "Yes" in 1993: How and Why?', *Electoral Studies*, 13(2), pp. 107–16.

Skenderovic, Damir (2007) 'Immigration and the Radical Right in Switzerland: Ideology, Discourse and Opportunities', *Patterns of Prejudice*, 41(2), pp. 155–76.

Smilov, Daniel and Toplak, Jurij (eds) (2007) *Political Finance and Corruption in Eastern Europe: The Transition Period* (Aldershot: Ashgate).

Smith, Anthony D. (1991) *National Identity* (London: Penguin).

Smith, Anthony D. (1992) 'National Identity and the Idea of European Unity', *International Affairs*, 68(1), pp. 55–76.

Smith, Karen E. (2005a) 'The Outsiders: the European Neighbourhood Policy', *International Affairs*, 81(4), pp. 757–73.

Smith, Karen E. (2005b) *Engagement and Conditionality: Incompatible or Mutually Reinforcing?* (London: Foreign Policy Centre).

Smith, Mark (2000) 'Nato Enlargement and European Security', in Lisbeth Aggestam and Adrian Hyde-Price (eds) *Security and Identity in Europe: Exploring the New Agenda* (Basingstoke: Palgrave Macmillan).

Smith, Martin J. (1993) *Pressure, Power and Policy: State Autonomy and Policy Networks in Britain and the United States* (New York: Harvester Wheatsheaf).

Smith, Michael (2004) 'CFSP and ESDP: From Idea to Institution to Policy', in Martin Holland (ed.), *Common Foreign and Security Policy: The First Ten Years* (London: Continuum).

Smith, Michael E. (2011) 'A Liberal Grand Strategy in a Realist World? Power, Purpose and the EU's Changing Global Role', *Journal of European Public Policy* 18(2), pp.144–16.

Sniderman, Paul M. and Hagendoorn, Paul (2007) *When Ways of Life Collide: Multiculturism and its Discontents in the Netherlands* (Princeton, NJ: Princeton University Press).

Snow, David A., Soule, Sarah and Kriesi, Hanspeter (eds) (2004) *The Blackwell Companion to Social Movements* (Oxford: Blackwell).

Snyder, James M. and Ting, Michael M. (2002) 'An Informational Rationale for Political Parties', *American Journal of Political Science*, 46(1), pp. 90–110.

Solivetti, Luigi M. (2012) 'Looking for a Fair Country: Features and Determinants of Immigrants' Involvement in Crime in Europe', *Howard Journal of Criminal Justice*, 51(2), pp. 133–159.

Soroka, Stuart and Wlezien, Christopher (2010) *Degrees of Democracy: Politics, Public Opinion, and Policy* (Cambridge: Cambridge University Press).

Sotiropoulos, Dimitri A. (2004) 'Southern European Public Bureaucracies in Comparative Perspective', *West European Politics*, 27(3), pp. 405–22.

Spanou, Calliope and Sotiropoulos, Dimitri A. (2011) 'The Odyssey of Administrative Reforms in Greece, 1981–2009: a Tale of Two Reform Paths', *Public Administration*, 89(3), pp. 723–737.

Sparks, Colin (1997) 'Post-communist Media in Transition', in John Corner, Philip Schlesinger and Roger Silverstone (eds), *International Media Research: A Critical Survey* (London: Routledge).

Sparks, Colin (2000) 'Media Theory after the Fall of European Communism: Why the Old Models from East and West Won't Do Anymore', in James Curran and Myung-Jin Park (eds), *De-Westernizing Media Studies* (London: Routledge).

Spence, David (2012) 'The Early Days of the European External Action Service: A Practitioner's View', *Hague Journal of Diplomacy*, 7(1), pp. 115–134.

Spies, Dennis and Franzmann, Simon T. (2011) 'A Two-Dimensional Approach to the Political Opportunity Structure of Extreme Right Parties in Western Europe', *West European Politics*, 34(5), pp. 1044–1069.

Spirova, Maria (2007) 'Bulgaria', *European Journal of Political Research*, 46(7–8).

Spirova, Maria (2008) *Political Parties in Post-Communist Societies* (Basingstoke: PalgraveMacmillan).

Spohn, Willfried and Triandafyllidou, Anna (eds) (2002) *Europeanization, National Identities and Migration: Changes in Boundary Constructions between Western and Eastern Europe* (London: Routledge).

Sprague-Jones, Jessica (2011) 'Extreme right-wing vote and support for multiculturalism in Europe', *Ethnic and Racial Studies*, 34(4), pp. 535–555.

Sprungk, Carina (2010) 'Ever More or Ever Better Scrutiny? Analysing the Conditions of Effective National Parliamentary Involvement in EU Affairs', *European Integration online Papers (EIoP)*, 14(02), http://eiop.or.at/eiop/texte/2010–002a.htm.

Stammers, Neil (2001) 'Social Democracy and Global Governance', in Luke Martell (ed.), *Social Democracy: Global and National Perspectives* (Basingstoke: Palgrave Macmillan).

Stan, Lavinia and Turcescu, Lucian (2011) *Church, State, and Democracy in Expanding Europe* (Oxford: Oxford University Press).

Stanyer, James and Wring, Dominic (eds) (2004) *Public Image, Private Lives: The Mediation of Politicians Around the Globe*, Parliamentary Affairs, Special issue, 57(1).

Starke, Peter (2007) *Radical Welfare State Retrenchment* (Basingstoke: Palgrave Macmillan).

Starke, Peter, Obinger, Herbert and Castles, Francis G. (2008) 'Convergence towards where: in what ways, if any, are welfare states becoming more similar?', *Journal of European Public Policy*, 15(7), pp. 975–1000.

Starke, Peter; Kaasch, Alexandra; van Hooren, Franca (2011) 'Explaining the variety of social policy responses to economic crisis: How parties and welfare state structures interact', TranState working papers, No. 154, http://hdl.handle.net/10419/50561.

Statham, Paul and Koopmans, Ruud (2009) 'Political Party Contestation over Europe in the Mass Media: Who Criticizes Europe, How, and Why?' *European Political Science Review*, 1(3), pp 435–463.

tefuriuc, Irina (ed.) (2009) *Government Coalitions in Multi-level Settings: Institutional Determinants and Party Strategy*. Special issue of Regional and Federal Studies, 19(1).

Steinmetz, Robert and Wivel, Anders (eds) (2010) *Small States in Europe* (Farnham: Ashgate).

Stephens, J.D., Huber, E. and Ray, L. (1999) 'The Welfare State in Hard Times', in Herbert Kitschelt, Peter Lange, Gary Marks and John D. Stephens (eds), *Continuity and Change in Contemporary Capitalism* (Cambridge: Cambridge University Press).

Stephenson, Paul (2009) 'Catching the Train to Europe: Executive Control of Policy Formulation inside Spain's Parliamentary European Union Affairs Committee', *South European Society and Politics*, 14(3), pp. 317–336.

Št tka, Václav (2012) 'Back to the Local? Transnational Media Flows and Audience Consumption Patterns in Central and Eastern Europe', in Sabina Mihelj and John Downey (eds.) *Central and Eastern European Media in Comparative Perspective* (Farnham: Ashgate).

Stoll, Heather (2010) 'Elite-Level Conflict Salience and Dimensionality in Western Europe: Concepts and Empirical Findings', *West European Politics*, 33(3), pp. 445–473.

Stolle, Dietlind and Hooghe, Marc (2005) 'Shifting Inequalities? Patterns of Exclusion and Inclusion in Emerging Forms of Political Participation', APSA Annual Meeting paper.

Stolle, Dietlind, Hooghe, Marc and Micheletti, Michele (2005) 'Politics in the Supermarket: Political Consumerism as a Form of Political Participation', *International Political Science Review*, 26(3), pp. 245–69.

Stone, Norman (2011) *The Atlantic and Its Enemies: A History of the Cold War* (Harmondsworth: Penguin).

Stone Sweet, Alec (2000) *Governing with Judges: Constitutional Politics in Europe* (Oxford: Oxford University Press).

Stone Sweet, Alec (2004) *The Judicial Construction of Europe* (Oxford: Oxford University Press).

Stone Sweet, Alec and Brunell, Thomas (2012) 'The European Court of Justice, State Noncompliance, and the Politics of Override', *American Political Science Review*, 106(1), pp. 203–214.

Strange, Gerard (2002) 'British Trade Unions and European Integration in the 1990s: Politics versus Political Economy', *Political Studies*, 50(2), pp. 332–53.

Stråth, Bo (ed.) (2001) *Europe and the Other and Europe as the Other* (Brussels: Peter Lang).

Street, John (2011) *Mass Media, Politics and Democracy, 2nd Edition* (Basingstoke: Palgrave Macmillan).

Strøm, Kaare (1990) *Minority Government and Majority Rule* (Cambridge: Cambridge University Press).

Strøm, Kaare, Müller, Wolfgang C., Bergman, Torbjörn (eds.) (2010) *Cabinets and Coalition Bargaining: The Democratic Life Cycle in Western Europe* (Oxford: Oxford University Press).

Strömbäck, Jesper (2008) *Four Phases of Mediatization: An Analysis of the Mediatization of Politics*, International Journal of Press/Politics, 13(3), pp. 228–246.

Strömbäck, Jesper and Kaid, Lynda Lee (eds.) (2008) *The Handbook of Election News Coverage Around the World* (Abingdon: Routledge).

Strömbäck, Jesper and Kiousis, Spiro (eds.) (2011) *Political Public Relations: Principles and Applications* (Abingdon: Routledge).

Sunstein, Cass R. (2007) *Republic.com 2.0* (Princeton, NJ: Princeton University Press).

Swank, Duane (2005) 'Globalization, Domestic Politics, and Welfare State Retrenchment in Capitalist Democracies', *Social Policy and Society*, 4(2), pp. 183–95.

Swenden, Wilfried and Maddens, Bart (eds.) (2009) *Territorial Party Politics in Western Europe* (Basingstoke: Palgrave Macmillan).

Szczerbiak, Aleks (2001) *Poles Together? The Emergence and Development of Political Parties in Postcommunist Poland* (Budapest: Central European University Press).

Szczerbiak, Aleks (2003) 'Old and New Divisions in Polish Politics: Polish Parties' Electoral Strategies and Bases of Support', *Europe–Asia Studies*, 55(5), pp. 729–46.

Szczerbiak, Aleks (2011) *Poland within the European Union: The New Awkward Partner* (London: Routledge).

Szczerbiak, Aleks and Taggart, Paul (2004) 'The Politics of European Referendum Outcomes and Turnout: Two Models', *West European Politics*, 27(4), pp. 557–83.

Szczerbiak, Aleks and Taggart, Paul (2008) *Opposing Europe: The Comparative Party Politics of Euroscepticism, Volumes I and II* (Oxford: Oxford University Press).

Szukala, Andrea (2003) 'France: The European Transformation of the French Model', in Wolfgang Wessels, Andreas Maurer and Jürgen Mittag (eds), *Fifteen into One? The European Union and its Member States*, 2nd edn (Manchester: Manchester University Press).

T

Taggart, Paul (2000) *Populism* (Buckingham: Open University Press).

Takens, Janet, van Hoof, Anita, Kleinnijenhuis, Jan and Atteveldt, Wouter (2011) 'Do New Parties Bring Personalization, a Narrow Issue Agenda and Populist Rhetoric? Evidence from Dutch Election Campaign Coverage from 1998–2006', in van Haaften, Ton *et al.* (eds.) *Bending Opinion: Essays on Persuasion in the Public Domain* (Leiden: Leiden University Press).

Tannam, Etain (2011) 'The European Union and Conflict Resolution: Northern Ireland, Cyprus and Bilateral Cooperation', *Government and Opposition*, 47(1), pp. 49–73.

Tarrow, Sidney G. (2005) *The New Transnational Activism* (Cambridge: Cambridge University Press).

Tatham, Michaël (2010) '"With or Without You"? Revisiting Territorial State-Bypassing in EU Interest Representation', *Journal of European Public Policy*, 17(1), pp. 76–99.

Tavits, Margit (2005) 'The Development of Stable Party Support: Electoral Dynamics in Post-Communist Europe', *American Journal of Political Science*, 49(2), pp. 283–98.

Tavits, Margit (2006) 'Party System Change: Testing a Model of New Party Entry', *Party Politics*, 12(1), pp. 99–119.

Tavits, Margit (2008a) *Presidents with Prime Ministers: Do Direct Elections Matter?* (Oxford: Oxford University Press).

Tavits, Margit (2008b) 'The Role of Parties' Past Behavior in Coalition Formation', *American Political Science Review*, 102(4), pp. 495–507.

Tavits, Margit and Annus, Taavi (2006) 'Learning to Make Votes Count: The Role of Democratic Experience', *Electoral Studies*, 25(1), pp. 72–90.

Tavits, Margit and Letki, Natalia (2009) 'When Left is Right: Party Ideology and Policy in Post-Communist Europe', *American Political Science Review*, 103(4), pp.555–569.

Taylor-Gooby, Peter (ed.) (2004) *New Risks, New Welfare: The Transformation of the European Welfare State* (Oxford: Oxford University Press).

Taylor-Gooby, Peter (2005) 'Is the Future American? Or, Can Left Politics Preserve European Welfare States through Growing "Racial" Diversity', *Journal of Social Policy*, 34(4), pp. 661–72.

Taylor-Gooby, Peter and Stoker, Gerry (2011) 'The Coalition Programme: A New Vision for Britain or Politics as Usual?', *Political Quarterly*, 82(1), pp. 4–15.

Teague, Paul and Donaghey, James (2003) 'European Economic Government and the Corporatist *Quid Pro Quo*', *Industrial Relations Journal*, 34(2), pp. 104–118.

Teló Mario (2006) *Europe: A Civilian Power? European Union, Global Governance, World Order* (Basingstoke: Palgrave Macmillan).

Temple, Mick (2006) 'Dumbing Down is Good for You', *British Politics*, 1(2), pp. 257–273.

ter Wal, Triandafyllidou, Anna, Steindler, Chiara and Kontochristou, Maria (2009) 'The Mohammed Cartoons Crisis 2006: the Role of Islam in the European Public Sphere', in Anna Triandafyllidou, Ruth Wodak, and Michał Krzy anowski (eds.) *The European Public Sphere and the Media: Europe in Crisis* (Basingstoke: Palgrave Macmillan).

Tesser, L. (2003) 'The Geopolitics of Tolerance: Minority Rights under EU Expansion in East-Central Europe', *East European Politics and Societies*, 17(3), pp. 483–532.

Thomassen, Jacques (2005) *The European Voter: A Comparative Study of Modern Democracies* (Oxford: Oxford University Press).

Thompson, Mark (2006) 'Television in Europe', *Political Quarterly*, 77(1), pp. 124–7.

Thomson, Robert (2001) 'The Programme to Policy Linkage: The Fulfillment of Election Pledges on Socio-economic Policy in the Netherlands, 1986–1998', *European Journal of Political Research*, 40(2), pp. 171–97.

Thomson, Robert (2010) 'Opposition through the Back Door in the Transposition of EU Directives', *European Union Politics*, 11(4), pp. 577–596.

Thomson, Robert, Stokman, Francis, Achen, Christopher and König, Thomas (eds) (2000) *The European Union Reader* (Cambridge; Cambridge University Press).

Thomson, Robert, Royed, Terry, Naurin, Elin, Artes, Joaquin, Ferguson, Mark J, Kostadinova, Petia and Moury, Catherine (2012) 'The Program-to-Policy Linkage: A Comparative Study of Election Pledges and Government Policies in Ten Countries', Paper presented to the Annual Meeting of the APSA, New Orleans. Available online at http://ssrn.com/abstract=2106482

Thomson, Robert, Stokman, Francis, Achen, Christopher and König, Thomas (eds) (2006) *The European Union Decides: Political Economy of Institutions and Decisions* (Cambridge: Cambridge University Press).

Thomson, Stuart (2000) *The Social Democratic Dilemma: Ideology, Governance and Globalization* (Basingstoke: Palgrave Macmillan).

Thorisdottir, Hulda, Jost, John T., Liviatan, I. and Shrout, Patrick E. (2007) 'Psychological Needs and Values Underlying Lefright Political Orientation: Cross-National Evidence from Eastern and Western Europe', *Public Opinion Quarterly*, 71(2), pp. 175–203.

Tiersky, Ronald and van Oudenaren, John (eds) (2010) *European Foreign Policies: Does Europe Still Matter?* (Lanham, MA: Rowman and Littlefield).

Tilly, Charles (1975) 'Reflecting on the History of European State-making', in Charles Tilly (ed.), *The Formation of the National State in Western Europe* (Princeton, NJ: Princeton University Press).

Tilly, Charles (1993) *Coercion, Capital and European States, AD 990–1992* (Oxford: Blackwell).

Tilly, Charles (2004) *Social Movements, 1768–2004* (London: Paradigm).

Timonen, Virpi (2003) *Restructuring the Welfare State: Globalization and Social Policy Reform in Finland and Sweden* (Cheltenham: Edward Elgar).

Toboso, Fernando and Scorsone, Eric (2010) 'How Much Power to Tax do Regional Governments Enjoy in Spain Since the 1996 and 2001 Reforms?', *Regional and Federal Studies*, 20(2), pp. 157–174.

Toens, Katrin (2009) 'Welfare Lobbyism in Europe: the German Case', in Conor McGrath (ed.) *Interest Groups and Lobbying in Europe* (Lampeter: Edwin Mellen Press).

Tomka, Miklós (2011) *Expanding Religion: Religious Revival in Post-Communist Central and Eastern Europe* (Berlin: De Gruyter).

Toole, James (2007) 'The historical foundations of party politics in post-communist East Central Europe', *Europe–Asia Studies*, 59(4), pp. 541–566.

Torfing, Jacob, Peters, B. Guy, Pierre, Jon and Sørensen, Eva (2012) *Interactive Governance: Advancing the Paradigm* (Oxford: Oxford University Press).

Tranøy, Bent Sofus (ed) (2011) Symposium on 'The Political Economy of the Icelandic Financial Crisis', *European Political Science*, 10(3), pp. 277–336.

Trappel, Josef and Enli, Gunn Sara (2011) 'Online Media: Changing Provision of News', in Trappel, Josef, Meier, Werner

A., D'Haenens, Leen, Steemers, Jeanette, Thomass, Barbara (eds.) *Media in Europe Today* (Bristol: Intellect).

Traxler, Franz (2010) The Long Term Development of Organized Business and its Implications for Corporatism: a Cross-National Comparison of Membership, Activities and Governing Capacities of Business Interest Associations, 1980–2003', *European Journal of Political Research*, 49, pp. 151–173.

Trechsel, Alexander H. and Vassil, Kristjan (2011) *Internet Voting in Estonia. A Comparative Analysis of Five Elections since 2005* (Florence: EUI/EUDO), available online at http://www.vvk.ee/public/dok/Internet_Voting_Report_20052011_Final.pdf.

Triandafyllidou, Anna (2003) 'The Launch of the Euro in the Italian Media', *European Journal of Communication*, 18(2), pp. 255–63.

Triandafyllidou, Anna (2010) *Irregular Migration in Europe: Myths and Realities* (Farnham: Ashgate).

Tsebelis, George, Jensen, Christian B., Kalandrakis, Anastassios and Kreppel, Amie (2001) 'Legislative Procedures in the European Union: An Empirical Analysis', *British Journal of Political Science*, 31(4), pp. 573–99.

Turner, Barry (2012) *Statesman's Yearbook 2013: The Politics, Cultures and Economies of the World* (Basingstoke: Palgrave Macmillan).

Tzelgov, Eitan (2011) 'Communist successor parties and government survival in Central Eastern Europe', *European Journal of Political Research*, 50(4), pp. 530–558.

U

Uba, Katrin and Uggla, Fredrick (2011) 'Protest Actions against the European Union, 1992–2007', *West European Politics*, 34(2), pp. 384–393.

Ueta, Takako and Remacle, Eric (eds) (2008) *Tokyo–Brussels Partnership: Security, Development and Knowledge-based Society* (Brussels: Peter Lang).

UNHCR (2012) *Asylum Levels and Trends in Industrialized Countries, 2011*, available at http://www.unhcr.org/4e9beaa19.html.

United Nations (2000) http://www.unhcr.ch/huricane/huricane.nsf/view01/59FCECC36567F2DA802568A20061B8AA?open document.

Upchurch, Martin, Taylor Graham, and Mathers, Andrew (2009) *The Crisis of Social Democratic Trade Unionism in Western Europe. The Search for Alternatives* (Farnham: Ashgate).

US Mission to Pristina (2007) http://pristinamsmission.gov.

V

Vachudova, Milada Anna (2009) Corruption and Compliance in the EU's Post-Communist Members and Candidates', *Journal of Common Market Studies*, 47(S1), pp. 43–62.

van Aelst, Peter and Walgrave, Stefaan (2001) 'Who is that (Wo)man in the Street? From the Normalisation of Protest to the Normalisation of the Protester', *European Journal of Political Research*, 39(4), pp. 461–86.

van Aelst, Peter and Walgrave, Stefaan (2011) 'Minimal or Massive? The Political Agenda-Setting Power of the Mass Media According to Different Methods', *The International Journal of Press/Politics*, 16(3), pp. 295–313.

van Biezen, Ingrid (2003) *Political Parties in New Democracies: Party Organization in Southern and East-Central Europe* (Basingstoke: Palgrave Macmillan).

van Biezen, Ingrid (2004) 'Political Parties as Public Utilities', *Party Politics*, 10(6), pp. 701–22.

van Biezen, Ingrid (2010a) 'State Intervention in Party Politics: the Public Funding and Regulation of Political Parties', *European Review*, 16(3), pp. 337–53.

van Biezen, Ingrid (2010b) 'Party and Campaign Finance', in Lawrence LeDuc, Righard G. Niemi and Pippa Norris (eds), *Comparing Democracies, 3: Elections and Voting in the 21st Century* (Thousand Oaks, CA: Sage Publications).

van Biezen, Ingrid and Kopecký, Petr (2007) 'The State and the Parties: Public Funding, Public Regulation and Rent-Seeking in Contemporary Democracies', Party Politics, 13(2), pp. 235–54.

van Biezen, Ingrid, Mair, Peter and Poguntke, Thomas (2012) 'Going, Going,…Gone? The Decline of Party Membership in Contemporary Europe', *European Journal of Political Research*, 51(1), pp. 24–56.

van Cuilenburg, Jan and McQuail, Dennis (2003) 'Media Policy Paradigm Shifts: Towards a New Communications Policy Paradigm', *European Journal of Communication*, 18(2), pp. 181–207.

van Deth, Jan and Janssen, Joseph (1994) 'Party Attachments and Political Fragmentation in Europe', *European Journal of Political Research*, 25, pp. 87–109.

van Deth, Jan, Montero, José Ramón and Westholm, Anders (eds) (2007) *Citizenship and Involvement in European Democracies* (London: Routledge).

van Ham, Peter (2009) 'EOSCE Relations: Partners or Rivals in Security', in Jørgensen, Knud Erik (ed.) *The European Union and International Organizations* (Abingdon: Routledge).

van Haute, Emilie (ed) (2011) *Party Membership in Europe: Exploration into the Anthills of Party Politics* (Brussels: Editions de l'Universite de Bruxelles).

van Hecke, Steven and Gerard, Emmanuel (eds) (2004) *Christian Democratic Parties in Europe since the End of the Cold War* (Leuven: Leuven University Press).

van Ingen, Erik and van der Meer, Tom (2011) 'Welfare state Expenditure and Inequalities in Voluntary Association Participation', *Journal of European Social Policy*, 21(4), pp. 302–322.

van Kempen, Hetty (2007) 'Media–Party Parallelism and Its Effects: a Cross-National Comparative Study', *Political Communication*, 24(3), pp. 303–32.

van Kersbergen, Kees (1995) *Social Capitalism: A Study of Christian Democracy and the Welfare State* (London: Routledge).

van Kersbergen, Kees (2000) 'The Declining Resistance of Welfare States to Changer', in Stein Kuhnle (ed.), *Survival of the European Welfare State* (London: Routledge/ECPR).

van Kersbergen, Kees and Krouwel, André (2008) 'A Double-Edged Sword! The Dutch Centre-Right and the "Foreigners Issue"', in Tim Bale (ed.), *Immigration and Integration Policy in Europe: Why Politics – and the Centre-Right – Matter* (London: Routledge).

van Kersbergen, Kees and Manow, Philip (eds.) (2009) *Religion, Class Coalitions, and Welfare States* (Cambridge: Cambridge University Press).

van Kersbergen, Kees and Manow, Philip (eds.) (2009) *Religion, Class Coalitions, and Welfare States* (Cambridge: Cambridge University Press).

van Kersbergen, Kees, Hemerijck, Anton and Manow, Philip (2000) 'Welfare without Work? Divergent Experiences of Reform in Germany and the Netherlands', in Stein Kuhnle (ed.), *The Survival of the European Welfare State* (London: Routledge).

van Kessel, Stijn (2011) 'Explaining the Electoral Performance of Populist Parties: the Netherlands as a Case Study', *Perspectives on European Politics and Society*, 12(1), pp. 68–88.

van Kessel, Stijn and Hollander, Saskia (2012) *Europe and the Dutch Parliamentary Election, September 2012*, European Parties Elections and Referendums Network, Election Briefing Paper, no. 71

van Noije, Lonneke, Kleinnijenhuis, Jan and Oegema, Dirk (2008) 'Loss of Parliamentary Control Due to Mediatization and Europeanization: a Longitudinal and Cross-Sectional Analysis of Agenda Building in the United Kingdom and the Netherlands', *British Journal of Politics and International Relations*, 38(3), pp. 455–478.

van Oorschot, Wim and Uunk, Wilfred (2007) 'Welfare Spending and the Public's Concern for Immigrants: Multilateral Evidence for Eighteen European Countries', *Journal of Comparative Politics*, 40(1), pp. 63–82.

van Ryzin, Gregg G. (2011) 'Outcomes, Process, and Trust of Civil Servants', *Journal of Public Administration Research and Theory*, 21(4), pp. 745–60.

van Spanje, Joost (2010) 'Contagious Parties: Anti-immigration Parties and their Impact on Other Parties' Immigratio Stances in Contemporary Western Europe', *Party Politics* 16(5), pp. 563–586.

van Zoonen, Liesbet (2006) 'The Personal, the Political and the Popular: A Woman's Guide to Celebrity Politics', *European Journal of Cultural Studies*, 9(3), pp. 287–301.

van de Donk, Wim, Loader, Brian, Nixon, Paul and Rucht, Dieter (eds) (2003) *Cyberprotest: New Media, Citizens and Social Movements* (London: Routledge).

van de Steeg, Marianne (2006) 'Does a Public Sphere Exist in the European Union? An Analysis of the Content of the Debate on the Haider Case', *European Journal of Political Research*, 45, pp. 609–34.

van de Walle, S. & Hammerschmid, G. (2011). 'The Impact Of The New Public Management: Challenges For Coordination And Cohesion In European Public Sectors'. *Halduskultuur – Administrative Culture*, 12(2): 190–209, also available at http://papers.ssrn.com/sol3/papers.cfm?abstract_id=1958168

van der Brug, Wouter (2010) 'Structural and Ideological Voting in Age Cohorts', West European Politics, 33(3), pp. 586–607.

van der Brug, Wouter, Fennema, Meindert and Tillie, Jan (2000) 'Anti-immigrant Parties in Europe: Ideological or Protest Vote?', *European Journal of Political Research*, 37(1), pp. 77–102.

van der Brug, Wouter, Hobolt, Sara, de Vreese, Claes H. (2009) 'Religion and Party Choice in Europe', *West European Politics*, 32(6), 1266–1283.

van der Brug, Wouter and Kritzinger, Sylvia (eds) (2012) 'Generational Differences in Electoral Behaviour', special symposium in *Electoral Studies*, 31(2), pp. 245–468.

van der Eijk, C. and Franklin, M. (eds) (1996) *Choosing Europe? The European Electorate and National Politics in the Face of Union* (Ann Arbor: University of Michigan Press).

van der Heijden, Hein-Anton (2011) *Social Movements, Public Spheres and the European Politics of the Environment: Green Power Europe?* (Basingstoke: Palgrave).

van der Meer, Tom and van Ingen, Erik (2009) 'Schools of Democracy? Disentangling the Relationship between Civic Participation and Political Action in 17 European countries', *European Journal of Political Research*, 48(2) pp. 281–308.

van der Wurff, Richard (2004) 'Supplying and Viewing Diversity: The Role of Competition and Viewer Choice in Dutch Broadcasting', *European Journal of Communication*, 19(2), pp. 215–37.

Vasilopoulou, Sofia (2011) 'European Integration and the Radical Right: Three Patterns of Opposition', *Government and Opposition*, 46(2), pp. 223–244.

Verheijen, Tony (ed.) (1999) *Civil Service Systems in Central and Eastern Europe* (Aldershot: Edward Elgar).

Verhoest, Koen, Roness, Paul G., Verschuere, Bram, Rubecksen, Kristin and MacCarthaigh, Muiris (2010) *Autonomy and Control of State Agencies Comparing States and Agencies* (Basingstoke: Palgrave Macmillan).

Verhulst, Joris and Walgrave, Stefaan (2007) 'Protest and Protesters in Advanced Industrial Democracies: The Case of the 15th February Global Anti-war Demonstrations', in Derrick A. Purdue (ed.), *Civil Societies and Social Movements: Potentials and Problems* (London: Routledge).

Verney, Susannah (ed.) (2011) 'Euroscepticism in Southern Europe: A Diachronic Perspective', special issue of *South European Society and Politics*, 16(1).

Versluis, Esther (2007) 'Even Rules, Uneven Practices: Opening the "Black Box" of EU Law in Action', *West European Politics*, 30(1), pp. 50–67.

Vertovec, Steven and Wessendorf, Susanne (2009) *The Multiculturalism Backlash: European Discourses, Policies and Practices* (Abingdon: Routledge).

Vink, Maarten (2010) 'Citizenship Attribution in Western Europe: International Framework and Domestic Trends', *Journal of Ethnic and Migration Studies*, 36(5), pp 713–34.

Vis, Barbara (2012) 'Under Which Conditions Does Spending on Active Labour Market Policies Increase? An fsQCA analysis of 53 governments between 1985 and 2003', *European Political Science Review*, 3(2), pp. 229–252.

Visser, Jelle (1998) 'Learning to Play: The Europeanization of Trade Unions', in Patrick Pasture and Johan Verberckmoes (eds), *Working Class Internationalism and the Appeal of National Identity: Historical Debates and Current Perspectives* (Oxford: Berg).

Visser, Jelle (2006) 'Union Membership Statistics in 24 Countries', *Monthly Labor Review*, January.

Vlachová, Mira (2001) 'Party Identification in the Czech Republic: Inter-party Hostility and Party Preference', *Communist and Post-Communist Studies*, 34(4), pp. 479–99.

Vliegenthart, Rens and Walgrave, Stefaan (2011) 'When the Media matter for politics: Partisan moderators of the mass media's agenda-setting influence on parliament in Belgium', *Party Politics*, 17(3), pp. 321–342.

Vliegenthart, Rens, Boomgaarden, Hajo G and van Spanje, Joost (2012) 'Anti-Immigrant Party Support and Media Visibility: a

Cross-Party, Over-Time Perspective', *Journal of Elections, Public Opinion and Parties*, 22(3), pp. 315–358.

Volden, Craig and Carrubba, Clifford J. (2004) 'The Formation of Oversized Coalitions in Parliamentary Democracies', *American Journal of Political Science*, 48(3), pp. 521–37.

Volkens, Andrea (2004) 'Policy Changes of European Social Democrats, 1945–1998', in Guiliano Bonoli and Martin Powell (eds), *Social Democratic Party Policies in Contemporary Europe* (London: Routledge).

Volkens, Andrea and Klingemann, Hans-Dieter, (2002) 'Parties, Ideologies, and Issues. Stability and Change in Fifteen European Party Systems 1945–1998', in Kurt Richard Luther and Ferdinand Müller-Rommel, (eds) *Political Parties in the New Europe: Political and Analytical Challenges*, (Oxford University Press, Oxford).

W

Wagner, Aiko and Weßels, Bernhard (2012) 'Parties and their Leaders. Does it Matter How they Match? The German General Elections 2009 in Comparison', *Electoral Studies*, 31(1), pp. 72–82.

Wagner, Markus (2011) 'The Right in the European Parliament Since 1979', *Perspectives on European Politics and Society*, 12(1), pp. 52–67.

Wagner, Markus (2012) 'When do Parties Emphasise Extreme Positions? How Strategic Incentives for Policy Differentiation Influence Issue Importance', *European Journal of Political Research*, 51, pp. 64–88.

Wagner, Markus, Johann, David and Kritzinger, Sylvia (2012) 'Voting at 16: Turnout and the quality of vote choice', *Electoral Studies*, 31(2), pp. 372–383.

Walczak, Agnieszka, van der Brug, Wouter, de Vries, Catherine (2012), 'Long- and Short-term Determinants of Party Preferences: Inter-generational Differences in Western and East Central Europe', *Electoral Studies*, 31(2), pp. 273–284.

Walgrave, Stefaan (2008) 'Again, the Almighty Mass Media? The Media's Political Agenda-Setting Power According to Politicians and Journalists in Belgium', *Political Communication*, 25(4), pp. 445–459.

Walgrave, Stefaan and van Aelst, Peter (2006) 'The Contingency of the Mass Media's Political Agenda Setting Power: Toward a Preliminary Agenda', *Journal of Communication*, 56, pp. 88–109.

Wallace, Helen (2000) 'Europeanisation and Globalisation: Complementary or Contradictory Trends', *New Political Economy*, 5(3), pp. 369–82.

Wallace, Helen, Pollack, Mark, and Young, Alasdair (eds) (2010) *Policy making in the European Union* (Oxford: Oxford University Press).

Ward, Stephen and Lusoli, Wainer (2003) 'Dinosaurs in Cyberspace?: British Trade Unions and the Internet', *European Journal of Communication*, 18(2), pp. 147–79.

Warwick, Paul (2011) 'Voters, Parties, and Declared Government Policy', *Comparative Political Studies*, 44(12), pp. 1675–1699.

Warwick, Paul V. (2012) 'Dissolvers, Disputers and Defectors: the Terminators of Parliamentary Governments', *European Political Science Review*, 42(2), pp 263–281.

Waters, Malcolm (2001) *Globalization* (London: Routledge).

Wattenberg, Martin P. (2011) *Is Voting for Young People?* (London: Longman).

Webb, Paul, Farrell, David M. and Holliday, Ian (eds) (2002) *Political Parties in Advanced Industrial Democracies* (Oxford: Oxford University Press).

Webb, Paul and Kolodny, Robin (2006) 'Professional Staff in Political Parties', in Richard Katz and William Crotty (eds), *Handbook of Party Politics* (London: Sage).

Webb, Paul and White, Stephen (2007) *Party Politics in New Democracies* (Oxford: Oxford University Press).

Wehner, Joachim (2006) 'Assessing the Power of the Purse: an Index of Legislative Budget Institutions', *Political Studies*, 54(4), pp. 767–85.

Weibull, Lennart and Nilsson, Åsa (2010) 'Four Decades of European Newspapers: Structure and Content', in Gripsund, Jostein and Weibull, Lennart (eds.) *Media, Markets and Public Spheres* (Bristol: Intellect).

Weiss, Linda (1998) *The Myth of the Powerless State: Governing the Economy in a Global Era* (Cambridge: Polity).

Weldon, Steven A. (2006) 'Downsize My Polity? Impacts of Size on Party Membership and Member Activism', *Party Politics*, 12(4), pp. 467–81.

Weller, Patrick, Barkis, Herman and Rhodes, R.A.W. (eds) (1997) *The Hollow Crown: Countervailing Trends in Core Executives* (Basingstoke: Palgrave Macmillan).

Welzel, Christian, Inglehart, Ronald and Deutsch, Franziska (2005) 'Social Capital, Voluntary Associations and Collective Action: Which Aspects of Social Capital Have the Greatest "Civic" Payoff?', *Journal of Civil Society*, 1(2), pp. 121–46.

Wessels, Wolfgang, Maurer, Andreas and Mittag, Jürgen (eds) (2003) *Fifteen into One? The European Union and its Member States*, 2nd edn (Manchester: Manchester University Press).

Wheeler, Mark (2009) 'Supranational Regulation: the EU Competition Directorate and the European Audio-visual Market Place', in Jackie Harrison and Bridgette Wessels (eds.) *Mediating Europe: New Media, Mass Communications and the European Public Sphere* (Oxford: Berghahn Books).

White, Jonathan (2011) *Political Allegiance after European Integration* (Basingstoke: Palgrave Macmillan).

White, Stephen, Lewis, Paul G. and Batt, Judy (eds) (2007) *Developments in Central and East European Politics* (Basingstoke: Palgrave Macmillan).

Whitefield, Stephen (2002) 'Political Cleavages and Post-communist Politics', *Annual Review of Political Science*, 5, pp. 181–200.

Whitman, Richard G. (2011) *Normative Power Europe: Empirical and Theoretical Perspectives* (Basingstoke: Palgrave Macmillan).

Whitman, Richard G. and Wolff, Stefan (2010a) 'The EU as a conflict manager? The case of Georgia and its implications', *International Affairs*, 86(1), pp. 87–107.

Whitman, Richard G. and Wolff, Stefan (2010b) *The European Union as a Global Conflict Manager* (Abingdon: Routledge).

Wiessala, Georg (2006) *Re-orienting the Fundamentals: Human Rights and New Connections in EU–Asia Relations* (Farnham: Ashgate).

Wilensky, Harold (2002) *Rich Democracies: Political Economy, Public Policy, and Performance* (Berkeley: University of California Press).

Wilke, Jürgen and Reinemann, Carsten (2001) 'Do the Candidates Matter? Long Term Trends of Campaign Coverage

– A Study of the German Press Since 1949', *European Journal of Communication*, 16(3), pp. 291–314.

Wilkinson, Richard and Pickett, Kate (2010) *The Spirit Level: Why Equality is Better for Everyone* (Harmondsworth: Penguin).

Williams, Garrath (2005) 'Monomaniacs or Schizophrenics?: Responsible Governance and the EU's Independent Agencies', *Political Studies*, 53(1), pp. 82–99.

Williams, Kevin (2006) 'Competing Models of Journalism? Anglo-American and European Reporting in the Information Age', *Journalistica*, 2 available online at http://ojs.stats biblioteket.dk/index.php/journalistica/article/view/1788/1610

Williams, Laron K. (2011) 'Unsuccessful Success? Failed No-Confidence Motions, Competence Signals, and Electoral Support', *Comparative Political Studies*, 44(11), pp. 1474–1499.

Williams, Michelle Hale (2006) *The Impact of Radical Right-Wing Parties in Western Democracies* (New York: Palgrave Macmillan).

Wilson, David and Game, Chris (2006) *Local Government in the United Kingdom*, 2nd edn (Basingstoke: Palgrave Macmillan).

Wincott, Daniel (2003) 'Beyond Social Regulation? New Instruments and/or a New Agenda for Social Policy at Lisbon?', *Public Administration*, 81(3), pp. 533–53.

Woldendorp, Jaap (2011) 'Corporatism in small North-West European countries 1970–2006: Business as Usual, Decline, or a New Phenomenon?' http://www.fsw.vu.nl/en/Images/WP_Woldendorp_2011_tcm31-199579.pdf.

Wolff, Stefan (2007) *Ethnic Conflict: A Global Perspective* (Oxford: Oxford University Press).

Wolinetz, Stephen (ed.) (1997) *Party Systems* (Aldershot: Ashgate).

Wolinetz, Stephen (ed.) (1998) *Political Parties* (Aldershot: Dartmouth).

Woll, Christina (2006) 'National Business Associations under Stress: Lessons from the French Case', *West European Politics*, 29(3), pp. 489–512.

Wollmann, Hellmut (2008) 'Reforming Local Leadership and Local Democracy: The Cases of England, Sweden, Germany and France in Comparative Perspective', *Local Government Studies*, 34(2), pp. 279–298.

Wollmann, Hellmut and Marcou, Gerard (eds.) (2010) *The Provision of Public Services in Europe: Between State, Local Government and Market* (Cheltenham: Edward Elgar).

Wong, Reuben and Hill, Christopher (eds) (2011) *National and European Foreign Policies: Towards Europeanization* (Abingdon: Routledge).

Wonka, Ardnt (2008) 'Decision-making Dynamics in the European Commission: Partisan, National or Sectoral?', *Journal of European Public Policy*, 15(8), pp. 1145–1163.

Wonka, Ardnt, Baumgartner, Frank R., Mahoney, Christine and Berkhout, Joost (2010) 'Measuring the Size and Scope of the EU Interest Group Population', *European Union Politics*, 11(3), pp. 463–476.

Woolcock, Stephen (2009) 'External trade policy: a further shift towards Brussels', in Polack, Mark, Young, Alasdair and Wallace, Helen. (eds) *Policy Making in the European Union* (Oxford: Oxford University Press).

Woolcock, Stephen (2010) *The Treaty of Lisbon and the European Union as an actor in international trade*, ECIPE Working Paper No. 01/2010 (Brussels: ECIPE).

Woolcock, Stepehn (2012) *European Union Economic Diplomacy: The Role of the EU in External Economic Relations* (Farnham: Ashgate).

Wright, Sue (2008) 'Citizenship Tests in a Post-National Era', special issue of *IJMS: International Journal on Multicultural Societies*, 10(1), available online at http://www.unesco.org/new/en/social-and-human-sciences/resources/periodicals/diversities/past-issues/vol-10-no-1-2008/

Wright, Vincent and Hayward, Jack (2000) 'Governing from the Centre: Policy Coordination in Six European Core Executives', in R.A.W. Rhodes (ed.), *Transforming British Government, 2: Changing Roles and Relationships* (Basingstoke: Palgrave Macmillan).

X, Y, Z

Yanai, Nathan (1999) 'Why do Political Parties Survive? An Analytical Discussion', *Party Politics*, 5(1), pp. 5–18.

Young, Alasdair and Wallace, Helen (2000) *Regulatory Politics in the Enlarging European Union: Weighing Civic and Producer Interests* (Manchester: Manchester University Press).

Youngs, Richard (2009) *Energy Security: Europe's New Foreign Policy Challenge* (Abingdon: Routledge).

Youngs, Richard (2010) *The EU's Role in World Politics: a Retreat from Liberal Internationalism* (Abingdon: Routledge).

Zaiotti, Ruben (2007) 'Of Friends and Fences: Europe's Neighbourhood Policy and the "Gated Community Syndrome"', *Journal of European Integration*, 29(2), pp. 143–62.

Zeff, Eleanor E. and Pirro, Ellen B. (2001) *The European Union and the Member States: Cooperation, Coordination and Compromise* (Boulder: Lynne Rienner).

Zeidenitz, S. and Barkow, B. (1999) *The Xenophobe's Guide to the Germans* (London: Oval).

Zielinski, Jakub (2002) 'Translating Social Cleavages into Party Systems: The Significance of New Democracies', *World Politics*, 54(2), pp. 184–211.

Zielinski, Jakub, Slomczynski, Kazimierz, M. and Shabad, Goldie (2005) 'Electoral Control in New Democracies: The Perverse Incentives of Fluid Party Systems', *World Politics*, 57(3), pp. 365–95.

Ziller, Jacques (2001) 'European Models of Government: Towards a Patchwork with Missing Pieces', *Parliamentary Affairs*, 54, pp. 102–19.

Zillien, Nicole and Hargittai, Eszter (2009) 'Digital Distinction: Status-Specific Types of Internet Usage', *Social Science Quarterly*, 90(2), pp. 274–291.

Zittel, Thomas (2004) 'Political Communication and Electronic Democracy: American Exceptionalism or Global Trend?', in Frank Esser and Barbara Pfetsch (eds), *Comparing Political Communication: Theories, Cases, and Challenges* (Cambridge: Cambridge University Press).

Zmerli, Sonja, Newton, Kenneth and Montero, José Ramón (2007) 'Trust in People, Confidence in Political Institutions and Satisfaction with Democracy', in Jan van Deth, José Ramón Montero, and Anders Westholm (eds), *Citizenship and Involvement in European Democracies: A Comparative Analysis* (London: Routledge).

Zohlnhöfer, Reimut and Obinger, Herbert (2006) 'Selling Off the "Family Silver": The Politics of Privatization', *World Political Science Review*, 2(1), article 2, available at http://www.bepress.com/wpsr/vol2/issl/art2

Zubek, Radoslaw (2006) 'Poland: a Core Ascendent?', in Vesselin Dimitrov, Klaus H. Goetz and Hellmut Wollman (2006), *Governing after Communism: Institutions and Policy Making* (Lanham: Rowman & Littlefield).

Zubek, Radoslaw (2008) *Core Executive and Europeanization in Central Europe* (Basingstoke: Palgrave Macmillan).

Zubek, Radoslaw (2011) 'Negative Agenda Control and ExecutivLegislative Relations in East Central Europe, 1997–2008', *Journal of Legislative Studies*, 17(2), 172–192.

Zürn, M. and Joerges, C. (eds) (2005) *Law and Governance in Postnational Europe* (Cambridge: Cambridge University Press).

Index

Entries and page numbers in bold refer to boxes or highlighted definitions.